D0208590

Investment under Uncertainty

Investment under Uncertainty

Avinash K. Dixit and Robert S. Pindyck

Princeton University Press
Princeton, New Jersey

Copyright © 1994 by Princeton University Press
Published by Princeton University Press, 41 William Street,
Princeton, New Jersey 08540
In the United Kingdom: Princeton University Press, Chichester,
West Sussex

Library of Congress Cataloging-in-Publication Data
Dixit, Avinash K.
   Investment under uncertainty / by Avinash K. Dixit and Robert S.
Pindyck
     p.   cm.
   Includes bibliographical references and index.
   ISBN 0-691-03410-9
   1. Capital investments—Decision making. I. Pindyck, Robert S.
II. Title.
HG4028.C4D58   1993
658.15′54—dc20   93-26321
                                                      CIP

This book has been composed in Times Roman

Princeton University Press books are printed on acid-free paper
and meet the guidelines for permanence and durability of the
Committee on Production Guidelines for Book Longevity of the
Council on Library Resources

Printed in the United States of America
10 9 8 7 6 5 4 3 2

To the future

Contents

Part III. A Firm's Decisions

Preface

THIS BOOK provides a systematic treatment of a new theoretical approach to capital investment decisions of firms, stressing the irreversibility of most investment decisions and the ongoing uncertainty of the economic environment in which those decisions are made. This new approach recognizes the option value of waiting for better (but never complete) information. It exploits an analogy with the theory of options in financial markets, which permits a much richer dynamic framework than was possible with the traditional theory of investment.

The new view of investment opportunities as options is the product of over a decade of research by many economists, and is still an active topic in journal articles. It has led to some dramatic departures from the orthodox theory. It has shown that the traditional "net present value" rule, which is taught to virtually every business school student and student of economics, can give very wrong answers. The reason is that this rule ignores irreversibility and the option of delaying an investment. For the same reason, the new theory also contradicts the orthodox textbook view of production and supply going back to Marshall, according to which firms enter or expand when the price exceeds long-run average cost, and exit or contract when price falls below average variable cost. Policy prescriptions based on the traditional theory, for example, the use of interest rate cuts to stimulate investment and antitrust policies based on price-cost margins, are also called into question.

In this book we have tried to present the new theory in a clear and systematic way, and to consolidate, synthesize, and in some places extend the various strands of this growing body of research. While there is a large and burgeoning literature of journal articles, including a survey article by each of us, a book format has distinct advantages. It offers us the space to develop the different themes in more detail and better order, and to place them in relation to one another. It also gives us the opportunity to introduce and explain the new techniques that underlie much of this work, but that are often unfamiliar to economists. We hope that the result is a better pedagogic treatment, of use to students, researchers, and practitioners. However, perhaps even more important than pedagogy is the ability of the book format to provide a broad vision of the subject, and of the mechanisms of the dynamic, uncertain economic world.

Our main aim is to clarify and explain the theory, but we think this is often best done by applying it to the real world. Therefore we often obtain numerical solutions for our theoretical models using data that pertain to some specific industries or products. We believe that the cumulative weight of these calculations constitutes strong prima facie evidence for the validity and the quantitative significance of the new theory of investment. However, more rigorous econometric testing, and the detailed work that is needed to devise improved decisionmaking tools for managers, await further research. We believe that this is an exciting and potentially important subject, and hope that our book will stimulate and aid such research.

Who Should Read This Book?

This book is intended for three broad audiences. The first audience consists of economists with an interest in the theory of investment, and in its policy implications. This includes graduate students engaged in the study of micro- and macroeconomic theory as well as industrial organization, and researchers at universities and other institutions with an interest in problems relating to investment. The second broad audience is students and researchers of financial economics, with an interest in corporate finance generally, and capital budgeting in particular. This would include graduate students studying problems in capital budgeting (that is, how firms should evaluate projects and make capital investment decisions), as well as anyone doing research in finance with an interest in investment decisions and investment behavior. Finally, the third audience is finance practitioners. This includes people working in financial institutions and concerned with the evaluation of companies and their assets, as well as corporate managers who must evaluate and decide whether to go ahead with large-scale investments for their firms.

Some parts of this book are fairly technical, but that should not deter the interested reader. The first two chapters provide a fairly brief and self-contained introduction to the theory of irreversible investment under uncertainty. These chapters convey many of the basic ideas, while avoiding technical details and any mathematical formalism. Reading these chapters is a low-risk investment that we can almost guarantee will have a high return. Even those practitioners whose knowledge of economics and finance textbooks is very rusty should be able to follow these two chapters without too much effort or difficulty.

We anticipate that many readers will want to go into the theory in more detail and address some of the technical issues, but lack some of the necessary mathematical tools. With those readers in mind, we have included two chapters (Chapters 3 and 4) that provide a self-contained introduction to the mathematical concepts and tools that underlie this work. (These tools have applicability that goes well beyond the theory of investment under uncertainty, and so we anticipate that some readers will find these chapters useful even if their applied interests lie elsewhere, for example, macroeconomics, international trade, or labor economics.)

However, we think that techniques are best learned by using them. Therefore we do not attempt to be very rigorous or thorough in the mathematics as such. We rely on intuition as far as possible, sketch some simple formal arguments in appendices, and refer the readers who wish greater mathematical rigor or depth to more advanced treatises. For most readers, we recommend reading Chapters 3 and 4 once, and proceeding to the later chapters where the techniques are used. We think they will emerge with a much better grasp of the mathematics in this way than by trying to master it first and in the abstract.

Finally, we expect that many readers will want to see the new view of investment developed in detail, including as many of its ramifications as possible, along with examples and applications. Chapters 5 through 12 provide just that, building up slowly from a basic and fairly simple model of irreversible investment in Chapter 5, to more complete models in Chapters 6 and 7 that account for decisions to start or stop producing, to the models in Chapters 8 and 9 that account for the interactions of firms within industries, and finally to the more advanced extensions of the theory and its applications in Chapters 10, 11, and 12.

Acknowledgments

This book is an outgrowth of the research that each of us has been doing over the past several years on the theory of investment. That research—and hence this book—have benefitted enormously from our interactions with colleagues and friends at our home institutions and elsewhere. To try to list all of the people from whom we received insights, ideas, and encouragement would greatly lengthen the book. However, there are some individuals who have been especially helpful through the comments, criticisms, and suggestions they provided after reading our research papers and draft chapters of this book, and they deserve special mention: Giuseppe Bertola, Olivier Blanchard, Alan Blinder, Ricardo Caballero, Andrew Caplin, John Cox, Bernard Dumas, Gene Grossman, Sandy Grossman, John Leahy, Gilbert Metcalf, Marcus Miller, Julio Rotemberg, and Jiang Wang. In addition, we want to thank Lead Wey for his outstanding research assistance throughout the development of this book. Our thanks, too, to Lynn Steele for editorial help in preparing the final draft of the manuscript.

The second printing of the book gave us the opportunity to correct several errors. We thank all the readers who brought these errors to our attention, most particularly Marco Dias of PUC, Rio de Janeiro, and David Nachman of Georgia State University. We are sure that more errors remain, but we practice the preaching of capital theory: manuscripts should not be improved to the point of perfection, but only to the point where the rate of further improvement equals the rate of interest.

Finally, we want to thank Peter Dougherty, our editor at Princeton University Press, for his encouragement and advice as we prepared the manuscript, and his guiding hand in seeing the book through to production.

Both of us also received financial support for which we are very grateful. Avinash Dixit acknowledges the support of the National Science Foundation and the Guggenheim Foundation. Robert Pindyck acknowledges support from the National Science Foundation and from MIT's Center for Energy and Environmental Policy Research.

Avinash K. Dixit

Robert S. Pindyck

Part I
Introduction

Chapter 1

A New View of Investment

ECONOMICS defines investment as the act of incurring an immediate cost in the expectation of future rewards. Firms that construct plants and install equipment, merchants who lay in a stock of goods for sale, and persons who spend time on vocational education are all investors in this sense. Somewhat less obviously, a firm that shuts down a loss-making plant is also "investing": the payments it must make to extract itself from contractual commitments, including severance payments to labor, are the initial expenditure, and the prospective reward is the reduction in future losses.

Viewed from this perspective, investment decisions are ubiquitous. Your purchase of this book was an investment. The reward, we hope, will be an improved understanding of investment decisions if you are an economist, and an improved ability to make such decisions in the course of your future career if you are a business school student.

Most investment decisions share three important characteristics in varying degrees. First, the investment is partially or completely *irreversible*. In other words, the initial cost of investment is at least partially sunk; you cannot recover it all should you change your mind. Second, there is *uncertainty* over the future rewards from the investment. The best you can do is to assess the probabilities of the alternative outcomes that can mean greater or smaller profit (or loss) for your venture. Third, you have some leeway about the *timing* of your investment. You can postpone action to get more information (but never, of course, complete certainty) about the future.

These three characteristics interact to determine the optimal decisions of investors. This interaction is the focus of this book. We develop the theory of irreversible investment under uncertainty, and illustrate it with some practical applications.[1]

The orthodox theory of investment has not recognized the important qualitative and quantitative implications of the interaction between irreversibility, uncertainty, and the choice of timing. We will argue that this neglect explains some of the failures of that theory. For example, compared to the predictions of most earlier models, real world investment seems much less sensitive to interest rate changes and tax policy changes, and much more sensitive to volatility and uncertainty over the economic environment. We will show how the new view resolves these anomalies, and in the process offers some guidance for designing more effective public policies concerning investment.

Some seemingly noneconomic personal decisions also have the characteristics of an investment. To give just one example, marriage involves an up-front cost of courtship, with uncertain future happiness or misery. It may be reversed by divorce, but only at a substantial cost. Many public policy decisions also have similar features. For instance, public opinion about the relative importance of civil rights of the accused and of social order fluctuates through time, and it is costly to make or change laws that embody a particular relative weight for the two. Of course the costs and benefits of such noneconomic decisions are difficult or even impossible to quantify, but our general theory will offer some qualitative insights for them, too.

1   The Orthodox Theory

How should a firm, facing uncertainty over future market conditions, decide whether to invest in a new factory? Most economics and business school students are taught a simple rule to apply to problems of this sort. First, calculate the present value of the expected stream of profits that this factory will generate. Second, calculate the present value of the stream of expenditures required to build the factory. Finally, determine whether the difference between the two—the *net present value* (NPV) of the investment—is greater than zero. If it is, go ahead and invest.

---

[1] Some decisions that are the opposite of investment—getting an immediate benefit in return for an uncertain future cost— are also irreversible. Prominent examples include the exhaustion of natural resources and the destruction of tropical rain forests. Our methods apply to these decisions, too.

Of course, there are issues that arise in calculating this net present value. Just how should the expected stream of profits from a new factory be estimated? How should inflation be treated? And what discount rate (or rates) should be used in calculating the present values? Resolving issues like these are important topics in courses in corporate finance, and especially capital budgeting, but the basic principle is fairly simple—calculate the NPV of an investment project and see whether it is positive.

The net present value rule is also the basis for the neoclassical theory of investment as taught to undergraduate and graduate students of economics. Here we find the rule expressed using the standard incremental or marginal approach of the economist: invest until the value of an incremental unit of capital is just equal to its cost. Again, issues arise in determining the value of an incremental unit of capital, and in determining its cost. For example, what production structure should be posited? How should taxes and depreciation be treated?

Much of the theoretical and empirical literature on the economics of investment deals with issues of this sort. We find two essentially equivalent approaches. One, following Jorgenson (1963), compares the per-period value of an incremental unit of capital (its marginal product) and an "equivalent per-period rental cost" or "user cost" that can be computed from the purchase price, the interest and depreciation rates, and applicable taxes. The firm's desired stock of capital is found by equating the marginal product and the user cost. The actual stock is assumed to adjust to the ideal, either as an ad hoc lag process, or as the optimal response to an explicit cost of adjustment. The book by Nickell (1978) provides a particularly good exposition of developments of this approach.

The other formulation, due to Tobin (1969), compares the capitalized value of the marginal investment to its purchase cost. The value can be observed directly if the ownership of the investment can be traded in a secondary market; otherwise it is an imputed value computed as the expected present value of the stream of profits it would yield. The ratio of this to the purchase price (replacement cost) of the unit, called Tobin's q, governs the investment decision. Investment should be undertaken or expanded if q exceeds 1; it should not be undertaken, and existing capital should be reduced, if $q < 1$. The optimal rate of expansion or contraction is found by equating the marginal cost of adjustment to its benefit, which depends on the difference between q and 1. Tax rules can alter this somewhat, but the basic principle is similar. Abel (1990) offers an excellent survey of this q-theory of investment. In all of this, the underlying principle is the basic net present value rule.

2   The Option Approach

The net present value rule, however, is based on some implicit assumptions that are often overlooked. Most important, it assumes that either the investment is reversible, that is, it can somehow be undone and the expenditures recovered should market conditions turn out to be worse than anticipated, *or*, if the investment is irreversible, it is a now or never proposition, that is, if the firm does not undertake the investment now, it will not be able to in the future.

Although some investments meet these conditions, most do not. Irreversibility and the possibility of delay are very important characteristics of most investments in reality. As a rapidly growing literature has shown, the ability to delay an irreversible investment expenditure can profoundly affect the decision to invest. It also undermines the simple net present value rule, and hence the theoretical foundation of standard neoclassical investment models. The reason is that a firm with an opportunity to invest is holding an "option" analogous to a financial call option—it has the right but not the obligation to buy an asset at some future time of its choosing. When a firm makes an irreversible investment expenditure, it exercises, or "kills," its option to invest. It gives up the possibility of waiting for new information to arrive that might affect the desirability or timing of the expenditure; it cannot disinvest should market conditions change adversely. This lost option value is an opportunity cost that must be included as part of the cost of the investment. As a result, the NPV rule "invest when the value of a unit of capital is at least as large as its purchase and installation cost" must be modified. The value of the unit must exceed the purchase and installation cost, by an amount equal to the value of keeping the investment option alive.

Recent studies have shown that this opportunity cost of investing can be large, and investment rules that ignore it can be grossly in error. Also, this opportunity cost is highly sensitive to uncertainty over the future value of the project, so that changing economic conditions that affect the perceived riskiness of future cash flows can have a large impact on investment spending, larger than, say, a change in interest rates. This may help to explain why neoclassical investment theory has so far failed to provide good empirical models of investment behavior, and has led to overly optimistic forecasts of effectiveness of interest rate and tax policies in stimulating investment.

The option insight also helps explain why the actual investment behavior of firms differs from the received wisdom taught in business schools. Firms invest in projects that are expected to yield a return in excess of a required, or "hurdle," rate. Observers of business practice find that such hurdle rates are typically three or four times the cost of capital.[2] In other words, firms do not invest until price rises substantially above long-run average cost. On the downside, firms stay in business for lengthy periods while absorbing operating losses, and price can fall substantially below average variable cost without inducing disinvestment or exit. This also seems to conflict with standard theory, but as we will see, it can be explained once irreversibility and option value are accounted for.

Of course, one can always redefine NPV by subtracting from the conventional calculation the opportunity cost of exercising the option to invest, and then say that the rule "invest if NPV is positive" holds once this correction has been made. However, to do so is to accept our criticism. To highlight the importance of option values, in this book we prefer to keep them separate from the conventional NPV. If others prefer to continue to use "positive NPV" terminology, that is fine as long as they are careful to include all relevant option values in their definition of NPV. Readers who prefer that usage can readily translate our statements into that language.

In this book we develop the basic theory of irreversible investment under uncertainty, emphasizing the option-like characteristics of investment opportunities. We show how optimal investment rules can be obtained from methods that have been developed for pricing options in financial markets. We also develop an equivalent approach based on the mathematical theory of optimal sequential decisions under uncertainty—dynamic programming. We illustrate the optimal investment decisions of firms in a variety of situations—new entry, determination of the initial scale of the firm and future costly changes of scale, choice between different forms of investment that offer different degrees of flexibility to meet future conditions, completion of successive stages of a complex multistage project, temporary shutdown and restart, permanent exit, and so forth. We also analyze how the actions of such firms are aggregated to determine the dynamic equilibrium of an industry.

To stress the analogy with options on financial assets, the opportunities to acquire real assets are sometimes called "real options." Therefore this book could be titled "The Real Options Approach to Investment."

---

[2]Summers (1987, p. 300) found hurdle rates ranging from 8 to 30 percent, with a median of 15 and a mean of 17 percent. The cost of riskless capital was much lower; allowing for the deductibility of interest expenses, the nominal interest rate was 4 percent, and the real rate close to zero. See also Dertouzas et al. (1990, p. 61). The hurdle rate appropriate for investments with systematic risk will exceed the riskless rate, but not by enough to justify the numbers used by many companies.

3   Irreversibility and the Ability to Wait

Before proceeding, it is important to clarify the notions of irreversibility, the ability to delay an investment, and the option to invest. Most important, what makes an investment expenditure a sunk cost and thus irreversible?

Investment expenditures are sunk costs when they are firm or industry specific. For example, most investments in marketing and advertising are firm specific and cannot be recovered. Hence they are clearly sunk costs. A steel plant, on the other hand, is industry specific—it can only be used to produce steel. One might think that because in principle the plant could be sold to another steel company, the investment expenditure is recoverable and is not a sunk cost. This is incorrect. If the industry is reasonably competitive, the value of the plant will be about the same for all firms in the industry, so there would be little to gain from selling it. For example, if the price of steel falls so that a plant turns out, ex post, to have been a "bad" investment for the firm that built it, it will also be viewed as a bad investment by other steel companies, and the ability to sell the plant will not be worth much. As a result, an investment in a steel plant (or any other industry-specific capital) should be viewed as largely a sunk cost.

Even investments that are not firm or industry specific are often partly irreversible because buyers in markets for used machines, unable to evaluate the quality of an item, will offer a price that corresponds to the average quality in the market. Sellers, who know the quality of the item they are selling, will be reluctant to sell an above-average item. This will lower the market average quality, and therefore the market price. This "lemons" problem (see Akerlof, 1970) plagues many such markets. For example, office equipment, cars, trucks, and computers are not industry specific, and although they can be sold to companies in other industries, their resale value will be well below their purchase cost, even if they are almost new.

Irreversibility can also arise because of government regulations or institutional arrangements. For example, capital controls may make it impossible for foreign (or domestic) investors to sell assets and reallocate their funds, and investments in new workers may be partly irreversible because of high costs of hiring, training, and firing. Hence most major capital investments are in large part irreversible.

Let us turn next to the possibilities for delaying investments. Of course, firms do not always have the opportunity to delay their investments. For example, there can be occasions in which strategic considerations make it imperative for a firm to invest quickly and thereby preempt investment by existing or potential competitors.[3] However, in most cases, delay is at least feasible. There may be a cost to delay—the risk of entry by other firms, or simply foregone cash flows—but this cost must be weighed against the benefits of waiting for new information. Those benefits are often large.

As we said earlier, an irreversible investment opportunity is much like a financial call option. A call option gives the holder the right, for some specified amount of time, to pay an exercise price and in return receive an asset (e.g., a share of stock) that has some value. Exercising the option is irreversible; although the asset can be sold to another investor, one cannot retrieve the option or the money that was paid to exercise it. A firm with an investment opportunity likewise has the option to spend money (the "exercise price"), now or in the future, in return for an asset (e.g., a project) of some value. Again, the asset can be sold to another firm, but the investment is irreversible. As with the financial call option, this option to invest is valuable in part because the future value of the asset obtained by investing is uncertain. If the asset rises in value, the net payoff from investing rises. If it falls in value, the firm need not invest, and will only lose what it spent to obtain the investment opportunity. The models of irreversible investment that will be developed in Chapter 2 and in later chapters will help to clarify the optionlike nature of an investment opportunity.

Finally, one might ask how firms obtain their investment opportunities, that is, options to invest, in the first place. Sometimes investment opportunities result from patents, or ownership of land or natural resources. More generally, they arise from a firm's managerial resources, technological knowledge, reputation, market position, and possible scale, all of which may have been built up over time, and which enable the firm to productively undertake investments that individuals or other firms cannot undertake. Most important, these options to invest are valuable. Indeed, for most firms, a substantial part of their market value is attributable to their options to invest and grow in the future, as opposed to the capital they already have in place.[4] Most of the economic and financial theory of investment has focused on how firms should (and do) exercise their options to invest. To better understand investment behavior it may be just as important to develop better models of how firms obtain investment opportunities, a point that we will return to in later chapters.

---

[3] See Gilbert (1989) and Tirole (1988, Chapter 8) for surveys of the literature on such strategic aspects of investment.

[4] For discussions of growth options as sources of firm value, see Myers (1977), Kester (1984), and Pindyck (1988b).

4 An Overview of the Book

In the rest of this chapter, we outline the plan of the book and give a flavor of some of the important ideas and results that emerge from the analysis.

4.A A Few Introductory Examples

The general ideas about "real options" expounded above are simple and intuitive, but they must be translated into more precise models before their quantitative significance can be assessed and their implications for firms, industries, and public policy can be obtained. Chapter 2 starts this program in a simple and gentle way. We examine a firm with a single discrete investment opportunity that can be implemented within a "window" of two decision periods. Between the two periods, the price of the output undergoes a permanent shift up or down. Suppose the investment would be profitable at the average price, and therefore a fortiori at the higher price, but not at the lower price. By postponing its decision to the second period, the firm can make it having observed the actual price movement. It invests if the price has gone up, but not if it has gone down. Thus it avoids the loss it would have made if it had invested in the first period and then seen the price go down. This value of waiting must be traded off against the loss of the period-1 profit flow. The result—the decision to invest or to wait—depends on the parameters that specify the model, most importantly the extent of the uncertainty (which determines the downside risk avoided by waiting) and the discount rate (which measures the relative importance of the future versus the present).

We carry out several numerical calculations to illustrate these effects and build intuition for real options. We also explore the analogy to financial options more closely. We introduce markets that allow individuals to shift the risk of the price going up or down, namely contingent claims that have different payoffs in the two eventualities. Then we construct a portfolio of these contingent claims that can exactly replicate the risk and return characteristics of the firm's real option to invest. The imputed value of the real option must equal that of the replicating portfolio, because otherwise there would be an arbitrage opportunity—an investor could make a pure profit by buying the cheaper and selling the dearer of the two identical assets.

We also examine some variants of the basic example. First, we expand the window of investment opportunity to three periods, where the price can go up or down between periods 2 and 3 just as it could between periods 1 and 2. We show how this changes the value of the option. Next, we examine uncertainty in the costs of the project and in the interest rate that is used to discount future profit flows. Finally, we consider choice between projects of different scales, a larger project having higher fixed costs but lower operating costs.

Even with these extensions and variations, the analysis remains at the level of an illustrative and very simple example rather than that of a theory with some claim to generality. In later chapters we proceed to develop a broader theoretical framework. But the example does yield some valuable insights that survive the generalization, and we summarize them here.

First, the example shows that the opportunity cost of the option to invest is a significant component of the firm's investment decision. The option value increases with the sunk cost of the investment and with the degree of uncertainty over the future price, the downside component of the risk being the most important aspect. These results are confirmed in more general models in Chapters 5–7.

Second, we will see that the option value is not affected if the firm is able to hedge the risk by trading in forward or futures markets. In efficient markets such risk is fairly priced, so any decrease in risk is offset by the decrease in return. The forward transaction is a financial operation that has no effect on the firm's real decisions. (This is another example of the Modigliani-Miller theorem at work.)

Third, when future costs are uncertain, their effect on the investment decision depends on the particular form of the uncertainty. If the uncertainty pertains to the price the firm must pay for an input, the effect is just like that of output price risk. The freedom not to invest if the input price turns out to have gone up is valuable, so immediate investment is less readily made. However, instead suppose that the project consists of several steps, the uncertainty pertains to the total cost of investment, and information about it will be revealed only as the first few steps of the project are undertaken. Then these steps have information value over and above their contribution to the conventionally calculated NPV. Thus it may be desirable to start the project even if orthodox NPV is somewhat negative. We return to this issue in Chapter 10 and model it in a more general theoretical framework.

Fourth, we will see that investment on a smaller scale, by increasing future flexibility, may have a value that offsets to some degree the advantage that a larger investment may enjoy due to economies of scale.

4.B Some Mathematical Tools

In reality, investment projects can have different windows of opportunity, and various aspects of the future can be uncertain in different ways. Therefore the simple two-period examples of Chapter 2 must be generalized greatly before they can be applied. Chapters 3 and 4 develop the mathematical tools that are needed for such a generalization.

Chapter 3 develops more general models of uncertainty. We start by explaining the nature and properties of *stochastic processes*. These processes combine dynamics with uncertainty. In a dynamic model without uncertainty, the current state of a system will determine its future state. When uncertainty is added, the current state determines only the probability distribution of future states, not the actual value. The specification in Chapter 2, where the current price could go either up or down by a fixed percentage with known probabilities, is but the simplest example. We describe two other processes that prove especially useful in the theory of investment—Brownian motion and Poisson processes—and examine some of their properties.

Chapter 4 concerns optimal sequential decisions under uncertainty. We begin with some basic ideas of the general mathematical technique for such optimization: dynamic programming. We introduce this by recapitulating the two-period example of Chapter 2, and showing how the basic ideas extend to more general multiperiod choice problems where the uncertainty takes the form of the kinds of stochastic processes introduced in Chapter 3. We establish the fundamental equation of dynamic programming, and indicate methods of solving it for the applications of special interest here. Then we turn to a market setting, where the risk generated by the stochastic process can be traded by continuous trading of contingent claims. We show how the sequential decisions can be equivalently handled by constructing a dynamic hedging strategy—a portfolio whose composition changes over time to replicate the return and risk characteristics of the real investment.

Readers who are already familiar with these techniques can skip these chapters, except perhaps for a quick glance to get used to our notation. Others not familiar with the techniques can use the chapters as a self-contained introduction to stochastic processes and stochastic dynamic optimization—even if their interests are in applications other than those discussed in the rest of the book.

4.C   The Firm's Investment Decision

These techniques are put to use in the chapters that follow. Chapters 5–7 constitute the core theory of a firm's investment decision. We begin in Chapter 5 by supposing that investment is totally irreversible. Then the value of the project in place is simply the expected present value of the stream of profits (or losses) it would generate. This can be computed in terms of the underlying uncertainty. Then the investment decision is simply the decision to pay the sunk cost and in return get an asset whose value can fluctuate. This is exactly analogous to the financial theory of call options—the right but not the obligation to purchase an asset of fluctuating value for a preset exercise price. Therefore the problem can be solved directly using the techniques developed in Chapter 4. The result is also familiar from financial theory. The option can be profitably exercised—is "in the money"—when the value of the asset rises above the exercise price. However, exercise is not optimal when the option is only just in the money, because by exercising it the firm gives up the opportunity to wait and avoid the loss it would suffer should the value fall. Only when the value of the asset rises sufficiently above the exercise price—the option is sufficiently "deep in the money"—does its exercise become optimal.

An alternative formulation of this idea would help the intuition of economists who think of investment in terms of Tobin's q, the ratio of the value of a capital asset to its replacement cost. In its usual interpretation in the investment literature, the value of a capital asset is measured as the expected present value of the profit flow it will generate. Then the conventional criterion for the firm is to invest when q equals or exceeds unity. Our option value criterion is more stringent; q must exceed unity by a sufficient margin. It must equal or exceed a critical or threshold value q^*, which itself exceeds unity, before investment becomes optimal.

We perform several numerical simulations to calculate the value of the option and the optimal exercise rule, and examine how these vary with the amount of the uncertainty, the discount rate, and other parameters. We find that for plausible ranges of these parameters, the option value effect is quantitatively very important. Waiting remains optimal even though the expected rate of return on immediate investment is substantially above the interest rate or the "normal" rate of return on capital. Return multiples of as much as two or three times the normal rate are typically needed before the firm will exercise its option and make the investment.

4.D   Interest Rates and Investment

Once we understand why and how firms should be cautious when deciding whether to exercise their investment options, we can also understand why interest rates seem to have so little effect on investment. Econometric tests of the orthodox theory generally find that interest rates are only a weak or insignificant determinant of investment demand. Recent history also shows that interest rate cuts tend to have only a limited stimulative effect on investment; the experience of 1991–1992 bears the latest witness to that. The options approach offers a simple explanation. A reduction in the interest rate makes the future generally more important relative to the present, but this increases the value of investing (the expected present value of the stream of profits) and the value of waiting (the ability to reduce or avoid the prospect of future losses) alike. The net effect is weak and sometimes even ambiguous.

The real options approach also suggests that various sources of uncertainty about future profits—fluctuations in product prices, input costs, exchange rates, tax and regulatory policies—have much more important effects on investment than does the overall level of interest rates. Uncertainty about the future path of interest rates may also affect investment more than the general level of the rates. Reduction or elimination of unnecessary uncertainty may be the best kind of public policy to stimulate investment. And the uncertainty generated by the very process of a lengthy policy debate on alternatives may be a serious deterrent to investment. Later, in Chapter 9, we construct specific examples that show how policy uncertainty can have a major negative effect on investment.

4.E Suspension and Abandonment

Chapters 6 and 7 extend the simple model. As future prices and/or costs fluctuate, the operating profit of a project in place may turn negative. In Chapter 5 we assumed that the investment was totally irreversible, and the firm was compelled to go on operating the project despite losses. This may be true of some public services, but most firms have some escape routes available. Chapters 6 and 7 examine some of these. In Chapter 6 we suppose that a loss-making project may be temporarily suspended, and its operation resumed later if and when it becomes profitable again. Now a project in place is a sequence of operating options; its value must be found by using the methods of Chapter 4 to value all these operating options, and then discount and add them. Then the investment opportunity is itself an option to acquire this compound asset.

In Chapter 7 we begin by ruling out temporary suspension, but we allow permanent abandonment. This is realistic if a live project has some tangible or intangible capital that disappears quickly if the project is not kept in operation—mines flood, machines rust, teams of skilled workers disband, and brand recognition is lost. If the firm decides to restart, it has to reinvest in all these assets. Abandonment may have a direct cost; for example, workers may have to be given severance payments. More importantly, however, it often has an opportunity cost—the loss of the option to preserve the capital so it can be used profitably should future circumstances improve. Therefore a firm with a project in place will tolerate some losses to keep this option alive, and only sufficiently extreme losses will induce it to abandon.

In fact we have here an interlinked pair of options. When the firm exercises its option to invest, it gets a project in place and an option to abandon. If it exercises the option to abandon, it gets the option to invest again. The two options must be priced simultaneously to determine the optimal investment and abandonment policies. The linkage has important implications; for example, a higher cost of abandonment makes the firm even more cautious about investing, and vice versa. We illustrate the theory using numbers that are typical of the copper industry, and find a very wide range of fluctuation of the price of copper between the investment and abandonment thresholds.

We also consider an intermediate situation, where both suspension and abandonment are available at different costs. A project in suspension requires some ongoing expenditure, for example, keeping a ship laid up, but restarting is cheap. Abandonment saves on the maintenance cost, and may even bring some immediate scrap value, but then the full investment cost must be incurred again if profit potential recovers. Now we must determine the optimal switches between three alternatives—an idle firm, an operating project, and a suspended project. We do this, and illustrate it for the case of crude oil tankers.

4.F Temporary versus Permanent Employment

While most of our attention in this book is on firms' capital investment choices, similar considerations apply to their hiring and firing decisions. Each of these choices entails sunk costs, each decision must be made in an uncertain environment, and each allows some freedom of timing. Therefore the above ideas and results can be applied. For example, a new worker will not be hired until the value of the marginal product of labor is sufficiently above the wage rate, and the required margin or multiple above the wage will be higher the greater the sunk costs or the greater the uncertainty.

The U.S. labor market in mid-1993 offered a vivid illustration of this theory in action. As the economy emerged from the recession of the early 1990s, firms increased production by using overtime and hiring temporary workers even for highly skilled positions. But permanent new full-time hiring was very slow to increase. The current level of profitability must have been high, since firms were willing to pay wage premiums of 50 percent for overtime work and to use agencies that supplied temporary workers and charged fees of 25 percent or more of the wage. But these same firms were not willing to make

the commitment involved in hiring regular new workers.[5] Our theory offers a
natural explanation for these observations. A high level of uncertainty about
future demand and costs prevailed at that time. The robustness and durability
of the recovery were unclear; it was feared that inflation would return and
lead the Federal Reserve to raise interest rates. Future tax policy was very
uncertain, as was the level of future health care costs that employers would
have to bear. Therefore we should have expected firms to be very cautious, and
wait for greater assurance of a continued prospect of high levels of profitability
before adding to their regular full-time labor force. In the meantime, they
would prefer to exploit the current profit opportunities using less irreversible
(even if more costly) methods of production, namely overtime and temporary
work. That is exactly what we saw.

4.G Hysteresis

When we consider investment and abandonment (or entry and exit) together,
a firm's optimal decision is characterized by two thresholds. A sufficiently
high current level of profit, corresponding to an above-normal rate of return
on the sunk cost, justifies investment or entry, while a sufficiently large level
of current loss leads to abandonment or exit. Now suppose the current level
of profit is somewhere between these two thresholds. Will we see an active
firm? That depends on the recent history of profit fluctuations. If the profit
is at its current intermediate level having most recently descended from a
high level that induced entry, then there will be an active firm. However, if
the intermediate level was most recently preceded by a low level that induced
exit, then there will not. In other words, the current state of the underlying
stochastic variable is not enough to determine the outcome in the economy;
a longer history is needed. The economy is *path dependent*.

   The idea of path dependence has been recently explored and illustrated,
most prominently by Arthur (1986) and David (1985, 1988). They allow an
even more extreme possibility: even very long-run properties of their systems
are altered by slight differences in initial conditions. Here we have a more
moderate kind of path dependence. The long-run distribution of the possible
states of the economy is unaltered, but the short- and medium-run evolution
can still be dramatically affected by initial conditions.

---

[5] Two articles describing these developments appeared in the New York Times on the same
day, Sunday, May 16, 1993: "Fewer Jobs Filled as Factories Rely on Overtime Pay," and "In a
Shaky Economy, Even Professionals Are Temps."

The path dependence can lead to the following kind of sequence of events. When the firm first arrives on the scene and contemplates investment, the current profit is in the intermediate range between the two thresholds. Therefore the firm decides to wait. Then profit rises past the upper threshold, so the firm invests. Finally, profit falls back to its old intermediate level, but that does not take it down to the lower threshold where abandonment would occur. Thus the underlying cause (current profitability) has been restored to its old level, but its effect (investment) has not.

Similar effects have long been known in physics and other sciences. The most familiar example comes from electromagnetism. Take an iron bar and loop an insulated wire around it. Pass an electric current through the wire: the iron will become magnetized. Now switch the current off. The magnetism is not completely lost; some residual effect remains. The cause (the current) was temporary, but it leaves a longer-lasting effect (the magnetized bar).

This phenomenon is called *hysteresis*, and by analogy the failure of investment decisions to reverse themselves when the underlying causes are fully reversed can be called economic hysteresis. A striking example occurred during the 1980s. From 1980 to 1984, the dollar rose sharply against other currencies. The cost advantage of foreign firms in US markets became very substantial, and ultimately led to a large rise in US imports. Then the dollar fell sharply, and by 1987 was back to its 1980 level. However, the import penetration was not fully reversed; in fact it hardly decreased at all. It took a larger fall in the dollar to achieve any significant reduction in imports.

4.H   Industry Equilibrium

In Chapters 8 and 9 the focus turns from a firm's investment decisions to the equilibrium of a whole industry composed of many such firms. One's first reaction might be that the competition among firms will destroy any one firm's option to wait, eliminating the effects of irreversibility and uncertainty that we found in Chapters 5–7. Competition does destroy each firm's option to wait, but this does not restore the present value approach and results of the orthodox theory. On the contrary, caution when making an irreversible decision remains important, but for somewhat different reasons.

Consider one firm contemplating its investment, knowing that the future path of industry demand and its own costs are uncertain, and knowing that there are many other firms facing similar decisions with similar uncertainty. The firm is ultimately concerned with the consequences of its decision for its own profits, but it must recognize how the similar decisions of other firms will affect it. In this respect, two types of uncertainty must be distinguished because they can have different implications for investment: aggregate uncertainty that affects all firms in the industry, and firm-specific or idiosyncratic uncertainty facing each firm.

To see this, first suppose that investment is totally irreversible, and consider an industry-wide increase in demand. Any one firm expects this to lead to a higher price, and so improve its own profit prospects, making investment more attractive. However, it also knows that several other firms are making a similar calculation. Their supply response will dampen the effect of the demand shift on the industry price. Therefore the upward shift of its own profit potential will not be quite as high as in the case where it is the only firm and has a monopoly on the investment opportunity. However, with investment being irreversible, a downward shift of industry demand has just as unfavorable an effect in the competitive case as in the monopoly case. Even though other competitive firms are just as badly affected, they cannot exit to cushion the fall in price. Thus the competitive response to uncertainty has an inherent asymmetry: the downside exerts a more potent effect than the upside. This asymmetry makes each firm cautious in making the irreversible investment. The ultimate effect is very similar, and in some models identical, to that of the option value for a firm possessing a monopoly on the investment opportunity and waiting to exercise it. In fact, the theory of a competitive industry can be formulated by giving each firm the option to invest, valuing these real options as in Chapters 5–7, and finally imposing the condition that in the competitive equilibrium this option value should be zero.

If we allow some reversibility, the exit of other firms does cushion the effect of adverse demand shocks on price. But then each firm's exit decision recognizes this asymmetric effect of demand shocks in an initially poor situation: their upside effect is more potent than the downside. Thus competitive firms are not quick to leave when they start to make operating losses; they wait a while to see if things improve or if their rivals leave. The overall effect is just like that for a single monopoly firm's abandonment decision that we found in Chapter 7. In fact, the competitive equilibrium model of joint entry and exit decisions with aggregate demand shocks that we analyze in Chapter 8 has exactly the same critical levels of high and low prices to trigger entry and exit as the corresponding monopoly model of Chapter 7.

Firm-specific uncertainty does not lead to this kind of asymmetry. If just one firm experiences a favorable shift of its demand, say some idiosyncratic switch of fashion, then it knows that this good fortune is not systematically shared by other firms, and therefore does not fear that entry of other firms will erode its profit potential in the same way. However, then the value of waiting reemerges in the older familiar form. The lucky firm does have a monopoly on the opportunity to enter with its low cost. Therefore it also has an option value of waiting; it can thereby avoid a loss if its low cost should turn out to be transitory. Thus firm-specific uncertainty in industry equilibrium also leads to investment decisions similar to those found in Chapters 5–7 for an isolated firm.

4.I   Policy Toward Investment

Some readers might interpret the result that uncertainty makes firms less eager to invest as indicating a need for government policy intervention to stimulate investment. That would be a hasty reaction. A social planner also gets information by waiting, and therefore should also recognize the opportunity cost of sinking resources into a project. A case for policy intervention will arise only if firms face a different value of waiting than does society as a whole, in other words, if some market failure is associated with the decision process.

Chapter 9 focuses on these issues. Our first result is a confirmation of the standard theory of general equilibrium. If markets for risk are complete, and if firms behave as competitive price- takers (in this stochastic dynamic context this must be interpreted to mean that each firm takes as given the stochastic process of the price and has rational expectations about it), then the equilibrium evolution of the industry is socially efficient. A social planner would show the same degree of hesitancy in making the investment decision.

If markets for risk are incomplete, beneficial policy interventions do exist, but the correct policy needs some careful calculation and implementation. The blunt tools that are often used for handling uncertainty can have adverse effects. We illustrate this by examining the consequences of price ceilings and floors. For example, price supports promote investment by reducing the downside risk. However, the resulting rightward shift of the industry supply function implies lower prices in good times. Averaging over good times and bad, we find that the overall result is a *lower* long-run average price. In other words, the policy is harming the very group it sets out to help. Price floor or ceiling policies, for example, urban rent controls and agricultural price supports, are usually criticized because they reduce overall economic efficiency. Our finding is perhaps a politically more potent argument against them: their distributional effect can be perverse, too.

We also study the effect of uncertainty concerning future policy itself. For example, if an investment tax credit is being discussed, firms will recognize more value in waiting, because there is a probability that the cost of investment to the firm will fall. We find that such policy uncertainty can have a powerful deterrent effect on immediate investment. If governments wish to stimulate investment, perhaps the worst thing they can do is to spend a long time discussing the right way to do so.

4.J Antitrust and Trade Policies

Chapters 8 and 9 paint a very different picture of competitive equilibrium than the one familiar from intermediate microeconomics textbooks. There we are told that firms will enter the industry if the price rises to equal the long-run average cost, and they will exit if the price falls as low as the average variable cost. Our theory implies a wider range of price variation on either side. For example, in the face of aggregate uncertainty, firms' entry as soon as the price rises to the long-run average cost will not constitute an industry equilibrium. Each firm knows that entry of other similar firms will stop the price from ever rising any higher, while future unfavorable shifts can push the price below this level. Also, a future price path that sometimes touches the long-run average cost and otherwise stays below this level can never offer a normal return on the firm's investment. Only if the price ceiling imposed by entry is strictly above the long-run average cost can the mix of intervals of supernormal profit and ones of subnormal profit average out to a normal return. Similarly, firms will exit only when the price falls sufficiently far below the average variable cost. They will tolerate some losses, knowing that the exit of other firms puts a lower bound on the price. The equilibrium level of this floor is determined by averaging out the prospects of future losses and profits to zero.

Thus we find that competitive equilibrium under uncertainty is not a stationary state even in the long run, but a dynamic process where prices can fluctuate quite widely. Periods of supernormal profits can alternate with periods of losses. A similar view of dynamic equilibrium as a stochastic process has become quite common in macroeconomics, but is surprisingly uncommon in microeconomics, particularly with regard to its implications for antitrust policy or international trade policy. The conceptual framework of such policies is generally static, and the recommendations in practice are based on observations of "snapshots" of an industry at a particular instant. We find that the dynamic view calls for a substantial rethinking of both the theory and the practice.

For example, in industrial organization theory, excess profits suggest collusion or entry barriers, calling for antitrust action. In our dynamic perspective, substantial periods of supernormal profits without new entry can occur even though all firms are small price takers. In international trade, when foreign firms continue their export operations at a loss, domestic firms allege predatory dumping and call for the standard trade policy response of countervailing import duties. However, our analysis suggests that the foreign firms may be simply and rationally keeping alive their option of future operation in our market, with no predatory intent whatever. Only a sufficiently long time series of data will allow us to test whether the supposed collusive or predatory actions are merely natural phases in the evolution of a competitive industry or genuine failures of competition.

4.K Sequential and Incremental Investment

In Chapters 10 and 11 we return to a single firm's investment decision and examine some other aspects of it that are important in applications. Chapter 10 deals with investments that consist of several stages, all of which must be completed in sequence before any output or profit flow can commence. The firm can constantly observe some indicator of the future profit potential, and this fluctuates stochastically. At any stage, the firm may decide to continue immediately, or wait for conditions to improve. At an early stage of the investment sequence, most of the cost remains to be sunk. Therefore the firm will go ahead with the program only if it sees a sufficiently high threshold level of the indicator of profitability. Gradually, as more steps are completed and less cost remains to be sunk, the next step is justified by an ever smaller threshold. In this sense, bygones affect the decisions to come.

In Chapter 10 we examine another effect of current decisions on the future, namely the learning curve. According to this theory, the cost of production at any instant is a decreasing function of cumulated output experience. Thus the current output flow contributes to a reduction in all future production costs. This additional value must be added to the current revenues before comparing them to the current costs of production to decide on the optimal level of production. We examine the dynamic output path under these conditions. We find that greater uncertainty lowers the value of future cost reductions, and that leads to a reduction in the pace of investment.

In Chapter 11 we turn to the study of incremental investment, where output and profit flow are available all the time as a function of the installed stock of capital. The aim is to characterize the optimal policy for capacity expansion. When production shows diminishing returns to capital, we can regard each new unit of capacity as a fresh project, which begins to contribute its marginal product from the date of its installation. Then the criterion derived in Chapter 6 for investment in such a project continues to apply. If production shows increasing returns to capital over an interval, then all the units of capacity in an appropriately constructed range must be regarded as a single project, and the criterion for its installation is again a natural generalization of that for a single project described in Chapter 6.

When the firm can choose its rate of capacity expansion, we must specify how the costs of this expansion depend on its volume and pace. Different assumptions in this respect imply different optimal policies. We construct a general model that places the alternatives in context, and in particular shows the relationship between the adjustment costs models that have been the mainstay of theoretical and empirical work over the last decade and the irreversibility approach that has been the focus of our book.

4.L   Empirical and Applied Research

In Chapter 12 we turn to some examples that illustrate applications and extensions of the techniques developed throughout the book. We also discuss the relevance of the theory for empirical work on investment behavior.

We begin Chapter 12 with a problem of great interest to oil companies—how to value an undeveloped offshore oil reserve, and how to decide when to invest in development and production. As we will see, an undeveloped reserve is essentially an option; it gives the owner the right to invest in development of the reserve and then produce the oil. By valuing this option we can value the reserve and determine when it should be developed. Oil companies regularly spend hundreds of millions of dollars for offshore reserves, so it is clearly important to determine how to value and best exploit them.

We then turn to an investment timing problem in the electric utility industry. The Clean Air Act calls for reductions in overall emissions of sulfur dioxide, but to minimize the cost of these reductions, it gives utilities a choice. They can invest in expensive "scrubbers" to reduce emissions to mandated levels, or they can buy tradeable "allowances" that let them pollute. There is considerable uncertainty over the future prices of allowances, and an investment in scrubbers is irreversible. The utility must decide whether to maintain flexibility by relying on allowances or invest in scrubbers. We show how this problem can be addressed using the options approach of this book.

To show how the principles and tools developed in this book have relevance beyond firms' investment decisions, we address a problem in public policy—when should the government adopt a policy in response to a threat to the environment, given that the future costs and benefits of the policy are uncertain? We will argue that the standard cost-benefit framework that economists have traditionally used to evaluate environmental policies is deficient. The reason is that there are usually important irreversibilities associated with environmental policy. These irreversibilities can arise with respect to environmental damage itself, but also with respect to the costs of adapting to policies to reduce the damage. Since the adoption of an environmental policy is rarely a now or never proposition, the same techniques used to study the optimal timing of an investment can be applied to the optimal timing of an environmental policy.

At the end of Chapter 12, we discuss some of the empirical implications of irreversibility and uncertainty for investment behavior. There is considerable anecdotal evidence that firms make investment decisions in a way that is at least roughly consistent with the theory developed in this book, for example, the use of hurdle rates that are much larger than the opportunity cost of capital as predicted by the capital asset pricing model. Some numerical simulations based on plausible parameters for costs and uncertainty are found to replicate features of reality. However, more systematic econometric testing of the theory is still at a very early stage. We review some work of this kind, point out its difficulties, and suggest ideas for future research.

5   Noneconomic Applications

Our focus in the book will be on investment decisions of firms and their implications for industry equilibrium. These matters are of primary interest to economists, their conditions (technology and resource availability) and criteria (maximization of the value of the firm) are generally agreed upon, and theory leads to quantifiable predictions about them. Investment decisions of consumers (purchase of durables) and workers (education and human capital) have obvious parallels. Research on these issues already exists, and we will sketch some of this literature in Chapter 12.

Many other personal and societal choices are made under the same basic conditions, namely irreversibility, ongoing uncertainty, and some leeway in timing. Therefore we can think about them in terms of some of the models and results outlined above, and offer some qualitative speculations. We believe there is scope for more serious research along these lines. This would amount to extending work such as that of Becker (1975, 1980) on economic approaches to social phenomena by incorporation of option values. Indeed, some recognition of this aspect can be read into Becker's own remarks on the subject, for example, in Becker (1962, pp. 22–23), but a more thorough and formal analysis along these lines remains a potentially fruitful project for the future. Although we cannot spare much space in an already lengthy book, we believe that readers will find some speculations along these lines both interesting and thought-provoking.

5.A   Marriage and Suicide

Marriage entails significant costs of courtship, and divorce has its own monetary and emotional costs. Happiness or misery within the marriage can be only imperfectly forecast in advance, and continues to fluctuate stochastically even after the event. Therefore waiting for a better match has an option value, and we should expect prospective partners to look for a sufficiently high initial threshold of compatibility to justify getting married. We should expect the option value to be higher in religions or cultures where marriage is less reversible. Therefore we should expect that, other things being equal, individuals in such societies will search more carefully (and on the average, search longer), and will insist on a higher threshold of the quality of the match. On the contrary, when divorce is easy, we should see couples entering into marriage (or equivalent arrangements) more readily.

Of course, other things are not equal. Societies that make divorce more difficult presumably attach higher value to marriage. Therefore we should expect them to counteract the rational search and delay on the part of individuals by social pressure, and provision of better "matchmaking technologies." Empirical tests of these ideas will have to be designed carefully to distinguish the separate and often opposing influences, but that only raises the interest and challenge of such research.

Perhaps the most extreme example of economics applied to sociological phenomena is the Beckerian theory of suicide developed by Hamermesh and Soss (1974). According to them, an individual will end his or her own life when the expected present value of the utility of the rest of life falls short of a benchmark or cutoff standard "zero." Most people react by saying that the model gives an excessively rational view of what is an inherently irrational action. Our theory suggests exactly the opposite. Whatever its merits or demerits as descriptive theory, the Hamermesh-Soss model is *not rational enough* from the prescriptive viewpoint, because it forgets the option value of staying alive. Suicide is the ultimate irreversible act, and the future has a lot of ongoing uncertainty. Therefore the option value of waiting to see if "something will improve" should be very large. The circumstances must be far more bleak than the cutoff standard of the Hamermesh-Soss model to justify pulling the trigger. This is true even if the expected direction of life is still downward; all that is needed is some positive probability on the upside.

Now return to the argument that most suicides are irrational, and ask exactly how they fail to be rational. There are several possibilities, but one seems especially pertinent. Suicides project the bleak present into an equally bleak future, ignoring uncertainty, and thereby ignoring the option value of life. Then religious or social proscriptions against suicide serve a useful function as measures to compensate for this failure of rationality. By raising the perceived cost of the act, these taboos lower the threshold of quality of life that leads to suicide when option value is ignored. This can correct the failure of the individuals' forethought, and bring their threshold in conformity with the optimal rule that recognizes the option value.

5.B Legal Reform and Constitutions

Finally, consider law reform. Different fundamental constitutional or legal principles often conflict with one another in specific contexts; for example, the civil rights of the accused often stand in the way of better enforcement of law and order. Public opinion as to the appropriate relative weight to be attached to these conflicting principles can shift over time. How quickly should the law respond to the latest swing of opinion? Given some legislative and administrative costs of changing laws, our theory suggests that the option to wait and see if the trend of opinion will reverse itself has some value. Reform should be delayed until the force of current opinion is sufficiently overwhelming to offset this value. But there is good reason to believe that the process is subject to a kind of myopia or "political market failure." At all times, people and politicians tend to believe that at last they have got it right; the balance of opinion that has just been reached will prevail forever. Therefore they will ignore future uncertainty and option values, and change the laws too frequently.

The time to anticipate and defeat this tendency is when the constitution is framed. Knowing that future generations will be too trigger-happy in changing laws, the founding fathers can artificially raise the cost of change, thereby making the politically flawed thresholds for legal change coincide with the truly optimal thresholds. Thus various supermajority requirements for constitutional change can be seen as a commitment device that corrects for the shortsightedness of future generations.

These are just a few examples of how the theory and techniques developed in this book are applicable to some fairly far-reaching problems. We have deliberately stated them in speculative and provocative ways, hoping to attract interest and research along these lines from a broader spectrum of social scientists. In the rest of the book, we will focus largely on investment, but ask the reader to keep in mind the much broader potential applicability of the theory.

Chapter 2

Developing the Concepts Through Simple Examples

FIRMS MAKE, implement, and sometimes revise their investment decisions continuously through time. Hence much of this book is devoted to the analysis of investment decisions as continuous-time problems. However, it is best to begin with some simple examples, involving a minimal amount of mathematics, in which investment decisions are made at two or three discrete points in time. In this way, we can convey at the outset an intuitive understanding of the basic concepts. In particular, we want to show how the irreversibility of an investment expenditure affects the decision to invest, and how it requires modification of the standard net present value (NPV) rule that is commonly taught in business schools. We also want to show how an opportunity to invest is much like a financial option, and can be valued and analyzed according.

This chapter begins by discussing these ideas in the context of a simple example in which an investment decision can be made in only one of two possible periods—now or next year. We will use this example to see how irreversibility creates an opportunity cost of investing when the future value of the project is uncertain, and how this opportunity cost can be accounted for when making the investment decision. We will also see how the investment decision can be analyzed using basic option pricing techniques. We will examine the characteristics of the firm's option to invest in some detail, and see how the value of that option, and the investment decision, depend on the degree of uncertainty over the future value of the project. Extending the example to three periods will provide more insight into the problem of investment timing, and set the stage for modelling investment problems in continuous time. Finally, we will briefly examine investment decisions when the *cost* of the investment (as opposed to its payoff) is uncertain, when future interest rates are uncertain, and when one must choose the scale of an investment.

1 Price Uncertainty Lasting Two Periods

Consider a firm that is trying to decide whether to invest in a widget factory. The investment is completely irreversible—the factory can only be used to make widgets, and should the market for widgets evaporate, the firm cannot "uninvest" and recover its expenditure. To keep matters as simple as possible, we will assume that the factory can be built instantly, at a cost I, and will produce one widget per year forever, with zero operating cost. Currently the price of a widget is \$200, but next year the price will change. With probability q, it will rise to \$300, and with probability $(1 - q)$, it will fall to \$100. The price will then remain at this new level forever. (See Figure 2.1.)

Again, to keep things simple, we will assume that the risk over the future price of widgets is fully diversifiable (that is, it is unrelated to what happens with the overall economy). Hence the firm should discount future cash flows using the risk-free rate of interest, which we will take to be 10 percent.

For the time being we will set $I = \$1600$ and $q = 0.5$. (Later we will see how the investment decision depends on I and q.) Given these values for I and q, is this a good investment? Should the firm invest now, or would it be better to wait a year and see whether the price of widgets goes up or down? Suppose we invest now. Calculating the net present value of this investment in the standard way (and noting that the *expected* future price of widgets is

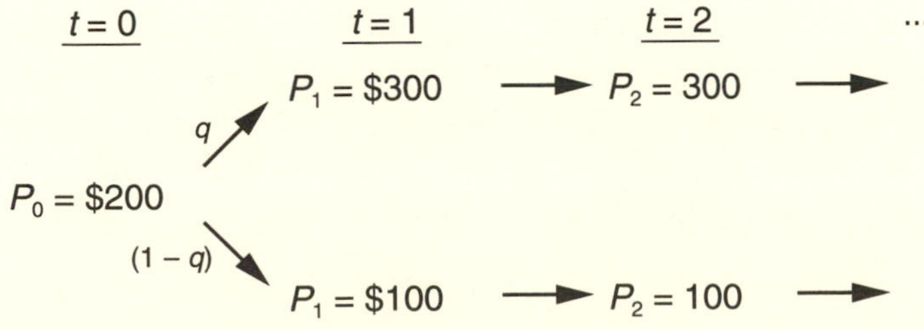

Figure 2.1. Price of Widgets

always $200), we get

$$\text{NPV} = -1600 + \sum_{t=0}^{\infty} \frac{200}{(1.1)^t} = -1600 + 2200 = \$600. \qquad (1)$$

It appears that the NPV of this project is positive. The current value of a widget factory, which we will denote by V_0, is equal to $2200, which exceeds the $1600 cost of the factory. Hence it would seem that we should go ahead with the investment.

This conclusion is incorrect, however, because the calculations above ignore a cost—the opportunity cost of investing now, rather than waiting and keeping open the possibility of not investing should the price fall. To see this, let us calculate the NPV of this project a second time, this time assuming that instead of investing now, we will wait one year and then invest only if the price of widgets goes up. (Investing only if the price goes up is in fact ex post optimal.) In this case the NPV is given by[1]

$$\text{NPV} = (0.5) \left[\frac{-1600}{1.1} + \sum_{t=1}^{\infty} \frac{300}{(1.1)^t} \right] = \frac{850}{1.1} = \$773. \qquad (2)$$

(Note that in year 0, there is no expenditure and no revenue. In year 1, the $1600 is spent only if the price rises to $300, which will happen with probability 0.5.) If we wait a year before deciding whether to invest in the factory, the project's NPV today is $773, whereas it is only $600 if we invest in the factory now. Clearly it is better to wait than to invest right away.

Note that if our only choices were to invest today or never invest, we would invest today. In that case there is no option to wait a year, and hence no opportunity cost to killing such an option, so the standard NPV rule applies. We would likewise invest today if next year we could disinvest and recover our $1600 should the price of widgets fall. Two things are needed to introduce an opportunity cost into the NPV calculation—irreversibility, and the ability to invest in the future as an alternative to investing today. There are, of course, situations in which a firm cannot wait, or cannot wait very long, to invest. (One example is the anticipated entry of a competitor into a market that is only large enough for one firm. Another example is a patent or mineral resource lease that is about to expire.) The less time there is to delay, and the greater the cost of delaying, the less will irreversibility affect the investment decision. We will explore this point later in this book as we develop more general models of investment.

---

[1] In all of the calculations below, we have rounded the results to the nearest dollar.

How much is it worth to have the flexibility to make the investment decision next year, rather than having to invest either now or never? (We know that having this flexibility is of some value, because we would prefer to wait rather than invest now.) The value of this "flexibility option" is easy to calculate; it is just the difference between the two NPV's, that is, $773 − $600 =$173. In other words, we should be willing to pay $173 more for an investment opportunity that is flexible than one that only allows us to invest now.

Another way to look at the value of flexibility is to ask the following question: How high an investment cost I would we be willing to accept to have a flexible investment opportunity rather than an inflexible "now or never" one? To answer this, we find the value of I, which we denote by $\overline{I}$, that makes the NPV of the project when we wait equal to the NPV when $I = \$1600$ and we invest now, that is, equal to $600. Substituting $\overline{I}$ for the $1600 and substituting $600 for the $773 in equation (2):

$$\text{NPV} = (0.5)\left[\frac{-\overline{I}}{1.1} + \sum_{t=1}^{\infty} \frac{300}{(1.1)^t}\right] = \$600. \tag{3}$$

Solving this for $\overline{I}$ yields $\overline{I} = \$1980$. In other words, the opportunity to build a widget factory *now and only now* at a cost of $1600 has the same value as an opportunity to build the widget factory *now or next year* at a cost of $1980.

Finally, suppose there exists a futures market for widgets, with the futures price for delivery one year from now equal to the expected future spot price, that is, $200.[2] Would the ability to hedge on the futures market change our investment decision? Specifically, would it lead us to invest now, rather than waiting a year? The answer is no. To see this, consider investing now and hedging the price risk with futures contracts. To hedge all price risk, we would need to sell short futures for 11 widgets; this would exactly offset any fluctuations in the NPV of our project next year. (If the price of widgets rises to $300, our project would be worth $3300, but we would lose $1100 on the futures contract. If the price fell to $100, our project would be worth only $1100, but we would earn an additional $1100 from the futures. Either way, we end up

[2]In this example, the futures price would equal the expected future price because we assumed that the risk is fully diversifiable. (If the price of widgets were positively correlated with the market portfolio, the futures price would be less than the expected future spot price.) Note that if widgets were storable and aggregate storage is positive, the marginal convenience yield from holding inventory would have to be 10 percent. The reason is that since the futures price equals the current spot price, the net holding cost (the interest cost of 10 percent less the marginal convenience yield) must be zero.

with a net project value of $2200.) But this would also mean that the NPV of our project today is $600 ($2200 less the $1600 cost of the investment), exactly what it is without hedging.[3]

Hence there is no gain from hedging, and we are still better off waiting until next year to make our investment decision. This result is a variant of the Modigliani-Miller (1958) theorem. Operating in the futures market is only a form of financial policy, and barring the possibility of bankruptcy, it has no real consequences for investment decisions or for the value of the firm's investment opportunities.

1.A   Analogy to Financial Options

Our investment opportunity is analogous to a call option on a common stock. It gives us the right (which we need not exercise) to make an investment expenditure (the exercise price of the option) and receive a project (a share of stock) the value of which fluctuates stochastically. In the case of our simple example, we have an option that is *"in the money,"* meaning that if it were exercised today it would yield a positive net payoff. (An option is said to be *"out of the money"* if exercising it today yields a negative net payoff.) We found that even though the option is "in the money," it is better to wait rather than exercise it now. Next year if the price rises to $300, we will exercise our option by paying $1600 and receive an asset which will be worth $V_1 = \$3300 = \sum_0^\infty 300/(1.1)^t$. If the price falls to $100, this asset will be worth only $1100, and so we will not exercise the option.

We found that the value of our investment opportunity (assuming that the actual decision to invest can indeed be made next year) is $773. It will be helpful to recalculate this value using standard option pricing methods, because later we will use such methods to analyze other investment problems.

To do this, let F_0 denote the value today of the investment opportunity, that is, what we should be willing to pay today to have the option to invest in the widget factory, and let F_1 denote the value of this investment opportunity next year. Note that F_1 is a random variable; it depends on what happens to the price of widgets. If the price rises to $300, then F_1 will equal $\sum_0^\infty 300/(1.1)^t - 1600 = \$1700$. On the other hand, if the price falls to $100, the option to invest

---

[3] Most futures markets only apply to horizons of a year or so. If there were a futures market for widgets over the indefinite future, an equivalent hedge would be to sell short one widget in each future year, that is, to sell forward the entire output stream. The result would be the same.

will go unexercised, and in that case F_1 will equal 0. Thus we know all possible values for F_1. The problem is to find F_0, the value of the option today.[4]

To solve this problem, we will create a portfolio that has two components: the investment opportunity itself, and a certain number of widgets. We will pick this number of widgets so that the portfolio is risk-free, that is, so that its value next year is independent of whether the price of widgets goes up or down. Since the portfolio will be risk-free, we know that the rate of return one can earn from holding it must be the risk-free rate of interest. (If the return on the portfolio were higher than the risk-free rate, arbitrageurs could earn unlimited amounts of money by borrowing at the risk-free rate and buying the portfolio. If the portfolio's return were less than the risk-free rate, arbitrageurs could earn money by selling short the portfolio and investing the funds at the risk-free rate.) By setting the portfolio's return equal to the risk-free rate, we will be able to calculate the current value of the investment opportunity.

Specifically, consider a portfolio in which one holds the investment opportunity, and sells short n widgets. (If widgets were a traded commodity, such as oil, one could obtain a short position by borrowing from another producer, or by going short in the futures market. For the moment, however, we need not be concerned with the actual implementation of this portfolio.) The value of this portfolio today is $\Phi_0 = F_0 - n P_0 = F_0 - 200 n$. The value of the portfolio next year is $\Phi_1 = F_1 - n P_1$. This depends on P_1. If P_1 turns out to be $300, so that $F_1 = 1700$, then $\Phi_1 = 1700 - 300 n$. If P_1 turns out to be $100, so that $F_1 = 0$, then $\Phi_1 = -100 n$. Now, let us choose n so that the portfolio is risk-free, that is, so that Φ_1 is independent of what happens to the price. To do this, just set

$$1700 - 300 n = -100 n, \tag{4}$$

or, $n = 8.5$. With n chosen in this way, $\Phi_1 = -850$, whether the price of widgets rises to $300 or falls to $100.

Now let us calculate the return from holding this portfolio. That return is the capital gain, $\Phi_1 - \Phi_0$, minus any payments that must be made to hold the short position. Since the expected rate of capital gain on a widget is zero (the expected price next year is $200, the same as this year's price), no rational investor would hold a long position unless he or she could expect to earn at least 10 percent. Hence selling widgets short will require a payment of

---

[4]In this example, all uncertainty is resolved next year. Therefore an option to wait has no value next year, and investment is made according to the conventional NPV criterion at that time. Waiting has relevance only this year. In later chapters we will consider more general situations where uncertainty is never fully resolved, and the option to wait retains value at all times.

$0.1\,P_0 = \$20$ per widget per year. (This is analogous to selling short a dividend-paying stock; the short position requires payment of the dividend, because no rational investor will hold the offsetting long position without receiving that dividend.) Our portfolio has a short position of 8.5 widgets, so it will have to pay out a total of \$170. The return from holding this portfolio over the year is therefore

$$\Phi_1 - \Phi_0 - 170 = \Phi_1 - (F_0 - n\,P_0) - 170$$
$$= -850 - F_0 + 1700 - 170$$
$$= 680 - F_0.$$

Because this return is risk-free, we know that it must equal the risk-free rate, which we have assumed is 10 percent, times the initial value of the portfolio, $\Phi_0 = F_0 - n\,P_0$:

$$680 - F_0 = 0.1\,(F_0 - 1700). \tag{5}$$

We can thus determine that $F_0 = \$773$. Note that this is the same value that we obtained before by calculating the NPV of the investment opportunity under the assumption that we follow the optimal strategy of waiting a year before deciding whether to invest.

We have found that the value of our investment opportunity, that is, the value of the option to invest in this project, is \$773. The payoff from investing (exercising the option) today is \$2200 – \$1600 = \$600. But once we invest, our option is gone, so the \$773 is an opportunity cost of investing. Hence the *full cost* of investing today is \$1600 + \$773 = \$2373 > \$2200. As a result, we should wait and keep our option alive, rather than invest today. We have thus come to the same conclusion as we did by comparing NPV's. This time, however, we calculated the value of the option to invest, and explicitly took it into account as one of the costs of investing.

Our calculation of the value of the option to invest was based on the construction of a risk-free portfolio, which requires that one can trade (hold a long or short position in) widgets. Of course, we could just as well have constructed our portfolio using some other asset, or combination of assets, the price of which is perfectly correlated with the price of widgets. But what if one cannot trade widgets, and there are no other assets that "span" the risk in a widget's price? In this case one could still calculate the value of the option to invest the way we did at the outset—by computing the NPV for each investment strategy (invest today versus wait a year and invest if the price goes up), and picking the strategy that yields the highest NPV. That is essentially the dynamic programming approach. In this case it gives exactly the same answer, because all price risk is diversifiable. Later in this book we will explore this connection between option pricing and dynamic programming in more detail.

1.B   Characteristics of the Option to Invest

We have seen how our investment decision is analogous to the decision to exercise an option, and we were able to value the option to invest in much the same way that financial call options are valued. To get more insight into the nature of the investment option, let us see how its value depends on various parameters. In particular, we will determine how the value of the option—and the decision to invest—depend on the direct cost of the investment, I, on the initial price of widgets, P_0, on the magnitudes of the up and down movements in price next period, and on the probability q that the price will rise next period.

Changing the Cost of the Investment

So far we have fixed the cost of the investment, I, at \$1600. How much would the option to invest be worth if I were above or below this number? We can find out by going through the same steps that we did before. Doing so, it is easy to see that the short position needed to obtain a risk-free portfolio depends on I as follows:[5]

$$n = 16.5 - 0.005\, I. \tag{6}$$

The current value of the option to invest is then given by

$$F_0 = 1500 - 0.455\, I. \tag{7}$$

Equation (7) gives the value of the investment opportunity as a function of the direct cost of the investment, I. We saw earlier that if $I = \$1600$, it is better to wait a year rather than invest today. Are there values of I for which investing today is the preferred strategy?

To answer this, recall that we should invest today as long as the payoff from investing is at least as large as the *full* cost, that is, the direct cost, I, plus the opportunity cost F_0. Since the payoff from investing today is $V_0 = \$2200$,

---

[5] As before, the value of the portfolio next year is $\Phi_1 = F_1 - n\, P_1$. If $P_1 = \$300$, $F_1 = 3300 - I$, so $\Phi_1 = 3300 - I - 300\, n$. If $P_1 = \$100$, and I is not so low that we would invest anyway, $F_1 = 0$, and $\Phi_1 = -100\, n$. Setting the Φ_1's for each price scenario equal gives the equation above for n.

we should invest today if $2200 > I + F_0$. Substituting in equation (7) for F_0, we should invest as long as

$$I + 1500 - 0.455\, I < 2200.$$

Thus, if $I < \$1284$, one should invest today rather than wait. The reason is that waiting means giving up revenue in the first year, and in this case the lost revenue exceeds the opportunity cost of committing resources rather than keeping the investment option open. However, if $I = \$1284$, $F_0 = \$916 = V_0 - I$, and one would be indifferent between investing today and waiting until next year. (This can also be seen by comparing the project's NPV if we invest today with the NPV if we wait until next year; in either case the NPV is \$916.) And if $I > \$1284$, one is better off waiting.

The dependence of F_0 on I is illustrated in Figure 2.2. This graph shows the value of the option, F_0, and the net payoff from investing today, $V_0 - I$, both as functions of I. For $I > \$1284$, $F_0 = 1500 - 0.455\, I > V_0 - I$, so the option should be kept alive, that is, we should wait until next year before deciding whether to invest. However, if $I < \$1284$, $F_0 = 1500 - 0.455\, I < V_0 - I$, so the option should be exercised now, and hence the value of the option is just its net payoff, $V_0 - I$.

In the terminology of options, when I is small, the net payoff from immediate investment becomes large, or the option is "deep in the money." At a critical point or threshold where it is sufficiently deep, the cost of waiting

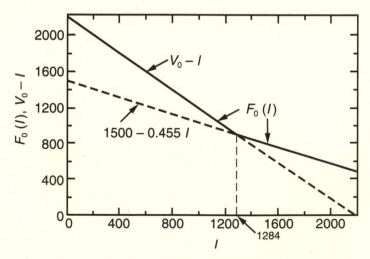

Figure 2.2.   *Option to Invest in Widget Factory*

(the sacrifice of the immediate profit) outweighs the benefit of waiting (the value of the ability to decide optimally after observing whether the price has gone up or down), and immediate exercise becomes optimal.

Changing the Initial Price

Let us again fix the cost of the investment, I, at \$1600, but now vary the initial price of widgets, P_0. To do this, we will assume that whatever P_0 happens to be, with probability 0.5 the price next year will be 50 percent higher, and with probability 0.5 it will be 50 percent lower. (See Figure 2.3.)

To value the option to invest, we again set up a risk-free portfolio in which we hold the option and sell short some number of widgets. The value of this portfolio today is $\Phi_0 = F_0 - n\,P_0$. Its value next year depends on P_1. The value of a widget factory next year is $V_1 = \sum_0^\infty P_1/(1.1)^t = 11\,P_1$, but we will only invest in the factory if its value exceeds \$1600, the cost of the investment. Hence $F_1 = \max[0, 11\,P_1 - 1600]$. Suppose P_0 is in the range where if the price goes up next year (that is, if $P_1 = 1.5\,P_0$) it will be worthwhile to invest, but if the price goes down it will not. (We will consider other possibilities shortly.) Then $\Phi_1 = 16.5\,P_0 - 1600 - 1.5\,n\,P_0$ if the price goes up, and $\Phi_1 = -0.5\,n\,P_0$ if the price goes down. Equating the Φ_1's for these two scenarios gives the value of n that makes the portfolio risk-free:

$$n = 16.5 - 1600/P_0. \tag{8}$$

Note that with n chosen this way, $\Phi_1 = -8.25\,P_0 + 800$ whether the price goes up or down.

Now let us calculate the return on this portfolio, remembering that the short position will require a payment of $0.1\,n\,P_0 = 1.65\,P_0 - 160$. That return is $6.60\,P_0 - F_0 - 640$. Since the return is risk-free, it must equal $0.1\,\Phi_0 =$

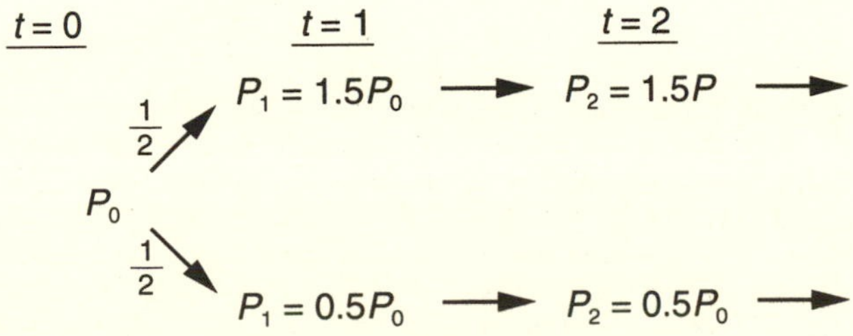

Figure 2.3. *Price of Widgets*

$0.1\, F_0 - 1.65\, P_0 + 160$. Solving for F_0 gives the value of the option to invest:

$$F_0 = 7.5\, P_0 - 727. \tag{9}$$

We have calculated the value of the investment option assuming that we would only want to invest if the price goes up next year. However, if P_0 is low enough we might never want to invest, and if P_0 is high enough it might be better to invest now rather than waiting. Below what price would we never invest? From the equation above, we see that $F_0 = 0$ when $7.5\, P_0 = 727$, or $P_0 = \$97$.

If P_0 is less than \$97, V_1 will be less than the \$1600 cost of the investment even if the price rises by 50 percent next year.

For what values of P_0 should we invest now rather than wait? Once again, we should invest now if the current value of a widget factory, V_0, exceeds its *total* cost, $\$1600 + F_0$. Hence the critical price, which we will denote by P_0^*, satisfies $V_0 = 1600 + F_0$, that is, $11\, P_0^* = 1600 + 7.5\, P_0^* - 727$, or $P_0^* = \$249$. If P_0 exceeds \$249, we are better off investing today rather than waiting. The option is sufficiently deep in the money that the cost of waiting (the sacrifice of period-0 profit) outweighs the benefit.[6]

We obtained this critical price by finding the value of the investment option, but we also could have found it by calculating (as a function of P_0) the NPV of the project assuming we invest today, and equating it to the NPV assuming we wait until next year and then decide whether to invest based on the outcome for price. (We leave this for you as an exercise.)

The value of the investment option is thus a piecewise-linear function of the current price, P_0, and the optimal investment rule likewise depends on P_0. If $P_0 \le \$97$, $F_0 = 0$, and one should never invest in the factory. If $\$97 < P_0 \le \$249$, then $F_0 = 7.5\, P_0 - 727$, and one should wait a year and invest if the price goes up. If $P_0 > \$249$, then $F_0 = 11\, P_0 - 1600$, and one should invest immediately. This solution is summarized in Table 2.1.

In Figure 2.4 we have plotted F_0 as a function of P_0. Suppose our only choice were to invest today or else never invest. Then the option to invest would be worth the maximum of zero and $11\, P_0 - 1600$, that is, the value

---

[6] You might think that immediate investment would be justified only if we would invest next year irrespective of whether the price went up or down. In fact, the critical price for immediate investment is lower. Assuming we wait, we will invest next year if $V_1 - 1600 = 11\, P_1 - 1600 > 0$, so if the price goes down, that is, $P_1 = 0.5\, P_0$, we would invest only if $5.5\, P_0 - 1600 > 0$, or $P_0 > \$291$, which exceeds $P_0^* = \$249$. The problem with the faulty intuition is that it ignores the profit we could earn this year by investing now. Indeed, for a P_0 of, say, \$260, it is better to invest today even though if we did wait, we would *not* invest next year if it turned out that the price went down.

Table 2.1.   *Value of Option to Invest and Investment Rule*

Region	Option Value	Optimal Investment Rule
$P_0 \leq 97$	$F_0 = 0$	Never invest.
$97 < P_0 \leq 249$	$F_0 = 7.5 P_0 - 727$	Invest in period 1 only if price has gone up.
$P_0 > 249$	$F_0 = 11 P_0 - 1600$	Invest in period 0.

of a widget factory today, V_0, less the $1600 cost of building the factory. (In financial jargon, this is the *intrinsic value* of the option—the maximum of zero and its value if it were exercised immediately.) Also, we would invest today as long as $11 P_0 > \$1600$, that is, as long as $P_0 > \$146$. When $P_0 > \$249$, the option to invest *is* worth its intrinsic value of $11 P_0 - 1600$, because then it is optimal to invest today rather than wait. Hence $11 P_0 - 1600$ is shown as a solid line for values of P_0 greater than $249. When $P_0 < \$249$, however, the option to invest is worth *more* than $11 P_0 - 1600$, and should be left unexercised, at least until next year.

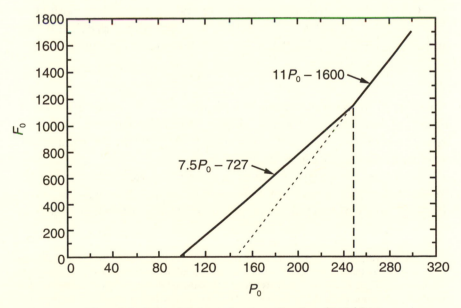

Figure 2.4.   *Value of Option to Invest as a Function of Initial Price*

Note from Figure 2.4 that F_0 is a convex function of P_0, and that F_0 is greater than or equal to the net payoff from exercising the option today, $V_0 - I$, up to the optimal exercise point (\$249 in this example). As we will see, the value of an option to invest typically has these characteristics.

Changing the Probabilities for Price

We can also determine how the value of the option to invest depends on q, the probability that the price of widgets will rise next year. (So far we have assumed that this probability is 0.5.) To do this, we will let the initial price, P_0, be some arbitrary value, but we will fix the cost of the investment, I, at \$1600. We can then follow the same steps as before to find the value of the option and the optimal investment rule.

The reader can verify that the short position in widgets needed to construct a risk-free portfolio is $n = 8.5$, and is independent of q. (The reason is that n depends on the possible values for the portfolio in period 1, Φ_1, and not on the probabilities that the portfolio will take on those values.) However, the payment required for this short position does depend on q, because the expected capital gain from holding a widget depends on q. To calculate this, let $\mathcal{E}_0(P_1)$ denote the expected price of widgets next year, calculated conditional on the knowledge of the period-0 price.[7] Thus $\mathcal{E}_0(P_1) = (q + 0.5) P_0$. Therefore the expected rate of capital gain on a widget is $[\mathcal{E}_0(P_1) - P_0]/P_0 = q - 0.5$. Hence the required payment per widget in the short position is $[0.1 - (q - 0.5)] P_0 = (0.6 - q) P_0$. Setting $\Phi_1 - \Phi_0 - (0.6 - q) n P_0 = 0.1 \Phi_0$, and setting $n = 8.5$, we find that if $P_0 > \$97$, the value of the option is

$$F_0 = 15 q P_0 - 1455 q. \tag{10}$$

Note that F_0 increases as q increases (as long as $P_0 > 97$). This is as we would expect, because a higher q means a higher probability that the price will go up and the option to invest will be exercised. If $P_0 \leq \$97$, we will never invest, whether or not the price goes up, and $F_0 = 0$.

How does the decision to invest depend on q? Recall that it is better to wait rather than invest today as long as $F_0 > V_0 - I$. In this case, $V_0 = P_0 + \sum_1^\infty (q + 0.5) P_0/(1.1)^t = (6 + 10 q) P_0$. Hence it is better to wait as

---

[7]We will use $\mathcal{E}$ to denote the expectation (mean) of a random variable, and a time subscript on $\mathcal{E}$ will indicate that the expectation is conditional on information available as of that time. Similarly, we will use $\mathcal{V}$ to denote variances. These symbols are used consistently throughout the book. Other notation is specific to each chapter or even section. A symbol glossary at the end of the book collects the significant symbols and states what they denote.

long as $15q\,P_0 - 1455\,q > (6 + 10q)\,P_0 - 1600$, that is, as long as $P_0 < P_0^* = (1600 - 1455\,q)/(6 - 5\,q)$. Also, P_0^* decreases as q increases, that is, a higher probability of a price increase induces the firm to invest more readily. Why? The cost of waiting is the revenue foregone by not selling a widget this period, which increases with P_0. Since a higher q makes a bad outcome next period less likely, it reduces the value of waiting. Thus a higher q implies that a smaller P_0 suffices to make the cost of waiting exceed the value of waiting.

Increasing the Uncertainty over Price

When we changed the probability q while keeping all the other parameters fixed, we changed the expected price in period 1. Suppose the expected price in period 1 remains fixed at the initial price level, P_0, but we increase the size of the up and down changes so that the *variance* of the period-1 price increases. What effect would such a *mean-preserving spread* in the distribution for P_1 have on the value of the investment option, F_0, and on the critical price, P_0^*, above which it is optimal to invest immediately rather than wait?

We will assume as before that q is 0.5, but now the price will either rise or fall in period 1 by 75 percent, rather than by 50 percent as before. Thus the variance of P_1 is greater, but its expected value is still P_0. To find F_0, we go through the same steps as before, creating a risk-free portfolio and equating its return to the risk-free return. Again, let the portfolio be long the investment option and short n widgets, so its value now is $\Phi_0 = F_0 - n\,P_0$. In period 1, the price will rise to $1.75\,P_0$, in which case the project will be worth $V_1 = 11\,P_1 = 19.25\,P_0$ so that Φ_1 will equal $19.25\,P_0 - 1600 - 1.75\,n\,P_0$, or the price will fall to $0.25\,P_0$, in which case Φ_1 will equal $-0.25\,n\,P_0$. Equating these two possible values of Φ_1 and solving for n gives

$$n = 12.83 - 1067/P_0. \tag{11}$$

(Then, $\Phi_1 = -3.21\,P_0 + 267$ irrespective of P_1.) Remembering that the short position will require a payment of $0.1\,n\,P_0 = 1.28\,P_0 - 107$, the return on the portfolio is $8.34\,P_0 - F_0 - 693$. Setting this equal to $0.1\,\Phi_0 = 0.1\,F_0 - 1.28\,P_0 + 107$ and solving for F_0 gives

$$F_0 = 8.75\,P_0 - 727. \tag{12}$$

If P_0 is $200, F_0 is $1023, which is substantially larger than the value of $773 that we found before when the price could only rise or fall by 50 percent. Why does an increase in uncertainty increase the value of the option to invest? Because it increases the upside potential payoff from the option, leaving the downside payoff unchanged at zero (since we will not exercise the option if the price falls).

We can also calculate the critical initial price, P_0^*, that is sufficient to warrant investing now rather than waiting. Again, just equate the current value of the widget factory, $V_0 = 11 P_0$, to its total cost, $1600 + F_0$. Utilizing equation (12) for F_0, this gives $P_0^* = \$388$, which is much larger than the value of $249 that we found before. Because the value of the option is larger, the opportunity cost of investing now rather than waiting is larger, so there is a greater incentive to wait.

A "Bad News Principle"

We can take this one step further by allowing both the probability q of an upward price move as well as the sizes of the upward and downward moves to vary. In so doing, we can determine how "good news" (an upward move) and "bad news" (a downward move) separately affect the critical price, P_0^*, that warrants immediate investment (in the above calculation the upward and downward moves had to increase or decrease together). We will see that P_0^* depends only on the size of the downward move, not the size of the upward move. The reason is that it is the ability to avoid the consequences of "bad news" that leads us to wait.[8]

Suppose that the initial price is P_0, but in period 1 the price becomes

$$P_1 = \begin{cases} (1+u)P_0 & \text{with probability } q, \\ (1-d)P_0 & \text{with probability } 1-q. \end{cases}$$

To keep things general, we will let the cost of the investment be I. In this case, the NPV if we invest now is

$$\text{NPV} = -I + P_0 + q \sum_{t=1}^{\infty} \frac{(1+u)P_0}{(1.1)^t} + (1-q) \sum_{t=1}^{\infty} \frac{(1-d)P_0}{(1.1)^t}$$

$$= -I + 10\,[1.1 + q(u+d) - d]\,P_0. \tag{13}$$

On the other hand, if we wait the NPV is

$$\text{NPV} = \frac{1}{1.1} \big\{ q \max[0, -I + 11(1+u)P_0] \\ + (1-q) \max[0, -I + 11(1-d)P_0] \big\}. \tag{14}$$

---

[8] This "bad news principle" was first spelled out by Bernanke (1983), and the ideas can also be found in Cukierman (1980).

It is easy to show (and should be intuitively clear) that the point of indifference between investing now and waiting occurs in the range of P_0 where investment in period 1 is warranted if the price goes up but not if it goes down.

In this case the NPV in equation (14) simplifies to

$$\text{NPV} = \frac{q}{1.1} \left[-I + 11 \left(1 + u \right) P_0 \right]. \tag{15}$$

Equating the NPV of equation (13) for investing now with the NPV of equation (15) for waiting and solving for P_0 gives

$$P_0^* = I \left(\frac{0.1}{1.1} \right) \left(\frac{0.1 + (1 - q)}{0.1 + (1 - q)(1 - d)} \right). \tag{16}$$

Equation (16) has one detail that is important to note—P_0^* does not depend in any way on u, the size of an upward move. It only depends on the size of a downward move, d, and the probability $(1 - q)$ of a downward move. Also, the larger is d, the larger is the critical price, P_0^*; it is the magnitude of the possible "bad news" that drives the incentive to wait.[9]

We can also examine the effect of a mean-preserving spread in P_1 in a more general way than we did before. Suppose we set $q = d/(u + d)$. Then $\mathcal{E}(P_1) = P_0$, and $\mathcal{V}(P_1) = u\, d\, P_0^2$. Hence if we increase u and d proportionally, we keep q and $\mathcal{E}(P_1)$ unchanged while increasing the variance of P_1. Observe from equation (16) that if d is larger but q is unchanged, P_0^* increases. Again, we find that a mean-preserving spread increases the incentive to wait.

2 Extending the Example to Three Periods

In our example, we made the unrealistic assumption that there is no uncertainty over the price of widgets after the first year. In most markets, future prices are always uncertain, and the amount of uncertainty increases with the time horizon. In other words, while the expected future price of widgets might always equal the current price, the variance of the future price will typically be greater the farther into the future we look. Later in this book we will model

---

[9]If current profit can be negative and the firm is contemplating a costly disinvestment or abandonment of a project, the bad news principle turns into a good news principle: the size and probability of an upturn are the driving forces behind the incentive to wait. Recalling our discussion of suicide in Chapter 1, we should emphasize this point. If the potential bad outcomes become even worse, that does not increase the incentive for immediate abandonment. However, if potential good outcomes become better, that increases the value of staying alive.

the stochastic evolution of price in just this way. At this point, however, we can obtain additional insight into the nature of the investment problem by extending our example so that there are three periods in which the investment decision might be made.

We will assume as before that at $t = 0$ the price of widgets begins at some level P_0, and at $t = 1$ it will either increase or decrease by 50 percent (to $P_1 = 1.5 P_0$ or $P_1 = 0.5 P_0$), each with probability 0.5. Then, at $t = 2$, it will again either increase or decrease by 50 percent with equal probability. Hence there are three possible values for P_2: 2.25 P_0, 0.75 P_0, and 0.25 P_0. The price then remains at this level for all $t \geq 2$. (See Figure 2.5.) We will again fix the direct cost of the investment, I, at \$1600.

By adding one more period of price uncertainty, our investment problem becomes quite a bit more complicated. One reason is that there are now five different possible investment strategies that might make sense and must be considered. In particular, it might be optimal to (i) invest immediately; (ii) wait a year and then invest if the price has gone up, but never invest if the price has gone down; (iii) wait a year and invest if the price has gone up, but if it went down wait another year and invest if it then goes up; (iv) wait two years and only invest if the price has gone up both times; or (v) never invest. Which rule is optimal will depend on the initial price and the cost of the investment, and the value of the investment option must be calculated for each possible rule. The second complicating factor is that while we can still compute the value of the investment option by constructing a risk-free portfolio, the makeup of that portfolio will not be constant over the two years; we will have to

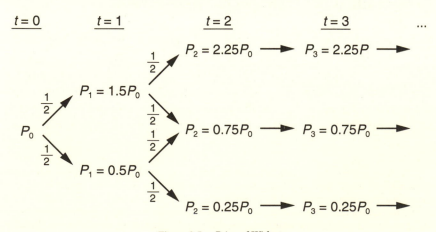

Figure 2.5.   *Price of Widgets*

change the number of widgets in the short position after the price changes at $t = 1$.[10]

We will again approach this problem using option pricing methods. We want to obtain the value of the option to invest at $t = 0$, F_0, as a function of the initial price, P_0, as well as the optimal investment rule. The trick is to work backwards. We will solve two separate investment problems looking forward from $t = 1$, first for $P_1 = 0.5\,P_0$, and then for $P_1 = 1.5\,P_0$, assuming in both cases that we have not yet invested. In each case we will determine F_1, the value of the investment option at $t = 1$, by constructing a risk-free portfolio and calculating its return. Given the two possible values for F_1 (one for $P_1 = 0.5\,P_0$ and one for $P_1 = 1.5\,P_0$), we then back up to $t = 0$ and determine F_0 by again constructing a risk-free portfolio and calculating its return.

Suppose that at $t = 1$, $P_1 = 0.5\,P_0$, and that P_0 is such that we would invest in period 2 if the price goes up, but not if it goes down. Now construct a portfolio that includes the option to invest and is short some number n_1 of widgets. The value of this portfolio is $\Phi_1 = F_1 - n_1\,P_1$. If the price goes up in period 2 (to $0.75\,P_0$), we will invest, so F_2 will equal $\sum_0^\infty 0.75\,P_0/(1.1)^t - 1600 = 8.25\,P_0 - 1600$, and Φ_2 will equal $8.25\,P_0 - 1600 - 0.75\,n_1\,P_0$. If the price goes down in period 2 (to $0.25\,P_0$), we will not invest, F_2 will equal 0, and Φ_2 will equal $-0.25\,n_1\,P_0$. Equating the expressions for Φ_2 under the two scenarios, we find that the portfolio will be risk-free if $n_1 = 16.5 - 3200/P_0$; then Φ_2 will equal $800 - 4.125\,P_0$ whether the price goes up or down. Calculating the portfolio's return ($\Phi_2 - \Phi_1 - 0.1\,n_1\,P_1$) and setting it equal to the risk-free return ($0.1\,\Phi_1$) gives us the value of the investment option: $F_1 = 3.75\,P_0 - 727.3$. Also, note from this that $F_1 = 0$ when $P_0 = 193.94$. Hence if the price has gone down in period 1 and $P_0 < 193.94$, we will never invest.

We must now repeat this exercise assuming that price has gone up in period 1, that is, that $P_1 = 1.5\,P_0$. You can verify that in this case the risk-free portfolio requires a short position of $n_1 = 16.5 - 1067/P_0$ widgets, and the value of the investment option is $F_1 = 11.25\,P_0 - 727.3$. In this case $F_1 = 0$ when $P_0 = 64.65$. Hence if $P_0 < 64.65$ we will never invest at all, even if the price goes up in both periods. Also, suppose we invest in period 1 rather than waiting until period 2. Then we would obtain a net value $V_1 - I = 11\,(1.5\,P_0) - 1600$. Setting this equal to F_1 and solving for P_0 gives $P_0 = 166.23$.

---

[10]The method of keeping a portfolio riskless by changing its composition through repeated trading is called a "dynamic hedging strategy," and is of considerable importance in financial economics. We will develop it in a general setting of continuous time in Chapters 4 and 5.

Hence if $P_0 > 166.23$, we should invest in period 1 if the price has gone up, rather than wait another year.

We now know F_1 and the optimal investment strategy (assuming we have not yet invested) for each of the two possible outcomes for P_1, so we can determine F_0 by once again constructing a risk-free portfolio and calculating its return. Since the optimal investment strategy depends on P_0, this must be done for different ranges of P_0, that is, for $64.65 < P_0 \leq 166.23$ (in which case we would invest in period 2 only if the price goes up in both periods), for $166.23 < P_0 \leq 193.94$ (in which case we would invest in period 1 if the price goes up, but if it goes down we would never invest), and for $P_0 > 193.94$ (in which case we would invest in period 1 if the price goes up, but if it goes down wait and invest if it goes up in period 2). The solution, which the reader might want to verify, is summarized in Table 2.2.

Figure 2.6 shows F_0 plotted as a function of P_0. As in the two-period model, it is a piecewise-linear function, but now there are more pieces, each corresponding to an optimal investment strategy. Also, suppose the only choice were to invest today or else never invest. Then the option to invest would be worth $11 P_0 - 1600$, and we would invest today as long as $11 P_0 > \$1600$, that is, as long as $P_0 > \$146$. When $P_0 > 301.19$, the option *is* worth this much, because then $F_0 = 9.2 P_0 - 1057.9 = 11 P_0 - 1600$, and it is optimal to invest today rather than wait. Hence $11 P_0 - 1600$ is shown as a solid

Table 2.2.   *Value of Option to Invest and Investment Rule*

Region	Option Value	Optimal Investment Rule
$P_0 \leq 64.65$	$F_0 = 0$	Never invest.
$64.65 < P_0 \leq 166.23$	$F_0 = 5.11 P_0 - 330.6$	Invest in period 2 only if price goes up in period 1 *and* in period 2.
$166.23 < P_0 \leq 193.94$	$F_0 = 7.5 P_0 - 727.3$	Invest in period 1 if price goes up. If price goes down in period 1, then never invest.
$193.94 < P_0 \leq 301.19$	$F_0 = 9.2 P_0 - 1057.9$	Invest in period 1 if price goes up. If price goes down in period 1, then wait and invest in period 2 if price goes up.
$P_0 > 301.19$	$F_0 = 11 P_0 - 1600$	Invest in period 0.

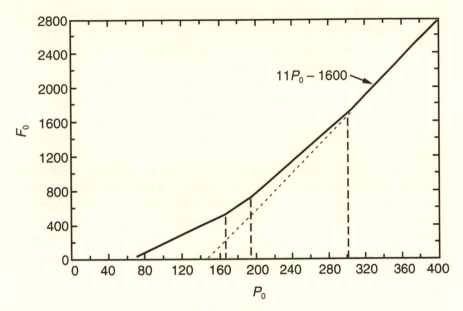

Figure 2.6. *Value of Option to Invest as a Function of Initial Price*

line for $P_0 > 301.19$, but is shown as a dotted line for $146 < P_0 < 301.19$. Finally, note once again that F_0 is a convex function of P_0, and that F_0 is greater than or equal to the net payoff from exercising the option today, $V_0 - I$, up to the optimal exercise point ($301.19 in this case).

As before, we could examine the dependence of F_0 and the optimal exercise point P_0^* on the cost of the investment, I, or on the variance of price changes. (Going through these calculations is now a bit more laborious, however, because three periods are involved instead of two.) For example, we could show that if the variance of the price changes increases, while the expected price changes remain the same, the value of the option F_0 will increase, as will the critical exercise price P_0^*. As an exercise, the reader might want to check this by letting P increase or decrease by 75 percent in each period, instead of by 50 percent as in Figure 2.5.

If we wanted to, we could now extend our example to four periods, allowing the price to again increase or decrease by 50 percent at $t = 3$. We could then work backwards, finding F_2 for each possible value of P_2, then finding F_1 for each possible value of P_1, and finally finding F_0. In like manner, we could then extend the example to five periods, to six periods, and so on. As we did this, we would find that the curve for F_0 would have more and more kinks. We will see in Chapter 5 that as the number of periods becomes large, the curve for F_0 will approach a smooth curve that starts at zero and rises to meet the curve showing the net payoff from immediate investment ($V_0 - I$). In fact the two curves meet tangentially, and the point where they meet defines the threshold P_0^* where immediate investment is optimal.

Adding more and more periods will make our example unreasonably complicated, however, and in any case would be less than satisfactory because ultimately we would like to allow the price to increase or decrease at every future time t. Thus we need a better approach to solving investment problems of this sort.

In Chapter 5 of this book we will extend our example by allowing the payoff from the investment to fluctuate *continuously* over time. As we will see, this continuous-time approach is quite powerful, and ultimately quite simple. However, it will require some understanding of stochastic processes, as well as Ito's Lemma (which is essentially a rule for differentiating and integrating functions of stochastic processes). These tools, which are becoming more and more widely used in economics and finance, provide a convenient way of analyzing a broad range of investment timing and option valuation problems. In the next two chapters we provide an introduction to these tools for readers who are unfamiliar with them.

3 Uncertainty over Cost

We now return to our simple two-period example and examine some alternative sources of uncertainty. In this section, we will consider uncertainty over the cost of the investment. Uncertainty over cost can be especially important for large projects that take time to build. Examples include nuclear power plants (where total construction costs are very hard to predict due to engineering and regulatory uncertainties), large petrochemical complexes, the development of a new line of aircraft, and large urban construction projects. Also, large size is not a requisite. Most R&D projects involve considerable cost uncertainty; the development of a new drug by a pharmaceutical company is an example.

In the context of our two-period example, suppose that the price of a widget is now $200, and we know that it will always remain $200. However, the direct cost of building a widget factory, I, is uncertain.

We will consider two different sources of uncertainty regarding I. The first, which we will call *input cost uncertainty*, arises because a widget factory requires steel, copper, and labor to build, and the prices of these construction inputs fluctuate stochastically over time. In addition, government regulations change unpredictably over time, and this can change the required quantities of one or more construction inputs. (For example, new safety regulations may add to labor requirements, or changing environmental regulations may require more capital.) Thus, although I might be known today, its value next year is uncertain.

As one might expect, this kind of uncertainty has the same effect on the investment decision as uncertainty over the future value of the payoff from the investment, V—it creates an opportunity cost of investing now rather than waiting for new information. As a result, a project could have a conventionally measured NPV that is positive, but it might still be uneconomical to begin investing.

As an example, suppose that I is $1600 today, but next year it will increase to $2400 or decrease to $800, each with probability 0.5. As before, the interest rate is 10 percent. Should we invest today, or wait until next year? If we invest today, the NPV is again given by equation (1), that is, $-1600 + 2200 = \$600$. This NPV is positive, but once again it ignores an opportunity cost. To see this, let us recalculate the NPV, but this time assuming we wait until next year, in which case it will be ex post optimal to invest only if I falls to $800. In this case the NPV is given by

$$\text{NPV} = (0.5) \left[\frac{-800}{1.1} + \sum_{t=1}^{\infty} \frac{200}{(1.1)^t} \right] = \frac{700}{1.1} = \$636. \qquad (17)$$

(In year 0 there is no expenditure and no revenue. In year 1, we invest only if I falls to $800, which will happen with probability 0.5.) If we wait a year before deciding whether to invest, the project's NPV today is $636, so waiting is clearly better than investing now.

At this point it might appear that uncertainty always leads one to postpone investments, or at least increase the hurdle rate that the investment must meet, but this is not the case. If investing provides information, uncertainty can *lower* the hurdle rate for a project. Consider uncertainty over the physical difficulty of completing a project. We will call this *technical uncertainty*: assuming factor costs are known, how much time, effort, and materials will ultimately be required to complete a project? This kind of uncertainty can only be resolved by actually undertaking and completing the project.[11] One

---

[11]This is a simplification in that, for some projects, cost uncertainty can be reduced by first performing additional engineering studies. The investment problem is then more complicated because one has three choices instead of two: start construction now, undertake an engineering study and then begin construction only if the study indicates costs are likely to be low, or abandon the project completely.

then observes actual costs (and construction time) unfold as the project proceeds. These costs may from time to time turn out to be greater or less than anticipated (as impediments arise or instead the work moves ahead faster than planned), but the total cost of the investment is only known for certain when the project is complete.

With this kind of uncertainty, a project can have an expected cost that makes its NPV negative, but if the variance of the cost is sufficiently high, it can still be economical to begin investing. The reason is that investing reveals information about cost, and thus about the expected net payoff from investing further. It therefore has a value beyond its direct contribution to the completion of the project. This additional value (called a *shadow value* because it is not a directly measurable cash flow) lowers the full expected cost of the investment.

The following simple example will help to illustrate this. Suppose that the price of a widget is and always will be $200, but the cost of building a widget factory is uncertain. To build a factory, one must initially spend $1000. With probability 0.5 the factory will then be complete, but with probability 0.5 an additional $3000 will be required to complete it. Since the expected cost of the factory is $1000 + (0.5)(3000) = 2500, and its value is $2200, the NPV of the investment seems to be negative, suggesting that we should not invest. But this ignores the value of the information obtained from completing the first stage of the project, and the fact that we can abandon the project should a second phase costing $3000 be required. The correct NPV is $-1000 + (0.5)(2200) = 100. This is positive, so one should invest in the first phase of the project.

We see, then, that the uncertainty over the cost of a project can lead one to postpone investing or to speed it up. If the resolution of uncertainty is independent of what the firm does, it has much the same effect as uncertainty over the payoff from investing, and creates an incentive to wait. But if the uncertainty can be partly resolved by investing, it has the opposite effect. We will return to uncertainty over cost later in this book, and examine its implications in more detail.

4   Uncertainty over Interest Rates

Next suppose that the cost of the investment and the payoff from investing are both known with certainty, but the interest rate used to discount future cash flows changes in an unpredictable manner. How will uncertainty over the interest rate affect the decision to invest?

Interest rate uncertainty can have two effects on an investment decision. First, unpredictable fluctuations in interest rates can increase the *expected value* of a future payoff from investing. For example, suppose the investment yields a perpetuity that pays $1 per year forever. The present value of this perpetuity is $1/r$, where r is the interest rate. If $r = 10$ percent, the value is $1/0.10 = 10. But suppose r is uncertain, and can equal either 5 percent or 15 percent, each with probability 0.5, so that $\mathcal{E}(r) = 10$ percent. Then the expected value of the perpetuity is $0.5(1/0.05) + 0.5(1/0.15) = $13.33 > 10. This makes the investment more attractive, and increases the incentive to invest.[12]

Nonetheless, uncertainty over future interest rates can still lead to a postponement of investment. The reason is that the second effect of interest rate uncertainty works in the opposite direction— it creates a value of waiting (to see whether interest rates rise or fall). This effect works in much the same way as uncertainty over the payoff from the investment.

To clarify this, let us again return to our two-period example. This time we will assume that the price of a widget is fixed at $200, and that the cost of building the widget factory is fixed at $2000. The only uncertainty is over interest rates. Today the interest rate is 10 percent, but next year it will change. There is a 0.5 probability that it will increase to 15 percent, and a 0.5 probability that it will decrease to 5 percent. It will then remain at this new level.

What will a widget factory be worth next year? If there were no uncertainty over interest rates, that is, if we knew that the interest rate will remain 10 percent, then the value of the factory next year would be

$$V_1 = \sum_{t=0}^{\infty} \frac{200}{(1.1)^t} = $2200.$$

In our example, the expected value of the interest rate next year and thereafter is 10 percent, but the actual value is unknown. So, the value of the factory next year will be

$$V_1 = \begin{cases} \sum_{t=0}^{\infty} 200/(1.15)^t = $1533 & \text{with probability 0.5,} \\ \sum_{t=0}^{\infty} 200/(1.05)^t = $4200 & \text{with probability 0.5.} \end{cases}$$

---

[12]In technical language, this result is an implication of *Jensen's Inequality*, combined with the fact that the present value of a future cash flow is a convex function of the interest rate. Jensen's Inequality says that if x is a random variable and $f(x)$ is a convex function of x, then $\mathcal{E}[f(x)] > f(\mathcal{E}[x])$. Thus if the expected value of x remains the same but the variance of x increases, $\mathcal{E}[f(x)]$ will increase. In the case at hand, if the expected value of next year's interest rate remains fixed but the uncertainty around that value increases, the expected present discounted value of a payoff received next year will increase.

Hence the expected value of V_1 is $(0.5)(1533) + (0.5)(4200) = \$2867$, which is higher than it is when future interest rates are certain.

We see, then, that uncertainty over the future interest rate (holding the expected value of the interest rate constant) increases the expected value of the project. But how does uncertainty affect the investment decision? First, note that if there were no uncertainty over interest rates, we would clearly want to invest today. The NPV of the project if we invest today is

$$\text{NPV} = -2000 + \sum_{t=0}^{\infty} \frac{200}{(1.1)^t} = \$200, \qquad (18)$$

whereas the NPV today if we wait until next year is only $\$2200/1.1 - \$2000 = \$0$.

The situation is different if interest rates are uncertain. If we invest now, the NPV is

$$\text{NPV} = -2000 + 200 + \frac{\mathcal{E}(V_1)}{1.1} = -1800 + \frac{2867}{1.1} = \$806. \qquad (19)$$

(If we invest today we can make and sell a widget now for $\$200$, and we will have a factory whose expected value next year is $\$2867$.) This NPV is positive, but suppose we wait until next year before deciding whether to invest. If the interest rate rises to 15 percent, the value of the factory will be only $\$1533$, which is less than the $\$2000$ cost of the investment. Hence we will only invest if the interest rate falls to 5 percent. Since there is a 0.5 probability that this will happen, the NPV assuming we wait is

$$\text{NPV} = (0.5) \left[\frac{-2000}{1.1} + \frac{1}{1.1} \sum_{t=0}^{\infty} \frac{200}{(1.05)^t} \right] = \$1000. \qquad (20)$$

This NPV is higher, so it is better to wait than invest now.

This is a simple analysis of interest rate uncertainty, but it has some important implications. First, mean-preserving volatility in interest rates will increase the expected value of a project, but will also create an incentive to wait rather than invest now. The reason is that, as with uncertainty over future cash flows, uncertainty over future interest rates creates a value to waiting for new information. Second, if an objective of public policy is to stimulate investment, the stability of interest rates may be more important than the level of interest rates. Policies that lead to lower but more volatile interest rates could end up depressing aggregate investment spending.[13] As we will illustrate in Chapter 9,

---

[13]Ingersoll and Ross (1992) have developed a continuous-time model of investment with interest rate uncertainty, and it leads to more or less the same conclusions.

the importance of stability and predictability may apply to other instruments of government policy as well, such as tax rates and trade policy.

5   Scale versus Flexibility

As students of economics or business learn early on, economies of scale can be an important source of cost savings. By building a large plant instead of two or three smaller ones, a firm might be able to reduce its average cost and increase its profitability. This suggests that firms should respond to growth in demand for their products by bunching their investments, that is, investing in new capacity only infrequently, but adding large and efficient plants each time.

What should firms do, however, when there is uncertainty over demand growth (as there usually is)? If the firm irreversibly invests in a large addition to capacity, and demand grows only slowly or even shrinks, it will find itself holding capital it does not need. Hence when the growth of demand is uncertain, there is a tradeoff between scale economies and the flexibility that is gained by investing more frequently in small increments to capacity as they are needed.

This problem is an important one for the electric utility industry. It is much cheaper per unit of capacity to build a large coal-fired power plant than it is to add capacity in small amounts. But at the same time, utilities face considerable uncertainty over the rate by which the demand for their electricity will grow.[14] Adding capacity in small amounts gives the utility flexibility, but is also more costly. Hence it is important to be able to value this flexibility. The options approach used in this book is well suited to do this. Here we will illustrate the basic idea with a simple example in which demand growth is certain, but there is uncertainty over relative fuel prices.[15]

Consider a utility that faces constant demand growth of 100 megawatts (MW) per year. Hence the utility must add to capacity; the question is how. There are two alternatives. The utility can build a 200-MW coal-fired plant (enough capacity for two years worth of additional demand) at a capital cost of $190 million (Plant A), or it can build a 100-MW oil-fired plant at a capital

---

[14]The reason is not just that there is uncertainty over the growth of total electricity demand, but also because utilities now often find themselves competing with other sources of electric power (such as cogeneration).

[15]This is a modified version of an example presented in Sawhill (1989).

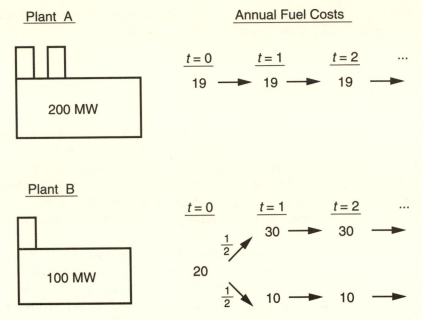

Figure 2.7.   *Choosing Among Electric Power Plants*

cost of $100 million (Plant B). At current coal and oil prices, the coal-fired plant is not only more economical in terms of its capital cost ($90 million per 100 MW of capacity), but also in terms of its operating cost; operating Plant A will cost $19 million per year for each 100 MW of power, whereas Plant B will cost $20 million per year. We will assume that the discount rate for the utility is 10 percent per year, and that each plant lasts forever. In this case, if fuel prices remain constant, Plant A is clearly the preferred choice.

Fuel prices are unlikely to remain constant, however. Since what matters is the relative price of oil compared to coal (and since the price of coal is in fact much less volatile than the price of oil), we will assume that the price of coal will remain fixed, but the price of oil will either rise or fall next year, with equal probability, and then remain constant. If it rises, the operating cost for Plant B will rise to $30 million per year, but if it falls, the operating cost will fall to $10 million per year. (See Figure 2.7.)

The choice of plant is now more complicated. Although Plant A's capital cost is lower because of its scale, and its operating cost is lower at the current oil price, Plant B affords the utility more flexibility because it only requires a commitment to one year's worth of demand growth— if the price of oil falls, the utility will not be stuck with the extra 100 MW of coal-burning capacity in the second year. To decide which choice is best, let us calculate for each the present value of the expected cost of generating 100 MW of power per year forever starting this year, and an additional 100 MW per year starting next year.

First, suppose we commit the full 200 MW to either coal or oil. Then, if we choose coal, the present value of the flow of cost is

$$PV_A = 180 + \sum_{t=0}^{\infty} \frac{19}{(1.1)^t} + \sum_{t=1}^{\infty} \frac{19}{(1.1)^t} = \$579. \tag{21}$$

Note that 180 is the capital cost for the full 200 MW, and that 19 is the annual operating cost for each 100 MW, the first of which begins now and the second next year. Next, suppose we choose oil. Since the expected operating cost for oil is \$20 million per year, the present value is

$$PV_B = 100 + \frac{100}{1.1} + \sum_{t=0}^{\infty} \frac{20}{(1.1)^t} + \sum_{t=1}^{\infty} \frac{20}{(1.1)^t} = \$611. \tag{22}$$

Thus it would seem that Plant A is preferred.

But this calculation ignores the flexibility afforded by the smaller oil-fired plant. Suppose we install 100 MW of oil-fired capacity now, but then if the price of oil goes up next year, we install 200 MW of coal-fired capacity, rather than another oil-fired plant. This would give us a total of 300 MW of capacity, so to make the cost comparison meaningful, we must net out the present value of the additional 100 MW, which would be utilized starting two years from now:

$$PV'_B = 100 + \sum_{t=0}^{\infty} \frac{20}{(1.1)^t}$$

$$+ \frac{1}{2}\left[\frac{100}{1.1} + \sum_{t=1}^{\infty} \frac{10}{(1.1)^t}\right]$$

$$+ \frac{1}{2}\left[\frac{180}{1.1} - \frac{90}{(1.1)^2} + \sum_{t=1}^{\infty} \frac{19}{(1.1)^t}\right] = \$555. \tag{23}$$

Note that the second line in equation (23) is the present value of the capital and operating cost for the second 100-MW oil plant (which is built only if the price of oil goes down), and the third line is the present value of the capital and operating cost of the *first 100 MW* of a 200-MW coal plant. This present value turns out to be \$555 million, so installing the smaller oil-fired plant and thereby retaining flexibility is the preferred choice.

One way to value this flexibility is to ask how much lower would the capital cost of Plant A have to be to make it the preferred choice. Let I_A be the capital cost of Plant A. Then the present value of the costs of installing and operating Plant A is

$$I_A + \sum_{t=0}^{\infty} \frac{19}{(1.1)^t} + \sum_{t=1}^{\infty} \frac{19}{(1.1)^t} = I_A + 399.$$

The present value of the cost of providing the 200 MW of power by installing Plant B now and then next year installing either Plant A or B (depending on whether the price of oil goes up or down) is

$$100 + \sum_{t=0}^{\infty} \frac{20}{(1.1)^t} + \frac{1}{2} \left[\frac{100}{1.1} + \sum_{t=1}^{\infty} \frac{10}{(1.1)^t} \right]$$

$$+ \frac{1}{2} \left[\frac{I_A}{1.1} - \frac{0.5\,I_A}{(1.1)^2} + \sum_{t=1}^{\infty} \frac{19}{(1.1)^t} \right]$$

$$= 320 + \frac{1}{2}\,(90.9 + 100) + \frac{1}{2}\,(0.496\,I_A + 190) = 510.5 + 0.248\,I_A.$$

To find the capital cost that makes the utility indifferent between these choices, just equate these present values and solve for I_A:

$$I_A + 399 = 510.5 + 0.248\,I_A,$$

or, $I_A^* = \$148.3$ million. Hence the economies of scale would have to be quite large (so that a 200-MW coal plant was less than 75 percent of the cost of two 100-MW oil plants) to make giving up the flexibility of the smaller plant economical.

6   Guide to the Literature

The net present value criterion and its application to investment decisions is an important topic in corporate finance courses, and is the starting point for much of what we do in this book. Readers unfamiliar with NPV calculations, including the use of the capital asset pricing model to determine risk-adjusted discount rates, may want to review a standard textbook in corporate finance. A good choice is Brealey and Myers (1992).

Although we largely ignore the implications of taxes in this book, they can affect the choice of discount rate for NPV calculations. Taggart (1991) provides a review of the various approaches to calculating discount rates (adjusted for risk and taxes) for use in the standard NPV model. Ruback (1986) shows that riskless after-tax nominal cash flows should always be discounted at the after-tax risk-free rate (for example, the Treasury bill rate times 1 minus the corporate tax rate), and Myers and Ruback (1992) derive a simple and robust rule for discounting risky cash flows in NPV calculations.

Throughout this book we will emphasize the connections between investment decisions and the valuation and exercising of financial options. Although certainly not necessary, some familiarity with options and option pricing techniques will be helpful when reading this book. Brealey and Myers (1992) provide a simple introduction; so do the expository surveys by Rubinstein (1987) and Varian (1987). For more detailed treatments, see Cox and Rubinstein (1985), Hull (1989), and Jarrow and Rudd (1983). Although somewhat dated, the survey article by Smith (1976) is also useful. Finally, for heuristic discussions of investments as options, see Kester (1984), Mason and Merton (1985), Trigeorgis and Mason (1987), and Chapter 12 of Copeland, Koller, and Murrin (1991).

Part II

Mathematical Background

Chapter **3**

Stochastic Processes and Ito's Lemma

THIS CHAPTER and the next provide the mathematical tools—stochastic calculus, dynamic programming, and contingent claims analysis—that will be used throughout the rest of this book. With these tools, we can study investment decisions using a continuous-time approach, which is both intuitively appealing and quite powerful. In addition, the concepts and techniques that we introduce here are becoming widely used in a number of areas of economics and finance, and so are worth learning even apart from their application to investment problems.

This chapter begins with a discussion of stochastic processes. We will begin with simple discrete-time processes, and then turn to the Wiener process (or Brownian motion), an important continuous-time process that is a fundamental building block for many of the models that we will develop in this book. We will explain the meaning and properties of the Wiener process, and show how it can be derived as the continuous limit of a discrete-time random walk. We will then see how the Wiener process can be generalized to a broad class of continuous-time stochastic processes, called Ito processes. Ito processes can be used to represent the dynamics of the value of a project, output prices, input costs, and other variables that evolve stochastically over time and that affect the decision to invest.

As we will see, these processes do not have a time derivative in the conventional sense, and as a result, cannot always be manipulated using the ordinary rules of calculus. To work with these processes, we must make use of Ito's Lemma. This lemma, sometimes called the Fundamental Theorem of stochastic calculus, is an important result that will allow us to differentiate and integrate functions of stochastic processes. We will provide a heuristic derivation of Ito's Lemma and then, through a variety of examples, show how it can be used to perform simple operations on functions of Wiener processes. We will also show how it can be used to derive and solve stochastic differential equations. Next, we will introduce jump processes—processes that make infrequent but discrete jumps, rather than fluctuate continuously—and show how they can be analyzed using a version of Ito's Lemma. Finally, in the Appendix to this chapter we introduce the Kolmogorov equations, which describe the dynamics of the probability density function for a stochastic process, and show how they can be applied.

1 Stochastic Processes

A stochastic process is a variable that evolves over time in a way that is at least in part random. The temperature in downtown Boston is an example; its variation through time is partly deterministic (rising during the day and falling at night, and rising towards summer and falling towards winter), and partly random and unpredictable.[1] The price of IBM stock is another example; it fluctuates randomly, but over the long haul has had a positive expected rate of growth that compensated investors for risk in holding the stock.

Somewhat more formally, a stochastic process is defined by a probability law for the evolution x_t of a variable x over time t. Thus, for given times $t_1 < t_2 < t_3$, etc., we are given, or can calculate, the probability that the corresponding values x_1, x_2, x_3, etc., lie in some specified range, for example

$$\text{prob}(a_1 < x_1 \le b_1, \ a_2 < x_2 \le b_2, \ \ldots).$$

When time t_1 arrives and we observe the actual value x_1, we can condition the probability of future events on this information.[2]

---

[1]One might argue that the randomness is a reflection of the limitations of meteorology, and that in principle it could be eliminated if we could build sufficiently complete and accurate meteorological models. Perhaps, but from an operational point of view, next week's temperature is indeed a random variable.

[2]In this book we will not attempt any detailed or rigorous treatment of stochastic processes, offering instead the minimal explanations and intuitions that suffice for our applications. For detailed and general treatments, see Cox and Miller (1965), Feller (1971), and Karlin and Taylor (1975).

The temperature in Boston and the price of IBM stock are processes that differ in an important respect. The temperature in Boston is a *stationary* process. This means, roughly, that the statistical properties of this variable are constant over long periods of time.[3] For example, although the expected temperature tomorrow may depend in part on today's temperature, the expectation and variance of the temperature on January 1 of next year is largely independent of today's temperature, and is equal to the expectation and variance of the temperature on January 1 two years from now, three years from now, etc. The price of IBM stock, on the other hand, is a *nonstationary* process. The expected value of this price can grow without bound, and, as we will soon see, the variance of price T years from now increases with T.

The temperature in Boston and the price of IBM stock are both *continuous-time* stochastic processes, in the sense that the time index t is a continuous variable. (Even though we might only measure the temperature or stock price at particular points in time, these variables vary continuously through time.) Although we will work mostly with continuous-time processes in this book, it is easiest to begin with some examples of *discrete-time* processes, that is, variables whose values can change only at discrete points in time. Similarly, the set of all logically conceivable values for x_t (often called the states) can be continuous or discrete. Our definition above is general enough to allow all these possibilities.

One of the simplest examples of a stochastic process is the *discrete-time discrete-state random walk*. Here, x_t is a random variable that begins at a known value x_0, and at times $t = 1, 2, 3, \ldots$, takes a jump of size 1 either up or down, each with probability $\frac{1}{2}$. Since the jumps are independent of each other, we can describe the dynamics of x_t with the following equation:

$$x_t = x_{t-1} + \epsilon_t, \tag{1}$$

where ϵ_t is a random variable with probability distribution

$$\text{prob}(\epsilon_t = 1) = \text{prob}(\epsilon_t = -1) = \tfrac{1}{2} \qquad (t = 1, 2, \ldots).$$

We call x_t a discrete-state process because it can only take on discrete values. For example, set $x_0 = 0$. Then for odd values of t, possible values of x_t are $(-t, \ldots, -1, 1, \ldots, t)$, and for even values of t, possible values of x_t are $(-t, \ldots, -2, 0, 2, \ldots, t)$. The probability distribution for x_t is found

---

[3]This ignores the very long-run possibilities of global warming or cooling.

from the binomial distribution. For t steps, the probability that there are n downward jumps and $t - n$ upward jumps is

$$\binom{t}{n} 2^{-t}.$$

Therefore, the probability that x_t will take on the value $t - 2n$ at time t is

$$\text{prob}(x_t = t - 2n) = \binom{t}{n} 2^{-t}. \tag{2}$$

We will use this probability distribution in the next section when we derive the Wiener process as the continuous limit of the discrete-time random walk. At this point, however, note that the range of possible values that x_t can take on increases with t, as does the variance of x_t. Hence x_t is a nonstationary process.

Because the probability of an upward or downward jump is $\frac{1}{2}$, at time $t = 0$ the expected value of x_t is zero for all t. (Likewise, at time t, the expected value of x_T for $T > t$ is x_t.) One way to generalize this process is by changing the probabilities for an upward or downward jump. Let p be the probability of an upward jump and $q = (1 - p)$ the probability of a downward jump, with $p > q$. Now we have a *random walk with drift*; at time $t = 0$, the expected value of x_t for $t > 0$ is greater than zero, and is increasing with t.

Another way to generalize this process is to let the size of the jump at each time t be a continuous random variable. For example, we might let the size of each jump be normally distributed with mean zero and standard deviation σ. Then, we refer to x_t as a *discrete-time continuous-state stochastic process*.

Another example of a discrete-time continuous-state stochastic process is the *first-order autoregressive process*, abbreviated as AR(1). It is given by the equation

$$x_t = \delta + \rho x_{t-1} + \zeta_t, \tag{3}$$

where δ and ρ are constants, with $-1 < \rho < 1$, and ζ_t is a normally distributed random variable with zero mean. This process is stationary, and x_t has the long-run expected value $\delta/(1 - \rho)$, irrespective of its current value. [This long-run expected value is found by setting $x_t = x_{t-1} = x$ in equation (3) and solving for x.] The AR(1) process is also referred to as a mean-reverting process, because x_t tends to revert back to this long-run expected value. We will examine a continuous-time version of this process later in this chapter.

Both the random walk (with discrete or continuous states, and with drift or without) and the AR(1) process satisfy the *Markov property*, and are therefore called *Markov processes*. This property is that the probability distribution for x_{t+1} depends only on x_t, and not additionally on what happened before time t. For example, in the case of the simple random walk given by equation (1), if $x_t = 6$, then x_{t+1} can equal 5 or 7, each with probability $\frac{1}{2}$. The values of x_{t-1}, x_{t-2}, etc., are irrelevant once we know x_t. The Markov property is important because it can greatly simplify the analysis of a stochastic process. We will see this shortly as we turn to continuous-time processes.

2 The Wiener Process

A Wiener process—also called a *Brownian motion*—is a continuous-time stochastic process with three important properties.[4] First, it is a *Markov process*. As explained above, this means that the probability distribution for all future values of the process depends only on its current value, and is unaffected by past values of the process or by any other current information. As a result, the current value of the process is all one needs to make a best forecast of its future value. Second, the Wiener process has *independent increments*. This means that the probability distribution for the change in the process over any time interval is independent of any other (nonoverlapping) time interval. Third, changes in the process over any finite interval of time are *normally distributed*, with a variance that increases linearly with the time interval.

The Markov property is particularly important. Again, it implies that only current information is useful for forecasting the future path of the process. Stock prices are often modelled as Markov processes, on the grounds that public information is quickly incorporated in the current price of the stock, so that the past pattern of prices has no forecasting value. (This is called the weak form of market efficiency. If it did not hold, investors could in principle "beat the market" through technical analysis, that is, by using the past pattern of prices to forecast the future.) The fact that a Wiener process has independent increments means that we can think of it as a continuous-time version of a random walk, a point that we will return to below.

The three conditions discussed above—the Markov property, independent increments, and changes that are normally distributed—may seem quite restrictive, and might suggest that there are very few real-world variables

---

[4]In 1827, the botanist Robert Brown first observed and described the motion of small particles suspended in a liquid, resulting from the apparent successive and random impacts of neighboring particles; hence the term Brownian motion. In 1905, Albert Einstein proposed a mathematical theory of Brownian motion, which was further developed and made more rigorous by Norbert Wiener in 1923.

that can be realistically modelled with Wiener processes. For example, while it probably seems reasonable that stock prices satisfy the Markov property and have independent increments, it is not reasonable to assume that price changes are normally distributed; after all, we know that the price of a stock can never fall below zero. It is more reasonable to assume that changes in stock prices are *lognormally* distributed, that is, that changes in the logarithm of the price are normally distributed.[5] But this just means modelling the logarithm of price as a Wiener process, rather than the price itself. As we will see, through the use of suitable transformations, the Wiener process can be used as a building block to model an extremely broad range of variables that vary continuously (or almost continuously) and stochastically through time.

It is useful to restate the properties of a Wiener process somewhat more formally. If $z(t)$ is a Wiener process, then any change in z, Δz, corresponding to a time interval Δt, satisfies the following conditions:

1. The relationship between Δz and Δt is given by

$$\Delta z = \epsilon_t \sqrt{\Delta t},$$

   where ϵ_t is a normally distributed random variable with a mean of zero and a standard deviation of 1.
2. The random variable ϵ_t is serially uncorrelated, that is, $\mathcal{E}[\epsilon_t \epsilon_s] = 0$ for $t \neq s$. Thus the values of Δz for any two different intervals of time are independent. [Thus $z(t)$ follows a Markov process with independent increments.]

Let us examine what these two conditions imply for the change in z over some finite interval of time T. We can break this interval up into n units of length Δt each, with $n = T/\Delta t$. Then the change in z over this interval is given by

$$z(s + T) - z(s) = \sum_{i=1}^{n} \epsilon_i \sqrt{\Delta t}. \tag{4}$$

The ϵ_i's are independent of each other. Therefore we can apply the Central Limit Theorem to their sum, and say that the change $z(s+T) - z(s)$ is normally distributed with mean zero and variance $n \Delta t = T$. This last point, which follows from the fact that Δz depends on $\sqrt{\Delta t}$ and not on Δt, is particularly important; *the variance of the change in a Wiener process grows linearly with the time horizon.*

---

[5] We always use natural logarithms, that is, those with base e.

We will make considerable use of this property later. Also, note that the Wiener process is nonstationary. Over the long run its variance will go to infinity.

By letting Δt become infinitesimally small, we can represent the increment of a Wiener process, dz, in continuous time as

$$dz = \epsilon_t \sqrt{dt}. \tag{5}$$

Since ϵ_t has zero mean and unit standard deviation, $\mathcal{E}(dz) = 0$, and $\mathcal{V}[dz] = \mathcal{E}[(dz)^2] = dt$. Note, however, that a Wiener process has no time derivative in a conventional sense; $\Delta z/\Delta t = \epsilon_t (\Delta t)^{-1/2}$, which becomes infinite as Δt approaches zero.

At times we may want to work with two or more Wiener processes, and we will be interested in their covariances. Suppose that $z_1(t)$ and $z_2(t)$ are Wiener processes. Then we can write $\mathcal{E}(dz_1 \, dz_2) = \rho_{12} \, dt$, where ρ_{12} is the *coefficient of correlation* between the two processes. Because a Wiener process has a variance and standard deviation per unit of time equal to 1 ($\mathcal{E}[(dz)^2]/dt = 1$), ρ_{12} is also the covariance per unit of time for the two processes.[6]

2.A Brownian Motion with Drift

We mentioned earlier that the Wiener process can easily be generalized into more complex processes. The simplest generalization of equation (5) is the *Brownian motion with drift*:

$$dx = \alpha \, dt + \sigma \, dz, \tag{6}$$

where dz is the increment of a Wiener process as defined above. In equation (6), α is called the drift parameter, and σ the variance parameter. Note that over any time interval Δt, the change in x, denoted by Δx, is normally distributed, and has expected value $\mathcal{E}(\Delta x) = \alpha \, \Delta t$ and variance $\mathcal{V}(\Delta x) = \sigma^2 \Delta t$.

Figure 3.1 shows three sample paths of equation (6), with trend $\alpha = 0.2$ per year, and standard deviation $\sigma = 1.0$ per year. Although the graph is shown in annual terms (over the time period 1950 to 2000), each sample path was generated by taking a time interval, Δt, of one month, and then calculating a trajectory for $x(t)$ using the equation

$$x_t = x_{t-1} + 0.01667 + 0.2887 \, \epsilon_t, \tag{7}$$

---

[6]Recall that if X and Y are random variables, their coefficient of correlation is $\rho_{XY} = \text{Cov}(XY)/(\sigma_X \sigma_Y)$. In this case $\sigma_X = \sigma_Y = 1$.

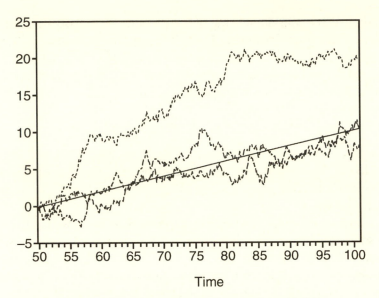

Figure 3.1. *Sample Paths of Brownian Motion with Drift*

with $x_{1950} = 0$. In equation (7), at each time t, ϵ_t is drawn from a normal distribution with zero mean and unit standard deviation. (Also note that the parameters α and σ have been put in monthly terms. A trend of 0.2 per year implies a trend of 0.0167 per month. A standard deviation of 1.0 per year implies a variance of 1.0 per year, and hence a variance of $\frac{1}{12} = 0.0833$ per month, so that the standard deviation in monthly terms is $\sqrt{0.0833} = 0.2887$.) Also shown is a trend line, that is, equation (7) with $\epsilon_t = 0$.

Figure 3.2 shows an optimal forecast of the same stochastic process. Here, a sample path was generated from 1950 to the end of 1974, again using equation (7), and then forecasts of $x(t)$ were constructed for 1975 to 2000. (For comparison, a realization, that is, continuation of the sample path, was also generated.) Recall that because of the Markov property, *only* the value of $x(t)$ for December 1974 is needed to construct this forecast. The forecasted value of x for a time T months beyond December 1974 is given by

$$\hat{x}_{1974+T} = x_{1974} + 0.01667\,T.$$

The graph also shows a 66-percent forecast confidence interval, that is, the forecasted trajectory for $x(t)$ plus or minus one standard deviation. (A 95-percent confidence interval would be given by the forecasted trajectory plus or minus 1.96 standard deviations.) Recall that since the variance of the

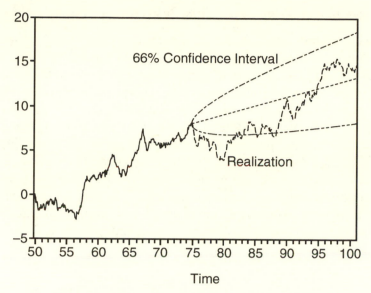

Figure 3.2. *Optimal Forecast of Brownian Motion with Drift*

Wiener process grows linearly with the time horizon, the standard deviation grows as the *square root* of the time horizon. Hence the 66-percent confidence interval for a forecast T months ahead is given by

$$x_{1974} + 0.01667T \pm 0.2887 \sqrt{T}.$$

One can similarly construct 90- or 95-percent confidence intervals.

One can also observe from Figures 3.1 and 3.2 that, in the long run, the trend is the dominant determinant of Brownian motion, whereas in the short run, the volatility of the process dominates. Again, this is an implication of the fact that the mean of $(x_t - x_0)$ is αt, and the standard deviation is $\sigma \sqrt{t}$; for large t, that is, the long run, $\sqrt{t} \ll t$, but for small t, the opposite holds. Another way to see this is to consider the probability that $x_t < x_0$ when $\alpha > 0$. This probability is very small for large t, but is about $\frac{1}{2}$ for small t.

The Brownian motion with drift is a fairly simple stochastic process, but it is important that it be clearly understood. At this point, the definition of a Wiener process and the properties of its generalization in equation (6) may seem somewhat arbitrary. Why, for example, should dx depend on the square root of dt, and not just on dt? And is it reasonable to expect changes in x over any finite interval to be normally distributed? One way to better motivate equation (6) and its properties is to show how it relates to a random walk in discrete time. We turn to this next.

2.B   Random Walk Representation of Brownian Motion

Here we show how equation (6) can be derived as the continuous limit of a discrete-time random walk.[7] To do this, we will divide time up into discrete periods of length Δt, and we will assume that in each period the variable x either moves up or down by an amount Δh. Let the probability that it moves up be p, and the probability that it moves down be $q = 1 - p$. Figure 3.3 shows the possible values of x in each of three periods, assuming it begins at the point x_0. For each possible combination of t and x, the probability of it being reached is also shown. Note that from each period to the next, Δx is a random variable that can take on the values $\pm\Delta h$. Also note that x follows a Markov process with independent increments—the probability distribution for its future value depends only on where it is now, and the probability that it will move up or down in each period is independent of what happened in previous periods.

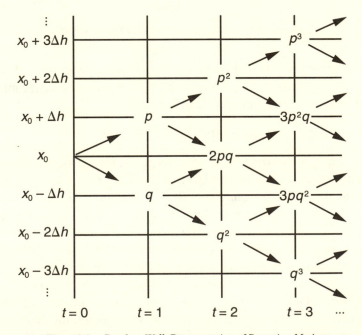

Figure 3.3.   *Random Walk Representation of Brownian Motion*

---

[7]This approach is developed in detail by Cox and Miller (1965). Our exposition is based on Dixit (1993a).

Let us examine the distribution for future values of x. First, observe that the mean of Δx is $\mathcal{E}[\Delta x] = (p - q)\,\Delta h$. Also,

$$\mathcal{E}[(\Delta x)^2] = p\,(\Delta h)^2 + q\,(-\Delta h)^2 = (\Delta h)^2.$$

Thus the variance of Δx is

$$\mathcal{V}[\Delta x] = \mathcal{E}[(\Delta x)^2] - (\mathcal{E}[\Delta x]^2) = [1 - (p - q)^2](\Delta h)^2 = 4pq\,(\Delta h)^2. \quad (8)$$

A time interval of length t has $n = t/\Delta t$ discrete steps. Since the successive steps of the random walk are independent, the cumulated change $(x_t - x_0)$ is a binomial random variable with mean

$$n\,(p - q)\,\Delta h = t\,(p - q)\,\Delta h/\Delta t,$$

and variance

$$n\,[1 - (p - q)^2]\,(\Delta h)^2 = 4pq\,t\,(\Delta h)^2/\Delta t.$$

To interpret this, consider a series of n independent trials, where a success in any one trial counts as 1 and occurs with probability p, while a failure counts as 0 and occurs with probability $q = 1 - p$. The number of successes in n independent trials has a binomial distribution with mean np and variance npq; see Feller (1968, pp. 223, 228). The expressions above are analogous. Now a success counts as Δh and a failure as $-\Delta h$, so the variance, for example, is $4(\Delta h)^2$ times that of the usual binomial expression.

So far the probabilities p and q and the increments Δh and Δt have been chosen arbitrarily, and shortly we will want to let Δt go to zero. As it does, we would like the mean and variance of $(x_t - x_0)$ to remain unchanged, and to be independent of the particular choice of p, q, Δh, and Δt. In addition, we would like to reach equation (6) in the limit. We can ensure that this will indeed be the case by setting

$$\Delta h = \sigma\sqrt{\Delta t}, \quad (9)$$

and

$$p = \tfrac{1}{2}\left[1 + \frac{\alpha}{\sigma}\sqrt{\Delta t}\right], \qquad q = \tfrac{1}{2}\left[1 - \frac{\alpha}{\sigma}\sqrt{\Delta t}\right]. \quad (10)$$

Then

$$p - q = \frac{\alpha}{\sigma}\sqrt{\Delta t} = \frac{\alpha}{\sigma^2}\,\Delta h.$$

Substitute these expressions for Δh and $p - q$ into the formulas above for the mean and variance of $(x_t - x_0)$, and let Δt approach zero. For any finite

t, the number of steps, n, then goes to infinity, and the binomial distribution converges to a normal distribution, with mean

$$t \frac{\alpha}{\sigma^2} \Delta h \frac{\Delta h}{\Delta t} = \alpha t$$

and variance

$$t \left[1 - \left(\frac{\alpha}{\sigma} \right)^2 \Delta t \right] \frac{\sigma^2 \Delta t}{\Delta t} \rightarrow \sigma^2 t.$$

These are exactly the values we need for Brownian motion; α is the drift, and σ^2 the variance, per unit time. In the limit as $\Delta t \rightarrow 0$, both the mean and variance of $(x_t - x_0)$ are independent of Δh and Δt.

We see, then, that Brownian motion is the limit of a random walk, when the time interval and step length go to zero together while preserving the relationship of equation (9). Furthermore, this relationship between Δh and Δt is not an arbitrary one; it is the only way to make the variance of $(x_t - x_0)$ depend on t and not on the number of steps. Thus it should now be clear why dx in equation (6) depends (via dz) on the square root of dt and not on dt. And it should also be clear why changes in x over finite periods are normally distributed; as the number of steps becomes very large, the binomial distribution approaches a normal distribution.

An interesting property of Brownian motion is that as $\Delta t \rightarrow 0$, the total distance travelled over any finite interval of time becomes infinite. This follows from the relationship between Δh and Δt. Since $|\Delta x| = \Delta h$ with certainty, $\mathcal{E}(|\Delta x|) = \Delta h$. Then the total expected length of the path over a time interval of length t is

$$n \Delta h = t \frac{\Delta h}{\Delta t} = \frac{t\sigma}{\sqrt{\Delta t}},$$

which goes to infinity as Δt goes to zero. Likewise, $\Delta x / \Delta t \rightarrow \pm\infty$, depending on whether $\Delta x = +\Delta h$ or $-\Delta h$. Thus the sample paths of a Brownian motion must have many ups and downs, and look very jagged, and such paths will not be differentiable. The derivative dx/dt will not exist, and we cannot speak of $\mathcal{E}(dx/dt)$. However, $\mathcal{E}[dx]$ will in general exist, and so will $(1/dt) \, \mathcal{E}[dx]$.

3   Generalized Brownian Motion—Ito Processes

The Wiener process can serve as a building block to model a broad range of stochastic variables. We will examine a number of examples, all of which are

special cases of the following generalization of the simple Brownian motion
with drift that we studied in the previous section:

$$dx = a(x, t) \, dt + b(x, t) \, dz, \tag{11}$$

where, again, dz is the increment of a Wiener process, and $a(x, t)$ and $b(x, t)$
are known (nonrandom) functions. The new feature is that the drift and variance coefficients are functions of the current state and time. The continuous-
time stochastic process $x(t)$ represented by equation (11) is called an *Ito
process*.

Consider the mean and variance of the increments of this process. Since
$\mathcal{E}(dz) = 0, \mathcal{E}(dx) = a(x, t) \, dt$. The variance of dx is equal to $\mathcal{E}[dx^2] - (\mathcal{E}[dx]^2)$,
which contains terms in dt, in $(dt)^2$, and in $(dt)(dz)$, which is of order $(dt)^{3/2}$.
For dt infinitesimally small, terms in $(dt)^2$ and $(dt)^{3/2}$ can be ignored, and to
order dt the variance is
$$\mathcal{V}[dx] = b^2(x, t) \, dt.$$

We refer to $a(x, t)$ as the expected instantaneous *drift rate* of the Ito process,
and to $b^2(x, t)$ as the instantaneous *variance rate*.

3.A   Geometric Brownian Motion

An important special case of equation (11) is the *geometric Brownian motion
with drift*. Here, $a(x, t) = \alpha x$, and $b(x, t) = \sigma x$, where α and σ are constants.
In this case equation (11) becomes

$$dx = \alpha \, x \, dt + \sigma \, x \, dz. \tag{12}$$

From our discussion of the simple Brownian motion of equation (6), we know
that percentage changes in x, $\Delta x / x$, are normally distributed. Since these
are changes in the natural logarithm of x, absolute changes in x, Δx, are
lognormally distributed.

The relation between x and its logarithm is somewhat more complicated
in this context. In the next section we will show that if $x(t)$ is given by equation
(12), then $F(x) = \log x$ is the following simple Brownian motion with drift:

$$dF = (\alpha - \tfrac{1}{2}\sigma^2) \, dt + \sigma \, dz, \tag{13}$$

so that over a finite time interval t, the change in the logarithm of x is normally
distributed with mean $(\alpha - \tfrac{1}{2}\sigma^2) \, t$ and variance $\sigma^2 t$. As for x itself, it can be
shown that if currently $x(0) = x_0$, the expected value of $x(t)$ is given by

$$\mathcal{E}[x(t)] = x_0 \, e^{\alpha t},$$

and the variance of $x(t)$ is given by[8]

$$V[x(t)] = x_0^2 \, e^{2\alpha t} \, (e^{\sigma^2 t} - 1).$$

This result for the expectation of a geometric Brownian motion can be used to calculate the expected present discounted value of $x(t)$ over some period of time. For example, note that

$$\mathcal{E}\left[\int_0^\infty x(t) \, e^{-rt} \, dt \right] = \int_0^\infty x_0 \, e^{-(r-\alpha)t} \, dt = x_0/(r - \alpha), \qquad (14)$$

provided the discount rate r exceeds the growth rate α. This will prove useful in later chapters when we will need to calculate the discounted present value of a profit flow that follows a geometric Brownian motion.

Geometric Brownian motion is frequently used to model securities prices, as well as interest rates, wage rates, output prices, and other economic and financial variables. Figure 3.4 shows three sample paths of equation (12), with a drift rate of $\alpha = 0.09$, that is, 9 percent per year, and $\sigma = 0.2$, that is, 20 percent per year. These particular numbers were chosen because they are approximately equal to the annual expected rate of growth and standard deviation of the New York Stock Exchange Index, expressed in real (constant-dollar) terms. As with Figure 3.1, the sample paths were generated by taking a time interval, Δt, of one month. Then, $x(t)$ is calculated using the equation

$$x_t = 1.0075 \, x_{t-1} + 0.0577 \, x_{t-1} \, \epsilon_t, \qquad (15)$$

with $x_{1950} = 100$. (Again, at each time t, ϵ_t is drawn from a normal distribution with zero mean and unit standard deviation.) Also shown is the trend line, that is, equation (15) with $\epsilon_t = 0$. Note that in one of these sample paths the "stock market" outperformed its expected rate of growth, but in the other two sample paths it clearly underperformed.

Figure 3.5 shows an optimal forecast of this process. As before, a sample path was generated from 1950 to the end of 1974, and then forecasts of $x(t)$ were constructed for 1975 to 2000. For comparison, a realization, that is, a continuation of the sample path, is also shown. Once again, because of the Markov property, only the value of $x(t)$ for December 1974 is needed to construct the forecast. The forecasted value of x is given by

$$\hat{x}_{1974+T} = (1.0075)^T \, x_{1974},$$

[8]See Aitchison and Brown (1957) for a detailed discussion of the lognormal distribution and its properties.

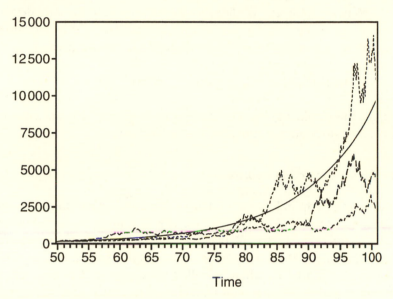

Figure 3.4. *Sample Paths of Geometric Brownian Motion*

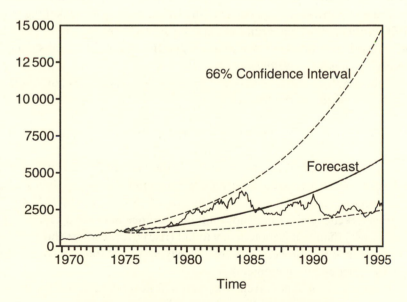

Figure 3.5. *Optimal Forecast of Geometric Brownian Motion*

where T is measured in months starting in January 1975. Also shown in the figure is a 66-percent forecast confidence interval. Since the standard deviation of percentage changes in x grows with the square root of the time horizon, the upper and lower bounds of this confidence interval are given by

$$(1.0075)^T (1.0577)^{\sqrt{T}} x_{1974} \quad \text{and} \quad (1.0075)^T (1.0577)^{-\sqrt{T}} x_{1974}.$$

Note that this confidence interval becomes quite wide. In this particular realization, the "stock market" underperformed its forecast.

3.B   Mean-Reverting Processes

As the sample paths in Figures 3.1 and 3.4 illustrate, Brownian motions tend to wander far from their starting points. This is realistic for some economic variables—for example, speculative asset prices—but not for others. Consider, for example, the prices of raw commodities such as copper or oil. Although such prices are often modelled as geometric Brownian motions, one could argue that they should somehow be related to long-run marginal production costs. In other words, while in the short run the price of oil might fluctuate randomly up and down (in response to wars or revolutions in oil-producing countries, or in response to the strengthening or weakening of the OPEC cartel), in the longer run it ought to be drawn back towards the marginal cost of producing oil. Thus one might argue that the price of oil should be modelled as a *mean-reverting process*.

The simplest mean-reverting process—also known as an *Ornstein-Uhlenbeck process*—is the following:

$$dx = \eta \, (\bar{x} - x) \, dt + \sigma \, dz. \tag{16}$$

Here, η is the speed of reversion, and $\bar{x}$ is the "normal" level of x, that is, the level to which x tends to revert. (If x is a commodity price, then $\bar{x}$ might be the long-run marginal cost of production of this commodity.) Note that the expected change in x depends on the difference between x and $\bar{x}$. If x is greater (less) than $\bar{x}$, it is more likely to fall (rise) over the next short interval of time. Hence this process, although satisfying the Markov property, does not have independent increments.

If the value of x is currently x_0 and x follows equation (16), then its expected value at any future time t is

$$\mathcal{E}[x_t] = \bar{x} + (x_0 - \bar{x}) \, e^{-\eta t}. \tag{17}$$

Also, the variance of $(x_t - \bar{x})$ is

$$\mathcal{V}[x_t - \bar{x}] = \frac{\sigma^2}{2\eta}(1 - e^{-2\eta t}). \tag{18}$$

[See the Appendix to this chapter for a derivation of equations (17) and (18).] Observe from these equations that the expected value of x_t converges to $\bar{x}$ as t becomes large, and the variance converges to $\sigma^2/2\eta$. Also, as $\eta \to \infty$, $\mathcal{V}[x_t] \to 0$, which means that x can never deviate from $\bar{x}$, even momentarily. Finally, as $\eta \to 0$, x becomes a simple Brownian motion, and $\mathcal{V}[x_t] \to \sigma^2 t$.

Figure 3.6 shows four sample paths of equation (16) for different values of η. In each case, $\sigma = 0.05$ in *monthly* terms, $\bar{x} = 1$, and $x(t)$ begins at $x_0 = 1$. The first is for $\eta = 0$, which corresponds to a simple Brownian motion without drift. Note that $x(t)$ tends to drift far from its initial value of 1. Sample paths are also shown for $\eta = 0.01, 0.02$, and 0.5. Note that the larger η is, the less $x(t)$ tends to drift away from $\bar{x}$. When $\eta = 0.5$, $x(t)$ makes only small and short-lived excursions away from $\bar{x}$.

Figure 3.7 shows an optimal forecast of this process, for $\eta = 0.02$. In this case a sample path was generated from 1950 to the end of 1980, and then forecasts of $x(t)$ were constructed for 1981 to 2000. For comparison, a realization, that is, a continuation of the sample path, is also shown, as is a

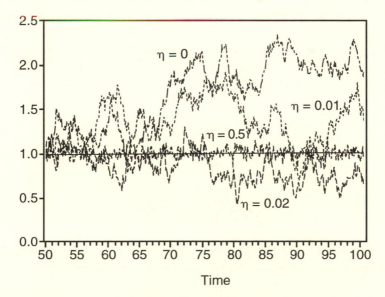

Figure 3.6. *Sample Paths of Mean-Reverting Process: $dx = \eta(\bar{x} - x)dt + \sigma dz$*

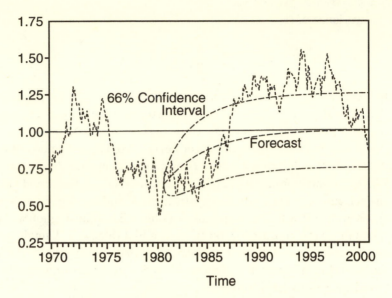

Figure 3.7. *Optimal Forecast of Mean-Reverting Process*

66-percent confidence interval for the forecast. Note that after four or five years, the variance of the forecast converges to $\sigma^2/2\eta = 0.0025/0.04 = 0.065$, so the 66-percent confidence interval ($\pm\,1$ standard deviation) converges to the forecast ± 0.25.

Equation (16) is the continuous-time version of the first-order autoregressive process in discrete time. Specifically, equation (16) is the limiting case as $\Delta t \to 0$ of the following AR(1) process:

$$x_t - x_{t-1} = \bar{x}\,(1 - e^{-\eta}) + (e^{-\eta} - 1)\,x_{t-1} + \epsilon_t, \tag{19}$$

where ϵ_t is normally distributed with mean zero and standard deviation σ_ϵ, and

$$\sigma_\epsilon^2 = \frac{\sigma^2}{2\eta}\,(1 - e^{-2\eta}).$$

Thus one could estimate the parameters of equation (16) using discrete-time data (the only data ever available) by running the regression

$$x_t - x_{t-1} = a + b\,x_{t-1} + \epsilon_t,$$

and then calculating $\bar{x} = -\hat{a}/\hat{b}$, $\hat{\eta} = -\log(1 + \hat{b})$, and

$$\hat{\sigma} = \hat{\sigma}_\epsilon \sqrt{\frac{\log(1 + \hat{b})}{(1 + \hat{b})^2 - 1}},$$

where $\hat{\sigma}_\epsilon$ is the standard error of the regression.

It is easy to generalize equation (16). For example, one might expect $x(t)$ to revert to $\bar{x}$ as in (16), but the variance rate to grow with x. Then one could use the following process:

$$dx = \eta(\bar{x} - x)\,dt + \sigma x\,dz. \tag{20}$$

Alternatively, proportional changes in a variable might be modelled as a simple mean-reverting process. This is equivalent to describing $x(t)$ by the process

$$dx = \eta x(\bar{x} - x)\,dt + \sigma x\,dz. \tag{21}$$

We will examine the implications of different mean-reverting processes for investment decisions later in this book.

Before closing this subsection, let us return to a question we asked earlier: are the prices of raw commodities and other goods best modelled as geometric Brownian motions or as mean-reverting processes? One way to answer this is to examine the data for the price variable in question, and in particular to estimate equation (19) and test whether the coefficient of x_{t-1} on the right-hand side is significantly different from zero. There are two problems with this. First, under the null hypothesis that this coefficient is indeed zero (so that x_t follows a random walk), its ordinary least squares estimator is biased towards zero, so one cannot use a standard t-test to determine whether the estimate is significantly different from zero. However, there are alternative tests, called *unit root tests*, that can easily be applied instead.[9] Second and more serious, it usually requires many years of data to determine with any degree of confidence whether a variable is indeed mean reverting.

As an illustration, Figures 3.8 and 3.9 show the prices of crude oil and copper, in constant 1967 dollars, over the past 120 years.[10] A cursory look at these figures suggests that these prices are mean reverting, but that the rate of mean reversion is very slow. This is indeed confirmed by running unit root tests on the data. Running these tests on the full 120 years of data, one can

---

[9]The tests were originally developed by Dickey and Fuller (1981), and have since been extended and refined. See Chapter 15 of Pindyck and Rubinfeld (1991) for an introduction to these tests.

[10]The data for 1870 to 1973 are from Manthy (1978); data after 1973 are from publications of the U.S. Energy Information Energy and U.S. Bureau of Mines. Prices were deflated by the Wholesale Price Index (now the Producer Price Index).

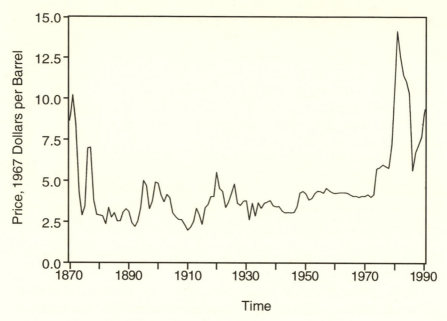

Figure 3.8. Price of Crude Oil in 1967 Dollars per Barrel

easily reject the random walk hypothesis; that is, the data confirm that the prices are mean reverting. However, if one performs unit root tests using data for only the past 30 or 40 years, one fails to reject the random walk hypothesis. This seems to be the case for many other economic variables as well; using 30 or so years of data, it is difficult to statistically distinguish between a random walk and a mean-reverting process.

As a result, one must often rely on theoretical considerations (for example, intuition concerning the operation of equilibrating mechanisms) more than statistical tests when deciding whether or not to model a price or other variable as a mean-reverting process. Another criterion that may enter into this modelling decision is analytical tractability. As we will see in later chapters, valuing a project and solving for an optimal investment rule is often much simpler when the underlying stochastic variables are modelled as geometric Brownian motions.[11]

---

[11]It is usually impossible to obtain analytical solutions for optimal investment rules when the underlying stochastic variables are modelled as mean reverting, so that one must instead use numerical solution techniques. For a strong argument *against* modelling the prices of oil and other exhaustible resources as geometric Brownian motions, see Lund (1991b).

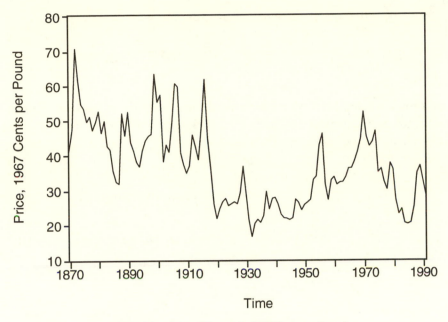

Figure 3.9. *Price of Copper in 1967 Cents per Pound*

4 Ito's Lemma

We have seen that the Ito process of equation (11) is continuous in time, but is not differentiable. However, we will often need to work with functions of Ito processes, and we will want to take the differentials of such functions. For example, we might describe the value of an option to invest in a copper mine as a function of the price of copper, which in turn might be represented by a geometric Brownian motion. In this case we would want to determine the stochastic process that the value of the option follows. To do this, and in general to differentiate or integrate functions of Ito processes, we will need to make use of *Ito's Lemma*.

Ito's Lemma is easiest to understand as a Taylor series expansion. Suppose that $x(t)$ follows the process of equation (11), and consider a function $F(x, t)$ that is at least twice differentiable in x and once in t. We would like to find the total differential of this function, dF. The usual rules of calculus define this differential in terms of first-order changes in x and t:

$$dF = \frac{\partial F}{\partial x} \, dx + \frac{\partial F}{\partial t} \, dt.$$

But suppose that we also include higher-order terms for changes in x:

$$dF = \frac{\partial F}{\partial x}\, dx + \frac{\partial F}{\partial t}\, dt + \frac{1}{2} \frac{\partial^2 F}{\partial x^2}\, (dx)^2 + \frac{1}{6} \frac{\partial^3 F}{\partial x^3}\, (dx)^3 + \cdots . \qquad (22)$$

In ordinary calculus, these higher-order terms all vanish in the limit. To see whether that is also the case here, expand the third and fourth terms on the right-hand side of equation (22). First, substitute equation (11) for dx to determine $(dx)^2$:

$$(dx)^2 = a^2(x, t)\, (dt)^2 + 2\, a(x, t)\, b(x, t)\, (dt)^{3/2} + b^2(x, t)\, dt. \qquad (23)$$

Terms in $(dt)^{3/2}$ and $(dt)^2$ go to zero faster than dt as it becomes infinitesimally small, so we can ignore these terms and write

$$(dx)^2 = b^2(x, t)\, dt.$$

As for the fourth term on the right-hand side of equation (22), every term in the expansion of $(dx)^3$ will include dt raised to a power greater than 1, and so will go to zero faster than dt in the limit. This is likewise the case for any higher-order terms, such as $(dx)^4$, etc. Hence Ito's Lemma gives the differential dF as

$$dF = \frac{\partial F}{\partial t}\, dt + \frac{\partial F}{\partial x}\, dx + \frac{1}{2} \frac{\partial^2 F}{\partial x^2}\, (dx)^2. \qquad (24)$$

We can also write this in expanded form by substituting equation (11) for dx:

$$dF = \left[\frac{\partial F}{\partial t} + a(x, t) \frac{\partial F}{\partial x} + \frac{1}{2} b^2(x, t) \frac{\partial^2 F}{\partial x^2} \right] dt + b(x, t) \frac{\partial F}{\partial x}\, dz. \qquad (25)$$

Compared to the chain rule for differentiation in ordinary calculus, equation (25) has one extra term. For some intuition, suppose for simplicity that the drift rate $a(x, t) = 0$, and that $\partial F/\partial t = 0$. Now $\mathcal{E}(dx) = 0$, but $\mathcal{E}(dF) \neq 0$. This is just an implication of Jensen's Inequality. $\mathcal{E}(dF)$ will be positive if F is a convex function of x (that is, $\partial^2 F/\partial x^2 > 0$), and negative if F is a concave function of x (that is, $\partial^2 F/\partial x^2 < 0$). For Ito processes, dx behaves like $\sqrt{dt}$, and $(dx)^2$ like dt, so the effect of convexity or concavity is of order

dt and cannot be ignored when writing the differential of F. The extra term in equation (25) captures exactly this effect.

We can easily extend this Taylor series expansion to functions of several Ito processes. For example, suppose that $F = F(x_1, \ldots, x_m, t)$ is a function of time and of the m Ito processes $x_1, \ldots, x_m$, where

$$dx_i = a_i(x_1, \ldots, x_m, t)\, dt + b_i(x_1, \ldots, x_m, t)\, dz_i, \qquad i = 1, \ldots, m, \quad (26)$$

with $\mathcal{E}(dz_i\, dz_j) = \rho_{ij}\, dt$. Then Ito's Lemma gives the differential dF as

$$dF = \frac{\partial F}{\partial t}\, dt + \sum_i \frac{\partial F}{\partial x_i}\, dx_i + \tfrac{1}{2} \sum_i \sum_j \frac{\partial^2 F}{\partial x_i \partial x_j}\, dx_i\, dx_j. \qquad (27)$$

Again, we can substitute (26) for dx_i and write this in expanded form as

$$dF = \left[\frac{\partial F}{\partial t} + \sum_i a_i(x_1, \ldots, t) \frac{\partial F}{\partial x_i} + \tfrac{1}{2} \sum_i b_i^2(x_1, \ldots, t) \frac{\partial^2 F}{\partial x_i^2} \right.$$

$$\left. + \tfrac{1}{2} \sum_{i \neq j} \rho_{ij}\, b_i(x_1, \ldots, t)\, b_j(x_1, \ldots, t) \frac{\partial^2 F}{\partial x_i \partial x_j} \right] dt \qquad (28)$$

$$+ \sum_i b_i(x_1, \ldots, t) \frac{\partial F}{\partial x_i}\, dz_i.$$

Example: **Geometric Brownian Motion.** Let us return to the geometric Brownian motion of equation (12). We will use Ito's Lemma to show that the process followed by $F(x) = \log x$ is indeed given by equation (13). Since $\partial F/\partial t = 0$, $\partial F/\partial x = 1/x$, and $\partial^2 F/\partial x^2 = -1/x^2$, we have from (24):

$$
\begin{aligned}
dF &= \frac{1}{x}\, dx - \frac{1}{2x^2}\, (dx)^2 \\
&= \alpha\, dt + \sigma\, dz - \tfrac{1}{2}\sigma^2\, dt = (\alpha - \tfrac{1}{2}\sigma^2)\, dt + \sigma\, dz.
\end{aligned}
\qquad (29)
$$

Hence over any finite time interval T, the change in $\log x$ is normally distributed with mean $(\alpha - \tfrac{1}{2}\sigma^2)\, T$ and variance $\sigma^2\, T$.

Why is the drift rate of $F(x) = \log x$ less than α? The reason is that $\log x$ is a concave function of x, so with x uncertain, the expected value of $\log x$ changes by less than the logarithm of the expected value of x. (Once again this is just a consequence of Jensen's Inequality.) Uncertainty over x is greater the longer the time horizon, so the expected value of $\log x$ is reduced by an amount that increases with time; hence the drift rate is reduced.

Example: **Correlated Brownian Motions.** As a second example, consider the function $F(x, y) = xy$, where x and y each follow geometric Brownian motions:

$$dx = \alpha_x \, x \, dt + \sigma_x \, x \, dz_x,$$

$$dy = \alpha_y \, y \, dt + \sigma_y \, y \, dz_y,$$

with $\mathcal{E}[dz_x \, dz_y] = \rho \, dt$. We will find the process followed by $F(x, y)$, and the process followed by $G = \log F$.

Since $\partial^2 F/\partial x^2 = \partial^2 F/\partial y^2 = 0$ and $\partial^2 F/\partial x \partial y = 1$, we have from (27):

$$dF = x \, dy + y \, dx + dx \, dy. \tag{30}$$

Now substitute for dx and dy and rearrange:

$$dF = (\alpha_x + \alpha_y + \rho \, \sigma_x \, \sigma_y) \, F \, dt + (\sigma_x \, dz_x + \sigma_y \, dz_y) \, F. \tag{31}$$

Hence F also follows a geometric Brownian motion. What about $G = \log F$? Going through the same steps as in the previous example, we find that

$$dG = (\alpha_x + \alpha_y - \tfrac{1}{2} \sigma_x^2 - \tfrac{1}{2} \sigma_y^2) \, dt + \sigma_x \, dz_x + \sigma_y \, dz_y. \tag{32}$$

From equation (32) we see that over any time interval T, the change in $\log F$ is normally distributed with mean $(\alpha_x + \alpha_y - \tfrac{1}{2} \sigma_x^2 - \tfrac{1}{2} \sigma_y^2) \, T$ and variance $(\sigma_x^2 + \sigma_y^2 + 2\rho \, \sigma_x \, \sigma_y) \, T$.

Example: **Present Discounted Value.** Suppose $F(x) = x^\theta$, where x follows the geometric Brownian motion of equation (12). We will show how to calculate the expected present discounted value

$$\mathcal{E}\left[\int_0^\infty F(x(t)) \, e^{-rt} \, dt \right].$$

First, use Ito's Lemma to write

$$\begin{aligned} dF &= \theta \, x^{\theta-1} [\alpha \, x \, dt + \sigma \, x \, dz] + \tfrac{1}{2} \theta(\theta - 1) x^{\theta-2} \sigma^2 x^2 \, dt \\ &= [\theta \, \alpha + \tfrac{1}{2} \theta(\theta - 1) \sigma^2] \, F \, dt + \theta \, \sigma \, F \, dz. \end{aligned} \tag{33}$$

Observe from equation (33) that F follows a geometric Brownian motion. Hence we can use equation (14) for the expectation of a geometric Brownian motion to write

$$\mathcal{E}[F(x, t)] = F(x_0) \, \exp\left[(\theta \, \alpha + \tfrac{1}{2} \theta \, (\theta - 1) \sigma^2)t \right], \tag{34}$$

and the present discounted value is

$$x_0^\theta / [r - \theta \, \alpha - \tfrac{1}{2} \theta(\theta - 1) \sigma^2],$$

provided the denominator is positive.

5 Barriers and Long-Run Distribution

Suppose x starts at x_0, and follows the simple Brownian motion of equation (6). Left to itself, at time t it will have a normal distribution with mean $(x_0 + \alpha t)$ and variance $\sigma^2 t$. However, now we constrain the process of x not to cross an upper reflecting barrier at $\bar{x}$. Using our random walk representation, this means that starting at $\bar{x} - \Delta h$, if x tries to take an upward step it is moved right back to $\bar{x} - \Delta h$. (A step down to $\bar{x} - 2\Delta h$ is allowed to occur without interference.) Similarly, we place a lower reflecting barrier at $\underline{x}$.

In economic applications, such barriers often occur because of equilibrating mechanisms in the market. For example, if x is the price of a commodity, it is subject to an upper barrier where new firms enter, and a lower barrier where incumbent firms will exit. We will encounter such models in Chapters 8 and 9.

Here we want to consider what happens when x follows such a process for a long time. The influence of the initial x_0 will disappear when one of the barriers is hit, because of the Markov property. As the motion goes back and forth trapped between the two barriers, we expect it will settle down to a stationary long-run process. We want to find the probability density of this distribution, which we denote by $\phi(x)$.

Once again we use the random walk representation. Consider any three adjacent points, say $x - \Delta h$, x, and $x + \Delta h$. In any one small time interval Δt, the probability mass $\phi(x - \Delta h)$ moves up with probability p, and the mass $\phi(x + \Delta h)$ moves down with probability q, where p and q are given by equation (10). These moves constitute the probability mass at x after the end of the interval. If the probability distribution is to be stationary, this must be just $\phi(x)$. Thus

$$\phi(x) = p\,\phi(x - \Delta h) + q\,\phi(x + \Delta h). \tag{35}$$

Now we substitute for p and q, expand the right-hand side by Taylor's theorem, and collect terms together. This gives

$$\phi(x) = \tfrac{1}{2}\left[1 + (\alpha/\sigma^2)\,\Delta h\right]\left[\phi(x) - \Delta h\,\phi'(x) + \tfrac{1}{2}(\Delta h)^2\,\phi''(x) + \cdots\right]$$
$$+ \tfrac{1}{2}\left[1 - (\alpha/\sigma^2)\,\Delta h\right]\left[\phi(x) + \Delta h\,\phi'(x) + \tfrac{1}{2}(\Delta h)^2\,\phi''(x) + \cdots\right]$$
$$= \phi(x) - (\alpha/\sigma^2)(\Delta h)^2\,\phi'(x) + \tfrac{1}{2}(\Delta h)^2\,\phi''(x) + \cdots .$$

The omitted terms all go to zero faster than $(\Delta h)^2$ (or Δt). So we cancel $\phi(x)$ from both sides, divide by $(\Delta h)^2$, and take limits as $\Delta h \to 0$. This gives the differential equation

$$\phi''(x) = \gamma\,\phi'(x),\tag{36}$$

where $\gamma = 2\alpha/\sigma^2$.

The general solution of this equation is easily seen to be

$$\phi(x) = A\,e^{\gamma x} + B,$$

where A and B are constants to be determined. For that we must consider what happens at the barriers $\bar{x}$ and $\underline{x}$. Consider the upper barrier. The mass of probability $\phi(\bar{x} - \Delta h)$ moves up with probability p, but is reflected right back to $\bar{x} - \Delta h$. Therefore the equation balancing the probability masses is modified to

$$\phi(\bar{x} - \Delta h) = p\phi(\bar{x} - \Delta h) + p\phi(\bar{x} - 2\,\Delta h).$$

Expanding this and simplifying as before, we find

$$\phi'(\bar{x}) = \gamma\,\phi(\bar{x}).$$

Substituting the general solution into this, we find $B = 0$. The same conclusion could have been obtained by considering the lower barrier $\underline{x}$.

Finally, the constant A must be chosen to ensure that the whole probability mass between $\underline{x}$ and $\bar{x}$ must sum to one. This gives

$$\phi(x) = \gamma\,\exp(\gamma\,x)\,/\,[\exp(\gamma\,\bar{x}) - \exp(\gamma\,\underline{x})].\tag{37}$$

The long-run stationary probability density is thus a simple exponential. It is natural that if the x process has a positive drift rate ($\alpha > 0$ and therefore $\gamma > 0$), the exponential should be rising toward the upper barrier, and if it has a negative drift rate, the density should be falling to the right. If $\gamma > 0$, we can in fact let the lower barrier $\underline{x}$ go to $-\infty$ and consider a process with only an upper barrier at $\bar{x}$; it will have a long-run stationary distribution whose density falls exponentially to the left of $\bar{x}$. Likewise, if $\gamma < 0$, we can let the upper barrier $\bar{x}$ go to ∞.

We will have occasion to make use of this distribution at several points in Chapters 8 and 9. On a couple of occasions we will generalize the argument to allow a jump process of "sudden death." More substantial extensions include the case where x follows a general Ito process, and examination of the actual dynamics of the probability distribution of x rather than only its long-run stationary state. Both these extensions require the development of a differential equation for the probability density—the Kolmogorov equation—and we treat this in an Appendix to this chapter.

6 Jump Processes

So far we have considered only diffusion processes, that is, stochastic processes that are everywhere continuous. Often, however, it is more realistic to model an economic variable as a process that makes infrequent but discrete jumps. An example would be entry by a new competitor in a market with few firms, so that price suddenly drops. Likewise, one might model the value of a patent as subject to unpredictable but sizable drops in response to competitors' success in developing related patents. Or, one might view the price of oil as a mixed Brownian motion–jump process; during normal times the price fluctuates continuously, but the price can also take large jumps or falls if a war or revolution begins or ends. In this section, we discuss *Poisson (jump) processes*, and we introduce a version of Ito's Lemma that will help us to work with them.

A Poisson process is a process subject to jumps of fixed or random size, for which the arrival times follow a Poisson distribution. We call these jumps "events." Letting λ denote the *mean arrival rate* of an event, during a time interval of infinitesimal length dt, the probability that an event will occur is given by $\lambda\, dt$, and the probability that an event will not occur is given by $1 - \lambda\, dt$. The event is a jump of size u, which can itself be a random variable.

Let q denote a Poisson process by analogy with the Wiener process; in other words

$$dq = \begin{cases} 0 & \text{with probability } 1 - \lambda\, dt, \\ u & \text{with probability } \lambda\, dt. \end{cases}$$

Then we write the stochastic process for the variable x as a Poisson differential equation, which corresponds to the Ito process of equation (11) as follows:

$$dx = f(x, t)\, dt + g(x, t)\, dq, \tag{38}$$

where $f(x, t)$ and $g(x, t)$ are known (nonrandom) functions.

Suppose that $H(x, t)$ is some (differentiable) function of x and t, and that we would like to derive an expression for the expected change in H, that is, $\mathcal{E}(dH)$. To do this, expand dH as follows:

$$\begin{aligned} dH &= \frac{\partial H}{\partial t}\, dt + \frac{\partial H}{\partial x}\, dx \\ &= \frac{\partial H}{\partial t}\, dt + \frac{\partial H}{\partial x} \left[f(x, t)\, dt + g(x, t)\, dq \right]. \end{aligned} \tag{39}$$

(Note that higher-order terms go to zero faster than dt because, unlike for the Ito process, dx does not depend on $\sqrt{dt}$.) Thus changes in x cause changes in H in two ways. First, $H(x, t)$ will change continuously and deterministically in response to the drift in x. Second, there is a possibility that a Poisson event will occur; if it does, x will change by the random amount $u\,g(x, t)$, and $H(x, t)$ will change accordingly. Since the probability that a Poisson event will occur over the interval dt is $\lambda\,dt$, we have

$$\mathcal{E}\left[\frac{\partial H}{\partial x}\,g(x, t)\,dq\right] = \mathcal{E}_u\{\lambda\,[H(x + u\,g(x, t), t) - H(x, t)]\}\,dt, \qquad (40)$$

where the expectation on the right-hand side of the equation is with respect to the size of the jump u. Hence the expectation of the differential of H is given by

$$\mathcal{E}[dH] = \left[\frac{\partial H}{\partial t} + f(x, t)\,\frac{\partial H}{\partial x}\right]\,dt + \mathcal{E}_u\{\lambda[H(x + g(x, t)\,u, t) - H(x, t)]\}\,dt.$$
$$(41)$$

We can use equation (41) in the same way that we used Ito's Lemma when working with continuous processes.

Sometimes we meet a combination of an Ito process and a jump process. The former goes on all the time; the latter occurs infrequently. Then the appropriate version of Ito's Lemma also combines the two effects. Thus, if

$$dx = a(x, t)\,dt + b(x, t)\,dz + g(x, t)\,dq,$$

then the expected value of the change in the function $H(x, t)$ is given by

$$\mathcal{E}[dH] = \left[\frac{\partial H}{\partial t} + a(x, t)\,\frac{\partial H}{\partial x} + \tfrac{1}{2}\,b^2(x, t)\,\frac{\partial^2 H}{\partial x^2}\right]\,dt \qquad (42)$$
$$+ \mathcal{E}_u\{\lambda[H(x + g(x, t)\,u, t) - H(x, t)]\}\,dt.$$

Note that the second-order derivative is relevant only for the variance contributed by the continuous part of the process. The jump part contributes the last term on the right-hand side involving a difference in values of H at discretely different points.

Example: **Present Value of Wages.**   Suppose an individual who lives forever receives a wage $W(t)$ which rises by a constant amount ϵ at random points in time. If λ is the mean arrival rate of raises, we can write the differential equation for the individual's wage as

$$dW = \epsilon\,dq, \qquad (43)$$

with $u = 1$ with probability 1. What is the present value of the individual's expected earnings stream?

We want to find

$$V(W) = \mathcal{E} \int_0^\infty W(t) e^{-\rho t} \, dt.$$

We can treat V as an asset and equate the normal return on it at rate ρ to the sum of the dividend (current wage) and the expected capital gain:

$$\rho V \, dt = W(t) \, dt + \mathcal{E}(dV).$$

In this case, $\mathcal{E}(dV) = (dV/dW) \lambda \epsilon \, dt = (\lambda \epsilon / \rho) \, dt$, so that

$$V(W) = \frac{W}{\rho} + \frac{\lambda \epsilon}{\rho^2}.$$

Thus V is equivalent to a perpetuity that pays out forever the current wage W plus the capitalized value of the average raise per unit time.

Example: **Value of a Machine.** Suppose a machine produces a constant flow of profit π as long as it operates. It requires no maintenance, but at some point in time it will break down and will have to be discarded. If λ is the arrival rate of a breakdown, and ρ is the discount rate, what is the machine's value?

The value of the machine follows the process

$$dV = -V \, dq,$$

where an "event" is $u = 1$ with probability 1. Then the asset return equation becomes

$$\rho V \, dt = \pi \, dt + \mathcal{E}(dV) = \pi \, dt - \lambda V \, dt.$$

Thus,

$$V = \frac{\pi}{\rho + \lambda}.$$

Hence we can treat the profit flow as a perpetuity, and value it by increasing the discount rate by an amount λ. This is a very general idea: if a profit flow can stop when a Poisson event with arrival rate λ occurs, then we can calculate the expected present value of the stream as if it never stops, but adding λ to the discount rate. We will come across this in many applications in later chapters.

7 Guide to the Literature

Our treatment of stochastic processes and Ito's Lemma has been at an introductory and heuristic level. For a more in-depth development of stochastic processes and their properties, see Cox and Miller (1965), Feller (1971), and Karlin and Taylor (1975, 1981). Cox and Miller (1965) and Karlin and Taylor (1981) provide particularly nice treatments of the Kolmogorov equations. Also, see Chapter 3 of Merton (1990) for a discussion of the use of continuous and jump processes in economic and financial modelling. For a much more rigorous approach to stochastic processes, see Karatzas and Shreve (1988).

For more detailed but still introductory discussions of Ito's Lemma and its application, see Merton (1971), Chow (1979), Malliaris and Brock (1982), and Hull (1989). [Merton (1971) also provides a nice discussion of Poisson processes, with examples.] For more rigorous treatments, see Kushner (1967), Arnold (1974), Dothan (1990), and Chapter 4 of Harrison (1985). Also, for a more detailed discussion of the calculation of expected present values, see Dixit (1993a).

Appendix

A   The Kolmogorov Equations

At times we will want to answer questions of the following sort: If $x(t)$ follows a particular stochastic process and its current value is x_0, what is the probability that it will be within a certain range at time t later? Or, what is the probability that $x(t)$ will have reached a point x_1 within a time $t \leq T$? To answer questions like these we will need to describe the probability distribution for x and its evolution over time. This can be done using the *Kolmogorov equations*.

We will derive the Kolmogorov equation for the simple Brownian motion with drift of equation (6), using the discrete-time random walk representation that we introduced in Section 2.B of this chapter. Recall that we broke a time interval of length t into $n = t/\Delta t$ discrete steps, and in each step, with probability p, x would increase by an amount Δh, and with probability $q = 1 - p$, it would decrease by Δh. Finally, to keep the variance of $(x_t - x_0)$ independent of the particular choice of Δt, we set $\Delta h = \sigma \sqrt{\Delta t}$.

Let $\phi(x_0, t_0; x, t)$ be the probability density function for $x(t)$, given that at an earlier time t_0 we have $x(0) = x_0$. Thus

$$\text{Prob}[a \leq x(t) \leq b \mid x(t_0) = x_0] = \int_a^b \phi(x_0, t_0; u, t)\, du.$$

Over the interval of time $t - \Delta t$ to t, the process can reach the point x in one of two ways, by increasing from the point $x - \Delta h$, or by decreasing from the point $x + \Delta h$. Hence

$$\phi(x_0, t_0; x, t) = p\phi(x_0, t_0; x - \Delta h, t - \Delta t) + q\,\phi(x_0, t_0; x + \Delta h, t - \Delta t). \quad (44)$$

We recognize this as a dynamic generalization of the stationary-state computation in the text; see equation (35).

Now expand $\phi(x_0, t_0; x - \Delta h, t - \Delta t)$ in a Taylor series around $\phi(x_0, t_0; x, t)$:

$$\phi(x_0, t_0; x - \Delta h, t - \Delta t) = \phi(x_0, t_0; x, t) - \Delta t\,\frac{\partial \phi}{\partial t} - \Delta h\,\frac{\partial \phi}{\partial x} + \tfrac{1}{2}(\Delta h)^2\,\frac{\partial^2 \phi}{\partial x^2} + \cdots.$$

Note that third- and higher-order terms are of order $(\Delta t)^{3/2}$, $(\Delta t)^2$, etc., and hence will go to zero faster than Δt. Expand $\phi(x_0, t_0; x + \Delta h, t - \Delta t)$ likewise, and substitute these expressions into equation (44):

$$\phi(x_0, t_0; x, t) = (p+q)\,\phi(x_0, t_0; x, t) - (p+q)\,\Delta t\,\frac{\partial \phi}{\partial t}$$

$$- (p-q)\,\Delta h\,\frac{\partial \phi}{\partial x} + \tfrac{1}{2}(p+q)(\Delta h)^2\,\frac{\partial^2 \phi}{\partial x^2}.$$

Finally, we use $p + q = 1$, and from equation (10), $p - q = (\alpha/\sigma)\sqrt{\Delta t}$. We also substitute $\Delta h = \sigma\sqrt{\Delta t}$, divide through by Δt, and rearrange:

$$\tfrac{1}{2}\sigma^2\,\frac{\partial^2}{\partial x^2}\,\phi(x_0, t_0; x, t) - \alpha\,\frac{\partial}{\partial x}\,\phi(x_0, t_0; x, t) = \frac{\partial}{\partial t}\phi(x_0, t_0; x, t). \quad (45)$$

Equation (45) is called the *Kolmogorov forward equation* for the Brownian motion with drift, and it describes the evolution over time of the probability density function $\phi(x_0, t_0; x, t)$. In a similar manner, one can derive the Kolmogorov forward equation for the general Ito process of equation (11):[12]

$$\tfrac{1}{2}\frac{\partial^2}{\partial x^2}[b^2(x, t)\,\phi(x_0, t_0; x, t)] - \frac{\partial}{\partial x}[a(x, t)\,\phi(x_0, t_0; x, t)] = \frac{\partial}{\partial t}\phi(x_0, t_0; x, t).$$
$$(46)$$

Equations (45) and (46) are called "forward" equations because they have as boundary conditions the initial value x_0 at time t_0, and are solved forward for the density function for future values of x. One can likewise describe the evolution of the density function backward in time, that is, taking $x(t)$ at time t as the boundary conditions and solving for the density function for previous

---

[12]See Karlin and Taylor (1981) for derivations and more detailed discussions of the Kolmogorov forward and backward equations.

values of x_0 at time $t_0 < t$. The *Kolmogorov backward equation* for the Ito process is

$$\frac{1}{2} b^2(x_0, t_0) \frac{\partial^2}{\partial x_0^2} \phi(x_0, t_0; x, t) + a(x_0, t_0) \frac{\partial}{\partial x_0} \phi(x_0, t_0; x, t)$$

$$= -\frac{\partial}{\partial t_0} \phi(x_0, t_0; x, t). \tag{47}$$

We will use the Kolmogorov equations later in this book, but at this point it is useful to consider a couple of examples.

Example: **Ornstein-Uhlenbeck Process.**   In this example we will return to the simple Ornstein-Uhlenbeck (mean-reverting) process of equation (16). For simplicity, set $\bar{x} = 0$, so that the equation becomes

$$dx = -\eta x \, dt + \sigma \, dz. \tag{48}$$

In the text we asserted that equations (17) and (18) give the mean and variance of $x(t)$. We can use the Kolmogorov forward equation to prove this claim.

Write the moment-generating function for $x(t)$ as

$$M(\theta, t) \equiv \mathcal{E}(e^{-\theta x}) = \int_{-\infty}^{\infty} \phi(x_0, t_0; x, t) \, e^{-\theta x} \, dx. \tag{49}$$

Then,

$$\frac{\partial M}{\partial t} = \int_{-\infty}^{\infty} \frac{\partial \phi}{\partial t} e^{-\theta x} \, dx. \tag{50}$$

The Kolmogorov forward equation for this process is

$$\frac{\partial \phi}{\partial t} = \frac{1}{2} \sigma^2 \frac{\partial^2 \phi}{\partial x^2} - \eta x \frac{\partial \phi}{\partial x} + \eta \phi. \tag{51}$$

Substitute this for $\partial \phi / \partial t$ in equation (50), and integrate by parts to get the following equation for $M(\theta, t)$:

$$\frac{1}{2} \sigma^2 \theta^2 M - \eta \theta \frac{\partial M}{\partial \theta} = \frac{\partial M}{\partial t}. \tag{52}$$

This partial differential equation must be solved subject to the boundary conditions:

$$M(0, t) = 1, \quad -M_\theta(0, 0) = x_0, \quad \text{and} \quad \mathcal{V}[x(0)] = M_{\theta\theta}(0, 0) - x_0^2 = 0.$$

The reader can verify that the equation has the following solution:

$$M(\theta, t) = e^{\sigma^2 \theta^2 / 4\eta} \left[1 - x_0 \theta e^{-\eta t} + \left(\tfrac{1}{2} x_0^2 - \frac{\sigma^2}{4\eta} \right) \theta^2 e^{-2\eta t} \right]. \quad (53)$$

Using the fact that $\mathcal{E}(x_t) = -M_\theta(0, t)$ and $\mathcal{E}(x_t^2) = M_{\theta\theta}(0, t)$, the reader can verify equations (17) and (18).

Example: **The Steady-State Distribution for a Renewable Resource.** The Kolomogorov equations are partial differential equations, and so are usually difficult to solve. However, we are often interested in the long-run steady-state characteristics of stochastic variables. Not all stochastic processes will have probability distributions that converge to some steady-state function (the geometric Brownian motion, for example, will not, but the Ornstein-Uhlenbeck process will). However, if a steady-state distribution exists, in most cases it can be readily found using the Kolmogorov forward equation, which then reduces to an ordinary differential equation.

As a simple first exercise, we begin by rederiving the negative exponential distribution for a long-run stationary Brownian motion between reflecting barriers directly from equation (45). This distribution is independent of the initial x_0, t_0, and the current t, so we get an ordinary differential equation for the function $\phi(x)$:

$$\tfrac{1}{2} \sigma^2 \phi''(x) - \alpha \phi'(x) = 0.$$

This is the same as equation (36) in the text, and the solution proceeds as there.

Now consider a more complicated stochastic process, which could be used to describe the evolution of a renewable resource stock, $x(t)$, subject to some rate of harvesting $q(x)$ that might depend on x:

$$dx = [f(x) - q(x)] dt + \sigma(x) dz. \quad (54)$$

Here, $f(x)$ is the *growth function* for the resource, and is concave, with

$$f(x_{\min}) = f(x_{\max}) = 0, \quad \text{and} \quad f(x) > 0 \quad \text{for} \quad x_{\min} < x < x_{\max}.$$

Much of the literature on renewable resources deals with deterministic versions of equation (54), and compares the socially optimal $q(x)$ with that resulting from a competitive market. However, as biologists and population ecologists have long recognized, most renewable resource stocks evolve

stochastically, and (54) is a natural representation.[13] Although $x(t)$ will fluctuate stochastically, it is of interest to study the probability density for x in
steady-state equilibrium.

In steady-state equilibrium, ϕ does not depend on x_0, t_0, or t in the forward equation (46). Write the stationary density function as $\phi_\infty(x)$. Then the
equation becomes (after integrating once):

$$\frac{1}{2}\frac{d}{dx}[\sigma^2(x)\,\phi_\infty(x)] = [f(x) - q(x)]\,\phi_\infty(x).$$

This can be rewritten as

$$\frac{d[\sigma^2(x)\,\phi_\infty(x)]}{\sigma^2(x)\,\phi_\infty(x)} = \frac{2}{\sigma^2(x)}[f(x) - q(x)]\,dx. \tag{55}$$

This can be integrated to give the following equation for the steady-state
density:[14]

$$\phi_\infty(x) = \frac{m}{\sigma^2(x)}\ \exp\left[2\int^x \frac{f(v) - q(v)}{\sigma^2(v)}\,dv\right], \tag{56}$$

where m is a constant of integration, chosen so that $\int_0^\infty \phi_\infty(x)dx = 1$.

As an example, suppose that $f(x)$ is the logistic function, that is,

$$f(x) = \alpha\,x\,(1 - x/K),$$

where K is the "carrying capacity" of the resource stock. Also, suppose that
there is no harvesting, that is, $q(x) = 0$, and that $\sigma(x) = \sigma x$. Then equation
(56) yields the following steady-state density that applies when $\sigma^2 < 2\alpha$:

$$\phi_\infty(x) = (2\alpha/\sigma^2 K)^{2\alpha/\sigma^2 - 1}\ x^{2\alpha/\sigma^2 - 2}\ e^{-2\alpha x/\sigma^2 K}\ /\ \Gamma(2\alpha/\sigma^2 - 1), \tag{57}$$

where Γ denotes the gamma function. From this we can determine that the
expected value of x in steady-state equilibrium is

$$\mathcal{E}(x_\infty) = K\ \left(1 - \frac{\sigma^2}{2\alpha}\right). \tag{58}$$

Note that stochastic fluctuations reduce the steady-state expected value
of x, and as σ^2 approaches 2α, $\mathcal{E}(x_\infty)$ approaches zero. Also, if $\sigma^2 \geq 2\alpha$,
stochastic fluctuations will drive the resource stock to extinction, that is, ϕ_∞
collapses and $x(t) \to 0$ with probability 1. [For a more detailed discussion of
this and related models of renewable resources, as well as a derivation of the
optimal stochastic harvesting rule $q^*(x)$, see Pindyck (1984).]

---

[13]See, for example, Beddington and May (1977) and Goel and Richter-Dyn (1974). For a
good overview of renewable resource economics in a deterministic context, see Clark (1976).
   [14]Merton (1975) also provides a derivation of this equation, and shows how it can be applied
to a neoclassical model of growth with a stochastically evolving population.

Chapter **4**

Dynamic Optimization under Uncertainty

TIME PLAYS a particularly important role for investment decisions. The payoffs to a firm's investment made today accrue as a stream over the future, and are affected by uncertainty as well as by other decisions that the firm or its rivals will make later. The firm must look ahead to all these developments when making its current decision. As we emphasized in Chapter 2, one aspect of this future is an opportunity to make the same decision later; therefore the option of postponement should be included in today's menu of choices. The mathematical techniques we employ to model investment decisions must be capable of handling all these considerations.

In this chapter we develop two such techniques: dynamic programming and contingent claims analysis. They are in fact closely related to each other, and lead to identical results in many applications. However, they make different assumptions about financial markets, and the discount rates that firms use to value future cash flows.

Dynamic programming is a very general tool for dynamic optimization, and is particularly useful in treating uncertainty. It breaks a whole sequence of decisions into just two components: the immediate decision, and a valuation function that encapsulates the consequences of all subsequent decisions, starting with the position that results from the immediate decision. If the planning horizon is finite, the very last decision at its end has nothing following it, and can therefore be found using standard static optimization methods. This solution then provides the valuation function appropriate to the penultimate

93

decision. That, in turn, serves for the decision two stages from the end, and so on. One can work backwards all the way to the initial condition. This sequence of computations might seem difficult, but advances in computing hardware and software have made it quite feasible, and in this book we will obtain solutions to several problems of this kind. If the planning horizon is infinite, what might seem like an even more difficult calculation is simplified by its recursive nature: each decision leads to another problem that looks exactly like the original one. This not only facilitates numerical computation, but also often makes it possible to obtain a theoretical characterization of the solution, and sometimes an analytical solution itself.

Contingent claims analysis builds on ideas from financial economics. Begin by observing that an investment project is defined by a stream of costs and benefits that vary through time and depend on the unfolding of uncertain events. The firm or individual that owns the right to an investment opportunity, or to the stream of operating profits from a completed project, owns an *asset* that has a value. A modern economy has markets for quite a rich menu of assets of all kinds. If our investment project or opportunity happens to be one of these traded assets, it will have a known market price. However, even if it is not directly traded, one can compute an implicit value for it by relating it to other assets that are traded.

All one needs is some combination or portfolio of traded assets that will exactly replicate the pattern of returns from our investment project, at every future date and in every future uncertain eventuality. (The composition of this portfolio need not be fixed; it could change as the prices of the component assets change.) Then the value of the investment project must equal the total value of that portfolio, because any discrepancy would present an arbitrage opportunity: a sure profit by buying the cheaper of the two assets or combinations, and selling the more valuable one. Implicit in this calculation is the requirement that the firm should use its investment opportunity in the most efficient way, again because if it did not, an arbitrager could buy the investment opportunity and make a positive profit. Once we know the value of the investment opportunity, we can find the best form, size, and timing of investment that achieves this value, and thus determine the optimal investment policy.

In the first section of this chapter we develop the basic ideas of dynamic programming. For continuity we start with the same two-period example that was the mainstay of Chapter 2, and then extend it to longer time spans, in discrete periods and in continuous time. There we consider the two special forms of uncertainty that were introduced in Chapter 3, namely Ito and Poisson processes. Section 2 develops the general ideas of contingent claims to uncertain future payoffs, and the determination of their prices by arbitrage. Again the focus is on Ito and Poisson processes. Section 3 explains the relationships between the two approaches. We also develop this relationship to obtain a simple method for discounting and valuing payoffs with varying degrees of risk.

Throughout, we emphasize the intuition behind the methods rather than formal proofs. A sketch of the technical details is placed in an appendix.

1 Dynamic Programming

In this section we introduce the basic ideas of dynamic programming. We start with the two-period example from Chapter 2, thus providing a simple concrete setting for the ideas and continuity with the previous analysis. Then we extend the ideas and develop the general theory of multiperiod decision strategies. Finally, we let time be continuous, and represent the underlying uncertainty with either Ito or Poisson processes. That is the setting for most of the applications that will appear in later chapters.

1.A The Two-Period Example

An extended example in Chapter 2 introduced the ideas of optimal timing of investment decisions and of option values. We began by comparing the present values that result from immediate investment and from waiting. Dynamic programming is in essence a systematic method of making such comparisons for more general dynamic decisions. In order to illustrate this, let us proceed to generalize our example.

As the first step, in this section we rework the simple two-period example from Chapter 2 in a more general way. Before, we chose specific numerical values for most of the parameters in the example; now we will let them have arbitrary values. Let I denote the sunk cost of investment in the factory that then produces one widget per period forever, and let r be the interest rate. Suppose the price of a widget in the current period 0 is P_0. From period 1 onward, it will be $(1 + u) P_0$ with probability q, and $(1 - d) P_0$ with probability $(1 - q)$.

First, suppose that the investment opportunity is available only in period 0; if the firm decides not to invest in period 0, it cannot change its mind in period 1. Let V_0 denote the expected present value of the revenues the firm gets if it invests. Weighting the two alternative possibilities for widget prices by their respective probabilities, discounting, and adding, we have

$$V_0 = P_0 + [q(1+u)P_0 + (1-q)(1-d)P_0]\left[\frac{1}{1+r} + \frac{1}{(1+r)^2} + \cdots\right]$$

$$= P_0 + [1 + q(u+d) - d]P_0 \frac{1/(1+r)}{1 - 1/(1+r)}$$

$$= P_0[1 + r + q(u+d) - d]/r.$$

(Note that we need $r > 0$ for convergence of the sum.) If $V_0 > I$, the investment is made and the firm gets $V_0 - I$; if $V_0 < I$, the investment is not made and the firm gets 0; if $V_0 = I$, the firm is indifferent between investing and not investing and gets zero in either case. Let Ω_0 denote the net payoff of the project to the firm, if it is forced in period 0 to decide whether to invest, on a now-or-never basis. Thus we have shown that

$$\Omega_0 = \max[V_0 - I, 0]. \tag{1}$$

Now consider the actual situation, where the investment opportunity remains available in future periods. Here the period-0 decision involves a different tradeoff: invest now, or wait and do what is best when period 1 arrives. To assess this, the firm must look ahead to its own actions in different future eventualities. From period 1 onward the conditions will not change, so there is no point postponing any profitable projects beyond period 1. Hence we need look ahead only as far as period 1.

Suppose the firm does not invest in period 0, but instead waits. In period 1 the price will be

$$P_1 = \begin{cases} (1+u)P_0 \text{ with probability } q, \\ (1-d)P_0 \text{ with probability } 1-q. \end{cases}$$

It will stay at this level for periods 2, 3, ... The present value of this stream of revenues, discounted back to period 1, is

$$V_1 = P_1 + P_1/(1+r) + P_1/(1+r)^2 + \cdots$$

$$= P_1(1+r)/r.$$

For each of the two possibilities (the price going up or down between periods 0 and 1), the firm will invest if $V_1 > I$, realizing a net payoff

$$F_1 = \max[V_1 - I, 0].$$

This outcome of future optimal decisions is sometimes called the *continuation value*. From the perspective of period 0, the period-1 price P_1, and therefore the values V_1 and F_1, are all random variables. Let $\mathcal{E}_0$ denote the expectation (probability-weighted average) calculated using the information available at period 0. Then we have

$$\mathcal{E}_0[F_1] = q \, \max[\, (1+u) \, P_0 \, (1+r)/r - I \,, 0]$$
$$+ (1-q) \, \max[\, (1-d) \, P_0 \, (1+r)/r - I \,, 0]. \tag{2}$$

This could be called the expected continuation value, or just the continuation value, with the expectation being understood.

Now return to the decision at period 0. The firm has two choices. If it invests immediately, it gets the expected present value of the revenues minus the cost of investment, $V_0 - I$. If it does not, it gets the continuation value $\mathcal{E}_0[F_1]$ derived above, but that starts in period 1 and must be discounted by the factor $1/(1+r)$ to express it in period-0 units. The optimal choice is obviously the one that yields the larger value. Therefore the net present value of the whole investment opportunity optimally deployed, which we denote by F_0, is

$$F_0 = \max \left\{ V_0 - I, \frac{1}{1+r} \, \mathcal{E}_0[F_1] \right\}. \tag{3}$$

The firm's optimal decision is the one that maximizes this net present value.

This captures the essential idea of dynamic programming. We split the whole sequence of decisions into two parts: the immediate choice, and the remaining decisions, all of whose effects are summarized in the continuation value. To find the optimal sequence of decisions we work backward. At the last relevant decision point we can make the best choice and thereby find the continuation value (F_1 in our example). Then at the decision point before that one, we know the expected continuation value and therefore can optimize the current choice. In our example there were just two periods and that was the end of the story. When there are more periods, the same procedure applies repeatedly.

The decision where the investment opportunity remains available at period 1 is less constrained than the one where it must be made on a now-or-never basis in period 0. Equation (1) shows the net payoff Ω_0 for this latter case; since that situation terminates the decision process at time 0, let us call it the *termination value* at time 0. Now we have the net worth F_0 of the less constrained decision problem from equation (3). The difference $(F_0 - \Omega_0)$ is just the value of the extra freedom, namely the *option to postpone* the decision.

In Chapter 2 we calculated the value of the investment opportunity, F_0, and the termination value, Ω_0, for some specific cases of this general model, where the parameters P_0, q, etc., were given numerical values. Readers can now refer back to those examples and place them in the context of the general theory. Here we point out one feature of those results, by reference to Figure 2.4, which shows these values as functions of the initial price, P_0. When P_0 exceeds the critical level of 249, the firm finds it optimal to invest at once. Then the option to postpone is worthless, and F_0 coincides with Ω_0, which equals $V_0 - I$ in this range of the price. When $P_0 < 249$, it is optimal to wait; then the graph of F_0 lies above that of Ω_0. A similar property holds as other parameters are varied in other figures in Chapter 2. The idea is that the critical point where immediate investment just becomes optimal is found where the lines representing the value of the full opportunity, F_0, and the termination value, Ω_0, meet.

To get a better idea of the factors that affect the value of the option to postpone, let us examine more closely the sources of the differences between F_0 and Ω_0. First, by postponing the decision the firm gives up the period-0 revenue P_0. This difference favors immediate action. Second, postponing the decision also means postponing the cost of investment; this favors waiting since the interest rate is positive. (More generally, the cost of investment could itself be changing over time, and that would bring new considerations; for example, if the firm expects capital equipment to get cheaper over time, that is an additional reason for waiting.) Third, and most important, waiting allows a separate optimization in each of the contingencies of a price rise and a price fall, whereas immediate action must be based on only the average of the two. This ability to tailor action to contingency, specifically to refrain from investment if the price goes down, gives value to the extra freedom to wait.[1]

1.B   Many Periods

We now generalize the two-period example above. Our applications in subsequent chapters are mostly to situations where time is continuous and the uncertainty takes the form of Wiener processes or more general diffusion processes for the state variables. However, in this subsection we develop the theory of dynamic programming in a setting where uncertainty is modelled using discrete-time Markov processes. Some general properties are easier to demonstrate in this format. Also, the setting of the rest of the book is a limiting case. Diffusion processes are Markov processes, and as we saw in Chapter 3,

---

[1]In technical terms, the maximum is a convex function, so by Jensen's Inequality the average of the separate maxima in equation (2) is greater than the maximum of the corresponding averages.

they can be regarded as limits of random walks in discrete time as the length of each time period and of each step of the walk both become small in a suitable way.

With our application to investment in mind, we will refer to the decisions of a firm, but the theory is of course perfectly general. The firm's current status as it affects its operation and expansion opportunities is described by a state variable x. For simplicity of exposition we take this to be a scalar (real number), but the theory extends readily to vector states of any dimension. At any date or period t, the current value of this variable x_t is known, but future values x_{t+1}, x_{t+2}, ... are random variables. We suppose that the process is Markov, that is, all the information relevant to the determination of the probability distribution of future values is summarized in the current state x_t.

At each period t, some choices are available to the firm, and we represent them by the control variable(s) u. In the above example where the only choice was whether to invest at once or wait, we could let u be a scalar binary variable, whose value 0 represents waiting and 1 represents investing at once. In other applications, for example, if the scale of investment is a matter of choice, u can be a continuous variable. If the firm has choices in addition to those bearing on investment, for example, hiring labor at time t, then u can be a vector. The value u_t of the control at time t must be chosen using only the information that is available at that time, namely x_t.

The state and the control at time t affect the firm's immediate profit flow, which we denote by $\pi_t(x_t, u_t)$. Here the relevant control variable u_t might be the quantity of labor hired or raw materials purchased. The x_t and u_t of period t also affect the probability distribution of future states. Here u_t can be the amount of investment or R&D, or even a decision to abandon the enterprise. Let $\Phi_t(x_{t+1} \mid x_t, u_t)$ denote the cumulative probability distribution function of the state next period conditional upon the current information (state and control variables).

The discount factor between any two periods is $1/(1 + \rho)$, where ρ is the discount rate. The aim is to choose the sequence of controls $\{u_t\}$ over time so as to maximize the expected net present value of the payoffs. Sometimes we will force the decision process to end at some period T, with a final payoff that depends on the state reached; we denote this *termination payoff* function by $\Omega_T(x_T)$.

We are ready to apply the basic dynamic programming technique. Remember the idea is to split the decision sequence into two parts, the immediate period and the whole continuation beyond that. Suppose the current date is t and the state is x_t. Let us denote by $F_t(x_t)$ the outcome—the expected net present value of all of the firm's cash flows—when the firm makes all decisions optimally from this point onwards.

When the firm chooses the control variables u_t, it gets an immediate profit flow $\pi_t(x_t, u_t)$. At the next period $(t+1)$, the state will be x_{t+1}. Optimal decisions thereafter will yield, in the notation we have established, $F_{t+1}(x_{t+1})$. This is random from the perspective of period t, so we must take its expected value $\mathcal{E}_t[F_{t+1}(x_{t+1})]$. That is what we called the continuation value.[2] Discounting back to period t, the sum of the immediate payoff and the continuation value is

$$\pi_t(x_t, u_t) + \frac{1}{1+\rho} \, \mathcal{E}_t[F_{t+1}(x_{t+1})].$$

The firm will choose u_t to maximize this, and the result will be just the value $F_t(x_t)$. Thus

$$F_t(x_t) = \max_{u_t} \left\{ \pi_t(x_t, u_t) + \frac{1}{1+\rho} \, \mathcal{E}_t[F_{t+1}(x_{t+1})] \right\}. \qquad (4)$$

The idea behind this decomposition is formally stated in Bellman's Principle of Optimality: *An optimal policy has the property that, whatever the initial action, the remaining choices constitute an optimal policy with respect to the subproblem starting at the state that results from the initial actions.* Here the optimality of the remaining choices u_{t+1}, u_{t+2}, etc., is subsumed in the continuation value, so only the immediate control u_t remains to be chosen optimally.

The result of this decomposition, namely equation (4), is called the *Bellman equation*, or the *fundamental equation of optimality*. To reiterate, the first term on the right-hand side is the immediate profit, the second term constitutes the continuation value, and the optimum action this period is the one that maximizes the sum of these two components.

In the two-period example, immediate investment gave $V_0 - I$, waiting had no period-0 payout but only a discounted continuation value $\mathcal{E}_0[F_1]/(1+r)$, and the optimal binary choice between these alternatives yielded the larger of these two. Thus our earlier equation (3) is a special case of the general Bellman equation (4).

---

[2]The expectation notation is generally clear enough. However, to make it precise that the information at time t includes the state and the control at that time, we state it formally once for reference:

$$\mathcal{E}_t[F_{t+1}(x_{t+1})] = \int F_{t+1}(x_{t+1}) \, d\Phi_t(x_{t+1} \mid x_t, u_t),$$

where the range of integration is that over which x_{t+1} is distributed, namely, the support of $\Phi_t(x_{t+1} \mid x_t, u_t)$.

If the many-period problem has a fixed finite time horizon T, we can similarly start at the end and work backward. At the end of the horizon the firm gets a termination payoff $\Omega_T(x_T)$. Then the period before,

$$F_{T-1}(x_{T-1}) = \max_{u_{T-1}} \left\{ \pi(x_{T-1}, u_{T-1}) + \frac{1}{1+\rho} \, \mathcal{E}_{T-1}[\Omega_T(x_T)] \right\}.$$

Thus we know the value function at $T - 1$. That in turn allows us to solve the maximization problem for u_{T-2}, leading to the value function $F_{T-2}(x_{T-2})$, and so on. At one time this was thought to be too complex a procedure to be practicable, and all kinds of indirect methods were devised. However, advances in computing have made the backward calculation remarkably usable, and several of our numerical simulations in later chapters use it. Later in this chapter we will offer an example of it.

1.C   Infinite Horizon

If there is no fixed finite time horizon for the decision problem, there is no known final value function from which we can work backward. Instead, the problem gets a recursive structure that facilitates theoretical analysis as well as numerical computation. The crucial simplification that an infinite horizon brings to equation (4) is independence from time t as such. Of course the current state x_t matters, but the calendar date t by itself has no effect. This works provided the flow profit function π, the transition probability distribution function Φ, and the discount rate ρ are themselves all independent of the actual label of the date, a condition that is satisfied or assumed in many economic applications.

In this setting, the problem one period hence looks exactly like the problem now, except of course for the new starting state. Therefore the value *function* is common to all periods, although of course it will be evaluated at different points x_t. Therefore we write the function as $F(x_t)$ without any time label on the function symbol. The Bellman equation for any t becomes

$$F(x_t) = \max_{u_t} \left\{ \pi(x_t, u_t) + \frac{1}{1+\rho} \, \mathcal{E}_t[F(x_{t+1})] \right\}.$$

Since x_t and x_{t+1} could be any of the possible states, write them in general form as x and x'. Then, for all x, we get

$$F(x) = \max_{u} \left\{ \pi(x, u) + \frac{1}{1+\rho} \, \mathcal{E}[F(x') \mid x, u] \right\}, \tag{5}$$

where we have now denoted the expectation as conditioned on the knowledge of the current period's x and u. This is the Bellman equation for the infinitely repeating, or recursive, dynamic programming problem.

Now that we have no fixed terminal date from which to work backward, we seem to have lost an explicit or constructive way to find the value function F. And without knowing the function F, we cannot find the optimal control u by solving the maximization problem on the right-hand side of the Bellman equation. Thus we need assurance that a solution actually exists, and a way to find it. Luckily, neither question is very difficult.

The recursive Bellman equation (5) can be thought of as a whole list of equations, one for each possible value of x, with a whole list of unknowns, namely all the values $F(x)$. If x took on only a finite number of discrete values x_i, this would be a simultaneous system with exactly as many equations as the number of unknowns $F(x_i)$. More generally, we can regard (5) as a *functional equation*, with the *whole function F* as its unknown.

Despite superficial appearances, this equation is not linear. The optimal choice of u depends on all the values $F(x')$ that appear, weighted by the appropriate probabilities, in the expectation on the right-hand side. When this optimal control is substituted back, the result can be nonlinear in the $F(x')$ values.

In general we do not know whether nonlinear functional equations have solutions, let alone unique ones. Fortunately, the recursive Bellman equation has a very special structure that allows one to prove existence and uniqueness of a solution function $F(x)$ under conditions typical of our economic applications. This is a technical side issue for our more practical concerns. We include a brief sketch of the ideas in Appendix A to this chapter, and interested readers can find excellent treatments in more theoretical books, for example, Stokey and Lucas with Prescott (1989, Chapters 4,9). But the technical argument does have an indirect payoff: it is essentially a practical solution method.

This takes the form of an iterative procedure. Start with *any* guess for the true value function, say $F^{(1)}(x)$. Use it on the right-hand side of equation (5) and find the corresponding optimal choice rule u^1, which can now be expressed as a function of x alone. Substituting it back, the right-hand side becomes a new function of x; call it $F^{(2)}(x)$. Now use it as the next guess of the true value function, and repeat the procedure. Then the successive guesses $F^{(3)}(x)$, $F^{(4)}(x)$, etc., will converge to the true function. Convergence is guaranteed no matter how bad the initial guess, but of course with a good initial guess the procedure will reach the desired accuracy of the approximation in fewer steps.

The key lies in the factor $1/(1 + \rho)$ on the right-hand side. This being less than 1, it scales down, or contracts, any errors in the guess from one step to the next. As long as the profit flows are bounded, any errors in the choice of u cannot blow up. Gradually, only the correct solution is left.

This procedure is very easy to understand, program, and compute. It can take a long time on the computer, especially if the discount rate ρ is very small so that each step does only a little scaling down. However, that is no longer a prohibitive consideration when individuals can leave their own personal computers running for days without tying up scarce mainframe resources. Therefore this method is increasingly used in many applications, and even in econometric work. We will give a numerical example of this method, too, later in the chapter.

1.D Optimal Stopping

One particular class of dynamic programming problems is very important for our applications. Here the choice in any period is binary. One alternative corresponds to stopping the process to take the termination payoff, and the other entails continuation for one period, when another similar binary choice will be available. In the investment model of Chapter 2 and the first section of this chapter, stopping corresponds to making the investment, and continuation corresponds to waiting. Here continuation does not generate any profit flow within the period. However, in other contexts there may be some such flow. For example, for a firm in bad economic conditions that is contemplating shutdown, continuation may give a profit flow (positive or negative), and termination may yield some scrap value of the plant and equipment, minus any severance payments the firm is required to make to its workers and other costs of site restoration, breaking contracts, etc.

Let $\pi(x)$ denote the flow profit, and $\Omega(x)$ the termination payoff. Then the Bellman equation becomes

$$F(x) = \max \left\{ \Omega(x), \; \pi(x) + \frac{1}{1 + \rho} \; \mathcal{E}[F(x') \mid x] \right\}. \tag{6}$$

For some range of values of x, the maximum on the right-hand side of this will be achieved by termination, and for other values of x it will be achieved through continuation. In general this division could be arbitrary; intervals where termination is optimal could alternate with ones where continuation is optimal. However, most economic applications will have more structure. There will be a single cutoff x^*, with termination optimal on one side and continuation on the other. For example, in the investment problem of Chapter 2 we had a critical level of the initial price, $P_0 = 249$, such that in period 0, investment was optimal to its right but waiting was optimal to its left. All of our applications will have a similar property, and in each case it will be intuitively clear which action is optimal on which side of the threshold or cutoff point. To complete the reader's understanding of this result, we should explain the general conditions that lead to it. We state these intuitively here, and explain them somewhat more formally in Appendix B.

For sake of definiteness we concentrate on the case where continuation is optimal for $x > x^*$ and stopping is optimal for $x < x^*$. Let us examine the forces that will make continuation more attractive relative to termination for higher values of x. First, the immediate profit from continuation should become larger relative to the termination payoff. Since the former is a flow and the latter is a stock, we need to express them in comparable terms. The precise condition turns out to be that

$$\pi(x) + (1 + \rho)^{-1} \mathcal{E}[\Omega(x')|x] - \Omega(x) \tag{7}$$

should be increasing as x increases. Second, any current advantage should not be likely to be reversed in the near future. For this, we need positive serial correlation, or persistence, in the stochastic process of evolution of x. To be more precise, if this period's x rises, the conditional distribution $\Phi(x'|x)$ of next period's values x' should give greater weight to larger values, that is, it should shift everywhere to the right. (In technical language, this is the concept of "first-order stochastic dominance.") These two conditions together are sufficient to ensure the desired result.

If the expression in (7) is decreasing as x increases, then continuation will be optimal to the left and termination to the right of x^*. Note that the second condition stays unchanged; we do not switch it to require negative persistence of the stochastic process.

We repeat that both of these properties will always be satisfied for our applications. The first is easily verified in each instance; the second is true for random walks, Brownian motion, mean-reverting autoregressive processes, and indeed in almost all economic applications we can think of.

For ease of notation in conveying the concept, we did not allow the profit or terminal payoff to depend on time t as such, but that extension presents no difficulty. The threshold simply becomes a function of time, $x^*(t)$. This will be the case in much of the rest of the chapter and in many of our applications.

1.E Continuous Time

Now return to the general control problem of Section 1.B, but suppose each time period is of length Δt. Ultimately we are interested in the limit where

Δt goes to zero and time is continuous. We write $\pi(x, u, t)$ for the *rate* of the profit flow, so that the actual profit over the time period of length Δt is $\pi(x, u, t)\,\Delta t$. Similarly, let ρ be the discount rate per unit time, so the total discounting over an interval of length Δt is by the factor $1/(1 + \rho\,\Delta t)$.

The Bellman equation (5) now becomes

$$F(x, t) = \max_u \left\{ \pi(x, u, t)\,\Delta t + (1 + \rho\,\Delta t)^{-1}\, \mathcal{E}[F(x', t + \Delta t)|x, u] \right\}.$$

Multiply by $(1 + \rho\,\Delta t)$ and rearrange to write

$$\rho\,\Delta t\, F(x, t) = \max_u \left\{ \pi(x, u, t)\,\Delta t\,(1 + \rho\,\Delta t) + \mathcal{E}[F(x', t + \Delta t) - F(x, t)] \right\}$$

$$= \max_u \left\{ \pi(x, u, t)\,\Delta t\,(1 + \rho\,\Delta t) + \mathcal{E}[\Delta F] \right\}.$$

Divide by Δt and let it go to zero. We get

$$\rho\, F(x, t) = \max_u \left\{ \pi(x, u, t) + \frac{1}{dt}\, \mathcal{E}[dF] \right\}, \tag{8}$$

where $(1/dt)\,\mathcal{E}[dF]$ is the limit of $\mathcal{E}[\Delta F]/\Delta t$. We must remember that the expectation is conditioned on the current x and u, and we must remember to include the influence of changes in both x and t when we calculate the change in $F(x, t)$ over the interval dt.

This form of the Bellman equation makes explicit the idea that the entitlement to the flow of profits is an asset, and that $F(x, t)$ is its value. On the left-hand side we have the normal return per unit time that a decision maker, using ρ as the discount rate, would require for holding this asset. On the right-hand side, the first term is the immediate payout or dividend from the asset, while the second term is its expected rate of capital gain (loss if negative). Thus the right-hand side is the expected total return per unit time from holding the asset. The equality becomes a no-arbitrage or equilibrium condition, expressing the investor's willingness to hold the asset. The maximization with respect to u means that the current operation of the asset is being managed optimally, of course bearing in mind not only the immediate payout but also the consequences for future values.

The limit on the right-hand side depends on the expectation corresponding to the random x' a time Δt later. There are two classes of stochastic processes in continuous time that allow such limits in a form conducive to further analysis and solution of the function $F(x, t)$ in the continuation region. Luckily they are particularly useful for many economic applications. In fact they are just the Ito and Poisson processes we discussed in Chapter 3. We will develop the theory of dynamic programming in their specific contexts in the next two subsections.

The above analysis is local to the short time interval $(t, t + dt)$, and the resulting equation holds for any t. We can complete the analysis by choosing a finite time horizon T and imposing a terminal payoff, or letting the horizon be infinite and using the recursive structure, or some other way. In any of these, rigorous mathematical proofs of existence and uniqueness of solutions become quite hard in continuous time. Since the details are immaterial for our applications, we omit them and refer the reader to Fleming and Rishel (1975) or Krylov (1980).

Our mathematics has been simplified in another respect. We have treated the limit to continuous time in a very casual and heuristic way, and will continue to do so. However, it is fair to warn the reader that some quite tricky issues are hidden, and must be handled carefully in more rigorous treatments. In discrete time, we stipulated that the action u_t taken in the current period t could depend on the knowledge of the current state x_t, but not on the random future state x_{t+1}. In continuous time the two coalesce. We have to be careful not to allow choices to depend on information about the future, even about "the next instant." Otherwise we would be acting with the benefit of hindsight, and could make infinite profits. Technically this can be avoided by requiring the uncertainty to be "continuous from the right" in time while the strategies are "continuous from the left." Then any jumps in the stochastic processes occur *at an instant*, while the actions cannot change until *just after the instant*. For a discussion and rigorous analysis, see Duffie (1988, pp. 139–40).

1.F Ito Processes

The first continuous-time stochastic process that yields a simple form for (8) is the Ito process we discussed in Chapter 3. Equation (11) of that chapter defined the formula for its increment, which we recapitulate here, but now allowing the drift and the diffusion parameters to depend on the control variable as well as the state variable:

$$dx = a(x, u, t)\, dt + b(x, u, t)\, dz, \tag{9}$$

where dz is the increment of a standard Wiener process. As before, we write the profit flow as $\pi(x, u, t)$ and the value of the firm (asset) as $F(x, t)$.

Let x be the known starting position at time t, and $x' = x + dx$ the random position at the end of a small interval of time Δt. Ito's Lemma for such a process was stated in equation (25) of Chapter 3. Applying it to the value function F, we have

$$\mathcal{E}[F(x + \Delta x, t + \Delta t)|x, u]$$
$$= F(x, t) + \left[F_t(x, t) + a(x, u, t) F_x(x, t) \right.$$
$$\left. \tfrac{1}{2} b^2(x, u, t) F_{xx}(x, t) \right] \Delta t + o(\Delta t),$$

where $o(\Delta t)$ represents terms that go to zero faster than Δt. Then the "return equilibrium" condition (8) becomes

$$\rho F(x, t) = \max_u \left\{ \pi(x, u, t) + F_t(x, t) + a(x, u, t) F_x(x, t) \right.$$
$$\left. + \tfrac{1}{2} b^2(x, u, t) F_{xx}(x, t) \right\}. \tag{10}$$

We can express the optimal u as a function of $F_t(x, t)$, $F_x(x, t)$, $F_{xx}(x, t)$ as well as x, t, and the various parameters that govern the functional form of π, a, and b. Substituting this expression for the optimal u back into the right-hand side of equation (10), we get a partial differential equation of the second order, with F as the dependent variable and x and t as the independent variables. In general this equation is very complicated. However, in many applications we can develop ways to solve it analytically or numerically.

The solution methods are generally analogous to those for discrete time. If there is a fixed time limit T when a termination payoff $\Omega(x_T, T)$ is enforced, then the equation has a boundary condition

$$F(x, T) = \Omega(x, T) \quad \text{for all } x.$$

We can start at time T and work our way backward to find $F(x, t)$ for all earlier times. In fact, in practice we have to choose a discrete grid of values of x and t on which to calculate the solution. We will offer two examples of this procedure, one later in this chapter when we directly solve the underlying dynamic programming problem, and one in Chapter 10 where we solve the partial differential equation itself.

If the time horizon is infinite and the functions π, a, and b do not depend explicitly on time, then neither does the value function depend on time, and equation (10) becomes an ordinary differential equation with x as its only independent variable:

$$\rho F(x) = \max_u \left\{ \pi(x, u) + a(x, u) F'(x) + \tfrac{1}{2} b^2(x, u) F''(x) \right\}. \tag{11}$$

Note that we have followed standard calculus notation and used primes to denote total derivatives of a function of one independent variable, and subscripts to denote partial derivatives of a function of several independent variables.

We will generally adhere to this, but will occasionally use subscripts even for total derivatives, for example if the function symbol needs a superscript for some other reason.

In most of our models of investment throughout Chapters 5–9, we will have occasion to formulate and solve equations like (11), and will develop appropriate solution methods for them gradually. We turn to one special kind of control, namely optimal stopping of an Ito process, that is of particular importance in all of our applications.

1.G   Optimal Stopping and Smooth Pasting

Here we consider a binary decision problem. At every instant, the firm can either continue its current situation to get a profit flow, or stop and get a termination payoff. Both the profit flow $\pi(x, t)$ and the termination payoff $\Omega(x, t)$ can depend on a state variable x and on time t, where x follows an Ito process

$$dx = a(x, t)\, dt + b(x, t)\, dz. \tag{12}$$

The most obvious example is of a firm deciding whether to cease operation and sell its equipment for its scrap value. Investment decisions can also be put in this form: continuation means waiting, and the flow payoff is zero; stopping means investing, and the termination payoff is just the expected present value of future profits from the project minus the cost of investment.

Intuition suggests that for each t there will be a critical value $x^*(t)$, with continuation optimal if x_t lies on one side of $x^*(t)$, and stopping optimal on the other side. We saw in Section 1.D that some conditions must be imposed on the profit flow and termination payoff functions to ensure this. Continuation will be relatively more attractive for larger values of x if the expression in (7) is an increasing function of x. In continuous time, if x follows the Ito process (12), then the analysis of Appendix B shows that

$$\pi(x) - \rho\, \Omega(x, t) + a(x, t)\, \Omega_x(x, t) + \tfrac{1}{2}\, b(x, t)^2\, \Omega_{xx}(x, t) + \Omega_t(x, t)$$

should be increasing in x for each t. Similarly, continuation will be less attractive relative to stopping for larger x if the expression is decreasing. In each of our applications, one of these conditions will hold. For sake of exposition we take up the former case.

Given such conditions, we can regard the critical values $x^*(t)$ for various t as forming a curve that divides the (x, t) space into two regions, with continuation optimal above the curve and termination optimal below it. Of course we do not know the equation of the curve $x = x^*(t)$ in advance, but must find it out as a part of the solution of the dynamic programming problem.

Now the Bellman equation for the optimal stopping problem, (6), becomes

$$F(x, t) = \max \left\{ \Omega(x, t), \, \pi(x, t) + (1 + \rho \, dt)^{-1} \, \mathcal{E}[F(x + dx, t + dt) \mid x] \right\}.$$

In the continuation region, the second term on the right-hand side is the larger of the two. Expanding it by Ito's Lemma and simplifying as above, we get the partial differential equation satisfied by the value function:

$$\tfrac{1}{2} b^2(x, t) \, F_{xx}(x, t) + a(x, t) \, F_x(x, t) + F_t(x, t) - \rho \, F(x, t) + \pi(x, t) = 0, \quad (13)$$

where subscripts denote partial derivatives.

This holds for $x > x^*(t)$, and we must look for boundary conditions that hold along $x = x^*(t)$. From the Bellman equation, we know that in the stopping region we have $F(x, t) = \Omega(x, t)$, so by continuity we can impose the condition

$$F(x^*(t), t) = \Omega(x^*(t), t) \quad \text{for all } t. \tag{14}$$

This is often called the "value-matching condition" because it matches the values of the unknown function $F(x, t)$ to those of the known termination payoff function $\Omega(x, t)$.

But the boundary itself is an unknown: the region in (x, t) space over which the partial differential equation (13) is valid is itself endogenous. The boundary of that region, namely the curve $x^*(t)$, is called a "free boundary," and the whole problem of solving the equation and determining its region of validity is called a free-boundary problem.

It is clear that we need a second condition in addition to (14) if we are to find $x^*(t)$ jointly with the function $F(x, t)$. The general mathematical theory of partial differential equations is of little help in this regard; the conditions applicable to free boundaries are specific to each application and must come from economic (or physical or biological, as the case may be) considerations. For us the right condition turns out to require that for each t, the values $F(x, t)$ and $\Omega(x, t)$, regarded as functions of x, should meet tangentially at the boundary $x^*(t)$, or

$$F_x(x^*(t), t) = \Omega_x(x^*(t), t) \quad \text{for all } t. \tag{15}$$

This is called the "high-order contact" or "smooth-pasting condition" because it requires not just the values but also the derivatives or slopes of the two functions to match at the boundary.

While continuity is very intuitive, continuity of slopes or smooth pasting is more subtle and remarkable. However, the argument for it is somewhat technical, so we relegate it to Appendix C. Here we merely illustrate how it works.

1.H   Example—Optimal Abandonment of a Machine

The chapters that follow are full of applications of dynamic programming and contingent claims analysis. Here, however, having developed the theory at a general and rather dry level, it would be useful to offer a concrete example. We do not solve it in detail, but merely state the solution backed by some intuition. We hope this illustrates the various steps in a specific context, and prepares the reader for more detailed applications to come.

Suppose the asset is a machine used to make widgets, with a total physical life of T years. Its profitability declines over this life, both because it wears out gradually and thus produces less output or requires more maintenance, and because technical progress elsewhere in the economy makes this machine less competitive with newer ones. There are also random shocks to its productivity, because of the general business cycle, or because of idiosyncratic variations in the demand for widgets. Let the state variable x be the current operating profit flow, and suppose it evolves according to

$$dx = a\,dt + b\,dz,$$

where $a < 0$ to reflect the gradual decline over the lifetime.

At any time during the physical life, the firm can abandon the machine. If the current profit flow becomes negative, this may seem an attractive alternative. Once abandoned, however, the machine will rust quickly and be very costly to restart should the profit flow recover. Therefore the abandonment decision will have to look ahead to such future possibilities. The firm will accept some losses to keep the machine in operating condition. Of course, accepting losses will be less compelling if the physical life of the machine is drawing to a close. Thus we must keep track of two variables, the current profit, x, and the age of the machine, t. Intuitively, we know that there will be a threshold curve $x^*(t)$ such that if the current x falls below this curve the machine will be abandoned.

The actual parameters used in the calculation are $T = 10$ years, $\rho = 10$ percent per year, $a = -0.1$ per year, and $b = 0.2$, which implies a standard deviation of 0.2 over one year, or a variance of 0.04 per year. To obtain a numerical solution, we use a discrete approximation to Brownian motion, with $\Delta t = 0.01$, or 3.65 days. Correspondingly, each discrete step of the profit variable x is $\Delta h = b\sqrt{\Delta t} = 0.02$.

We solve the dynamic programming problem directly using the method outlined at the end of Section 1.B, starting at T when there is no future consideration, and marching backward one time step at a time. Figure 4.1 shows the solution. Part (a) shows the optimal threshold curve—the free boundary—

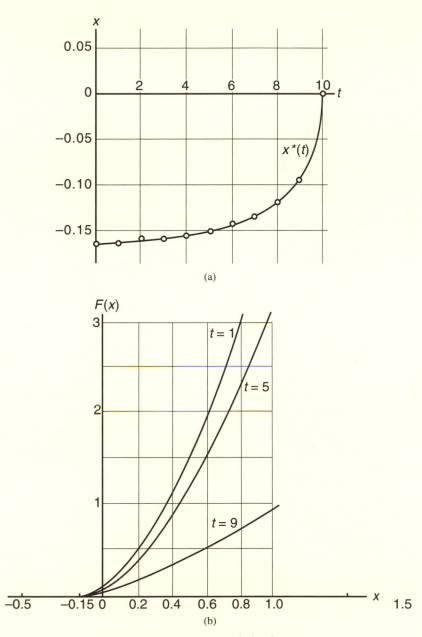

Figure 4.1. *Depreciation and Abandonment*

$x^*(t)$ in (t, x) space. At each t, if the current x is above this curve, the machine
is kept in operation and has a value $F(x, t)$ that satisfies the differential equation corresponding to (13), namely,

$$\tfrac{1}{2} b^2 \, F_{xx}(x, t) + a \, F_x(x, t) + F_t(x, t) - \rho \, F(x, t) + x = 0.$$

Below the curve, the machine is abandoned for the termination value 0. (We
could have also obtained a solution by specifying some other scrap value
function.) Note how the curve goes to 0 as the age of the machine approaches
the physical limit of 10 years—there is no reason to keep alive a loss-making
project in the hope of a future turnaround if the machine is going to die
very soon anyway. The greater the remaining physical life of the machine, the
greater is the willingness to absorb some losses. However, this effect ultimately
levels off. With a 10-year horizon, a brand-new machine will be kept operating
even if the current loss is about 0.15.

   Part (b) of the figure shows graphs of the value function $F(x, t)$ as a
function of x for some particular values of t. As we would expect, the greater
is x, the greater is the value of the machine. However, the machine has value
even if $x = 0$, because, given the simple Brownian motion that we assumed
for x, there is the possibility that x will rise in the future. Note that the value-
matching and smooth-pasting conditions hold: for each of the chosen t, both
$F(x, t)$ and $F_x(x, t)$ fall to zero as x approaches $x^*(t)$.

   What if the machine has a very long physical life that we can regard as
effectively infinite? Now we can leave calendar time out of the picture and
solve a recursive functional equation for $F(x)$, or we can remove time from
the partial differential equation (13) and write it as an ordinary differential
equation

$$\tfrac{1}{2} b^2 \, F''(x) + a \, F'(x) - \rho \, F(x) + x = 0.$$

The solution and the threshold x^* can be found using the value-matching and
smooth-pasting conditions $F(x^*) = 0$, $F'(x^*) = 0$. In Chapters 5–7 we will
develop this procedure in some detail, so here we merely invite interested
readers to try it out. The result in our numerical example is that the critical x^*
for abandonment equals -0.17. Thus a 10-year life is already quite close to
infinity as far as the effect of the future on the willingness to absorb current
losses is concerned.

1.I Poisson Processes

We introduced Poisson (jump) processes in Chapter 3. Over a short interval
dt of time, the probability of a jump in the random variable x is $\lambda \, dt$, where λ is

called the mean arrival rate. If a jump occurs, it is of size $g(x, t) u$, where $g(x, t)$ is a known function and u is a random variable. With probability $(1 - \lambda dt)$ there is no random jump, and x moves by a deterministic amount $f(x, t) dt$. We write this compactly by analogy with the notation for Brownian motion as

$$dx = f(x, t) dt + g(x, t) dq, \tag{16}$$

where dq is a random variable that equals u with probability λdt and 0 otherwise.

Now consider dynamic programming when the state variable follows a Poisson process. We illustrate this for the optimal stopping problem, since this will be our most common application in this context. Once again the values of x will fall into two subsets, one where immediate stopping is optimal with the termination value $\Omega(x, t)$, and the other where continuation is optimal for at least the next short interval dt, with the flow payoff $\pi(x, t)$. What happens to the asset value return equation (8) in this case?

First suppose u is a known nonrandom number. Then there are two possibilities for the change in value dF, depending on whether a jump from x to $x + g(x, t)u$ takes us into the stopping region or not. If it does, then

$$dF = \lambda dt [\Omega(x + g(x, t)u) - F(x, t)] + (1 - \lambda dt) [F(x + f(x, t) dt) - F(x, t)].$$

Using this in (8) and letting dt go to zero, we have

$$\rho F(x, t) = \pi(x, t) + \lambda [\Omega(x + g(x, t)u) - F(x, t)] + F_x(x, t) f(x, t). \tag{17}$$

If $x + g(x, t)u$ remains in the continuation region, we get a similar equation but with $\Omega(x + g(x, t)u)$ replaced by $F(x + g(x, t)u)$. More generally, when u is random, we must allow both of these cases, and obtain a combined equation by taking the expectation over the distribution of u.

Note a new feature: unlike the partial differential equation (13) for the Ito process case, the equation (17) is not *local* to the continuation region. We cannot hope to solve it separately and then paste it to the terminal payoff at the stopping boundary. Therefore the problem for the general Poisson process is quite hard.

However, there are some simple cases. Suppose the jump, if one occurs, is always to the same known point, say x_0. Then we have

$$[\rho + \lambda] F(x, t) = \pi(x, t) + \lambda F(x_0, t),$$

if x_0 is in the continuation region, and a similar equation but with $\Omega(x_0, t)$ if it is in the stopping region. For example, if x_0 corresponds to a sudden stoppage of the flow payoff, then $\Omega(x_0, t) = 0$ and $F(x, t) = \pi(x, t)/(\rho + \lambda)$. Here the Poisson arrival rate λ simply acts like an addition to the discount rate ρ.

In later chapters we will develop some applications where the underlying uncertainty follows a simple Poisson process amenable to analysis. In a couple of instances we will have a combined model, where the variable x undergoes a Poisson jump with a specified hazard rate, and follows an Ito process if there is no jump. Then the equations and their solutions combine the features outlined here.

2   Contingent Claims Analysis

When we studied the optimal stopping problem in dynamic programming, we interpreted $F(x, t)$ as the market value of an asset that entitles the owner to the firm's future profit flows $\pi(x, t)$. The equation (8) expressed the condition that for an investor who holds this asset for a short interval of time, the immediate profit flow and the expected capital gain together provide a total rate of return ρ. We specified this discount rate exogenously, but in practice it has the interpretation as the opportunity cost of capital, and therefore it should equal the return the investor could have earned on other investment opportunities with comparable risk characteristics. Now we make the idea more explicit, and extend it to provide a better treatment of risk.

Financial economics has developed sophisticated theories describing the decisions of investors, the market equilibria resulting from the aggregation of such decisions, and the equilibrium prices of assets. The basic setting is an economy with a rich menu of traded assets with different return and risk characteristics. To value a new asset, we try to replicate its return and risk characteristics through a portfolio of existing traded assets. The price of the new asset must then equal the market value of this portfolio. Any discrepancy would be exploited by arbitrageurs who look for sure profits by buying whichever is cheaper, repackaging it, and selling it in the more valuable form. Therefore price discrepancies for equivalent assets or portfolios could not persist in equilibrium. The asset held in the continuation region of our analysis can be analyzed in this way. Much of this theory has assumed that the underlying uncertainty can be described by an Ito process, and we shall begin likewise.

2.A   Replicating Portfolio

We begin with the simplest setting. Suppose the profit flow depends on a variable x; think of it as the firm's output price. Since we will be dealing with proportional rates of return, it is convenient to assume that x follows a geometric Brownian motion

$$dx = \alpha \, x \, dt + \sigma \, x \, dz, \tag{18}$$

where α is the growth rate parameter, σ the proportional variance parameter, and dz the increment of the standard Wiener process. We allow for a more general process later.

Now we assume that the firm's output can itself be traded as an asset in financial markets. This would literally be the case if the output is a commodity like oil or copper. In the next section we will show that it is sufficient that the risk in the dynamics of x, namely the dz term above, can be replicated by some portfolio of traded assets.

Like any asset, the output is held by investors only if it provides a sufficiently high return. Part of the return comes in the form of the expected price appreciation, α. Another part may also come in the form of a dividend, directly (the product might be a tree that grows more wood) or indirectly (the holder of oil or copper might be a firm that plans to use these as inputs and finds it convenient to hold its own inventory rather than rely on the spot market; then the dividend is the implicit "convenience yield"). We will discuss the role of this convenience yield in some detail in Chapters 5 and 6; here we simply stipulate that there is a dividend and denote its rate by δ. Let $\mu = \alpha + \delta$ denote the total expected rate of return.

This expected return must be enough to compensate the holders for risk. Of course it is not risk as such that matters, but only nondiversifiable risk. The whole market portfolio provides the maximum available diversification, so it is the covariance of the rate of return on the asset with that on the whole market portfolio that determines the risk premium.

Throughout our analysis we will assume that the riskless rate of return r is exogenously specified, for example as the return on government bonds.[3] Then the fundamental condition of equilibrium from the capital asset pricing model (CAPM) says that

$$\mu = r + \phi \, \sigma \, \rho_{xm}, \tag{19}$$

where ϕ is an aggregate market parameter (the market price of risk) that is

[3]In reality even government bonds have some risk because of inflation; we neglect this complication. For a fuller general equilibrium model that determines the term structure of interest rates, see Cox, Ingersoll, and Ross (1985).

exogenous to our analysis, and ρ_{xm} is the coefficient of correlation between returns on the particular asset x and the whole market portfolio m.[4]

We find the value $F(x, t)$ of a firm with profit flow $\pi(x, t)$ (really the value of the asset that entitles the owner to the profit flow stream) by replicating its return and risk characteristics using traded assets of known value. Specifically, consider investing a dollar in the riskless asset and also buying n units of the firm's output; we will choose n shortly to achieve the desired replication. This portfolio costs $(1 + nx)$ dollars. Hold it for a short interval of time dt. In this time, the riskless asset pays the sure return $r\,dt$, while the other asset pays a dividend $n\,\delta x\,dt$ and has a random capital gain of $n\,dx = n\alpha x\,dt + n\sigma x\,dz$. Thus the total return per dollar invested is

$$\frac{r + n(\alpha + \delta)x}{1 + nx}\,dt + \frac{\sigma\,nx}{1 + nx}\,dz.$$

Compare this with holding ownership of the firm for the same short interval of time dt. This costs $F(x, t)$ to buy. The dividend is the profit $\pi(x, t)\,dt$; this involves no uncertainty since x is known when the initial decision is being made.[5] The asset also yields a random capital gain, which we calculate using Ito's Lemma as

$$dF = \left[\,F_t(x, t) + \alpha x\,F_x(x, t) + \tfrac{1}{2}\sigma^2 x^2\,F_{xx}(x, t)\,\right]dt + \sigma\,x\,F_x(x, t)\,dz.$$

The total return per dollar invested is

$$\frac{\pi(x, t) + F_t(x, t) + \alpha x\,F_x(x, t) + \tfrac{1}{2}\sigma^2 x^2\,F_{xx}(x, t)}{F(x, t)}\,dt + \frac{\sigma\,x\,F_x(x, t)}{F(x, t)}\,dz.$$

If our portfolio is to replicate the risk of owning the firm, we must therefore choose

$$nx/(1 + nx) = x\,F_x(x, t)/F(x, t).$$

However, in the market, two assets with identical risk must earn equal return. Therefore this choice must also ensure

$$\frac{\pi(x, t) + \alpha x\,F_x(x, t) + \tfrac{1}{2}\sigma^2 x^2\,F_{xx}(x, t)}{F(x, t)} = \frac{r + n(\alpha + \delta)x}{1 + nx}.$$

---

[4] For more on the capital asset pricing model, see any standard text on financial economics; Brealey and Myers (1992) is relatively elementary, and Huang and Litzenberger (1990) is more advanced.

[5] To be rigorous, in continuous time $\pi(x, t)$ can change even over this short interval, and the evolution of it is random. However, the difference made by this consideration is of magnitude dt^2 and we can ignore it.

Substituting for $nx/(1 + nx)$, the right-hand side becomes

$$r \left[1 - \frac{x\, F_x(x, t)}{F(x, t)} \right] + (\alpha + \delta)\, \frac{x\, F_x(x, t)}{F(x, t)}.$$

On simplification, the return equation becomes a partial differential equation for the value:

$$\tfrac{1}{2} \sigma^2 x^2\, F_{xx}(x, t) + (r - \delta)\, x\, F_x(x, t) + F_t(x, t) - r\, F(x, t) + \pi(x, t) = 0. \quad (20)$$

This is strikingly similar to the corresponding equation (13) that we derived by dynamic programming methods. Indeed, the analogy is almost exact if we rewrite the dynamic programming equation for the geometric Brownian motion process using $a(x, t) = \alpha x$ and $b(x, t) = \sigma x$. The only remaining difference is that the riskless interest rate r is used in place of the exogenously specified discount rate ρ, and the coefficient of the F_x term has an $r - \delta$ instead of α. We will discuss this correspondence between the dynamic programming and contingent claims valuation approaches in Section 3.

An alternative and equivalent way to derive the same result is to construct a portfolio that consists of the firm and n units of a *short position* in the asset x. Then n is chosen to make this portfolio riskless. This is algebraically somewhat simpler, so we will generally use this method in the future. However, the one given above demonstrates the concept of constructing a *replicating portfolio* more directly and clearly.

2.B   The Use of Spanning Assets

Even if the risk in x is not directly traded in the market, it suffices to be able to trade some other asset whose risk tracks or spans the uncertainty in x. Now we show how this works. In the process we generalize the above analysis by letting x follow an arbitrary Ito process of equation (12) above. We also demonstrate the alternative approach to replication mentioned above.

We suppose there is a traded asset whose stochastic fluctuations are perfectly correlated with the stochastic process for x. (This traded asset could be a simple asset such as a stock or futures contract, or a *dynamic portfolio* of simple assets, that is, a portfolio of assets whose contents are adjusted continuously so that the value of the portfolio is perfectly correlated with the process for x.) To remind ourselves that the traded asset is tracking or spanning the risk in x, we call it the spanning (i.e., replicating asset. Let X denote its market price. Then the stochastic process of X must take the form

$$dX = A(x, t)\, X\, dt + B(x, t)\, X\, dz. \quad (21)$$

Note two points. First, the coefficients $A(x, t)$ and $B(x, t)$ are functions of the state variable, x, not the price of the replicating asset, X. This is in keeping with the notion that the state variable summarizes all the information about the current state of the economy. Second, the coefficients $A(x, t)$ and $B(x, t)$ of the asset price process (21) need bear no relation to the $a(x, t)$ and $b(x, t)$ of the state evolution process (12); but the two Wiener process increments dz must be the same if X is to track the stochastic fluctuations in x. (When we say same, we mean that the two must have identical realizations, not merely that they have the same probability law.)

Suppose the replicating asset also pays a flow dividend at rate $D(x, t)$. Then one dollar invested in this asset over the small interval of time from t to $(t + dt)$ generates the total return:

$$[D(x, t) + A(x, t)]\, dt + B(x, t)\, dz.$$

Next we ask what rate of return will make an investor willing to hold this replicating asset. The capital asset pricing model (CAPM) formula for the required expected return, which we denote by $\mu_X(x, t)$, is

$$\mu_X(x, t) = r + \phi\, \rho_{xm}\, B(x, t). \tag{22}$$

To understand this, compare it to the earlier formula (19) for x. The market price of risk ϕ is an aggregate parameter, so it is the same in the two cases. The standard deviation of the return on X is $B(x, t)$, and since the changes dX and dx are perfectly correlated, the correlation coefficient between the rates of return on X and the market is the same as that between x and the market, namely ρ_{xm}. Finally, note that in an equilibrium where the asset X is actually held, we must have

$$\mu_X(x, t) = D(x, t) + A(x, t). \tag{23}$$

Now consider a portfolio that consists of the firm and n units of a short position in the asset X. This costs $[F(x, t) - n\, X]$ dollars to buy. Hold it for a short interval of time dt. During this time the firm pays a dividend of $\pi(x, t)\, dt$. Further, since a unit of X pays a dividend of $D(x, t)\, X dt$, the holder of a short position must pay this to some corresponding holder of the long position. The capital gain on the portfolio is

$$dF - n\, dX = \left[F_t + a\, F_x + \tfrac{1}{2} b^2\, F_{xx} - n\, A X \right] dt + [b\, F_x - n\, B\, X]\, dz,$$

where we have used Ito's Lemma, and have omitted the arguments of the functions for brevity. To make this portfolio riskless, we must choose $n = b\, F_x / (B X)$.

When that is done, we can set the expected return on our portfolio equal to the riskless return on its dollar cost, namely $r\,[F - nX]\,dt$. Doing this, and simplifying, we find that $F(x, t)$ satisfies the partial differential equation

$$\tfrac{1}{2}\,b^2(x, t)\,F_{xx}(x, t)$$
$$+ \{a(x, t) - [b(x, t)/B(x, t)]\,[\mu_X(x, t) - r]\}\,F_x(x, t)$$
$$- r\,F(x, t) + F_t(x, t) + \pi(x, t) = 0. \tag{24}$$

This has basically the same form as the earlier (20).

The merit of the contingent claims valuation approach in this context is that all the coefficients of these equations are either known from the specification of the model—such as $a(x, t)$—or can be observed or estimated from the market, as with $\mu_X(x, t)$. Then the partial differential equation can be solved to obtain the value of the firm.

2.C Smooth Pasting

The above analysis assumes only that the various assets are held during a very short interval of time dt. What happens after time $t + dt$ is of no concern, and does not affect the validity of the partial differential equations (24) or (20). However, solutions to these equations require boundary conditions, and therefore some attention to longer time spans.

If the firm that is being valued above has a fixed time horizon T when it is forced to take a termination payoff $\Omega(x_T, T)$, then we can solve the partial differential equation subject to the boundary condition $F(x, T) = \Omega(x, T)$ for all x. Likewise, the firm may be *forced* to take the termination payoff at an earlier time t if the state variable hits a threshold $x^*(t)$. Here the boundary condition is clearly

$$F(x^*(t), t) = \Omega(x^*(t), t) \quad \text{for all } t.$$

This is exactly the value-matching condition (14) we found in the section on dynamic programming.

Sometimes the firm can *choose* its termination optimally, knowing its termination payoff function $\Omega(x, t)$. This decision will be made so as to maximize the firm's value. We know from our dynamic programming analysis that such choice determines a threshold or free boundary $x^*(t)$, and that the appropriate additional condition (15) is the "smooth-pasting" property,

$$F_x(x^*(t), t) = \Omega_x(x^*(t), t) \quad \text{for all } t.$$

2.D   Poisson Processes

Suppose the state variable x follows the Poisson jump process of equation (16), rather than an Ito diffusion process. Can we create a replicating portfolio and use it as we did above to obtain an equation analogous to (20)?

In principle, it might be possible to find an asset that duplicates the stochastic dynamics of $x(t)$. For example, if $x(t)$ is the price of oil (and we believed that it followed a Poisson process), the replicating asset could be a near-term futures contract on oil. More generally, however, we would have to replicate $x(t)$ with a dynamic portfolio of assets, the components of which were continuously adjusted as $x(t)$ fluctuates. If $x(t)$ follows a diffusion process, this is feasible, because the path of x is itself continuous, so the portfolio can be adjusted as x moves over time from one value to another. It is not feasible if x follows a Poisson process and takes discrete jumps.

This means that when working with Poisson processes, we will usually have to make one of two assumptions. First, we can assume that stochastic changes in x associated with the Poisson process are uncorrelated with market portfolio. Then there is no adjustment for risk, and equation (20) will again hold, but with $\delta \equiv r - \alpha$. (Note that this is equivalent to dynamic programming with the discount rate equal to the risk-free rate, r.) Alternatively, we can use dynamic programming, with an exogenous discount rate, ρ.

3   Relationship between the Two Approaches

By now the reader should begin to see the close parallels between dynamic programming and contingent claims valuation. The value function of dynamic programming and the asset value in contingent claims analysis satisfy very similar partial differential equations. The Bellman equation of dynamic programming has an interpretation in terms of asset value and the willingness of investors to hold the asset. The boundary conditions in the contingent claims approach are based on the idea that investors want to choose the option exercise date optimally to maximize the value of their assets.

However, there are some differences, too. The dynamic programming approach started by specifying the discount rate, ρ, exogenously as a part of the objective function. In the contingent claims approach the required rate of return on the asset was derived as an implication of the overall equilibrium in capital markets. Only the riskless rate of return, r, was taken to be exogenous (and even that can be endogenized if the theory is taken to an even more general equilibrium level of analysis). Thus the contingent claims approach offers a better treatment of the discount rate.

Balancing this consideration, the contingent claims approach requires the existence of a sufficiently rich set of markets in risky assets. The crucial requirement is that the stochastic component dz of the return on the asset we are trying to value be exactly replicated by the stochastic component of the return on some traded asset (or dynamic portfolio of traded assets). This can be quite demanding—we require not only that the stochastic components obey the same probability law, but also that they are perfectly correlated, namely that each and every path (realization) of one process is replicated by the other. Dynamic programming makes no such demand; if risk cannot be traded in markets, the objective function can simply reflect the decision maker's subjective valuation of risk. The objective function is usually assumed to have the form of the present value of a flow "utility" function calculated using a constant discount rate, ρ. This is restrictive in its own way, but it too can be generalized. Of course we have no objective or observable knowledge of private preferences, so testing the theory can be harder.

Thus we see that the two methods have offsetting advantages and disadvantages, and together they can handle quite a large variety of applications. In specific applications one may be more convenient in practice than the other, and different readers may develop a better feel for one rather than the other, but there is no difference of principle between the two on their common ground. In the chapters that follow, we will often track the two approaches in parallel, and switch from one to the other as convenient. For example, in Chapter 5 we will first use dynamic programming and then use contingent claims analysis to solve a very basic investment problem—when to make a sunk expenditure I in return for a factory currently worth V, where V follows a geometric Brownian motion. This will let us explore the differences in the two approaches in more detail.

3.A   Equivalent Risk-neutral Valuation

A further exploration of the relationship between dynamic programming and contingent claims valuation leads to a useful way of writing down and interpreting solutions to partial differential equations for asset values. We will illustrate this in the familiar context of a firm whose profit flow $\pi(x, t)$ depends on a state variable x. We will also force termination at a finite time T, with a terminal payoff $\Omega(x_T, T)$. We will assume that the state variable follows a geometric Brownian motion

$$dx = \alpha x \, dt + \sigma x \, dz.$$

These special assumptions will allow us to develop the exposition in the simplest possible way, but the reader will see that the underlying ideas are much more generally valid.

Suppose at time t the current state is x. Let $F(x, t)$ denote the value of the firm, namely, the title to the stated stream of profits. We will derive this in each of the two ways developed before in this chapter.

Begin with dynamic programming. Here we stipulate an exogenous discount rate, ρ. Then $F(x, t)$ is just the expected present value

$$F(x, t) = \mathcal{E}_t \left[\int_t^T e^{-\rho(\tau - t)} \pi(x_\tau, \tau) \, d\tau + e^{-\rho(T-t)} \Omega(x_T, T) \right], \qquad (25)$$

where $\mathcal{E}_t$ denotes the expectation based on the information as of time t.

If we consider the situation a short time dt later, the state variable will have moved to $(x + dx)$, and the value of the asset will have changed to $F(x + dx, t + dt)$. To express this in time-t equivalent units, we must discount it by the factor $e^{-\rho \, dt}$. Further, dx is a random increment from the perspective of time t, so we must take an expectation. Thus

$$F(x, t) = \pi(x, t) \, dt + e^{-\rho \, dt} \mathcal{E}_t[F(x + dx, t + dt)]. \qquad (26)$$

This idea of splitting the whole time interval from t to T into two parts— the immediate short interval dt and the continuation beyond that—is the whole essence of dynamic programming. Thus equation (26) is a Bellman equation, but of a trivial kind. In this instance no action is taken during the interval dt, so there is no maximization on the right-hand side.

Expand the right-hand side of (26) using Ito's Lemma, and omit terms that go to zero faster than dt as $dt \to 0$. This yields

$$\pi(x, t) \, dt + e^{-\rho \, dt} \mathcal{E}_t[F(x + dx, t + dt)]$$

$$= \pi(x, t) \, dt + (1 - \rho \, dt) \left[F(x, t) + F_t(x, t) \, dt + F_x(x, t) \alpha x \, dt \right.$$

$$\left. + \tfrac{1}{2} F_{xx}(x, t) \sigma^2 x^2 \, dt \right]$$

$$= F(x, t) + \left[\tfrac{1}{2} \sigma^2 x^2 F_{xx}(x, t) + \alpha x F_x(x, t) + F_t(x, t) \right.$$

$$\left. - \rho F(x, t) + \pi(x, t) \right] dt.$$

Substituting in (26) and simplifying, we see that $F(x, t)$ satisfies the following partial differential equation:

$$\tfrac{1}{2} \sigma^2 x^2 F_{xx}(x, t) + \alpha x F_x(x, t) + F_t(x, t) - \rho F(x, t) + \pi(x, t) = 0. \qquad (27)$$

This is just the dynamic programming equation (12) for the present case of geometric Brownian motion. The boundary condition is

$$F(x, T) = \Omega(x, T) \quad \text{for all } x, \tag{28}$$

which our expression (25) satisfies by construction. In other words, that expression is the solution to the partial differential equation.

Had we begun by deriving the equation and the boundary condition, and then started looking for a solution, that would have seemed a formidable task. However, this is a very lucky and exceptional instance where we knew the solution (25) even before we derived the equation. Of course it needs a lot of work to evaluate the expectation. We know that given the initial x at time t, the state at any future time is lognormally distributed. Also, for $\tau \geq t$, the logarithm of x_τ has mean $\log x + (\alpha - \frac{1}{2}\sigma^2)(\tau - t)$ and variance $\sigma^2(\tau - t)$. If $\pi(x, t)$ and $\Omega(x_T)$ have very convenient functional forms, for example, powers or exponentials, it is possible to evaluate the expression (25) explicitly. Otherwise one must resort to numerical solutions. However, the expression has some conceptual use, as we will soon see.

The result that (25) is the solution to the differential equation (27) with the boundary condition (28) is a special case of a very general result known as the Feynman-Kac formula; see Karatzas and Shreve (1988, pp. 267ff) for a more detailed and rigorous discussion of it.[6]

Now consider the problem of valuing the firm from the perspective of contingent claims valuation. Here we already showed that the value satisfies the partial differential equation (20), which we restate for ease of reference:

$$\frac{1}{2}\sigma^2 x^2 F_{xx}(x, t) + (r - \delta) x F_x(x, t) + F_t(x, t) - r F(x, t) + \pi(x, t) = 0.$$

Recall that r is the riskless interest rate, and $\delta = \mu - \alpha$ is the dividend or convenience yield on the x asset. The boundary condition is again (28).

Here we do not know the solution in advance. However, we can write it down immediately by noticing the formal analogy between this partial differential equation and the one obtained using the dynamic programming

---

[6]In quantum electrodynamics the result proves to have immense practical utility. In fact it underlies Feynman's (1949) diagrammatic technique for summing probabilities over all possible paths of a particle. His approach, developed before dynamic programming and Ito's Lemma had been thought of, was an amazing achievement. Since the dependent variable—the probability amplitude—in quantum electrodynamics is complex valued, the analogy with dynamic programming and contingent claims valuation may not extend beyond the mathematical formalism. If it does, then in addition to all his achievements in physics, Feynman could be claimed as the father of financial economics.

approach, (27). The exogenously specified discount rate ρ for the latter is now replaced by the riskless market rate r, and the growth rate α of the geometric Brownian motion of x is replaced by $(r - \delta)$. In other words, we can evaluate the future payoff by discounting it at the riskless rate r, provided we are willing to pretend that x follows a process with a different growth rate parameter $\alpha' = r - \delta$.

Therefore the solution is

$$F(x, t) = \mathcal{E}'_t \left[\int_t^T e^{-r(\tau-t)} \pi(x'_\tau, \tau) \, d\tau + e^{-r(T-t)} \Omega(x'_T, T) \right], \qquad (29)$$

where x' is an artificial variable that starts at the same initial point x at time t, but thereafter follows a new geometric Brownian motion

$$dx' = \alpha' x' \, dt + \sigma x' \, dz \equiv (r - \delta) x' \, dt + \sigma x' \, dz. \qquad (30)$$

The expectation $\mathcal{E}'_t$ is taken with respect to this stochastic process, from the perspective of the information (namely the value of x) at time t.

We have here an instance of "equivalent risk-neutral valuation," a procedure with much wider applicability and interest in financial economics; see Duffie (1988, Section 17) and Huang and Litzenberger (1990, Chapter 8) for rigorous and general theory.

3.B   Examples

We illustrate the procedure with some simple examples. In each case we find the initial value $F(x, 0)$.

First consider the simplest case where there is no profit flow, and the terminal payoff is $\Omega(x) = x$. Then

$$F(x, 0) = e^{-\rho T} \mathcal{E}_0[x_T].$$

Taking the equivalent risk-neutral perspective, the expectation of the x' process is

$$\mathcal{E}'_0[x'_T] = x \, e^{(r-\delta) T}.$$

Therefore

$$F(x, 0) = e^{-r T} x \, e^{(r-\delta) T} = x \, e^{-\delta T} = e^{-\mu T} x \, e^{\alpha T}.$$

In other words, we recognize that x grows at rate α, and discount its future value at the risk-adjusted rate μ. This is obvious, but serves as a simple way to clarify the general formula and build up the reader's confidence in it.

Next suppose $\Omega(x) = x^\beta$ for some given β. Now, using standard results on the lognormal distribution,

$$\mathcal{E}'_0[(x'_T)^\beta] = x^\beta \, \exp\left[\, \beta \, (r - \delta) \, T + \tfrac{1}{2}\sigma^2 \, \beta(\beta - 1) \, T \,\right],$$

and

$$F(x, 0) = x^\beta \, \exp\left[\, \left(\tfrac{1}{2}\sigma^2 \, \beta(\beta - 1) + (r - \delta) \, \beta - r\right) T \,\right].$$

For $\beta = 1$ this reduces to $x \, e^{-\delta T}$ as above. For $\beta = 0$, we get just $e^{-r T}$; the payoff $x^0 \equiv 1$ is riskless and therefore discounted at the rate r. Finally, if β is a root of the quadratic equation

$$\tfrac{1}{2}\sigma^2 \, \beta(\beta - 1) + (r - \delta) \, \beta - r = 0,$$

then we get $F(x, 0) = x^\beta$. Here the force of growth is exactly offset by that of discounting; thus we can just evaluate the terminal payoff function at the initial state x and call that the asset value. We will see this used later in Chapter 6 and elsewhere.

For a somewhat trickier example, consider the case of risk neutrality and no discounting, and for numbers a and b, define

$$\Omega(x) = \begin{cases} 1 \text{ if } a \leq x \leq b, \\ 0 \text{ otherwise.} \end{cases}$$

Now $F(x, 0)$ is simply the probability that the geometric Brownian motion, starting at the initial value x, will after time T end up in the interval (a, b). By letting b converge to a, we get the limit of $F(x, 0)/(b-a)$ as the corresponding probability density.

Either of our approaches shows that this function satisfies the partial differential equation

$$\tfrac{1}{2}\sigma^2 x^2 \, F_{xx}(x, t) + \alpha \, x \, F_x(x, t) + F_t(x, t) = 0.$$

In other words, we have derived the backward Kolmogorov equation (see the Appendix to Chapter 3) as a corollary of our asset-pricing formula.

4   Guide to the Literature

Dynamic programming was developed by Richard Bellman and others in the 1950s. It is a standard tool in economic analysis and operations research, and is treated in several textbooks. For a particularly simple exposition aimed at economists, see Dixit (1990, Chapter 11). Other good expositions can be found in Dreyfus (1965), Harris (1987), and Kamien and Schwartz (1991). For an outstanding and very thorough treatment, with several applications to dynamic general equilibrium theory, growth theory, labor economics, and other topics, see Stokey and Lucas with Prescott (1989).

In this book we use dynamic programming only in the context of optimal control and stopping of Brownian motion. For more details but still at an intuitive level, see Dixit (1993a). For very rigorous treatments, see Fleming and Rishel (1975) and Krylov (1980).

Contingent claims analysis was systematically developed following the pioneering papers of Black and Scholes (1973) and Merton (1971, 1973), although an early contribution by Samuelson (1965) is noteworthy in that it introduced stochastic calculus and the smooth-pasting condition. Contingent claims analysis has now become an established part of the literature on financial economics, and has textbooks devoted to it, for example, Cox and Rubinstein (1985), Hull (1989), and Jarrow and Rudd (1983). A beginner can benefit from the expositions of Rubinstein (1987) and Varian (1987) in a special symposium in the Journal of Economic Perspectives. Cox and Ross (1976) and Cox, Ross, and Rubinstein (1979) develop contingent claims valuation using the random walk representation of Brownian motion that we discussed earlier in this chapter. More advanced treatments include Duffie (1988, 1992), Dothan (1990), and Huang and Litzenberger (1990).

For a pioneering rigorous treatment of equivalent risk-neutral valuation and related ideas, see Harrison and Kreps (1979). Precursors of these ideas can be found in Arrow (1970) and Cox and Ross (1976).

Bernstein (1992) is an excellent and very enjoyable history of the development of these ideas.

Appendix

A Recursive Dynamic Programming

Here we sketch some technical arguments that prove the existence and uniqueness of the solution of the Bellman equation (5) for infinite-horizon dynamic programming. We restate the equation for ease of reference:

$$F(x) = \max_u \left\{ \pi(x, u) + \frac{1}{1 + \rho} \, \mathcal{E}[F(x') \mid x, u] \right\}. \tag{5}$$

We seek a function $F(x)$ that satisfies (5). We regard the right-hand side as an operator, or a function of a function. Given a function $F(x)$, the right-hand side defines a new function of x. The solution is a function that, when operated on in this way, leads to itself. In technical terms, we seek a fixed point of the operator.

Follow an iterative procedure that starts with any initial choice $F^{(1)}(x)$. Use this on the right-hand side of (5). Now the right-hand side is fully known, so the results of applying the operator can be calculated for every x. Call the result a new function $F^{(2)}(x)$. Next use it on the right-hand side to get the next iterate $F^{(3)}(x)$, and so on. What happens to the sequence of such functions $F^{(m)}(x)$ as m goes to infinity?

Suppose that instead of $F^{(1)}(x)$, we use a different starting function, say, $Z^{(1)}(x) = F^{(1)}(x) + k$ for some positive constant k. Substituting into the right-hand side of (5), first note that

$$(1 + \rho)^{-1} \, \mathcal{E}[\, Z^{(1)}(x') \mid x, u \,] = (1 + \rho)^{-1} \{ \, \mathcal{E}[\, F^{(1)}(x') \mid x, u \,] + k \, \}.$$

Thus we get an extra term $(1 + \rho)^{-1} k$ on the right-hand side. This does not alter the maximizing choice of u, nor the value of any of the other terms. Thus, for all x, the result of applying the operator to $Z^{(1)}(x)$ will be a new function

$$Z^{(2)}(x) = F^{(2)}(x) + (1 + \rho)^{-1} k.$$

Proceeding in this way,

$$Z^{(m)}(x) = F^{(m)}(x) + (1 + \rho)^{-(m-1)} k.$$

In other words, changes or "errors" in the initially chosen function decay geometrically in the proportion $1/(1 + \rho)$ at each step of our iteration. Then it is intuitively clear, and not too hard to prove rigorously, that the iteration proceeds to the same limiting function $F(x)$ regardless of the initial choice. In the limit, $F^{(m+1)}(x)$ becomes the same as $F^{(m)}(x)$; the limiting function $F(x)$ is a fixed point of the iteration step. It obviously satisfies the functional equation (5). The property of geometric reduction in errors (technically the "contraction mapping property") has allowed us to prove existence and uniqueness of the solution, and the iterative procedure constitutes a numerical algorithm.

B   Optimal Stopping Regions

Here we consider the case of a binary choice between continuation and stopping. The Bellman equation is (6), which we repeat for ease of reference:

$$F(x) = \max \left\{ \Omega(x), \pi(x) + \frac{1}{1+\rho} \, \mathcal{E}[F(x') \mid x] \right\}. \tag{6}$$

Continuation is optimal for those values of x for which the maximum on the right-hand side of (6) is attained at the second argument, that is,

$$\pi(x) + (1+\rho)^{-1} \int F(x') \, d\Phi(x'|x) > \Omega(x),$$

and immediate termination is optimal when the opposite inequality holds. Call the corresponding divisions of the range of x the "continuation region" and the "stopping region," respectively. We are interested in the structure of these regions.

For arbitrary specifications of $\pi(x)$, $\Omega(x)$, and $\Phi(x'|x)$, the regions could be any sequence of alternating intervals. Thus continuation may be optimal for a lowest range of values of x, stopping optimal for a range above that, then continuation again, and so on. However, one expects that in many problems of economic interest, there will be a clean division of the range into low and high values separated by a threshold, say, x^*, such that continuation is optimal for $x < x^*$ and stopping optimal for $x > x^*$ (or perhaps the other way around). We find some conditions on the payoff and distribution functions that yield such a division.

Subtract $\Omega(x)$ from both sides of (6), and denote $F(x) - \Omega(x)$ by $G(x)$ for brevity. Then

$$G(x) = \max \left[0, \pi(x) - \Omega(x) + (1+\rho)^{-1} \int F(x') \, d\Phi(x'|x) \right]$$

$$= \max \left[0, \pi(x) - \Omega(x) + (1+\rho)^{-1} \int \Omega(x') \, d\Phi(x'|x) \right.$$

$$\left. + (1+\rho)^{-1} \int G(x') \, d\Phi(x'|x) \right] \tag{31}$$

Now make two assumptions that together suffice to establish the desired property.

Assumption [1]: The expression

$$\pi(x) + (1 + \rho)^{-1} \int \Omega(x')\, d\Phi(x'|x) - \Omega(x)$$

is a monotonic function of x; for definiteness, make it increasing.

This is just the difference between the value of waiting for exactly one period before stopping, and that of stopping right away. The nice point is that the advantage of waiting for exactly one period translates into an advantage of waiting until an optimally chosen stopping time. If the function is increasing, we expect continuation to be optimal for high x and termination for low x; if decreasing, the other way around.

Assumption [2]: There is positive persistence of uncertainty, in the sense that the cumulative probability distribution $\Phi(x'|x)$ of future values x' shifts uniformly to the right when the current value x increases.

If this failed, a larger current relative advantage for high x would be more likely to be reversed in the near future. This assumption will hold for all the processes we will consider.

Given these two assumptions, the solution function $G(x)$ for (31) must be increasing. To see this, note that the second argument of the max operator on the right-hand side consists of two parts. The first, which is just the expression in Assumption 1, has been directly assumed to be increasing. The other, namely the integral, is increasing if $G(x)$ is. To see this, note that by Assumption [2], a larger x shifts the probability weights attached to the increasing set of values $G(x')$ to the right, and therefore raises the expected value. Thus, starting with an increasing function, the right-hand side yields another increasing function. Then the fixed point of the iteration step, namely the solution of (31), is itself an increasing function.[7]

We have proved that the second argument in (31) is increasing. Therefore there is a unique x^* such that the second argument is positive if and only if $x > x^*$. Then continuation is optimal to the right of x^*, and stopping is optimal to the left, as we set out to prove.

In continuous time, we must replace ρ by $\rho\, dt$ and $\pi(x)$ by $\pi(x)\, dt$. Suppose $x' = x + dx$, and x follows the geometric Brownian motion $dx =$

---

[7]To be technically precise, the operator is closed on the convex cone of nondecreasing functions, and therefore has a fixed point in this subspace. That is also a fixed point on the whole space of functions. However, we have already shown in Section A of the Appendix that the latter fixed point is unique.

$\mu x \, dt + \sigma x \, dz$. Then, on expanding $\Omega(x')$ using Ito's Lemma and simplifying, Assumption [1] becomes simply the requirement that

$$\pi(x) - \rho \, \Omega(x) + \mu x \, \Omega'(x) + \tfrac{1}{2} \sigma^2 x^2 \, \Omega''(x)$$

be monotonic.

C   Smooth Pasting

Here we consider the optimal stopping problem with a finite horizon and time dependence, when the state variable follows an Ito process. We demonstrate somewhat more formally the value-matching and smooth-pasting conditions for (14) and (15) that determine the free boundary that separates the continuation and stopping regions.

Over a short interval of time dt, the Bellman equation (6) becomes

$$F(x, t) = \max \{ \, \Omega(x) \, , \, \pi(x, t) \, dt + (1 - \rho \, dt) \, F(x, t) + \mathcal{E}[dF] \, \}.$$

Stopping is optimal if the first term in the braces on the right-hand side is the larger of the two, and continuation is optimal if the second expression is larger.

Fix a particular t. For definiteness we consider the case where continuation is optimal for $x > x^*(t)$ and stopping for $x < x^*(t)$. First suppose, contrary to the assertion in (14), that $F(x^*(t), t) < \Omega(x^*(t), t)$. By continuity, we will have $F(x, t) < \Omega(x, t)$ for x just slightly to the right of $x^*(t)$. The second expression on the right-hand side differs from $F(x, t)$ only by terms of order dt, so for sufficiently small dt, it, too, will be less than $\Omega(x, t)$ over this range. Then immediate stopping will be optimal for such x, contrary to the definition of $x^*(t)$ as the threshold. Next suppose that $F(x^*(t), t) > \Omega(x^*(t), t)$. By continuity, we will have $F(x, t) > \Omega(x, t)$ for x just slightly to the left of $x^*(t)$. Then, for sufficiently small dt, continuation will yield a value that is also greater than $\Omega(x, t)$, so stopping cannot be optimal there, contrary to the definition of $x^*(t)$.

The argument for the smooth-pasting condition also proceeds by contradiction. We develop it with the aid of Figure 4.2. Again consider just the case where continuation is optimal to the right of $x^*(t)$ and stopping to the left. If the functions $F(x, t)$ and $\Omega(x, t)$ do not meet tangentially at $x^*(t)$, they must meet at a kink. This cannot be an upward-pointing kink as in part (a) of the figure; else by continuity $\Omega(x, t)$ would exceed $F(x, t)$ for x slightly greater than $x^*(t)$, and termination rather than continuation would be optimal for such x, contrary to the definition of $x^*(t)$ as the threshold. Next consider a downward-pointing kink as in part (b) of the figure. Here we show that $x^*(t)$

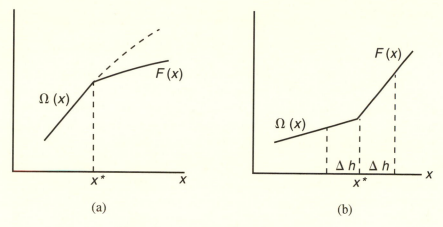

Figure 4.2. *Argument to Prove Smooth Pasting*

cannot be a point of indifference between the two choices; continuation for a short interval of time Δt is definitely the better policy. The intuitive idea is that by waiting a little bit longer, we can observe the next step of x and choose positions on either side of the kink. An average of the two does better than the kink point itself. This is true even though that average must be discounted because it occurs time Δt later. The reason is that for Brownian motion the steps are proportional to the square root of Δt, and so is their effect on the value, while the effect of discounting is proportional to Δt. When Δt is small, the former effect is relatively much larger. This argument needs to be spelled out in a little more algebraic detail.

As in Chapter 3, we treat the process of x as a random walk that can take steps of size $\Delta h = b(x,t)\sqrt{\Delta t}$ up or down with respective probabilities

$$p = \tfrac{1}{2}[1 + a(x,t)\sqrt{\Delta t}/b(x,t)], \qquad q = \tfrac{1}{2}[1 - a(x,t)\sqrt{\Delta t}/b(x,t)].$$

[In Chapter 3 the drift and diffusion coefficients α and σ were constant; here they are more general—functions $a(x,t)$ and $b(x,t)$.]

Now consider the alternative policy: continuation for time Δt, followed by further continuation if the next step of x is upward, and stopping to take the termination payoff if it is downward. With the appropriate probability weighting and discounting, this yields

$$\pi(x^*(t),t)\Delta t + (1+\rho\Delta t)^{-1}\big[pF(x^*(t)+\Delta h, t+\Delta t) + q\Omega(x^*(t)-\Delta h, t+\Delta t)\big].$$

Expand this in a Taylor series around $(x^*(t),t)$, using the value-matching condition just above, and remembering that Δt is of order $(\Delta h)^2$. The first two terms are

$$F(x^*(t), t) + \tfrac{1}{2} \left[F_x(x^*(t), t) - \Omega_x(x^*(t), t) \right] \Delta h.$$

If the functions meet with a downward-pointing kink as in part (b) of Figure 4.2, then $F_x > \Omega_x$ at $x^*(t)$, so the second term is positive. Therefore the alternative policy does better than the common value of continuation or termination at $x^*(t)$, contradicting its definition as the threshold where the optimal policy is a matter of indifference between the two.

Part III
A Firm's Decisions

Chapter **5**

Investment Opportunities and Investment Timing

WITH THE mathematical preliminaries behind us, we can now turn to the analysis of investment decisions under uncertainty. In this chapter and throughout this book, our main concern will be with investment expenditures that have two very important characteristics. First, the expenditures are at least partly irreversible; in other words, *sunk costs* that cannot be recovered. Second, these investments can be delayed, so that the firm has the opportunity to wait for new information to arrive about prices, costs, and other market conditions before it commits resources.

As the simple examples in Chapter 2 suggested, the ability to delay an irreversible investment expenditure can profoundly affect the decision to invest. In particular, it invalidates the simple net present value rule as it is commonly taught to students in business schools: "Invest in a project when the present value of its expected cash flows is at least as large as its cost." This rule is incorrect because it ignores the opportunity cost of making a commitment now, and thereby giving up the option of waiting for new information. As we saw in Chapter 2, that opportunity cost must be included as part of the total cost of investing. In this chapter and those that follow, we will examine this opportunity cost and its implications for investment at a greater level of generality and in more detail.

In this chapter, we will set forth and analyze in considerable detail one of the most basic continuous-time models of irreversible investment. In this model, which was originally developed by McDonald and Siegel (1986), a firm must decide when to invest in a single project. The cost of the investment, I, is known and fixed, but the value of the project, V, follows a geometric Brownian motion. The simple net present value rule is to invest as long as $V > I$, but as McDonald and Siegel demonstrated, this is incorrect. Because *future* values of V are unknown, there is an opportunity cost to investing today. Hence the optimal investment rule is to invest when V is at least as large as a critical value V^* that exceeds I. As we will see, for reasonable parameter values, this critical value may be *two or three times* as large as I. Hence the simple NPV rule is not just wrong; it is often *very* wrong.

After describing the basic model in more detail, we will show how the optimal investment rule (that is, the critical value V^*) can be found by dynamic programming. An issue that arises, however, is the choice of discount rate. If capital markets are "complete" (in a sense that will be made clear), the investment problem can be viewed as a problem in option pricing, and solved using the techniques of contingent claims analysis. We will re-solve the optimal investment problem in this way, and then examine the characteristics of the firm's option to invest and its dependence on key parameters. Finally, we will extend the model by considering alternative stochastic processes for the value of the project, V. In particular, we will find and characterize the optimal investment rules that apply when V follows a mean-reverting process, and then when it follows a mixed Brownian motion/Poisson jump process.

1   The Basic Model

Our starting point is a model first developed by McDonald and Siegel (1986). They considered the following problem: At what point is it optimal to pay a sunk cost I in return for a project whose value is V, given that V evolves according to the following geometric Brownian motion:

$$dV = \alpha V \, dt + \sigma V \, dz, \tag{1}$$

where dz is the increment of a Wiener process. Equation (1) implies that the current value of the project is known, but future values are lognormally distributed with a variance that grows linearly with the time horizon; the exact formulas are in Section 3(a) of Chapter 3. Thus although information arrives over time (the firm observes V changing), the future value of the project is *always* uncertain.

Equation (1) is clearly an abstraction from most real projects. For example, suppose the project is a widget factory with some capacity. If variable costs are positive and managers have the option to shut down the factory temporarily when the price of output is below variable cost, and/or the option to abandon the project completely, V will not follow a geometric Brownian motion even if the price of widgets does. (We will develop models in which the output price follows a geometric Brownian motion and the project can be temporarily shut down and/or abandoned in Chapters 6 and 7.) If variable cost is positive and managers do *not* have the option to shut down (perhaps because of regulatory constraints), V can become negative, which is again in conflict with the assumption of lognormality. In addition, one might believe that a competitive product market will prevent the price from wandering too far from long-run industry-wide marginal cost, or that stochastic changes in price are likely to be infrequent but large, so that V should follow a mean-reverting or jump process. For the time being we ignore these possibilities in order to provide the simplest introduction to the basic ideas and techniques. We allow exogenously specified mean reversion in Section 5(a) of this chapter, and consider industry equilibrium in Chapters 8 and 9.

Note that the firm's investment opportunity is equivalent to a perpetual call option—the right but not the obligation to buy a share of stock at a prespecified price. Therefore the decision to invest is equivalent to deciding when to exercise such an option. Thus, the investment decision can be viewed as a problem of option valuation (as we saw in the simple examples presented in Chapter 2).[1] Alternatively, it can be viewed as a problem in dynamic programming. We will derive the optimal investment rule in two ways, first using dynamic programming, and then using option pricing (contingent claims) methods. This will allow us to compare these two approaches and the assumptions that each requires. We will then examine the characteristics of the solution.

In what follows, we will denote the value of the investment opportunity (that is, the value of the option to invest) by $F(V)$. We want a rule that maximizes this value. Since the payoff from investing at time t is $V_t - I$, we want to maximize its expected present value:

$$F(V) = \max \mathcal{E}[(V_T - I)e^{-\rho T}], \tag{2}$$

where $\mathcal{E}$ denotes the expectation, T is the (unknown) future time that the investment is made, ρ is a discount rate, and the maximization is subject to

---

[1] The investment opportunity is analogous to a perpetual call option on a dividend-paying stock. (The payout stream from the completed project is equivalent to the dividend on the stock.) A solution to this option valuation and exercise problem was first found by Samuelson (1965).

equation (1) for V. For this problem to make sense, we must also assume that $\alpha < \rho$; otherwise the integral in equation (1) could be made indefinitely larger by choosing a larger T. Thus waiting longer would always be a better policy, and the optimum would not exist. We will let δ denote the difference $\rho - \alpha$; thus we are assuming $\delta > 0$.

1.A The Deterministic Case

Although we will be mostly concerned with the ways in which the investment decision is affected by uncertainty, it is useful to first examine the case in which there is no uncertainty, that is, σ in equation (1) is zero. As we will see, there can still be a value to waiting.

If $\sigma = 0$, $V(t) = V_0 e^{\alpha t}$, where $V_0 = V(0)$. Thus given a current V, the value of the investment opportunity assuming we invest at some arbitrary future time T is

$$F(V) = (V e^{\alpha T} - I) e^{-\rho T}. \tag{3}$$

Suppose $\alpha \leq 0$. Then $V(t)$ will remain constant or fall over time, so it is clearly optimal to invest immediately if $V > I$, and never invest otherwise. Hence $F(V) = \max[V - I, 0]$.

What if $0 < \alpha < \rho$? Then $F(V) > 0$ even if currently $V < I$, because eventually V will exceed I. Also, even if V now exceeds I, it may be better to wait rather than invest now. To see this, maximize $F(V)$ in equation (3) with respect to T. The first-order condition is

$$\frac{dF(V)}{dT} = -(\rho - \alpha) V e^{-(\rho-\alpha)T} + \rho I e^{-\rho T} = 0,$$

which implies[2]

$$T^* = \max \left\{ \frac{1}{\alpha} \log \left[\frac{\rho I}{(\rho - \alpha)V} \right], \ 0 \right\}. \tag{4}$$

Note that if V is not too much larger than I, we will have $T^* > 0$. The reason for delaying the investment in this case is that in present value terms, the cost of the investment decreases by a factor of $e^{-\rho T}$, whereas the payoff is reduced by the smaller factor of $e^{-(\rho-\alpha)T}$.

For what values of V is it optimal to invest immediately? By setting $T^* = 0$, we see that one should invest immediately if $V \geq V^*$, where

$$V^* = \frac{\rho}{\rho - \alpha} I > I. \tag{5}$$

---

[2]The reader can verify that the second-order condition is satisfied at this point provided $\alpha > 0$, which is true in the present case.

Finally, by substituting expression (4) into equation (3), we obtain the following solution for $F(V)$:

$$F(V) = \begin{cases} [\alpha I/(\rho - \alpha)] [(\rho - \alpha)V/\rho I]^{\rho/\alpha} & \text{for } V \leq V^*, \\ V - I & \text{for } V > V^*. \end{cases} \qquad (6)$$

Figure 5.1 shows $F(V)$ as a function of V for $I = 1$, $\rho = 0.10$, and $\alpha = 0$, 0.03, and 0.06. In each case, the tangency point of $F(V)$ with the line $V - I$ is at the critical value $V^* = \rho I/(\rho - \alpha)$. Note that $F(V)$ increases when α increases, as does the critical value V^*. Growth in V creates a value to waiting, and increases the value of the investment opportunity.

1.B The Stochastic Case

We will now return to the general case in which $\sigma > 0$. The problem is to determine the point at which it is optimal to invest I in return for an asset worth V. Since V evolves stochastically, we will not be able to determine a time T as we did above. Instead, our investment rule will take the form of

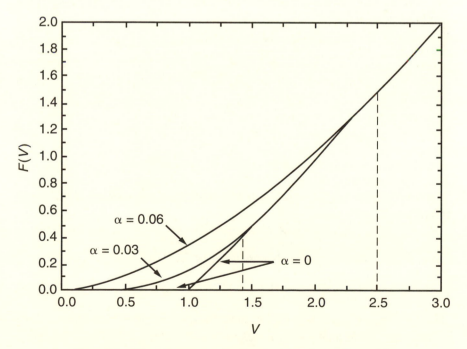

Figure 5.1. *Value of Investment Opportunity, $F(V)$, for $\sigma = 0$, $\rho = 0.1$*

a critical value V^* such that it is optimal to invest once $V \geq V^*$. As we will see, a higher value of σ will result in a higher V^*, that is, a greater value to waiting. It is important to keep in mind, however, that in general both growth ($\alpha > 0$) *and* uncertainty ($\sigma > 0$) can create a value to waiting and thereby affect investment timing.

In the next two sections, we will solve this investment problem in two ways, following the techniques described in Chapter 4. First, we will use dynamic programming, and then we will solve the same problem over again using contingent claims methods. This will enable us to carefully compare these two approaches.

2   Solution by Dynamic Programming

In the terminology of Chapter 4, we have an optimal stopping problem in continuous time. Because the investment opportunity, $F(V)$, yields no cash flows up to the time T that the investment is undertaken, the only return from holding it is its capital appreciation. Hence, as we saw in Chapter 4, in the continuation region (values of V for which it is not optimal to invest) the Bellman equation is

$$\rho \, F \, dt = \mathcal{E}(dF). \tag{7}$$

Equation (7) just says that over a time interval dt, the total expected return on the investment opportunity, $\rho \, F \, dt$, is equal to its expected rate of capital appreciation.

We expand dF using Ito's Lemma, and we use primes to denote derivatives, for example, $F' = dF/dV$, $F'' = d^2F/dV^2$, etc. Then

$$dF = F'(V) \, dV + \tfrac{1}{2} F''(V) \, (dV)^2.$$

Substituting equation (1) for dV into this expression and noting that $\mathcal{E}(dz) = 0$ gives

$$\mathcal{E}[dF] = \alpha \, V \, F'(V) \, dt + \tfrac{1}{2} \sigma^2 \, V^2 \, F''(V) \, dt.$$

Hence the Bellman equation becomes (after dividing through by dt):

$$\tfrac{1}{2} \sigma^2 \, V^2 \, F''(V) + \alpha \, V \, F'(V) - \rho \, F = 0. \tag{8}$$

It will be easier to analyze the solution and to compare it to that obtained using contingent claims analysis if we make the substitution $\alpha = \rho - \delta$. To ensure existence of an optimum (for reasons already explained in connection with the deterministic case), we assume that $\alpha < \rho$, or $\delta > 0$. With this notation, the Bellman equation becomes the following differential equation that must be satisfied by $F(V)$:

$$\tfrac{1}{2}\sigma^2 V^2 F''(V) + (\rho - \delta) V F'(V) - \rho F = 0. \tag{9}$$

In addition, $F(V)$ must satisfy the following boundary conditions:

$$F(0) = 0, \tag{10}$$

$$F(V^*) = V^* - I, \tag{11}$$

$$F'(V^*) = 1. \tag{12}$$

Condition (10) arises from the observation that if V goes to zero, it will stay at zero [this is an implication of the stochastic process (1) for V]. Therefore the option to invest will be of no value when $V = 0$. The other two conditions come from consideration of optimal investment. V^* is the price at which it is optimal to invest, or in the language of Chapter 4, the free boundary of the continuation region. Then (11) is the value-matching condition; it just says that upon investing, the firm receives a net payoff $V^* - I$. Finally, condition (12) is the "smooth-pasting" condition, discussed in Chapter 4 and its Appendix C. If $F(V)$ were not continuous and smooth at the critical exercise point V^*, one could do better by exercising at a different point.

Note that equation (9) is a second-order differential equation, but there are three boundary conditions that must be satisfied. The reason is that although the position of the first boundary ($V = 0$) is known, the position of the second boundary is not. In other words, the "free boundary" V^* must be determined as part of the solution. That needs the third condition.

Equation (11) has another useful interpretation. Write it as $V^* - F(V^*) = I$. When the firm invests, it gets the project valued V, but gives up the *opportunity* or option to invest, which is valued at $F(V)$. Thus its gain, net of the opportunity cost, is $V - F(V)$. The critical value V^* is where this net gain equals the direct or tangible cost of investment, I. Equivalently, we could write the equation as $V^* = I + F(V^*)$, setting the value of the project equal to the full cost (direct cost plus opportunity cost) of making the investment. We will discuss this point in more detail later.

To find $F(V)$, we must solve equation (9) subject to the boundary conditions (10)–(12). In this case a solution is easy to find; we can guess a functional form, and determine by substitution if it works. We first state the solution and derive some of its properties, and then discuss it in more detail.

To satisfy the boundary condition (10), the solution must take the form

$$F(V) = AV^{\beta_1}, \tag{13}$$

where A is a constant that is yet to be determined, and $\beta_1 > 1$ is a known constant whose value depends on the parameters σ, ρ, and δ of the differential equation.

The remaining boundary conditions, (11) and (12), can be used to solve for the two remaining unknowns—the constant A, and the critical value V^* at which it is optimal to invest. By substituting (13) into (11) and (12) and rearranging, we find that

$$V^* = \frac{\beta_1}{\beta_1 - 1} I, \tag{14}$$

and

$$A = (V^* - I)/(V^*)^{\beta_1} = (\beta_1 - 1)^{\beta_1 - 1} / [(\beta_1)^{\beta_1} I^{\beta_1 - 1}]. \tag{15}$$

Equations (13)–(15) give the value of the investment opportunity and the optimal investment rule, that is, the critical value V^* at which it is optimal to invest. We will examine the characteristics of this solution in some detail later. For the time being, the most important point is that since $\beta_1 > 1$, we have $\beta_1/(\beta_1 - 1) > 1$ and $V^* > I$. Thus the simple NPV rule is incorrect; uncertainty and irreversibility drive a wedge between the critical value V^* and I. The size of the wedge is the factor $\beta_1/(\beta_1 - 1)$, and it becomes important to examine its magnitude for realistic values of the underlying parameters, and its response to changes in these parameters. To do that we must examine the solution (13) in more detail.

2.A   The Fundamental Quadratic

Since the second-order homogeneous differential equation (9) is linear in the dependent variable F and its derivatives, its general solution can be expressed as a linear combination of any two independent solutions. If we try the function AV^{β}, we see by substitution that it satisfies the equation provided β is a root of the quadratic equation

$$\tfrac{1}{2}\sigma^2\beta(\beta - 1) + (\rho - \delta)\beta - \rho = 0. \tag{16}$$

The two roots are

$$\beta_1 = \tfrac{1}{2} - (\rho - \delta)/\sigma^2 + \sqrt{\left[(\rho - \delta)/\sigma^2 - \tfrac{1}{2}\right]^2 + 2\rho/\sigma^2} \; > 1,$$

and

$$\beta_2 = \tfrac{1}{2} - (\rho - \delta)/\sigma^2 - \sqrt{\left[(\rho - \delta)/\sigma^2 - \tfrac{1}{2}\right]^2 + 2\rho/\sigma^2} \; < 0,$$

so the general solution to equation (9) can be written as

$$F(V) = A_1 \, V^{\beta_1} + A_2 \, V^{\beta_2},$$

where A_1 and A_2 are constants to be determined. In our problem, the boundary condition (10) implies that $A_2 = 0$, leaving the solution (13).

To answer our economic questions concerning the multiple $\beta_1/(\beta_1 - 1)$, we must therefore examine the quadratic equation (16) in more detail. Since this equation, or something closely similar, will appear in almost every chapter, it helps to establish a standard terminology and obtain some general results at the outset.

We will generally denote the variable in the equation by β, and the whole quadratic expression (the left-hand side) by Q. Thus Q is a function of the variable β, as well as the parameters σ, ρ, and δ. We will not show this dependence explicitly unless it is important to do so.

Although the roots of a quadratic are known in explicit algebraic form, it helps to show them geometrically. Figure 5.2 shows Q as a function of β. The coefficient of β^2 in $Q(\beta)$ is positive, so the graph is an upward-pointing parabola that goes to ∞ as β goes to $\pm\infty$. Also, $Q(1) = -\delta < 0$ (remember we are assuming $\delta > 0$) and $Q(0) = -\rho < 0$. Therefore the graph crosses the horizontal axis at one point to the right of 1 and another to the left of 0. That is, one root, call it β_1, exceeds 1, and the other, β_2, is negative.

We focus on the positive root β_1. How does it change if a parameter, say σ, changes? This is answered by standard comparative statics. Differentiate

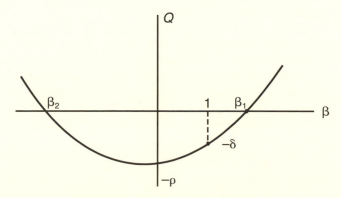

Figure 5.2. *The Fundamental Quadratic*

the quadratic expression totally:

$$\frac{\partial Q}{\partial \beta} \frac{\partial \beta_1}{\partial \sigma} + \frac{\partial Q}{\partial \sigma} = 0,$$

where all derivatives are evaluated at β_1. Figure 5.2 shows that $\partial Q / \partial \beta > 0$ at β_1. Also

$$\partial Q / \partial \sigma = \sigma \beta (\beta - 1) > 0$$

at $\beta_1 > 1$. Therefore $\partial \beta_1 / \partial \sigma < 0$. In other words, as σ increases, β_1 decreases, and therefore $\beta_1 / (\beta_1 - 1)$ increases. The greater is the amount of uncertainty over future values of V, the larger is the wedge between V^* and I, that is, the larger is the excess return the firm will demand before it is willing to make the irreversible investment.

Readers can likewise verify two other properties of this quadratic. First, β_1 increases as δ increases, so a higher δ means a lower wedge $\beta_1 / (\beta_1 - 1)$. Second, β_1 decreases as ρ increases, so a higher ρ implies a larger wedge. We will discuss these results in greater detail and offer some numerical values in Section 4 of this chapter.

Some limiting results concerning β_1 are also informative. We merely state them; they are easily verified using the algebraic formula. First, as $\sigma \to \infty$, we have $\beta_1 \to 1$ and $V^* \to \infty$, that is, the firm never invests if σ is infinite. Next consider what happens as $\sigma \to 0$. We have

If $\alpha > 0$, then $\beta_1 \to \rho / (\rho - \delta)$ and $V^* \to (\rho / \delta) I$.

If $\alpha \leq 0$, then $\beta_1 \to \infty$ and $V^* \to I$.

These results conform to those of the deterministic case that we examined earlier.

2.B   Relationship to Neoclassical Investment Theory

To push this analysis a bit further, suppose that the project itself is an infinitely lived factory that produces a profit flow, π_t, that follows the process

$$d\pi = \alpha \pi \, dt + \sigma \pi \, dz.$$

Hence V is given by

$$V_t = \mathcal{E} \int_t^\infty \pi_s \, e^{-\rho(s-t)} \, ds = \frac{\pi_t}{\rho - \alpha},$$

and dV is given by equation (1). The usual Marshallian rule is to invest as long as $V_t \geq I$, or $\pi_t \geq (\rho - \alpha)I$. However, equation (14) tells us that instead the firm should invest when

$$\pi_t \geq \pi^* = \frac{\beta}{\beta - 1}(\rho - \alpha)I > (\rho - \alpha)I. \tag{17}$$

Another way to look at this is in terms of the Jorgensonian approach to investment.[3] From the quadratic equation (16) satisfied by β_1, we have

$$\frac{\beta_1}{\beta_1 - 1}(\rho - \alpha) = \rho + \tfrac{1}{2}\sigma^2 \beta_1.$$

Thus the critical profit level π^* can be written as

$$\pi^* = (\rho + \tfrac{1}{2}\sigma^2 \beta_1)I > \rho I. \tag{18}$$

Since we have assumed zero depreciation, ρI is the Jorgensonian user cost of capital; the Jorgensonian rule is to invest when $\pi_t = \rho I$. Equation (18) says that when future profits are uncertain, the threshold π^* must exceed this user cost of capital.

In the absence of uncertainty, the Jorgensonian investment rule has the firm investing when $\pi_t = \rho I$, *not* when $\pi_t = (\rho - \alpha)I$. As we saw before, this can be viewed as an optimal timing rule. Once again, the firm must choose T to maximize

$$\max_T \left(\frac{\pi_0 e^{\alpha T}}{\rho - \alpha} - I\right) e^{-\rho T} = \frac{\pi_0 e^{-(\rho - \alpha)T}}{\rho - \alpha} - I e^{-\rho T}. \tag{19}$$

The solution is to invest at a time T when

$$\pi_T = \pi_0 e^{\alpha T} = \rho I. \tag{20}$$

(The reader can verify that $\alpha > 0$ is the second-order condition for this maximization.) Therefore the firm should wait to invest even if there is no uncertainty, because waiting allows the postponement (and thus discounting) of the payment I.[4] As equation (18) shows, with uncertainty there is an additional $\tfrac{1}{2}\sigma^2 \beta_1$ term, so that the firm must wait even longer before investing. This additional term can be thought of as a correction to the neoclassical investment model.

---

[3] Jorgenson (1963) showed that absent uncertainty, the firm should invest when the marginal profit from an extra unit of capital equals the user cost of capital. Our thanks to Giuseppe Bertola for suggesting this viewpoint in this context.

[4] To our knowledge, this point was first noted by Marglin (1963, Chapter 2).

2.C   Relationship to Tobin's q

Tobin (1969) introduced a magnitude q, defined as the ratio of "the value of existing capital goods, or of titles to them" to "their current reproduction cost." This has become a central concept in the orthodox theory of investment. The idea is that if this ratio exceeds unity, a firm can increase its market value by increasing its capital stock. Hence we should see a firm investing when the value of q for the firm is above 1, but not when it is less than 1. Furthermore, we can aggregate by calculating a q based on the average market value of firms in an industry (or the whole economy) and the corresponding average replacement cost of capital. We should then observe at the aggregate level that investment spending is positively related to the value of this q.

A number of issues arise with respect to the measurement and interpretation of q. An important one is that what should matter for investment is *marginal* q, that is, the q that applies to the firm or industry's incremental investment project, as opposed to the *average* q that applies to the entire value and capital stock of the firm or industry. We will address the concept of marginal q in more detail in Chapters 11 and 12. Here we want to emphasize a different problem. As stated, the numerator in q is the market value of *existing* assets. What is relevant for the investment decision is the effect of the *next* project on the value of the firm. We have seen that to get this, the cost of using up the option to invest must be subtracted from the value of a project. Therefore, when a project of value V and option value $F(V)$ is installed, the value of the firm should increase by $V - F(V)$, not V. Correspondingly, q should be defined as the ratio $[V - F(V)]/I$. Then the critical value of q that justifies investment will indeed be 1, as we see from equation (11), which defines the critical V^*.

However, it is difficult to allocate the portion of a firm's market value that comes from the marginal unit of capital. Partly because of this, q has come to be defined, or at least measured, somewhat differently, namely, as the ratio of the expected present value of profits that would flow from a completed investment, to the cost of its construction. This corresponds to using the value of an existing asset, where the option to invest has already been exercised and its opportunity cost is a bygone. In our notation, this means defining q as V/I. We can express the correct investment criterion in terms of this notion of q: the threshold q^* that justifies investment is given by

$$q^* = \beta_1/(\beta_1 - 1) > 1. \tag{21}$$

As V fluctuates, there will be stretches of time when the conventionally measured q exceeds 1 without attracting investment. This gives a new perspective on the effect of irreversibility on the firm's investment decision.

In Chapters 11 and 12, we will have occasion to discuss the literature on investment that uses the q concept. Some articles have used the first of the above definitions of q, and others the second. Therefore we will have to be careful to distinguish them. We will call the first—net of the option value, and having 1 as the upper limit—the "value of the firm" concept, and the second—omitting the option value, and having $\beta_1/(\beta_1 - 1)$ as the critical level—the "value of assets in place" concept.

3 Solution by Contingent Claims Analysis

If the firm doing the investing is publicly held and its managers want their decisions to reflect the shareholders' interests, they should try to maximize the market value of the firm. How do we know that the investment rule derived above will do this? One problem with this investment rule is that it is based on an arbitrary and constant discount rate, ρ. It is not clear where this discount rate should come from, or even that it should be constant over time. As we saw in Chapter 4, we can use contingent claims (option pricing) methods to derive a slightly modified investment rule that will indeed maximize the market value of the firm. In this section, we will go through the required steps in detail.

3.A Reinterpreting the Model

The use of contingent claims analysis requires one important assumption: stochastic changes in V must be *spanned* by existing assets in the economy. Specifically, capital markets must be sufficiently "complete" so that, at least in principle, one could find an asset or construct a dynamic portfolio of assets (that is, a portfolio whose holdings are adjusted continuously as asset prices change), the price of which is perfectly correlated with V. This is equivalent to saying that markets are sufficiently complete that the firm's decisions do not affect the opportunity set available to investors.[5]

The assumption of spanning should hold for most commodities, which are typically traded on both spot and futures markets, and for manufactured

---

[5]For a more rigorous and detailed discussion of spanning and its implications, see Huang and Litzenberger (1990) and Duffie (1992). Duffie and Huang (1985) lay out the full set of conditions needed for spanning.

goods to the extent that prices are correlated with the values of shares or portfolios. However, there may be cases in which this assumption will not hold; an example might be a project to develop a new product that is unrelated to any existing ones, or an R&D venture, the results of which may be hard to predict.

We will assume in this section that spanning holds, that is, that in principle the uncertainty over future values of V can be replicated by existing assets. With this assumption, we can determine the investment rule that maximizes the firm's market value without making any assumptions about risk preferences or discount rates. Also, the use of contingent claims analysis will make it easier to interpret certain properties of the solution. Of course, if spanning does not hold, dynamic programming can still be used to maximize the present value of the firm's expected flow of profits, subject to an arbitrary discount rate. See the discussion in Chapter 4, Section 3 for more on the relationship between the two approaches.

We follow the theory of contingent claims valuation outlined in Chapter 4, Section 2, but repeat some details for reinforcement and clarity. Let x be the price of an asset or dynamic portfolio of assets perfectly correlated with V, and denote by ρ_{xm} the correlation of x with the market portfolio. Since x is perfectly correlated with V, $\rho_{xm} = \rho_{Vm}$. We will assume that this asset or portfolio pays no dividends, so its entire return is from capital gains. Then x evolves according to

$$dx = \mu x\, dt + \sigma x\, dz, \tag{22}$$

where μ, the drift rate, is the expected rate of return from holding this asset or portfolio of assets. According to the Capital Asset Pricing Model (CAPM), μ should reflect the asset's systematic (nondiversifiable) risk. As explained in Chapter 4, μ will be given by

$$\mu = r + \phi\, \rho_{xm}\, \sigma,$$

where r is the risk-free interest rate, and ϕ is the market price of risk.[6] Thus, μ is the risk-adjusted expected rate of return that investors would require if they are to own the project. We will assume that α, the expected percentage rate of change of V, is less than this risk-adjusted return μ. (As we will see, the firm would never invest if this were not the case. No matter what the current

---

[6]That is, $\phi = (r_m - r)/\sigma_m$, where r_m is the expected return on the market, and σ_m is the standard deviation of that return. If we take the New York Stock Exchange Index as the market, $r_m - r \approx 0.08$ and $\sigma_m \approx 0.2$, so $\phi \approx 0.4$. For a more detailed discussion of the Capital Asset Pricing Model, see Brealey and Myers (1991) or Duffie (1992).

level of V, the firm would always be better off waiting and simply holding on to its option to invest.) We will let δ denote the difference between μ and α, that is, $\delta = \mu - \alpha$. Thus we are assuming $\delta > 0$, and this plays the same role as the corresponding assumption in the dynamic programming formulation of Section 2.

The parameter δ plays an important role in this model. We discussed its role as an explicit or implicit dividend in Chapter 4; here we elaborate on those remarks. It will be helpful to draw upon the analogy with a financial call option. If V were the price of a share of common stock, δ would be the dividend rate on the stock. The total expected return on the stock would be $\mu = \delta + \alpha$, that is, the dividend rate plus the expected rate of capital gain. If the dividend rate δ were zero, a call option on the stock would always be held to maturity, and never exercised prematurely. The reason is that the entire return on the stock is captured in its price movements, and hence by the call option, so there is no cost to keeping the option alive. However, if the dividend rate is positive, there is an opportunity cost to keeping the option alive rather than exercising it. That opportunity cost is the dividend stream that one forgoes by holding the option rather than the stock. Since δ is a proportional dividend rate, the higher is the price of the stock, the greater is the flow of dividends. At some high enough price, the opportunity cost of foregone dividends becomes great enough to make it worthwhile to exercise the option.

For our investment problem, μ is the expected rate of return from owning the completed project. It is the equilibrium rate established by the capital market, and includes an appropriate risk premium. If $\delta > 0$, the expected rate of capital gain on the project is less than μ. *Hence δ is an opportunity cost of delaying construction of the project, and instead keeping the option to invest alive.* If δ were zero, there would be no opportunity cost to keeping the option alive, and one would never invest, no matter how high the NPV of the project. That is why we assume $\delta > 0$. On the other hand, if δ is very large, the value of the option will be very small, because the opportunity cost of waiting is large. As $\delta \to \infty$, the value of the option goes to zero; in effect, the only choices are to invest now or never, and the standard NPV rule again applies.

The parameter δ can be interpreted in other ways. For example, it could reflect the process of entry and capacity expansion by competitors. (However, in Chapter 8 we will discuss more complete models that endogenize the process of rivals' entry, and find that the resulting equilibrium *cannot* be well described by simply raising the δ for each firm.) Or it can simply reflect the cash flows from the project. If the project is infinitely lived, then equation (1) can represent the evolution of V during the operation of the project, and δV is the rate of cash flow that the project yields. Since we are assuming that δ is constant, this is consistent with future cash flows being a constant proportion of the project's market value.[7]

When some other parameter of the model (such as σ) varies, we must ask what happens to δ. Various possibilities can be imagined. We will always suppose that the riskless interest rate r is fixed by the larger considerations of the whole capital market, independently of what happens to any one asset (or firm or even industry). The aggregate market price of risk ϕ is likewise held fixed. Now suppose σ increases. This raises the risk-adjusted discount rate μ. To preserve equilibrium in the market for x, either α or δ must change. Two extreme cases are logically possible. First, α might be a fundamental fact about x, so that δ must respond to the change in μ (for example, the dividend rate might depend on the quantity of the commodity held). Alternatively, δ might be a basic behavioral parameter, and the price process of x must change so that α does the adjusting. A third possibility is that both α and δ take up part of the adjustment. In our numerical or comparative static exercises we will often regard δ as a basic parameter independent of σ, but will mention alternative possibilities where they make a material difference to the results.

3.B   Obtaining a Solution

Let us now turn to the valuation of our investment opportunity, and the optimal investment rule. Once again, we will let $F(V)$ be the value of the firm's option to invest. We will determine $F(V)$ in much the same way that we did in the two-period example of Chapter 2 or the general theory of Chapter 4, Section 2 —by constructing a risk-free portfolio, determining its expected rate of return, and equating that expected rate of return to the risk-free rate of interest.

Consider the following portfolio: Hold the option to invest, which is worth $F(V)$, and go short $n = F'(V)$ units of the project (or equivalently, of the asset or portfolio x that is perfectly correlated with V). The value of this portfolio is $\Phi = F - F'(V) V$. Note that this portfolio is dynamic; as V

---

[7]A constant payout rate, δ, and required expected return, μ, imply an infinite project life. Letting π denote the flow of profit from the project,

$$V_0 = \int_0^T \pi_t e^{-\mu t}\, dt = \int_0^T \delta V_0 e^{(\mu - \delta)t} e^{-\mu t}\, dt,$$

which implies $T = \infty$. If the project has a finite life, equation (1) cannot represent the evolution of V during the operating period. However, it can represent its evolution prior to construction of the project, which is all that matters for the investment decision. See Majd and Pindyck (1987, pp. 11–13), for a more detailed discussion of this point.

changes, $F'(V)$ may change from one short interval of time to the next, so that the composition of the portfolio will be changed. However, over each short interval of length dt, we hold n fixed.

The short position in this portfolio will require a payment of $\delta V\,F'(V)$ dollars per time period; otherwise no rational investor will enter into the long side of the transaction. We discussed this in Chapter 2, Section 1(a), and recapitulate the calculation briefly. An investor holding a long position in the project will demand the risk-adjusted return μV, which equals the capital gain αV *plus* the dividend stream δV. Since the short position includes $F'(V)$ units of the project, it will require paying out $\delta V\,F'(V)$. Taking this payment into account, the total return from holding the portfolio over a short time interval dt is[8]

$$dF - F'(V)\,dV - \delta V\,F'(V)\,dt.$$

To obtain an expression for dF, use Ito's Lemma:

$$dF = F'(V)\,dV + \tfrac{1}{2}\,F''(V)\,(dV)^2.$$

Hence the total return on the portfolio is

$$\tfrac{1}{2}\,F''(V)\,(dV)^2 - \delta V\,F'(V)\,dt.$$

From equation (1) for dV, we know that $(dV)^2 = \sigma^2 V^2\,dt$ so the return on the portfolio becomes

$$\tfrac{1}{2}\,\sigma^2 V^2\,F''(V)\,dt - \delta V\,F'(V)\,dt.$$

Note that this return is risk-free. Hence to avoid arbitrage possibilities, it must equal $r\,\Phi\,dt = r\,[F - F'(V)\,V]\,dt$:

$$\tfrac{1}{2}\,\sigma^2 V^2\,F''(V)\,dt - \delta V\,F'(V)\,dt = r\,[F - F'(V)\,V]\,dt.$$

Dividing through by dt and rearranging gives the following differential equation that $F(V)$ must satisfy:

$$\tfrac{1}{2}\,\sigma^2 V^2\,F''(V) + (r - \delta)\,V\,F'(V) - r\,F = 0. \tag{23}$$

Observe that this equation is almost identical to equation (9) obtained using dynamic programming. The only difference is that the risk-free interest

---

[8]Since $n = F'(V)$ is held fixed over this short interval, we do not have any terms involving $dF'(V)$.

rate r replaces the discount rate ρ. The same boundary conditions (10)–(12) will also apply here, and for the same reasons as before. Thus the solution for $F(V)$ again has the form

$$F(V) = AV^{\beta_1},$$

except that now r replaces ρ in the quadratic equation for the exponent β_1, and therefore

$$\beta_1 = \tfrac{1}{2} - (r - \delta)/\sigma^2 + \sqrt{\left[(r - \delta)/\sigma^2 - \tfrac{1}{2}\right]^2 + 2r/\sigma^2}. \qquad (24)$$

The critical value V^* and the constant A are again given by equations (14) and (15).

Hence the contingent claims solution to our investment problem is equivalent to a dynamic programming solution, under the assumption of risk neutrality (that is, the discount rate ρ is equal to the risk-free rate).[9] Thus whether or not spanning holds, we can obtain a solution to the investment problem, but without spanning, the solution will be subject to an assumed discount rate. In either case, the solution will have the same form, and the effects of changes in σ or δ will likewise be the same. One point is worth noting, however. Without spanning, there is no theory for determining the "correct" value for the discount rate ρ (unless we make restrictive assumptions about investors' or managers' utility functions). The CAPM, for example, would not hold, and so it could not be used to calculate a risk-adjusted discount rate in the usual way.

4   Characteristics of the Optimal Investment Rule

Let us assume that spanning holds, and examine the characteristics of the optimal investment rule and the value of the investment opportunity, as given

---

[9]This result was first demonstrated by Cox and Ross (1976). Also, note that equation (23) is the Bellman equation for the maximization of the net payoff to the risk-free portfolio that we constructed. Since the portfolio is risk-free, the Bellman equation for that problem is

$$r\,\Phi\,dt = -\delta V\,F'(V)\,dt + \mathcal{E}(d\Phi), \qquad (i)$$

that is, the return on the portfolio equals the per-period cash flow that it pays out [which is negative, since $\delta V\,F'(V)$ must be paid in to maintain the short position], plus the expected rate of capital gain. By substituting $\Phi = F - F'(V)V$ and expanding dF as before, one can see that equation (23) follows from (i). Also, note that in equation (i), $\delta = \mu - \alpha$ and not $r - \alpha$, so one must still have an estimate of the risk-adjusted expected return that applies to V. This is an example of the "equivalent risk-neutral valuation" procedure discussed in Chapter 4, Section 3.A.

by equations (13), (14), (15), and (24). Some numerical solutions will help to illustrate the results and show how they depend on the values of the various parameters. As we will see, these results are qualitatively the same as those that come out of standard option pricing models.

Unless otherwise noted, in what follows we set the cost of the investment, I, equal to 1, $r = 0.04$, $\delta = 0.04$, and $\sigma = 0.2$ (at annual rates). (Note that we do not need to know μ or α, but only the difference between them, δ.) Payout rates on projects vary enormously from one project to another, so this value of 4 percent for δ should be viewed as reasonable, but not necessarily representative. As for σ, the standard deviation of the rate of return on the stock market as a whole has been about 20 percent on average. Although this represents a diversified portfolio of assets, it also includes the effects of leverage on equity returns, and so might be a reasonable number for an average asset.

Given these parameter values, $\beta_1 = 2$, $V^* = 2I = 2$, and $A = \frac{1}{4}$. Thus the simple NPV rule, which says that the firm should invest as long as V is at least as large as I, is grossly in error. For this reasonable set of parameter values, V must be at least *twice* as large as I before the firm should invest. The value of the firm's investment opportunity is $F(V) = \frac{1}{4}V^2$ for $V \leq 2$, and $F(V) = V - 1$ for $V > 2$ (since the firm exercises its option to invest and receives the net payoff $V - 1$ when $V > 2$).

Figure 5.3 plots $F(V)$ as a function of V for these parameter values, and also for $\sigma = 0$ and $\sigma = 0.3$. In each case, the tangency point of $F(V)$ with the line $V - I$ gives the critical value V^*. The figure also shows that the simple NPV rule must be modified to include the opportunity cost of investing now rather than waiting. That opportunity cost is exactly $F(V)$. When $V < V^*$, $F(V) > V - I$ and therefore $V < I + F(V)$: the value of the project is less than its *full* cost, the direct cost I plus the opportunity cost $F(V)$. [When $\sigma = 0$, $V^* = I$, and $F(V) = 0$ for $V \leq I$.]

Note that $F(V)$ increases when σ increases, as does the critical value V^*. Thus greater uncertainty increases the value of a firm's investment opportunities, but (for that very reason) decreases the amount of actual investing that the firm will do. As a result, when a firm's market or economic environment becomes more uncertain, the market value of the firm can go up, even though the firm does less investing and perhaps produces less.

The dependence of V^* on σ is also shown more directly in Figure 5.4. Observe that V^* increases sharply with σ. *Thus investment is highly sensitive to volatility in project values, irrespective of investors' or managers' risk preferences, and irrespective of the extent to which the riskiness of V is correlated with the market.* Firms can be risk neutral, and stochastic changes in V can

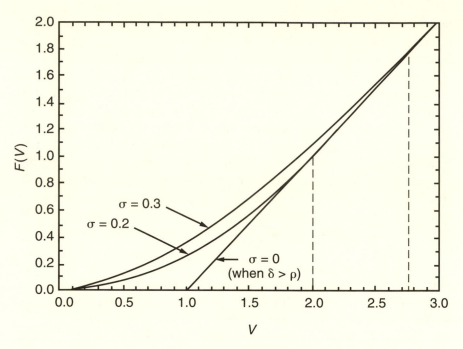

Figure 5.3.   *Value of Investment Opportunity,* $F(V)$, *for* $\sigma = 0,$ 0.2, *and* 0.3

be completely diversifiable; an increase in σ will still increase V^* and hence tend to depress investment.[10]

Figures 5.5 and 5.6 show how $F(V)$ and V^* depend on δ. Observe that an increase in δ from 0.04 to 0.08 results in a decrease in $F(V)$, and hence a decrease in the critical value V^*. (In the limit as $\delta \to \infty$, $F(V) \to 0$ for $V < I$, and $V^* \to I$, as Figure 5.6 shows.) The reason is that as δ becomes larger (holding everything else constant except for α), the expected rate of growth of V falls, and hence the expected appreciation in the value of the option to invest and acquire V falls. In effect, it becomes costlier to wait rather than invest now. To see this, consider an investment in an apartment building, where δV is the net flow of rental income. The total return on the building, which must equal the risk-adjusted market rate, has two components—this income flow plus the expected rate of capital gain. Hence the greater the income flow relative to the total return on the building the more one forgoes

---

[10]Note that for $\sigma = 0$, we have $V^* = 1$ if $\delta \geq 0.04$, but $V^* > 1$ if $\delta < 0.04$. This bears out our earlier discussion of the Jorgensonian criterion.

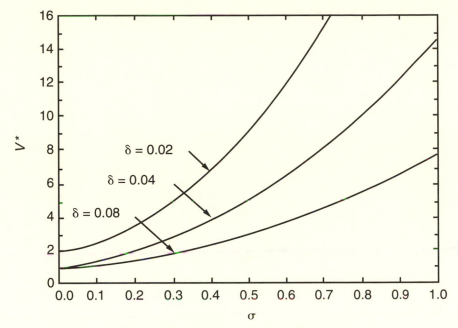

Figure 5.4. *Critical Value V* as a Function of σ*

by holding an option to invest in the building rather than owning the building itself.

We have treated σ and δ as independent parameters. If instead we allow δ to adjust as σ changes, then each unit increase in σ requires an increase in δ of $\phi \rho_{xm}$ units, because

$$\delta = \mu - \alpha = r + \phi \sigma \rho_{xm} - \alpha.$$

Readers can now specify desired values for these parameters, and then combine the two calculations above to obtain the effect of changes in σ for this case.

If the risk-free rate, r, is increased, $F(V)$ increases, and so does V^*. The reason is that the present value of an investment expenditure I made at a future time T is Ie^{-rT}, but the present value of the project that one receives in return for that expenditure is $Ve^{-\delta T}$. Hence if δ is fixed, an increase in r reduces the present value of the cost of the investment but does not reduce its payoff. However, note that while an increase in r raises the value of a firm's investment options, it also results in fewer of those options being exercised. Hence higher (real) interest rates reduce investment, but for a different reason

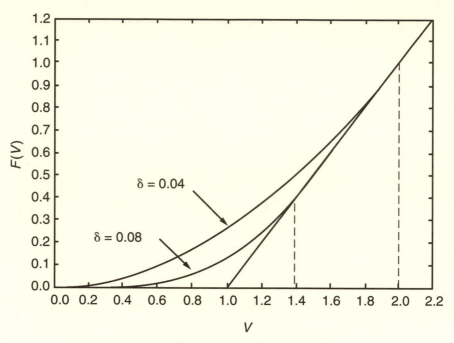

Figure 5.5. *Value of Investment Opportunity, F(V), for δ = 0.04 and 0.08*

than in the standard model. In the standard model, an increase in the interest rate reduces investment by raising the cost of capital; in this model, it increases the value of the option to invest and hence increases the opportunity cost of investing now. (Figure 5.7 shows the dependence of V^* on r for δ equal to 0.04 and 0.08.)

Once again in this calculation we held δ fixed as r increased. If instead we hold α fixed, then δ increases one for one with r. Now a lower r reduces β_1 and increases the critical level V^*. In this sense, a lower interest rate *discourages* investment. This is a pure manifestation of the option idea: a low interest rate makes the future relatively more important, therefore it increases the opportunity cost of exercising the option to invest.

Figure 5.8 provides another way of seeing how the optimal investment rule depends on the parameter values. It also lets us cast our results in terms of Tobin's q. Here we use the "value of assets in place" definition that ignores the opportunity cost of exercising the option, as explained in Section 2(c) above. Then $q^* = V^*/I = \beta_1/(\beta_1 - 1)$ is the critical value of this q, that is, the multiple of I required to invest. The figure shows contours of constant q^* plotted for different values of the parameter combinations $2r/\sigma^2$ and $2\delta/\sigma^2$.

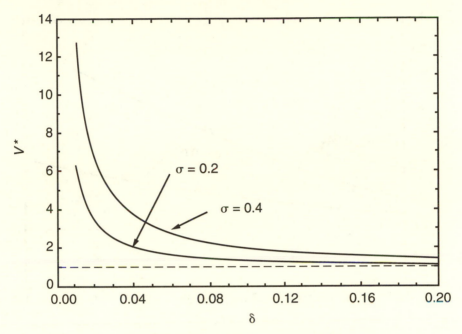

Figure 5.6. *Critical Value V^* as a Function of δ*

We have scaled r and δ by $2/\sigma^2$ because, as the reader can verify by substituting $\beta_1 = q^*/(q^* - 1)$ into equation (16), q^* must satisfy

$$\frac{2r}{\sigma^2} = q^* \left(\frac{2\delta}{\sigma^2} \right) - \frac{q^*}{q^* - 1}.$$

As the figure shows, the multiple is large when δ is small or r is large.

These comparative statics results are the same as those that apply to financial call options. Our option to invest is analogous to a perpetual call option on a dividend-paying stock, where V is the price of the stock, δ is the (proportional) dividend rate, and I is the exercise price of the option. The value of the call option on the stock and the optimal exercise rule will depend on the parameters σ, δ, and r as illustrated by Figures 5.1–5.7. [11]

We repeat that it is important to be careful when interpreting comparative statics results, because different parameters are unlikely to be independent of each other. For example, an increase in the risk-free rate, r, is likely to result

---

[11] For more detailed discussions of financial call options and their comparative statics, see Cox and Rubinstein (1985) and Hull (1989).

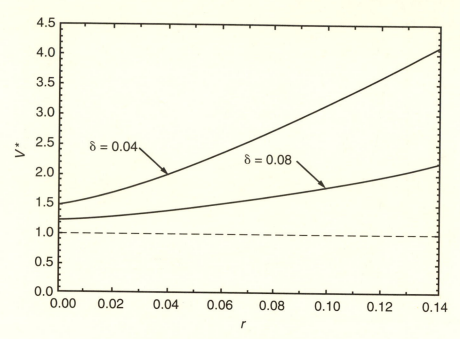

Figure 5.7. *Critical Value V* as a Function of r*

in an increase in the risk-adjusted expected return, μ, which, if the drift rate α is constant, implies an increase in δ. Likewise, an increase in σ is likely to be accompanied by an increase in μ, which again implies an increase in δ if α is constant. These interdependencies should be kept in mind when analyzing how a change in a market-driven parameter (such as r) will affect the value of the investment opportunity and the optimal investment rule.

Another issue that should be kept in mind when performing comparative statics experiments is that our model assumes that the parameters α, σ, etc., are fixed numbers. If α and σ are changing over time or in response to changes in the state variable V (either deterministically or stochastically) and the firm knows this, it should take this into account when determining the optimal investment rule. For example, it may be that α and σ in equation (1) should be replaced with functions $\alpha(V, t)$ and $\sigma(V, t)$. This will complicate the problem considerably. If time affects the parameters, the value of the investment opportunity will likewise be a function of both V and time t, and equation (23) will become a partial differential equation. Even if α and σ are functions of V alone, as with a mean-reverting process for V, the ordinary

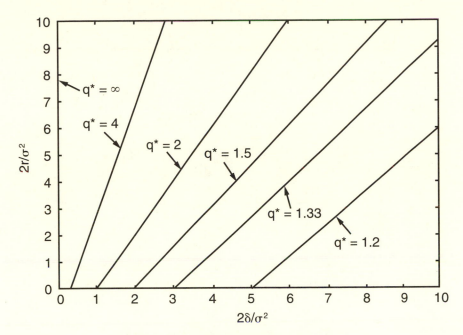

Figure 5.8. *Curves of Constant $q^* = \beta_1/(\beta_1 - 1)$*

differential equation for $F(V)$ will become more complicated and typically need numerical solution; we will soon see an example of this.[12]

Figures 5.9 and 5.10 show sample paths for $V - I$ and $F(V) = \frac{1}{4}V^2$. In both cases we assume that $\mu = 0.08$, so that with $\delta = 0.04$, the drift rate α is 0.04. (As before, $r = 0.04$ and $\sigma = 0.2$, both at annual rates.) We begin each set of sample paths in 1980 with $V_0 = I = 1$. Taking a time interval of one month, we then calculate V_t using the equation

$$V_t = 1.003\,27\,V_{t-1} + 0.0577\,V_{t-1}\,\epsilon_t, \tag{25}$$

[12]Or, one might believe that σ fluctuates stochastically over time, for example, according to the mean-reverting process

$$d\sigma = \eta\,(\bar{\sigma} - \sigma)\,dt + \xi\,\sigma\,dw,$$

where dw is the increment of a Wiener process that is uncorrelated with dz. The value of the investment opportunity will then be a function of two state variables, V and σ, and will satisfy a partial differential equation. Problems of this sort have been studied by Hull and White (1987), Scott (1987), and Wiggins (1987).

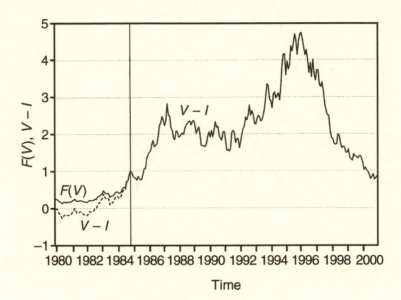

Figure 5.9.   *Sample Path of F(V) and V − I*

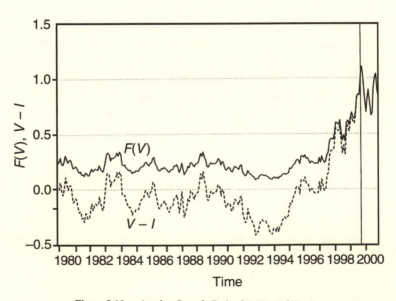

Figure 5.10.   *Another Sample Path of F(V) and V − I*

where at each time t, ϵ_t is drawn from a normal distribution with zero mean and unit standard deviation. (Note that the coefficient $0.0577 = 0.20/\sqrt{12}$ is the *monthly* standard deviation.)

Since $V_0 = I = 1$, the standard NPV rule would call for investing immediately. However, $F(V_0) = 0.25$, so $V_0 < I + F(V_0)$, and the firm should wait rather than invest. In Figure 5.9, the firm happens to wait approximately five years before V reaches $V^* = 2$. This waiting time can vary considerably from one sample path to the next. In the sample path shown in Figure 5.10 for example, the firm must wait much longer—nearly 20 years—before V reaches the critical value of 2.[13]

5 Alternative Stochastic Processes

The use of a geometric Brownian motion as a model for V is convenient, but in some cases may not be realistic. In this section we will examine the value of the investment opportunity and the optimal investment rule when V follows alternative stochastic processes. We will first consider the case of a mean-reverting process, and then a Poisson jump process.

5.A Mean-Reverting Process

Suppose V follows the mean-reverting process

$$dV = \eta\,(\bar{V} - V)\,V\,dt + \sigma\,V\,dz, \tag{26}$$

so that the expected percentage rate of change in V is $(1/dt)\,\mathcal{E}(dV/V) = \eta\,(\bar{V} - V)$, and the expected absolute rate of change is $(1/dt)\,\mathcal{E}(dV) = \eta\,\bar{V}\,V - \eta\,V^2$, a parabola that equals zero at $V = 0$ and $V = \bar{V}$ and has a maximum at $V = \bar{V}/2$. As we will see, an advantage of this particular process is that we will be able to obtain an analytical solution to the investment problem.

To find the optimal investment rule, we will use contingent claims analysis. Let μ be the risk-adjusted discount rate for the project (that is, μ reflects the systematic risk in the stochastic fluctuations in V). In this case the expected

---

[13]The expectation and variance of this "waiting time" can be computed analytically. We will not need these expressions, but refer the interested reader to some simple cases in Dixit (1993a, pp. 54–57), and the more rigorous theory in Karlin and Taylor (1981, pp. 242–244) or Harrison (1985, pp. 11–14).

rate of growth of V is not constant, but is instead a function of V. Hence the "shortfall," $\delta = \mu - (1/dt)\,\mathcal{E}(dV)/V$, is likewise a function of V:[14]

$$\delta(V) = \mu - \eta\,(\bar{V} - V). \tag{27}$$

The differential equation (23) will again apply, but with equation (27) substituted for δ. Hence $F(V)$ must satisfy

$$\tfrac{1}{2}\sigma^2 V^2 F''(V) + [r - \mu + \eta\,(\bar{V} - V)]\,V\,F'(V) - r\,F = 0. \tag{28}$$

Also, $F(V)$ must satisfy the same boundary conditions (10)–(12) as before, and for the same reasons. [Note that $V = 0$ is an absorbing barrier for the process (26), so $F(0) = 0$.]

Finding a solution to equation (28) is a little more complicated than it was for equation (23). We define a new function $h(V)$ by

$$F(V) = A V^\theta\, h(V), \tag{29}$$

where A and θ are constants that will soon be chosen in such a way as to make $h(V)$ satisfy a differential equation with a known solution. Substituting this expression for $F(V)$ into equation (28) and rearranging gives the following equation:

$$
\begin{aligned}
V^\theta\, h(V) &\left[\tfrac{1}{2}\sigma^2\theta(\theta - 1) + (r - \mu + \eta\bar{V})\theta - r\right] \\
&+ V^{\theta+1}\left[\tfrac{1}{2}\sigma^2 V\, h''(V) + (\sigma^2\theta + r - \mu + \eta\bar{V} - \eta V)\,h'(V)\right. \\
&\left. - \eta\theta\, h(V)\right] = 0.
\end{aligned}
\tag{30}
$$

Equation (30) must hold for any value of V, so the bracketed terms in both the first and second lines of the equation must equal zero. First we choose θ to set the bracketed terms in the first line of the equation equal to zero:

$$\tfrac{1}{2}\sigma^2\,\theta(\theta - 1) + (r - \mu + \eta\bar{V})\theta - r = 0.$$

This quadratic equation has two solutions for θ, one of which is positive and the other negative. To satisfy the boundary condition that $F(0) = 0$, we use the positive solution:

$$\theta = \tfrac{1}{2} + (\mu - r - \eta\bar{V})/\sigma^2 + \sqrt{\left[(r - \mu + \eta\bar{V})/\sigma^2 - \tfrac{1}{2}\right]^2 + 2r/\sigma^2}. \tag{31}$$

---

[14]We have not developed a model that explains *why* V is mean reverting, and unless there is a payout stream that is mean reverting, V will have a rate of return that is below the equilibrium rate μ. See McDonald and Siegel (1984) for a discussion of this point.

From the second line of equation (30), we have

$$\tfrac{1}{2}\sigma^2 V h''(V) + (\sigma^2\theta + r - \mu + \eta\bar{V} - \eta V)h'(V) - \eta\theta h(V) = 0. \qquad (32)$$

By making the substitution $x = 2\eta V/\sigma^2$, we can transform equation (32) into a standard form. Let $h(V) = g(x)$, so that $h'(V) = (2\eta/\sigma^2)g'(x)$ and $h''(V) = (2\eta/\sigma^2)^2 g''(x)$. Then (32) becomes

$$x g''(x) + (b - x)g'(x) - \theta g(x) = 0, \qquad (33)$$

where

$$b = 2\theta + 2(r - \mu + \eta\bar{V})/\sigma^2.$$

Equation (33) is known as Kummer's Equation. Its solution is the confluent hypergeometric function $H(x; \theta, b(\theta))$, which has the following series representation:[15]

$$H(x; \theta, b) = 1 + \frac{\theta}{b}x + \frac{\theta(\theta+1)}{b(b+1)}\frac{x^2}{2!} + \frac{\theta(\theta+1)(\theta+2)}{b(b+1)(b+2)}\frac{x^3}{3!} + \cdots. \qquad (34)$$

We have verified that the solution to equation (28) is indeed of the form of equation (29). The solution is

$$F(V) = AV^\theta H\left(\frac{2\eta}{\sigma^2}V; \theta, b\right), \qquad (35)$$

where A is a constant that is yet to be determined. We can find A, as well as the critical value V^* at which it is optimal to invest, from the remaining two boundary conditions, that is, $F(V^*) = V^* - I$ and $F_V(V^*) = 1$. Because the confluent hypergeometric function is an infinite series, A and V^* must be found numerically.

We can gain some insight into the effects of mean reversion by looking at several numerical solutions. Unless otherwise stated, we will set $I = 1$, $r = 0.04$, $\mu = 0.08$, and $\sigma = 0.2$. We will vary η and $\bar{V}$. Note, however, that the dependence of $(1/dt)\mathcal{E}(dV)/V$ on η depends on the scaling of $\bar{V}$. We will work with values of $\bar{V}$ in the range of 0.5 to 1.5, so a value of η of 0.5 or above implies a very high rate of mean reversion.

Figure 5.11 shows the value of the investment opportunity $F(V)$ and the critical value V^* for $\eta = 0.05$ (which implies a relatively low rate of mean

---

[15] See Abramowitz and Stegun (1964), Section 7.9 of Pearson (1990), or Slater (1960) for discussions of the confluent hypergeometric function and its properties.

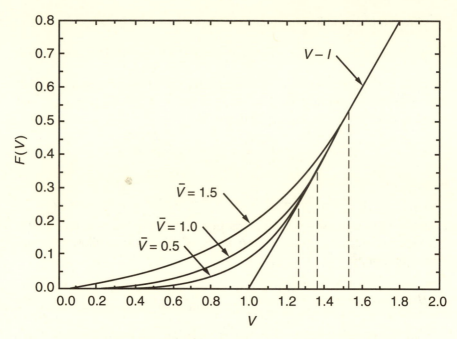

Figure 5.11. *Mean Reversion—$F(V)$ for $\eta = 0.05$ and $\bar{V} = 0.5$, 1.0, and 1.5*

reversion) and $\bar{V} = 0.5$, 1.0, and 1.5. For comparison, note that if η were zero, the model would correspond to the basic one in the previous section, with $\alpha = 0$ and hence $\delta = \mu = 0.08$; in that case, V^* would equal 1.39. In Figure 5.11, η is small enough so that for each value of $\bar{V}$, V^* is fairly close to 1.39. As we would expect, the larger is $\bar{V}$, the larger is $F(V)$ and the higher is V^*. Other things equal, a larger $\bar{V}$ implies a higher expected rate of growth of V, so that an option to buy V will be worth more.

Figures 5.12 and 5.13 also show the value of the investment opportunity $F(V)$ and the critical value V^* for $\bar{V} = 0.5$, 1.0, and 1.5, but in Figure 5.12, $\eta = 0.1$, and in Figure 5.13, $\eta = 0.5$. As these figures show, when $\bar{V}$ is 1.5 (larger than I), a larger value of η increases $F(V)$, but when $\bar{V}$ is 0.5 (smaller than I), a larger value of η reduces $F(V)$. [If $\bar{V} < I$ and η is large, it is unlikely that V will exceed I for very much time, and the option to invest will not be worth much. On the other hand, if $\bar{V} > I$ and η is large, even if V is initially small, it is likely to quickly rise above I and remain above I most of the time, so that $F(V)$ will be large.]

Figures 5.12 and 5.13 also show that if $\bar{V}$ and η are large, $F(V)$ will no longer be uniformly convex; it will be concave for small values of V. This

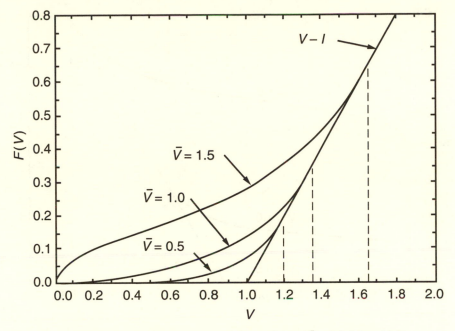

Figure 5.12. *Mean Reversion—$F(V)$ for $\eta = 0.1$ and $\bar{V} = 0.5$, 1.0, and 1.5*

is a result of the particular stochastic process (26) that we used to describe the evolution of V. That process has an absorbing barrier at $V = 0$ [so that $F(0) = 0$], but the absolute rate of mean reversion rises rapidly for small but positive values of V, so that $F(V)$ likewise rises rapidly. This is most evident in Figure 5.13 for the case of $\bar{V} = 1.5$; $F(0) = 0$, but the expected rate of growth of V becomes large once V is even slightly greater than zero, so that $F(V)$ rises rapidly.

Figure 5.14 shows the critical value V^* as a function of the mean-reversion parameter η for $\bar{V} = 0.5$, 1.0, and 1.5. Observe that V^* increases with η when $\bar{V}$ is large, but decreases with η when $\bar{V}$ is small. This is an implication of what we saw before; when $\bar{V}$ is large, a larger η increases $F(V)$ (and hence V^*), but when $\bar{V}$ is small, a larger η reduces $F(V)$. Figure 5.14 suggests that $\bar{V} = I$ is the dividing line, but in fact, whether V^* rises or falls with η also depends on the risk-adjusted expected rate of return, μ. In Figure 5.14, $\mu = 0.08$. Figure 5.15 also shows V^* as a function of η, but for $\mu = 0.04$. Other things equal, a lower value of μ implies a lower value for the expected rate of capital gain "shortfall," $\delta = \mu - (1/dt)E(dV)/V$, and hence a larger value of $F(V)$. This increase in $F(V)$ will be most pronounced when η is small. (When η is

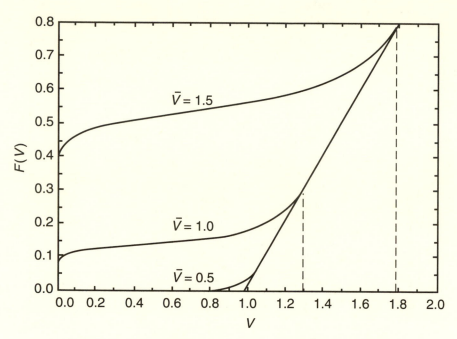

Figure 5.13. *Mean Reversion—F(V) for $\eta = 0.5$ and $\bar{V} = 0.5$, 1.0, and 1.5*

large, V is in any case expected to revert quickly to $\bar{V}$.) Hence if μ is small, V^* will decrease with η unless $\bar{V}$ is substantially larger than I.

Finally, Figures 5.16 and 5.17 illustrate the dependence of V^* on μ. Figure 5.16 shows V^* as a function of μ for $\bar{V} = 1.0$ and $\eta = 0.05$, 0.1, and 0.5, and Figure 5.17 shows the same, but for $\bar{V} = 1.5$. Note that in all cases, V^* declines with μ; again, a higher μ implies a higher capital gain "shortfall" $\delta(V)$, and hence a lower $F(V)$ and lower V^*. However, the rate of decline depends on $\bar{V}$ and η. When η is small, V^* begins at a higher value (again, if η were zero, the model would reduce to that of the previous section, with $\alpha = 0$ and $\delta = \mu$ so that $\lim_{\mu \to 0} V^* = \infty$), and declines more rapidly (because the rate of reversion to $\bar{V}$ and hence the expected rate of capital gain for V is small). Also, as we would expect, the larger is $\bar{V}$, the larger is V^* [and $F(V)$], whatever the values of η and μ.

Our choice of the mean-reverting process (26) for V was convenient in that it led to a quasianalytical solution for the value of the investment opportunity and the optimal investment rule. This should not be viewed as particularly restrictive. We could just as well have specified some alternative mean-reverting process for V (for example, one in which the absolute, rather

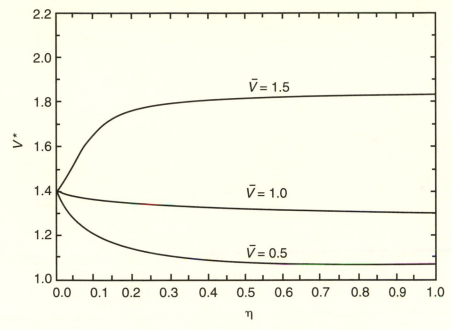

Figure 5.14.   *Critical Value V^* as a Function of η for $\mu = 0.08$ and $\bar{V} = 0.5$, 1.0, and 1.5*

than percentage, rate of mean reversion is linear in V). Depending on the process, the resulting differential equation for $F(V)$ might or might not have a known series solution; in any case it could be solved numerically, usually with little difficulty.

5.B   Combined Brownian Motion and Jump Process

Let us now return to our basic model in which V follows a geometric Brownian motion, and extend it in a different way. This time we will allow for the possibility that at some random point in time, V will take a Poisson jump downward. This version of the model could describe a situation in which a company has a patent that gives it the option to invest in a project whose value is V, but other companies are also doing research which, if successful, will allow them to invest in a similar project. If and when one of those other companies is successful, the resulting competition will reduce profits, and hence V.

To modify our basic model, we will assume that V follows the mixed Brownian motion/jump process:

$$dV = \alpha V\, dt + \sigma V\, dz - V\, dq, \tag{36}$$

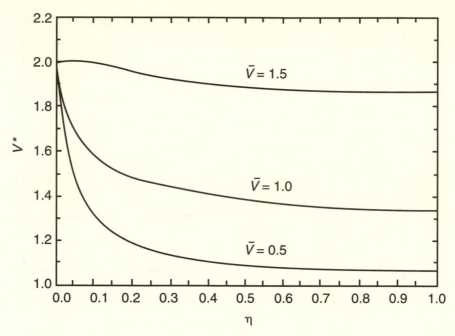

Figure 5.15.   *Critical Value V^* as a Function of η for $\mu = 0.04$ and $\bar{V} = 0.5$, 1.0, and 1.5*

where dq is the increment of a Poisson process with mean arrival rate λ, and dq and dz are independent [so that $\mathcal{E}(dzdq) = 0$]. We will assume that if an "event" occurs, q falls by some fixed percentage ϕ (with $0 \leq \phi \leq 1$) with probability 1. Thus equation (36) says that V will fluctuate as a geometric Brownian motion, but over each time interval dt there is a small probability $\lambda\, dt$ that it will drop to $(1 - \phi)$ times its original value, and it will then continue fluctuating until another event occurs. (Poisson jump processes of this kind are described in Chapter 3.)

It is important to be clear about the meaning of equation (36). First, note that the expected percentage rate of change in V is not α, but instead is $(1/dt)\,\mathcal{E}(dV)/V = \alpha - \lambda\phi$, because over each interval of time dt there is a probability $\lambda\, dt$ that V will fall by $100\,\phi$ percent. Thus increases in λ reduce the expected rate of capital gain on V by increasing the chance of a sudden drop in V. Second, because a Poisson event occurs only infrequently, most of the time the variance of dV/V over a short interval of time dt is just that of the Brownian motion part, $\sigma^2\, dt$. However, if the event occurs, it contributes a very large deviation, so its contribution to the variance calculated given the information at t cannot be neglected. Using the random walk approximation

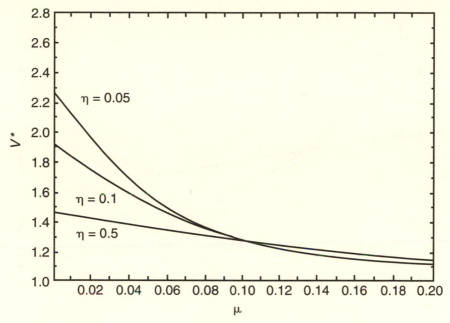

Figure 5.16. *Critical Value V^* as a Function of μ for $\bar{V} = 1.0$ and $\eta = 0.05$, 0.1, and 0.5*

for Brownian motion, let us for simplicity set $\alpha = 0$ and write

$$dV = \begin{cases} \sigma V \sqrt{dt} & \text{with probability } \frac{1}{2}(1 - \lambda\, dt), \\ -\sigma V \sqrt{dt} & \text{with probability } \frac{1}{2}(1 - \lambda\, dt), \\ -\phi V & \text{with probability } \lambda\, dt. \end{cases}$$

Then

$$\mathcal{E}[dV] = -\lambda\, dt\, \phi V,$$

$$\mathcal{E}[(dV)^2] = (1 - \lambda\, dt)\, \sigma^2 V^2\, dt + \lambda\, dt\, \phi^2 V^2,$$

$$\mathcal{V}[dV] = \mathcal{E}[(dV)^2] - \{\mathcal{E}[dV]\}^2$$

$$= (1 - \lambda\, dt)\, \sigma^2 V^2\, dt + \lambda\, dt\, \phi^2 V^2 - \lambda^2 \phi^2 V^2\, (dt)^2$$

$$= \sigma^2 V^2\, dt + \lambda \phi^2 V^2\, dt,$$

ignoring terms in $(dt)^2$, etc.

Note that this variance has two components. The first component, $\sigma^2 V^2\, dt$, is the *instantaneous* (or "local") variance of dV, which comes from

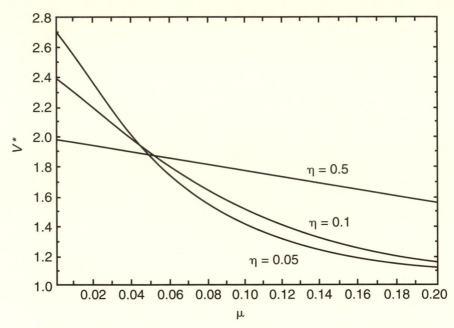

Figure 5.17.   *Critical Value V^* as a Function of μ for $\bar{V} = 1.5$ and $\eta = 0.05, 0.1,$ and 0.5*

the Brownian motion part of the process, and is conditional on no jump occurring. The second component, $\lambda \phi^2 V^2 dt$, accounts for the possibility of a jump. Shortly we will want to use Ito's Lemma to find the differential of a function of V. As we saw in Chapter 3, when applying Ito's Lemma to a combined Brownian motion/jump process, it is only the first component of this variance that contributes to the new term involving second-order derivatives. The jump part contributes a different term involving a difference in values at discretely different points.

Finally, in order to gauge the effects of changing λ, we will want to know the expected value of T, the amount of time that V fluctuates continuously before dropping. To determine $\mathcal{E}(T)$, we use the fact that the probability that no event occurs in the interval $(0, T)$ is $e^{-\lambda T}$. Therefore the probability that the first event occurs in the short interval $(T, T+dT)$ is $e^{-\lambda T} \lambda \, dT$. Therefore the expected time until V takes a Poisson jump is

$$\mathcal{E}[T] = \int_0^\infty \lambda \, T \, e^{-\lambda T} \, dT = 1/\lambda. \qquad (37)$$

We will now proceed to solve for the optimal investment rule using dynamic programming. We will assume that the firm is risk neutral, so that its discount rate is $\rho = r$. Then the Bellman equation for $F(V)$, the value of the investment opportunity, is

$$r\, F\, dt = \mathcal{E}(dF).$$

We now expand dF using the version of Ito's Lemma for combined Brownian and Poisson processes (see Section 5 of Chapter 3):

$$r\, F\, dt = \alpha\, V\, F'(V)dt + \tfrac{1}{2}\sigma^2\, V^2\, F''(V)dt$$
$$- \lambda\{\, F(V) - F[(1 - \phi)\, V]\,\}\, dt. \tag{38}$$

Replacing α with $r - \delta$, this can be rewritten as

$$\tfrac{1}{2}\sigma^2\, V^2\, F''(V) + (r - \delta)\, V\, F'(V)$$
$$- (r + \lambda)\, F(V) + \lambda\, F[(1 - \phi)V] = 0. \tag{39}$$

The same boundary conditions (10)–(12) apply as before.

The solution to (39) is again of the form $F(V) = A\, V^{\beta_1}$, but now β_1 is the positive solution to a slightly more complicated nonlinear equation:

$$\tfrac{1}{2}\sigma^2\, \beta\, (\beta - 1) + (r - \delta)\, \beta - (r + \lambda) + \lambda\, (1 - \phi)^\beta = 0. \tag{40}$$

The value of β that satisfies (40) and also satisfies the condition $F(0) = 0$ can be found numerically. Then, given β_1, V^* and A can again be found from equations (14) and (15), which in turn follow from boundary conditions (11) and (12).[16]

Figure 5.18 shows the critical value V^* as a function of σ for $\phi = 0$, 0.4, and 1. (In each case, $\lambda = 0.1$, $r = \delta = 0.04$, and $I = 1$.) Note that the larger is ϕ, the smaller is V^*. The reason is that a larger value of ϕ implies a smaller value of the investment opportunity (when an event occurs, V will fall by a larger fraction), which means a smaller opportunity cost of investing now rather than waiting.

Table 5.1 shows β_1, V^*, and A for various values of λ, for the case in which $\phi = 1$ (so that V falls to zero when an event occurs). (In this table,

---

[16]If $\phi = 1$ (so that the event is that V falls to zero, where it remains forever), equation (40) simplifies to a quadratic equation, which is just like our earlier equation except that the Poisson parameter λ gets added to the interest rate in the constant term. The positive solution is

$$\beta_1 = \tfrac{1}{2} - (r - \delta)/\sigma^2 + \sqrt{[(r - \delta)/\sigma^2 - \tfrac{1}{2}]^2 + 2(r + \lambda)/\sigma^2}.$$

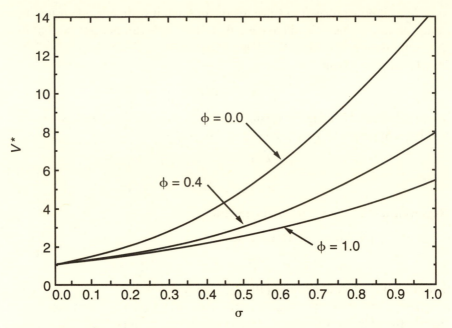

Figure 5.18. *Critical Value V* as a Function of σ for Mixed Poisson/Brownian Motion, with* λ = 0.1

$r = \delta = 0.04$, $\sigma = 0.2$, and $I = 1$.) A positive value of λ affects the value of the investment opportunity in two ways. First, it reduces the expected rate of capital gain on V (from α to $\alpha - \lambda$), which reduces $F(V)$. Second, it increases the variance of percentage changes in V over finite intervals of time, and this tends to increase $F(V)$. As Table 5.1 shows, the *net* effect is to reduce $F(V)$, and therefore to reduce the critical value V^*. Furthermore, this net effect is quite strong; small increases in λ lead to a substantial drop in V^*. For example, using equation (37) we know that if $\lambda = 0.2$, the expected time for V to remain positive, $\mathcal{E}(T)$, is 5 years, but compared to when λ is zero, A falls by more than half, and V^* drops from 2 to 1.33.

As we said earlier, it is important to be careful when interpreting comparative statics results. In this case we have increased λ while holding α fixed. One could argue that the market-determined expected rate of return on V (which in this case is the risk-free rate, r) should remain constant, so that an increase in λ should be accompanied by a commensurate increase in α (otherwise no investor would choose to hold this project). Suppose $\phi = 1$. Then if α increases exactly as much as λ, so that $\alpha - \lambda$ remains constant, we would have to replace the terms $(r - \delta)$ in equation (40) with $(r + \lambda - \delta)$. In this case

Table 5.1. Dependence of β_1, V^*, and A on λ
(Note: $I = 1$, $\phi = 1$, $r = \delta = 0.04$, and $\sigma = 0.2$.)

λ	β_1	V^*	A
0	2.00	2.00	0.250
0.05	2.70	1.59	0.169
0.1	3.19	1.46	0.138
0.2	4.00	1.33	0.105
0.3	4.65	1.27	0.009
0.5	5.72	1.21	0.007
1.0	7.73	1.15	0.005

an increase in λ would be equivalent to an increase in the risk-free rate r, and would lead to an *increase* in $F(V)$ and V^*.[17]

The particular jump process given by equation (36) leads to a differential equation for $F(V)$ that is easy to solve. One could, of course, specify alternative processes for V. For example, a firm holding a patent might face many potential competitors, each of which is trying to develop its own patent. The success of a competitor might cause V to fall by some *random*, rather than fixed, amount. Over time, additional competitors may succeed in entering the market, so that V continues to fall. The calculation of the optimal investment rule for a model of this sort will be more difficult, however, and would likely require a numerical solution method.

6   Guide to the Literature

Antecedents of the McDonald-Siegel (1986) model include Myers (1977), who showed that firms' investment options are a component of their market value, Tourinho (1979), who showed that natural resource reserves can be viewed as options to produce the resource and valued accordingly, and work by

---

[17]Merton (1976) derived a formula for the value of a call option on a non-dividend-paying stock whose price follows a mixed Brownian motion/Poisson jump process, and showed that if the "event" is that the stock price drops to zero, the original Black-Scholes (1973) formula applies, but with $r' \equiv r + \lambda$ replacing the risk-free rate, r. He kept the expected rate of capital gain on the stock constant, that is, replaced the drift rate α with $\alpha + \lambda$. Then an increase in λ will increase the value of the option.

Cukierman (1980) and Bernanke (1983). The last two authors also developed models in which firms have an incentive to postpone irreversible investment decisions so that they can wait for new information to arrive. However, in their models, this information makes the future value of a project less uncertain; our focus in this chapter has been on situations in which information arrives over time, but the future is always uncertain. Brock, Rothschild, and Stiglitz (1988) examine capital-theoretic implications of uncertainty, and Demers (1991) is a more recent contribution to the study of investment when information arrives over time.

To derive optimal investment rules using contingent claims analysis, we had to assume that uncertainty over the payoff from the investment was spanned by existing assets. Duffie and Huang (1985) lay out the full set of conditions required for dynamic spanning; Huang and Litzenberger (1990), Duffie (1992), and Dothan (1990) provide detailed discussions at the graduate textbook level. Also, we saw that the basic investment option is analogous to a perpetual call option on a dividend-paying stock, and has the same properties as such a financial option. For detailed treatments of the valuation and optimal exercising of financial options, see Cox and Rubinstein (1985), Hull (1989), or Jarrow and Rudd (1983), and see Smith (1976) for an overview of option pricing methods and results.

Our results for the basic case in which V follows a geometric Brownian motion are also described and interpreted in the survey articles by Dixit (1992) and Pindyck (1991b), upon which this chapter draws. Also, Merton (1977) and Mason and Merton (1985) discuss the connections between financial options and investment decisions. Unless there are bankruptcy costs, the Modigliani–Miller theorem holds, so the firm's real investment decisions are independent of its financial structure.

For a general overview of neoclassical investment theory, including implications of adjustment costs, see Nickell (1978).

Chapter **6**

The Value of a Project and the Decision to Invest

THE BASIC model of irreversible investment in Chapter 5 demonstrated a close analogy between a firm's option to invest and a financial call option. In the case of a call option, the price of the stock underlying the option is assumed to follow an exogenously specified stochastic process, usually a geometric Brownian motion. In our model of real investment, the corresponding state variable was the value of the project, V, for which we stipulated an exogenous stochastic process.

However, as we explained at the beginning of Chapter 5, letting V follow an exogenous stochastic process, and particularly a geometric Brownian motion, is an abstraction from reality. First, if the project is a factory and there are variable costs of operation, V will not follow a geometric Brownian motion. Second and more important, the value of a project depends on future prices of outputs and inputs, interest rates, etc. These in turn can be explained in terms of the underlying demand and technology conditions in various markets. Hence fluctuations in V can be traced back to uncertainty in these more basic variables. How deep one goes depends on the purpose of the analysis. To understand a firm's behavior, we might be satisfied to work with an exogenous process for the output and input prices. At the industry level, we must make the output price endogenous. At an even more general equilibrium level, the input prices must also be determined simultaneously by considering all industries' factor demands. In this chapter we take some first steps along this route.

For most of the time in this chapter, we consider a firm that has the privileged opportunity or monopoly right to invest in a single discrete project that will produce a given output flow. The basic uncertainty is over the demand for this output, but given a fixed scale, there is an immediate correspondence between demand and price. Therefore we allow the output price P to be exogenous, and determine the value V of the project, and the value F of the option to invest, in terms of the stipulated stochastic process for P. The methods are the same as those employed in Chapter 5, namely, contingent claims analysis or dynamic programming. We will see that once again, the value of the option to invest includes a holding premium, which implies a stiffer test for investment than the traditional Marshallian criterion.

In Section 1, we begin with the simplest case where production has no operating costs. Then the value of a completed project is just the discounted present value of the revenue flow, and the formulas of Chapter 5 that were expressed in terms of V translate immediately into corresponding formulas in terms of P.

In Section 2 we introduce an operating cost C. Hence the project will generate a flow of operating profit equal to $(P - C)$ per period. This raises a new issue—the output price can go below C from time to time, which would make the operating profit negative. We must specify what happens then. We will consider two, somewhat extreme, possibilities. The first, which is the subject of this chapter, is that the project can be costlessly shut down if P falls below C, and later costlessly restarted if P rises above C. In effect, this makes the project an infinite sequence of instantaneous operating options, each of which is exercised if $P > C$, and can be valued accordingly. The other extreme possibility, which we will consider in Chapter 7, prohibits such temporary suspension by supposing that the full investment cost I must be incurred over again if operations are ever resumed. Then some losses will be sustained to keep the option of future operations alive, but if the losses grow sufficiently large, the project will be abandoned. Of course reality lies somewhere between these two extremes. Ongoing projects generally build up specific assets—workers' skills, customers' loyalty, etc.—that will gradually disappear, or "rust," if operation is suspended. Thus resumption involves a cost, but less than the cost of starting anew, and the difference depends on the nature of the product and the duration of the suspension. Our analysis of the extreme cases yields results that can be suitably combined to fit particular applications that lie in between.

In Section 3 we allow some instantaneous variation of inputs like labor and raw materials, to vary the output flow from the project in response to transient price fluctuations. Now the profit flow becomes a nonlinear function of the price, which alters the effect of uncertainty on investment.

All of the analysis up to this point assumes that the project, once installed, goes on producing the output flow forever. This unrealistic assumption is made only to convey the basic ideas of option values in a simpler manner. In Section 4 we relax this assumption by introducing depreciation. We show that the effect on option values depends not on the mortality of one project, but on how we specify the opportunities available to the firm after its initial project has reached the end of its life. We also show that option values remain of considerable significance even with fairly rapid depreciation.

In the concluding section of this chapter we consider a situation where two variables that affect the firm's investment decision—the output price and the investment cost—are both random. Here the value of the option to invest is a function of both of these independent variables, and therefore it satisfies a partial differential equation. In general such equations are difficult and must be solved numerically. A special feature of homogeneity helps us reduce the problem to an ordinary differential equation and solve it analytically. Now investment is optimal only when the ratio of output price to investment cost exceeds a threshold influenced by the option value of waiting.

Throughout this chapter, the insights about option values which we gained from the analysis of Chapter 5 will remain valid and valuable as we introduce new features into the model. The techniques developed there will also continue to be useful. In future chapters we will continue the program of generalizing the models and posing new issues. In Chapter 7 we will consider the possibility of temporarily mothballing or permanently abandoning a project if its cash flow turns negative. Then, in Chapters 8 and 9 we will move to the level of industry equilibrium, where each firm has the opportunity to invest in a single project. In Chapter 10 we will return to the perspective of a single firm, but generalize the nature of the project, letting it consist of a number of investment steps, all of which must be completed before the profit flows begin. Finally, in Chapter 11 we consider incremental investment, where each unit of addition to capacity begins to yield its marginal revenue product as soon as it is installed.

1 The Simplest Case: No Operating Costs

In this section the firm's investment project, once completed, will produce a fixed flow of output forever. For convenience, we will choose the units so that the quantity of output from the project is equal to one unit per year.

Suppose the inverse demand function giving price P in terms of quantity Q is $P = Y D(Q)$, where Y is a stochastic shift variable. In this section the variable costs of production are assumed to be zero, so the firm's profit flow is just $P = Y D(1)$. Hence, without further loss of generality, we can take P itself as the stochastic variable.

For most of the time in this chapter we will assume the simplest stochastic process for P, and one closest to the framework of Chapter 5, namely, the geometric Brownian motion:

$$dP = \alpha P\, dt + \sigma P\, dz. \tag{1}$$

The profit flow is P in perpetuity, and its expected value grows at the trend rate α. If future revenues are discounted at the rate μ, then the expected present value V of the project when the current price is P is just given by $V = P/(\mu - \alpha)$. In this case V, being a constant multiple of P, also follows a geometric Brownian motion with the same parameters α and σ. Hence the investment problem reduces to the model we studied in Chapter 5, but we will rework it directly in terms of P to set the stage for the generalizations to come.

1.A The Risk-Adjusted Rate of Return

The capital asset pricing model allows us to determine the risk-adjusted discount rate μ. For this we need the stochastic fluctuations in P to be "spanned" by financial markets, that is, there is a traded asset, or one could construct a dynamic portfolio of assets, that is perfectly correlated with P. For simplicity of exposition we suppose that the project output is directly tradeable. In this case, the discount rate μ will be the market risk-adjusted expected rate of return on P. As in Chapter 5 we have the CAPM formula

$$\mu = r + \phi\,\sigma\,\rho_{pm}, \tag{2}$$

where r is the discount rate appropriate to riskless cash flows, ρ_{pm} is the coefficient of correlation between the asset that tracks P and the whole market portfolio, and ϕ is the market price or risk. For the value of the project, V, to be bounded, we must have $\mu > \alpha$. As in Chapter 5, we will denote the difference $\mu - \alpha$ by δ.

Investors will hold the output or asset perfectly correlated with P only if they get a total expected rate of return, μ, from it. Of this, α comes in the form of expected capital gain. The rest, δ, must accrue as some kind of dividend. If the output of the project is a storable commodity (for example, oil or copper),

δ will represent the *net marginal convenience yield from storage*, that is, the flow of benefits (less storage costs) that the marginal stored unit provides.[1] We will generally let δ be an exogenously specified parameter. However, in practice, the convenience yield can vary (stochastically over time and/or in response to market-wide variables such as total storage), and our models can be adapted to account for this.[2]

When some underlying parameter changes, the equilibrium relationship $\mu - \alpha = \delta$ must continue to hold, but which of the three magnitudes adjust to restore equilibrium depends on the underlying technology and behavior. We assume that the riskless rate r and the market price of risk ϕ, being properties of the whole market, are totally exogenous to our analysis. Now, when the σ of the P asset increases, μ must increase. If δ is a fundamental market constant, then α must change one for one with μ. However, if α is a fundamental market constant, then δ must adjust; for example, the total amount of storage might change. When we study the effects of changes in σ on the firm's investment decision, our answer will depend on which of these viewpoints we adopt. Generally we will take δ to be the basic parameter and let α adjust. When another specification leads to an important different result, we will point this out.

1.B Valuing the Project

Our project is a contingent or derivative asset, whose payoffs depend on the value of the more basic asset P. Then we can derive the value of the project as a function $V(P)$ of the price of the basic asset. We follow the procedure of contingent claims valuation that was discussed in different contexts in Chapters 4 and 5. We construct a riskless portfolio by taking suitable combinations of the asset to be valued (the project) and basic asset (P). Since this portfolio is riskless, it must earn the riskless rate of return. That condition yields a differential equation for the unknown value of our project. The equation can then be solved given appropriate boundary conditions.

---

[1] These benefits can include an increased ability to smooth production, avoid stockouts, and facilitate the scheduling of production and sales. Convenience yield is the reason that firms hold inventories in the first place, even when the expected capital gain on those inventories is below the risk-adjusted rate, or even negative. As one would expect, for most commodities, marginal convenience yield varies inversely with the total amount of storage. For empirical studies of convenience yield and its role in commodity price formation, see Pindyck (1993 c,d).

[2] See, for example, Gibson and Schwartz (1990, 1991), who show how oil-producing projects can be valued when the price of oil follows a geometric Brownian motion, and the rate of convenience yield also follows a stochastic process. Also, Brennan (1991) estimates and tests alternative functions and stochastic processes for convenience yield and its dependence on price and time.

Suppose we construct a portfolio at time t that contains one unit of the project, and a short position of n units of output, where we will choose n to make the portfolio riskless. We consider holding this portfolio over the small interval of time $(t, t + dt)$.

The holder of the project will get the revenue or profit flow $P\,dt$ over the time interval of length dt. Also, a holder of each unit of the short position must pay to the holder of the corresponding long position an amount equal to the dividend or convenience yield that the latter would have earned, namely, $\delta\,P\,dt$. Thus holding our portfolio yields a net dividend $(P - n\,\delta\,P)\,dt$. It also yields a (stochastic) capital gain, which is equal to

$$dV - n\,dP = \{\alpha(P)\,P\,[V'(P) - n] + \tfrac{1}{2}\sigma(P)^2\,P^2\,V''(P)\}\,dt$$
$$+ P\,[V'(P) - n]\,\sigma(P)\,dz.$$

(Note that we have used Ito's Lemma to express dV in terms of the price process.) Now choose $n = V'(P)$ so that the terms in dz disappear and the portfolio becomes riskless.[3] The total return to the portfolio is then

$$[\,P - \delta\,P\,V'(P) + \tfrac{1}{2}\sigma^2\,P^2\,V''(P)\,]\,dt.$$

Equating this to the riskless return $r\,[V(P) - n\,P]\,dt$ and collecting terms, we have the differential equation

$$\tfrac{1}{2}\sigma^2\,P^2\,V''(P) + (r - \delta)\,P\,V'(P) - r\,V(P) + P = 0. \qquad (3)$$

Simple substitution shows that the homogeneous part of the equation has solutions of the form $V(P) = AP^\beta$, provided β is a root of the fundamental quadratic equation

$$\mathcal{Q} \equiv \tfrac{1}{2}\sigma^2\,\beta(\beta - 1) + (r - \delta)\,\beta - r = 0. \qquad (4)$$

This is very familiar from Chapter 5; there we gave a detailed account of its roots and their dependence on the three parameters r, δ, and σ. Most

---

[3]The composition of the portfolio is held constant over the short interval $(t, t + dt)$; thus n remains equal to $V'(P(t))$ even though $V'(P)$ itself changes over this interval as P changes. Over a longer period of time, the "dynamic hedging strategy" will adjust the portfolio at successive short intervals. Thus over $(t + dt, t + 2dt)$ we will set n at $V'(P(t + dt))$, and so on, rather like a chained price index. Rigorous formulation of such strategies in the limiting case of continuous time as $dt \to 0$ needs great care; see Harrison and Kreps (1979) and Duffie (1988, pp. 138–147).

importantly for our immediate purpose, given our economic conditions $r > 0$ and $\delta > 0$, the two roots satisfy $\beta_1 > 1$ and $\beta_2 < 0$.

Then the general solution of the homogeneous part of the equation is a linear combination of the two independent solutions $B_1 P^{\beta_1}$ and $B_2 P^{\beta_2}$. To it we add any particular solution of the full equation; the easiest to spot is P/δ. Therefore

$$V(P) = B_1 \, P^{\beta_1} + B_2 \, P^{\beta_2} + P/\delta,$$

where the constants B_1 and B_2 remain to be determined.

1.C Fundamentals and Speculative Bubbles

The term P/δ in the solution has an immediate interpretation: it is just the expected present value of the revenue stream P_t when the initial level is P. This is because $\mathcal{E}[P_t] = P \, e^{\alpha t}$, and discounting at the appropriate risk-adjusted rate μ gives[4]

$$\int_0^\infty P \, e^{\alpha t} \, e^{-\mu t} \, dt = P/(\mu - \alpha) = P/\delta.$$

This might be called the fundamental component of the value of the project, in the sense that it is justified by the prospective profit flows. The other two terms must be speculative components of value. We can eliminate them by invoking economic considerations to rule out speculation.

First, it makes sense to require that $V(0) = 0$. If the price is ever zero in the geometric Brownian motion (1), it will forever remain zero; in technical terms, zero is an absorbing barrier for the process. With no prospect of a profit flow, the asset should have zero value. However, since $\beta_2 < 0$, that power of P goes to infinity as P goes to zero. To prevent the value from diverging, we must set the corresponding coefficient $B_2 = 0$.

The other term, $B_1 \, P^{\beta_1}$, is not so easy to get rid of. It represents a component of V attributable to speculative bubbles as $P \to \infty$. People might value the asset above its fundamentals if they expected to be able to resell it later at a sufficient capital gain. That is exactly what this first term ensures.

To see this, we show that an asset that is always valued at P^{β_1} yields its appropriate risk-adjusted return from its expected capital gain alone. By Ito's

---

[4]See also the approach based on "equivalent risk-neutral valuation" in Chapter 4, Section 3(a).

Lemma we have

$$d(P^{\beta_1})/P^{\beta_1} = \{\,\beta_1\,P^{\beta_1-1}\,dP + \tfrac{1}{2}\,\beta_1\,(\beta_1-1)\,P^{\beta_1-2}\,\sigma^2\,P^2\,dt\,\}/P_1^{\beta}$$
$$= \{\,\beta_1\alpha + \tfrac{1}{2}\,\beta_1\,(\beta_1-1)\,\sigma^2\,\}\,dt + \beta_1\,\sigma\,dz$$
$$= \{\,r + (\mu-r)\,\beta_1\,\}\,dt + \beta_1\,\sigma\,dz$$
$$= \{\,r + \phi\,\beta_1\,\rho_{pm}\,\sigma\,\}\,dt + \beta_1\,\sigma\,dz,$$

where the third line follows from the fact that β_1 satisfies the quadratic equation $\mathcal{Q} = 0$, and the last line uses the CAPM formula (2). Thus the standard deviation of the return on P^{β_1} is exactly β_1 times that of P. The covariance of P^{β_1} with the market portfolio also becomes β_1 times that of P with the market portfolio. With the covariance and the variance both multiplied by the same factor, the correlation coefficient between P^{β_1} and the market portfolio is the same as that between P and the market portfolio, namely, ρ_{pm}. Therefore the risk-adjusted rate of return for P^{β_1} is $(r + \phi\,\rho_{pm}\,\beta_1\sigma)$, which is exactly the expected rate of return in the last line above.[5]

In the remainder of this chapter we will rule out such speculative bubbles. Then we are left with the fundamental component of value found by direct integration above, namely,

$$V(P) = P/\delta. \tag{5}$$

1.D   Valuing the Option to Invest

Once we know the value V of an installed project as a function of the current price P, we can obtain the diffusion process of V from that of P by using Ito's Lemma. Then, in principle, the methods of Chapter 5 would allow us to find the value F of the option to invest in the project as a function of V. However, the drift and diffusion parameters of the process of V are generally quite complicated expressions, making it hard to solve the differential equation linking F and V. An alternative and generally simpler approach is to find the value of the option to invest as a function of the price, $F(P)$, using the above solution for $V(P)$ as the boundary condition that holds at the optimal exercise threshold.

We will now employ this method for our simple project. Once again we follow the steps of contingent claims valuation. Now the portfolio will consist

---

[5]The fact that the risk-adjusted discount rate for P^{β} equals the expected rate of growth of P^{β} when β is a root of the fundamental quadratic was also shown using the equivalent risk-neutral valuation procedure in Chapter 4, Section 3.A.

of one option to invest and a short position of $n = F'(P)$ units of the output. Following the same steps as before, the reader can check that we get the differential equation

$$\tfrac{1}{2} \sigma^2 P^2 F''(P) + (r - \delta) P F'(P) - r F(P) = 0. \tag{6}$$

This is just like equation (3) for the value of the project, but of course the option has no dividend or profit flow. This is a homogeneous linear equation of second order, so its solution is a linear combination of any two linearly independent solutions, say,

$$F(P) = A_1 P^{\beta_1} + A_2 P^{\beta_2},$$

where A_1 and A_2 are constants to be determined. This solution is valid over the range of prices for which it is optimal to hold the option. Since higher prices make investment more attractive, the range in question extends from zero to an investment threshold P^*. Of course P^* is itself an unknown to be determined as a part of the solution. Thus we have three unknowns, A_1, A_2, and P^*, and need three conditions to complete the solution.

The limiting behavior of $F(P)$ near zero gives us one condition. When P is very small, the prospect of it rising to the exercise threshold P^* is quite remote. Therefore the option should be almost worthless at this extreme. To ensure that $F(P)$ goes to zero as P goes to zero, we should set the coefficient of the negative power of P equal to zero; thus $A_2 = 0$.

For the other two conditions, we consider the behavior of $F(P)$ at P^*. At this threshold it becomes optimal to exercise the option, and thereby acquire an asset (the project) of value $V(P)$ by incurring the exercise price (sunk cost) of investment I. As in Chapter 5, two conditions govern this. First, the value of the option must equal the net value obtained by exercising it; this is the *value-matching* condition:

$$F(P^*) = V(P^*) - I. \tag{7}$$

Second, the graphs of $F(P)$ and $V(P) - I$ should meet tangentially at P^*; this is the *smooth-pasting* condition:

$$F'(P^*) = V'(P^*). \tag{8}$$

Using the specific functional forms of $F(P)$ and $V(P)$, we can write the value-matching and smooth-pasting conditions as

$$A_1 (P^*)^{\beta_1} = P^*/\delta - I,$$

$$\beta_1 A_1 (P^*)^{\beta_1 - 1} = 1/\delta.$$

These yield

$$P^* = \frac{\beta_1}{\beta_1 - 1}\, \delta\, I. \tag{9}$$

For reference we also state the solution for A_1; it is

$$A_1 = (\beta_1 - 1)^{\beta_1 - 1}\, I^{-(\beta_1 - 1)} / (\delta\beta_1)^{\beta_1}. \tag{10}$$

Using the relation (5), we can express the price threshold equivalently in terms of a value threshold,

$$V^* = \frac{\beta_1}{\beta_1 - 1}\, I.$$

This is exactly the equation (14) of Chapter 5. Thus our approach expressing both the value of the project and the value of the option in terms of the underlying price has produced the same result as we could have obtained by starting with the value of the project directly. In the present instance, V is just a constant multiple of P, and the equivalence of the two approaches is easy to demonstrate directly. However, the result is perfectly general. We will generally find it somewhat more convenient to work in terms of P, as it is economically the more basic variable.

The important point stressed in Chapter 5 was that $V^* > I$; the option value of waiting to invest implies an action threshold where the expected value from investing exceeds the cost. Here the corresponding idea is that $P^*/\delta > I$ or $P^* > \delta\, I$. We could call $\delta\, I$ the flow-equivalent (per unit of time) cost of investment: that is the level the initial profit flow must have if its subsequent expected value is to cover the cost of investing.[6]

In Chapter 5 we discussed at length the factor by which V^* exceeds I, namely the "option value multiple" $\beta_1/(\beta_1 - 1)$. We calculated its magnitude for a range of variation of the parameters r, σ, and δ. We do not need to repeat those points here, but we will perform corresponding calculations for the new and more general models to be developed later in this chapter.

Likewise, in Chapter 5 we defined Tobin's q in the sense of the ratio of the value of assets in place to their replacement cost, namely V/I. This allows us to interpret the effect of waiting as the possibility that no investment occurs even though q exceeds 1, as long as it remains below $\beta_1/(\beta_1 - 1)$. We can now similarly define $q = P/(\delta\, I)$ and obtain the same interpretation.

---

[6]If we leave out the uncertainty and the trend in price, we get $\delta = r$ and the flow-equivalent cost becomes just the interest cost or the opportunity cost of the amount invested, $r\, I$.

1.E   Dynamic Programming

If the risk in P cannot be spanned by existing assets, then we cannot construct a riskless portfolio and use it to obtain a differential equation for $V(P)$. As explained in Chapters 4 and 5, we can instead use dynamic programming with an exogenously specified discount rate ρ, although we will not be able to relate this discount rate to the riskless rate and the market price of risk using CAPM. Here is a quick summary of the steps.

The value of the project at time t can be expressed as the sum of the operating profit over the interval $(t, t+dt)$ and the continuation value beyond $t + dt$. Thus

$$V(P) = P\,dt + \mathcal{E}[V(P + dP)\,e^{-\rho\,dt}].$$

Expanding the right-hand side using Ito's Lemma, we have

$$V(P) = P\,dt + [\,\alpha\,P\,V'(P) + \tfrac{1}{2}\sigma^2\,P^2\,V''(P)\,]\,dt + (1 - \rho\,dt)\,V(P) + o(dt),$$

where $o(dt)$ collects terms that go to zero faster than dt. Simplifying, dividing by dt, and proceeding to the limit as $dt \to 0$, we get the differential equation

$$\tfrac{1}{2}\sigma^2\,P^2\,V''(P) + \alpha\,P\,V'(P) - \rho\,V(P) + P = 0.$$

This is exactly like equation (3) that we had earlier, except that r is replaced by the (arbitrary) discount rate ρ and $(r - \delta)$ by α. The equation can be solved by similar methods, and ruling out bubble solutions, we get $V(P) = P/(\rho - \alpha)$. For this to make economic sense we need $\rho > \alpha$.

Then the option to invest can be analyzed similarly. Start with a P in the range $(0, P^*)$, where the option continues to be held. Split the future into the immediate interval $(t, t + dt)$ and the continuation beyond that. Expanding and simplifying as above yields the differential equation

$$\tfrac{1}{2}\sigma^2\,P^2\,F''(P) + \alpha\,P\,F'(P) - \rho\,F(P) = 0.$$

Now consider the quadratic equation

$$Q \equiv \tfrac{1}{2}\sigma^2\,\beta(\beta - 1) + \alpha\,\beta - \rho = 0.$$

Since $\rho > \alpha$, the larger root β_1 of this exceeds 1. Since $\rho > 0$, the other root β_2 is negative. Then the solution for the option value takes the form $F(P) = A_1\,P^{\beta_1}$, where the constant A_1 remains to be determined.

Finally we use value matching and smooth pasting between $F(P)$ and $V(P)$ at P^* to complete the solution. The result is

$$P^* = \frac{\beta_1}{\beta_1 - 1} (\rho - \alpha) I,$$

which is the natural analog of (9) above.

For most of the rest of this chapter we will assume that spanning holds and use contingent claims methods, leaving to the reader the obvious modifications that apply when dynamic programming is used instead. Occasionally, for variety and simplicity of exposition, we will do the opposite.

2   Operating Costs and Temporary Suspension

Suppose once again that the output price follows the geometric Brownian motion of equation (1). Then α, σ, μ, and $\delta \equiv \mu - \alpha$ are all constants. If the option of investing in the project is ever going to be exercised, we need $\mu > \alpha$, or $\delta > 0$, and we will assume that this is indeed the case. We will also assume that operation of the project entails a flow cost C, but that the operation can be temporarily and costlessly suspended when P falls below C, and costlessly resumed later if P rises above C. Therefore, at any instant the profit flow from this project is given by

$$\pi(P) = \max [P - C, 0]. \tag{11}$$

McDonald and Siegel (1985) pointed out another useful way to look at such a project. It gives the owner an infinite set of options. The option at time t, if exercised, means paying C to receive the P that prevails at that instant. Since each option can only be exercised at its specified instant, these are European call options.[7] They also showed that the project can be valued by valuing each of these options (using the standard Black-Scholes formula), and then summing these values by integrating over t. We will find it easier to value the project as a simple contingent claim that depends on P. We will go through the steps of obtaining $V(P)$ in the following subsection, and then afterwards we will turn to the problem of valuing the option to invest.

---

[7]A European option can be exercised only at the time of expiration. An American option can be exercised at any time up to and including the time of expiration.

2.A The Value of the Project

Once again we consider the portfolio that consists of a unit of the project and $n = V_P(P)$ units of a short position in the asset that spans P. When held for the short time interval $(t, t + dt)$, the owner of this portfolio can exercise the current operation option. That is profitable if $P > C$; the resulting profit flow rate is just $\pi(P) = \max(P - C, 0)$. The other aspects of the portfolio (capital gains, dividend payment for the short position, etc.) are as before. Therefore the differential equation for the value of the project is

$$\tfrac{1}{2}\sigma^2 P^2 V''(P) + (r - \delta)PV'(P) - rV(P) + \pi(P) = 0.$$

This is solved by familiar methods. The homogeneous part has two independent solutions P^{β_1} and P^{β_2} exactly as above. The only new feature is that the nonhomogeneous part, or forcing function $\pi(P)$, is defined differently when $P < C$ and when $P > C$. Therefore we solve the equation separately for $P < C$ and $P > C$, and then stitch together the two solutions at the point $P = C$.

In the region $P < C$, we have $\pi(P) = 0$ and only the homogeneous part of the equation remains. Therefore the general solution is just a linear combination of the two power solutions corresponding to the two roots:

$$V(P) = K_1 \, P^{\beta_1} + K_2 \, P^{\beta_2},$$

where the constants K_1 and K_2 remain to be determined. In the region $P > C$, we take another linear combination of the power solutions of the homogeneous part, and add on any particular solution of the full equation. A simple substitution shows that $(P/\delta - C/r)$ satisfies the equation. Therefore the general solution for $P > C$ is

$$V(P) = B_1 \, P^{\beta_1} + B_2 \, P^{\beta_2} + P/\delta - C/r,$$

where the constants B_1 and B_2 are to be determined.

These solutions have straightforward economic interpretations. In the region $P < C$, operation is suspended and the project yields no current profit flow. However, there is positive probability that the price process will at some future time move into the region $P > C$, when operation will resume and profits will accrue. The value $V(P)$ when $P < C$ is just the expected present value of such future flows.

Next consider the region $P > C$. Suppose for a moment that the firm is forced to continue operation of the project forever, even during those times when the risky revenues fall below C. What is the net worth of such a project? The expected value of the revenues grows at the rate α, and is discounted back at the appropriate risk-adjusted rate μ, so the expected present value is $P/(\mu - \alpha) = P/\delta$. The sure constant cost stream C is discounted at the riskless rate r, yielding a present value C/r. The net worth $(P/\delta - C/r)$ constitutes the last two terms in the solution above. Since that solution did not impose any requirement to continue operating despite losses, the other two terms must be the additional value of the option to suspend operations in the future should P fall below C.

The constants in the solutions are determined using considerations that apply at the boundaries of the regions. Begin with $P < C$. As P becomes very small, the event of its rising above C becomes unlikely except perhaps in the very remote future. The expected present value of future profits should then go to zero, and so should the value of the project. However, with β_2 negative, P^{β_2} goes to ∞ as P goes to 0. Therefore the constant multiplying this term, namely, K_2, should be zero. Now turn to $P > C$. When P becomes very large, the suspension option is unlikely to be invoked except perhaps in the very remote future, so its value should be zero. For this we should rule out the positive power of P, by making $B_1 = 0$.[8] This leaves

$$V(P) = \begin{cases} K_1 \, P^{\beta_1} & \text{if } P < C, \\ B_2 \, P^{\beta_2} + P/\delta - C/r & \text{if } P > C. \end{cases} \tag{12}$$

This still leaves two constants, for which we consider the point $P = C$ where the two regions meet. Since the Brownian motion of P can diffuse freely across this boundary, the value function cannot change abruptly across it. In fact the solution $V(P)$ must be continuously differentiable across C. For a heuristic argument see Dixit (1993a, Section 3.8); a rigorous proof is in Karatzas and Shreve (1988, Theorem 4.4.9). Equating the values and derivatives of the two component solutions at C, we have

$$K_1 \, C^{\beta_1} = B_2 \, C^{\beta_2} + C/\delta - C/r,$$

$$\beta_1 \, K_1 \, C^{\beta_1 - 1} = \beta_2 \, B_2 \, C^{\beta_2 - 1} + 1/\delta.$$

---

[8]Note that these arguments are ruling out speculative bubbles just as we did before.

These are two linear equations in the unknowns K_1 and B_2; they readily yield the solution

$$K_1 = \frac{C^{1-\beta_1}}{\beta_1 - \beta_2} \left(\frac{\beta_2}{r} - \frac{\beta_2 - 1}{\delta} \right), \tag{13}$$

$$B_2 = \frac{C^{1-\beta_2}}{\beta_1 - \beta_2} \left(\frac{\beta_1}{r} - \frac{\beta_1 - 1}{\delta} \right). \tag{14}$$

Since the term in K_1 captures the expected profit from the option to resume operations in the future, and that in B_2 the value of future suspension options, both the constants should be positive. For that, we need

$$r > \beta_1 (r - \delta) \quad \text{and} \quad r > \beta_2 (r - \delta).$$

To verify these, evaluate the quadratic expression $Q(\beta)$ at $\beta = r/(r - \delta)$. We have

$$Q(r/(r - \delta)) = \tfrac{1}{2} \sigma^2 r\delta/(r - \delta)^2 > 0.$$

Therefore $r/(r - \delta)$ must lie either to the right of the larger root β_1 or to the left of the smaller root β_2. First suppose $r > \delta$, so $r/(r - \delta) > 0$. Then

$$r/(r - \delta) > \beta_1 > \beta_2,$$

and we are done. Next, suppose $r < \delta$, so $r/(r - \delta) < 0$. Then

$$r/(r - \delta) < \beta_2 < \beta_1,$$

and multiplying by the negative number $(r - \delta)$, which reverses the inequality, we have the desired result again.

A numerical example will help to illustrate this solution. Unless otherwise noted, we set $r = \delta = 0.04$, and $C = 10$. Figure 6.1 shows $V(P)$ as a function of P for $\sigma = 0, 0.2$, and 0.4. When $\sigma = 0$, there is no possibility that P will rise in the future, so in this case the project will never produce (and has no value) for $P < 10$. If $P > 10$, $V(P) = (P - 10)/0.04 = 25\,P - 250$. However, if $\sigma > 0$, the project always has some value as long as $P > 0$; although the firm may not be producing today, it is likely to produce at some point in the future. Also, since the upside potential for future profit is unlimited while the downside is limited to zero, the greater is σ, the greater is the expected future flow of profit, and the higher is $V(P)$.

Figure 6.2 shows $V(P)$ for $\sigma = 0.2$ and $\delta = 0.02, 0.04$, and 0.08. For any fixed risk-adjusted discount rate, a higher value of δ means a lower expected rate of price appreciation, and hence a lower value for the project.

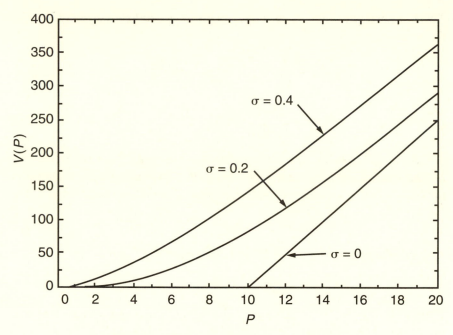

Figure 6.1. *Value of Project, $V(P)$, for $\sigma = 0$, 0.2, 0.4*
(Note: $r = \delta = 0.04$, and $C = 10$)

2.B   The Value of the Option to Invest

Now that we know the value of the project, $V(P)$, we can find the value of the option to invest in the project, $F(P)$, as well as the optimal investment rule. Since the price P follows the geometric Brownian motion (1), we can go through the same steps as in the previous section to establish that the value of the option to invest takes the form

$$F(P) = A_1\, P^{\beta_1} + A_2\, P^{\beta_2}.$$

Since $P = 0$ is an absorbing barrier, so that $F(0) = 0$, we know that $A_2 = 0$. At the optimal exercise point P^* we have the value-matching and smooth-pasting conditions linking $F(P)$ with the appropriate $V(P)$ from equation (12). Of course the option will not be exercised when $P < C$; there is no reason to incur the investment cost I only to keep the project idle for some time. This can be verified formally: $A_1\, P^{\beta_1}$ cannot satisfy value matching and smooth pasting with $K_1\, P^{\beta_1} - I$. Therefore in equation (12) we use the solution for $V(P)$ in the operating region, that is, for $P > C$. The value-matching and

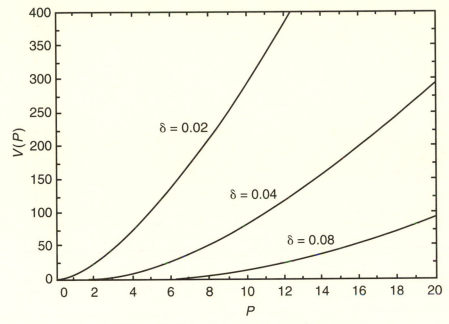

Figure 6.2.   *Value of Project, V(P), for δ = 0.02, 0.04, 0.08*
(Note: $r = 0.04$, $\sigma = 0.2$, and $C = 10$)

smooth-pasting conditions then give

$$A_1 (P^*)^{\beta_1} = B_2 (P^*)^{\beta_2} + P^*/\delta - C/r - I, \tag{15}$$

$$\beta_1 A_1 (P^*)^{\beta_1 - 1} = \beta_2 B_2 (P^*)^{\beta_2 - 1} + 1/\delta. \tag{16}$$

Recall that B_2 is known from (14), so the pair of equations (15) and (16) can be solved for A_1 and P^*. Eliminating A_1, we are left with an equation for the investment threshold:

$$(\beta_1 - \beta_2) B_2 (P^*)^{\beta_2} + (\beta_1 - 1) P^*/\delta - \beta_1 (C/r + I) = 0. \tag{17}$$

Equation (17), which is easily solved numerically, gives the optimal investment rule. The reader can check first, that (17) has a unique positive solution for P^* that is larger than $(C + rI)$, which is the Marshallian full cost (operating cost plus interest on the capital cost of investment), and second, that $V(P^*) > I$, so that the project must have a NPV that exceeds zero before it is optimal to invest.

Returning to our numerical example, this solution for $F(P)$ and P^* is shown graphically in Figure 6.3 for $r = \delta = 0.04$, $\sigma = 0.2$, and $I = 100$.

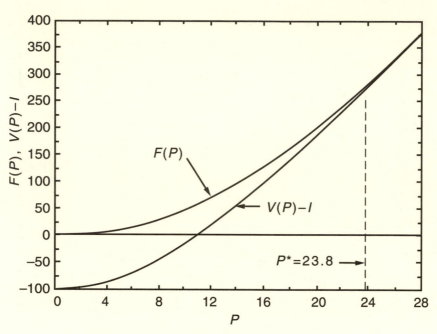

Figure 6.3. *Value of Investment Opportunity, F(P), and V(P)−I*
(Note: $r = \delta = 0.04$, $\sigma = 0.2$, and $I = 100$)

The figure plots $F(P)$ and $V(P) - I$. Recall that from the value-matching condition, P^* satisfies $F(P^*) = V(P^*) - I$, and from the smooth-pasting condition, P^* is at a point of tangency of the two curves.

It is useful to examine how these curves shift when σ or δ is changed. As we saw before, an increase in σ results in an increase in $V(P)$ for any P. (As we explained, the project is a set of call options on future production, and the greater the volatility of price, the greater the value of these options.) However, although an increase in σ raises the value of the project, it also increases the critical price at which it is optimal to invest, that is, $\partial P^*/\partial \sigma > 0$. The reason is that for any P, the value of the investment option (and thus the opportunity cost of investing), $F(P)$, increases even more than $V(P)$. Hence as with the simpler model developed in Chapter 5, increased uncertainty reduces investment. This is illustrated in Figure 6.4, which shows $F(P)$ and $V(P) - I$ for $\sigma = 0$, 0.2, and 0.4. When $\sigma = 0$, the critical price is 14, which just makes the value of the project equal to its cost of 100. As σ is increased, both $V(P)$ and $F(P)$ increase; P^* is 23.8 for $\sigma = 0.2$, and 34.9 for $\sigma = 0.4$.

An increase in δ also increases the critical price P^* at which the firm should invest. There are two opposing effects. If δ is larger, so that the expected rate of increase of P is smaller, options on future production are worth less, so $V(P)$ is smaller. At the same time, the opportunity cost of waiting to invest rises [the expected rate of growth of $F(P)$ is smaller], so there is more incentive to exercise the investment option, rather than keep it alive. The first effect dominates, so that a higher δ results in a higher P^*. This is illustrated in Figure 6.5, which shows $F(P)$ and $V(P) - I$ for $\delta = 0.04$ and 0.08. (In both cases, $r = 0.04$, and $\sigma = 0.2$.) Note that when δ is increased, $V(P)$ and hence $F(P)$ fall sharply, and the tangency at P^* moves to the right.

This result might at first seem to contradict what the simpler model of Chapter 5 told us. Recall that in that model, an increase in δ reduces the critical value of the project, V^*, at which the firm should invest. However, while in this model P^* is higher when δ is larger, the corresponding value of the project, $V(P^*)$, is lower. This can be seen from Figure 6.6, which shows P^* as a function of σ for $\delta = 0.04$ and 0.08, and Figure 6.7, which shows $V(P^*)$. If, say, σ is 0.2 and δ is increased from 0.04 to 0.08, P^* will rise from 23.8 to

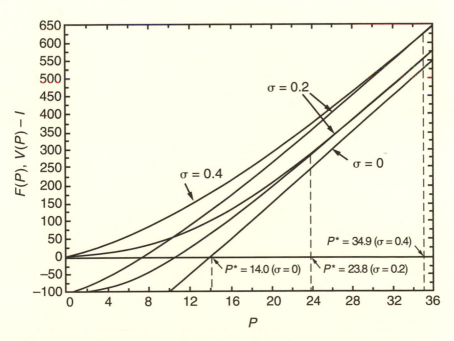

Figure 6.4. *Value of Investment Opportunity, $F(P)$, and $V(P)-I$, for $\sigma = 0$, 0.2, and 0.4*

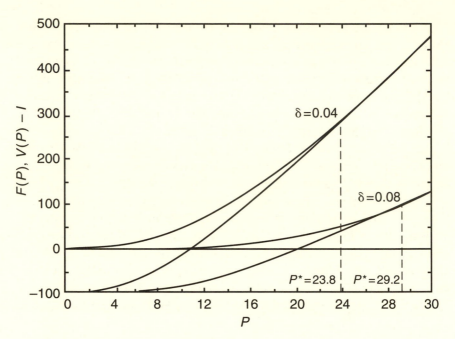

Figure 6.5.   *Value of Investment Opportunity,* $F(P)$, *and* $V(P) - I$, *for* $\delta = 0.04$ *and* 0.08

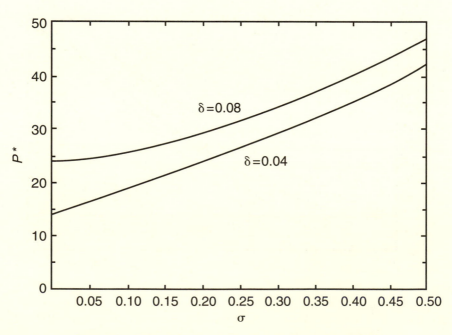

Figure 6.6.   *Critical Price* P^* *as a Function of* σ *for* $\delta = 0.04$ *and* 0.08

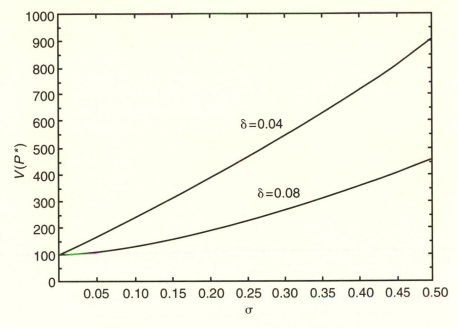

Figure 6.7. $V(P^*)$ as a Function of σ for $\delta = 0.04$ and 0.08

29.2, but even at the higher P^*, V is lower. Thus $V^* = V(P^*)$ is declining with δ, just as in the simpler model.

3   A Project with Variable Output

The basic model of this chapter can be extended and generalized in several ways. One is to allow a more general price process, for example, a mean-reverting process such as the one we discussed in Chapter 5, or an even more general Ito process. The only difference this makes is that in the differential equations for the value of the project and that of the option, the coefficients become more complicated functions of P. In almost all such cases we must rely on numerical solutions. Since there are no new general economic insights to be had from such calculations, we will not develop this line of models here.

A different direction of extension is worth some attention. Suppose the single discrete project, once installed, allows some flexibility in its operation at any instant, by varying some inputs, such as labor or raw materials, that do not require any irreversible commitments that extend over time. Then the optimal amounts of these at any instant will depend on the output price at that instant; the project will have an upward-sloping supply curve. The resulting profit flow will also depend on the price. Looking ahead to this, the firm's investment decision will be affected. We now examine this in more detail.

At each instant, we have the choice of some operating variables, say, labor or some intermediate inputs, denoted by the vector v. These generate output according to a production function $h(v)$ and entail a variable cost $C(v)$. The optimal choice of v maximizes the operating profit. We can capture the result in a reduced-form instantaneous profit function:

$$\pi(P) \equiv \max_{v} [\, P h(v) - C(v) \,]. \tag{18}$$

In Section 2 we studied a basic model where, at each instant, the firm had a simple binary choice of whether or not to operate. Now we can think of that as a special case of this more general formula. Suppose the variable v can take on just two values, 0 and 1, where the former corresponds to suspension and the latter to operation. Define

$$h(v) = 1, \quad C(v) = C \qquad \text{if } v = 1,$$
$$h(v) = 0, \quad C(v) = 0 \qquad \text{if } v = 0.$$

Then we have the model developed in Section 2 with $\pi(P) = \max[P - C, 0]$.

Another very familiar example is the Cobb-Douglas production function. Suppose v is a scalar, and

$$h(v) = v^{\theta}, \qquad 0 < \theta < 1.$$

Let us concentrate on output price uncertainty by setting the input price constant at c. (We will analyze an example of joint price and cost uncertainty in the final section of this chapter.) Then instantaneous profit maximization gives the input demand function

$$v = [\theta \, P/c]^{1/(1-\theta)},$$

and the instantaneous supply function for output

$$h(v) = [\theta \, P/c]^{\theta/(1-\theta)}.$$

Generalization to several variable inputs is straightforward and yields almost identical expressions.

The profit flow when the variable input is chosen optimally is

$$\pi(P) = (1 - \theta) \, (\theta/c)^{\theta/(1-\theta)} \, P^{1/(1-\theta)}. \tag{19}$$

For brevity of notation we write this as $\pi(P) = K P^{\gamma}$, where $\gamma = 1/(1 - \theta) > 1$.

The power of P in the expression for the maximized profit $\pi(P)$ exceeds 1; thus $\pi(P)$ is a convex function of P. This is a standard "duality" property; see Dixit (1990) or Varian (1991). The intuition is that, without any instantaneous variability in operations, output is constant and revenue and profits change linearly with P. When instantaneous variation is possible, the optimal choice must make profit increase faster when P increases, and decrease slower when P falls. This makes $\pi(P)$ convex. This has important consequences regarding the effect of uncertainty on investment.

Now let us find the value of the project, that is, the value of the whole sequence of operating options. Here, of course, the option at each instant is exercised, but with a different choice of v as P varies. If we had allowed a flow fixed cost of production at each instant, there would have been a lower bound on P (the familiar Marshallian minimum average cost) below which the operation would be suspended.

We will continue to assume that the price follows the geometric Brownian motion of equation (1). Then familiar steps produce the differential equation for the value of the project

$$\tfrac{1}{2}\sigma^2 P^2 V''(P) + (r - \delta) P V'(P) - r V(P) + K P^\gamma = 0. \tag{20}$$

The homogeneous part of this is the same as before, but the nonhomogeneous term is different. We try a particular solution of the form $K_1 P^\gamma$. Substituting and solving for K_1, we find the solution

$$K P^\gamma / \left[r - (r - \delta)\gamma - \tfrac{1}{2}\sigma^2 \gamma(\gamma - 1) \right].$$

This may look complicated, but it has a natural economic interpretation: it is just the expected present value of a profit stream $K P^\gamma$ calculated using the appropriate risk-adjusted discount rate. This can be seen as another application of the equivalent risk-neutral valuation formula of Chapter 4, Section 3(a). It says that we can use the riskless discount rate provided we change the stochastic process of P to have a different growth rate $(r - \delta)$. Then for any future t, using results for the lognormal distribution of P_t, we have

$$\mathcal{E}'[K (P_t)^\gamma] = K P^\gamma \exp\left\{ \left[\gamma(r - \delta) + \tfrac{1}{2}\sigma^2 \gamma(\gamma - 1) \right] t \right\},$$

where P is the initial price, and $\mathcal{E}'$ denotes expectation calculated relative to this new process. Multiplying by e^{-rt} and integrating, we get the present value in the previous equation.

To see the result more directly, we use Ito's Lemma to write the expected growth rate of P^γ, which we denote by α', as

$$\alpha' = \mathcal{E}[dP^\gamma]/P^\gamma = \left\{ \gamma\, P^{\gamma-1}\, \mathcal{E}[dP] + \tfrac{1}{2}\gamma\,(\gamma-1)\, P^{\gamma-2}\sigma^2\, P^2\, dt \right\}/P^\gamma$$

$$= \left\{ \gamma\alpha + \tfrac{1}{2}\gamma\,(\gamma-1)\sigma^2 \right\} dt.$$

In Section 1.C above we calculated the risk-adjusted discount rate appropriate to any power of P. Using that formula, the rate μ' for a profit flow proportional to P^γ is

$$\mu' = r + \gamma\,(\mu - r).$$

Then the return shortfall or convenience yield on P^γ must be

$$\delta' = \mu' - \alpha'$$

$$= r - (r - \delta)\gamma - \tfrac{1}{2}\sigma^2\gamma(\gamma-1). \tag{21}$$

With this, our particular solution is just $K\,P^\gamma/\delta'$, which is the expected present value of the profit stream calculated using the appropriately risk-adjusted discount rate.

Once again we rule out bubble solutions and set the value of the project equal to the fundamental:

$$V(P) = K\,P^\gamma/\delta'. \tag{22}$$

For all this to make economic sense we need $\delta' > 0$. That can be looked at from another perspective. We can recognize the expression for δ' as just the negative of our fundamental quadratic evaluated at γ. Therefore by requiring that $\delta' > 0$, we are requiring $\mathcal{Q}(\gamma) < 0$. Then γ must lie between the two roots of the quadratic, specifically $\gamma < \beta_1$. In turn, this amounts to a restriction $\theta < (\beta_1 - 1)/\beta_1$ on the permissible power in the Cobb-Douglas production function.

The solution for the value of the option takes the familiar form

$$F(P) = A_1\,P^{\beta_1}.$$

Finally, the usual conditions of value matching and smooth pasting,

$$F(P^*) = V(P^*) - I, \qquad F'(P^*) = V'(P^*),$$

can be solved to characterize the threshold of price P^* that triggers the investment:

$$\frac{K\,(P^*)^\gamma}{\delta'} = \frac{\beta_1}{\beta_1 - \gamma}\,I. \tag{23}$$

The left-hand side is the expected present value of profits; this must exceed the cost of investment by the "option value multiple" $\beta_1/(\beta_1 - \gamma)$. Under the conditions we have established, $\beta_1 > \gamma > 0$, so the multiple again exceeds unity.

Now we can examine the effect of uncertainty on investment. In earlier work, we regarded δ as a parameter independent of σ; let us continue to do that for a while. We already know one effect of an increase in σ: it lowers β_1 and therefore increases the multiple, $\beta_1/(\beta_1 - \gamma)$. This contributes to increasing P^*. Greater volatility raises the value of the option to invest, and therefore requires a higher current threshold of profitability to bring forth investment. However, now we have an added effect. As σ increases, holding δ fixed, we see from equation (21) that δ' decreases. Then equation (23) shows that this added effect leads to a lower P^*, and therefore it contributes a greater inducement to invest.

This new aspect arises from the convexity of profit in price. As we look farther ahead into the future, the variance of the distribution of price increases. By Jensen's Inequality, the expected value of a convex function increases. Ito's Lemma makes this precise: there is an added term $\frac{1}{2}\sigma^2\gamma(\gamma - 1)$ in the expected growth rate of the profit flow. Therefore a larger σ means a larger expected present value of the profit stream, and thus a greater incentive to invest. We will come across this "Jensen's Inequality effect" on investment again in Chapter 11.

4 Depreciation

We have assumed thus far that the investment, once made, lasts forever. In reality, physical decay or technological obsolescence limit the life of a project. In other words, capital depreciates through age, or use, or advance of competing technologies. It is not difficult in principle to modify our analysis to take this aspect into account, although that does complicate the algebra to some extent. In this section we will indicate how such modification can be made for relatively simple patterns of decay that are commonly used in economic theory.

Depreciation also has conceptual relevance for our "real options" approach to investment. One would expect that an opportunity to invest in a depreciating project would be less valuable, and therefore that allowance for depreciation would reduce the importance of the issues we have stressed. Our analysis will show that this intuition must be interpreted with care. The value of an option to take an action depends on the degree of irreversibility of the action. This depends not only on the life expectancy of one project, but also on the opportunities that may or may not remain available after the first project comes to the end of its life.

4.A Exponential Decay

We begin with a form of depreciation that is most often used in economic theory largely for its analytical convenience. Here the lifetime is random and follows a Poisson process. At any time T, if the project has lasted that long, there is probability $\lambda\,dT$ that it will die during the next short interval of time dT. Now, from the initial perspective, the probability that the project dies before T, or the cumulative probability distribution function of the random lifetime T, is $1 - e^{-\lambda T}$. The corresponding probability density function of T is $\lambda\,e^{-\lambda T}$.

Suppose that during its lifetime the project will produce a unit flow of output with no variable costs. The initial price is P, and its subsequent path P_t follows a geometric Brownian motion with growth rate α. The risk-adjusted discount rate appropriate to P is μ.

If the project lasts exactly T years, the expected present value of its profit flows is

$$\mathcal{E}\int_0^T e^{-\mu t} P_t\,dt = \int_0^T P\,e^{\alpha t}\,e^{-\mu t}\,dt$$

$$= P[1 - e^{-(\mu-\alpha)T}]/(\mu - \alpha)$$

$$= P[1 - e^{-\delta T}]/\delta,$$

where as before we have abbreviated $\mu - \alpha = \delta$, and δ is the return shortfall or the convenience yield on a traded asset that replicates the risk in P. Now we can use the probability density of the lifetime for a Poisson process to obtain the expected value of the project:

$$V(P) = \int_0^\infty \lambda\,e^{-\lambda T}\,P\,\frac{1 - e^{-\delta T}}{\delta}\,dT$$

$$= \frac{\lambda P}{\delta}\left[\frac{1}{\lambda} - \frac{1}{\lambda + \delta}\right]$$

$$= P/(\lambda + \delta).$$

Formally, we can regard the project as infinite-lived, but augment the rate at which future profits are discounted by adding the Poisson death parameter, so that the discount rate increases from μ to $\mu + \lambda$. This conforms to our general analysis of Poisson processes in Chapters 3 and 4.

This formula has alternative interpretations. First, the project might have an infinite life, but it might function less and less well as it ages, producing an output flow $e^{-\lambda t}$ at time t after installation. That will yield the same discounted present value as the expected value calculated above. Second, the machine might need an increasing stream of maintenance expenditures as it ages. We can then regard $P e^{-\lambda t}$ as a proxy or reduced-form expression for the profit flow it can produce at time t.

Next we value an option to invest in such a project. We must distinguish two possibilities. The option may give the firm the right to invest in this project just once; after the project dies, the firm has no further rights. Or the firm may have the right to invest in perpetuity; after one project dies it gets the original opportunity to invest back again. We begin with the first case.

Let $F(P)$ denote the value of the option. As before, we construct a portfolio consisting of one unit of the option, and $F'(P)$ units of a short position in the asset that spans the risk in P. Note that such a traded asset is quite exogenous to the project or the firm; it does not die with the project. Therefore its convenience yield is $\delta = \mu - \alpha$. Then the calculation goes through as before, and yields the functional form for the option value

$$F(P) = A_1\, P^{\beta_1},$$

where A_1 is a constant to be determined, and β_1 is the positive root of the familiar quadratic equation (4).

The investment threshold P^* and the constant A_1 are jointly determined by solving the value-matching and smooth-pasting conditions

$$F(P) = V(P) - I, \qquad F'(P) = V'(P),$$

where I is the sunk cost of investment. A simple calculation gives

$$P^* = \frac{\beta_1}{\beta_1 - 1}\, (\delta + \lambda)\, I. \tag{24}$$

This is almost identical to our earlier formula (9) for the investment threshold for an infinite-lived project. The only difference is that the δ on the right-hand side is replaced by $\delta + \lambda$. This can be understood by considering the special case of risk neutrality and zero trend in the price. Then $\delta = r$, and $r\,I$ is just the annualized or flow equivalent of the cost of the infinite-lived investment. Then at the threshold the profit flow should be a multiple of this cost flow, to reflect the value of the option that is sacrificed when the investment is made. When we introduce depreciation, the flow equivalent cost is increased by the Poisson death parameter because the sunk cost of investment must be recouped over a shorter expected lifetime. However, the same option value multiple applies to this new flow cost: the equation for β_1 is unaffected by depreciation. Therefore the intuition that depreciation would reduce the importance of option values is not valid in this context.

Since the opportunity to invest is available only once, its exercise is just as irreversible even though the project has a finite life. If we take the alternative perspective where the physical life is infinite but the output flow decreases exponentially, then the depreciation has no bearing on the irreversibility of the action.

Matters are different if the option to invest is available in perpetuity, so that the firm regains the right to start another identical project after the first one expires. Of course the randomly evolving price might be too low to justify investment at the instant the first project dies, but the firm once again has the option, and can start a second project when the price rises again to the threshold. We now turn to this case.

In this analysis we must consider revenues and values that are various nonlinear functions of P, and the risk-adjusted discount rate appropriate to each is different. We take the dynamic programming perspective with an exogenously specified discount rate ρ. However, a similar analysis can be conducted using the contingent claims approach provided the Poisson risk of the project's death is fully diversifiable; this point was discussed in the context of Poisson processes in Chapter 4.

Let P^* denote the investment threshold, and let $F(P)$ denote the value of the option to invest. While unexercised, that is, in the range $0 < P < P^*$, this option merely has an expected capital gain

$$\mathcal{E}[dF(P)] = [\alpha\, P\, F'(P) + \tfrac{1}{2}\sigma^2\, P^2\, F''(P)]\, dt.$$

Setting this equal to the normal return $\rho\, F(P)\, dt$, we get a familiar differential equation for $F(P)$, and an equally familiar solution

$$F(P) = A_1\, P^{\beta_1},$$

where A_1 is a constant to be determined, and β_1 is the positive root of the quadratic

$$\tfrac{1}{2}\sigma^2\, \beta(\beta - 1) + \alpha\, \beta - \rho = 0. \tag{25}$$

As usual, we have considered the limit as $P \to 0$ to rule out the term with the negative root.

Let $J(P)$ denote the value of an installed project along with that of all future replacement options. First consider the range $P < P^*$. Over the next short interval of time dt, the profit flow is $P\, dt$. Then with probability $\lambda\, dt$, the current project will die and the firm will go back to holding the option worth $F(P)$. Thus

$$J(P) = P\,dt + (1 - \lambda\,dt)\,e^{-\rho\,dt}\,\mathcal{E}[J(P + dP)] + \lambda\,dt\,e^{-\rho\,dt}\,\mathcal{E}[F(P + dP)].$$

Expanding the right-hand side using Ito's Lemma and simplifying, we have

$$\tfrac{1}{2}\sigma^2\,P^2\,J''(P) + \alpha\,P\,J'(P) - (\rho + \lambda)\,J(P) + P + \lambda\,A_1\,P^{\beta_1} = 0.$$

This has the solution

$$J(P) = B_1\,P^{\beta_1'} + P/(\rho + \lambda - \alpha) + A_1\,P^{\beta_1},$$

where B_1 is a constant to be determined, and β_1' is the positive root of the quadratic

$$\tfrac{1}{2}\sigma^2\,\beta(\beta - 1) + \alpha\,\beta - (\rho + \lambda) = 0. \tag{26}$$

Over the range $P > P^*$, a similar analysis applies, but if the current project dies a new one will be immediately started. Therefore

$$J(P) = P\,dt + (1 - \lambda\,dt)\,e^{-\rho\,dt}\,\mathcal{E}[J(P + dP)] + \lambda\,dt\,e^{-\rho\,dt}\,\mathcal{E}[J(P + dP) - I].$$

This becomes

$$\tfrac{1}{2}\sigma^2\,P^2\,J''(P) + \alpha\,P\,J'(P) - \rho\,J(P) + P - \lambda\,I = 0.$$

The solution is

$$J(P) = B_2\,P^{\beta_2} + P/(\rho - \alpha) - \lambda\,I/\rho,$$

where B_2 is a constant to be determined, and β_2 is the negative root of the quadratic (25).

Now the two branches of $J(P)$ must meet tangentially at the common point P^* of their ranges of validity. Also, since P^* is the investment threshold, $F(P)$ must satisfy value matching and smooth pasting with $J(P) - I$ at P^*. Thus we have four equations to determine the constants C_1, B_1, B_2, and the threshold P^*. This completes the solution.

The seemingly complicated procedure yields a very simple answer. Since the two branches of the function $J(P)$ to the left and right of P^* meet tangentially at P^*, we can use either branch for the value-matching and smooth-pasting conditions that link $F(P)$ and $J(P) - I$ at P^*. The left-hand branch gives the solution more easily. The value-matching condition is

$$A_1\,P^{\beta_1} = B_1\,P^{\beta_1'} + P/(\rho + \lambda - \alpha) + A_1\,P^{\beta_1} - I,$$

Table 6.1. *Option Value Multiples with Depreciation*

		σ		
λ	0.1	0.2	0.3	0.4
0.00	1.4215	2.0000	2.7631	3.7321
0.01	1.3706	1.8632	2.5000	3.2966
0.05	1.2651	1.5954	2.0000	2.4868
0.10	1.2077	1.4561	1.7500	2.0938
0.15	1.1759	1.3813	1.6193	1.8927

or

$$B_1 P^{\beta_1'} + P/(\rho + \lambda - \alpha) = I.$$

The smooth-pasting condition is

$$\beta_1' B_1 P^{\beta_1'-1} + 1/(\rho + \lambda - \alpha) = 0.$$

Solving these and writing $\rho - \alpha = \delta$, we find

$$P^* = \frac{\beta_1'}{\beta_1' - 1} (\delta + \lambda) I. \tag{27}$$

Contrast this with the formula (24) for the case where the option gave the right to invest in the project just once. The flow-equivalent cost part is identical, but the option value multiple is different. The root β_1' comes from an equation (26) different from equation (25) for β_1. The latter has the depreciation parameter λ added to the discount rate ρ. Therefore $\beta_1' > \beta_1$ and $\beta_1'/(\beta_1' - 1) < \beta_1/(\beta_1 - 1)$, so that in this case depreciation does lower the option value multiple. If the option to invest is perpetually available, its exercise on any one occasion is a less irreversible act when the project depreciates faster.

We illustrate in Table 6.1 the numerical significance of this effect. As in the central case of our earlier calculations in this chapter, we take $\rho = r = 0.04$ and $\alpha = 0$. We then show the option value multiple $\beta_1'/(\beta_1' - 1)$ for various values of σ and λ. Depreciation has a significant effect on the option value multiples. But the multiples remain substantially above 1, particularly when σ is not too low.

4.B Sudden Death

Next to the exponential or Poisson decay, the form of depreciation most popular in economic analysis is a fixed finite life during which the project continues in perfect health, followed by a sudden instantaneous death.[9]

Let T denote the fixed finite life. The project continues to produce a unit of output, and therefore the profit flow $\{P_t\}$, for T years, at which point it suddenly stops functioning. Let the initial price be P. The value of the project at installation is the discounted present value of expected profits over its lifetime:

$$
\begin{aligned}
V(P) = \mathcal{E} \int_0^T & e^{-\mu t} P_t \, dt \\
&= P[1 - e^{-(\mu - \alpha) T}]/(\mu - \alpha) \\
&= P[1 - e^{-\delta T}]/\delta,
\end{aligned}
$$

where we have used the risk-adjusted discount rate μ and recognized that the expected value of the price, and therefore the profit flow, grows exponentially at rate α.

In equation (5) we found the value $V(P) = P/\delta$ for an infinite-lived project. The above formula is now seen as a very natural generalization; the infinite-life case is obtained by taking the limit as T goes to ∞.

The value of an option to invest can now be found following the same steps as in the previous section, and distinguishing the cases of a one-time and a perpetual option. We leave this as an exercise.

4.C The General Case

We can subsume the above common forms of depreciation into a very general analysis. Suppose the project produces a profit flow $\pi(P, t)$. The Poisson

---

[9]In economic theory such depreciation by sudden death is sometimes labelled "one-hoss shay." The term comes from the poem "The Deacon's Masterpiece; or the Wonderful One-hoss Shay" by Oliver Wendell Holmes, Sr.:

> Have you heard of the wonderful one-hoss shay
> Which was built in such a logical way
> That it ran a hundred years to a day
> And then, of a sudden, it ...
> ... went to pieces all at once

We give this quotation in an attempt to demonstrate that economists are not entirely devoid of culture.

decay case has π declining exponentially, while in the "one-hoss shay" case π stays constant for a while and then drops to zero. More generally, π might decline gradually over time, either because capital suffers gradual physical decline, or because the project, embodying the technology at its date of construction, must compete with later and newer projects. In the latter case, the project will suspend operation at the endogenous date when $\pi(P, t)$ drops to zero; this phenomenon is sometimes termed "economic obsolescence." This was modelled in the framework of a deterministic and monotonic advance in technology by Solow, Tobin, von Weizsacker, and Yaari (1967) and Bliss (1968); we suggest its extension to the case of uncertainty as a research exercise for interested readers.

The value of such a project can be expressed as a present value integral, but for general forms of π that is hard to evaluate. We describe an alternative approach. It has the added advantage of yielding a general formula for the value of a project at any moment during its lifetime, and not just at the initial date of construction.

Let $V(P, t)$ denote the value of a project as a function of the current price P and the current time t. We consider the usual portfolio that holds the project and goes short n units of an asset perfectly correlated with P, for a short interval of time dt. Over this interval, the portfolio earns dividends $\pi(P, t)\, dt - n\,\delta\, P\, dt$, where as usual $\delta = \mu - \alpha$ is the "return shortfall" or convenience yield on the P asset, and the second term in the expression for the dividend represents the payment the holder of the short position must make to the holder of the corresponding long position. The portfolio has a capital gain given by

$$dV(P, t) - n\,dP = [V_P(P, t) - n]\,dP + [\tfrac{1}{2}\sigma^2 P^2 V_{PP}(P, t) + V_t(P, t)]\,dt,$$

where we are using subscripts to denote partial derivatives since V now has two independent variables; thus $V_P = \partial V / \partial P$, etc. By choosing $n = V_P(P, t)$ we can make the portfolio riskless. Then we can set its total expected return equal to the riskless return:

$$\pi(P, t) - \delta\, P\, V_P(P, t) + \tfrac{1}{2}\sigma^2 P^2 V_{PP}(P, t) + V_t(P, t)$$
$$= r\,[V(P, t) - P\, V_P(P, t)],$$

or

$$\tfrac{1}{2}\sigma^2 P^2 V_{PP}(P, t) + (r - \delta)\, P\, V_P(P, t) + V_t(P, t) - r\, V(P, t) + \pi(P, t) = 0.$$

This is a partial differential equation that can be solved numerically. If there is a known maximum possible lifetime T, then the solution can be started at $t = T$ with the condition $V(P, T) = 0$ for all P, and completed backward. We will illustrate such solutions in another context in Chapter 10.

Here we point out the economic significance of the new term $V_t(P, t)$ that enters the picture. The value of the project can now change for two reasons: a different initial value of the stochastic price, and pure passage of time because that changes the future profile of profit flows. The latter effect is exactly what economists mean by depreciation. Thus $-V_t(P, t)$ gives us a quantitative measure of economic depreciation. This concept was well elucidated by Samuelson (1964) in the context of certainty and perfect foresight, and here we have a natural extension that incorporates uncertainty and rational expectations.

5 Price and Cost Uncertainty

Thus far we have allowed only one random variable, namely, the output price (or a demand shift variable), keeping all other parameters bearing on the investment decision known and constant. We did this to develop the analytical methods in a relatively simple setting. The same methods can be employed in more general situations where two or more random variables affect the firm's decision. For example, if both the investment cost I and the output price P are uncertain, then we have to express the value of the project and the value of the option to invest as functions of both of these variables, $V(P, I)$ and $F(P, I)$. Then we have to find the whole region of values of (P, I) where investment will occur, the whole region where it will not occur, and the critical boundary or threshold curve separating the two regions. Needless to say, this is mathematically more difficult. With two independent variables, the value functions satisfy partial differential equations, and their solution can require numerical methods of some complexity.[10] However, some examples with special features—in particular, some form of homogeneity—can be solved by reducing the problem to one state variable. We now illustrate this.

Consider a unit-sized project whose investment cost I and the revenue flow P are both uncertain. We can even allow the uncertainty in these two variables to be correlated due to some common macroeconomic shocks. Thus we assume that P and I follow the geometric Brownian motions:

$$dP/P = \alpha_P \, dt + \sigma_P \, dz_P, \qquad dI/I = \alpha_I \, dt + \sigma_I \, dz_I,$$

---

[10]To be precise, we must solve free-boundary problems for elliptic partial differential equations.

where

$$\mathcal{E}[dz_P^2] = dt, \qquad \mathcal{E}[dz_I^2] = dt, \qquad \mathcal{E}[dz_P\,dz_I] = \rho\,dt.$$

Once an investment is made, further uncertainty in the evolution of the investment cost is irrelevant. The value of a live project when the current price is P is simply $V(P) = P/(\mu_P - \alpha_P) = P/\delta_P$, where $\mu_P = r + \phi\,\rho_{pm}\,\sigma_P$ is the risk-adjusted discount rate appropriate to P, and $\delta_P = \mu_P - \alpha_P$ is the "convenience yield" or "rate-of-return shortfall" in P.

The value of the option to invest, however, depends on both P and I. Intuitively, we expect that the option will be held when P is low or I is high, and exercised when P becomes sufficiently high for given I, or I becomes sufficiently low for given P. Figure 6.8 shows the suggested regions in (I, P) space corresponding to waiting and investing, and the boundary separating the two. Our aim is to make this intuition more precise, and develop an analytical method to find the boundary and thereby determine the optimal investment rule.

By now, the steps should be very familiar. Let $F(P, I)$ be the value of the option. We find a differential equation for it. We assume that both the risks in output price and investment cost are spanned by existing assets, and work with assets whose prices are P and I, respectively.[11] Call these assets "output" and "capital" for brevity. Consider a portfolio consisting of one unit of the option, m units short in the output, and n units short in capital. By Ito's

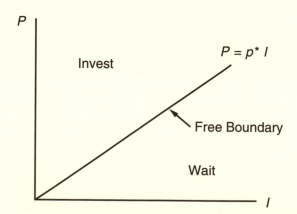

Figure 6.8.   *Investment with Price and Cost Uncertainty*

---

[11]Otherwise a dynamic programming approach leads to a very similar differential equation.

Lemma, we have

$$d(F - mP - nI) = (F_P - m)\,dP + (F_I - n)\,dI$$
$$+ \tfrac{1}{2}\,(F_{PP}\,\sigma_P^2\,P^2 + 2\,F_{PI}\,\rho\,\sigma_P\,\sigma_I\,P\,I + F_{II}\,\sigma_I^2\,I^2)\,dt.$$

Note that the dP and dI on the right-hand side are stochastic. However, we can choose $m = F_P$ and $n = F_I$ to get rid of these terms and make the portfolio riskless. Then the holder of the portfolio over the interval $(t, t + dt)$ will have the sure capital gain

$$\tfrac{1}{2}\,(F_{PP}\,\sigma_P^2\,P^2 + 2\,F_{PI}\,\rho\,\sigma_P\,\sigma_I\,P\,I + F_{II}\,\sigma_I^2\,I^2)\,dt.$$

He must also make a payment corresponding to the convenience yields on output and capital, $(m\,\delta_P\,P + n\,\delta_I\,I)\,dt$, to hold the short position. Equating the sum of these two components to the riskless return $r\,(F - mP - nI)\,dt$ and collecting terms, we get the basic equation

$$\tfrac{1}{2}\,(\sigma_P^2\,P^2\,F_{PP} + 2\,\rho\,\sigma_P\,\sigma_I\,P\,I\,F_{PI} + \sigma_I^2\,I^2\,F_{II}) + (r - \delta_P)\,P\,F_P$$
$$+ (r - \delta_I)\,I\,F_I - r\,F = 0. \tag{28}$$

As there are two independent variables (P, I), this is a partial differential equation. It applies over the region of the (P, I) space where it is optimal to hold the option unexercised. Over the region where the option is immediately exercised, we have

$$F(P, I) = V(P) - I = P/\delta_P - I.$$

At the boundary between the two regions, this becomes a value-matching condition. The two functions must also meet tangentially at the boundary, yielding two smooth-pasting conditions

$$F_P(P, I) = V'(P) = 1/\delta_P, \qquad F_I(P, I) = -1.$$

The differential equation, together with these boundary conditions, should fix the position of the boundary itself, and also yield a solution for the function F in the waiting region.

The fact that the boundary itself is an unknown makes problems of this kind quite difficult. In fact the theory of partial differential equations has little to say about this class of "free boundary" problems in general. Analytical solutions are rarely available, and numerical solution methods are mostly ad hoc, each tailored to fit a particular situation. This is in principle no different from the problem even when only the price is uncertain; the investment threshold P^* is itself unknown and becomes the free-boundary point that separates the one-dimensional range of values of P where investment occurs from the range where it does not occur. In one dimension it is much easier to find the solution, whether analytically or numerically. Luckily, in the present case the natural homogeneity of the problem allows us to reduce it to one dimension.

If the current values of both P and I are doubled, that will merely double the value of the project and also the cost of investing. The optimal decision should therefore depend only on the ratio $p \equiv P/I$, and therefore the boundary in Figure 6.8 should be a ray through the origin. Correspondingly, the value of the option should be homogeneous of degree 1 in (P, I), enabling us to write

$$F(P, I) = I \, f(P/I) = I \, f(p),$$

where f is now the function to be determined.

Successive differentiation gives

$$F_P(P, I) = f'(p), \qquad F_I(P, I) = f(p) - p \, f'(p),$$

and

$$F_{PP}(P, I) = f''(p)/I, \qquad F_{PI}(P, I) = -p \, f''(p)/I,$$
$$F_{II}(P, I) = p^2 \, f''(p)/I.$$

Substituting this in the partial differential equation (28) and grouping terms, we find

$$\tfrac{1}{2} \left(\sigma_P^2 - 2\rho \, \sigma_P \, \sigma_I + \sigma_I^2 \right) p^2 \, f''(p) + (\delta_I - \delta_P) \, p \, f'(p) - \delta_I \, f(p) = 0. \quad (29)$$

This is an ordinary differential equation for the unknown function $f(p)$ of the scalar independent variable p. Moreover, it has exactly the same form as the familiar (6) for the case when only the price is uncertain. Its boundary conditions are also similar. The value-matching condition becomes

$$f(p) = p/\delta_P - 1.$$

The two smooth-pasting conditions become

$$f'(p) = 1/\delta_P, \qquad f(p) - p \, f'(p) = -1.$$

Of these three conditions, any one can be derived from the other two. We can select the value-matching condition and the first smooth-pasting condition as the two that are exactly parallel to the pure price uncertainty case, and complete the solution as before. The fundamental quadratic is

$$Q = \tfrac{1}{2} \left(\sigma_P^2 - 2\rho \, \sigma_P \, \sigma_I + \sigma_I^2 \right) \beta(\beta - 1) + (\delta_I - \delta_P) \beta - \delta_I = 0.$$

Let β_1 denote the larger root of this; if δ_I and δ_P are both positive (which we assume), then $\beta_1 > 1$. Then we find

$$P^*/I^* = p^* = \frac{\beta_1}{\beta_1 - 1}\, \delta_P. \tag{30}$$

This ray through the origin separates the regions of waiting and investment in the (P, I) space. Its slope has the standard option value multiple interpretation.[12] Thus if either σ_P or σ_I increase, β_1 will decrease, and the multiple $\beta_1/(\beta_1 - 1)$ will increase. However, the multiple will decrease if ρ increases; holding their variances fixed, a greater covariance between changes in P and I implies less uncertainty over their ratio, and hence a reduced incentive to wait.

6   Guide to the Literature

This chapter presented more complete models of investment, and also extended the important idea that the value of a firm is largely the value of a set of options. In Chapter 5 we saw that a firm has valuable options to invest. Some of these will be exercised and some not, so that the value of the firm will equal the value of its existing projects (that is, its capital in place) plus the value of its options to invest in new projects in the future. In this chapter we saw that an existing project can also be viewed as a set of options—options to produce and earn profits should price be sufficiently high relative to operating cost—and can be valued accordingly. This idea appears in Marcus and Modest (1984) in the context of agricultural production decisions, but was first spelled out in detail by McDonald and Siegel (1985). They showed that if price follows a geometric Brownian motion, a unit-output project with fixed operating cost can be valued as the sum of an infinite set of European call options. The approach used in this chapter is more general and more tractable—we simply valued the project as a single contingent claim, and thereby derived a differential equation for $V(P)$ in the same way that we derived an equation for the value of the investment option, $F(P)$, in Chapter 5. We then used the solution for $V(P)$ in the boundary conditions to find the solution for $F(P)$, along with the optimal investment rule. This approach was developed in Pindyck (1988b) in the context of incremental investment.

---

[12]It may seem puzzling that the riskless interest rate has disappeared from the quadratic equation and hence from the solution. In fact, r remains, concealed in μ_P, δ_P, and δ_I.

We have seen that an important starting point for the valuation of projects and investment opportunities is the underlying stochastic process for the output price, $P(t)$. We assumed that if price follows a geometric Brownian motion, its expected rate of growth is less than the risk-adjusted expected return, μ. For a storable commodity, this difference would have to reflect the convenience yield accruing to holders of inventory. This point was raised by McDonald and Siegel (1984), and the stochastic structure of convenience yield itself is examined in Gibson and Schwartz (1990) and Brennan (1991).

This chapter introduced a number of free boundary problems, some of which could be solved analytically, and some of which require numerical solution methods. For readers seeking more background on the mathematics of these problems and their solution, we suggest Guenther and Lee (1988) and Fasano and Primicerio (1983).

Bertola (1988, Chapter 1) has a very general model with simultaneous uncertainty in the output price, the price of capital goods, and prices of variable inputs.

Most of these methods rely on discretization of the state variables, and we have adopted the same approach for numerical solutions of multivariable problems in Chapters 4 and 10. Some recent work on numerical methods is based on an alternative, called the finite element method. Here the whole region of space of the independent variables is split into small cells, the function we are trying to obtain is approximated by a low-order polynomial in each cell, and the different approximations are pasted together at the edges of the cells. This method looks promising for many economic applications. Interested readers should consult books by Johnson (1990) and Judd (1992).

Chapter 7

Entry, Exit, Lay-Up, and Scrapping

IN THE previous chapter we showed how one can first value a project, and then value the option to invest in the project and determine the optimal investment rule. Our starting point was a stochastic process for the evolution of the price of the project's output, and hence uncertainty over the future flow of operating profits. This flow of profits could sometimes become negative, and we assumed that at such times the firm could suspend operation, and resume it later if the profit flow turned positive, without paying any lump-sum stopping or restarting costs.

For many projects, this assumption of costless suspension and restarting is unrealistic. In some cases it is almost impossible to suspend and later restart the operation of a project. An example is a research laboratory engaged in the development of a new pharmaceutical product; suspending the laboratory's operation may mean losing its team of research scientists and hence the ability to resume development of the product in the future. In other cases it is possible to suspend and later restart the operation, but only at a substantial cost. For example, if the operation of an underground mine is suspended, a sunk cost and an ongoing fixed cost must be incurred to prevent the mine from flooding with water so that it can be later reopened, and an additional sunk cost must be incurred to actually reopen it.

This chapter begins with a model that is the opposite extreme of the one developed in the last chapter. We will assume that if the operation is ever suspended, the firm must incur the whole investment cost over again to restart it. (This is as if capital "rusts" and crumbles once it is unused.) Instead of suspension, now an active firm must contemplate outright abandonment. Of course it will not take this step the moment its operating profit flow turns negative. Since restarting is costly, there will be an option value of keeping the operation alive, and abandonment will be optimal only at a sufficiently large threshold level of operating losses. We will assume that the firm retains whatever market power it had to start with, and does not lose its *right* to invest if it abandons operation. (In Chapter 8 we will consider the other extreme of a perfectly competitive industry, where any of a large number of potential firms can invest, and any active firm can abandon without retaining any special privilege of reentry.)

In most cases, reality lies between the extremes of costless temporary suspension and immediate total rusting. The capital sunk in most projects rusts when not used, but does so gradually. Machinery or ships rust literally; mines are subject to cave-ins and flooding; other intangibles like customer loyalty and brand-name recognition fade.[1] Then restarting is costly, but not quite as costly as new investment. In some cases, the cost of restarting rises with the duration of the suspension. To model this, we must consider an option to restart (as distinct from the option to start ab initio), and introduce the elapsed time since the last suspension as an explicit state variable affecting the value of this new option. The resulting partial differential equation can be solved numerically, but we will not treat this case here.

Later in this chapter we will consider another intermediate possibility. "Rusting" of idle capital can be prevented by undertaking "maintenance"— literal in the case of machinery, ships, and mines, and figurative in the case of intangibles like customer loyalty. Instead of abandoning, a firm may choose to keep its project alive by maintaining capital but not actively producing output. For example, ships are "mothballed" or "laid up." This incurs an ongoing maintenance cost, but saves the prospect of future reinvestment cost. The tradeoff between these alternatives depends on the relative magnitudes of the two costs, and on the likelihood of a quick return of favorable operating conditions.

Mathematically, in addition to the state variable (for example, price) that evolves stochastically and affects the profitability of operation, the possibility of abandonment introduces a second discrete state variable, which takes on

---

[1] A scientist undertaking a new research project must invest capital—acquiring familiarity with the literature, learning new mathematical techniques or laboratory skills, etc. Our own experience is that such capital rusts very quickly if we set the project aside for as little as a few weeks.

the value 0 if the project is not operating, and the value 1 if it is operating. The firm's strategy consists of a pair of decisions to switch between these two. In each discrete state the firm has a call option on the other. An idle firm can exercise the option to invest. This gets it the flow of operating profit, plus an option to abandon. We must find the rules for optimal exercise of these options simultaneously in terms of the underlying random variable (price). Similarly, when we consider the third alternative of "mothballing" or "lay-up," there are three discrete states, with optimal switches among them to be calculated.

1   Combined Entry and Exit Strategies

We confine the discussion to the case of demand uncertainty, assuming a geometric Brownian motion price process. Interested readers can develop extensions to other processes along the lines of Section 5 of Chapter 5, and to uncertainty in other variables along the lines of Section 5 of Chapter 6. We retain the setup and notation of Chapter 6 wherever possible. The investment and abandonment decisions are made by a firm that takes price as given, and we again assume that the price follows a geometric Brownian motion,

$$dP = \alpha P \, dt + \sigma P \, dz. \tag{1}$$

If the firm invests (that is, enters the market), it obtains a project that produces one unit of output per period, and lasts forever or until abandoned. Variable costs of operation C are known and constant. The riskless rate of interest is exogenously fixed at r. We will assume that stochastic fluctuations in price are spanned by other assets in the economy (although, as we have seen, if this were not the case, a solution could be obtained by dynamic programming). The appropriately risk-adjusted discount rate for the firm's revenues is

$$\mu = r + \phi \rho_{PM} \sigma, \tag{2}$$

where ϕ is the market price of risk, and ρ_{PM} is the coefficient of correlation between the price P and the entire market portfolio. As usual, we let $\delta = \mu - \alpha$ denote the rate-of-return shortfall on price, and we assume that $\delta > 0$.

The firm must incur a lump-sum cost I to invest in the project, and a lump-sum cost E to abandon it. This latter cost might include legally required termination payments to workers, or costs of restoring the site of a mine to its natural condition. It might be the case that part of the investment cost I is not sunk, so that E is negative, reflecting the portion of the investment that can be recouped upon exit. Of course we need $I + E > 0$ to rule out a "money machine" of rapid cycles of investment and abandonment.

In Chapter 6 we began by finding the value V of a live project, and then went on to the value F of the option to invest. Now that sequence becomes a full circle. The live project is really a composite asset, part of which is an option to abandon. If that option is exercised, the firm goes back to the inactive state. In other words, it acquires another asset, namely, the option to invest. When this option is exercised in turn, it leads back to a live project. Thus the values of a live firm and an idle firm are interlinked, and must be determined simultaneously.

Intuition suggests that an idle firm will invest when demand conditions become sufficiently favorable, and an active firm will abandon when they become sufficiently adverse. Indeed, we will see that the optimal strategy for investment and abandonment, or for holding or exercising the two options, will take the form of two threshold prices, say, P_H and P_L, with $P_H > P_L$. An idle firm will find it optimal to remain idle as long as P remains below P_H, and will invest as soon as P reaches the threshold P_H. An active firm will remain active as long as P remains above P_L, but it will abandon if P falls to P_L. In the range of prices between the thresholds P_L and P_H, the optimal policy is to continue with the staus quo, whether it be active operation or waiting. We now proceed to verify this intuition. Of course we must find the values of these thresholds in terms of the exogenous data.

1.A   Valuing the Two Options

The value of the firm is now a function of the exogenous state variable P, and of the discrete state variable that indicates whether the firm is currently idle (0) or active (1). To clarify this, we will change the notation slightly, letting $V_0(P)$ denote the value of the option to invest (that is, the value of an idle firm), and letting $V_1(P)$ denote the value of an active firm. Note that $V_1(P)$ is the sum of two components, the entitlement to the profit from operation, and the option to abandon should the price fall too far.

Over the range of prices $(0, P_H)$, an idle firm holds on to its option to invest. As in Chapter 6, an arbitrage argument tells us that $V_0(P)$ satisfies a differential equation over this interval. The boundary conditions link values and derivatives of $V_0(P)$ to those of $V_1(P)$ at P_H. Similarly, over the range of prices (P_L, ∞), an active firm remains active, holding its option to abandon. $V_1(P)$ satisfies a corresponding differential equation, and the boundary conditions link the values and derivatives of $V_1(P)$ to those of $V_0(P)$ at P_L. This system of equations and boundary conditions contains just enough information to complete the solution.

We begin with the idle firm. To obtain a differential equation for $V_0(P)$, construct a portfolio with one unit of the option to invest, and a short position of $V_0'(P)$ units of output. The steps that follow are exactly the same as those in Chapters 5 and 6, so we omit them and leave them as an exercise for the reader. The resulting equation is

$$\tfrac{1}{2}\sigma^2 P^2 V_0''(P) + (r - \delta) P V_0'(P) - r V_0(P) = 0. \tag{3}$$

This has the general solution

$$V_0(P) = A_1 P^{\beta_1} + A_2 P^{\beta_2},$$

where A_1 and A_2 are constants to be determined, and β_1 and β_2 are the roots of the quadratic equation familiar from Chapters 5 and 6:

$$\beta_1 = \tfrac{1}{2} - (\rho - \delta)/\sigma^2 + \sqrt{\left[(\rho - \delta)/\sigma^2 - \tfrac{1}{2}\right]^2 + 2\rho/\sigma^2} \; > 1,$$

and

$$\beta_2 = \tfrac{1}{2} - (\rho - \delta)/\sigma^2 - \sqrt{\left[(\rho - \delta)/\sigma^2 - \tfrac{1}{2}\right]^2 + 2\rho/\sigma^2} \; < 0.$$

Since the option to invest gets very far out of the money and therefore becomes nearly worthless as P goes to 0, the coefficient A_2 corresponding to the negative root β_2 must be zero. That leaves

$$V_0(P) = A_1 P^{\beta_1}. \tag{4}$$

Remember that this is valid over the interval $(0, P_H)$ of prices.

Next consider the value of the active firm. The calculation is similar, except that the live project part of the portfolio pays a net cash flow $(P-C)\,dt$. Then we get

$$\tfrac{1}{2}\sigma^2 P^2 V_1''(P) + (r - \delta) P V_1'(P) - r V_1(P) + P - C = 0. \tag{5}$$

The general solution to this equation is

$$V_1(P) = B_1 P^{\beta_1} + B_2 P^{\beta_2} + P/\delta - C/r.$$

As in Chapter 6, we interpret the last two terms as the value of the live project when the firm is required to keep it operating forever despite any losses, and the first two terms as the value of the option to abandon. The likelihood of abandonment in the not-too-distant future becomes extremely small as P

goes to ∞, so the value of the abandonment option should go to zero as P becomes very large. Hence the coefficient B_1 corresponding to the positive root β_1 should be zero. This leaves

$$V_1(P) = B_2 \, P^{\beta_2} + P/\delta - C/r. \tag{6}$$

This is valid for P in the range (P_L, ∞).

At the investment threshold P_H, the firm pays the lump-sum cost I to exercise its investment option, giving up this asset of value $V_0(P_H)$ to get the live project which has value $V_1(P_H)$. For this we have the conditions of value matching and smooth pasting:

$$V_0(P_H) = V_1(P_H) - I, \qquad V_0'(P_H) = V_1'(P_H). \tag{7}$$

Likewise, at the abandonment threshold P_L, the value-matching and smooth-pasting conditions are

$$V_1(P_L) = V_0(P_L) - E, \qquad V_1'(P_L) = V_0'(P_L). \tag{8}$$

Using equations (4) and (6) for $V_0(P)$ and $V_1(P)$, these conditions can be written as

$$-A_1 \, P_H^{\beta_1} + B_2 \, P_H^{\beta_2} + P_H/\delta - C/r = I, \tag{9}$$

$$-\beta_1 \, A_1 \, P_H^{\beta_1 - 1} + \beta_2 \, B_2 \, P_H^{\beta_2 - 1} + 1/\delta = 0, \tag{10}$$

$$-A_1 \, P_L^{\beta_1} + B_2 \, P_L^{\beta_2} + P_L/\delta - C/r = -E, \tag{11}$$

$$-\beta_1 \, A_1 \, P_L^{\beta_1 - 1} + \beta_2 \, B_2 \, P_L^{\beta_2 - 1} + 1/\delta = 0. \tag{12}$$

These four equations determine the four unknowns—the thresholds P_H, P_L and the coefficients A_1 and B_2 in the option values.

The equations are very nonlinear in the thresholds, so that an analytic solution in closed form is impossible. However, it can be proved that a solution exists, is unique, and has economically intuitive basic properties. The thresholds satisfy $0 < P_L < P_H < \infty$, and the coefficients of the option value terms, A_1 and B_2, are positive.[2] Some other important general economic insights can be inferred by analytic methods, but further results require numerical solution. We proceed to these in turn.

---

[2]The proofs are lengthy and not in themselves interesting, so we omit them. Interested readers should consult Dixit (1989a, Appendix A).

1.B Comparison with Myopic Decisions

The theory of investment and abandonment as typically presented in intermediate microeconomics textbooks is based on the Marshallian concepts of long-run average cost and short-run variable cost. For our unit-sized firm, the long-run average cost is the sum of the operating cost and the interest on the sunk cost of investment, $(C + rI)$. The textbook theory tells a firm to invest if the price exceeds this. Similarly, an active firm should abandon if the price falls short of the variable cost C. When there is an explicit lump-sum cost E of abandonment, the firm should also take into account the interest on this cost, so that the threshold becomes $(C - rE)$.

In other words, the traditional Marshallian concept is to compare the rate of return on the investment, $(P - C)/I$, and that on disinvestment, $(C - P)/E$, to the normal return r. Implicit in this view is an assumption of static expectations or myopia—that is, the current price is assumed to prevail forever. This may be appropriate for analyzing a price change that came as a surprise, and when the firm knows for sure that it will never happen again. However, such price changes are rare. In most real-world situations, the demand (and cost) conditions facing a firm change all the time, and the firm must make its investment and disinvestment decisions taking into account that the future is and always will be uncertain. Hence a more natural theoretical approach is to assume that the firm has rational expectations about the probabilistic law of motion for its uncertain environment. Our model above does just that—the firm's decisions are optimal given the stochastic process (1) for the price.

Let us now ask what difference it makes to give the firm rational rather than static expectations. How does the optimal investment threshold P_H compare with the Marshallian threshold $(C + rI)$, and the optimal abandonment threshold P_L compare with the Marshallian threshold $(C - rE)$? To answer this, we begin by defining the function

$$G(P) \equiv V_1(P) - V_0(P)$$
$$= -A_1 P^{\beta_1} + B_2 P^{\beta_2} + P/\delta - C/r. \tag{13}$$

This function can be formally defined for all P. Note, however, that $V_1(P)$ defines the value of an active firm only over the interval (P_L, ∞), and $V_0(P)$ defines the value of an idle firm only over $(0, P_H)$. Therefore over the range (P_L, P_H), we can interpret $G(P)$ as the firm's *incremental value of becoming active*, that is, how much more it is worth in the active rather than inactive state.

For small values of P, the dominant term in $G(P)$ is the one with the negative power β_2 of P; it is decreasing and convex. For large values of P, the dominant term is the one with the power $\beta_1 > 1$; this term is negative, decreasing, and concave. For intermediate values, the third term contributes to the increasing portion of $G(P)$. Thus the general form of $G(P)$ is as shown in Figure 7.1.

The boundary conditions that apply at the thresholds can be written in terms of $G(P)$. The value-matching conditions (9) and (11) become

$$G(P_H) = I, \qquad G(P_L) = -E,$$

while the smooth-pasting conditions (10) and (12) can be written

$$G'(P_H) = 0, \qquad G'(P_L) = 0.$$

Refering to Figure 7.1, these conditions imply that the graph of $G(P)$ should have an S shape over the range from P_L to P_H, and should be tangential to the horizontal line at height I at the upper end, and tangential to the horizontal line at $-E$ at the lower end.[3] Note that $G(P)$ is concave at P_H and convex at P_L.

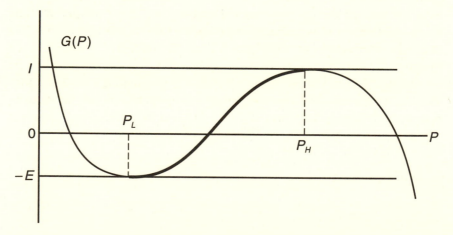

Figure 7.1. *Determination of the Thresholds P_L and P_H*

---

[3]This can be made into a geometric method for computing the thresholds, given good interactive graphics software. Superimpose the horizontal lines I, $-E$ on the graph of $G(P)$, and adjust the coefficients A_1 and B_2 until you get the tangencies. The abscissas of the tangency points are the optimal thresholds P_H, P_L.

Now consider the upper threshold. Subtracting the differential equation (3) for $V_0(P)$ from equation (5) for $V_1(P)$, we have

$$\tfrac{1}{2}\sigma^2 G''(P) + (r - \delta) G'(P) - r G(P) + P - C = 0.$$

Evaluating this for $P = P_H$, and using the boundary conditions that must hold at P_H, we find

$$-r\,I + P_H - C = -\tfrac{1}{2}\sigma^2 G''(P_H) > 0,$$

or $P_H > C + r I$. Similarly at the other end, we have $P_L < C - r E$. In other words, the optimal thresholds with rational expectations are spread farther apart than the Marshallian ones with static expectations. When inactive firms take into account the uncertainty over future prices, they are more reluctant to invest, and if they are already active, they are more reluctant to abandon. This is of course a manifestation of the option value of the status quo that we discussed in Chapters 5 and 6.[4] We will discuss its implications below, after we have examined its quantitative significance in numerical simulations.

1.C Comparative Statics

Although the equations defining the thresholds are highly nonlinear and do not have closed-form solutions, the total differentials corresponding to small changes in exogenous parameters are, as usual, linear. This makes it relatively straightforward to obtain qualitative comparative statics results for at least some parameters. On the other hand, several parameters of interest, notably r, $\delta = \mu - \alpha$, and σ, enter into the quadratic equation whose roots are the powers β_1 and β_2, so changes in these parameters can have complicated effects on the function G. This makes the analytical comparative static expressions difficult to interpret, and we must resort to numerical simulations. The other parameters, namely, I, E, and C, have simpler effects, and serve to illustrate the general method. We consider the investment cost I in detail; the other two are similar.

Working with the function G remains useful, and it helps to show its dependence on the option value coefficients. Thus we write $G(P, A_1, B_2)$. The value-matching and smooth-pasting conditions are

$$G(P_H, A_1, B_2) = I, \qquad G(P_L, A_1, B_2) = -E, \tag{14}$$

$$G_P(P_H, A_1, B_2) = 0, \qquad G_P(P_L, A_1, B_2) = 0. \tag{15}$$

---

[4] Some macroeconomists may find it a pleasing irony that going from static to rational expectations implies more inertia, not less.

Now suppose that I changes by dI, and consider how the four endogenous variables A_1, B_2, P_L, and P_H respond. Begin by differentiating the value-matching conditions (14) totally. Denote the partial derivatives of G by subscripts as usual, and write $G_A(P_H, A_1, B_2) = G_A(H)$, etc., for brevity. We get

$$G_A(H)\, dA_1 + G_B(H)\, dB_2 = dI,$$

$$G_A(L)\, dA_1 + G_B(L)\, dB_2 = 0.$$

Note that the terms $G_P(H)\, dP_H$ and $G_P(L)\, dP_L$ have vanished because of the smooth-pasting conditions (15). Therefore the general comparative static system in the four endogenous changes dA_1, dB_2, dP_L, and dP_H in fact separates into a simpler system. First we solve the above two equations for the changes in the option value coefficients dA_1, dB_2. Then we can totally differentiate the smooth-pasting conditions to get the changes in the thresholds dP_H, dP_L.

Noting that $G_A(H) = -P_H^{\beta_1}$, etc., the solution is

$$dA_1 = -P_L^{\beta_2}\, dI/\Delta, \qquad dB_2 = -P_L^{\beta_1}\, dI/\Delta,$$

where

$$\Delta = P_H^{\beta_1}\, P_L^{\beta_2} - P_H^{\beta_2}\, P_L^{\beta_1},$$

which is positive because $P_H > P_L$ and $\beta_1 > 0 > \beta_2$.

Now differentiate the smooth-pasting condition at P_H in (15) to write

$$G_{PP}(H)\, dP_H + G_{PA}(H)\, dA_1 + G_{PB}(H)\, dB_2 = 0,$$

which yields

$$G_{PP}(H)\, dP_H = -[\, \beta_1\, P_H^{\beta_1-1}\, P_L^{\beta_2} - \beta_2\, P_H^{\beta_2-1}\, P_L^{\beta_1}\,]\, dI\,/\,\Delta.$$

Since $G(P)$ is concave at P_H, $G_{PP}(H)$ is negative and then $dP_H > 0$ when $dI > 0$. The investment threshold rises with the investment cost, as we should expect. Similarly, P_L falls as E rises.

Similarly, the lower smooth-pasting condition gives

$$G_{PP}(L)\, dP_L = -(\beta_1 - \beta_2)\, P_L^{\beta_1+\beta_2-1}\, dI\,/\,\Delta.$$

Since $G_{PP}(L) > 0$, we have $dP_L < 0$ when $dI > 0$: the abandonment threshold falls when the investment cost rises. This important interaction between the costs and thresholds should also be intuitive upon reflection. The firm abandons an ongoing project with some reluctance because of its option value. By keeping the project alive, it avoids having to incur the investment cost once again should the price process turn sufficiently favorable in the future. Therefore, the larger is the investment cost, the larger is this option value and the greater is the reluctance to abandon. The mirror image result, namely, that the investment threshold P_H rises as the abandonment cost E increases, is perhaps even clearer. The firm is more reluctant to undertake the project if it might have to incur a larger cost to shut it down in the future.

If we evaluate these comparative static derivatives as I and E both go to zero, we find P_H, P_L both go to C, but $dP_H/dI \to \infty$ and $dP_L/dI \to -\infty$, and likewise with respect to E. Thus the entry and exit thresholds begin to spread apart very rapidly even for small costs of entry and exit. Expanding the four equations of the set (14) and (15) in Taylor series and carrying through some tedious algebra, Dixit (1991a) finds that

$$\log(P_H/P_L) = k\,(I + E)^{1/3}, \tag{16}$$

where k is a constant. In other words, entry and exit costs that are small and of third order (proportional to ϵ^3 where ϵ is small) produce a gap between the entry and exit thresholds that is of first order (proportional to ϵ). Thus very small sunk costs have a disproportionately large effect on the firm's decisions.

Moreover, the effect of small costs on the thresholds is entirely symmetric: the entry threshold is affected by the exit cost just as strongly as by the entry cost. For larger magnitudes, each type of cost will affect its "own" threshold more strongly. The reason is intuitively clear. Consider a firm contemplating entry. The entry cost must be paid immediately, while the exit cost affects the firm's entry decision only through the prospect that it will have to pay that some time in the future. Because of discounting, the immediate effect is the stronger one. However, if the costs are very small, the thresholds are very close together, and the Brownian motion is almost sure to reach the other threshold very quickly. Therefore the difference made by discounting is small, and vanishes in the limit.

We leave it as an exercise for the reader to verify that both P_H and P_L rise as C rises: as one would expect, a project with higher *operating* cost is undertaken more reluctantly and abandoned sooner.

1.D An Example: Entry and Exit in the Copper Industry

We have seen that uncertainty over future demand conditions increases the firm's zone of inaction; that is, it causes the optimal investment and abandonment thresholds to be spread farther apart than the traditional Marshallian ones. How much larger does this zone of inaction become in practice? Is it really necessary to account for irreversibility and uncertainty as we have, or might the simple Marshallian rules provide a good enough approximation for most investment and abandonment decisions? To answer these questions, it is useful to look at a specific example.

We will examine the decision to invest in a new copper production facility—a combined mine, smelter, and refinery—and the decision to permanently abandon a facility that is currently operating. The price of copper has historically been quite volatile. (The standard deviation of annual percentage changes in the price of copper has been 20 to 50 percent over the past two decades.) In addition, opening or closing a mine or smelter involves large sunk costs, so that copper producers need to make these entry and exit decisions very carefully, taking uncertainty into account.

In reality, a producer with an operating copper mine has an alternative option to permanent abandonment or continued operation. A copper mine can be temporarily "mothballed," and later reactivated should the price rise. Mothballing and reactivation involve sunk costs (construction is needed to prevent the mine from flooding or caving in while it is inactive, and an additional expenditure is needed to reactivate the mine), as well as an ongoing fixed cost (to pump out water, prevent unauthorized entry, etc.). However, if reactivation in the not-too-distant future is likely, this can still be cheaper than abandoning and later building a new mine from scratch. In the next section, we will expand our basic model of entry and exit to include the possibilities of mothballing and reactivation. For the time being, however, we will ignore this additional option and consider only investment and abandonment.[5] Likewise, a producer could open or shut down a mine but not a refinery, but for simplicity we will treat the production of refined copper as one integrated operation.

We will consider a facility that produces 10 million pounds of refined copper per year. To keep the analysis simple, we will ignore the fact that the mine's reserves are limited and will eventually run out; we will assume instead that the mine can operate forever. (This is not too extreme an assumption, since most copper mines can operate for at least 20 or 30 years.) A reasonable number for the cost of building such a mine, smelter, and refinery is $I = \$20$ million, and for the cost of abandonment (largely for cleanup and environmental restoration) is $E = \$2$ million. (These and all other numbers are in 1992 constant dollars.) Average variable cost of production varies across firms in the United States, and even more so across different countries. We will set

---

[5] Brennan and Schwartz (1985) use contingent claims methods to value a copper mine, and focus on the options to mothball and later reactivate the mine.

variable cost at $C = \$0.80$ per pound, about the average for U.S. producers in 1992, but we will also vary this cost to determine its impact on the entry and exit thresholds. (For comparison, the average price of copper was about $1.00 in 1992, but over the 1985–1992 period it fell to as low as $0.60 per pound and rose to over $1.50 per pound.)

A reasonable value for the *real* risk-adjusted annual rate of return for a copper mine or refinery is $\mu = 0.06$, for the average rate of convenience yield (or return shortfall) is $\delta = \mu - \alpha = 0.04$, and for the real risk-free interest rate is $r = 0.04$. Finally, we will take 0.2 as a base value for the volatility parameter, σ, but we will also consider values of that parameter in the range of 0.1 to 0.4, consistent with estimates that differ in different periods of time.[6]

Given these parameter values, equations (9) to (12) can be solved numerically for the constants A_1 and B_2 and the entry and exit thresholds P_H and P_L. Figure 7.2 shows the critical entry and exit thresholds, P_H and P_L, as functions of the volatility parameter σ. Observe that for $\sigma = 0.2$, these thresholds are about $1.35 and $0.55, respectively. For comparison, if there were no uncertainty over future prices ($\sigma = 0$), the thresholds would be $0.88 and $0.79.[7] Hence a very moderate amount of uncertainty causes the zone of inaction to increase dramatically—from $0.88 - 0.79 = \$0.09$ to $1.35 - 0.55 = \$0.80$. Observe that this zone increases as σ increases; if σ is 0.4, the width of this zone is about $1.30.

Figures 7.3 and 7.4 show the dependence of the entry and exit thresholds on the operating cost, C, and on the sunk cost of exiting, E. Observe that as the operating cost increases, both P_H and P_L increase. A higher operating cost reduces the expected flow of profit from, and hence the value of, the project, so that a higher price is required before the firm is willing to invest. In addition, the firm will abandon at a higher threshold price, because it will lose more money when C is higher.

---

[6] See, for example, Bodie and Rosanski (1980) and Brennan (1991) regarding σ. The use of $\delta = 0.04$ for the rate of convenience yield is close to its average value over the past two decades, but one should keep in mind that this parameter has fluctuated widely over time. There have been sustained periods when it has been close to zero, and shorter periods (when the total stock of inventories has been low) during which it has been as high as 30 or 40 percent per year. We have assumed a constant δ to simplify the analysis. For discussions of convenience yield and its behavior, in general and for copper, see Brennan (1991) and Pindyck (1993c,d).

[7] Since the project produces 10 million pounds of copper per year, the NPV of investing (expressed in millions of dollars) is $-20 + 10 P/0.04 - 8/0.04$. (The revenue flow is discounted at rate $\mu = 0.06$ but is expected to grow at rate $\alpha = 0.02$, and the operating cost is discounted at the riskless rate $r = 0.04$.) If $\sigma = 0$, the firm should invest if this NPV > 0, that is, if $P > \$0.88$. Likewise, once the firm is in the market, the NPV of exiting is $-2 - P/0.04 + 8/0.04$, which is positive when $P < \$0.79$.

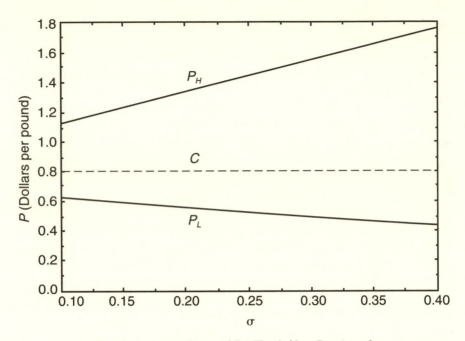

Figure 7.2.   *Copper: Entry and Exit Thresholds as Functions of σ*

Observe that when the abandonment cost E increases, the entry thresh-old P_H also increases. The reason is that for any price P, a higher E reduces the value of the option to abandon an active project, and hence reduces the value of the project, which in turn implies that the price must be higher before the firm is willing to invest in the first place. Likewise, an increase in E reduces the abandonment threshold P_L; the firm must pay more to exercise its aban-donment option, so the price must fall more before it is willing to abandon. Observe, however, that while P_H rises and P_L falls when E increases, they do not rise and fall by very much. The reason is that the value of the option to abandon is largely determined by σ and by the much larger entry cost I, and does not change very much as E is varied.

Figure 7.5 shows the value of an idle firm, $V_0(P)$, and the value of an active firm, $V_1(P)$, both as functions of the price P. (We have used the base case parameter values: $I = \$20$ million, $E = \$2$ million, $C = \$0.80$ per pound, $r = \delta = 0.04$, and $\sigma = 0.2$.) Also shown are the thresholds P_H and P_L. Note that at $P = P_L$, $V_0(P)$ exceeds $V_1(P)$ by the abandonment cost $E = 2$, since at that price it is optimal to exercise the abandonment option, giving up $E + V_1$ and receiving V_0. Likewise, at $P = P_H$ it is optimal to invest, so $V_1 = V_0 + I$.

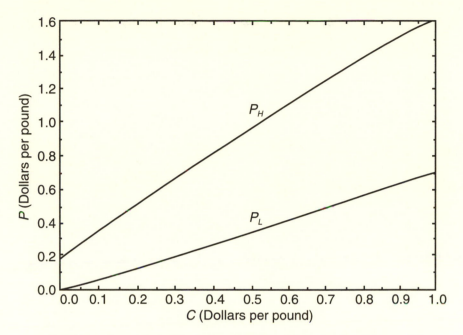

Figure 7.3. *Entry and Exit Thresholds as Functions of Operating Cost C, for* $\sigma = 0.2$

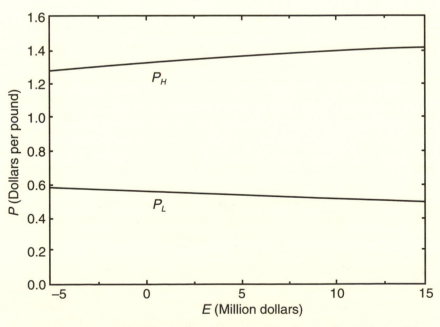

Figure 7.4. *Entry and Exit Thresholds as Functions of Abandonment Cost E, for* $\sigma = 0.2$

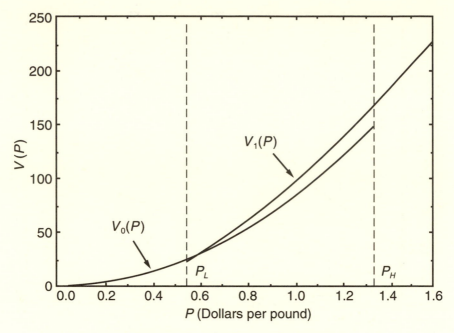

Figure 7.5. $V_0(P)$ and $V_1(P)$ as Functions of P

Finally, Figure 7.6 shows the function $G(P) = V_1(P) - V_0(P)$. Note the S shape of this curve in the region of inaction between P_L and P_H, and the tangency with the horizontal line at I at $P = P_H$, and with the horizontal line at $-E$ at $P = P_L$.

This example can help us understand the behavior of copper producers in the United States and elsewhere during the past two decades. During periods of very low prices (for example, in the mid-1980s, when copper prices had fallen to their lowest levels in real terms since the Great Depression), firms often continued to operate unprofitable mines and smelters that had been opened when prices were high. At other times when prices were high, firms failed to invest in new mines or reopen seemingly profitable ones that had been closed when prices were low. This response of producers to uncertainty had a feedback effect on the price level itself. The reluctance of firms to close down mines during the mid-1980s when demand was weak allowed the price of copper to fall even more than it would have otherwise.

We have assumed here that the price process of copper is exogenous to the firm. In Chapter 8 we will see how the price of a competitively produced commodity can be made endogenous in an equilibrium model of industry

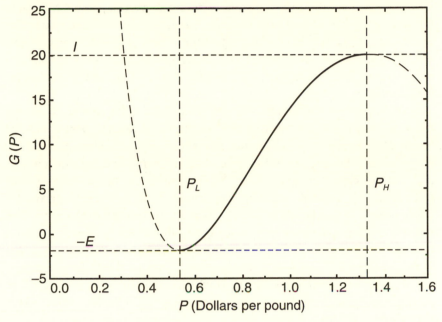

Figure 7.6. $G(P) = V_1(P) - V_0(P)$

behavior. At that point we will return to this example of entry and exit in the copper industry, but in the context of a competitive equilibrium where price is endogenous.

2 Lay-Up, Reactivation, and Scrapping

As mentioned above, a copper producer has other options besides permanently abandoning an operating mine when the price of copper falls. Instead, the mine could be put into a state of temporary suspension, allowing it to be reactivated in the future at a sunk cost much less than the cost of building a new mine from scratch. Plants that are "mothballed" or ships that are "laid up" are examples of this state of temporary suspension.

Mothballing, like permanent abandonment, requires a sunk cost, which we will denote by E_M. In addition, once a plant is mothballed, maintaining the capital requires a cost flow M. The operation can be reactivated in the future at a further sunk cost R. Mothballing only makes sense if the maintenance cost M is less than the cost C of actual operation, and if the reactivation cost R is less than the cost of fresh investment I; we will assume that these conditions are indeed met. Our objective is to determine how the value of an operating project, the value of the opportunity to invest in such a project, and the decision rules for investment, mothballing, reactivation, and scrapping are affected by the various costs I, E_M, M, and R, as well as the volatility of the output price.

As before, we will assume that the price follows the geometric Brownian motion (1). The firm must decide whether and when a plant should be mothballed, taking into account this uncertainty over future prices. Intuition suggests the following general scheme. Starting from a state in which it does not have any kind of capital installed, the firm will make the investment if the price rises to a threshold P_H. The firm will mothball an operating project if the price falls to another threshold P_M. Given a project in mothballs, the firm will reactivate it if the price rises to yet a third threshold P_R. Since the cost of reactivation is less than that of investing from scratch, we expect $P_R < P_H$. If instead the price falls, making reactivation a sufficiently unlikely or remote event, there is a fourth threshold P_S at which the mothballed project will be scrapped altogether to save on maintenance cost. Then the firm will revert to the original idle state.

Of course all these thresholds P_H, P_M, P_R, and P_S are endogenous, and must be determined in terms of the basic parameters. Even more fundamentally, we must ask if the firm will find it optimal to use the mothballing option at all. If the maintenance cost M is sufficiently high, or the reactivation cost R not sufficiently less than the full investment cost I, then the firm might find it better to scrap an operating project directly if the price hits a lower threshold P_L; in that case we are back to the model of the previous section. We must determine endogenously whether mothballing figures in the firm's optimal strategy.

2.A   Rules for Optimal Switches

In the previous section we denoted the cost of abandoning a live project by E. Now we are letting E_M be the cost of mothballing an operating project, and E_S be the cost of scrapping a project already in mothballs. (In the case of a mine, the former may be the cost of firing the miners and the latter the cost of site restoration. With a ship, the latter may be negative, representing the scrap value.) To keep the exposition simple, we will assume that $E_M + E_S = E$, so the cost of directly abandoning an active project is just the sum of the costs of mothballing it first and then abandoning the mothballed project. In practice, going from an operational project to total scrapping may be more or less costly when done via the stage of mothballing. Costs of preparing a ship and moving it to and from the lay-up location may have to be incurred twice, but there may be some saving in labor firing costs if the more gradual route allows the labor force reduction to be achieved by retirement or quits. We leave it to the reader to examine the issues raised by such nonadditivity of costs.

Similar considerations apply to the investment cost I. In principle, one can imagine installing a project in the mothballed state at a cost J, say, and then activating it later at a cost R. However, we see little reason why this indirect route should ever be cheaper than simply investing in an operating project. Hence the firm will never find it optimal to take this route; it will never invest into a mothballed project. By postponing investment until the instant of operation, it can delay spending the first tranche J of capital cost, and save on the flow M of maintenance cost.[8]

This leaves us one less switch to consider among the possible six switches that are conceivable across the three states. Of the remaining five switches—idle to live, live to mothballed, mothballed to scrap, mothballed to live, and live to scrap—the first four are used if mothballing is actually a part of the optimal strategy. Otherwise only the first and last are used. We proceed for a while on the assumption that when price falls to a certain point, mothballing *is* used, and then determine its limits of validity during the course of the analysis.

We will continue to denote the idle and operating states by the labels 0 and 1, respectively, and we introduce the additional label m for the mothballed state. We find the value of the firm in each state as the appropriate combinations of the expected profit or cost streams and the options to switch. The method is exactly the same as that used earlier in this chapter, and in Chapters 5 and 6, so we will sketch out the analysis and omit many of the details.

The firm can be in the idle state over the interval $(0, P_H)$ of prices. Then its value is once again given by equation (4) above:

$$V_0(P) = A_1 \, P^{\beta_1},$$

where A_1 is a constant to be determined. This is just the value of the option to invest. We have as usual eliminated the term in the negative power β_2 by using the fact that $V_0(P)$ must go to zero as P goes to zero.

---

[8] In an oligopolistic industry there may be strategic reasons for holding a project in mothballs, but we do not consider that market structure here.

Similarly, the operating state can prevail over the interval (P_M, ∞), with the value of the firm again given by equation (6) above:

$$V_1(P) = B_2\, P^{\beta_2} + P/\delta - C/r,$$

where the constant B_2 remains to be determined. In the model developed in the previous section, $B_2\, P^{\beta_2}$ represented the value of the option to abandon. Now this term is the value of the option to mothball. As before, the other two terms give the expected present value of continuing operations forever. Of course the mothballing option derives its value from further possibilities of reactivation or scrapping.

The mothballed state can continue over some range of prices (P_S, P_R). Since neither zero nor infinity is included in this range, we cannot eliminate either the positive or the negative power in the option value part of the solution. Therefore the value of the mothballed project is given by

$$V_m(P) = D_1\, P^{\beta_1} + D_2\, P^{\beta_2} - M/r, \qquad (17)$$

where the constants D_1 and D_2 remain to be determined. The first term in equation (17) is the value of the option to reactivate the mothballed project. The second term is the value of the option to scrap the project. Finally, the last term is simply the capitalized maintenance cost, assuming the project remains in the mothballed state forever.

At each switching point, we have appropriate value-matching and smooth-pasting conditions. For the original investment, these conditions are

$$V_0(P_H) = V_1(P_H) - I, \qquad V_0'(P_H) = V_1'(P_H).$$

For mothballing, the conditions are

$$V_1(P_M) = V_m(P_M) - E_M, \qquad V_1'(P_M) = V_m'(P_M).$$

For reactivation,

$$V_m(P_R) = V_1(P_R) - R, \qquad V_m'(P_R) = V_1'(P_R).$$

Finally, for scrapping,

$$V_m(P_S) = V_0(P_S) - E_S, \qquad V_m'(P_S) = V_0'(P_S).$$

This system of eight equations determines the four thresholds P_H, P_M, P_R, P_S and the four option value coefficients A_1, B_2, D_1, D_2. We can solve the equations formally, but then we must ask whether the solution makes economic sense, and thereby determine the limits on the range of parameters where the mothballing option is actually used.

The most promising starting point is the interaction between mothballing and reactivation. Using the functional forms above, the four equations at these two thresholds become

$$-D_1 P_R^{\beta_1} + (B_2 - D_2) P_R^{\beta_2} + P_R/\delta - (C - M)/r = R, \qquad (18)$$

$$-\beta_1 D_1 P_R^{\beta_1 - 1} + \beta_2 (B_2 - D_2) P_R^{\beta_2 - 1} + 1/\delta = 0, \qquad (19)$$

$$-D_1 P_M^{\beta_1} + (B_2 - D_2) P_M^{\beta_2} + P_M/\delta - (C - M)/r = -E_M, \qquad (20)$$

$$-\beta_1 D_1 P_M^{\beta_1 - 1} + \beta_2 (B_2 - D_2) P_M^{\beta_2 - 1} + 1/\delta = 0. \qquad (21)$$

We can regard this as a system of four equations in the four unknowns D_1, $(B_2 - D_2)$, P_R, and P_M, and solve it on its own. Furthermore, the system has exactly the same form as the one we worked with in the previous section for the case of investment and abandonment without the mothballing option; compare equations (18) to (21) with equations (9) to (12) above. We need only reinterpret R as the cost of investment, E_M as the cost of abandonment, and $(C - M)$ as the cost of operation. Then P_R is like the investment threshold from the previous section, and P_M is like the abandonment threshold.

To continue with the analogy to the earlier model, let us define $H(I, E, C)$ as the upper threshold and $L(I, E, C)$ as the lower threshold that solve the investment-abandonment system, each expressed as a function of the lump-sum and flow costs. Remember our comparative static results: both functions H and L are increasing in the flow cost argument C, the function H is increasing in the lump-sum cost arguments I and E, while the function L is decreasing in these two. Now the reactivation and mothballing thresholds of our present model can be written in the form

$$P_R = H(R, E_M, C - M), \qquad P_M = L(R, E_M, C - M).$$

Turn now to the remaining four equations in the eight-equation system above. The value-matching and smooth-pasting conditions for new investment are familiar:

$$-A_1 P_H^{\beta_1} + B_2 P_H^{\beta_2} + P_H/\delta - C/r = I, \qquad (22)$$

$$-\beta_1 A_1 P_H^{\beta_1 - 1} + \beta_2 B_2 P_H^{\beta_2 - 1} + 1/\delta = 0. \qquad (23)$$

Those conditions at the scrapping threshold become

$$(D_2 - A_2) P_S^{\beta_1} + D_2 P_S^{\beta_2} - M/r = -E_S, \qquad (24)$$

$$\beta_1 (D_1 - A_1) P_S^{\beta_1 - 1} + \beta_2 D_2 P_S^{\beta_2 - 1} = 0. \qquad (25)$$

These equations have six unknowns—the thresholds P_H, P_S and the coefficients A_1, B_2, $(D_1 - A_1)$, and D_2. However, the solution to the first group of four equations above gave us two relations among the coefficients; we know $D_1 = (D_1 - A_1) + A_1$ and $(B_2 - D_2)$. Therefore we can complete the solution.

This system is too complicated to grasp analytically, so we will present some numerical simulations that provide more insight into the nature of the solution. However, intuition suggests some general properties of the solution. First, if M and R are both zero, then mothballing is tantamount to costless suspension, and we are back to the basic McDonald-Siegel (1985) model of Chapter 6. Then the mothballing and reactivation triggers both converge to C, and the scrapping trigger collapses to zero. Now consider raising R and M gradually, one at a time.

When R is raised holding M constant, the reactivation threshold P_R will rise and the mothballing threshold P_M will fall, just as the investment and abandonment thresholds did earlier in this chapter when the investment cost increased. The threshold P_H for new investment will rise; when reactivation is more costly, the option of mothballing is less useful, and therefore the firm is more reluctant to invest. Finally, the scrapping threshold P_S will also rise; when reactivation is more costly, the firm will not hold on to a laid-up project as willingly when the price falls.

As we keep on increasing R, the mothballing threshold P_M falls and the scrapping threshold P_S rises. For mothballing to be a part of the optimal strategy, we must have $P_M > P_S$. Therefore the value of R where these two thresholds meet defines the boundary of the parameter space where mothballing ceases to be relevant. Write P_C for the common value of the two at this boundary. Adding the value-matching conditions (20) and (24) satisfied by the common P_C, and likewise for the smooth-pasting conditions (21) and (25), we find

$$-A_1 \, P_C^{\beta_1} + B_2 \, P_C^{\beta_2} + P_C/\delta - C/r = -(E_M + E_S) = -E,$$

$$-\beta_1 \, A_1 \, P_C^{\beta_1-1} + \beta_2 \, B_2 \, P_C^{\beta_2-1} + 1/\delta = 0.$$

These are exactly the abandonment equations (11) and (12) that, together with the corresponding pair for investment (9) and (10), were satisfied by the thresholds P_H and P_L earlier in this chapter when mothballing was not available at all. Thus the whole story fits together as it should. For high enough values of R, the firm ignores the possibility of mothballing and switches optimally between idle and active states as before.

Next hold R fixed and raise M. This reduces $(C - M)$, the flow cost saving from mothballing. Therefore both P_R and P_M fall; the firm will mothball a live project less readily, and reactivate a mothballed project more readily. However, P_H and P_S will rise; the firm will be more reluctant to invest at all, and will scrap a mothballed project more readily. Once again a falling P_M and a rising P_S will meet when M rises to a critical level; for any higher values of M, mothballing will not be used.

There will also be a trade-off between the critical values of R and M that define the boundaries of the use of mothballing. When R is larger, the critical value of M will be smaller, and vice versa.

2.B Numerical Results

Now we turn to numerical solutions to verify these intuitions. The parameters of greatest interest are the flow maintenance cost M and the reactivation cost R. To focus on them, we will assume for the rest of this exposition that the lay-up and scrapping costs E_M and E_S are both zero; then so is their sum, the cost of direct abandonment, E. Shortly we will present another numerical example that illustrates the effects of making these parameters nonzero.

We normalize to $C = 1$. We assume a risk-neutral firm, with $r = 0.05$. The price process has $\alpha = 0$ and $\sigma = 0.2$. Then $\mu = r = 0.05$, and $\delta = \mu - \alpha = 0.05$. The lump-sum cost of investing is $I = 2$, and there is no lump-sum cost of disinvesting, so $E = 0$. With these numbers, and ignoring the possibility of mothballing, the investment and abandonment thresholds turn out to be $P_H = 1.5977$ and $P_L = 0.7135$.

Now allow mothballing, and consider two cases, $M = 0.01$ and $M = 0.05$. For each, we consider a range of values of R. The resulting values of the four thresholds are shown in Table 7.1. The effects of varying R for fixed M can be seen separately in each case detailed there. In Case 1, the maintenance cost is low; $M = 0.01$. Now mothballing is used over some range of prices until the critical limit of $\overline{R} \approx 1.76$; once R exceeds this $\overline{R}$, mothballing is never used. As R rises over the range 0 to $\overline{R}$, (1) P_H rises to its level in the absence of mothballing, (2) P_M falls and P_S rises until, when $R = \overline{R}$, the two meet at P_L, (3) P_R rises, only to become irrelevant once R reaches $\overline{R}$.

In Case 2, the maintenance cost is higher: $M = 0.05$. Now mothballing is relevant over a shorter range; $\overline{R}$ is only a little larger than 1.

The general pattern is easier to see from Figure 7.7. Fixing M at a relatively low value, the various thresholds are shown as functions of R by the thicker curves. Mothballing is part of the optimal strategy when $R < \overline{R}$. When $R \geq \overline{R}$, the two thresholds P_M and P_S merge into P_L. When a higher value of M is considered, the curves shift to the positions shown by the thinner lines. The P_M curve shifts down, the P_S curve shifts up, and the two meet at

Table 7.1. *Mothballing and Scrapping Thresholds*
(Parameters: $r = 0.05$, $\delta = 0.05$, $\sigma = 0.2$, $C = 1$, $I = 2$, $E = 0$)

		Case 1: Lower cost $M = 0.01$		
R	P_H	P_R	P_M	P_S
0.2	1.557	1.202	0.8322	0.2937
0.4	1.568	1.272	0.7987	0.3171
0.6	1.576	1.325	0.7770	0.3424
0.8	1.582	1.372	0.7608	0.3713
1.0	1.587	1.413	0.7478	0.4061
1.2	1.591	1.451	0.7369	0.4498
1.4	1.594	1.487	0.7276	0.5085
1.6	1.597	1.521	0.7195	0.5955
1.7634	1.598	1.548	0.7135	0.7135
		Case 2: Higher cost $M = 0.05$		
R	P_H	P_R	P_M	P_S
0.1	1.577	1.108	0.8246	0.5240
0.2	1.583	1.157	0.7968	0.5430
0.3	1.587	1.194	0.7783	0.5612
0.4	1.590	1.225	0.7644	0.5793
0.5	1.592	1.253	0.7530	0.5978
0.6	1.594	1.278	0.7434	0.6170
0.7	1.596	1.301	0.7351	0.6371
0.8	1.597	1.323	0.7278	0.6584
0.9	1.597	1.343	0.7212	0.6811
1.0307	1.598	1.370	0.7135	0.7135

a lower value $\overline{R}$. The P_H curve shifts up to reach its final constant level at this new lower $\overline{R}$. The P_R curve shifts down, only to end when mothballing ceases to be used. Note also that as R increases starting at zero, the restarting and mothballing thresholds spread apart very rapidly. Since we have set the mothballing cost $E_M = 0$, the sum of the costs of the pair of switches, namely, $R + E_M$, is small, and we have an instance of the cube root formula (16) above.

One further numerical experiment is of interest, namely, making both R and M small to drive the mothballing model to the limit of our model in Chapter 6. This does happen, but the approach to the limit is very slow, in

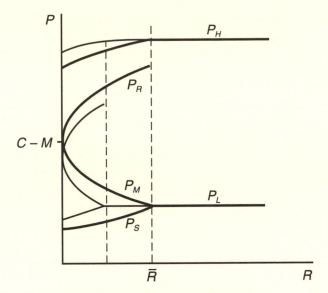

Figure 7.7. *Mothballing and Scrapping*

keeping with the general insight that even small sunk costs matter a great deal when there is ongoing uncertainty. Thus, keeping $C = 1$, etc., as above, even when we reduce the costs associated with mothballing to $M = 0.001$ and $R = 0.02$, we find $P_R = 1.089$ and $P_M = 0.919$, each about 10 percent away from their common limiting value, namely 1. The scrapping threshold becomes $P_S = 0.0963$, again significantly above its limit of zero.

2.C   Example: Building, Mothballing, and Scrapping Oil Tankers

The numerical solutions presented above help to illustrate the qualitative dependence of the optimal thresholds on the various cost parameters. However, it is useful to also examine optimal investment, mothballing, reactivation, and scrapping decisions for a real-world example. As with our copper industry example, this can give us a better appreciation for the importance of sunk costs and uncertainty, and also show how the model can be applied in practice.

We will apply our model to the oil tanker industry. Oil tankers provide a particularly good example since the potential or actual owners of tankers face considerable profit uncertainty, as well as substantial sunk costs. The uncertainty arises because the market for oil tankers is very competitive, and tanker rates (the revenue per day for the use of a tanker, that is, the price P

in our model) fluctuate considerably as oil prices fluctuate, as the geographical distribution of oil production and consumption change, and as the supply of tankers changes. Also, sunk costs are important because of the considerable expense of building a new tanker and maintaining or reactivating one that is mothballed.

There are four general sizes of oil tankers—small tankers, with capacities around 35,000 deadweight tons (dwt), medium tankers, with capacities around 85,000 dwt, large tankers, with capacities around 140,000 dwt, and, since the mid-1970s, "Very Large Crude Carriers" (VLCC's), with capacities of about 270,000 dwt. Revenue rates and construction, operating, and other costs do not increase linearly with tanker capacity, so the economics of investment, mothballing, etc., will vary across these different categories of tankers. We will focus on one particular category—medium tankers with an 85,000-dwt capacity.[9]

The average cost of building a new tanker with an 85,000-dwt capacity is about $I = \$40$ million. (All costs and revenues are expressed in 1992 dollars.) The one-time cost of mothballing a tanker is $E_M = \$200,000$, the cost of scrapping a mothballed tanker is $E_s = -\$3.4$ million (that is, the tanker has a positive scrap value), and the cost of reactivating a mothballed tanker of this size is $R = \$790,000$. The annual cost of maintaining a mothballed tanker is $M = \$515,000$. Finally, given fuel and labor costs, the annual 1992 operating cost for this tanker is $C = \$4.4$ million. In 1992, this tanker would earn a gross revenue of about $P = \$7.3$ million per year. We have assumed that P follows a geometric Brownian motion, and the drift α and volatility σ for that process can be estimated from the sample mean and sample variance of an actual time series for gross revenue. Using quarterly data for 1980 through mid-1992, we found that $\alpha = 0$ and $\sigma = 0.15$. Finally, we use a value of 0.05 for both the real risk-free interest rate r, and the risk-adjusted rate μ (so that $\delta = 0.05$.)[10]

Figure 7.8 shows the critical thresholds P_H, P_R, P_M, and P_S as functions of the one-time reactivation cost R. Note that for our base value of $790,000,

---

[9]For a general introduction to the oil tanker industry, see Rawlinson and Porter (1986). Goncalves (1992) has also used contingent claims methods to examine optimal investment decisions for tankers, as well as the relation between spot and long-term contract prices.

[10]We obtained time series data for revenue, costs, and other industry variables from Marsoft, Inc., of Boston. Our thanks to Dr. Arlie G. Sterling, the President of Marsoft, for making this data available and giving us advice on a variety of economic issues related to this industry. Thanks are also due to Victor Norman and Siri Pettersen Strandenes of the Norwegian School of Economics and Business, Bergen, who also provided data and advice.

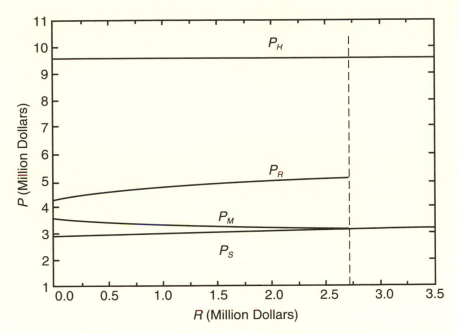

Figure 7.8. *Critical Thresholds as Functions of Reactivation Cost R*

the 1992 average gross revenue of $7.3 million per year would have been sufficiently high to reactivate a mothballed tanker, but well below the threshold revenue of about $9.5 million per year needed to invest in a new tanker. Consistent with this result, there was indeed little or no investment in new tankers during 1992. Observe that P_R and P_S rise as R is increased, and P_M falls, but not very fast. Mothballing remains a viable option as long as this cost of reactivation is below about $2.7 million. The investment threshold P_H also rises as R rises (although so slowly that it is hard to discern from the graph); a higher R reduces the value of a tanker, and therefore raises the revenue that a firm must expect to receive before it is willing to invest.[11]

Figure 7.9 shows the optimal thresholds as functions of the one-time cost of mothballing an operating tanker, E_M. Observe that the qualitative

---

[11] Unlike Figure 7.7, the curves for P_R and P_M do not meet on the vertical axis in the cube root form, because in drawing the earlier figure we assumed the cost of mothballing to be zero, which is not the case in this numerical example.

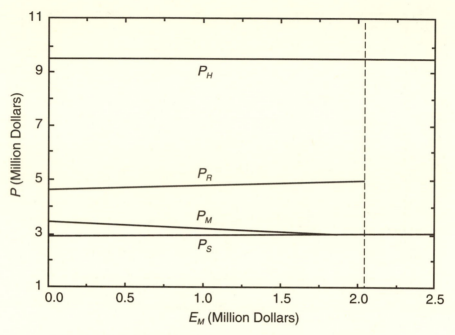

Figure 7.9. *Critical Thresholds as Functions of One-Time Cost of Mothballing E_M*

dependence of the thresholds on E_M is the same as it is on R. Values of E_M above \$1 million are unrealistic (recall that our base value is \$200,000), but we have included this larger range for illustrative purposes. Note that mothballing remains an option as long as E_M is below \$2.1 million.

Figure 7.10 shows the optimal thresholds as functions of annual cost of maintaining a mothballed tanker, M. As the figure makes clear, this is a critical parameter in determining whether mothballing is a viable option for the firm; note that mothballing remains an option only up to an M of about \$720,000, and our base value of \$515,000 is not far from this value. Remember that higher values of M reduce the value of a tanker and thereby raise the threshold for investment. A higher value of M also makes mothballing less desirable and therefore reduces P_r and P_m, and raises P_s.

Figure 7.11 shows the four critical thresholds as functions of the annual cost of operation, C. As with a higher value of M, a higher operating cost reduces the value of the tanker, and thereby raises the threshold P_H required for investment. As one would expect, however, changes in the operating cost have a much greater effect on the value of a tanker, and hence on P_H, than

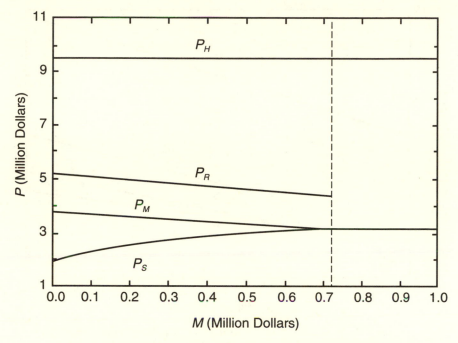

Figure 7.10. *Critical Thresholds as Functions of Annual Maintenance Cost M*

do changes in the maintenance cost M. Also, because a higher operating cost reduces the value of an operating tanker, it raises the threshold P_R at which a mothballed tanker is reactivated, and raises the thresholds P_M and P_R, so that the revenue P need not fall as far before the firm is willing to mothball or scrap its tanker.

Finally, Figure 7.12 shows the critical thresholds as functions of σ, the standard deviation of annual percentage changes in the revenue P. Observe that the thresholds, and especially P_H and P_S, are quite sensitive to σ. As we saw earlier with our copper example, for large values of σ, the zone of inaction widens considerably. Also, note that if σ is less than about 0.1, P_M and P_S coincide, and mothballing is not an option used by the firm. The reason is that mothballing is useful only if there is a reasonable probability of a substantial increase in revenue in the near future (so that the tanker will be reactivated). With $\sigma < 0.1$, the probability of a sufficiently large increase in revenue is too small to make mothballing economical, given the costs of mothballing, reactivation, and maintenance.

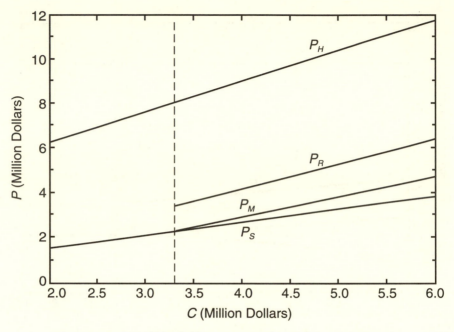

Figure 7.11. *Critical Thresholds as Functions of Annual Cost of Operation C*

3   Guide to the Literature

The pioneering article on the joint decisions to invest and abandon is Brennan and Schwartz (1985). They construct a very general model of the decision to open, close, and mothball a mine producing a natural resource whose price fluctuates over time. The finiteness of the total stock in the mine introduces addditional complexities beyond all the issues considered in this chapter. In fact the very complexity of the model conceals some important concepts. Having obtained the system of equations characterizing the price thresholds for investment and abandonment, Brennan and Schwartz immediately resort to numerical solutions. They obtain the ratio of the entry and exit threshold prices, and show that it exceeds 1 for reasonable parameter values.

Dixit (1989a) isolates the entry and exit decision from issues of lay-up or finite stocks. This allows some analytical results and insights. In particular, the entry and exit threshold prices can separately be compared to the myopic or Marshallian criteria of full and variable costs, respectively. This clarifies the role of the time value of the separate options to invest and to abandon,

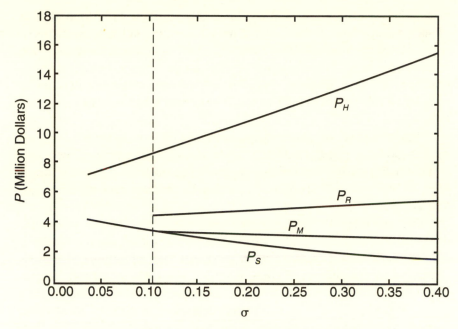

Figure 7.12. *Critical Thresholds as Functions of Volatility σ*

or more generally, the option value of the status quo. Our exposition closely follows Dixit's treatment.

Some of the earliest work on optimal mothballing decisions was by Mossin (1968), who developed a model in which operating revenue follows a trendless random walk with upper and lower reflecting barriers, and in which there is no possibility of scrapping. He calculated the optimal revenue levels at which it is optimal to mothball and reactivate the project. The more general model of Brennan and Schwartz (1985) includes the possibility of mothballing as well as active operation and abandonment. However, they confuse the transition to the two states from an active state, by using the same lower threshold symbol for mothballing as for abandonment. When they come to numerical solutions they specialize to a model where the maintenance cost is zero; then scrapping is never used and they consider switches between just two states—operation and mothballing. Once again our approach follows the subsequent but somewhat clearer analysis of Dixit (1988).

The models we studied in this chapter are instances of the general problem of optimal switching among a number of alternatives in response to changing economic conditions. Each switch is an exercise of an option, and each switch yields an asset that combines a payoff flow with the option of switching again. Thus we have a set of linked or compound options, and must price them simultaneously. There is a large body of literature analyzing such compound options, either from a general theoretical perspective or aiming at specific applications. Geske (1979) is an early example of this kind in financial economics; subsequent articles include Geske and Johnson (1984) and Carr (1988).

Turning to real investment decisions, Kulatilaka and Marcus (1988) develop a model of switches between two modes with three time periods, and indicate how it can be extended to many modes and switches. They also survey the early literature on real options by placing the different models within their framework.

Fine and Freund (1990) examine a general two-period model where the firm must choose its capacity before uncertainty is resolved, and it can choose either specific capital (suitable for a particular kind of output) or flexible capital (which can produce all kinds of output, albeit at greater cost). Triantis and Hodder (1990) have a similar model in continuous time. He and Pindyck (1992) go further by allowing subsequent expansion of capacity. In all these models, option value is even more important, because by waiting the firm preserves the opportunity of making a better investment later, and not just that of not investing at all, as was the case in the models of Chapters 5 and 6.

Bentolila and Bertola (1990) examine employment decisions of firms when there are hiring and firing costs. Dixit (1989b,c) considers production and import-export choices when exchange rates fluctuate. This builds on earlier work by Baldwin and Krugman (1989); see also Krugman (1989). Dumas (1992) and Krugman (1988) develop such models at a general equilibrium level to endogenize the exchange rate process. Kogut and Kulatilaka (1993) consider multinational firms' decisions to shift production from one country to another in response to exchange rate movements. Van Wijnbergen (1985) constructed a two-period model of capital outflows from less-developed countries in a context of policy uncertainty.

Part IV
Industry Equilibrium

Chapter 8

Dynamic Equilibrium in a Competitive Industry

IN CHAPTERS 5 through 7, we examined a variety of investment and disinvestment decisions for a single firm. Throughout, we assumed that the firm has a monopoly right to invest in a given project, and we ignored the possibility of other firms entering in competition.[1] The profit flows of an operational project were subject to ongoing shocks. Since we were assuming that the project would yield a fixed output flow, we could model these shocks as an exogenous price process. We found that the textbook Marshallian present value criteria or comparisons of price and cost were very far from the true optimal choices of the firm. With moderate amounts of uncertainty, investment was justified only when the current price exceeded the long-run average cost, or the current rate of return on the sunk cost of investment exceeded the cost of capital, usually by a large margin. Similarly, abandonment was triggered not when the price fell below average variable cost, or when the current operating profit became negative, but only when the loss became sufficiently large. The reason was the option value of waiting before making irreversible decisions in conditions of evolving uncertainty.

---

[1]In Chapter 5 we mentioned that the rate of return shortfall on the value of a project, $\delta = \mu - \alpha$, where μ is the competitive expected return on an asset with equivalent risk, could reflect the possibility of entry by other firms. However, we did not explicitly model entry, nor did we offer any justification for why it should lead to a constant rate of return shortfall.

In practice, most firms do not enjoy monopoly rights to invest, but instead must consider the possible entry of new competitors, or expansion of existing ones. This raises a fundamental doubt concerning our earlier conclusions. The opportunity to wait, and its value, depend on what the firm's competitors do. With free entry, should this value not be reduced to zero? Would that not restore the Marshallian criteria comparing price to the long-run average cost in the case of investment, and to the average variable cost for disinvestment? Thus the reader might suspect that the theory of an individual firm would not survive an extension of the scope of the analysis to the level of industry equilibrium.

In this chapter and the following one, we take up these questions. The answers are largely reassuring. What happens to the value of waiting depends not only on the nature of competition, but also on the nature of the uncertainty. We find that when uncertainty is firm-specific, a firm's value of waiting survives, and our firm-level analysis can readily be extended to the industry equilibrium. For aggregate or industry-wide uncertainty, the value of waiting for any one firm does drop to zero, but that does not restore the Marshallian criteria of price-cost comparisons. The optimal investment and disinvestment threshold prices differ from costs just the same way as they did in our firm-level analysis of Chapters 5–7, albeit for a different reason. We can no longer specify the stochastic process of the price exogenously. Price is an endogenous variable of industry equilibrium. We must trace the uncertainty to a deeper level, namely, the demand and cost conditions. The endogenous feedback of new entry on price is what generates the gap between the Marshallian and the optimal rules when uncertainty is industry-wide.

The earlier analysis of the monopoly firm also serves a useful pedagogical purpose, as well as a substantive one. All of our industry-level analysis is conducted using the same techniques (dynamic programming and contingent claims analysis) that were developed and illustrated in the preceding chapters. Thus that work provides a simpler setting for readers to become familiar with the new methods.

This chapter concerns the basic theory of industry equilibrium. In other words, we take the firm's decision model of Chapters 5–7, and build it as directly as possible into a model of industry equilibrium. Then in the next chapter we take up various extensions and implications. We allow for heterogeneity among firms, and we consider a simple example of imperfect competition among a small number of firms in the industry.

Finally, and perhaps most importantly, in Chapter 9 we also examine issues of policy regarding investment. If firms' irreversible choices under uncertainty are significantly influenced by the option value of the status quo and therefore characterized by considerable inertia, should the government attempt to encourage investment? How will various policy instruments affect investment? In particular, what will be the effect of government policies to reduce uncertainty (for example, through the use of price controls)? What will be the effect of uncertainty concerning the government's own actions (for example, uncertainty over future tax rates and regulatory changes)? Such questions must be examined at the industry level if they are to be useful guides to policy in many practical situations; therefore these chapters are the right place for their study.

Before we start on this program, we should say a few words about the nature of irreversibilities in relation to industry-wide and firm-specific forms of uncertainty. Investment is partially or totally irreversible when some or all of its costs are sunk. In Chapter 1, Section 3 we offered some general reasons why this happens. Perhaps the most prominent was the specificity of the plant and equipment itself. This applies with greater force in the case of industry-wide uncertainty than for firm-specific uncertainty. A steel plant cannot be used outside the steel industry. If one steel firm suffers an idiosyncratic negative shock, it can sell its plant to another firm and get fairly good value for it, so the irreversibility is less severe. However, if the whole industry suffers a negative shock, then the resale value of the plant is small and the irreversibility is large. Thus we should expect that our theory has greater significance in the context of aggregate uncertainty. Of course, even for firm-specific shocks, some investment expenditures are sunk, for example, any research or exploration costs incurred in the process of discovering the firm-specific random shock. Also, even nonspecific capital (such as automobiles, computers, and office equipment) is subject to a loss in resale value due to asymmetric information about product quality [that is, the "lemons" problem, illustrated by Akerlof (1970)].

1 The Basic Intuition

Before turning to the mathematical models, we enlarge on the intuition for the results to come. First suppose the uncertainty is firm-specific. Thus different firms experience independent shocks to demand (for example, a shift of fashion in an industry with differentiated products) or cost (for example, a chance improvement in entrepreneurial skills). As in the previous chapters, suppose each firm's shock has positive serial correlation; in actual models we will specify these shocks as Brownian motions. Even though the firms are identical ex ante, a firm that experiences a favorable shock does sneak a lead over its rivals, and therefore does have the opportunity to wait and see how permanent this lead is before committing sunk capital. Thus our option value analysis survives, and can be built into a model of industry equilibrium.

Now consider industry-wide uncertainty, for example, demand shocks when the product is homogeneous. For the moment, suppose investment is totally irreversible. In this environment, favorable and unfavorable shocks to industry demand or cost have asymmetric effects on the price. An unfavorable demand shock would lead to a lower price along the existing firms' supply curve. However, a favorable shock, if sufficiently large, causes entry or expansion of firms. This shifts the supply curve to the right, dampening the price increase. Thus the stochastic process of demand shocks translates into the stochastic process of price shocks in an asymmetric way. The upside is limited because of new entry, while the downside is unaffected. Our previous analysis of a monopoly firm's investment decision assumed a more symmetric Brownian motion process. Now we must modify it to allow an asymmetric price process. The asymmetry reduces the expected payoff from investment, and that is why the threshold price that justifies investment turns out to exceed the Marshallian long-run average cost. Similarly, when exit or abandonment is possible, the exit of other firms puts a floor on the price process, making each firm more willing to accept a period of losses.

Most of this chapter is an elaboration of this intuition. For that purpose we use a model that has two-fold merit in this context: it is a natural generalization of the monopoly firm model of Chapters 5–7, and it brings out the intuition in the simplest way possible.

We consider an industry with a large number of firms. Each firm is risk neutral,[2] acts competitively, and has rational expectations about the underlying stochastic processes and the decision rules of other firms. Each firm has the capacity to produce the flow of one unit of output, which it can activate by incurring a sunk cost. There are no variable costs of production, and the elasticity of demand is large enough to ensure that each firm that has paid its sunk cost will in fact want to produce at its capacity level.[3]

The prices of different firms' outputs can change unpredictably because of aggregate industry demand shocks, or because of firm-specific demand shocks that reflect changing relative tastes for the firms' products. Hence one firm's output can sell at a price that includes an exogenous premium or

---

[2]Extension to a CAPM setting is straightforward and merely introduces some extra notation in this context, so we leave it to interested readers.

[3]With Q firms, this requires a price elasticity in excess of $1/Q$, so the restriction entailed by this assumption is very weak.

discount relative to the market average. This premium or discount follows a known stochastic process, and changes in it constitute the firm-specific shocks. In addition, the market demand curve itself is subject to aggregate shocks that follow another stochastic process. More specifically, we assume that the price for any one firm's unit of output is given by

$$P = XY D(Q), \tag{1}$$

where X is the firm-specific shock, Y is the industry-wide shock, Q is the current output flow, and $D(Q)$ is a decreasing function, comprising the non-stochastic part of the industry's inverse demand curve. As each firm produces one unit of output, Q equals the number of currently active firms, which we treat as a continuous variable.[4]

Now we can state the intuition concerning the asymmetric effects of uncertainty in a different and more precise way in the context of this specification. We know from the general theory of choice under uncertainty that greater uncertainty will increase the expected value of an action if the payoff is convex in the random variable, and decrease it if the payoff is concave. Let us consider the simple case where the underlying uncertainty is symmetric, interpreted as equal up or down shifts of the future values of X or Y with equal probabilities. We will contrast the effects of this uncertainty in the firm-specific (X-shock) case and industry-wide (Y-shock) case.

Consider firm-specific uncertainty first. The X-shock translates proportionately into price uncertainty, which in turn translates proportionately into profit flow uncertainty. If the firm invests immediately, the distribution of its future profit flows is a linear function of X, and its expected value is unaffected by an increase in uncertainty. However, if the firm waits, it is able to reduce its downside risk by choosing not to invest if the price falls, while preserving the upside potential to invest if the price rises. Thus the consequence of waiting is that the payoff to the firm is a convex function of X, so the expected value of waiting rises with uncertainty in X. This contrast between the effects of uncertainty on the expected values of the payoff from investing immediately versus waiting explains why greater uncertainty raises the "option value" premium on waiting.

Now consider industry-wide uncertainty. The firm knows that if Y rises, this makes entry just as attractive for other firms as for itself. However, when

---

[4]Our treatment of the resulting continuum of random variables and their laws of large numbers is decidedly heuristic, but the results are intuitively clear, and a formal rigorous treatment would be far too lengthy and difficult for the present purpose. See Judd (1985) for the basis of the rigorous theory.

other firms enter, the industry supply curve shifts to the right, and the price rises less than proportionately with Y. Therefore price is a concave function of Y, and then so is the profit flow. Greater uncertainty in Y now reduces the expected value of investing relative to that of not investing. That is why the firm requires a higher current profitability (in excess of the Marshallian normal return) before it will invest.

We should stress the similarity as well as the difference between the two scenarios. In each, the underlying symmetric demand shock translates into an asymmetric profit flow shock; but this happens in very different ways in the two cases. In the case of firm-specific uncertainty, the downside of the profit shock is cushioned by the possibility of waiting. Thus greater uncertainty makes waiting more valuable relative to investing at once. In the case of industry-wide uncertainty, any one firm in the mass of competitive potential firms has a zero value of waiting. However, the upside profit potential is cut off by the prospect of entry of other firms. Therefore greater uncertainty reduces the value of investing relative to that of not investing at all.

In reality there are several other factors that can affect the convexity or concavity of profit flows as a function of the underlying shock variable. If the firm can adjust some variable inputs instantaneously, then its profit flow becomes a convex function of the price, as we saw in Chapter 6, Section 3. In addition, in Chapter 11 we will see that when the firm can add to its capital stock, and its output flow is given by a production function, there can be other ways by which the marginal profitability of an incremental investment becomes convex in price. However, the above intuition still operates similarly. For example, with firm-specific uncertainty, the possibility of waiting cuts off the downside risk and makes the profit flow an *even more* convex function of the underlying shock variable. In most of Chapters 8 and 9, however, we will leave aside these additional sources of convexity. We will define each firm as the possessor of a technology to install and operate a single discrete project of fixed size, and focus on the two kinds of asymmetries explained just above.

2   Aggregate Uncertainty

Despite the simplicity of the underlying intuition, the general model of uncertainty is quite difficult to set up and solve formally. The ideas are easier to explain by constructing some special cases that together span the complexity of the general one, so that is how we will proceed. In this section and the next, we consider only the industry-wide shock Y. Then, in Section 4, we deal with purely firm-specific uncertainty. Finally, some insights that do depend in an essential way on the joint presence of the two kinds of uncertainty are examined in the context of a simple but general model in Section 5.

When all uncertainty is industry-wide, the multiplicative factor X in the general demand curve (1) is constant, so we can just set it equal to 1. Then the industry's inverse demand curve becomes

$$P = Y D(Q). \tag{2}$$

The aggregate shock Y will follow the geometric Brownian motion process

$$dY = \alpha Y \, dt + \sigma Y \, dz. \tag{3}$$

On the production side, we assume that there is a large number of risk-neutral competitive firms. Each firm can undertake a single irreversible investment, requiring an initial sunk cost I. Once this investment is made, it yields a flow of one unit of output forever with no variable cost of production. We embed such firms in an industry by supposing that each unit of output is very small relative to the total industry output Q, so that each firm is an infinitesimal price taker. When Q firms are active, the short-run equilibrium price can be determined from equation (2) above.

As we discussed before, this is the simplest continuation of the model of Chapters 5–7 that serves our present purpose. Later and in Chapter 9, we introduce various generalizations, where each firm has some variable cost, short-run output variability, exit possibilities, etc., where the shocks affect demand in more general ways, and where the industry has some imperfect competition.

To set the stage for the competitive industry equilibrium, think of the usual textbook static model. The industry price—a single number—is parametric to each firm. The sum of the individual firms' optimum quantity responses to the price constitutes the industry's supply function. The equilibrium price is determined by the condition equating industry demand and supply. In our dynamic world with uncertainty, the corresponding equilibrium concept is one of rational expectations. Each firm takes as exogenous the whole stochastic process of the price. So we start with a price process, let all firms respond to it, and then find the process that clears the market at each instant. This is a function or a mapping that takes us from one stochastic process to another. We have an equilibrium if we get the same price process that we started with, or in other words, a *fixed point* of the mapping.

Since a stochastic process as a whole is a complex mathematical object—a vector in an uncountably infinite-dimensional function space—finding such a fixed point in full generality is far too difficult. Luckily, the solution to our problem can be found using a much simpler method.

In an interval of time when no new entry takes place, Q is fixed, so P is proportional to Y and equation (3) gives

$$dP = \alpha\, P\, dt + \sigma\, P\, dz. \tag{4}$$

A potential entrant observes this process, and interprets a high price as a signal of a high level of demand. Intuition suggests that there should be an upper threshold level $\overline{P}$ which, if reached, will trigger new entry. As soon as any one new firm enters, Q increases, and price decreases along the demand curve that applies for that instant. Thus, if the price ever climbs to $\overline{P}$, it is immediately brought back to a slightly lower level. In technical terms, the threshold $\overline{P}$ becomes an upper *reflecting barrier* on the price process.

Of course firms rationally anticipate all this. Thus the price process from the perspective of any one firm is a modification of the geometric Brownian motion process of equation (4). That process is valid as long as $P < \overline{P}$. However, the price cannot go any higher; an upper reflecting barrier is imposed at $\overline{P}$.

In Chapters 5–7 we studied a monopoly firm's entry decision when it faced a geometric Brownian price process. Now we see that a competitive firm's entry decision is a similar problem, except that the price process has a ceiling at $\overline{P}$ imposed by this firm's rational expectation of other firms' entry decisions. So we must reexamine a firm's optimal entry decision, taking into account this new price process.

The solution is again characterized by a threshold P^*, such that the firm on which we focus will choose to enter if the price rises to P^*. Since all firms are identical, industry equilibrium requires this firm's entry threshold to equal its rational expectation of all other firms' threshold. So we start with a trial $\overline{P}$, and solve one firm's decision problem to find its P^*. The fixed point of the process, namely, $P^* = \overline{P}$, determines the industry equilibrium. Note how the intuition or guess that the equilibrium price process is a geometric Brownian motion with a reflecting ceiling has simplified the calculation. We need to look for the fixed point of a chain of reasoning that takes us from one number to another, instead of a mapping on a whole function space of general stochastic processes.

2.A   The Value of an Active Firm

The first step in the equilibrium calculation is to find the value of an established firm facing a price process of the stipulated type. Since the future price path depends on the current price level P, the expected present value of the firm's future profits is a function of P, which we denote by $v(P)$. If the price process were not restricted upward by the reflecting barrier, we would have $v(P) = P/\delta$, where $\delta = r - \alpha$ is the shortfall between the discount rate (the risk-free interest rate in this case) and the expected rate of growth of P when it is below the barrier.[5] The reflecting barrier at $\overline{P}$ cuts off some of the upside potential for prices and profits, so the firm's value must in fact be less than P/δ. We will find a formula for the correction.

Start at an initial price $P < \overline{P}$. In a sufficiently small interval of time dt, the price process is almost sure to stay below the ceiling. Then we can carry out the usual dynamic programming or contingent claims analysis to obtain the familiar differential equation

$$\tfrac{1}{2}\sigma^2 P^2 v''(P) + (r - \delta) P v'(P) - r v(P) + P = 0. \tag{5}$$

The general solution to the equation should also be familiar:

$$v(P) = B\, P^{\beta_1} + P/\delta, \tag{6}$$

where B is a constant to be determined, and β_1 is the positive root of the fundamental quadratic

$$\mathcal{Q} \equiv \tfrac{1}{2}\sigma^2 \beta(\beta - 1) + (r - \delta)\beta - r = 0.$$

In fact $\beta_1 > 1$ under the usual conditions $r > 0$ and $\delta > 0$.

This conforms to the intuition stated above: P/δ would be the value of the firm in the absence of the price ceiling, so $B\, P_1^\beta$ must be the correction due to the ceiling. Therefore B should be negative. The interpretation also explains why we left out the term involving the negative root of the quadratic. If the current price P is very small, the barrier $\overline{P}$ is unlikely to be reached except in the far future. Then the correction arising from the barrier should become small. However, a negative power of P goes to infinity as P goes to zero; therefore, that term should not appear in the solution.

To determine the value of the constant B we look at the upper end point. From a starting point very close to the reflecting barrier $\overline{P}$, the price is almost sure to fall during the next small time interval. If the value function has a negative (respectively, positive) slope at this point, there will be sure arbitrage profits (respectively, losses) to be made. To rule this possibility out, we must have

$$v'(\overline{P}) \equiv \beta_1 B\, \overline{P}^{\beta_1 - 1} + 1/\delta = 0. \tag{7}$$

---

[5]Recall that we have assumed that the firm is risk neutral. Alternatively, we could have assumed that spanning holds, and that μ is the competitive risk-adjusted discount rate for an asset or portfolio of assets perfectly correlated with dz in equation (4); then δ would equal $\mu - \alpha$. For a review of this point, see Chapter 6, especially Section 1.B.

This looks like a smooth-pasting condition, but it is not a consequence of any optimization. Such a condition holds at any reflecting barrier for a diffusion process.[6]

Now we can solve for B from equation (7) to get

$$B = -\overline{P}^{1-\beta_1} / (\beta_1 \, \delta).$$

Note that $B < 0$; as explained earlier, the barrier cuts off some upside price potential, so the correction to the value is a reduction. Substituting for B into (6), we have

$$v(P) = \frac{P}{\delta} - \frac{1}{\delta\beta_1} \, P^{\beta_1} \, \overline{P}^{1-\beta_1}. \tag{8}$$

2.B   Equilibrium

The quick way to find the industry's equilibrium is to use a dynamic zero excess profit condition. At $\overline{P}$, the common entry threshold for all firms, each firm is just indifferent between entering and staying out, so the value of being in, $v(\overline{P})$, must exactly equal the entry cost I. Using equation (8) above, this gives

$$\overline{P} = \frac{\beta_1}{\beta_1 - 1} \, \delta \, I. \tag{9}$$

Most remarkably, this is the same entry price as that for a unit-sized monopolist firm facing the same demand process; compare this to equation (9) of Chapter 6. The two situations differ in two ways. The monopolist of Chapter 6 was not threatened by entry, so there was no upper barrier on the price process; now there is. However, the monopolist had a positive option value of waiting, while any of several identical potential firms of this chapter must have zero value of waiting. It so happens that the two differences exactly offset each other.

This coincidence between a competitive firm's and a monopolist's entry threshold is in the context of a very special example. In Chapter 9 we will find a very general result of this kind—a competitive firm can make the correct investment decision by acting myopically in the matter of future competitive entry, and acting as if it were going to be the last firm ever to enter this industry. That result also rests on a similar exact offset of two effects, one on the value of investing and the other on the value of waiting.

---

[6]See Malliaris and Brock (1982, p. 200) or Dixit (1993a, Section 3.5).

To understand the solution more fully, we must go into the details of the fixed-point process for constructing the equilibrium. Consider a firm contemplating entry. Write $f(P)$ for the value of its option to enter. As in Chapter 6, this takes the form

$$f(P) = A P^{\beta_1},$$

where A is a constant to be determined, and β_1 is as above. If the firm decides to enter when the price is P, it pays the investment cost I and receives in return an asset that we just valued at $v(P)$. The optimal entry threshold P^* satisfies two familiar conditions. First, value matching:

$$f(P^*) = v(P^*) - I,$$

and second, smooth pasting:

$$f'(P^*) = v'(P^*).$$

Using the functional forms for the functions $f(P)$ and $v(P)$, we have

$$A(P^*)^{\beta_1} = B(P^*)^{\beta_1} + P^*/\delta - I,$$

and

$$\beta_1 A(P^*)^{\beta_1-1} = \beta_1 B(P^*)^{\beta_1-1} + 1/\delta.$$

Note that we have already solved for the constant B in terms of the assumed upper barrier $\overline{P}$, but some expressions convey more insight when B is retained as such.

These two equations can be solved for the threshold P^* and the constant A; we have

$$P^* = \frac{\beta_1}{\beta_1 - 1} \, \delta I, \tag{10}$$

and

$$A = B + \frac{1}{\beta_1 \delta} (P^*)^{1-\beta_1}$$

$$= \frac{1}{\beta_1 \delta} \left[(P^*)^{1-\beta_1} - \overline{P}^{1-\beta_1} \right]. \tag{11}$$

Observe two features of the solution: the barrier $\overline{P}$ affects the solution only via the constant B in the value function $v(P)$, and the constant A in the option value function $f(P)$ responds one for one to changes in B. These have important implications for the equilibrium.

First, equation (10) shows that the entry threshold P^* is independent of B and therefore of the barrier $\overline{P}$. Of course, for the solution to make economic sense, the barrier must not be lower than the entry threshold. Given that, the exact level of the barrier is immaterial to the entry decision of the firm.[7] This remarkable property can be understood using the relation between the constants A and B. Any shift of the upper barrier has equal effects on the two, and thus equal effects on the value of an active firm and the option value of a potential firm. Roughly speaking, a cutoff of the upside price potential has equal effects on the value of entering at once and the value of waiting just a little longer, so it does not alter the trade-off between the two.

Since the barrier does not matter as long as it is high enough, we can let it go to infinity without affecting the entry threshold. That limit corresponds to the decision of a unit-sized monopoly firm that faced an identical demand curve but faced no threat of entry by other firms and therefore no upper barrier to the price process. This explains the coincidence of the entry thresholds of the monopoly and competitive industry cases. Once again, we alert the reader to a very general result of this kind to come in Chapter 9.

To solve explicitly for the competitive industry equilibrium, we set $P^* = \overline{P}$ in equation (10); this reproduces equation (9), which was derived before by a quick intuitive argument. Moreover, setting $P^* = \overline{P}$ in equation (11) gives $A = 0$. Therefore the option value of an idle firm $f(P)$ is identically zero. This was the intuitive starting point of our quick calculation; now we have verified it using a more rigorous theoretical argument.

The difference between a monopoly and a competitive firm is shown graphically in Figure 8.1. The range of prices facing a competitive firm is bounded above because of the entry of others; the monopolist's price range is not restricted. The monopolist has a positive value of waiting, and a positive value of investing over a range leading up to its optimal entry threshold. A competitive firm always has a zero value of waiting. Its value of investing is negative for most of its price range, and only just climbs to zero at the upper end of the range of possible prices.

The difference can be understood by relating the entry threshold to the Marshallian concept of the normal rate of return. This is most simply discussed in the case of $\alpha = 0$, so that the process is trendless, and as we are assuming risk-neutral firms, $\delta = r$. Now the unit-sized monopoly also faces a trendless price process; given the current price P, the expectation of the price at any future point in time is also P. If such a firm invests when the price is $P_0 = r\,I$,

---

[7]In Chapter 9 we will see the effect of price ceilings that are low enough to matter.

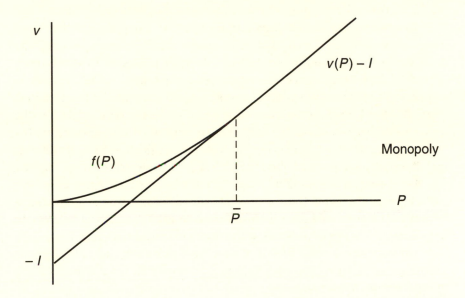

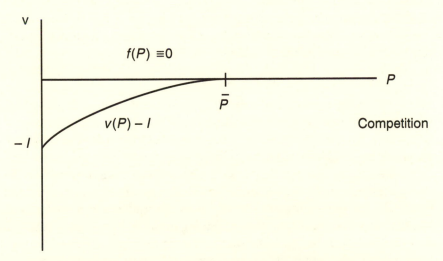

Figure 8.1. *Entry Decisions of Monopoly and Competitive Firms Compared*

it will earn a normal return on its sunk cost. However, we saw in Chapter 6 that it does not invest until the price rises to P^*, which is $\beta_1/(\beta_1 - 1)$ times P_0. We explained this in terms of the option value of waiting.

Now we see that a unit-sized competitive firm also waits until the price rises to the same level, even though its option value of waiting is zero. The explanation lies in the difference between the price processes in the two cases. The competitive firm's price process has an upper barrier, which reduces its expectation of future prices and returns. Specifically, since the firm knows that all other firms face the same choice and make the same decisions, the price will never rise above the level that prevails at its instant of entry; the current price when it enters is not the average but the best price it will ever get. If competitive firms adopted the rule of entering when the price reached P_0, they would earn a normal return only at those instants when entry was taking place—they would earn lower returns at all other instants. The average return over time would then be insufficient to justify the initial investment expenditure. On the other hand, when the entry threshold exceeds P_0, each firm will experience some period of supernormal returns and some periods of subnormal returns. The equilibrium $\overline{P}$ is exactly the level that ensures a normal return on average.

Since the entry threshold cum industry equilibrium price coincides with the threshold for a monopoly with the same parameters α, σ, r, and δ, we need not present detailed numerical calculations for the competitive equilibrium case; instead we refer the reader to those in Chapters 5 and 6. However, a few summary numbers are useful. Table 8.1 shows β_1 and the current rate of return on investment at the threshold,

$$\overline{P}/I = \beta_1 \delta/(\beta_1 - 1),$$

for $r = 0.05, \alpha = 0$ and 0.03, and $\sigma = 0, 0.2$, and 0.4. Note that when $\alpha = \sigma = 0$, the return $\overline{P}/I$ equals the Marshallian return, that is, the interest rate $r = 0.05$. This is also the case when $\alpha = 0.03$ and $\sigma = 0$. [As discussed in Chapter 5, when α is positive there is a value to waiting even if there is no uncertainty, and indeed in this case $\beta_1/(\beta_1 - 1) = 2.5$, but since δ falls as α increases, the return remains equal to r.] For either value of α, as σ is increased to 0.2 and 0.4, β falls and the required return $\overline{P}/I$ rises to about two or three times its Marshallian value. Hence the general finding from Chapters 5 and 6, that the firm's optimal decisions differ substantially from the implications of the textbook present value approach, has an exact parallel for a competitive industry. Its equilibrium differs substantially from the picture offered by the Marshallian theory presented in most elementary and intermediate microeconomics textbooks.

Table 8.1. *Required Return for Competitive Entry*
Note: $r = 0.05$

α	σ	β_1	$\overline{P}/I$
0	0	∞	0.050
0	0.2	2.16	0.093
0	0.4	1.44	0.165
0.03	0	1.67	0.050
0.03	0.2	1.35	0.077
0.03	0.4	1.16	0.143

3   Industry Equilibrium with Exit

The above basic model closely followed that of the monopoly firm in Chapter 6, and gave us very analogous results for the competitive industry with aggregate uncertainty. Most of the extensions of this model are left for Chapter 9. In this chapter we take up just one that fits more naturally here. We introduce exit, and construct a model that closely follows that of the monopoly firm's entry and exit decisions in Chapter 7. Once again, the results for the competitive industry with aggregate uncertainty are thoroughly parallel.

For exit to be a meaningful option, we need two conditions. First, the operating profit flow must sometimes become negative; we make this possible by introducing a variable cost C for each unit-sized firm. Second, temporary suspension of operation and resumption without a cost penalty must be ruled out; we do so. We also introduce a lump-sum cost of exit E. As before, this can comprise any legally required severance payments or costs of restoring land. It can also be negative (but numerically less than cost I), representing any nonsunk portion of the entry cost.

Now the intuition is that the exit of other firms will generate a floor—a lower reflecting barrier—on the price process, just as their entry generated a ceiling—an upper reflecting barrier. Each firm will have rational expectations about the price process it faces, namely, a geometric Brownian motion between these two barriers. The firm's own entry and exit decisions will again take the form of upper and lower thresholds on the price. The equilibrium levels of the two barriers will be found from a fixed-point argument: each firm's thresholds should equal the barriers generated by the behavior of all firms in the industry.

The calculation is somewhat more complicated than in the previous case of totally irreversible entry, because we cannot first find the value of an active firm and then the option value of an inactive firm. An active firm's choices include the option to exit, so the two values must be found simultaneously.

An active firm faces the price process of equation (4) with barriers $\overline{P}$ and $\underline{P}$. Let $v_1(P)$ denote its value when the current price P is in the interior of the range $[\underline{P}, \overline{P}]$. This satisfies the familiar differential equation

$$\tfrac{1}{2} \sigma^2 P^2 v_1''(P) + (r - \delta) P v_1'(P) - r v_1(P) + P - C = 0. \tag{12}$$

The form of the solution is equally familiar from Chapter 7:

$$v_1(P) = B_1 P^{\beta_1} + B_2 P^{\beta_2} + P/\delta - C/r. \tag{13}$$

The last two terms give the expected present value of profits corresponding to a price process without barriers. The slight new twist is that since the equation holds only over the finite range of prices $(\underline{P}, \overline{P})$, we cannot use considerations of limits as P goes to zero or infinity to eliminate either of the other terms. The first term, corresponding to the positive root β_1, represents the reduction in value due to the ceiling on the price process. The second term, corresponding to the negative root β_2, is the value of the firm's option to exit. At the upper reflecting barrier we have the arbitrage condition [similar to equation (7) for the entry-only case above]

$$v_1'(\overline{P}) = \beta_1 B_1 \overline{P}^{\beta_1-1} + \beta_2 B_2 \overline{P}^{\beta_2-1} + 1/\delta = 0. \tag{14}$$

Denote an inactive firm's value by $v_0(P)$. Then similar arguments give

$$v_0(P) = A_1 P^{\beta_1} + A_2 P^{\beta_2}, \tag{15}$$

where now the first term is the value of the activation option, and the second term is the increase in value that results from the floor on the price process. At the lower reflecting barrier we have

$$v_0'(\underline{P}) = \beta_1 A_1 \underline{P}^{\beta_1-1} + \beta_2 A_2 \underline{P}^{\beta_2-1} = 0. \tag{16}$$

Now suppose the entry threshold is P_H and the exit threshold P_L. These satisfy the usual value-matching and smooth-pasting conditions

$$v_0(P_H) = v_1(P_H) - I, \tag{17}$$

$$v_1(P_L) = v_0(P_L) - E, \tag{18}$$

$$v_0'(P_H) = v_1'(P_H), \tag{19}$$

$$v_1'(P_L) = v_0'(P_L). \tag{20}$$

For given barriers $\overline{P}$ and $\underline{P}$, these four equations, together with the conditions at the two reflecting barriers, can be solved for the constants A_1, A_2, B_1, B_2 and the thresholds P_H, P_L. Finally, the fixed point requirements $P_H = \overline{P}$ and $P_L = \underline{P}$ complete the determination of the equilibrium.

Let us begin by finding the thresholds. Note that the four value-matching and smooth-pasting conditions can be written

$$(B_1 - A_1) P_H{}^{\beta_1} + (B_2 - A_2) P_H{}^{\beta_2} + P_H/\delta - C/r = I, \qquad (21)$$

$$\beta_1 (B_1 - A_1) P_H{}^{\beta_1 - 1} + \beta_2 (B_2 - A_2) P_H{}^{\beta_2 - 1} + 1/\delta = 0, \qquad (22)$$

$$(B_1 - A_1) P_L{}^{\beta_1} + (B_2 - A_2) P_L{}^{\beta_2} + P_L/\delta - C/r = -E, \qquad (23)$$

$$\beta_1 (B_1 - A_1) P_L{}^{\beta_1 - 1} + \beta_2 (B_2 - A_2) P_L{}^{\beta_2 - 1} + 1/\delta = 0. \qquad (24)$$

Regard these as four equations in four unknowns: the thresholds P_H, P_L and the "composite" constants $(B_1 - A_1)$, $(B_2 - A_2)$. In this form the equations are exactly identical to the system of equations (9)–(12) in Chapter 7 that defined the entry and exit thresholds for a monopoly firm. Therefore the present system yields the same thresholds, independently of the barriers $\overline{P}$, $\underline{P}$. As in the previous model with totally irreversible entry, the barriers do not affect the threshold. Of course, for the exercise to be meaningful, the barriers must be wide enough to span the thresholds, that is, we need $\underline{P} \leq P_L$ and $P_H \leq \overline{P}$. Otherwise the exact position of the barriers is immaterial. Once again the reason is that the exact position affects each pair of option value constants A_1, B_1 and A_2, B_2 equally. Therefore the differences $(B_1 - A_1)$, $(B_2 - A_2)$, governing the trade-offs between immediate action and waiting for entry or exit, are unaltered.

Finally, turn to the equilibrium. For this we simply set $\overline{P} = P_H$ and $\underline{P} = P_L$ in the above system of equations (21)–(24). This being identical with the corresponding system for a monopolist—equations (9)–(12) of Chapter 7, we do not need to repeat the numerical calculations conducted there. The remarks there concerning the magnitude of the range of inertia continue to apply. The ceiling and floor on the competitive equilibrium price process differ substantially from the Marshallian long-run average cost and average variable cost, respectively, and are very far apart from each other. We will soon offer a dramatic numerical example of this.

It remains to find the separate values of active and idle firms. For this, we combine the two equations at the barriers, (14) and (16), with the two smooth-pasting conditions (19) and (20), to get $v_0'(\overline{P}) = 0 = v_0'(\underline{P})$, or

$$\beta_1 A_1 \overline{P}{}^{\beta_1 - 1} + \beta_2 A_2 \overline{P}{}^{\beta_2 - 1} = 0,$$

$$\beta_1 A_1 \underline{P}{}^{\beta_1 - 1} + \beta_2 A_2 \underline{P}{}^{\beta_2 - 1} = 0.$$

Regard these as a pair of linear equations in A_1, A_2. The coefficient matrix

$$\begin{pmatrix} \beta_1 \, \overline{P}^{\beta_1-1} & \beta_2 \, \overline{P}^{\beta_2-1} \\ \beta_1 \, \underline{P}^{\beta_1-1} & \beta_2 \, \underline{P}^{\beta_2-1} \end{pmatrix}$$

is nonsingular as long as $\overline{P} > \underline{P}$. Then the only solution is $A_1 = A_2 = 0$. Therefore the value of an idle firm is identically zero, as it should be, given competitive conditions and identical firms. This completes the solution.

3.A   Entry, Exit, and Price in the Copper Industry

We now return to our example of entry and exit in the copper mining industry from Chapter 7, restating some of the numerical results to give the readers a better feel for the magnitudes involved. In fact, the use of industry data to illustrate the story of a firm having a monopoly right to invest was something of an anomaly in Chapter 7; now the same numbers have a more satisfactory interpretation in the context of industry equilibrium. In the central case studied, we assumed that the capital cost of building an average-sized mine, smelter, and refinery (producing 10 million pounds of copper per year) was $I = \$20$ million, and the cost of site restoration upon abandonment was $E = \$2$ million. The variable cost was $C = \$0.80$ per pound, but was allowed to vary around this figure. The price volatility parameter σ was 0.2 in annual units, and was also allowed to vary around this range. The riskless interest rate was $r = 0.04$, and the return shortfall was $\delta = 0.04$. With these numbers, the Marshallian entry threshold price would be \$0.88 and the exit threshold \$0.792. As shown in Table 8.2, however, the correct entry and exit thresholds are \$1.35 and \$0.55, respectively. The table also shows the Marshallian and the actual thresholds for other values of C and σ.

Figures 8.2 and 8.3 show, for the central case of $C = \$0.80$ per pound and $\sigma = 0.2$, sample paths for the price of copper. Observe that this price fluctuates as a geometric Brownian motion between the upper and lower reflecting barriers, which are the entry and exit thresholds of \$1.35 and \$0.55. These thresholds are shown in the figures as horizontal lines; also shown are the Marshallian thresholds of \$0.88 and \$0.79. (In the figures, time is measured in years, and each year was divided into 50 increments for purposes of generating sample paths.) Figure 8.2 shows a "fortunate" (from the point of view of a copper producer) sample path, in which the price spends much of the time at the upper end of its range, while Figure 8.3 shows an "unfortunate" realization.

These figures show particular realizations of price, but we could ask what percentage of the time the price should be expected to stay in different regions

Table 8.2. *Entry and Exit Thresholds in Copper Mining*
(Note: see text for parameters)

c	σ	Upper threshold		Lower threshold	
		Marshallian	Correct	Marshallian	Correct
0.8	0.1	0.88	1.12	0.792	0.63
0.8	0.2	0.88	1.35	0.792	0.55
0.8	0.4	0.88	1.75	0.792	0.45
0.4	0.2	0.48	0.80	0.392	0.26
0.6	0.2	0.68	1.06	0.592	0.40
0.8	0.2	0.88	1.35	0.792	0.55
1.0	0.2	1.08	1.60	0.992	0.70

of its range over the long run. We can answer this question by calculating the long-run stationary distribution for price. Begin by observing that P follows the geometric Brownian motion of equation (4) between its reflecting barriers $\underline{P}$ and $\overline{P}$. Therefore, using Ito's Lemma, we know that $p \equiv \log P$ follows a simple Brownian motion with the drift parameter $\alpha' = \alpha - \frac{1}{2}\sigma^2$ and the variance parameter σ, between corresponding reflecting barriers $\underline{p} = \log \underline{P}$ and $\overline{p} = \log \overline{P}$. Now we can use the result of Chapter 3, Section 5 to find the long-run distribution of p. It is an exponential distribution, with density $K e^{\gamma x}$, where $\gamma = 2\alpha'/\sigma^2$, and the constant of proportionality K is chosen to achieve a total probability mass of unity. With this, it is easy to calculate what proportion of time p spends in various subsets of the range $(\underline{p}, \overline{p})$. The results can then be translated into the corresponding ranges for P.

For our base case parameter values, we find that, on average, price will be between the upper Marshallian and entry thresholds of $0.88 and $1.35 about 58.5 percent of the time. Thus more than half the time, copper producers will be earning what in traditional microeconomic analysis we would call a supernormal profit. Price will be between the two Marshallian thresholds of $0.79 and $0.88 about 11.3 percent of the time (in which case we can say that firms are earning positive but subnormal profits). Finally, price will be between the exit threshold of $0.55 and the lower Marshallian threshold of $0.79, so that firms are incurring losses, about 30.2 percent of the time.

These figures show very dramatically how the dynamics of a competitive industry under conditions of uncertainty will differ from the textbook picture. For almost 90 percent of the time, we expect the copper industry to be in a

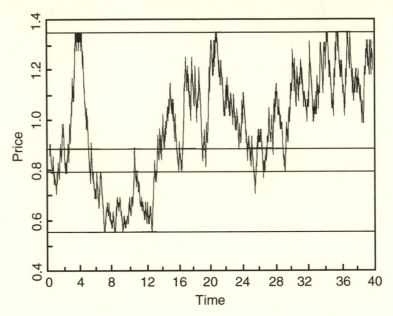

Figure 8.2.   *Sample Path of Copper Price*

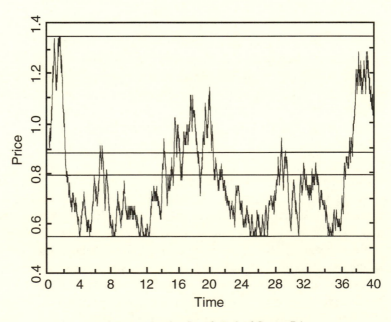

Figure 8.3.   *Another Sample Path of Copper Price*

state that according to the Marshallian theory simply ought not to exist. Either price will be above long-run average cost without attracting new entry, or it will be below average variable cost without inducing exit. To someone who tries to interpret such observations using the perspective of the Marshallian textbook, supernormal profits without entry will suggest entry barriers, and continued operation of loss-making firms will suggest cutthroat competition or predation. Our theory says that such episodes, even covering long stretches and most of the life of the industry, can be consistent with perfect competition, when the competitive process is appropriately interpreted in the stochastic dynamic context. We will return to the policy implications of this in Chapter 9.

4   Firm-Specific Uncertainty

In this section we treat the other extreme case where all uncertainty in the demand curve (1) is purely firm-specific. Now the industry-wide shock Y is set equal to 1, and any one firm's inverse demand curve becomes

$$P = X D(Q). \tag{25}$$

Recall the intuition concerning firm-specific uncertainty that we outlined in the introduction to Chapter 8. When one firm gets a good shock to its profitability, it knows that on average this luck is not shared by its competitors. Therefore it need not invest at once; it has some leeway to wait and see whether this good fortune is transitory. Our first model aims to make this idea more precise.

This opportunity to wait is relevant only if each firm is able to make its decision *after* observing the current level of its potential profitability. To capture this aspect in its purest form, one would define an industry consisting of a fixed population of potential firms, each of whom can continuously observe its firm-specific shock, and then decide whether to invest. However, that fails to capture another basic feature of competitive equilibrium, namely, free entry. Therefore we need another prior stage of decision making, namely, that of becoming one of these potential firms who get to observe their current profit potential. This decision must be made *without* knowledge of the specific shock.

Therefore we construct a two-stage model as follows. By paying an entry cost R, any firm can get an initial draw of its demand shock X from a known distribution. Thereafter this variable will follow a geometric Brownian motion process that is firm-specific, or independent across firms. Each firm can start actual operation by paying a further sunk investment cost I.

An example will help fix the idea. Consider a pharmaceutical company that can develop a new drug by incurring the research cost R. This yields an initial estimate of its efficacy and profitability. The firm patents the drug, but unless the profit estimate is sufficiently high, it will not incur the additional investment expenditure I that is necessary to begin production. Over time the profit estimate may increase as new uses are found for the drug, or decrease as other drugs to treat the same condition are discovered by other firms.

We characterize the competitive equilibrium of such an industry in the long run. There are numerous competitive firms facing independent shocks, and there is substantial uncertainty and volatility at the firm level. However, different firms' shocks are independent, and the operation of the law of large numbers ensures that industry aggregates are nonrandom.[8] Thus a nonrandom total volume of output can be produced by firms whose identities change through time but whose aggregate population distribution remains stationary. However, the firm-level uncertainty leaves a mark on the industry equilibrium: the parameters of the distribution of active firms, and therefore the actual values at which the nonrandom industry quantity and price settle, do depend on the extent of uncertainty faced by each firm.

The idea that relatively tranquil industry-wide conditions conceal much firm-level uncertainty has been emphasized in recent empirical work. Davis and Haltiwanger (1990) and others have demonstrated quite impressively the large gross hirings and firings that underlie small net changes in employment in the U.S. economy. The models that are constructed for applications of this kind generally contain too much context-specific detail to let the general intuition stand out. Our simple model can help the reader develop a better conceptual understanding and more general intuition for such phenomena.

We begin by specifying the nature of uncertainty in X so as to fit with the firm's two stages of decisions. A new entrant gets an initial draw of X from a known distribution. Thereafter its X evolves as a geometric Brownian motion

$$dX = \alpha \, X dt + \sigma \, X dz. \qquad (26)$$

We have interpreted X as an idiosyncratic demand shock (random fluctuations of taste shifts giving rise to price premia for slightly different varieties in the industry). What ultimately matters is the shock to profitability, and we could also think of X as a technology shock that appears in a reduced form in the formula for the firm's profit flow after the instantaneously variable choices have been optimized out, as discussed in Chapter 6, Section 3.

---

[8]Recall that we are not giving a formal rigorous treatment of this.

There is free entry into the industry, and anyone can get the initial draw by paying R. However, there is no obligation to start production at once. A further sunk investment I must be incurred to activate the process, and the firm can wait to see if X evolves to a more favorable level before making this irreversible commitment.

We will characterize the long-run stochastic equilibrium of such an industry. In fact we will postulate such an equilibrium, and then determine endogenously the various stationary magnitudes (price, number of firms, etc.) that constitute the equilibrium. Suppose N is the nonrandom stream of new entrants who pay the fee R and learn their initial X. Then their shocks will evolve independently and stochastically. A nonrandom flow M will reach the activation decision. We also want to keep the total number of active firms, Q, constant. To permit this, we assume that all firms, whether waiting or active, face an exogenous Poisson process of death with parameter λ. This process is also independent across firms. Then in a stationary equilibrium M must equal λQ.

All uncertainty being idiosyncratic, we specify that each firm is risk neutral and makes its decisions to maximize its expected net worth. Let r denote the risk-free interest rate at which future profit flows are discounted.

4.A The Activation Decision

In the long-run stationary equilibrium with a large and constant number Q of active firms, each new entrant or waiting firm takes this Q as given. Its profit flow is $X D(Q)$. It continually observes X, and decides when to pay its investment cost I and become an active producer. This is formally identical to the basic single-firm model we studied in Chapter 6, Section 1. Equation (9) of that section gave us the price threshold P^* that triggered investment. In the notation of this chapter, that becomes a threshold X^* on the firm's shock, and the defining equation becomes

$$X^* D(Q) = \frac{\beta_1}{\beta_1 - 1} (r + \lambda - \alpha) I, \tag{27}$$

where β_1 is the positive root of the fundamental quadratic

$$Q \equiv \tfrac{1}{2} \sigma^2 \beta(\beta - 1) + \alpha \beta - (r + \lambda) = 0.$$

The condition that ensures convergence of the expected profit flow is $r + \lambda > \alpha$; note that the Poisson death probability acts like a discount rate in achieving convergence, as we saw in the discussion of Poisson processes in Chapter 3,

Section 5 and Chapter 4, Section 1.I. Assuming the convergence condition to be met, we have $\beta_1 > 1$ as in the familiar models of Chapters 5 and 6.

Our intuitive discussion in the introduction to this chapter tells us the reason why equation (27) is exactly analogous to the corresponding formulas for the monopolist's entry decision in Chapters 5 and 6. When uncertainty is firm-specific, a firm that gets a favorable X does have an edge over its competitors. The favorable X is specific to this firm; if it does not invest at once, a rival cannot "steal" its X and jump in. Therefore a positive value of waiting does survive, and the firm's optimal decision shows familiar inertia.

Of course this is an incomplete account of the industry equilibrium until we show that Q can be determined in a way that is consistent with the above story. That needs more steps in the development of the model.

4.B The Entry Decision

With X^* determined as above, we can find the value of a potential firm that observes its current X in an industry with Q active firms:

$$V(X, Q) = \begin{cases} A(Q)\, X^{\beta_1} & \text{if } X \leq X^*, \\[2mm] X D(Q)/(r + \lambda - \alpha) - I & \text{if } X \geq X^*. \end{cases} \tag{28}$$

This is also familiar from Chapters 5–7. The upper line is the option value for a waiting firm, and the lower line is the expected present value of profits that the potential firm will get by immediate activation, net of the costs of the activation. Of course the latter formula applies in the region where immediate activation is optimal, and the former in the region where waiting is optimal. In fact X^* is determined by starting with these two expressions and value matching and smooth pasting. That also yields

$$A(Q) = \frac{(\beta_1 - 1)^{\beta_1 - 1}}{\beta_1{}^{\beta_1}} \frac{1}{(r + \lambda - \alpha)^{\beta_1}}\, D(Q)^{\beta_1}\, I^{1 - \beta_1}. \tag{29}$$

A higher Q lowers $D(Q)$. Therefore from (29) it lowers $A(Q)$, and from (27) it raises X^*. Finally, from (28) we see that a higher Q lowers the whole value function $V(X)$. Figure 8.4 shows a typical value function and its shift as Q changes. The intuition is that if there are more active firms in the industry, any one new entrant perceives a smaller prospective profit flow and therefore requires a higher firm-specific shock to profit before committing itself to activation.

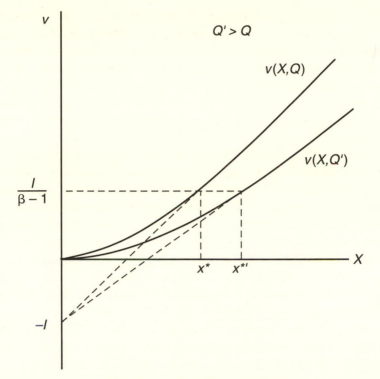

Figure 8.4. *A Firm's Value Function*

A potential entrant can then calculate its expected payoff $\mathcal{E}_X[V(X, Q)]$, conditioned using the known distribution of the initial draw of X. Free entry ensures

$$\mathcal{E}_X[V(X, Q)] = R, \tag{30}$$

where R is the initial entry cost. We just saw that the left-hand side is monotonic in Q; therefore this equation determines the equilibrium Q.

As an example, suppose the distribution of the initial draw is uniform over the interval $(0, \widehat{X})$. If the activation threshold X^* turns out to be larger than $\widehat{X}$, the zero expected net value condition (30) is

$$A(Q)\, \widehat{X}^{\beta_1} / (1 + \beta_1) = R.$$

In simple cases, for instance, if $D(Q)$ is isoelastic, this admits an explicit (but algebraically messy) solution for Q. If $X^* < \widehat{X}$, we get

$$\frac{A(Q)}{1 + \beta_1}\, (X^*)^{\beta_1 + 1} + \frac{D(Q)}{2\,(r + \lambda - \alpha)}\, [\,\widehat{X}^2 - (X^*)^2\,] - I\,(\widehat{X} - X^*) = R\,\widehat{X}.$$

This must be solved numerically.

Even now the argument is not complete. The number of active firms Q arises from a complex chain of initial entry decisions, independent random fluctuations of the firms' shock variables X, subsequent entry decisions, and independent random deaths. We must show how these interact in a consistent way to produce the industry's equilibrium Q.

4.C The Distribution of Firms

Recall the actual life history of any one firm that has just paid the entry cost R. It begins with an X randomly drawn from its known distribution. If the initial X exceeds the threshold X^*, the firm pays the investment cost I and becomes an active producer at once. Otherwise it lets its X evolve, and activates if and when X^* is reached. Throughout this process, the firm faces a constant and exogenous probability rate λ of death.

Such new entrants arrive at rate N. The full stochastic dynamics of each of them—the probability that it will be alive and occupy a position X at time t—can be examined using the Kolmogorov equation, which we developed in the Appendix to Chapter 3. Here our aim is more limited. For industry equilibrium, only the total numbers of firms in various states matter—how many are active, and how many are waiting with what values of X. Therefore the law of large numbers allows us to restrict attention to a long-run stationary equilibrium. This means that the rates of Poisson death by exit, and of activation, are constant through time. Likewise, the numbers of firms with various current levels of X are constant through time. Of course the actual identities of the firms occupying these positions keep changing, but for our purpose any firm is like any other with the same X.

The method of calculating this long-run distribution of firms is the same as that of Chapter 3, Section 5, but now we must include two new features, namely, fresh entry and Poisson deaths. It proves more convenient to work in terms of the logarithm, $x = \log X$. Let $g(x)$ denote the density function of the initial draw of x, and $G(x)$ the corresponding cumulative distribution. Note that the range of x extends to $-\infty$ to the left. Let $x^* = \log X^*$. Of the newly entering firms, $N[1 - G(x^*)]$ immediately get a draw large enough to justify activation. The rest join the mass of firms that do not complete the second step of committing the investment cost at once, but wait to reach the activation threshold.

For both groups, x continues to evolve. Applying Ito's Lemma to (26), we see that x follows the Brownian motion

$$dx = v\,dt + \sigma\,dz, \tag{31}$$

where $v = \alpha - \frac{1}{2}\sigma^2$. Also, both groups suffer exogenous "deaths" under the Poisson process with parameter λ.

Begin with the waiting firms, which are distributed over the range $(-\infty, x^*)$. Let $N\phi(x)$ denote the density of such firms at location x; the factor N just scales this by the rate of entry and leads to a simpler equation for $\phi(x)$. For the density to remain constant through time, the rate at which firms arrive at x (having received positive shocks from below or negative shocks from above) must equal the rate at which firms at x move away (having received shocks of the Brownian motion process or Poisson death). We express this equation of "balanced flow" of firms in a more precise way.

For this purpose, we use the binomial approximation to Brownian motion that proved so useful in Chapter 3, Section 2(b). Divide time into short intervals of duration dt, and the x space into short segments, each of length $dh = \sigma\sqrt{dt}$. Of the firms located in one such segment, in one short time interval a proportion $\lambda\,dt$ will die. Of the rest, a fraction p will move one segment to the right, and a fraction q will move to the left, where

$$p = \frac{1}{2}\left[1 + \frac{v}{\sigma}\sqrt{dt}\right], \qquad q = \frac{1}{2}\left[1 - \frac{v}{\sigma}\sqrt{dt}\right].$$

Now consider the segment centered at x. It starts out with $N\phi(x)\,dh$ firms. In the next unit time period dt, all of these move away with either Poisson or Brownian shocks. New entrants, as well as firms from the left and right, arrive to take their places. Figure 8.5 shows these flows schematically.

For balance we need

$$N\phi(x)\,dh = N\,dt\,g(x)\,dh + p\,(1 - \lambda\,dt)\,N\phi(x - dh)\,dh$$
$$+ q\,(1 - \lambda\,dt)\,N\phi(x + dh)\,dh. \tag{32}$$

Cancelling the common factor $N\,dh$, expanding the $\phi(x \pm dh)$ on the right hand side by Taylor's theorem, and simplifying, we get the differential equation

$$\frac{1}{2}\sigma^2\phi''(x) - v\phi'(x) - \lambda\phi(x) + g(x) = 0. \tag{33}$$

This equation is slightly different from the one of Chapters 5–7 because it pertains to a simple rather than geometric Brownian motion. However, the method of solution is very similar. It is easy to verify that the general solution has the form

$$\phi(x) = C_1 \exp[\gamma_1 x] + C_2 \exp[\gamma_2 x] + \phi_0(x),$$

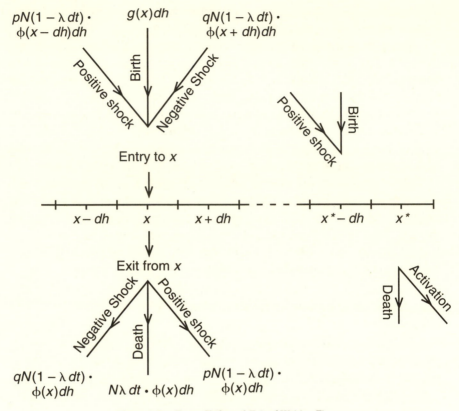

Figure 8.5. *Entry, Shift, and Exit of Waiting Firms*

where the last term is a particular solution of the full equation, and the first two terms arise from the general solution of the homogeneous part. The constants C_1 and C_2 remain to be determined, while γ_1 and γ_2 are roots of the quadratic

$$\mathcal{Q} \equiv \tfrac{1}{2}\sigma^2 \gamma^2 - \nu\gamma - \lambda = 0;$$

thus one is positive and the other is negative.

The first condition for determination of the constants C_1 and C_2 is found from the consideration that the total mass of waiting firms, that is,

$$\int_{-\infty}^{x^*} \phi(x)\, dx,$$

must be finite. That helps rule out the negative root in the solution of the homogeneous part, as a negative exponential would go to infinity as $x \to -\infty$.

For the second condition, observe that the firms that hit x^* become active and are lost to this distribution. Consider the segment of the x space just to the left of x^*, centered at $x = x^* - dh$. For this segment, we must modify the balance equation (32) above. It does not get any incomers from the right, therefore

$$N \phi(x) \, dh = N \, dt \, g(x) \, dh + p \, (1 - \lambda \, dt) \, N \, \phi(x - dh) \, dh.$$

Similar simplification now gives $\phi(x) = 0$. Letting dh go to zero, we have the condition $\phi(x^*) = 0$.

We can also calculate the rate at which waiting firms hit x^* and so become active. These are just the fraction $p \, (1 - \lambda \, dt)$ of the $N \, \phi(x - dh) \, dh$ firms located in the segment just to the left of x^*. Using Taylor's theorem again, the leading term in this expression is

$$\tfrac{1}{2} N \, [\phi(x^*) - \phi'(x^*) \, dh] \, dh = -\tfrac{1}{2} N \, \phi'(x^*) \, (dh)^2 = -\tfrac{1}{2} N \phi'(x^*) \, \sigma^2 \, dt.$$

Since these firms activate in the time interval dt, the rate of activation is $-\tfrac{1}{2} \sigma^2 \, N \, \phi'(x^*)$.

We illustrate this calculation for a case amenable to an analytical solution. Suppose the distribution of X is uniform over the interval $(0, \widehat{X})$. Then $x = \log X$ has an exponential distribution over $(-\infty, \widehat{x})$, where $\widehat{x} = \log \widehat{X}$. Thus

$$G(x) = g(x) = \exp(x - \widehat{x}).$$

We will simply assume that the rest of the parameters of the problem are such that the activation threshold x^* turns out to be less than $\widehat{x}$, leaving the other case, which is simpler because none of the entering firms activate immediately, to the reader.

A particular integral of (33) is easily verified to be

$$\phi_0(x) = e^{x - \widehat{x}} / [\lambda + v - \tfrac{1}{2} \sigma^2].$$

The denominator of this must be positive for it to make economic sense. This just says that the quadratic expression Q evaluated at $\gamma = 1$ is negative. Then the positive root γ_1 must in fact exceed unity. We assume this, and for typographic convenience write that root as γ.

Then the general solution of (33) is

$$\phi(x) = C \, e^{\gamma x} + \phi_0(x).$$

The constant C is to be determined from the condition $\phi(x^*) = 0$. This yields

$$\phi(x) = \frac{1}{\lambda + \nu - \frac{1}{2}\sigma^2} \left[e^{x - \hat{x}} - e^{\gamma(x - x^*)} e^{x^* - \hat{x}} \right]. \tag{34}$$

From this we can calculate some aggregates for the waiting firms. Their total number is

$$M \equiv N \int_{-\infty}^{x^*} \phi(x) \, dx = \frac{N}{\lambda + \nu - \frac{1}{2}\sigma^2} \frac{\gamma - 1}{\gamma} e^{x^* - \hat{x}}.$$

The rate of activation is

$$-\tfrac{1}{2}\sigma^2 N \phi'(x^*) = N \frac{\frac{1}{2}\sigma^2 (\gamma - 1)}{\lambda + \nu - \frac{1}{2}\sigma^2} e^{x^* - \hat{x}}.$$

We could similarly find the distribution of the mass of active firms. These will extend over the entire range $x \in (-\infty, \infty)$, because some firms may have activated and then had their X decline. They are also augmented by that part of the new entry flow that finds its initial X above X^* and activates immediately, and by the activation flow at x^*. Their numbers are diminished by the flow of Poisson deaths.

In fact we only need the total number of active firms, not the distribution of their X values, to find the industry equilibrium. The new entry flow that activates immediately is $N[1 - G(x^*)]$. The activation flow was found from the solution for waiting firms above as $-\frac{1}{2}\sigma^2 \phi'(x^*)$. The population of active firms being Q, the death flow is λQ. To keep the numbers constant, we need

$$\lambda Q = N [1 - G(x^*) - \tfrac{1}{2}\sigma^2 \phi'(x^*)]. \tag{35}$$

We can calculate x^* and Q from earlier conditions of equilibrium: the activation condition (27) and the free entry condition (30). Therefore this equation defines N. Since new entrants are indifferent to their choice because of the free entry condition (30), we can adopt the usual convention of long-run equilibrium analysis and suppose that just enough of them do enter. Thus the "stochastically stationary" equilibrium depicted above can be sustained.

In our special case where X has the uniform distribution, the condition (35) becomes

$$\lambda Q = N \left[1 - e^{x^* - \hat{x}} \frac{\lambda + \nu - \frac{1}{2}\sigma^2 \gamma}{\lambda + \nu - \frac{1}{2}\sigma^2} \right].$$

This allows us to calculate the rate of new entry N, either relative to the mass of active firms Q, or relative to the total mass of active and waiting firms, $(Q + M)$.

The various algebraic expressions get complicated, but some general principles stand out. When the firms in an industry are subject to specific shocks, the investment decisions of each are importantly influenced by the option value of waiting for better realizations of its own shock. At the industry level, the shocks and the responses of firms can aggregate into long-run stationary conditions, so that the industry output and price are nonrandom. However, the equilibrium levels of these variables are affected by the parameters of firm-specific uncertainty. Also, behind the aggregate certainty lies a great deal of randomness and fluctuations: firms enter, invest, and exit in response to the shocks to their individual fortunes.

In reality, industry-wide and firm-specific shocks occur together. Therefore we will proceed to combine the models studied thus far in this chapter into a single general model that encompasses both kinds of shocks. Then in Chapter 12 we will consider an application to some real data.

5 A General Model

Now we examine industry equilibrium in a more general model where the two kinds of uncertainty, firm-specific and industry-wide, coexist. To allow for the added notational and mathematical complexities of the joint uncertainty, we make some simplifications in each. Our treatment closely follows Caballero and Pindyck (1992).

We assume that the firms are risk neutral (or that the industry-wide risk is uncorrelated with the risk of the economy's capital market as a whole), leaving the more general case for the reader. We suppose that the industry demand is isoelastic; thus the demand equation (1) becomes

$$P = XY Q^{-\epsilon}, \tag{36}$$

where $1/\epsilon$ is the price elasticity of demand. We also omit the second activation stage from the above model of firm-specific uncertainty; thus $I = 0$ and $X^* = 0$.

As before, each firm has the capacity to produce a unit of output and has no variable costs of production; thus, P is also its profit flow. Also as before, we can think of this as the reduced form of a more general structure in which any variable inputs (those without irreversibility or adjustment cost) are chosen at their optimal levels. We continue to treat firms as infinitesimal and their number as a continuous variable; then Q equals this number.

The two shocks follow independent geometric Brownian motion processes.[9] Let dz_x and dz_y be increments of independent standard Wiener processes; thus $\mathcal{V}(dz_x) = \mathcal{V}(dz_y) = dt$ and $\mathcal{E}(dz_x\, dz_y) = 0$. Then the firm-specific shock follows

$$dX = \alpha_x\, X dt + \sigma_x\, X dz_x, \tag{37}$$

and the industry-wide shock follows

$$dY = \alpha_y\, Y\, dt + \sigma_y\, Y\, dz_y. \tag{38}$$

New entrants pay the sunk cost R and get an initial X chosen from the known distribution. Let $\overline{X}$ denote the expected value of this initial X. There are no further costs of activation, and the profit flow is always positive. Therefore all entrants will become active at once.

In the model of Section 2 we had only industry-wide uncertainty, and the equilibrium was characterized by an upper reflecting barrier on the price. With added firm-specific uncertainty, the natural generalization is a similar barrier on the industry-wide factors in the expression (36) for the price, namely,

$$W = Y\, Q^{-\epsilon}. \tag{39}$$

The idea is that as long as W is below a threshold level $\overline{W}$, no new firms will enter, while existing firms continue to suffer Poisson deaths, so $dQ = -\lambda\, Q$. The geometric Brownian motion of Y and the Poisson death process of Q will induce a geometric Brownian motion on W, namely,

$$dW = (\alpha_y + \epsilon\lambda)\, W dt + \sigma_y\, W dz_y. \tag{40}$$

However, if W rises to the threshold $\overline{W}$, enough new firms will enter to prevent it rising any further, thus making $\overline{W}$ an upper reflecting barrier on the process (40). Of course $\overline{W}$ must be determined endogenously as a part of the system of equations for the equilibrium. We now proceed to verify this conjecture.

The value of an active firm is

$$V(X, W) = \mathcal{E} \int_0^\infty X_t\, W_t\, e^{-(r+\lambda)t}\, dt,$$

---

[9]The assumption of independence is natural. Decompose X into two components, one in the direction of Y and the other orthogonal to it. The former, being perfectly correlated with the Y shock, would have to be industry-wide and so should be included in Y itself. That leaves the firm-specific shock independent of Y.

where the discount rate is increased by λ to allow for Poisson deaths in the now-familiar manner. This satisfies the differential equation

$$\tfrac{1}{2}\left[\,\sigma_x^2\, X^2\, V_{XX} + \sigma_y^2\, W^2\, V_{WW}\,\right] + \left[\,\alpha_x\, X V_X + \alpha_w\, W V_W\,\right] - (r+\lambda)\, V + XW = 0,$$

where α_w is an abbreviation for $(\alpha_y + \epsilon\lambda)$.

This value function will be homogeneous of degree 1 in X: a firm that is lucky enough to have twice as large an initial draw of its specific shock will forever have the expectation of twice as large a profit flow and therefore twice as large a value. However, the value function will not be homogeneous of degree 1 in W; if the industry-wide shock is larger, the threshold that draws fresh entry will be reached sooner and so the period of proportionately larger profit flow will not last as long. Thus we can write $V(X, W) = X v(W)$. Substituting into the above partial differential equation for V yields an ordinary differential equation for v, namely

$$\tfrac{1}{2}\,\sigma_y^2\, W^2\, v''(W) + \alpha_w\, W v'(W) - (r+\lambda - \alpha_x)\, v(W) + W = 0. \tag{41}$$

This takes us back to the familiar ground of Chapters 6 and 7. The solution is

$$v(W) = \frac{W}{r + \lambda - \alpha_x - \alpha_w} - A\, W^{\beta_1},$$

where A is a constant to be determined, and β_1 is the positive root of the quadratic

$$\tfrac{1}{2}\,\sigma_y^2\, \beta(\beta - 1) + \alpha_w\, \beta - (r + \lambda - \alpha_x) = 0.$$

As usual we have eliminated the term involving the negative root by considering the limit as W goes to zero. The interpretation of the solution should also be familiar from our earlier treatment of purely aggregate uncertainty. The first term on the right-hand side in the solution represents the expected present value of profit flow if W could continue its process without any fear of fresh entry, and the second term is the reduction in value because actual fresh entry places the ceiling on the W process. Also as usual, for the solution to make economic sense, we need the denominator in the first term on the right-hand side, namely, $(r + \lambda - \alpha_x - \alpha_w)$, to be positive. This in turn yields $\beta_1 > 1$.

The constant is determined, as was done earlier in this chapter in equation (7), from the "smooth-pasting" condition at the reflecting barrier: $v'(\overline{W}) = 0$. This yields

$$v(W) = \frac{1}{r + \lambda - \alpha_x - \alpha_w}\,[\, W - W^{\beta_1}\, \overline{W}^{1-\beta_1}\, /\, \beta_1\,]. \tag{42}$$

The actual value of a firm with a given X is $V(X, W) = Xv(W)$. A prospective entrant, however, observes only W. Therefore the expected value from the entrant's perspective is $\overline{X}v(W)$. The threshold $\overline{W}$ is defined by the condition of free entry, so this expected value must equal the cost of entry R at that point. Substituting and simplifying, we find

$$\overline{X}\overline{W} = \frac{\beta_1}{\beta_1 - 1} (r + \lambda - \alpha_x - \alpha_w) R. \tag{43}$$

This is a very natural generalization that combines the corresponding equations for the case of pure industry-wide uncertainty—equation (10) of Section 2 above—and pure firm-specific uncertainty—equation (27) of Section 4 above. Its properties should by now be too familiar to need comment.

For further theoretical details of this model we refer the reader to Caballero and Pindyck (1992). In Chapter 12 we will discuss an empirical application of it.

6   Guide to the Literature

Lucas and Prescott (1971) considered the rational expectations equilibrium of investment in a competitive industry using a discrete-time Markov chain model. They established the optimality of the equilibrium. Lippman and Rumelt (1985) combined entry and exit in a similar model.

Edleson and Osband (1988) showed that a competitive firm's entry and exit thresholds in equilibrium were not the Marshallian ones. The coincidence between a monopoly firm's option-value thresholds and a competitive firm's free entry threshold was first noted by Leahy (1992). Our exposition mostly follows Dixit (1993b).

Dumas (1992) presented an early model of general equilibrium where each firm made costly switching decisions under Brownian motion uncertainty; this was in the context of international relocation of productive capital, and the aim was to characterize the equilibrium dynamics of real exchange rates.

Caballero (1991) attempted to study industry equilibrium by the shortcut of modelling just one firm's decision, parametrically varying the price elasticity of its demand, and interpreting perfect competition as the limit when the elasticity goes to infinity. He argued that the traditional present value criterion would be restored in this limit. However, one must recognize that the level of price about which to make the demand more elastic is itself endogenous, and moreover, it acts as a ceiling or reflecting barrier. These effects can be understood only by conducting a proper industry-level analysis. See Pindyck (1993a) for a more specific and detailed discussion of this point. Caballero and Pindyck (1992) later joined forces to produce the model of industry equilibrium with combined firm-specific and aggregate uncertainty that forms the basis of our treatment above.

Chapter 9

Policy Intervention and Imperfect Competition

IN THE previous chapter we developed a basic model of competitive industry equilibrium in which each firm makes its irreversible investment decisions in an environment of ongoing uncertainty, knowing that all other firms are similarly situated and are making similar decisions. We considered industry-wide as well as firm-specific uncertainty, and found that both had the effect of making firms less eager to invest, but for different reasons. With industry-wide uncertainty, each firm knows that others will enter or expand in response to favorable developments just as it does. The resulting increase in supply will dampen the price increase, thereby reducing the firm's upside profit potential, and therefore the expected value of its own investment. With firm-specific uncertainty, each firm can take advantage of its own good fortune. However, then it must compare immediate investment against the alternative of waiting to reassess the situation. Waiting allows it to see if its good fortune is transient, and thus reduce the downside risk of investment. Thus uncertainty makes waiting more valuable, and discourages immediate investment.

In this chapter we extend the simple model that was used to make these points, and pursue its further implications. The first issue is with respect to the social optimality of this industry equilibrium. Many would argue that if firms are hesitant to invest in the face of ongoing uncertainty, the government should act to provide additional investment incentives. We find that this argument is often wrong, and at the very least must be severely qualified. The equilibrium of the basic model displays a great deal of inertia, but has no inherent distortion or market failure, so the inertia is socially optimal. A planner facing the same uncertainty and contemplating the same irreversible investment decisions should hesitate just as much. Policy intervention is justified only if some kind of market failure coexists with the uncertainty and irreversibility. A natural one in this context is the failure of markets to share risk, and we discuss the issues that it raises. However, we also find that some policies to reduce risk, for example, price controls, can have counterproductive and even surprising side effects.

The mathematical apparatus for examining social optimality has a useful by-product: it allows us to extend the simple model of Chapter 8 in a variety of useful ways. Earlier we had assumed multiplicative demand shocks, and identical firms each with unit output capacity and zero variable costs of production. Using the new techniques, we can remove all of these restrictions. The only difference this makes is that in industry equilibrium the ceiling (reflecting barrier) on the price process is no longer constant, but can change with the currently active number of firms.

Finally, we relax the assumption of perfect competition, and consider the industry equilibrium when the number of potential competitors is small. The stochastic choice problem then becomes a stochastic game. Such games are quite difficult with regard to both their general theory and their solution in our specific context, but we develop a simple special model that brings out some useful insights. A more general analysis of this kind is a promising topic for future research.

Even more promising areas of research related to the work of these chapters comprise econometric work to test these theories, and empirical work to apply them where appropriate. In Chapter 12 we provide a brief survey of the little work of this kind known to us, and we suggest avenues for further empirical research.

1 Social Optimality

Our industry consists of firms that operate in a well-functioning capital market where any risk is efficiently priced. The output market is competitive, and the firms have rational expectations. This is just the standard Arrow-Debreu framework where complete markets efficiently coordinate decisions involving time and uncertainty. Therefore we should expect the industry equilibrium to be socially optimal. We now demonstrate this optimality explicitly.

In the process we develop a new method of solving for the industry equilibrium that proves useful in its own right. The social optimum is the solution to a simple dynamic optimization problem. When it replicates the market equilibrium, we can find the latter by solving this same optimization problem. In all but the simplest of models, this method of finding equilibrium is far easier than trying to find a fixed point of the endogenous stochastic process of prices. We will demonstrate this by extending the simple model of Chapter 8 to allow for heterogeneous firms, each having an upward-sloping short-run supply curve, and to handle nonmultiplicative shocks to demand.

1.A   The Correspondence between Optimum and Equilibrium

We begin by characterizing the social optimum in the basic model of Chapter 8 with aggregate uncertainty. Recall that in that model, the industry's inverse demand curve is

$$P = Y D(Q), \tag{1}$$

where the multiplicative shift variable Y follows the geometric Brownian motion

$$dY = \alpha Y \, dt + \sigma Y \, dz. \tag{2}$$

The industry output Q equals the number of producing units, which is treated as a continuous variable. Each unit can be activated by incurring a sunk cost I. Suppose the decision to add capacity to the industry is taken by a social planner. In this context, we can treat the productive units as firms in a decentralized interpretation or implementation of the social optimum.

The area under the demand curve at any instant is given by

$$Y U(Q) = Y \int_0^Q D(q) \, dq. \tag{3}$$

This can be thought of as the flow of total social utility generated by the output flow Q when the shift variable takes the value Y; then $Y U'(Q) = Y D(Q)$ is the marginal social utility. In the decentralized implementation, this is just the price. Since there are no variable costs, the social planner aims to maximize the expected present value of social utility, net of the costs of capacity expansion.

The social utility at any instant t is $Y_t U(Q_t)$. If an amount ΔQ_t is added to capacity at this instant, a cost equal to $I \Delta Q_t$ is incurred. The social planner's objective function is therefore

$$\mathcal{E} \left\{ \int_0^\infty Y_t \, U(Q_t) \, e^{-\mu t} \, dt - \sum_t I \, \Delta Q_t \, e^{-rt} \right\},$$

where the sum is taken over all those instants when capacity additions take place. The uncertain revenues are discounted at the rate μ that includes the systematic risk, while the certain costs are discounted at the riskless rate r. The planner maximizes this social net present value, given the initial conditions, say, $Y_0 = Y$ and $Q_0 = Q$.

This is a dynamic programming problem. Here we will solve it somewhat heuristically so as to get quickly to the results. In Chapter 11 we will examine a similar problem of a single firm's capacity expansion in somewhat greater formal detail.[1]

Let $W(Q, Y)$ denote the maximized value of the objective function, that is, the Bellman value function, where the arguments are the initial state (Q, Y). As usual in dynamic programming, we break up the problem into the immediate future and the continuation beyond it. The social planner's immediate concern is whether to expand the capacity by some amount dQ. This would cost $I\,dQ$, and would increase the value function by $W_Q(Q, Y)\,dQ$. Therefore the addition is not justified if $W_Q(Q, Y) < I$. We expect intuitively that higher values of Y will justify further capacity additions. Therefore for each Q there will be a threshold, which we denote by $Y(Q)$, such that the marginal addition dQ will be optimal only when Y reaches $Y(Q)$. Moreover, the curve $Y(Q)$ will be upward sloping. Of course we must obtain $Y(Q)$ as a part of the solution.

In the region below this curve, where $Y < Y(Q)$, the firm will not add capacity for the next short interval of time dt. Therefore the Bellman equation of dynamic programming will become

$$W(Q, Y) = Y U(Q)\, dt + e^{-\rho\,dt}\, \mathcal{E}[W(Q, Y + dY)].$$

Expanding the right-hand side using Ito's Lemma and simplifying as we did so often in Chapters 5 and 6, we see that the Bellman function satisfies the differential equation

$$\tfrac{1}{2} \sigma^2 Y^2\, W_{YY}(Q, Y) + (r - \delta)\, Y\, W_Y(Q, Y) - r\, W(Q, Y) + Y U(Q) = 0. \quad (4)$$

For each Q, we can regard this as an ordinary differential equation linking W to Y. Again we draw on the experience of work in Chapters 5 and 6 to write down the solution

$$W(Q, Y) = B(Q)\, Y^{\beta_1} + Y U(Q)/\delta, \quad (5)$$

---

[1] After reading Chapter 11, Section 1, readers may find it useful to return to this section and compare the methods and the results.

where $B(Q)$ is a function to be determined,[2] δ is defined as $\mu - \alpha$, and β_1 is the positive root of the fundamental quadratic,

$$\mathcal{Q} \equiv \tfrac{1}{2}\sigma^2 \beta(\beta - 1) + (r - \delta)\beta - r = 0.$$

Assuming $r > 0$ and $\delta > 0$, as needed for convergence, we have $\beta_1 > 1$. Also, as before, we have considered the limit as $Y \to 0$ to eliminate the term with the negative root β_2.

To complete the solution we must find the optimal capacity expansion policy. At the boundary where the marginal dQth unit is added, the increase $W_Q(Q, Y)$ in the Bellman function equals the cost I of the marginal unit (the value-matching condition). Therefore

$$B'(Q)\, Y^{\beta_1} + Y\, U'(Q)/\delta = I. \tag{6}$$

Moreover, the derivatives of the gain W_Q and the cost I with respect to Y must be equal (the smooth-pasting condition). So $W_{QY}(Q, Y)$ must be zero, or

$$\beta\, B'(Q)\, Y^{\beta_1 - 1} + U'(Q)/\delta = 0. \tag{7}$$

We can solve these two equations to find the threshold $Y(Q)$; it satisfies

$$Y(Q)\, U'(Q) = \frac{\beta_1}{\beta_1 - 1}\, \delta\, I. \tag{8}$$

The equation has a very natural interpretation. The left-hand side is just the derivative with respect to Q of the flow of total social utility given by equation (3), and thus equals $Y\, D(Q)$, the price. We see, then, that the socially optimal threshold is defined very neatly in terms of a critical level of the price. More remarkably, this critical price is just the competitive equilibrium entry threshold $\overline{P}$ that we found in equation (9) of Chapter 8. The social optimum and the competitive equilibrium are one and the same. This confirms the intuition that led us down this avenue in the first place.[3]

The social optimality perspective, although formally equivalent to the perspective of a competitive equilibrium, has some practical advantages. For example, if the demand shock is not multiplicative, the entry threshold price varies with the current capacity. A pure equilibrium approach would require

---

[2]Since Q enters the differential equation (4) like a parameter, the constant of integration also depends on Q.

[3]We have merely verified the coincidence of the equilibrium and the optimum for a special example. For a general and rigorous proof, see Lucas and Prescott (1971).

us to look for a fixed point in the space of functions $\overline{P}(Q)$, which can be very difficult. The social optimization approach extends far more easily to such contexts; we will illustrate some of these in the next section.

Returning to the simple model, we can also eliminate Y between equations (6) and (7) to get $B'(Q)$, and integrate this to find $B(Q)$ and thus complete the solution for $W(Q, Y)$. We have

$$B'(Q) = -(\beta_1 - 1)^{\beta_1 - 1} \left(\frac{U'(Q)}{\delta} \right)^{\beta_1} I^{1-\beta_1} / \beta_1^{\beta_1}.$$

The precise expression is not of great interest here, but the interpretation of $B(Q)$ has considerable importance. In equation (5), the second term, $Y U(Q)/\delta$, is the expected present value of $Y U(Q)$ if Q is held fixed at its current level while Y follows its Brownian motion process. Therefore the first term, $B(Q) Y^{\beta_1}$, must be the value of society's ability to invest and thereby increase Q optimally in response to the evolution of Y. In other words, the first term is the value placed by society on its options to expand this industry. When a marginal expansion is actually carried out, society gains $Y U'(Q)/\delta$ in the form of expected present value of the extra output, but loses the value $-B'(Q) Y^{\beta_1}$ of the marginal option thus exercised [note $B'(Q)$ is negative]. Then the value-matching condition (6) equates the balance of these two effects (the net benefit) of the action to its cost I.

We can use the notation of Chapters 5 and 6 and write

$$v(Q, Y) = Y U'(Q)/\delta, \qquad f(Q, Y) = -B'(Q) Y^{\beta_1}.$$

Then $v(Q, Y)$ is the value of the marginal unit after it is installed, and $f(Q, Y)$ the value of the option to install it. The optimal threshold is found from the value-matching and smooth-pasting conditions exactly analogous to those of equations (7) and (8) in Chapter 6, namely

$$f(Q, Y) = v(Q, Y) - I, \qquad f_Y(Q, Y) = v_Y(Q, Y).$$

Then the value of this whole industry to society, when Q units are already installed and the current level of the stochastic variable is Y, is given by

$$W(Q, Y) = \int_0^Q v(q, Y) \, dq + \int_Q^\infty f(q, Y) \, dq,$$

that is, the sum of the values in place of all the installed units, and the sum of the values of options to install all the future units. The reader can easily check that our solution in equation (5) for $W(Q, Y)$ achieves exactly this.

In Chapter 11 we will consider a firm that can expand its capacity incrementally, and find a similar option value component in the total value of the firm. There we will recapitulate this intuition and build on it.

1.B   A More General Model

The social optimality perspective allows us to generalize the model of industry equilibrium, and in the process bring out an important principle that governs competitive firms' irreversible investment decisions.

Suppose industry demand takes the very general form

$$P = D(Q, Y). \tag{9}$$

Thus we no longer restrict the demand shift variable Y to enter multiplicatively. The expression for the area under the demand curve then becomes

$$U(Q, Y) = \int_0^Q D(q, Y) \, dq. \tag{10}$$

Differentiating, we have $U_Q(Q, Y) = D(Q, Y)$.

We also let firms have more general and flexible technologies. Each firm can vary its rate of output instantaneously, and firms differ in their abilities to do so. Suppose firm n has the variable cost function $c(q, n)$, where q is its rate of output. These functions have the standard properties of increasing total and marginal costs, $c_q > 0$, $c_{qq} > 0$, and the firms are labelled in order of increasing cost, so $c_n > 0$ and $c_{qn} > 0$.

Suppose N firms are currently active; we regard this as a continuous variable. A social planner, or the discipline of a competitive market, will ensure that aggregate production Q is allocated across firms—with firm n producing $q(n)$—in such a way as to minimize cost. Thus the aggregate cost function $C(Q, N)$ will achieve the following minimum:

$$\min_{q(n)} \int_0^N c(q(n), n) \, dn \qquad \text{subject to} \qquad \int_0^N q(n) \, dn = Q.$$

The first-order conditions for this minimization are

$$c_q(q(n), n) = \omega \qquad \text{for all } n \in [0, N],$$

where ω is the Lagrange multiplier.[4] By the envelope theorem, we have

$$C_Q(Q, N) = \omega.$$

----

[4] If N is large relative to Q, there may be a corner solution where some firms with the largest initial marginal cost $c_q(0, n)$ have zero output. This will complicate the algebra slightly without changing anything of economic significance; therefore we omit this consideration.

In other words, the marginal cost is equalized across firms, and the aggregate marginal cost equals each firm's marginal cost. That theorem also gives

$$C_N(Q, N) = c(q(N), N) - \omega q(N).$$

The aggregate output flow is also a matter of choice. The social planner will choose this to maximize the net social surplus (excess of utility over cost), which we denote by $S(N, Y)$. When the demand shift variable is at Y and there are N active firms, this means

$$S(N, Y) = \max_Q [U(Q, Y) - C(Q, N)].$$

The first-order condition for this is $U_Q(Q, Y) = C_Q(Q, N)$, or

$$D(Q, Y) = c_q(q(n), n) = \omega \qquad \text{for all } n \in [0, N].$$

Thus price equals each firm's marginal cost, which is the standard condition of short-run equilibrium in a competitive market.

By the envelope theorem, we have

$$S_N(N, Y) = -C_N(N, Y) = \omega q(N) - c(q(N), N)$$

$$= D(Q, Y) q(N) - c(q(N), N).$$

This is just the last firm's operating profit flow, and we abbreviate it as $\pi(N, Y)$.

Now consider the social planner's investment problem. A new firm can be established by making an irreversible investment I. For notational simplicity we assume risk neutrality, although the equivalent risk-neutral valuation procedure of Chapter 4, Section 3 can handle risk aversion. By natural extension of the previous special case, the social objective is

$$\mathcal{E} \left\{ \int_0^\infty S(N_t, Y_t) e^{-rt} dt - \sum_t I \Delta N_t e^{-rt} \right\},$$

where the sum is taken over all those instants when new firms are established. Let $W(N, Y)$ denote the result of the maximization as a function of the initial state (N, Y), namely, the Bellman value function. By retracing the steps of the argument of the multiplicative shock case in the previous subsection, we can write down its form

$$W(N, Y) = B(N) Y^{\beta_1} + T(N, Y),$$

where $T(N, Y)$ is the expected present value of the surplus that would result if N were kept constant at its initial value forever, and the first term is the value of society's expansion options.

The critical level of Y that would make it optimal to establish the marginal dNth firm is then given by the familiar value-matching and smooth-pasting conditions

$$W_N(N, Y) \equiv B'(N)\, Y^{\beta_1} + T_N(N, Y) = I,$$

and

$$W_{NY}(N, Y) \equiv \beta_1\, B'(N)\, Y^{\beta_1 - 1} + T_{NY}(N, Y) = 0.$$

Eliminating $B'(N)$ between these two equations, we get

$$T_N(N, Y) - \frac{Y}{\beta_1}\, T_{NY}(N, Y) = I. \tag{11}$$

This is the implicit function defining the threshold Y as a function of N.

To interpret it, observe that

$$T(N, Y) = \mathcal{E}\left\{ \int_0^\infty S(N, Y_t)\, e^{-rt}\, dt \right\}.$$

Differentiating under the integral sign, we get

$$T_N(N, Y) = \mathcal{E}\left\{ \int_0^\infty S_N(N, Y_t)\, e^{-rt}\, dt \right\}.$$

We saw above that $S_N(N, Y)$ was simply the operating profit $\pi(N, Y)$ of the Nth firm. Thus $T_N(N, Y)$ is just the expected value of this operating profit, calculated holding N constant while Y_t follows its stochastic process starting at the given initial Y.

Then T_{NY} is the marginal effect on this expected value of starting at a higher level of the stochastic variable Y. Since higher Y raises the profit, T_{NY} is positive. Therefore in equation (11) we must have $T_N > I$. In other words, at the threshold that justifies establishing the marginal firm dN when there are N actual firms, the marginal expected value of so doing exceeds the cost of the action. The reason is also familiar: the excess is just the opportunity cost to society of exercising the option.

Thus the general model in many respects replicates the analysis and the results of the earlier simple case. However, one result does not survive; only in very special cases will the threshold level found from (11) imply a constant price $D(Q, Y)$. Generally, the threshold price will be a function of the current number of firms, N.

Once again, since there are no distortions or market failures, the social planner's problem yields the same result as would a direct solution for the competitive equilibrium, but now we see the merit of our indirect approach.

If the entry threshold price is a function $\overline{P}(N)$, then the endogenous price process of the equilibrium is much more complicated. Its ceiling (reflecting barrier) shifts as new firms enter. To find the equilibrium, we must solve a fixed-point problem in a complicated function space. The social optimality problem remains a simple dynamic optimization calculation.

There is more. The formula (11) conceals an important and simple principle that governs the entry decisions of competitive firms. Suppose N firms are already in the industry, and the next marginal firm is contemplating entry. Suppose it has rational expectations about the stochastic evolution of Y, but it assumes itself to be the last entrant, ignoring the fact that other firms will enter after it if and when Y rises to suitable levels. It will calculate the expected present value of its profits as

$$v(N, Y) = \mathcal{E} \left\{ \int_0^\infty \pi(N, Y_t) e^{-rt} \, dt \right\} = T_N(N, Y).$$

It will carry out the usual calculation for the value $f(N, Y)$ of its option to enter, and find

$$f(N, Y) = b(N) \, Y^{\beta_1},$$

where $b(N)$ is determined jointly with the entry threshold $Y(N)$ from the value-matching and smooth-pasting conditions

$$f(N, Y) = v(n, Y) - I, \qquad f_Y(N, Y) = v_Y(N, Y).$$

It is easy to check that, on eliminating $b(N)$, these reduce to equation (11), exactly the equation for the threshold in the social optimum cum competitive equilibrium, where each firm recognizes the possibility of future entry and of the effect of such entry on the price process and on its own profit flow.

In other words, each firm can make its entry decision by finding the expected present value of its profits *as if it were the last firm that would enter this industry*, and then making the standard option value calculation. While the firm should entertain rational expectations about the stochastic process of Y, *it can be totally myopic in the matter of other firms' entry decisions*. Not only does it reach the same decision as it would if it correctly anticipated their entry decisions, but it gets to this answer with a far simpler calculation.

When the Nth firm pretends that it will be the last one to enter this industry, it is ignoring two things. First, it is thinking its profit flow will be given by the stochastic evolution of $\pi(N, Y)$ as Y changes, holding N fixed. Thus it is ignoring the reduction in the upside of its profit caused by the subsequent entry that would occur in response to Y rising to new heights. Other things equal, this would make investment seem more attractive to this firm than it would if it took entry into account. However, it is also ignoring the fact that the prospect of future entry reduces its value of waiting. It is pretending that it has the luxury of postponing its decision, and acting as though there is a positive value to its option to wait. Other things equal, this makes investment seem less attractive than it would otherwise. These two effects exactly offset each other, so that in this case, two wrongs make a right in the firm's optimal choice. We noted a special case of this in Chapter 8, Section 2(b), where the exact level of a price ceiling was immaterial to the calculation of a firm's entry threshold price, as long as the ceiling was at least as high as this threshold. Now we see the general version of the effect. This remarkable property of the competitive equilibrium was discovered by Leahy (1992).

1.C   Implications for Antitrust and Trade Policy

We have seen that the standard correspondence between social optimality and competitive equilibrium holds in the kind of model we have constructed so far. As long as there are no externalities, and the relevant risks can be traded in efficient markets, dynamics and uncertainty are not by themselves sufficient reasons for policy intervention. True, the market outcome shows a great deal of inertia—ranges of shocks where no investment takes place—and in popular perception the hesitancy of firms to invest might seem reason enough for the government to intervene and speed up the pace of investment. However, the inertia is optimal—a social planner would not want to invest any faster.

There are other features of our stochastic dynamic market equilibrium that are often thought to be inefficiencies requiring corrective policies. That is because the conventional textbook view of equilibrium is static, based on the Marshallian long-run picture. In that view, firms enter an industry when the price rises above the long-run average cost, and exit when price falls below the average variable cost. A price in excess of long-run average cost is then regarded as evidence of entry barriers, calling for antitrust measures. Similarly, a price below average variable cost is often regarded as a sign of predatory dumping, usually by foreign firms, and thus a justification for trade sanctions.

We want to emphasize that such conclusions are liable to be fundamentally mistaken, because in reality economic conditions are never tranquil. It is essential to think of the industry equilibrium in such a situation as itself changing in response to evolving uncertainty, that is, a stochastic process. The natural competitive dynamics of an industry in the face of ongoing uncertainty will have phases when a "snapshot" of the industry has features that the static theory would interpret as deviations from competitive behavior. This idea of regarding competitive equilibrium as a stochastic process has become quite common in macroeconomics; it is time for industrial organization theory and antitrust policy to recognize the same reality.

Suppose such an industry comes to the attention of policy authorities at an instant when the price is between the Marshallian long-run level P_0 and the equilibrium threshold $\overline{P}$. They see established firms making supernormal profits, but no new entry taking place. Using conventional microeconomics or industrial organization theory, they would suspect the presence of monopoly power or entry barriers, and might take antitrust action. That would be wrong; the process viewed as a whole is fully competitive, long-run expected returns are normal, and the equilibrium is socially optimal.

Likewise, if the price is below the minimum average variable cost, that need not signal predatory dumping by the firms that are incurring the losses. Remember that if market conditions are sufficiently volatile, the lower threshold price at which firms should optimally exit will be well below the minimum average variable cost. Thus in such a situation we may simply be observing firms rationally riding out a bad period to keep their sunk capital alive.[5]

The numerical example of the copper industry in Chapter 8 showed us that the market price is likely to be outside the Marshallian range for most of the time. Thus not just snapshots but time series of a few years' duration may also be insufficient. Only by observing the evolution of the industry for a very long time can we hope to spot genuine departures from the competitive norm. Basing policies on snapshots can result in serious mistakes despite the policymaker's best intentions. In the picture presented above, prices above long-run average costs and the resulting temporary large profits are merely due to the swings of demand in a competitive industry that permits only a normal profit as a long-run average. However, governments often try to control the supposedly excessive profits of firms, and protect consumers from these supposedly excessive prices. Urban residential rent controls are a common instance of such policies.

In Section 2 we will develop a model that describes the effect of such policies on investment in a true dynamic context. We will find that price controls can depress investment and thereby reduce industry supply to such an extent that the average price in the long run actually goes *up*. Thus a policy of price

---

[5]Of course, even if there were no uncertainty whatsoever over future market conditions, price could be below the minimum average variable cost if firms are moving down the steep part of a learning curve. Finally, price could be below the minimum average variable cost because of a combination of volatile economic conditions and a learning curve—for example, in the case of semiconductors.

controls can have perverse effects even from the perspective of the group it is designed to help. Conversely, if the government introduces price floors to support firms in bad periods, firms will react accordingly. They will enter the industry in greater numbers, and that can then make the bad times even worse, leading to a large drain of government revenues. Agricultural price supports, a long-standing policy fixture in the United States and in Europe (through the Common Agricultural Policy), often have such effects.

1.D   Market Failures and Policy Responses

We found above that uncertainty and irreversibility do not by themselves constitute market failures that warrant government intervention. It is important to emphasize this point, because public policy debates often err on this matter. The existence of adjustment costs is itself often thought to be an economic problem requiring policy action when industries and workers suffer adverse shocks, especially those arising from international competition. Calls for government action in such cases should be based on some other genuine market failure.

This does not mean that markets always work perfectly and government intervention is never called for. Some forms of market failure do arise naturally in a dynamic environment with uncertainty. In particular, markets for risk are often incomplete. The reasons for this have to do with asymmetric information or the sheer complexity of complete contracts. Labor income risk is particularly difficult to insure against. When such separate causes of market failure coexist with our basic issue of irreversible choices under ongoing uncertainty, the two interact to produce some new and interesting kinds of suboptimal outcomes.

We do not have the space here to provide a detailed description of models that demonstrate such market failures. Therefore we will merely outline the economic intuition behind them, and refer the interested reader to the work on which our discussion is based, Dixit and Rob (1993a,b).

The failure of risk markets is most frequent and natural in the context of labor income. Now labor supply decisions, for example, educational and occupational choices, also involve substantial sunk costs or irreversibilities, and must be made in an environment with ongoing uncertainty. Thus they are in essence investment decisions, and our general framework is naturally suited to their analysis. That is the setting we use.

Consider an economy that offers two alternative occupations, which we will call sectors and which may be different industries or cities. The relative attractiveness of the two fluctuates over time, for example, because of random technological shocks. A shift from one sector to the other requires some sunk costs that can include (depending on the circumstances) retraining, travel, purchase and sale of a house, moving household effects, time and effort involved in making new friends, and many other tangible and intangible costs. Therefore an individual will not make the switch unless the relative attractiveness of the other sector is sufficiently high to offset not just the normal return on these costs, but also the option value of the status quo.

The relative price between the outputs of the two sectors is determined in equilibrium by the standard equality of demand and supply. Call the sectors 1 and 2. In the absence of any labor mobility, the incomes of workers in each sector move in proportion to the technological productivity shock for that sector. This comprises the income risk that people face. Now suppose sector 2 receives a favorable shock. When an individual moves from sector 1 to sector 2 in response, this raises the output of 2 and so lowers its equilibrium price relative to 1. That dampens the initial increase of incomes in sector 2 relative to 1. In other words, when one person moves to the favored sector, that reduces the extent of income risk faced by all the others in both sectors.

If the risk were efficiently allocated using complete markets, this price change would be only a pecuniary externality. However, because risk markets are incomplete, the reduction in risk has real effects: it is a beneficial externality conveyed by the mover on all others in society. Since the mover does not take this social benefit into account in his private calculation, the resulting labor mobility is suboptimally low. A government that can encourage some extra mobility (perhaps by subsidizing job changes and any retraining that might be involved) can achieve a better outcome for society as a whole.[6]

This mechanism operates via the endogenous relative price. Therefore it is less significant the more elastic is demand. In the limiting case of a small economy that is open to world trade, the relative price is determined (perhaps as a stochastic process) by world market conditions, and the shift of labor across sectors in the economy has no impact on this price. Then the degree of mobility in equilibrium is the second-best optimal given the limitations on the risk markets. Unless the government can devise new ways to share risk, it cannot improve upon the outcome of uncoordinated private choices.

Various kinds of taxation do provide indirect risk sharing. In an open economy, trade taxes are such an instrument. Suppose the government levies

---

[6]In the light of this analysis, it is ironic that governments often pursue policies that actually reduce labor mobility, for example, public housing policies that favor long-time residents of a city. It is then necessary to undertake a variety of social insurance measures that ameliorate the greater income risk that the locked-in individuals face.

a tax (or offers a subsidy) so that the domestic relative price is not the same as the world relative price. Now the incomes in the two sectors are tied to the domestic output prices, and are further affected by the distribution of tax revenues (or the contributions to the subsidy proceeds). This changes the allocation of risk. Then it is not hard in principle to find a policy that will improve risk bearing and thus generate a social improvement. However, the precise nature of the policy is highly situation specific; a simple recipe such as an import tariff cannot be guaranteed to be beneficial across any broad range of circumstances.

2   Analyses of Some Commonly Used Policies

Governments do employ some policies that alter the uncertainty facing firms and consumers in their economic decisions. The policies are usually motivated by some immediate political or economic reason—a belief that firms are charging excessive prices, or a perceived need to stimulate investment. Now the simplest economic analysis teaches us that policies implemented with one aim often have other side effects; these are often surprisingly detrimental. This problem is all the more severe in the stochastic dynamic environment that is the theme of our book. In this section we illustrate this by analyzing two such policies.

2.A   Price Controls

Governments often attempt to reduce price volatility by imposing controls. The immediate aim is usually to protect consumers from excessively high prices, as in the case of urban rent ceilings or the U.S. natural gas and oil price controls of the 1970s, or to protect the incomes of producers, as with the European Common Agricultural Policy and the plethora of agricultural price supports in the United States. Economists are generally critical of such measures. They emphasize the harmful side effects, for example, the scarcity and poor quality of rental housing in cities with rent controls, and the wheat mountains and wine lakes in Europe. The economic analysis underlying these arguments is the standard textbook supply-and-demand framework. If the price is kept below the market-clearing level, there will be too little supply, and if it is kept above, too much. However, this is a very static picture, while the effects in reality are mostly dynamic, operating through the *investment* decisions of landlords or farmers. Our approach to investment under uncertainty permits a richer analysis of the effects of price controls, and yields a deeper understanding of their side effects.

We continue to use our basic model. To recapitulate, each firm has the capacity to produce one unit output when active, a sunk cost of investment I, and a variable cost of production C. For simplicity of notation, we assume risk neutrality and the riskless discount rate r. The industry demand curve is

$$P = Y D(Q), \tag{12}$$

where the aggregate shock Y follows the geometric Brownian motion

$$dY = \alpha Y \, dt + \sigma Y \, dz.$$

The simplest and unified treatment of price ceiling and floor policies can be given if the industry equilibrium involves both entry and exit. Therefore we adopt the model of Chapter 7, where a firm that is not producing must lose its sunk investment. Then we know that the industry equilibrium in the absence of any controls is characterized by an entry threshold and an exit threshold. For reasons that will be evident soon, we write the former as $\overline{S}$ and the latter as $\underline{S}$.

Now suppose the government imposes a ceiling $\overline{P}$ and/or a floor $\underline{P}$ on the price. We take this to mean that if at the existing level of Q and Y in the industry the price given by (12) that would clear the market exceeds $\overline{P}$, then the firm can collect only $\overline{P}$ and the excess demand is rationed. If the price that would clear the market is below $\underline{P}$, then the firms receive $\underline{P}$, and government becomes the buyer of last resort to absorb the excess supply. We assume in the background that such government purchases are either destroyed, or exported or given to other countries, with no future feedback on demand or supply in our economy. (This is broadly true for European agricultural policies.) Nor shall we be concerned here with the effects on the government budget.

In Chapter 8 we studied an aspect of a firm's entry and exit choices when such policies are in effect. In fact we found that as long as $\overline{P}$ exceeds the natural entry threshold $\overline{S}$, the actual level of $\overline{P}$ has no effect on $\overline{S}$ at all. A lower ceiling reduces the value of investing immediately and the value of waiting by equal amounts, leaving unaffected the trade-off that governs the investment threshold. A similar situation holds when the floor $\underline{P}$ is actually lower than the natural exit threshold $\underline{S}$.

Now we must allow the ceilings and floors to bind, and see how that will affect firms' choices and the industry's equilibrium. For simplicity of exposition we do this separately for ceilings and floors; then the two treatments are in principle easy to combine into a joint analysis.

First suppose the price floor is too low to affect the picture, say, $\underline{P} = 0$, but that the ceiling $\overline{P}$ sometimes binds. That is, sometimes the price that would clear the market exceeds $\overline{P}$. We will call this hypothetical market-clearing price the *shadow price*. We assume that the firms, both actual and potential, can observe the degree of scarcity (landlords see how many prospective tenants are going around looking for apartments, or read about it in the newspapers), so that they can calculate the shadow price. This will influence their decisions. Even though a unit of output currently gets only the controlled price $\overline{P}$, if the shadow price is much higher, they know that the control is likely to stay binding, and therefore the price is unlikely to fall below $\overline{P}$, for a long time. Therefore a higher shadow price will make investment more attractive even though it does not alter the actual current profit flow. Then there will be a threshold $\overline{S}$ that will trigger new investment. As the ceiling $\overline{P}$ is gradually lowered, the shadow price threshold $\overline{S}$ will rise. When the ceiling approaches the Marshallian long-run average cost $(C + r\,I)$, the shadow price threshold will approach infinity—if the controls are going to allow only a normal return, firms will invest only when they are assured that this state of affairs will last forever.

Suppose $\overline{P}$ is in this range of its effectiveness. Now we must determine thresholds such that $\underline{S} < \overline{P} < \overline{S}$. For this, we consider the value v of an actual firm as a function of the prevailing shadow price S.

When the shadow price S is in the range $(\underline{S}, \overline{P})$, it is also the actual price, and the firm's profit flow is $(S - C)$. Then, following familiar steps, its value is

$$v(S) = S/\delta - C/r + A_1\,S^{\beta_1} + A_2\,S^{\beta_2}. \tag{13}$$

The first two terms give the expected value of profits if neither exit nor the binding ceiling were ever going to be relevant; note that with S rising at the expected rate α, the revenue flow is discounted at rate $r - \alpha = \delta$. The other two terms are the expected present values of the consequences of reaching the exit threshold and the price ceiling in the future. The powers β_1 and β_2 are the roots of the familiar quadratic, and the constants A_1 and A_2 remain to be determined. To aid in this, we have the value-matching and smooth-pasting conditions at the exit threshold:

$$v(\underline{S}) = 0, \qquad v'(\underline{S}) = 0.$$

When the ceiling is binding, that is, the shadow price lies in the range $(\overline{P}, \overline{S})$, the profit flow is $(\overline{P} - C)$, and

$$v(S) = (\overline{P} - C)/r + B_1\,S^{\beta_1} + B_2\,S^{\beta_2}. \tag{14}$$

Again the first two terms are the value of receiving this profit flow forever; note that the constant revenue $\overline{P}$ must be discounted at rate r, not δ. The other two terms are the effects of reaching the limits of the range, and the constants B_1, B_2 remain to be determined. To help do that, we have the value-matching and smooth-pasting conditions at the entry threshold:

$$v(\overline{S}) = I, \qquad v'(\overline{S}) = 0.$$

Finally, the value function must be continuously differentiable at the $\overline{P}$ where the two regimes meet. Thus the expressions for $v(S)$ from (13) and (14) evaluated at $\overline{P}$ must be equal, and the same must hold for the corresponding expressions for $v'(S)$.

In all we have six equations to determine the two thresholds $\overline{S}$, $\underline{S}$ and the four constants A_1, A_2, B_1, B_2. These need numerical solution, which we soon illustrate.

First we develop some useful information about the equilibrium. Just like the actual price in Chapter 8, the shadow price S here follows a geometric Brownian motion with parameters α and σ and reflecting barriers at $\underline{S}$ and $\overline{S}$. Then we can find the long-run distribution of S, using the same methods as we did there. The logarithm of S follows a simple Brownian motion with the drift coefficient $\alpha' = \alpha - \frac{1}{2}\sigma^2$ and the variance coefficient σ. Therefore it has an exponential distribution between its barriers $\log \underline{S}$ and $\log \overline{S}$, with the density proportional to $e^{\gamma x}$, where $\gamma = 2\alpha'/\sigma^2$. In turn, the density of S can be seen to be proportional to $S^{\gamma-1}$. Then the probability that the ceiling is binding, that is, the proportion of time S will lie above $\overline{P}$, is given by

$$[\overline{S}^{\gamma} - \overline{P}^{\gamma}] / [\overline{S}^{\gamma} - \underline{S}^{\gamma}], \tag{15}$$

if $\gamma \neq 0$. As $\overline{P}$ decreases from the no-policy entry threshold to the Marshallian long-run average cost, this probability rises from 0 to 1.

Using the density function we can also compute the long-run average $\mathcal{E}[P]$ of the actual price that will prevail in the long run. Since the actual price equals the shadow price S in the interval $(\underline{S}, \overline{P})$ and equals the ceiling price $\overline{P}$ in the interval $(\overline{P}, \overline{S})$, the expectation becomes

$$\mathcal{E}[P] = \left\{ \int_{\underline{S}}^{\overline{P}} S\, S^{\gamma-1}\, dS + \int_{\overline{P}}^{\overline{S}} \overline{P}\, S^{\gamma-1}\, dS \right\} \Big/ \int_{\underline{S}}^{\overline{S}} S^{\gamma-1}\, dS$$

$$= \{ [\overline{P}^{\gamma+1} - \underline{S}^{\gamma+1}]/(\gamma + 1) + \overline{P}[\overline{S}^{\gamma} - \overline{P}^{\gamma}]/\gamma \}$$

$$/\{ [\overline{S}^{\gamma} - \underline{S}^{\gamma}]/\gamma \}, \tag{16}$$

again provided $\gamma \neq 0$.

If $\gamma = 0$ these two expressions must be interpreted as limits, taken using L'Hospital's Rule. The probability of the ceiling being binding becomes

$$[\log \overline{S} - \log \overline{P}] / [\log \overline{S} - \log \underline{S}],$$

and the expectation of the price becomes

$$\mathcal{E}[P] = \left\{ [\overline{P} - \underline{S}] + \overline{P}[\log \overline{S} - \log \overline{P}] \right\} / [\log \overline{S} - \log \underline{S}].$$

Now we turn to the numerical simulation. Since price ceilings are more likely to be applied to an industry in which demand and the free market price have been rising, we let $\alpha = 0.02$. We take $\sigma = 0.2$ and $r = 0.05$, which are typical of the values we have used in earlier chapters. Finally, we set $C = 1$ (this is a choice of units that normalizes the average variable cost), and $I = 2$, which makes the Marshallian long-run average cost 1.1.

Table 9.1 shows the results. In the absence of any controls (or equivalently, when the ceiling is at an irrelevantly high level, in effect at infinity) the entry threshold is 1.5324 and the exit threshold is 0.6790. As the ceiling is lowered, the most important effect is on the entry threshold of the shadow price. It increases gradually at first, but then more and more rapidly. By the time the ceiling is halfway between the natural threshold and the long-run average cost, the effect gathers momentum. The long-run average frequency with which the ceiling is binding also increases. The exit threshold also rises, but this is quantitatively much less significant.

This analysis gives us a clearer idea of the mechanism by which price controls discourage investment. Under price controls, firms wait to observe a

Table 9.1. *Effects of Price Ceiling*

(Parameters: $\alpha = 0.02$, $\sigma = 0.2$, $r = 0.05$, $I = 2$, $C = 1$.)

$\overline{P}$	$\underline{S}$	$\overline{S}$	Probability	$\mathcal{E}[P]$
∞	0.6790	1.5324	0.0000	1.0484
1.50	0.6790	1.5338	0.0273	1.0485
1.40	0.6795	1.5608	0.1307	1.0494
1.30	0.6823	1.6573	0.2736	1.0517
1.20	0.6930	1.9948	0.4802	1.0564
1.15	0.7066	2.6123	0.6275	1.0607
1.12	0.7212	4.0995	0.7467	1.0658
1.11	0.7280	6.0406	0.8001	1.0692
1.10	0.7364	∞	1.0000	1.1000

greater pressure of demand before they act. This dynamic decrease of supply in turn implies that the pressure of demand will be high enough to keep the ceiling binding more often. In effect, the policy generates its own "need."

Perhaps the most interesting and surprising result is the effect of controls on the long-run average price. As the ceiling is lowered, this price *increases*. In other words, the policy fails to achieve its intended goal of reducing the prices to consumers; its effect in the long-run average sense is just the opposite! The reason is that while the incidence of prices above the ceiling is cut off, the proportion of times the price stays at the new ceiling is increased because of the reduction in investment and therefore in long-run supply. In Figure 9.1 we see this shift of the distribution of prices: as $\overline{P}$ is lowered, the density to its right disappears, but there is a larger point mass of probability at $\overline{P}$, and some of the left tail also disappears. The effect on the average price is ambiguous from the picture, but from the numerical simulations we find that the effect is "perverse."

The analysis of a price floor follows similar steps. As we raise $\underline{P}$ from 0 to the level that the exit threshold $\underline{S}$ would have in the absence of any policy, the floor remains nonbinding. Beyond this point, it starts to bind for the relatively low states of demand. That in turn changes the entry and exit thresholds. As the price floor rises, the downside risk of investment is reduced. Therefore firms are more willing to enter and less eager to leave, so both thresholds fall. When the price floor reaches C, the exit threshold $\underline{S}$ drops to zero; incumbent firms that have the guarantee of their variable costs being covered will never leave. When the price floor is between the variable cost C and the Marshallian

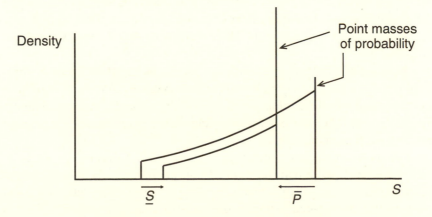

Figure 9.1. *Effect of Ceiling on Price Distribution*

long-run average cost $(C + rI)$, the exit threshold $\underline{S}$ stays at zero, while the entry threshold $\overline{S}$ remains above $(C+rI)$. This is because firms contemplating new investment still need some periods of supernormal profit to balance the periods of below-normal profits. Finally, as the price floor rises to $(C + rI)$, the entry threshold falls to that same level.

To characterize the equilibrium in more detail, we proceed as before. First suppose the price floor $\underline{P}$ is high enough to be sometimes binding, but below C. When the shadow price S lies in the interval $(\underline{S}, \underline{P})$, the firm's profit flow is $(\underline{P} - C)$ and its value is

$$v(S) = (\underline{P} - C)/r + A_1\, S^{\beta_1} + A_2\, S^{\beta_2}.$$

In the interval $(\underline{P}, \overline{S})$, the floor does not bind, the actual price equals the shadow price, the profit flow is $(S - C)$, and the value is

$$v(S) = S/\delta - C/r + B_1\, S^{\beta_1} + B_2\, S^{\beta_2}.$$

Then the value-matching and smooth-pasting conditions at $\underline{S}$ and $\overline{S}$, and the continuous differentiability at $\underline{P}$, complete the solution. We can also compute the probability that the floor will bind in the long run, and the long-run average price, as before.

Next suppose the price floor $\underline{P}$ lies in the range $(C, C + rI)$. Here $\underline{S} = 0$. For S in the range $(0, \underline{P})$, we get

$$v(S) = (\underline{P} - C)/r + A_1\, S^{\beta_1}.$$

This is just like the above solution except that only the positive root is retained by consideration of the limit as S goes to 0. For S in the range $(\underline{P}, \overline{S})$, the solution is exactly as above. Now the value-matching and smooth-pasting conditions at $\overline{S}$ and the requirement of continuous differentiability at $\underline{P}$ give four equations to determine the three constants A_1, B_1, and B_2 and the threshold $\overline{S}$.

Calculation of the long-run average price is different in this case. Since firms never leave once they have entered, the long-run number of firms goes to infinity and the distribution of the shadow price has the whole probability piled up at zero. Then in the limit the ceiling is always binding, and the average price equals the ceiling price.

We show a numerical simulation in Table 9.2. The parameters are as in the ceiling case, except that since price floors are more likely to be prevalent in industries with declining demand, we set $\alpha = -0.02$. Once again the most remarkable feature is the decline in the long-run average price as the floor is raised from its lowest nonbinding level up to the variable cost C. The reason

Table 9.2. *Effects of Price Floor*

(Parameters: $\alpha = -0.02$, $\sigma = 0.2$, $r = 0.05$, $I = 2$, $C = 1$.)

$\underline{P}$	$\underline{S}$	$\overline{S}$	Probability	$\mathcal{E}[P]$
0	0.7462	1.6667	0	1.0309
0.75	0.7462	1.6668	0.0126	1.0309
0.80	0.7398	1.6665	0.1804	1.0303
0.85	0.7184	1.6645	0.3511	1.0287
0.90	0.6722	1.6584	0.5291	1.0256
0.95	0.5735	1.6433	0.7238	1.0201
0.97	0.4982	1.6323	0.8185	1.0164
0.99	0.3543	1.6090	0.9160	1.0099
1.00	0	1.5960	1	1.00
1.02	0	1.5492	1	1.02
1.04	0	1.4899	1	1.04
1.06	0	1.4189	1	1.06
1.08	0	1.3257	1	1.08
1.09	0	1.2596	1	1.09
1.10	0	1.1000	1	1.10

is the same: the price is higher in the lowest states of demand, but this is more than offset by the effect of the induced extra entry leading to a lower price in the higher states of demand. The effect is quantitatively somewhat more modest, but it is unmistakable. Thus the long-run effect of the price floor policy may be harmful even to those it is intended to help. The observation that farmers in many countries are so dependent on farm price supports and yet so dissatisfied with their outcomes may have this explanation. Of course once the price floor rises above the variable cost level, it is always binding. Then the average price equals the floor and rises one-for-one with it, but this is a rather pathological state of affairs.

2.B Policy Uncertainty

Governments can not only deploy measures to reduce the uncertainty facing potential investors, they can also create uncertainty through the prospect of policy change. This feature of the policy process is particularly relevant in the United States, where changes in tax policy are constantly suggested and discussed, and even after a specific new tax legislation is introduced in the Congress it goes through months and even years of debate and modification. It is commonly believed that expectations of shifts of policy can have powerful effects on decisions to invest. Our theory of investment under uncertainty can examine the validity of this belief. However, policy uncertainty is not likely to be well captured by a Brownian motion process; it is more likely to be a Poisson jump. We now develop an example, based on Metcalf and Hassett (1993), to show how such policy uncertainty affects investment.

We adapt our basic model of Chapter 6. Begin with a firm contemplating a discrete investment with sunk cost I. The project will produce one unit of output flow forever after with no variable costs of production. The output price follows the geometric Brownian motion

$$dP = \alpha P \, dt + \sigma P \, dz.$$

The firm is risk neutral and r is the discount rate. Let $\delta = r - \alpha$. Then the expected present value of revenues from a completed project, when the initial price is P, is given by P/δ.

The policy instrument we consider is an investment tax credit at a given rate θ. When this policy is in effect, the sunk cost of investment to the firm is lowered to $(1 - \theta) I$. However, the government can switch between two policy regimes, one where the credit is not available, and the other where it is. We will identify the state without the tax credit by the subscript 0, and that with the tax credit by the subscript 1.

The switches between the two policy regimes are Poisson processes. Starting with a state when the credit is not in effect, the probability that it will be implemented in the next short interval of time dt is $\lambda_1 \, dt$, and when the credit is initially in effect, the corresponding probability that it will be withdrawn is $\lambda_0 \, dt$.

Intuition suggests the following form for the firm's investment policy. Over an interval of low values of P, say, $(0, P_1)$, the firm will not invest irrespective of whether the credit is in effect. Over an interval (P_1, P_0), the firm will invest if the credit is in effect, but if not, the firm will find it preferable to wait in the hope that such a policy will be implemented. Beyond P_0, the prospect of immediate revenues will be so large that the firm will invest irrespective of the current policy.

To determine the thresholds P_1 and P_0, we proceed as usual. Consider the net payoff to the investment opportunity as a function of the price, $V_0(P)$ in the absence of the credit and $V_1(P)$ when the credit is in effect. We obtain expressions and equations for these, and conditions they satisfy at the thresholds.

Over the range (P_0, ∞), the firm always invests at once, so we have

$$V_0(P) = P/\delta - I, \tag{17}$$

and

$$V_1(P) = P/\delta - (1 - \theta) I. \tag{18}$$

Over the range (P_1, P_0), the firm invests at once if the credit is in effect, so $V_1(P)$ is given by (18) as above. However, $V_0(P)$ is more complicated. Over the next short interval of time dt, with probability $\lambda_1 dt$ the credit will be implemented, the firm will invest, and its value will become $V_1(P + dP)$. Otherwise its value will be $V_0(P + dP)$. Thus

$$V_0(P) = e^{-r dt} \left\{ \lambda_1 dt \, \mathcal{E}[V_1(P + dP)] + (1 - \lambda_1 dt) \, \mathcal{E}[V_0(P + dP)] \right\}.$$

Expanding the right-hand side using Ito's Lemma, retaining leading terms in dt, and simplifying as usual, we have

$$\tfrac{1}{2} \sigma^2 P^2 V_0''(P) + (r - \delta) P V_0'(P) - r V_0(P) + \lambda_1 [V_1(P) - V_0(P)] = 0. \tag{19}$$

This is the usual differential equation for a firm waiting to invest, except for the additional term involving λ_1, which captures the expected capital gain from institution of the credit in the immediate future. Note that in the range of prices (P_1, P_0), we know the expression for $V_1(P)$. Then we can obtain the general solution to the differential equation:

$$V_0(P) = B_1 \, P^{\beta(1)_1} + B_2 \, P^{\beta(1)_2} + \frac{\lambda_1 \, P}{\delta \, (\delta + \lambda_1)} - \frac{\lambda_1 \, (1 - \theta) I}{r + \lambda_1}, \tag{20}$$

where B_1 and B_2 are constants to be determined, and $\beta(1)_1$ and $\beta(1)_2$ are the positive and negative roots of the familiar quadratic

$$\mathcal{Q}(1) \equiv \tfrac{1}{2} \sigma^2 \beta(\beta - 1) + (r - \delta) \beta - (r + \lambda_1) = 0.$$

The seemingly complicated notation for the quadratic and the roots serves to distinguish them from some other related expressions and roots that will appear soon.

Finally we address the region $(0, P_1)$. Here the firm waits in both policy regimes, and each regime can switch to the other. Following the same steps as above that led to the differential equation (19) for the waiting firm, we have a pair of differential equations:

$$\tfrac{1}{2} \sigma^2 P^2 V_0''(P) + (r - \delta) P V_0'(P) - r V_0(P) + \lambda_1 [V_1(P) - V_0(P)] = 0,$$

$$\tfrac{1}{2} \sigma^2 P^2 V_1''(P) + (r - \delta) P V_1'(P) - r V_1(P) + \lambda_0 [V_0(P) - V_1(P)] = 0.$$

These yield two linear combinations that can be solved easily. Define two new functions, say,

$$V_a(P) = V_1(P)/\lambda_0 + V_0(P)/\lambda_1, \qquad V_s(P) = V_1(P) - V_0(P).$$

Then

$$\tfrac{1}{2}\sigma^2 P^2 V_a''(P) + (r - \delta) P V_a'(P) - r V_a(P) = 0,$$

$$\tfrac{1}{2}\sigma^2 P^2 V_s''(P) + (r - \delta) P V_s'(P) - (r + \lambda_0 + \lambda_1) V_s(P) = 0.$$

Each of these equations yields a solution with powers of P that are the roots of a familiar quadratic equation. In each case we have an interval of P that extends to 0, so we include only the positive root. Thus

$$V_a(P) = C_a \, P^{\beta(0)_1}, \qquad V_s(P) = D_s \, P^{\beta(2)_1},$$

where C_a and D_s are constants to be determined, $\beta(0)_1$ is the positive root of

$$Q(0) \equiv \tfrac{1}{2}\sigma^2 \beta(\beta - 1) + (r - \delta)\beta - r = 0,$$

and $\beta(2)_1$ is the positive root of

$$Q(2) \equiv \tfrac{1}{2}\sigma^2 \beta(\beta - 1) + (r - \delta)\beta - (r + \lambda_0 + \lambda_1) = 0.$$

Mnemonically, $\beta(0)$ comes from the quadratic $Q(0)$ where the constant term includes neither λ_0 nor λ_1, $\beta(1)$ comes from the quadratic $Q(1)$ whose constant term has λ_1 alone, and $\beta(2)$ comes from the quadratic $Q(2)$ whose constant term has both λ_0 and λ_1. As before, the subscript 1 refers to the positive root and 2 to the negative root. Then the relevant roots satisfy the following chain of inequalities:

$$\beta(2)_1 > \beta(1)_1 > \beta(0)_1 > 1 > 0 > \beta(1)_2.$$

With this notation, we can write down the solutions for $V_0(P)$ and $V_1(P)$ in the range $(0, P_1)$ as

$$V_0(P) = \left\{ \lambda_0 \lambda_1 C \, P^{\beta(0)_1} - \lambda_1 D \, P^{\beta(2)_1} \right\} / (\lambda_0 + \lambda_1), \qquad (21)$$

and

$$V_1(P) = \left\{ \lambda_0 \lambda_1 C \, P^{\beta(0)_1} + \lambda_0 D \, P^{\beta(2)_1} \right\} / (\lambda_0 + \lambda_1). \qquad (22)$$

Now we can relate the expressions for the value in the different regimes. At the threshold P_1, the firm invests if the credit is in effect, so the expressions for $V_1(P)$ to the left (22) and right (18) should satisfy the value-matching and smooth-pasting conditions. For $V_0(P)$ this is not a decision threshold, but the function has to be continuously differentiable across it, so (21) and (20) should have equal values and derivatives there. Finally, for the optimum choice of the threshold P_0, the expressions for $V_0(P)$ to the left (20) and the right (17) should satisfy the value-matching and smooth-pasting conditions. In all we have six equations to determine the thresholds P_1, P_0 and the four constants B_1, B_2, C_a, and D_s.

We illustrate this calculation with a numerical solution. Take $\alpha = 0$, $\sigma = 0.1$ and $r = 0.05$, values that were fairly typical in our earlier calculations. Then $\delta = r - \alpha = 0.05$. Let $I = 20$; this is just a choice of units that gives the Marshallian investment threshold $\delta I = 1$, and allows easier interpretation of the numbers to come. With these numbers, and no tax credit policy at all, the optimal investment threshold would be $P^* = 1.3702$. Thus the normal option value premium over the Marshallian threshold is 0.37.

We consider a 10-percent tax credit, so $\theta = 0.1$. If this credit were always in effect, the threshold would be lowered by 10 percent to 1.2331. However, when the two regimes can switch back and forth in a Poisson process, both thresholds are affected. We examine the effects on the two thresholds, P_0 when the credit is not currently in effect, and P_1 when it is currently in effect, as the probability rates of enactment (λ_1) and removal (λ_0) vary over a range from 0 to 0.5 in each case. The results are shown in Tables 9.3 and 9.4.

First consider the situation when the credit is not currently in effect. Table 9.3 shows that as the probability of enactment λ_1 within the next year increases, the threshold P_0 increases. This is intuitively obvious; the prospect of a reduced cost of investment increases the value of waiting. The impressive aspect is the magnitude of this effect. The usual option value premium over the normal return of 1, if the credit had never been mentioned, was 0.37; a 30-percent probability of enactment of the 10-percent tax credit more than doubles this premium to 0.81. Remember that the tax credit had the aim of lowering the premium to 0.23. However, while the policy is being discussed and enactment is uncertain, the effect is to depress investment very strongly.

Even when the credit is *not* in place, the threshold P_0 is affected by the probability λ_0 of its *removal*. This is because the firm calculates that at the random future time when the tax credit is enacted, the economic conditions might be very unfavorable, and the credit might be removed before they improve sufficiently for it to invest. This reduces the value of waiting now. However, the effect is quantitatively negligible.

Next consider the situation when the credit is currently in effect. Now the relevant threshold is P_1 in Table 9.4. We see that it decreases as λ_0 increases:

Table 9.3.   *Investment Threshold when Tax Credit is not in Effect (P_0)*
(Parameters: $\alpha = 0$, $\sigma = 0.1$, $r = 0.05$, $I = 20$.)

	λ_1					
λ_0	0.0	0.1	0.2	0.3	0.4	0.5
0.0	1.371	1.498	1.642	1.813	2.003	2.201
0.1	1.371	1.494	1.641	1.813	2.003	2.201
0.2	1.371	1.492	1.640	1.813	2.003	2.201
0.3	1.371	1.491	1.639	1.812	2.003	2.201
0.4	1.371	1.491	1.638	1.812	2.003	2.201
0.5	1.371	1.490	1.638	1.812	2.002	2.200

the prospect of losing the credit induces firms to invest more readily now. This effect is quantitatively not as strong as the delaying effect of λ_1 on P_0 above. Here we need an increase in λ_0 from 0 all the way to 0.5 before the premium is halved from 0.233 to 0.117.

Moreover, an increase in λ_1 increases P_1. The point is that with a higher enactment probability, even if the tax credit now in effect is removed, it is likely to be restored fairly quickly, so the imperative to invest immediately is less strong. Of course this issue is irrelevant if $\lambda_0 = 0$, but becomes quite significant for larger values of λ_0. If $\lambda_1 = 0.5$, then the investment-promoting effect of the prospect of removal of the current credit (higher λ_0) is very small.

Table 9.4.   *Investment Threshold when Tax Credit is in Effect (P_1)*
(Parameters: $\alpha = 0$, $\sigma = 0.1$, $r = 0.05$, $I = 20$.)

	λ_1					
λ_0	0.0	0.1	0.2	0.3	0.4	0.5
0.0	1.233	1.233	1.233	1.233	1.233	1.233
0.1	1.177	1.196	1.209	1.216	1.221	1.224
0.2	1.152	1.176	1.193	1.204	1.212	1.216
0.3	1.135	1.162	1.182	1.195	1.204	1.210
0.4	1.125	1.153	1.174	1.188	1.198	1.205
0.5	1.117	1.145	1.167	1.183	1.194	1.201

These results suggest that uncertainty about the enactment of stimulus policies is likely to have a very detrimental effect on investment. In fact, if a government wishes to accelerate investment, the best thing it can do is to enact a tax credit right away, threaten to remove it soon, and swear never to restore it (high λ_0 and low λ_1). The credibility of such a policy is, of course, open to doubt.

While our analysis is conducted at the firm level, we can find its industry implications using the methods of Chapter 8. If we consider a competitive industry consisting of numerous such firms, the price threshold for each firm's investment decision will simply become the ceiling for the industry's price process in the stochastic dynamic equilibrium. Now the increase in P_0 will be interpreted as the effect of the reduction in industry supply due to the individual firms' reluctance to invest. While the debate on whether to institute a tax credit proceeds in the administration, the Congress, and the media, firms wait upon the outcome and their waiting implies a cost to consumers in the form of higher prices.

Metcalf and Hassett (1993) have a more general model where the scale of investment is itself a matter for choice. They find that policy uncertainty not only raises the threshold at which the firm invests, but also lowers the scale of its investment. When we develop the theory of investments of varying scale in Chapter 11, the reader will be able to handle this extension as an exercise.

3 Example of an Oligopolistic Industry

We have thus far considered two extreme market structures, namely monopoly in Chapters 5–7 and perfect competition in Chapter 8 and Chapter 9 to this point. The reason is practical rather than fundamental. Oligopolistic industries in our stochastic dynamic setting present formidable difficulties. The development of stochastic game theory for such applications is quite recent, and tractable models using that theory are rarer still. We will develop a particularly simple example, based on Smets (1991), that brings out some of the issues. More general and more richly detailed treatments must await further research.

The general point is not difficult to state. On the one hand, uncertainty and irreversibility imply an option value of waiting, and therefore greater hesitancy in each firm's investment decisions. The fear of preemption by a rival, on the other hand, suggests the need to act quickly. Which of these considerations is the more important depends on the parameters of the problem, and on the current state of the underlying shock. Our simple model serves to illustrate this tension.

We consider two firms, each with the potential to produce a unit output flow, which it can activate by incurring the sunk cost I. There are no variable costs of production, and we suppose that the industry demand is sufficiently elastic to ensure capacity production. Thus industry output is 0, 1, or 2 depending on the number of active firms. The price is given by the demand function (1), which we restate here:

$$P = Y D(Q),$$

and the multiplicative shock Y follows the geometric Brownian motion (2). For simplicity of notation we assume that the firms are risk neutral, or that the risk in Y has zero correlation with the overall market risk. Thus the discount rate for all future costs and revenues, certain or uncertain, is the riskless rate r.

Dynamic games are usually solved backwards, and this one is no exception. We begin by supposing that one of the firms has already invested, and find the optimal decision of the other, which we now call the follower. Then we look at the situation where neither firm has invested, and consider the decision of either as it contemplates whether to go first, knowing that the other will react in the way just calculated.

The follower's profit flow will be $Y D(2)$. Following familiar steps, we can find the threshold level Y_2 that will trigger its investment. It satisfies

$$Y_2 D(2) = \frac{\beta_1}{\beta_1 - 1} \delta I, \tag{23}$$

where β_1 and δ have the usual meanings.

If $Y \geq Y_2$, the follower will invest at once, and get the value $Y D(2)/\delta - I$. If $Y < Y_2$, the follower will wait until the threshold is first hit, and at that point get $Y_2 D(2)/\delta - I$. Therefore its expected present value is

$$\mathcal{E}[e^{-rT}][Y_2 D(2)/\delta - I],$$

where T is the (random) first time when the stochastic process of the demand shock reaches Y_2 starting at Y. We calculate this expectation in the Appendix. Using it, the follower's value can be stated as

$$V_2(Y) = \begin{cases} Y D(2)/\delta - I & \text{if } Y \geq Y_2, \\ (Y/Y_2)^{\beta_1}[Y_2 D(2)/\delta - I] & \text{if } Y < Y_2. \end{cases} \tag{24}$$

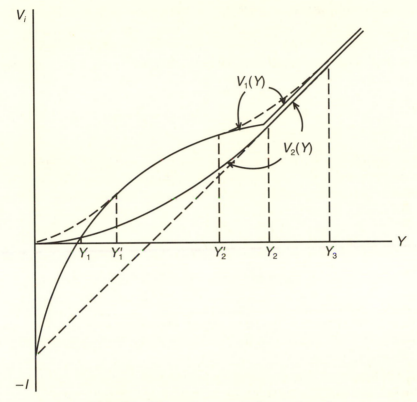

Figure 9.2. *Values of Leader and Follower in Duopoly*

The form of this function can be seen in Figure 9.2. Note that the two branches meet tangentially at Y_2; this is a smooth-pasting-like property of present values of Brownian motion at points of a switch of regimes.[7]

Now suppose neither firm has invested, and one of them is contemplating becoming the leader. [Of course this need not actually arise for some range(s) of values of Y, but we must consider the hypothetical scenario precisely in order to determine when immediate investment for at least one firm is optimal and so find just these ranges of Y.]

In making this calculation, this firm will take into account the action of the other firm after it sees that its rival has invested. That is just the follower's

---

[7]In fact this is just an alternative way of deriving and expressing our very first investment rule and the value formula in Chapter 5, equation (6).

decision we studied above. So if $Y \geq Y_2$, the follower will invest at once, the leader's profit flow will also be $Y\,D(2)$, and its value will be the same as the follower's. If $Y < Y_2$, then the follower will wait until Y_2 is hit. In the meantime, the leader will have the larger profit flow $Y\,D(1)$, and its expected value will be

$$\mathcal{E}\left[\int_0^T e^{-rt} Y\,D(1)\,dt\right] + \mathcal{E}[e^{-rT}]\,Y_2\,D(2)/\delta - I,$$

where, as before, T is the first time the stochastic process of the demand shock reaches Y_2 starting at Y. Again we compute the expectations in the Appendix and state the result here. The leader's value is

$$V_1(Y) = \begin{cases} V_2(Y) = Y\,D(2)/\delta - I & \text{if } Y \geq Y_2, \\ (1/\delta)Y\,D(1)\left[1 - (Y/Y_2)^{\beta_1 - 1}\right] \\ \quad + (Y/Y_2)^{\beta_1}\,Y_2\,D(2)/\delta - I & \text{if } Y < Y_2. \end{cases} \tag{25}$$

This has a more complicated shape, which is shown in Figure 9.2. It is concave over the range $Y < Y_2$, and its slope is discontinuous at Y_2.[8] The latter is of course a consequence of the fact that the follower's decision changes discontinuously at Y_2.

For a range of Y to the left of Y_2, the leader's value exceeds that of the follower because it enjoys a higher profit flow before the follower invests. However, for a range of very low values of Y, the leader's value is less than the follower's because the leader incurs the investment cost up front but has a low profit flow initially. The two curves cross at the point Y_1.

We have not designated one particular firm as the leader, and each firm's own profit considerations should govern whether it wants to lead or follow. The outcomes are different depending on the initial circumstances.

If the initial Y is below Y_1, neither firm will invest. When Y_1 is reached, one will invest at once and the other will wait until Y_2, but the two are indifferent between these two roles.

Note that at Y_1, we have $V_1(Y_1) = V_2(Y_1) > 0$. Then equation (25) gives

$$\frac{Y_1\,D(1)}{\delta}\left[1 - \left(\frac{Y_1}{Y_2}\right)^{\beta_1}\right] + \left(\frac{Y_1}{Y_2}\right)^{\beta_1}\frac{Y_2\,D(2)}{\delta} - I > 0,$$

---

[8] If β_1 is large enough, $V_1(Y)$ can actually peak to the left of Y_2 and then approach Y_2 with negative slope, but this does not affect the qualitative results that follow.

or

$$\frac{Y_1 \, D(1)}{\delta} > I + \left(\frac{Y_1}{Y_2}\right)^{\beta_1} \frac{D(1) - D(2)}{\delta} > I.$$

Thus $Y_1 \, D(1) > \delta \, I$; the first investment does not occur until the current profit flow of the first investor provides a supernormal return on the sunk cost. The reason is similar to that in the case of perfect competition. Even though the value of waiting is zero, the firm contemplating being the first to invest recognizes that future entry by the other firm will reduce the upper end of the distribution of profit flows. Therefore it requires enough of a current premium in compensation. Unlike the perfectly competitive case, though, the expected present value of the firm at this point is positive. With just two firms and no free entry, this makes intuitive sense.

Extending this analysis to N firms is simple in principle but messy in practice. However, the results should be evident without doing the formal work. At the smallest Y that triggers investment by the first firm, say, Y_1, we will have $Y_1 \, D(1) > \delta \, I$ and $V_1(Y_1) = \cdots = V_N(Y_1)$. The common value will go to zero as N goes to infinity.

Next suppose Y starts somewhere in the range (Y_1, Y_2). Then each firm stands to gain by seizing the leader's role. Neither can afford the option of waiting, because the other will invest if it does not.

Note that if both firms invest at once, each will have a value $Y \, D(2)/\delta - I$. This is even lower than the follower's $V_2(Y)$ while Y is in the range (Y_1, Y_2), so simultaneous investment is a "mistake" from their joint perspective. Of course such mistakes can occur in game equilibria. If the game were played in discrete time, the equilibrium would be in mixed strategies, where each independently chooses a probability of investing at once. Given that the other firm is choosing the equilibrium mix, each is indifferent between investing and not investing. However, with positive probability (the product of the two individual investment probabilities) the two invest together and get the lower value. In continuous time we would like the probability of such coincidences to go to zero. Doing that correctly requires some delicate limiting considerations. We omit these details, and refer the interested readers to Fudenberg and Tirole (1985).

We merely state the outcome in the resulting continuous-time equilibrium. One firm, chosen at random, gets to invest at once, and therefore gets the leader's (larger) value. The other then waits until Y_2 is hit and so gets the follower's (lesser) value. There are really two equilibria of this kind, where the two roles are interchanged between the firms. Since the firms are economically identical, the two equilibria are indistinguishable for our purpose.

In practice, some minor unspecified difference between the firms can govern which one invests first.

Matters are different if the roles of leader and follower are exogenously preassigned to the firms. Now the follower cannot invest until the leader has done so, and the leader has the ability to wait and recognizes an option value of doing so. The option values have the usual forms, $A_1 Y^{\beta_1}$ for a range of Y that includes zero, and $B_1 Y^{\beta_1} + B_2 Y^{\beta_2}$ for a range that includes neither zero nor infinity, where β_1 is the positive root and β_2 the negative root of the usual quadratic in the parameters. Figure 9.2 shows these option values as dashed curves smoothly pasted to the leader's value of investing at once. They meet the latter at the points Y_1', Y_2', and Y_3 as shown. Then the designated leader will invest at once if Y is in the range (Y_1', Y_2') (when the follower will wait until Y_2 is reached), and when Y exceeds Y_3 (when the other will follow at once). For values of Y either below Y_1' or in the range (Y_2', Y_3), the leader will prefer to wait. For some parameter values, the option value curve lies entirely above $V_1(Y)$; then the leader waits for the whole of $(0, Y_3)$

4   Guide to the Literature

The general idea of the optimality of competitive equilibrium in a dynamic and uncertain environment as long as markets are complete goes back to Arrow and Debreu. Lucas and Prescott (1971) present the earliest specific model of investment that demonstrates this explicitly. The fact that irreversible costs of shifting capital or labor do not by themselves constitute a market failure was given a much-needed emphasis in the context of economic adjustment to changing international trade conditions by Mussa (1982), but he considered only a deterministic response to a single unexpected shock.

Lucas and Prescott (1974) studied a stochastic dynamic equilibrium with costly intersectoral movements of labor. They assumed risk neutrality, so the equilibrium was again socially optimal. Dixit and Rob (1993a,b) introduced risk aversion and incomplete risk markets, and examined some policies that can improve upon the suboptimal equilibrium in these circumstances.

The fact that competitive firms would make the optimal entry decision even if they acted myopically and ignored all future entry was discovered by Leahy (1992).

Our treatment of the dynamic effects of price controls follows Dixit (1991b). See also Newbery and Stiglitz (1981) for a thorough analysis of price stabilization policies in agriculture.

Our treatment of policy uncertainty was based on Metcalf and Hassett (1993). Additional work on tax policy and investment from a real options perspective includes Majd and Myers (1986), and MacKie-Mason (1990). Using different technical approaches, Rodrik (1991) examined the effects of uncertainty over policy reforms designed to stimulate investment (for example, a tax incentive), and showed that if each year there is some probability that the policy will be reversed, the resulting uncertainty can eliminate any stimulative effect that the policy would otherwise have on investment. Aizenman and Marion (1991) developed a similar model in which the tax rate can rise or fall, and showed that this uncertainty can reduce irreversible investment in physical and human capital, and thereby suppress growth.

The trade-off between the strategic incentive to invest early in an oligopoly and the value of flexibility in the face of uncertainty has been studied by several writers using a two-period model; examples are Appelbaum and Lim (1985), Spencer and Brander (1992), and Kulatilaka and Perotti (1992). The last of these pairs of authors make an interesting new point. In a quantity-setting duopoly the first mover gets a larger market share. Therefore the leader's profit is a more convex function of a demand shock variable than is the follower's. As a result, an increase in uncertainty increases the relative value of early investment.

Models of duopoly in a continuous-time framework are rarer, because the underlying theory of stochastic games in continuous time is itself an ongoing research topic. A recent paper by Dutta and Rustichini (1991) offers a promising framework, and Smets (1991) builds a duopoly model using it. Our treatment follows his.

Appendix

A Some Expected Present Values

Here we establish the formulas stated in section 3 for

$$\mathcal{E}[e^{-rT}] \qquad \text{and} \qquad \mathcal{E}\left\{ \int_0^T e^{-rT} Y \, dt \right\},$$

when Y follows the geometric Brownian motion (2), and T is the random first time the process reaches a fixed level Y_2 starting from the general initial position Y. For a more general approach to the calculation of such expressions, see, for example, Harrison (1985, p. 42) or Karlin and Taylor (1975, p. 362).

Write $f(Y)$ for the first of these expectations. As long as $Y < Y_2$, we can choose dt sufficiently small that hitting the level Y_2 in the next short time interval dt is an unlikely event. Then the problem restarts from a new level $(Y + dY)$. Therefore we have the dynamic programming-like recursion expression

$$f(Y) = e^{-r\,dt}\, \mathcal{E}[\,f(Y + dY)\,].$$

Expanding the right-hand side, recalling that Y follows the process (2), and using Ito's Lemma, this becomes

$$f(Y) = [1 - r\,dt + o(dt)]\,[f(Y) + \alpha\, Y\, f'(Y)\,dt + \tfrac{1}{2}\sigma^2\, Y^2\, f''(Y)\,dt + o(dt)].$$

Simplifying and letting $dt \to 0$, we get the differential equation

$$\tfrac{1}{2}\sigma^2\, Y^2\, f''(Y) + \alpha\, Y\, f'(Y) - r\, f(Y) = 0.$$

This has the general solution

$$f(Y) = A_1\, Y^{\beta_1} + A_2\, Y^{\beta_2},$$

where β_1 is the positive root and β_2 the negative root of the standard quadratic.

The constants A_1 and A_2 are determined by a pair of boundary conditions. As Y approaches Y_2, T is likely to be small and e^{-rT} close to 1; therefore $f(Y_2) = 1$. When Y is very small, T is likely to be large and e^{-rT} close to 0; therefore $f(0) = 0$. Using these, we get $A_2 = 0$ and $A_1\, Y_2^{\beta_1} = 1$, so

$$f(Y) = (Y/Y_2)^{\beta_1}.$$

This is used in equations (24) and (25) in the text.

Similarly, define

$$g(Y) = \mathcal{E}\left\{ \int_0^T Y_t\, e^{-rt}\, dt \right\}.$$

This satisfies the differential equation

$$\tfrac{1}{2}\sigma^2\, Y^2\, g''(Y) + \alpha\, Y\, g'(Y) - r\, g(Y) + Y = 0.$$

This has the general solution

$$g(Y) = B_1\, Y^{\beta_1} + B_2\, Y^{\beta_2} + Y/(r - \alpha),$$

and the boundary conditions are $g(Y_2) = 0$, $g(0) = 0$. Therefore

$$B_2 = 0 \quad \text{and} \quad B_1 = -Y_2^{1-\beta_1}/(r - \alpha),$$

which is used in (25) in the text.

Part V

Extensions and Applications

Chapter **10**

Sequential Investment

IN THIS and the following chapters we return to the investment decisions of a single firm. In Chapters 5, 6, and 7, we developed a series of models in which the firm must decide when (and whether) to invest in a single project. In Chapter 5 we assumed that the value of that project evolved as an exogenous stochastic process, and we derived the optimal investment rule. In Chapter 6 we allowed the price of the project's output to evolve as an exogenous stochastic process, and then, given a variable cost of production, we derived both the value of the project and the investment rule. Finally, in Chapter 7 we extended the model to allow for the mothballing and later reactivation of the project, as well as scrapping.

In all three of those chapters we considered a single, discrete project, and hence a single initial investment decision. In many situations, however, investment decisions are made *sequentially*, and in a particular order. For example, investing in new oil production capacity is a two-stage process. First, reserves of oil must be obtained, either through exploration or outright purchase. Second, development wells and pipelines must be built so that the oil can be produced from these reserves. An oil company might invest in the first stage (for example, by buying proved reserves of oil), but decide to wait rather than immediately invest in the second stage. Investing in a new line of aircraft is also a multistage process that begins with engineering, and continues with prototype production, testing, and the final tooling stages. An investment in a new drug by a pharmaceutical company begins with research that (with some probability) leads to a new compound, and continues with extensive testing until FDA approval is obtained, and concludes with the construction of a production facility and the marketing of the product. Both the aircraft company

319

and the pharmaceutical company could decide to go ahead with the first stages of these investments, and then wait on the later stages.

Even investments that appear to involve only a single decision can turn out to be sequential. The reason is that many projects (and especially large ones) take considerable time to complete, and can be halted midway and temporarily or permanently abandoned. As a result, we can think of such projects as having many stages; each dollar spent gives the firm an option—which it may or may not exercise—to go ahead and spend the next dollar.

The key characteristic of sequential investments is the ability to temporarily or permanently stop investing if the value of the completed project falls, or if the expected cost of completing the investment rises. (If one had no choice but to complete the project once it had been started, investing would once again involve only a single decision.) This possibility of stopping midstream makes these investments analogous to *compound options*; each stage completed (or dollar invested) gives the firm an option to complete the next stage (or invest the next dollar). The investment problem boils down to finding a contingent plan for making these sequential (and irreversible) expenditures.

In this chapter we examine several different kinds of sequential investment problems. In each case we will try to draw analogies, as we have done throughout this book, with the valuation and exercising of financial options. We begin with some fairly simple two- and three-stage sequential investments, and use them to illustrate a basic approach to valuing the firm's option to invest and finding the optimal investment rule. Next, we turn to problems of continuous investment—the firm spends money a dollar at a time, it takes time to complete the project, and the firm can always stop investing in response to changing market conditions. In studying these investment problems, we will draw distinctions between uncertainty over the value of the completed project (due, for example, to uncertainty over the price of the project's output), and uncertainty over the cost of actually completing the project.

In each of these investment problems, the firm does not earn any cash flows from the project until the project is complete. (Investing in only the engineering and prototype production stages of a new aircraft is not sufficient for the firm to actually sell airplanes and earn money.) We will also examine the related problem of a firm moving down a learning curve. Here current production serves two functions: it yields an immediate profit flow, and also lowers future costs. The latter is like an investment. In Chapter 11 we discuss modelling of incremental investment in the usual sense, where each unit of capital contributes to the profit flow as soon as it is installed.

The mathematical models of this chapter and the next involve two state variables. One is the number of stages completed or the amount of capital installed; the other is the price or some other indicator of profitability of investment. Then the differential equations that emerge from dynamic programming or contingent claims analysis are partial differential equations, with the value of the project or the option as the dependent variable, and the two state variables as the independent ones. Solution of such equations typically requires numerical methods. For the class of models we consider, such solution is relatively easy. In an appendix to this chapter we briefly discuss the numerical procedure, and in the text we apply it to our specific model.

1 Decisions to Start and Complete a Multistage Project

In Chapter 6 we worked backwards to find the value of a project together with the optimal investment rule. Given a stochastic process for the project's output price, P, we derived the value of the project, $V(P)$. Then, given $V(P)$, we were able to find the value of the option to invest in the project, $F(P)$, and the critical price P^* at which it is optimal to invest. Recall that we needed $V(P)$ to find $F(P)$ and P^* because $V(P^*)$ appeared in two of the boundary conditions that accompany the differential equation for $F(P)$. We can use this same approach of working backwards to solve sequential investment problems in which the investment occurs in two or more discrete stages.

To see how this can be done, consider a two-stage investment in new oil production capacity. First, reserves of oil must be obtained, through exploration or purchase, at some cost I_1. Second, development wells (and possibly pipelines) must be built, at an additional cost I_2. Suppose that the price of oil, P, follows some specified exogenous stochastic process. Then the firm begins with an option, worth $F_1(P)$, to invest in reserves. Making this investment buys the firm another option, worth $F_2(P)$, to invest in development wells. Making this second investment yields production capacity, worth $V(P)$.

We can work backwards to find the optimal investment rules. First, as we have shown in Chapter 6, $V(P)$ is the value of the firm's operating options, and can be calculated accordingly. Next, $F_2(P)$ can be found in exactly the same way that we obtained the value of a single option to invest in Chapter 6; it will satisfy a differential equation subject to boundary conditions for an endpoint [for example, $F_2(0) = 0$], and for "value matching" and "smooth pasting" at the critical price P_2^* at which the firm should make this investment in development wells. Finally, $F_1(P)$ can be found. It will satisfy a similar differential equation and boundary conditions, but now there will be another critical price, P_1^*, at which the first-stage investment should be made. Note that because the payoff from the first-stage investment is $F_2(P)$, that is, the value of the option to invest in the second stage, we need to know $F_2(P)$ in order to solve for $F_1(P)$ and the critical price P_1^*. That is why we solve the investment problem by working backwards.

Intuitively, we should expect P_1^* to be greater than P_2^*. As we saw in Chapters 5 and 6, the higher the sunk cost required to obtain a risky payoff, the higher the critical value of the payoff (in this case the higher the critical price) that triggers the investment. So, if a project has two stages (costing, say, $5 million each), going ahead with the investment will require a higher critical price if both stages remain to be completed than it will if one stage is already finished, making the remaining sunk costs smaller.

The extension to a three-stage project should be obvious. Now, let $F_1(P)$ denote the value of the option to invest in the first stage, $F_2(P)$ the value of the option to invest in the second stage, and $F_3(P)$ the value of the option to invest in the third stage. We work backwards as before. First, find the value of the finished project, $V(P)$. Second, use this to find $F_3(P)$ and the critical price P_3^*. Third, use $F_3(P)$ to find $F_2(P)$ and the critical price P_2^*. Finally, use $F_2(P)$ to find $F_1(P)$ and the critical price P_1^* at which it is optimal to invest in the first stage.

We have assumed that the output price P is the (exogenous) stochastic state variable, so that V, F_1, F_2, etc., are all functions of P. However, in some cases there is no such thing as an actual output price until after the project has been completed and the output flow commences. The actual price of a home videocassette recorder, or of a personal computer, for example, was not observable when no such thing was being sold. The firms investing in these technologies and production facilities formed an estimate of this price based on some observable indicators, for example, what users were willing to pay for related services, or from surveys. In our models, P should likewise be interpreted as just such an observable indicator of profitability when the relevant price is not directly observable. For simplicity, we will go on referring to this state variable as the price.

At this point, the mechanics of actually carrying out the calculations described above may not be quite as clear as the overall approach. We will therefore work through the mechanics in some detail for the case of a two-stage project.

1.A The Investment Rule for a Two-Stage Project

Let us examine the two-stage project in more detail. We will assume as in Chapter 6 that the project, once completed, produces one unit of output period at an operating cost C. The output can be sold at a price P, which follows a geometric Brownian motion:

$$dP = \alpha P \, dt + \sigma P \, dz. \tag{1}$$

We will assume that the price uncertainty is spanned by capital markets, so that contingent claims methods can be used. Let μ denote the risk-adjusted discount rate that applies to P, and let $\delta = \mu - \alpha$. As in Chapter 6, we will assume that the operation can be temporarily and costlessly suspended when P falls below C, and costlessly resumed when P rises above C, so that the profit flow is given by $\pi(P) = \max[P - C, 0]$.

We will assume that investing in the first stage of the project requires a sunk cost I_1, and investing in the second stage requires a sunk cost I_2. We can now solve the investment problem by working backwards, first finding the value of the complete project $V(P)$, next finding the value of the option to invest in the second stage, $F_2(P)$, along with the critical price P_2^* for that investment, and finally finding the value of the option to invest in the first stage, $F_1(P)$, and the corresponding critical price P_1^*.

The Value of the Project

We already know how to find $V(P)$; we worked through this in some detail in Section 2 of Chapter 6. At this point, we will just summarize the steps.

Recall that $V(P)$ must satisfy the following differential equation:

$$\tfrac{1}{2}\sigma^2 P^2 V''(P) + (r - \delta) P V'(P) - r V(P) + \pi(P) = 0, \tag{2}$$

subject to $V(0) = 0$, and the continuity of $V(P)$ and $V_P(P)$ at $P = C$. The solution is

$$V(P) = \begin{cases} A_1 \, P^{\beta_1} & \text{if } P < C, \\ B_2 \, P^{\beta_2} + P/\delta - C/r & \text{if } P > C. \end{cases} \tag{3}$$

The constants β_1 and β_2 are the solutions to the fundamental quadratic equation, that is,

$$\beta_1 = \tfrac{1}{2} - (r - \delta)/\sigma^2 + \sqrt{\left[(r - \delta)/\sigma^2 - \tfrac{1}{2}\right]^2 + 2r/\sigma^2} \; > 1,$$

$$\beta_2 = \tfrac{1}{2} - (r - \delta)/\sigma^2 - \sqrt{\left[(r - \delta)/\sigma^2 - \tfrac{1}{2}\right]^2 + 2r/\sigma^2} \; < 0.$$

The constants A_1 and B_2 are determined from the continuity of $V(P)$ and $V'(P)$ at $P = C$, and are equal to

$$A_1 = \frac{C^{1-\beta_1}}{\beta_1 - \beta_2} \left(\frac{\beta_2}{r} - \frac{\beta_2 - 1}{\delta} \right), \tag{4}$$

$$B_2 = \frac{C^{1-\beta_2}}{\beta_1 - \beta_2} \left(\frac{\beta_1}{r} - \frac{\beta_1 - 1}{\delta} \right). \tag{5}$$

Equations (3), (4), and (5) give us the value of the completed project, $V(P)$, for any P.

The Second-Stage Investment

We find the value of the option to invest in the second stage of the project, $F_2(P)$, along with the critical price P_2^* at which it is optimal to invest, in the same way that we solved the investment problem for the single-stage project in Chapter 6. The value of the option must satisfy the differential equation

$$\tfrac{1}{2}\sigma^2 P^2 F_2''(P) + (r - \delta) P F_2'(P) - r F(P) = 0, \tag{6}$$

subject to the boundary conditions

$$F_2(0) = 0, \tag{7}$$

$$F_2(P_2^*) = V(P_2^*) - I_2, \tag{8}$$

$$F_2'(P_2^*) = V'(P_2^*). \tag{9}$$

We can guess and then confirm that $P_2^* > C$, so we use the solution for $V(P)$ in the operating region, that is, for $P > C$, in the boundary conditions (8) and (9). We then obtain the solution

$$F_2(P) = D_2 P^{\beta_1}. \tag{10}$$

From boundary conditions (8) and (9) we determine that

$$D_2 = \frac{\beta_2 B_2}{\beta_1} (P_2^*)^{(\beta_2 - \beta_1)} + \frac{1}{\delta \beta_1} (P_2^*)^{(1-\beta_1)}, \tag{11}$$

and that P_2^* is the solution to the equation

$$(\beta_1 - \beta_2) B_2 (P_2^*)^{\beta_2} + (\beta_1 - 1) P_2^*/\delta - \beta_1 (C/r + I_2) = 0. \tag{12}$$

Recall from Chapter 6 that equation (12) must be solved numerically for P_2^*.

The solution given by equation (10) applies for $P < P_2^*$. When $P \geq P_2^*$ the firm exercises its option to invest, and $F_2(P) = V(P) - I_2$. This is important for what follows, so we restate it formally:

$$F_2(P) = \begin{cases} D_2 P^{\beta_1} & \text{for } P < P_2^*, \\ V(P) - I_2 & \text{for } P \geq P_2^*. \end{cases} \tag{13}$$

The First-Stage Investment

Given $F_2(P)$ and P_2^*, we can now back up to the first stage of the project and find the value of the option to invest, $F_1(P)$, and the critical price P_1^*. By going through the usual steps, we can determine that $F_1(P)$ will also satisfy the differential equation (6), but now subject to the boundary conditions

$$F_1(0) = 0, \tag{14}$$

$$F_1(P_1^*) = F_2(P_1^*) - I_1, \tag{15}$$

$$F_1'(P_1^*) = F_2'(P_1^*). \tag{16}$$

The solution has the usual form:

$$F_1(P) = D_1 \, P^{\beta_1}. \tag{17}$$

We can now use boundary conditions (15) and (16) to find the constant b and the critical price P_1^*. However, when substituting $F_2(P)$ on the right-hand side of these boundary conditions, we need to know whether P_1^* is greater or smaller than P_2^*; note from equation (13) that if $P_1^* < P_2^*$, $F_2(P_1^*) = D_2 \, (P_1^*)^{\beta_1}$, but if $P_1^* > P_2^*$, $F_2(P_1^*) = V(P_1^*) - I_2$.

As we explained earlier, intuitively we would expect P_1^* to be greater than P_2^*; now we demonstrate this formally. Suppose $P_1^* \leq P_2^*$. Then $F_2(P_1^*) = D_2 \, (P_1^*)^{\beta_1}$, and the boundary condition (16) implies that $D_2 = D_1$, which is contradicted by the boundary condition (15). Hence we must have $P_1^* > P_2^*$.

Since $P_1^* > P_2^*$, and since in this model the investment can be completed instantaneously (before P has a chance to change), we know that once P reaches P_1^* and the firm invests, *it will complete both stages of the project.* In other words, it will never be the case that the firm will invest in the first stage, and then wait rather than also investing in the second stage. This result may seem anticlimactic, and the reader may be wondering why we bothered to solve this two-stage problem. Why did we not simply combine the two stages, let $I = I_1 + I_2$, and then use the solution to the investment problem that was derived in Chapter 6? There are two related reasons for our choice. First, in the real world, investing takes time, so that firms often do complete the early stages of a project and then wait before proceeding with the later stages. Second, the two stages may require different technical or managerial skills, or they may be advantageously located in different countries, or they may be subject to different tax treatments. For these reasons one firm may sell a partially completed project to another. Our method contains the calculation of the price of such a partially completed project. We will come back to this point shortly, but first let us complete the solution to our problem.

Because the firm should invest in both stages of the project if it should invest at all, we can rewrite boundary conditions (15) and (16) as

$$F_1(P_1^*) = V(P_1^*) - I_2 - I_1, \tag{18}$$

$$F_1'(P_1^*) = V'(P_1^*). \tag{19}$$

Substituting the solution for $V(P)$ in the operating region, these boundary conditions tell us that

$$D_1 = \frac{\beta_2 B_2}{\beta_1}(P_1^*)^{(\beta_2 - \beta_1)} + \frac{1}{\delta\beta_1}(P_1^*)^{(1-\beta_1)}, \tag{20}$$

and that P_1^* is the solution to the equation

$$(\beta_1 - \beta_2) B_2 (P_1^*)^{\beta_2} + (\beta_1 - 1) P_1^*/\delta - \beta_1 (C/r + I_2 + I_1) = 0. \tag{21}$$

Note that these equations are identical to equations (11) and (12), except that P_1^* replaces P_2^*, and $I_2 + I_1$ replaces I_2. It can be shown that these equations also imply that $P_1^* > P_2^*$, and that $D_1 < D_2$. As we would expect, the option to invest in the second stage of a project (given that the first stage has already been completed) is worth more than the option to invest in the first stage (for which the payoff is the option to invest in the second stage).

We have found that the solution to the multistage investment problem has exactly the same form as the solution to the single-stage problem that we solved in Chapter 6. The only thing that changes is the amount of the investment; the solution for the first stage uses the total investment cost $I_1 + I_2$, and the solution for the second stage uses the second-stage cost I_2. Figure 10.1 shows $F_1(P)$, $F_2(P)$, and the critical prices P_1^* and P_2^*, for the example that we worked out in Section 2 of Chapter 6, but with the total cost of the investment $I = 100$ broken down into two parts, $I_1 = I_2 = 50$. The other parameters are the same as those used in Chapter 6, that is, $\sigma = 0.20$ and $r = \delta = 0.04$.

1.B Summary and Discussion

We have seen how we can work backwards to determine the values of the options to invest in each stage of a multistage project, together with the critical prices that trigger investment. Extending the steps that we took above to projects with three or more stages should be straightforward. The idea is to start at the end, and then work backwards, using the solution for each stage in the boundary conditions for the previous stage. Note, however, that this just boils down to solving the model of Chapter 6 for different values of the

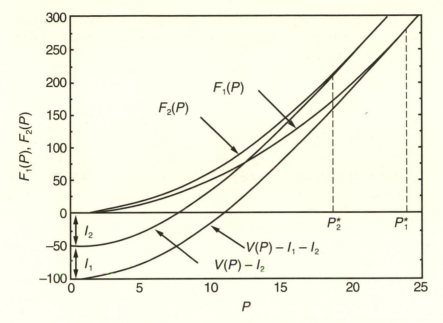

Figure 10.1. *Critical Prices and Option Values for a Two-Stage Project*
(P_1^* is critical price for investment in first stage, and P_2^* that for second stage.)

remaining sunk cost required to complete the project. The value of the option to invest in any stage j of an N-stage project is of the form

$$F_j(P) = D_j \, P^{\beta_1},$$

and the coefficient D_j and critical price P_j^* are found by solving equations (11) and (12), with P_j^* replacing P_2^* and $I_j + I_{j+1} + \cdots + I_N$ replacing I_2.

Of what use is this result, however, if investment in the first stage always implies immediate investment in all succeeding stages? Indeed, if investment is instantaneous and there are no other impediments to investing in all stages at once, there is no need to go through these steps—we can simply take the total cost, I, of all of the different stages of the investment, and then use the results of Chapter 6, or equivalently, use equations (11) and (12), with I replacing I_2.

In practice, it is often the case that it is not possible (or desirable) to invest at once in every stage of a project. First, most multistage projects take considerable time to complete. (Investments in new oil production capacity, in the development of a new line of aircraft, or in the development of a new drug are all examples of this.) Hence price might rise above the critical level that triggers the first stage of investment, and then while that first stage is underway, fall below the critical level needed to trigger the second stage. Then the firm should wait rather than proceed with the later stages of the project; it is clearly important to know the critical prices for each stage.

Second, even if investment can proceed very quickly, it may be important nonetheless to know the values of the options to invest in later stages of the project together with the critical prices. The reason is that the firm might decide to invest in the early stages, and then sell off the rights to the later stages rather than do the investing itself. An example is the development of a new drug by a small biotechnology company. The company might be very adept at doing the R&D needed to develop and patent the drug (the first stage of the project), but then find it best to license or sell the patent to a large pharmaceutical company that is better able to test, produce, and market the drug (the later stages of the project).

Third, there can be other considerations that lead a company to invest in the first stages of a project but then delay the later stages. For example, the firm might have a unique opportunity to buy land or mineral rights (the first stage), but then want to wait before developing the land or exploiting the mineral rights. Or, government regulations might force the company to delay the later stages of an investment (for example, regulations requiring the testing of new drugs).

We will focus on the first of these reasons—the fact that most multistage investments take considerable time to complete. In the next section we will turn to a slightly more complicated model in which the investment occurs continuously—the firm invests a dollar at a time, so that there are effectively an infinite number of stages to the project—and the investment also takes a minimum amount of time to complete.

2   Continuous Investment and Time to Build

We turn now to a model developed by Majd and Pindyck (1987) in which a firm invests continuously (each dollar spent buys an option to spend the next dollar) until the project is completed, investment can be stopped and later restarted costlessly, and there is a maximum rate at which outlays and construction can proceed (that is, it takes "time to build"). Hence the solution of the model provides a rule for optimal sequential investment that accounts for the time required to actually undertake the investment.

In this model, the firm receives nothing until the project is completed. The payoff upon completion is V, the value of the operating project. Also, it is assumed that V follows an exogenous geometric Brownian motion process, that is,

$$dV = \alpha V \, dt + \sigma V \, dz. \tag{22}$$

(Later we will see how the model can be expanded so that the price of the project's output, rather than V itself, follows an exogenous stochastic process.) We will assume that spanning applies, and we let μ equal the market risk-adjusted expected rate of return from owning and operating the project. We assume as usual that $\alpha < \mu$, and let $\delta = \mu - \alpha$.

Like Rome, this project cannot be built in a day; k is the maximum rate at which the firm can (productively) invest. Investment is also irreversible, so the rate of investment, $I(t)$, has the constraint $0 \le I(t) \le k$. If no investment is made, the previously installed capital does not decay. If V falls to a sufficiently low level the firm can suspend investment, and if V rises later, resume at the point it left off. Denote by K the total *remaining* expenditure required to complete the project. Then the dynamics of K are given by

$$dK = -I \, dt. \tag{23}$$

We therefore have two state variables that affect the optimal investment decision. The first is the remaining investment required to complete the project, K, which follows equation (23). The second is the current market value of the completed project, V, which follows equation (22). The problem is to find the optimal investment rule, $I^*(V, K)$.

Because there are no adjustment costs or other costs associated with changing the rate of investment, the problem will have a "bang-bang" solution—at any point in time, the optimal rate of investment will be either 0 or k. As a result, the optimal investment rule reduces to a critical cutoff value for the completed project, $V^*(K)$, such that when $V \ge V^*(K)$ the firm invests at the maximum rate k, and there is no investment otherwise.

As always, the firm has an option to invest that it may or may not exercise. We will denote by $F(V, K)$ the value of this option, assuming it is exercised optimally, that is, assuming that the firm follows the optimal investment rule by investing when $V \ge V^*$, and not investing otherwise. Then, as in earlier chapters, we will find $F(V, K)$ and obtain the critical value $V^*(K)$ as part of the solution. We can do this using dynamic programming, or, if spanning holds, using contingent claims analysis. We will assume that spanning holds and use contingent claims analysis to derive a partial differential equation that must be satisfied by $F(V, K)$; the solution to this equation will give us $V^*(K)$.

2.A   An Equation for $F(V, K)$

For review, we will derive the differential equation for $F(V, K)$. Consider a portfolio containing the option to invest and a short position in F_V units of V (or F_V units of an asset or dynamic portfolio of assets perfectly correlated with V). The value of this portfolio is $\Phi = F(V, K) - F_V V$, and the instantaneous change in this value is

$$d\Phi = dF - F_V\, dV$$
$$= F_V\, dV + \tfrac{1}{2} F_{VV}\, (dV)^2 + F_K\, dK - F_V\, dV$$
$$= \tfrac{1}{2}\sigma^2 V^2\, F_{VV}\, dt - I\, F_K\, dt.$$

The short position requires a payment flow of $\delta\, F_V\, V\, dt$, and, to the extent that investment is taking place, an additional outflow of $I\, dt$. Hence the total return on the portfolio is $d\Phi - I\, dt - \delta\, F_V V\, dt$, and since the portfolio is risk-free, this must equal $r\, \Phi\, dt$. Substituting for $d\Phi$, dividing through by dt, and rearranging gives the following partial differential equation for $F(V, K)$:

$$\tfrac{1}{2}\sigma^2 V^2\, F_{VV} - (r - \delta)\, V\, F_V - r\, F - I\, F_K - I = 0. \tag{24}$$

Equation (24) is also the Bellman equation from dynamic programming when the discount rate is the risk-free rate, r. As an exercise, the reader might want to confirm this by rederiving equation (24) using dynamic programming.

Note that equation (24) is linear in I, so that the optimal investment rule is indeed to either invest at the maximum rate k or not invest at all. When there is no investment, that is, $I = 0$, the term in F_K disappears, and equation (24) simplifies to an ordinary differential equation that can be solved analytically. However, when $I = k$, the equation will have to be solved numerically for both $F(V, K)$ and the critical boundary $V^*(K)$.

The solution to equation (24) must also satisfy the following boundary conditions:

$$F(V, 0) = V, \tag{25}$$

$$F(0, K) = 0, \tag{26}$$

$$\lim_{V \to \infty} F_V(V, K) = e^{-\delta K/k}, \tag{27}$$

along with the value-matching and smooth-pasting conditions that $F(V, K)$ and $F_V(V, K)$ be continuous at $V = V^*$. Condition (25) just says that when K reaches zero, the project is completed, and the firm receives the payoff V. Also, as V becomes very large relative to the total required expenditure K, it becomes very unlikely that the investment will ever be halted prior to completion. However, the project will still take time K/k to complete, and during this time the expected rate of increase in V is only $\mu - \delta$. Hence for very large V, a \$1 increase in V leads to an increase in $F(V, K)$ equal to

$$1 - \int_0^{K/k} \delta\, e^{(\mu-\delta)t}\, e^{-\mu t}\, dt = e^{-\delta K/k}.$$

This is just condition (27) above.

2.B Obtaining a Solution

When $V < V^*$ and $I = 0$, equation (24) has the analytical solution

$$F(V, K) = A V^{\beta_1}, \tag{28}$$

where

$$\beta_1 = \tfrac{1}{2} - (r - \delta)/\sigma^2 + \sqrt{\left[(r - \delta)/\sigma^2 - \tfrac{1}{2}\right]^2 + 2r/\sigma^2}.$$

This solution might seem troubling in that it does not appear to depend on K. In fact it does depend on K, through the "constant" A. As we will see, A must be found in conjunction with the boundary $V^* = V^*(K)$, and hence will vary with K.

When $V > V^*$ and $I = k$, equation (24) is a partial differential equation of the parabolic type that must be solved numerically. To do this, we first eliminate A using equation (28) together with the value-matching and smooth-pasting conditions:

$$F(V^*, K) = (V^*/\beta_1)\, F_V(V^*, K). \tag{29}$$

Then we numerically solve equation (24) (setting $I = k$), along with equation (29) and boundary conditions (25) to (27) using a finite difference method. This procedure transforms the variables V and K into discrete increments, and the partial differential equation (24) into a finite difference equation. The resulting equations can be solved algebraically, beginning at the terminal condition $K = 0$ and proceeding backwards in increments of ΔK, and finding the free boundary $V^*(K)$ at each value of K along with $F(V, K)$ for each value of V. The details of this numerical procedure are discussed in the Appendix to this chapter.[1]

2.C   A Numerical Example

As an example, consider a project that requires a total investment of $6 million ($K$), which can be spent productively at a rate no faster than $1 million per year ($k$). As for the other parameters, we set $r = 0.02$, $\delta = 0.06$, and $\sigma = 0.20$ (all at annual rates).

As explained in the Appendix, the solution procedure requires a discretization of the variables V and K. For this example, we will assume that investment outlays are made quarterly, that is, K is measured in discrete units of $0.25 million. (The solution procedure uses the logarithm of V rather than V itself; we take increments of $\log V$ of 0.15.)

The numerical solution is summarized in Table 10.1. Each entry in the table is the value of the investment option, $F(V, K)$, corresponding to a particular level of V and K. (To save space, only values of K in increments of $1 million are shown in the table.) Entries with an asterisk correspond to the critical value $V^*(K)$. For example, a project with $4 million of investment expenditures remaining has a critical value $V^* = \$7.03$ million, that is, if $V \geq \$7.03$ million the firm should make the next quarterly installment of investment at once; otherwise it should not. Also, if $V^* = \$7.03$ million, the value of the firm's investment option is $1.65 million. (Note that this is less than $V - K = \$7.03 - \$4 = \$3.03$. The reason is that the firm only receives V upon completion of the project, which will not occur for at least four years.)

Table 10.1 can be used to make optimal sequential investment decisions as the construction of this project proceeds, that is, as K falls from $6 million to zero. Unlike the simple model discussed in the previous section, here there is no guarantee that once investment begins it will continue until the project is completed. Because the project takes time, V can fall during construction to a point where investment will at least temporarily stop. Finally, note that this table can be used to evaluate any project requiring a total outlay of $1, $2, \ldots , \$6$ million, as long as the same values for r, δ, σ, and k apply.

Table 10.2 illustrates how the solution depends on the parameters σ and δ. The table shows the critical cutoff value, $V^*(K)$, for the initial investment decision (that is, when $K = \$6$ million), for $\sigma = 0.10$, 0.20, and 0.40, and for $\delta = 0.02$, 0.06, and 0.12. (The middle entry in this table corresponds to the

---

[1]Hawkins (1982) developed a model of a revolving credit agreement that is similar in structure to this one, but yields analytical solutions in both regions.

Table 10.1. *Numerical Example of Optimal Investment Rule*

(Note: Entries show value of the investment option, $F(V, K)$. Starred entries indicate the optimal investment rule; the value of V corresponding to each starred entry is the cutoff value, $V^*(K)$. Parameter values are $r = 0.02$, $\sigma = 0.20$, $\delta = 0.06$, and maximum rate of investment $k = \$1$ million per year.)

Value of the completed project, V	Total remaining investment, K						
	$6	$5	$4	$3	$2	$1	$0
$42.52	$23.70	$26.47	$29.37	$32.42	$35.62	$38.98	$42.52
36.60	19.62	22.12	24.75	27.50	30.39	33.42	36.60
31.50	16.10	18.38	20.76	23.26	25.88	28.62	31.50
27.11	13.07	15.16	17.34	19.62	22.00	24.50	27.11
23.34	10.46	12.38	14.39	16.48	18.67	20.95	23.34
20.09	8.22	10.00	11.85	13.78	15.79	17.89	20.09
17.29	6.23	7.94	9.67	11.46	13.32	15.26	17.29
14.88	4.63	6.18	7.78	9.46	11.19	13.00	14.88
12.81	3.20	4.65	6.17	7.73	9.36	11.05	12.81
11.02	2.02*	3.34	4.77	6.25	7.79	9.37	11.02
9.49	1.22	2.23*	3.57	4.98	6.43	7.93	9.49
8.17	0.74	1.34	2.54	3.88	5.26	6.69	8.17
7.03	0.44	0.81	1.65*	2.93	4.26	5.62	7.03
6.05	0.27	0.49	1.00	2.12	3.39	4.70	6.05
5.21	0.18	0.29	0.60	1.42*	2.65	3.91	5.21
4.48	0.10	0.18	0.36	0.86	2.00	3.23	4.48
3.86	0.06	0.11	0.22	0.52	1.45	2.64	3.86
3.32	0.04	0.06	0.13	0.31	0.98*	2.13	3.32
2.86	0.02	0.04	0.08	0.19	0.59	1.70	2.86
2.46	0.01	0.02	0.05	0.11	0.36	1.32	2.46
2.12	0.01	0.01	0.03	0.07	0.21	1.00	2.12
1.82	0.00	0.01	0.02	0.04	0.13	0.73*	1.82
1.57	0.00	0.01	0.01	0.02	0.08	0.44	1.57
1.35	0.00	0.00	0.00	0.02	0.05	0.27	1.35
1.16	0.00	0.00	0.00	0.01	0.03	0.16	1.16
1.00	0.00	0.00	0.00	0.01	0.02	0.10	1.00
0.00	0.00	0.00	0.00	0.00	0.00	0.00	0.00*

Table 10.2. *Dependence of Critical Value on σ and δ*

(Note: V^{**} is present value of V^* assuming investment proceeds at maximum rate $k = \$1$ million per year. V^* and V^{**} are for $K = \$6$ million.)

Volatility, σ	Critical value	Rate of return shortfall, δ		
		0.02	0.06	0.12
0.10	V^*	11.02	9.03	12.43
	V^{**}	9.77	6.30	6.05
0.20	V^*	20.09	11.02	12.81
	V^{**}	17.82	7.69	7.03
0.40	V^*	121.51	24.53	20.09
	V^{**}	107.77	17.11	9.78

"base case" shown in Table 10.1.) Observe that for any value of δ, V^* increases when σ is increased, and can increase dramatically when σ is increased above 0.20. This is quite similar to the results we obtained for the simple model presented in Chapter 5.[2]

The dependence of V^* on δ, however, is less obvious. In the model of Chapter 5, an increase in δ always reduced the critical value V^*, increasing the incentive to invest rather than wait. Recall that the reason for this is that δ is the shortfall in the expected rate of return from holding the option to invest rather than the completed project itself, and hence represents an opportunity cost of waiting, rather than investing now. In Table 10.2, however, V^* first decreases as δ goes from 0.02 to 0.06, but then (when $\sigma = 0.10$ or 0.20) increases as δ is

---

[2]We should also remind readers of our discussion in Chapters 5 and 6 concerning the parameter δ. As long as someone is holding the asset that tracks the risk in P, the equilibrium condition $\delta = \mu - \alpha$ must be satisfied. When σ changes, how this condition goes on being fulfilled depends on the hidden assumptions concerning the behavior of the holders of this asset. It is reasonable to assume that the risk-free rate r is exogenous, being determined by government policy or the behavior of a much wider class of investors. Then an increase in σ raises $\mu = r + \phi \sigma \rho_{pm}$, where ϕ is the market price of risk and ρ_{pm} the correlation coefficient between the asset tracking P and the market portfolio. If the holders of the P-asset have an exogenous convenience yield δ that remains unchanged, then somehow α must change to preserve equilibrium. In this case σ and δ can be treated as independent parameters. That is the interpretation we have taken here. However, if α is exogenously fixed, then the convenience yield δ must change to take up the slack. We leave this case for interested readers.

further increased to 0.12. The reason is that it takes time to build the project, which has an opposite effect on the incentive to invest. The payoff V is only received upon completion, and is expected to grow only at the rate $\mu - \delta$. Time to build therefore reduces the present value of the payoff, and reduces it by a larger amount as δ increases. This in turn reduces the incentive to invest, that is, increases the current critical value V^*. As Table 10.2 shows, for high values of δ this second effect can dominate, so that V^* increases when δ is increased.

We can net out this second effect by calculating the present value of V^*, assuming that the investment expenditures are made at the maximum rate k, so that it takes $T = K/k$ years to complete the project. The discount rate is μ but V has an expected rate of growth α, so this present value, V^{**}, is simply

$$V^{**} = V^* \, e^{-(\mu - \alpha)K/k} = V^* \, e^{-\delta K/k}. \tag{30}$$

Table 10.2 also shows values of V^{**}. Note that for any value of σ, V^{**} always decreases as δ is increased.

How large a wedge do irreversibility and the ability to delay drive between the payoff of the investment and its cost? One way to answer this is to compare V^{**} to the present value of the investment expenditures needed to complete the project. Assuming that these expenditures are made continuously over the period $T = K/k$, their present value is

$$K^* = \int_0^{K/k} k e^{-r\tau} \, d\tau = (1 - e^{-rK/k}) \, \frac{k}{r}. \tag{31}$$

For our example, $K^* = \$5.65$ million. Thus as Table 10.2 shows, V^{**} is higher than K^* for any values of σ and δ, and is much higher if σ is large and/or δ is small.

We can also examine the ways in which uncertainty and time to build interact in affecting the investment decision by calculating V^* for different values of k. Figure 10.2 shows V^* as a function of k for $K = \$6$ million, and $\delta = 0.03$ and 0.12.[3] Observe that when δ is small, changes in k have only a small effect on V^*. The reason is that then the expected rate of growth of V is close to μ, the risk-adjusted market rate, so the ability to speed up construction has little effect on the value of the investment option or on the investment decision. However, if δ is large, V^* can be fairly sensitive to k.

---

[3] As explained in the Appendix, the calculations of V^* are subject to numerical error because of the finite difference approximation. Absent such errors, the points plotted in Figures 10.2 and 10.3 would lie on smooth curves.

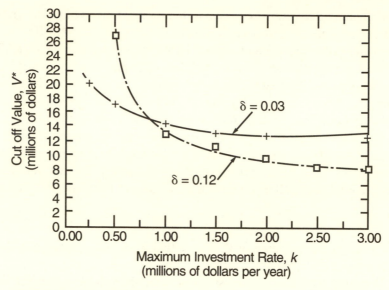

Figure 10.2.   *Critical Value, V*, as Function of Maximum Rate of Investment, k*
($r = 0.02$, $\sigma = 0.20$, and $K = \$6$ million)

Then, lower values of k (that is, longer minimum construction times) imply a lower present value of the payoff from completing the project, and hence a higher *current* critical value V^*. As above, this second effect could have been muted by considering V^{**}; we leave this for the readers.

We have assumed that k is constant, which may be unrealistic for some projects, where the maximum rate of investment can depend on the stage of the construction. However, this model can easily be modified to allow the maximum rate of investment to be a (known) function of the total remaining investment, K. This just means substituting a function of K rather than a constant for I in equation (24). The same numerical procedure can be used to obtain a solution. Likewise, it is not necessary to maintain the assumption that $I \geq 0$. There might be some positive lower bound on the rate of investment (for example, to maintain a construction site), so that the constraint becomes $l \leq I \leq k$, with l or k possibly dependent on K. This constraint can be interpreted in two ways: either that the firm is forced to proceed at this minimal rate once it embarks on the project, or that any smaller expenditure is tantamount to abandonment because existing stages will "rust" if not properly maintained. The optimal decision rules will be different in the two cases: the initial entry threshold will be stricter if there is no way out later.

2.D   The Value of Construction Time Flexibility

How valuable is the ability to speed up construction of a project? Many projects can be built with alternative construction technologies that differ in terms of flexibility over the rate of construction. Technologies offering greater flexibility tend to be more costly, so the increased cost must be balanced against the value of the greater construction time flexibility. We can use this model to determine the value of that greater flexibility. Since greater construction time flexibility corresponds to a higher k, we simply calculate the value of the investment opportunity, $F(V, K)$, for different values of k. The change in F corresponding to a change in k then measures the incremental value of extra flexibility. Of course this value of extra flexibility will depend on V and K, as well as the other parameters. [4]

Figure 10.3 shows this calculation for the base case parameter values $r = 0.02$, $\sigma = 0.20$, and $\delta = 0.06$. It plots $F(V, K; k)$ as a function of k holding V constant (first at \$10 million and then at \$15 million) and holding K constant (at \$6 million). For each value of V, the incremental value of construction time flexibility is given by $\Delta F/\Delta k$, that is, by the slope of the curve. As the figure shows, the incremental value of flexibility is always positive, but falls as k increases. Also, the horizontal lines in the figure show the value of the investment opportunity when there is maximum flexibility, that is, $k = \infty$; when $V = 10$, this value is 4.0, and when $V = 15$, it is 9.0.[5]

Consider two different construction technologies with the same $V = 10$, the same total cost $K = 6$, but different maximum rates of investment: $k = 0.5$ for the first, and 1.0 for the second. As can be seen from the figure, the incremental value of the more flexible technology is $\Delta F/\Delta k = 0.98/0.5 \approx 2$. Hence one should be willing to pay up to \$2 million to have access to the more flexible technology. The incremental value is higher if V is higher; if $V = 15$, the incremental value is about 5.5. Of course, in general greater flexibility might be accompanied by a different total required investment, K. In that case, we can rank the technologies by comparing $F(V, K; k)$ for each.

---

[4] Another measure of the incremental value of flexibility is the change in $F(V, K; k)/K$ (the value of the investment opportunity per dollar of total required investment) corresponding to a change in the minimum construction time K/k. Note, however, that $F(V, K; k)$ is not linear homogeneous in K, so that this measure will also depend on K.

[5] When $k = \infty$, the model reduces to the one we studied in Chapter 5. By using the results from Chapter 5, the reader can check that with $r = 0.02$, $\sigma = 0.20$, $\delta = 0.06$, and $K = 6$, the critical value is $V^* = 8.6$. Since $V = 10$ and 15 both exceed this, the value of the investment opportunity is just $V - K$, that is, 4.0 or 9.0.

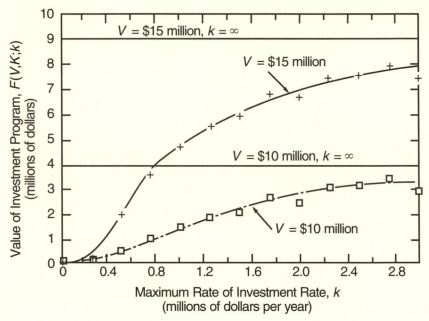

Figure 10.3. *Valuing Construction Time Flexibility*

[Shows $F(V, K; k)$ as function of k for $r = 0.02$, $\sigma = 0.20$, and $K = \$6$ million]

2.E   A Simple Extension

In Chapter 6 we argued that it is often more natural to think of a project's output price, rather than the value of the project, as following an exogenous stochastic process. Also, an advantage of starting with price as the stochastic variable is that we could determine how the value of the project depends on price, and hence how it (as well as the investment decision) is affected by price uncertainty.

The same arguments apply to this model of continuous investment with time to build. Fortunately, it is easy to modify the model so that the price of output is the exogenous stochastic state variable. As before, assume that there is a constant operating cost C, and that operation of the project can be temporarily and costlessly suspended when P falls below C, and costlessly resumed when P rises above C. We will also again assume that P follows the geometric Brownian motion of equation (1). Then, as shown in Chapter 6 and reviewed at the beginning of this chapter, the value of the project, $V(P)$, is given by equation (3).

Once we know $V(P)$, we can proceed pretty much as before. We write the value of the investment option as $F(P, K)$, and then by going through the usual step obtain the following partial differential equation:

$$\tfrac{1}{2}\sigma^2 P^2 F_{PP} - (r - \delta) P F_P - r F - I F_K - I = 0. \tag{32}$$

Note that this equation is the same as equation (24) except that P replaces V. Boundary conditions (25) to (27) now become

$$F(P, 0) = V(P), \tag{33}$$

$$F(0, K) = 0, \tag{34}$$

$$\lim_{P \to \infty} F_P(P, K) = (1/\delta)\, e^{-\delta K/k}. \tag{35}$$

Also, the value-matching and smooth-pasting conditions again apply; $F(P, K)$ and $F_P(P, K)$ must be continuous at the critical price $P = P^*(K)$.

A solution for $F(P, K)$ along with the critical price $P^*(K)$ can be obtained numerically in the same manner as before. The main difference is boundary condition (33). Numerical values for $V(P)$ must be calculated for the entire range of P used in the solution procedure. Then, at the terminal boundary ($K = 0$), $F(P, 0)$ is set equal to $V(P)$ for each value of P. Moving backwards in increments of ΔK, $F(P, K)$ and the boundary $P^*(K)$ are found for each K as before. The result will be a table similar to Table 10.1, except that the left-most column will contain prices, and the right-most column will contain project values $V(P)$ that correspond to those prices.

3 The Learning Curve and Optimal Production Decisions

Continuous sequential investment problems of the sort that we examined in the previous section are actually quite general. One closely related problem is the decision to produce when a firm faces a learning curve and uncertainty over future demand. When there is a learning curve, current production has two benefits. As always, it results in output that can be sold at some market price, but in addition, it moves the firm down the learning curve, reducing its *future* production costs.[6] Hence with a learning curve, part of the firm's

---

[6]For theoretical discussions of the learning curve and its implications for pricing and production in a deterministic setting, see Spence (1981), Kalish (1983), and Pindyck (1985). A variety of empirical studies have demonstrated the importance of learning curves for a wide range of industries; for an example, see Lieberman (1984).

cost of current production is actually an investment, the payoff from which is the reduction in future costs. Furthermore, it is an irreversible investment; if the firm regrets its production decision, it cannot "unproduce" and recover its costs. Finally, if the price of the firm's output fluctuates stochastically, the future payoffs from this investment will be uncertain.

A firm's production decisions when it faces a learning curve and a stochastically evolving output price are thus closely related to the kind of continuous investment decisions we just examined. At each instant the firm must observe price and decide whether to produce (and thereby invest in future cost reductions), knowing that it can later cease producing should the price fall sufficiently, and then resume producing should the price rise. To show how an optimal production rule can be found and to illustrate the close parallel with the investment problem, we make use of a recent model by Majd and Pindyck (1989).

In this model the firm sells its output at a price P that follows the geometric Brownian motion of equation (1). Marginal production cost is constant with respect to the rate of output, x, up to a capacity constraint arbitrarily set at unity. However, there is a learning curve; marginal cost declines with cumulative output, Q, until it reaches a minimum level, $\bar{c}$. Letting c denote the initial marginal cost, and Q_m the level of cumulative output at which learning ceases, we can write the marginal cost function as

$$C(Q) = \begin{cases} c\,e^{-\gamma Q} & \text{if } Q < Q_m, \\ c\,e^{-\gamma Q_m} = \bar{c} & \text{if } Q \geq Q_m. \end{cases} \tag{36}$$

As in Chapter 6, we will assume that the firm can, with no additional cost, shut down when P is low and later resume production if and when P rises sufficiently. But unlike our model in Chapter 6, now it may be optimal to continue producing even if the current profit flow is negative. The reason is that the value of current production depends both on the current cash flow and on the amount by which future costs are lowered. (In other words, there is a shadow value to current production which measures the benefit of moving down the learning curve.)

We will assume that uncertainty over P is spanned by existing assets in the economy, and that μ is the risk-adjusted discount rate for future revenue. As usual, we let $\delta = \mu - \alpha$. Now we can use our standard contingent claims method to value the firm and determine its optimal (value-maximizing) operating strategy. The value of the firm will depend on P and also on how far it has moved down the learning curve (that is, on cumulative output, Q). As in the model of the previous section, there are two state variables, in this case P and

Q, and one control variable, in this case x, subject to $0 \leq x \leq 1$. The problem is to find the value of the firm, $V(P, Q)$, along with the optimal production rule, $x^*(P, Q)$.

The reader should be able to easily verify that $V(P, Q)$ must satisfy the following partial differential equation:

$$\tfrac{1}{2}\sigma^2 P^2 V_{PP} + (r - \delta) P V_P + x V_Q - r V + x[P - C(Q)] = 0. \qquad (37)$$

Since this is linear in x, the optimal x is either 0 or 1. In fact

$$x^*(P, Q) = \begin{cases} 1 & \text{if } P + V_Q \geq C(Q), \\ 0 & \text{otherwise.} \end{cases} \qquad (38)$$

This formalizes our earlier intuition. A unit of current production yields an immediate benefit P, and a future benefit in the form of lower costs of future production, which is captured in the increment to the value of the firm, V_Q. Production is justified if the sum of these benefits exceeds the current cost $C(Q)$.

Once the problem is solved and the function $V(P, Q)$ is known, we have a threshold curve or free boundary, $P^*(Q)$, such that

$$P > P*(Q) \qquad \text{if and only if} \qquad P + V_Q(P, Q) > C(Q).$$

Then the optimal production rule becomes $x = 1$ if $P \geq P^*(Q)$ and $x = 0$ if $P < P^*(Q)$. Also, since cost falls as Q increases, we will have $dP^*/dQ < 0$. We now proceed to derive this solution.

The solution to (37) must satisfy the following boundary conditions:

$$V(0, Q) = 0, \qquad (39)$$

$$\lim_{P \to \infty} V_P(P, Q) = 1/\delta, \qquad (40)$$

$$P^*(Q) - C(Q) + V_Q(P, Q) = 0, \qquad (41)$$

$$V(P, Q_m) = \overline{V}(P), \qquad (42)$$

along with the value-matching condition that $V(P, Q)$ is continuous at $P = P^*$.

Conditions (39) and (40) are analogous to boundary conditions (26) and (27) in the model of investment with time to build in the preceding section; (39) just says that if $P = 0$, it remains 0, so that $V = 0$, and (40) says that if P becomes very high, the firm will almost surely always produce, and then the incremental value of a \$1 increase in price is just the present value of \$1 per period forever, discounted at $\mu - \alpha = \delta$. Condition (41) follows from the maximization of value with respect to production x; it is just the intuitive definition of $P^*(Q)$ above, and replaces the smooth-pasting condition. Finally, condition (42) is analogous to boundary condition (25) in the model of investment with time to build. It says that once Q reaches Q_m and production cost becomes constant, cumulative production can no longer affect the value of the firm, so that V is a function only of P. What is V in this case? We already derived it in Section 2 of Chapter 6 or equation (3) above:

$$\overline{V}(P) = \begin{cases} A_1 \ P^{\beta_1} & \text{if } P < \overline{c}, \\ B_2 \ P^{\beta_2} + P/\delta - \overline{c}/r & \text{if } P > \overline{c}, \end{cases} \tag{43}$$

where β_1 and β_2 are, respectively, the positive and negative roots of the fundamental quadratic, and A_1 and B_2 are constants given in equations (4) and (5) above.

When $P < P^*$ and $x = 0$, equation (37) has the usual analytical solution

$$V(P, Q) = a \ P^{\beta_1}. \tag{44}$$

When $P > P^*$ and $x = 1$, (37) does not have an analytical solution and must be solved numerically. Once again, a finite difference method is used, whereby the partial differential equation is transformed into a difference equation that can be solved algebraically. This method is essentially the same as that used in the preceding section, and described in the Appendix.

3.A   Characteristics of the Solution

Table 10.3 shows a solution for the following parameter values: initial marginal cost $c = 40$, final marginal cost $\overline{c} = 10$, $Q_m = 20$ (so that $\gamma = 0.0693$), $r = \delta = 0.05$ and $\sigma = 0.20$.[7] The table shows, for various amounts of cumulative production, the value of the firm as a function of price, as well as the critical price required for the firm to produce. For example, when cumulative production is zero (so that marginal cost is 40), the firm should produce when the price is $25.53 or more, and at this price the value of the firm is $178.53. When the price is below $25.53 the firm does not produce, but still has value

---

[7] Recall that σ is the annual standard deviation of percentage price changes. If the output of this firm happened to be an industrial commodity (for example, copper, cotton, or lumber), σ should in fact be significantly larger than 0.20. Also, note that if all price risk is diversifiable so that $\mu = r$, then setting $r = \delta$ implies that $\alpha = 0$, but if there is systematic risk so that $\mu > r$, $\alpha > 0$.

Table 10.3. *Value of Firm and Optimal Production Rule*

[Note: Entries show value of the firm $V(P, Q)$. Starred entries indicate optimal production rule; the price corresponding to each starred entry is the critical price $P^*(V)$. Parameter values are $r = \delta = 0.05$. $c = 40$, $\bar{c} = 10$, $Q_m = 20$, and $\sigma = 0.20$.]

Price in Dollars	Cumulative Production in Units (current marginal cost in dollars)					
	0.00 (40.00)	4.00 (30.32)	8.00 (22.98)	12.00 (17.41)	16.00 (13.20)	20.00 (10.00)
27.66	212.39	270.08	316.33	348.03	366.04	371.76
26.58	194.75	250.10	295.70	327.24	345.23	350.95
25.53	178.53*	231.15	276.00	307.36	325.31	331.03
24.53	163.76	213.24	257.21	288.33	306.25	311.98
23.57	150.22	196.35	239.29	270.15	288.03	293.75
22.65	137.79	180.50	222.24	252.78	270.61	276.32
21.76	126.40	165.70	206.03	236.20	253.96	259.67
20.91	115.94	151.97	190.65	220.39	238.06	243.77
20.09	106.35	139.32*	176.09	205.32	222.89	228.60
19.30	97.56	127.80	162.35	190.97	208.42	214.12
18.54	89.49	117.23	149.42	177.33	194.62	200.32
17.81	82.09	107.53	137.31	164.38	181.49	187.18
17.12	75.30	98.64	126.01	152.11	169.00	174.67
16.44	69.07	90.48	115.54	140.50	157.13	162.69
15.80	63.36	83.00	105.92*	129.55	145.86	151.50
15.18	58.12	76.13	97.16	119.26	135.19	140.79
14.59	53.31	69.83	89.12	109.61	125.09	130.65
14.01	48.90	64.06	81.75	100.62	115.55	121.06
13.46	44.86	58.76	74.99	92.29	106.57	112.00
12.94	41.15	53.90	68.79	84.61*	98.13	103.47
12.43	37.74	49.44	63.10	77.62	90.22	95.45
11.94	34.62	45.35	57.88	71.20	82.84	87.93
11.47	31.76	41.60	53.09	65.31	76.00	80.89
11.02	29.13	38.16	48.70	59.91	69.68*	74.33
10.59	26.72	35.00	44.67	54.95	63.92	68.24
10.18	24.51	32.11	40.98	50.41	58.63	62.61*
9.78	22.48	29.45	37.59	46.24	53.78	57.43
9.39	20.62	27.02	34.48	42.41	49.33	52.68

because the price may rise in the future. As Q increases, the value of the firm rises (because costs have been reduced), and P^* falls. The critical price falls to the long-run cost of \$10 as Q reaches 20; at that point the firm has reached the bottom of the learning curve and the shadow value of cumulative production is zero.

Of course, even if there is no uncertainty, when there is a learning curve a firm should produce at a price that can be substantially below current marginal cost because of the shadow value of cumulative production.[8] To see how uncertainty affects the firm's production decision, we can examine this shadow value, V_Q, and its dependence on P and σ. Figure 10.4 shows, for $Q = 0$, V_Q as a function of P for $\sigma = 0$, 0.05, 0.1, 0.2, 0.3, and 0.5. Also shown is the line $c - P$; note from equation (41) that P^* satisfies $P = C(Q) - V_Q$, and so, when $Q = 0$, is given by the intersection of this line with the V_Q curve. When $\sigma = 0$, $\alpha = r - \delta = 0$, so V_Q is zero up to the critical price of \$19.00 (if P is below this price the firm will never produce), and then is constant at \$21.00.[9] Note from this figure that the larger is σ, the larger is P^*. For example, when σ is 0.5, P^* is about \$31.

The effect of uncertainty on V_Q depends on the current price. The possibility of future increases in price raises V_Q, and the possibility of decreases reduces it. At low prices, the possibility of increases in price dominates, so uncertainty increases V_Q. To see this, note that if $\sigma = 0$, the price can never increase (because $\delta = r$), so future cost savings have no value when price is low. However, if $\sigma > 0$, the price may later rise enough to justify production, so reductions in future cost have some value. The greater is σ, the greater is the probability that the firm will begin to produce over some finite horizon, and thus the greater is the present value of reductions in future cost. At high prices the effect is just the opposite. Suppose P is high and the firm is producing. If $\sigma > 0$, the price may fall to the point where the firm shuts down, and the higher is σ, the sooner this is likely to occur. Thus for high prices, a higher σ implies a lower V_Q.

It is this higher price region that is relevant for the production decision. Thus, as Figure 10.4 shows, an increase in σ raises P^*. This result can also be understood by remembering that with a learning curve, part of the firm's production cost is actually an irreversible investment in reduced future costs.

---

[8] As Spence (1981) has shown, if the discount rate is zero (and there is no uncertainty), a competitive firm should produce when price exceeds the long-run marginal cost that will prevail when the firm reaches the bottom of its learning curve.

[9] When $\sigma = 0$, V_Q and P^* can be found analytically by integrating the flow of discounted profit.

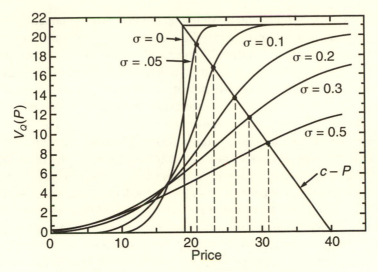

Figure 10.4. *Shadow Value of Cumulative Production*
(for $r = \delta = 0.05$, $\sigma = 0, 0.05, 0.1, 0.2, 0.3$, and 0.5)

When future price is uncertain, so is the payoff from this investment. As usual, this implies an opportunity cost to investing now rather than waiting to see how price will evolve. The net benefit of this investment—which is measured by V_Q—thus falls, pushing the critical price up closer to where it would be if there were no learning curve.

4   Cost Uncertainty and Learning

In most of the investment problems that we have examined so far, it is the future payoffs from the investment that are uncertain. However, sometimes the cost of an investment is more uncertain than the payoffs. Nuclear power plants, for which construction costs are hard to predict due to engineering and regulatory uncertainties, are an example. Although the future value of a completed nuclear plant is also uncertain (because electricity demand and costs of alternative fuels are uncertain), construction cost uncertainty is greater than revenue uncertainty, and has deterred utilities from building new plants. Other examples include the development of a new line of aircraft, urban construction projects, and many R&D projects, such as the development of a new drug by a pharmaceutical company.

When projects take time to complete, the firm faces a sequential invest-ment problem that can involve two different kinds of cost uncertainty, both of which were discussed briefly in Chapter 2. The first is *technical* uncertainty, and relates to the physical difficulty of completing the project: Assuming prices of construction inputs are known, how much time, effort, and materials will ultimately be required? Technical uncertainty can only be resolved by under-taking the project; actual costs and construction time unfold as the project proceeds. These costs may be greater or less than anticipated if impediments arise or if the work progresses more quickly than planned, but the total cost of the investment is only known for certain when the project is complete.

The second kind of uncertainty, which we will call *input cost* uncertainty, is external to what the firm does. It arises when the prices of labor, land, and materials needed to build a project fluctuate unpredictably, or when unpre-dictable changes in government regulations change the cost of construction. Prices and regulations change regardless of whether or not the firm is invest-ing, and are more uncertain the farther into the future one looks. Hence input cost uncertainty may be particularly important for projects that take time to complete or are subject to voluntary or involuntary delays.

Both technical and input cost uncertainty increase the value of an invest-ment opportunity for the same reason that uncertainty over future cash flows increases it—the net payoff from the investment is a convex function of the cost of the investment. However, as we saw in Chapter 2, these two types of uncertainty affect the investment decision differently. Technical uncertainty makes investing more attractive; a project can have an expected cost that makes its conventional NPV negative, but it can still be economical to begin investing. The reason is that investing reveals information about cost, and therefore has a shadow value beyond its direct contribution to the completion of the project; this shadow value lowers the full expected cost of the invest-ment. (In Chapter 2, we illustrated this in the context of a simple two-period example.)

On the other hand, input cost uncertainty makes it less attractive to invest now. A project with a conventional NPV that is positive might still be uneconomical, because costs of construction inputs change whether or not investment is taking place, so there is a value of waiting for new information before committing resources. Also, this effect is magnified when fluctuations in construction costs are correlated with the economy, or, in the context of the Capital Asset Pricing Model, when the "beta" of cost is high. The reason is that a higher beta raises the discount rate applied to expected future costs, which raises the value of the investment opportunity as well as the benefit from waiting rather than investing now.

Since technical and input cost uncertainty have different effects on investment, it can be important to incorporate both in the analysis. Here we summarize a model developed by Pindyck (1993b) that yields decision rules for irreversible investments subject to both types of cost uncertainty. The basic idea is that the project in question has an actual cost of completion that is a random variable, $\tilde{K}$; only the expected cost $K = \mathcal{E}(\tilde{K})$ is known. As in the model of Section 2, the project takes time to complete—the maximum rate at which the firm can (productively) invest is k. Upon completion, the firm receives an asset (for example, a factory or new drug) whose value, V, is known with certainty.

To allow for both technical and factor cost uncertainty, we will assume that the expected cost K evolves according to

$$dK = -I\,dt + v\,(I\,K)^{1/2}\,dz + \gamma\,K\,dw, \qquad (45)$$

where dz and dw are the increments of uncorrelated Wiener processes.[10] It is unlikely that the technical difficulty of completing a project will have much to do with the state of the overall economy, but this may not be the case for the evolution of construction costs. Hence we will assume that all risk associated with dz is diversifiable, (that is, dz is uncorrelated with the economy and the stock market), but dw may be correlated with the market.

Note that the second term on the right-hand side of equation (45) describes technical uncertainty. If $\gamma = 0$, K can change only if the firm is investing, and the instantaneous variance of dK/K increases linearly with I/K. When the firm is investing, the expected change in K over an interval Δt is $-I\,\Delta t$, but the realized change can be greater or less than this, and K can even increase. As the project proceeds, progress will at times be slower and at times faster than expected. The variance of $\tilde{K}$ falls as K falls, but the actual total cost of the project, $\int_0^{\tilde{T}} I\,dt$, is only known when the project is completed. The last term on the right-hand side of equation (45) describes input cost uncertainty. If $v = 0$, the instantaneous variance of dK/K is constant

---

[10]This is a special case of the following controlled diffusion process:

$$dK = -I\,dt + g(I, K)\,dz,$$

where $g_I \geq 0$, $g_{II} \leq 0$, and $g_K \geq 0$. For this equation to make economic sense, certain conditions should hold: (i) $F(K; V, k)$ is homogeneous of degree 1 in K, V, and k; (ii) $F_K < 0$, that is, an increase in the expected cost of an investment always reduces its value; (iii) the instantaneous variance of dK is bounded for all finite K and approaches zero as $K \to 0$; and (iv) if the firm invests at the maximum rate k until the project is complete, $\mathcal{E}_0 \int_0^{\tilde{T}} k\,dt = K$, so that K is indeed the expected cost to completion. Equation (45) meets these conditions.

and independent of I. Now K will fluctuate even when there is no investment; ongoing changes in the costs of labor and materials will change K irrespective of what the firm does.

The problem is to find an investment policy that maximizes the value of the investment opportunity, $F(K) = F(K; V, k)$:

$$F(K) = \max_{I(t)} \mathcal{E}_0 \left[V e^{-\mu \tilde{T}} - \int_0^{\tilde{T}} I(t) e^{-\mu t} \, dt \right], \tag{46}$$

subject to equation (45), $0 \leq I(t) \leq k$, and $K(\tilde{T}) = 0$. Here μ is an appropriate risk-adjusted discount rate, and the time of completion, $\tilde{T}$, is stochastic.

4.A   Solving the Investment Problem

We will assume that spanning holds, so that μ can be eliminated from the problem. Let x be the price of an asset or dynamic portfolio of assets perfectly correlated with w, so that dx follows

$$dx = \alpha_x x \, dt + \sigma_x x \, dw. \tag{47}$$

Then, the reader should be able to confirm that $F(K)$ must satisfy the following differential equation:

$$\begin{aligned}
\tfrac{1}{2} v^2 \, I \, K \, F''(K) &+ \tfrac{1}{2} \gamma^2 \, K^2 \, F''(K) - I \, F'(K) \\
&- \phi_x \, \gamma \, K \, F'(K) - I = r \, F(K),
\end{aligned} \tag{48}$$

where $\phi_x \equiv (r_x - r)/\sigma_x$, and r_x is the risk-adjusted expected rate of return on x, namely, $r_x = r + \phi \, \rho_{xm} \, \sigma_x$, where ϕ is the market price of risk and ρ_{xm} is the correlation coefficient between the x-asset and the market portfolio. Thus $\phi_x = \phi \, \rho_{xm}$. Since ϕ is an economy-wide parameter, the only project-specific parameter needed to determine ϕ_x is ρ_{xm}.

Because equation (48) is linear in I, the rate of investment that maximizes $F(K)$ is always either zero or the maximum rate k:

$$I = \begin{cases} k & \text{for } \tfrac{1}{2} v^2 \, K \, F''(K) - F'(K) - 1 \geq 0, \\ 0 & \text{otherwise.} \end{cases} \tag{49}$$

Equation (48) therefore has a free boundary at a point K^*, such that $I(t) = k$ when $K \leq K^*$ and $I(t) = 0$ otherwise. The value of K^* is found along with $F(K)$ by solving (48) subject to the following boundary conditions:

$$F(0) = V, \tag{50}$$

$$\lim_{K \to \infty} F(K) = 0, \tag{51}$$

$$\tfrac{1}{2}v^2 K^* F''(K^*) - F'(K^*) - 1 = 0, \tag{52}$$

along with the value-matching condition that $F(K)$ is continuous at K^*. Condition (50) says that at completion, the payoff is V. Condition (51) says that when K is very large, the probability is very small that over some finite time it will drop enough to begin the project. Condition (52) follows from (49), and is equivalent to the smooth-pasting condition that $F'(K)$ is continuous at K^*.

When $I = 0$, equation (48) has the simple analytical solution

$$F(K) = A K^{\beta_2}, \tag{53}$$

where β_2 is the *negative* root [from boundary condition (51)] of the fundamental quadratic equation

$$\tfrac{1}{2}\gamma^2 \beta(\beta - 1) - \phi_x \gamma \beta - r = 0.$$

The remaining boundary conditions are used to determine A along with K^* and the solution for $F(K)$ for $K < K^*$. This is done numerically, which is not difficult once equation (48) has been appropriately transformed.[11] A family of solutions for $K < K^*$ can be found, each of which satisfies condition (50), but a unique solution, together with the value of A, is determined from condition (52) and the continuity of $F(K)$ at K^*.

4.B Characteristics of the Solution

When only technical uncertainty is present, equation (48) reduces to

$$\tfrac{1}{2}v^2 I K F''(K) - I F'(K) - I = r F(K). \tag{54}$$

Then K can change only when investment is occurring, so if $K > K^*$ and the firm is not investing, K will never change, and $F(K) = 0$. When $r = 0$, equation (54) has an analytical solution:

$$F(K) = V - K + v^2 \left(\frac{V}{2}\right)^{-2/v^2} \left(\frac{K}{v^2 + 2}\right)^{(v^2+2)/v^2}, \tag{55}$$

---

[11]When $I = k$, equation (48) has a first-degree singularity at $K = 0$. To eliminate this, make the substitution $F(K) = f(y)$, where $y = \log K$. Then equation (48) becomes

$$f''(y) - f'(y) - \frac{2k\, f'(y)}{v^2 k + \gamma^2 e^y} = \frac{2k + 2r\, f(y)}{v^2 k e^{-y} + \gamma^2},$$

and boundary conditions (50) to (52) are transformed accordingly.

Table 10.4.   *Critical Cost to Completion, K*, as a Function of v and γ*

[Note: K^* is found by solving equation (48) and its boundary conditions for
$F(K)$. The parameters v and γ measure the degrees of technical and input
cost uncertainty respectively. Other parameter values are $V = 10$, $k = 2$,
$r = 0.05$, and $\phi = 0$.]

				γ		
v	0	0.1	0.2	0.3	0.4	0.5
0	8.9257	6.6113	4.9463	3.7524	2.8857	2.2559
0.1	8.9844	6.6504	4.9756	3.7720	2.9016	2.2681
0.2	9.1309	6.7578	5.0537	3.8330	2.9468	2.3032
0.3	9.3750	6.9385	5.1855	3.9307	3.0225	2.3608
0.4	9.7168	7.1875	5.3711	4.0674	3.1274	2.4438
0.5	10.156	7.5098	5.6104	4.2480	3.2617	2.5488
0.6	10.693	7.9053	5.8984	4.4629	3.4277	2.6758
0.7	11.328	8.3691	6.2402	4.7168	3.6230	2.8271
0.8	12.051	8.8965	6.6309	5.0146	3.8477	3.0005
0.9	12.861	9.5020	7.0801	5.3467	4.1016	3.1982
1.0	13.770	10.166	7.5732	5.7178	4.3848	3.4180

and the critical value K^* is given by

$$K^* = (1 + \tfrac{1}{2}v^2)\, V.$$

Equation (55) has a simple interpretation. When $r = 0$, $V - K$ would be the
value of the investment opportunity were there no possibility of abandoning
the project. The last term is the value of the put option, that is, the option to
abandon the project should costs turn out to be higher than expected. Note
that for $v > 0$, $K^* > V$, and K^* is increasing in v. The more uncertainty there
is, the greater is the value of the investment opportunity, and the larger is the
maximum expected cost for which beginning to invest is economical.

Let us return now to the general case, which requires numerical solution.
Since increases in v and γ have opposite effects on K^*, it is useful to determine
the net effect for combinations of these parameters. Table 10.4 shows K^* as
a function of both v and γ, for $\phi = 0$, $V = 10$, $k = 2$, and $r = 0.05$. Note
that K^* decreases with γ and increases with v, but is much more sensitive to
changes in γ. Whatever the value of v, a γ of 0.5 reduces K^* to about one-
fourth of its value when $\gamma = 0$. Also, this drop in K^* would be even larger

if there were a systematic component to the input cost uncertainty. Thus for many investments, and particularly for large industrial projects for which input costs fluctuate, increasing uncertainty is likely to depress investment. The opposite will be the case only for investments like R&D programs, for which technical uncertainty is far more important.

The application of this model requires estimates of v and γ. This requires estimating confidence intervals around projected cost for each source of uncertainty. To break cost uncertainty into technical and input cost components, note that the first is independent of time, whereas the variance of cost due to the second component grows linearly with the time horizon. Thus, a value for γ is found by estimating the standard deviation of cost T years into the future assuming no investment takes place prior to that time. This estimate, $\hat{\sigma}_T$, could come from experience with construction costs, or from an accounting model of cost combined with variance estimates for individual inputs. Then, $\hat{\gamma} = \hat{\sigma}_T/\sqrt{T}$. To estimate v we can make use of the fact that if $\gamma = 0$, the variance of the cost to completion is given by[12]

$$V(\tilde{K}) = \left(\frac{v^2}{2 - v^2}\right) K^2. \tag{56}$$

[Thus if one standard deviation of a project's cost is 25% (50%) of the expected cost, v would be 0.343 (0.63).] Using (56) and an initial estimate of expected cost, $K(0)$, a value for v can be based on an estimate of the time-independent standard deviation of $\tilde{K}$.

5 Guide to the Literature

The model of continuous investment with time to build that was presented in Section 2 has as its antecedent the model of optimal abandonment developed by Myers and Majd (1984). They valued a project when construction could be permanently abandoned at any point in time, and, using a similar numerical solution method, found the optimal abandonment rule. More recent studies of investment with time to build include Bar-Ilan and Strange (1992). Time

---

[12]Let $G(K) = \mathcal{E}_t\left[\int_t^{\tilde{T}} k\, d\tau | K\right]^2$. Then $G(K)$ must satisfy the following Kolmogorov equation:

$$\tfrac{1}{2}v^2 k K G''(K) - k G'(K) + 2k K = 0,$$

subject to the boundary conditions $G(0) = 0$ and $G(\infty) = \infty$. [See Karlin and Taylor (1981), page 203.] The solution to this is $G(K) = 2K^2/(2 - v^2)$, so the variance is given by (56).

to build (and related delays) is usually ignored in theoretical and empirical models of investment, but as Kydland and Prescott (1982) have shown, it can have important macroeconomic implications.

The model of cost uncertainty presented in Section 4 is related to several earlier studies. The value of information gathering was explored by Roberts and Weitzman (1981), who developed a similar model of sequential investment in which a project can be stopped in midstream, and the process of investing reduces both the expected cost to completion and the variance of that cost. They derive an optimal stopping rule, and show that it may pay to go ahead with the early stages of an investment even though the NPV of the entire project is negative. Weitzman, Newey, and Rabin (1981) then used that model to evaluate demonstration plants for synthetic fuels, and showed that learning about costs could justify some of these investments. MacKie-Mason (1991) extended the Roberts and Weitzman analysis by allowing for investors (who pay the cost of a project) and managers (who decide whether to continue or abandon the project) to have conflicting interests and asymmetric information. He showed that asymmetric learning about cost leads to inefficient overabandonment of projects.

Grossman and Shapiro (1986) also studied investments for which the total effort required to reach a payoff is unknown. They modelled the payoff as a Poisson process, with an arrival rate specified as a function of the cumulative effort expended. They allowed the rate of progress to be a concave function of effort, and focused on the rate of investment, rather than on whether one should proceed or not. Also related is the work of Baldwin (1982), who analyzed sequential investment decisions when investment opportunities arrive randomly and the firm has limited resources. She valued the sequence of opportunities and showed that a simple NPV rule leads to overinvestment, that is, there is a value to waiting for better opportunities. Likewise, if cost evolves stochastically, it may pay to wait for cost to fall. Finally, Zeira (1987) developed a model in which a firm learns about its payoff function as it accumulates capital.

All of these models of learning and cost uncertainty belong to a broad class of optimal search problems analyzed by Weitzman (1979). In what he characterized as a "Pandora's box" problem, one must decide how many investment opportunities with uncertain outcomes should be undertaken, and in what order. In this case, each dollar spent on a project is a single investment opportunity, and the uncertain outcome is the amount of progress that results. The model presented in Section 4 is more general in that expected outcomes can evolve stochastically even when no investment is taking place (input cost uncertainty), but is more restrictive in that the order in which dollars are spent is predetermined.

In the Appendix, we briefly explain the numerical procedure used to solve the partial differential equation for the model of investment with time to build in Section 2. Readers who wish to develop some expertise in solving partial differential equations could begin with one of the following textbooks: Haberman (1987), Guenther and Lee (1988), or Carrier and Pearson (1976). Numerical methods for solving the PDE's that arise in option pricing problems are discussed in Brennan and Schwartz (1978), Geske and Shastri (1985), and Hull and White (1990), among others.

Appendix

A Numerical Solution of Partial Differential Equation

This appendix shows how the partial differential equation (24) and its associated boundary conditions for the model of continuous investment with time to build can be solved numerically. The procedure used here is a variant of the explicit form of the finite difference method. Other numerical procedures could be used, and some might be more efficient or more accurate. Our objective here is simply to illustrate one approach.

To improve the accuracy of this procedure and make it possible to calculate $F(V, K)$ over a sufficiently large range for V, we begin by making the following transformation:

$$F(V, K) \equiv e^{-rK/k} G(X, K), \tag{57}$$

where $X \equiv \log V$. The partial differential equation (for $V > V^*$) and boundary conditions then become

$$\tfrac{1}{2}\sigma^2 G_{XX} + (r - \delta - \tfrac{1}{2}\sigma^2) G_X - k G_k - k e^{rK/k} = 0, \tag{58}$$

$$G(X, 0) = e^X, \tag{59}$$

$$\lim_{X \to \infty} \left[e^{-X} e^{-rK/k} G_X(X, K) \right] = e^{-\delta K/k}, \tag{60}$$

$$G(X^*, K) = (1/v) G_X(X^*, K). \tag{61}$$

Note that the coefficients of the PDE are no longer functions of V.

The finite difference method transforms the continuous variables V and K into discrete variables, and replaces the partial derivatives in the PDE with finite differences. The explicit form of this method corresponds to a specific choice of finite differences for this substitution. Let $G(X, K) \equiv G(i\Delta X, j\Delta K) \equiv G_{i,j}$, where $-b \leq i \leq m$ and $0 \leq j \leq n$. Now make the substitutions:

$$G_{XX} \approx [G_{i+1,j} - 2G_{i,j} + G_{i-1,j}]/(\Delta X)^2,$$

$$G_X \approx [G_{i+1,j} - G_{i-1,j}]/2\Delta X,$$

$$G_K \approx [G_{i,j+1} - G_{i,j}]/\Delta K.$$

The PDE then becomes the difference equation

$$G_{i,j} = p^+ G_{i+1,j-1} + p^o G_{i,j-1} + p^- G_{i-1,j-1} - n_{j-1}, \tag{62}$$

where

$$p^+ = \frac{\Delta K}{2k\Delta X} \left[\sigma^2/\Delta X + r - \delta - \tfrac{1}{2}\sigma^2\right],$$

$$p^o = 1 - \sigma^2 \Delta K/k(\Delta X)^2,$$

$$p^- = \frac{\Delta K}{2k\Delta X} \left[\sigma^2/\Delta X - r + \delta + \tfrac{1}{2}\sigma^2\right],$$

$$n_j = \Delta K\, e^{rj\Delta K/k}.$$

Note that $p^+ + p^o + p^- = 1$.[13] The terminal boundary condition then becomes

$$G_{i,j=0} = e^{i\Delta X}, \tag{63}$$

and the upper boundary condition becomes

$$\lim_{X\to\infty} \left[e^{-X-rK/k} G_X(X, K)\right] = e^{-\delta K/k},$$

or,

$$G_X(m\Delta X, K) = e^{m\Delta X + (r-\delta)j\Delta K/k}.$$

Using the finite difference approximation above for G_X, this becomes

$$[G_{m+1,j} - G_{m-1,j}]/2\Delta X = e^{m\Delta X + (r-\delta)j\Delta K/k},$$

[13] This is a three-point random walk representation of the Brownian motion of X, analogous to the two-point form we used in Chapter 3 and elsewhere. Or, as Brennan and Schwartz (1978) have shown, one can interpret the difference equation (62) in terms of a jump process with probabilities p^+ and p^-, respectively, of upwards and downwards jumps.

or,

$$G_{m+1,j} = 2\Delta X\, e^{m\Delta X+(r-\delta)j\Delta K/k} + G_{m-1,j}.$$

Now substitute this for $G_{m+1,j}$ in equation (62) (setting $i = m$):

$$G_{m,j+1} = p^+\, G_{m+1,j} + p^o\, G_{m,j} + p^-\, G_{m-1,j} - n_j,$$

or,

$$G_{m,j+1} = p^+\left[2\,\Delta X\, e^{m\Delta X+(r-\delta)j\Delta K/k}\right] + p^o\, G_{m,j} + (p^+ + p^-)\, G_{m-1,j} - n_j. \tag{64}$$

Finally, the free-boundary condition becomes

$$G_{i^*,j} = \frac{1}{v\Delta X + 1}\, G_{i^*+1,j}. \tag{65}$$

The solution proceeds backwards from the terminal boundary, as illustrated in Figure 10.5. First, the values of G along the terminal boundary ($j = 0$) are calculated using equation (63). Stepping back to $j = 1$, equation (64) is used to calculate $G_{m,1}$, and equation (62) is used to calculate the values of G for $i = m-1, m-2$, etc. Each time a value for G is calculated, equation (65) is used to check whether the free boundary has been reached. Because

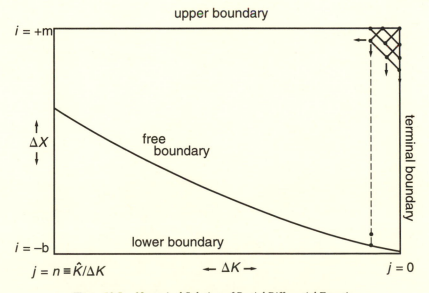

Figure 10.5. *Numerical Solution of Partial Differential Equation*

of numerical error due to the discretization, equation (65) will never hold exactly, so one checks whether it holds to within some specified bound ϵ:

$$G_{i^*,j} - \frac{1}{v\Delta X + 1} G_{i^*+1,j} \leq \epsilon, \tag{66}$$

where ϵ is chosen arbitrarily. (Setting $\epsilon = \Delta X/2$ tends to work well.) Once this check identifies the free boundary, equation (28) is used to determine the value of the coefficient a, as well as the values of G below the free boundary. We can summarize this procedure as follows:

1. First, fill in the terminal boundary using equation (63).
2. Then, for $j = 1$ to $j = n$, use equation (64) to calculate $G_{m,j}$, and then move down the column, using equation (62) to calculate $G_{i,j}$ for $i < m$.
3. Finally, at the free boundary, calculate the value of the coefficient a and use equation (28) to fill in the values of $G_{i,j}$ in the lower region.

Note that the solution for $V^*(K)$ will be subject to some numerical error because of the finite difference approximation, and that is why the points plotted in Figures 10.2 and 10.3 do not lie on smooth curves. In general, this numerical error will be smaller the smaller the size of the increments ΔX and ΔK.

Chapter 11

Incremental Investment and Capacity Choice

THE MODELS of individual firms' investment decisions that were developed in Chapters 5–7, and the models of industry equilibrium in Chapters 8 and 9, were based on a simple discrete unit of investment, namely, a single project of a given fixed size. In Chapter 10 we continued to examine a single project, but we accounted for the fact that completion of a project often requires a sequence of steps, each of which increases the sunk cost that is committed to the project. In this chapter, we examine a firm's investment decisions in a more general context. We allow each firm to hold and operate a large number of projects, to add new projects, and perhaps to retire old ones. Its existing projects continue to produce output and profit flows even as the firm contemplates adding new ones. In other words, we think of the firm as choosing an investment policy to alter its *stock* of capital. Its current output flow depends on its installed capital stock, and perhaps on flows of instantaneously variable inputs like labor and raw materials, through a production function.

We begin by considering how a firm irreversibly invests in its capital stock. When the production function shows diminishing returns to scale, we can conceptually line up successive units of capital in decreasing order of their marginal productivity, and think of them as distinct investment projects. Now suppose the output price, or the prices of some variable inputs, or some other parameter that affects productivity, is uncertain. For each of our conceptually discrete projects, we find a threshold of profitability that justifies the investment. This turns out to have the usual option value interpretation:

the expected present value of the project's marginal contribution must be a multiple $\beta_1/(\beta_1 - 1)$ of the cost of investment, where β_1 is the usual root of the fundamental quadratic that involves the discount rate and the drift and volatility coefficients of the price process. Successive units of capital, with successively lower marginal products, will require higher and higher thresholds. Thus we will find a "threshold curve" linking the stock of capital and the threshold value for the stochastic state variable. When this state variable is below the curve, no investment is made, while if the variable rises above the curve, just enough is invested to bring us back to the curve.

We define a version of Tobin's q, based on the value of assets in place but applying to the marginal unit of capital. Then the firm's optimal investment policy is to add a marginal unit when this "marginal q" rises to $\beta_1/(\beta_1 - 1)$.

If there are regions of increasing returns in the production function, then a threshold that justifies investment of one unit of capital may also justify several additional units that have higher marginal products. Thus the investment policy will yield some sudden jumps in the stock of capital to cross regions of increasing returns. In Section 2 we will find the exact condition that determines the threshold and the size of such jumps; it will turn out to be a natural analog of the standard option value multiplier condition, but now expressed in terms of the average product of the discrete jump in capital, instead of the marginal product of the next small unit.

In previous chapters, where each firm simply had to decide whether to go ahead with a single project, the cost of investment was a number, and it did not matter whether we thought of it as a fixed cost of decision making, or a sunk cost representing the irreversibility of investment, or an adjustment cost that is higher when the firm tries to install a given addition to its capital stock in a shorter span of time. However, now the firm is choosing the time path of its stock of capital, and we must specify in more detail how the cost of investment depends on the scale and rate of investment. The distinctions just mentioned become important; optimal investment policy takes very different forms depending on the nature of the cost.

The models presented in the first two sections of this chapter treat irreversible investment without any costs of adjustment or fixed costs of decision making. Thus the sunk cost of any addition to the stock of capital is proportional to the size of that addition. In Section 3 we consider a more general model that includes all three kinds of costs. We show how these other costs affect the investment decision, and we show the relation to and the differences between our approach and the traditional q-theory of investment.

We will confine the discussion to a single firm. It is not difficult in principle to take the analysis to a competitive equilibrium level as we did in Chapters 8 and 9, but the algebraic complications quickly mount up, and it seems more important to focus on the new issues raised by variable capacity in the simplest setting possible.

1   Gradual Capacity Expansion with Diminishing Returns

We begin with a model of a firm's capacity expansion, based on Pindyck (1988b) and Bertola (1989). It is a simple generalization of the model of Chapter 6. As there, we assume that the firm has a monopoly right to invest in the industry. Each unit of capital costs κ, and investment in the unit is irreversible. When the firm has K units of capital in place, the flow of output Q is given by the production function $Q = G(K)$. The industry demand function is $P = Y\,D(Q)$, where the shift variable Y follows the geometric Brownian motion

$$dY = \alpha\,Y\,dt + \sigma\,Y\,dz. \tag{1}$$

For simplicity, we assume that there are no variable costs, so the profit flow is

$$\pi = Y\,D(G(K))\,G(K) = Y\,H(K), \tag{2}$$

and the marginal revenue product of capital is $Y\,H'(K)$. In this section we assume that there are diminishing returns to capital in the sense that the marginal revenue product is decreasing in K, or the revenue function is concave in K, so $H''(K) < 0$. This could be the case because of physical diminishing returns in production $[G''(K) < 0]$, or because of a downward-sloping industry demand curve $[D'(Q) < 0]$, or some combination of the two. (In fact, even if there were physical increasing returns, we could have a decreasing marginal revenue product as long as the demand curve had a sufficiently large negative slope.)

More generally, we can regard the profit flow as the outcome of an instantaneous optimization problem where variable inputs such as labor or raw materials are chosen holding the level of capital fixed. The only new feature is that the stochastic variable need not enter multiplicatively. We will consider this extension later in this section, and point out its implications for the effect of uncertainty on investment.

The investment decision can as usual be examined in one of two essentially equivalent ways: dynamic programming and contingent claims analysis. We treated the single-project decision using both approaches in Chapters 5 and 6, and showed their similarity. Since then we have been using either one or the other to suit expository convenience. However, the present setting with incremental capacity choice is somewhat new, so we will once again discuss both approaches explicitly.

1.A   Optimal Investment via Dynamic Programming

Given the initial capital stock K and the initial level of the stochastic demand shift variable Y, the firm wants to choose the path of its capital stock, K_t, to maximize the expected present value of its operating profits, net of the cost of investing. Let ρ be the rate at which future profits are discounted. Write $W(K, Y)$ for the maximized value function or the Bellman function of the firm's choice problem. Of course this function is not known in advance but must be determined as part of the solution.[1]

Consider a short interval of time dt. Actual decisions are made continuously and the interval dt is an arbitrary construct, so we will be interested in the limit as $dt \to 0$. The profit flow during this interval is $\pi\, dt$; the effect of discounting over the interval is of order dt^2 and thus can be ignored. Suppose the firm increases its capital stock from K to K' at the end of this interval. The demand shift variable changes over the interval from Y to $Y + dY$. Of course, given the firm's information at time t, it does not know what dY will be, but knows its probability distribution from equation (1). Therefore it calculates the expected value of this increase in the capital stock as

$$Y\, H(K)\, dt + e^{-\rho\, dt}\, \{\, \mathcal{E}[W(K', Y + dY)] - \kappa\, (K' - K)\, \}. \tag{3}$$

The firm will choose K' to maximize the right-hand side of this expression. Then the resulting maximum will be just the initial value $W(K, Y)$ of the Bellman function.

We assumed that the function $H(K)$ is concave. Then it is easy to show that the Bellman function W must also be concave in K. To see why, consider any two starting capital stocks, say, K_a and K_b, and suppose the optimal investment policy leads to $\{K_{at}\}$ and $\{K_{bt}\}$ as the respective capacity expansion paths corresponding to a particular realization path of the stochastic variable, $\{Y_t\}$. Now let θ be any number between zero and one, and consider the firm's

---

[1]We considered a mathematically very similar problem from a social planner's perspective in Chapter 9, Section 1.A. There our concern was to establish a correspondence between the social optimum and the equilibrium of a competitive industry. We developed the model in the quickest heuristic way to reach that goal. Now we want more detailed characterization of the firm's investment policy, and will need to examine the model in an appropriately greater detail. Readers will grasp the method and the results more quickly by recalling some of the intuition we developed in Chapter 9, and then going back to rethink that model in the light of detail that emerges now.

investment problem when the initial capital stock is $\theta\,K_a + (1-\theta)\,K_b$. Define an investment policy by the following rule: if the stochastic variable evolves on the path $\{Y_t\}$, expand capacity on the θ-averaged path $\{\theta\,K_{at} + (1-\theta)\,K_{bt}\}$. The separate paths labelled a and b being feasible, at any time t each of K_{at} and K_{bt} cannot use any more information than is revealed in the path of the stochastic variable up to the time t. Then the same is true of the θ-averaged path, so it is feasible, too.

Because the function H is concave, the policy just defined yields the revenue flow

$$Y_t\,H(\theta\,K_{at} + (1-\theta)\,K_{bt}) \geq \theta\,Y_t\,H(K_{at}) + (1-\theta)\,Y_t\,H(K_{bt}).$$

The investment cost flow is just the θ-weighted average of the cost flows for the two separate policies for cases a and b. Discounting, and taking expectations over the possible realizations $\{Y_t\}$, we have

$$W(\theta\,K_a + (1-\theta)\,K_b, Y) \geq \theta\,W(K_a, y) + (1-\theta)\,W(K_b, Y),$$

or W is concave in K.

This concavity ensures that the maximization of (3) can be characterized by the familiar Kuhn-Tucker conditions of calculus. The derivative of the expression in (3) with respect to K' is

$$e^{-\rho\,dt}\,\{\,\mathcal{E}[W_K(K', Y + dY)] - \kappa\,\}.$$

As $dt \to 0$, this tends to $W_K(K', Y) - \kappa$. Irreversibility requires $K' \geq K$.

If $W_K(K, Y)$ is already $\leq \kappa$, the maximand will be decreasing with respect to K' throughout the range $K' \geq K$. Then the optimum policy will be to keep $K' = K$, that is, not to make any addition to capacity. If $W_K(K, Y) > \kappa$, the optimum policy will be to set K' at the level defined by the first-order condition $W_K(K', Y) = \kappa$ by instantaneously installing the amount of capital $(K' - K)$.

Suppose for a moment that the full problem has been solved, and the function W is known. Then the investment policy described above can be visualized as follows. In (K, Y) space, draw the curve defined by

$$W_K(K, Y) = \kappa. \tag{4}$$

We show the result in Figure 11.1. It is shown upward-sloping because a higher Y raises the profit from any given level of capital, and therefore should justify a larger capital stock and hence more investment. For now we leave matters at this intuitive level. Formal confirmation will follow, and the labels in the figure anticipate some of that work to come.

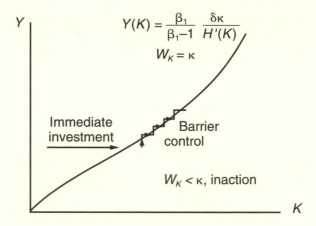

Figure 11.1. Investment Policy with Diminishing Returns

Below or to the right of the curve, we have $W_K < \kappa$ and no investment is made. As Y fluctuates stochastically, the point (K, Y) moves vertically up or down. If it ever rises to meet the curve and tries to cross it, just enough investment is made to stop it from crossing; this is shown in Figure 11.1 as a series of small steps indicating a phase of gradual investment. In technical terms this policy is sometimes called a "barrier control," because it prevents the point representing the state of the controlled system from crossing a certain barrier curve in the (K, Y) space. If after a phase of barrier control Y falls to take us back below the curve, investment stops until Y rises to hit the barrier again.

If the initial point is above or to the left of the curve $W_K = \kappa$, the stock of capital is instantly increased by a discrete amount large enough to move the point horizontally to the curve. Thereafter the policy of barrier control takes over. Thus, except possibly at the initial time 0, the point (K, Y) will never be seen above the curve.[2] Correspondingly, a discrete jump in the capital stock can only occur at the initial instant. Thereafter, the capital stock is either constant over a period of time while Y is low enough to keep us below the curve, or it responds continuously to small increments of Y at the curve.

If the derivative of K with respect to t were finite, we would call it the *flow* or the *rate* of investment I. However, this is problematic for barrier policy. As we explained in our discussion of Brownian motion in Chapter 3, the time path of Y is not differentiable. At the barrier any upward move of Y leads to a

---

[2]At the initial instant the point (K, Y) may be above the curve either because nonoptimal policies were followed in the past or because some unexpected shock just moved the curve.

corresponding rightward move of K, so the time path of K at such locations is also nondifferentiable; the time derivative dK/dt is infinite. Thus the barrier control policy does not generate a finite rate of investment through time, but occasional small bursts of investment as the barrier is hit. Of course in a more macroscopic view of time, we can calculate the average rate of investment, that is, the average rate of change of capital over a long interval of time.

Now we proceed to develop the argument and the optimal policy in somewhat greater detail. We begin with the region of inaction below the curve $W_K = \kappa$, where the policy is to be one of zero investment. Here we must substitute $K' = K$ in (3) to get the initial value $W(K, Y)$. Thus

$$W(K, Y) = Y H(K) dt + e^{-\rho dt} \mathcal{E}[W(K, Y + dY)].$$

Expanding the right-hand side by Ito's Lemma and keeping terms to order dt, we get

$$\begin{aligned} W(K, Y) &= Y H(K) dt + (1 - \rho dt) [W(K, Y) + \alpha Y W_Y(K, Y) dt \\ &\quad + \tfrac{1}{2}\sigma^2 Y^2 W_{YY}(K, Y)] dt \\ &= W(K, Y) + [Y H(K) - \rho W(K, Y) + \alpha Y W_Y(K, Y) \\ &\quad + \tfrac{1}{2}\sigma^2 Y^2 W_{YY}(K, Y)] dt. \end{aligned}$$

Therefore $W(K, Y)$ satisfies the differential equation

$$\tfrac{1}{2}\sigma^2 Y^2 W_{YY}(K, Y) + \alpha Y W_Y(K, Y) - \rho W(K, Y) + Y H(K) = 0. \qquad (5)$$

Since W is a function of two variables, this is really a partial differential equation. Luckily it does not involve any derivatives with respect to K. Thus we can regard it as an ordinary differential equation that links W to Y, and think of K as a parameter that shifts the whole functional relationship. Any constants of integration are also affected by K, and thus they should be regarded as functions of K.

The general solution of (5) is then familiar from Chapters 6 and 7:

$$W(K, Y) = B_1(K) Y^{\beta_1} + B_2(K) Y^{\beta_2} + Y H(K)/(\rho - \alpha),$$

where β_1 and β_2 are, respectively, the positive and negative roots of the fundamental quadratic

$$Q \equiv \tfrac{1}{2}\sigma^2 \beta(\beta - 1) + \alpha \beta - \rho = 0,$$

and $B_1(K)$, $B_2(K)$ are "constants" of integration to be determined.

The region of zero investment in Figure 11.1 includes the limit as Y goes to zero. To keep $W(K, Y)$ finite there, we must leave out the negative power of Y in the solution. Therefore we set $B_2(K) = 0$. We also abbreviate $\rho - \alpha = \delta$. Then the solution becomes

$$W(K, Y) = B_1(K)\, Y^{\beta_1} + Y\, H(K)/\delta. \qquad (6)$$

The remaining "constant," $B_1(K)$, is determined by considering the other boundary of the region of zero investment, namely, the curve $W_K(K, Y) = \kappa$. Solving for Y in terms of K, write the equation of this curve as $Y = Y(K)$. Then

$$W_K(K, Y(K)) = B_1'(K)\, Y(K)^{\beta_1} + Y(K)\, H'(K)/\delta = \kappa, \qquad (7)$$

where $B_1'(K)$ denotes the derivative of $B_1(K)$ with respect to K. This is just what we have been calling a value-matching condition. The other condition for optimality is the smooth-pasting condition, which requires that the derivative of $W_K(K, Y)$ with respect to Y should equal the derivative of κ with respect to Y as Y increases to the threshold $Y(K)$. Since the derivative of κ is zero, we have

$$W_{KY}(K, Y(K)) = \beta_1\, B_1'(K)\, Y(K)^{\beta_1 - 1} + H'(K)/\delta = 0. \qquad (8)$$

These two conditions can be combined to determine not only $B_1'(K)$ but also the location of the investment threshold $Y(K)$, that is, the free boundary

$$Y(K) = \frac{\beta_1}{\beta_1 - 1}\, \frac{\delta\kappa}{H'(K)} \qquad (9)$$

and

$$B_1'(K) = -\left(\frac{\beta_1 - 1}{\kappa}\right)^{\beta_1 - 1} \left(\frac{H'(K)}{\beta\delta}\right)^{\beta_1}. \qquad (10)$$

Observe that as K increases, $H'(K)$ decreases and therefore $Y(K)$ increases. This confirms our earlier intuition that the threshold curve should be upward-sloping.

The formula for the threshold is strikingly familiar. Suppose we install a marginal unit of capital dK when the existing stock is K and the stochastic shock has the value Y. The contribution of this marginal unit to the profit flow is $Y\, H'(K)\, dK$. Since Y is expected to grow at the rate α, and future profits are discounted at the rate ρ, the expected present value of this contribution is $Y\, H'(K)\, dK/(\rho - \alpha)$. The cost of installing the marginal unit is $\kappa\, dK$. Then equation (9) says that the marginal addition to the firm's capital stock is justified when the expected present value exceeds the cost by the multiple

$\beta_1/(\beta_1 - 1)$. This is exactly the multiple that reflected the option value of the status quo in the criterion for making a single discrete investment in Chapter 5. Here we have a natural generalization of that result to the case of a marginal addition to existing capacity.

The interpretation of equation (6) should now be transparent. The term $Y H(K)/\delta$ is the expected present value of the profits the firm would get if it kept its capital stock constant at the initial level K forever. Then the other term, $B_1(K) Y^{\beta_1}$, must be the value of the firm's optimal future capacity expansion, that is, the current value of its options to expand capacity in the future. When the firm exercises its option to install the $(K + dK)$th unit of capital, it gives up the marginal option value, which is why $B_1'(K)$ in equation (10) is negative. Then equation (7) says that at the threshold that justifies the incremental investment dK, its expected contribution to the capitalized profit flow should equal its cost of installment *plus* the opportunity cost of the option to wait.

Using the solution for $B_1'(K)$, we can find $B_1(K)$ itself by integration:

$$B_1(K) = \int_K^\infty [-B_1'(k)]\, dk = \left(\frac{\beta_1 - 1}{\kappa}\right)^{\beta_1 - 1} \int_K^\infty \left(\frac{H'(k)}{\beta_1 \delta}\right)^{\beta_1} dk. \tag{11}$$

For this integral to converge, $H'(K)$ must decrease sufficiently rapidly. The Cobb-Douglas case

$$H(K) = K^\theta, \qquad H'(K) = \theta K^{\theta-1}, \qquad 0 < \theta < 1$$

will illustrate the point. Now the integrand is a constant times $K^{-\beta_1(1-\theta)}$. For convergence of the integral, the power must exceed 1 in numerical value, so we must have $\beta_1 > 1/(1-\theta)$. In other words, θ must be sufficiently less than 1, which means returns to capital must be decreasing sufficiently quickly. These returns to capital are in revenue terms, and combine the effects coming from the production function and those from the demand curve; see equation (2). We can see, then, that this convergence requirement makes good economic sense. If returns to scale were constant instead of decreasing, a threshold level of the shift variable Y that made a unit of investment desirable would make a larger expansion of capacity proportionately even more desirable, so there would be no finite solution for the firm's optimal capacity.

We will proceed assuming that the convergence condition holds. If the marginal product of capital falls to zero at some sufficiently high level $\overline{K}$, then the upper limit of integration can be replaced by $\overline{K}$ and convergence is not a problem. This is the case, for example, in the model developed by Pindyck (1988b), where a linear demand curve is assumed.

The behavior of the threshold curve for small K deserves some comment. In growth theory it is common to assume that as $K \to 0$, $H'(K) \to \infty$; this is called the Inada condition. If this condition holds for our firm, then $Y(K) \to 0$. This is the case shown in Figure 11.1. However, if the marginal product $H'(K)$ stays bounded for small K, then $Y(K)$ will stay positive; installation of even the first unit of capital will require a strictly positive threshold level of the stochastic variable.

The most noteworthy feature of the solution is that we can regard the successive marginal increments to capital as distinct little projects, each contributing its marginal product independently of the others. Then we can find the optimal investment threshold for each using the standard option pricing approach, and string them together to obtain the solution of the full capacity expansion problem. Why can we treat each unit of capital independently of the others?

The marginal unit of capital labelled K_2 can be treated independently of the one labelled $K_1 < K_2$ because of diminishing returns. The marginal product of the unit K_2 is $H'(K_2)$ only when all previous units are in place. Diminishing returns ensures this: the threshold for K_1 is lower than that for K_2, so the unit labelled K_1 is going to be installed before that labelled K_2.[3] Conversely, the unit at K_1 can be treated independently of the unit at $K_2 > K_1$ because of the cancellation of two effects that we saw in Chapter 9. When the decision on the unit at K_1 is made according to the rule (9), the firm is acting as if this is the last unit it is going to install. It is thereby ignoring two things. First, it is ignoring the reduction in the productivity of capital that future expansion will cause. This makes it more willing to invest. Second, it is ignoring the need to have the unit at K_1 in place to pave the way for the next unit to come, thereby pretending that it has a greater leeway to wait. The two effects exactly cancel, allowing the firm to act on the unit at K_1 as if there were no further expansion opportunities.

Although all the interesting action is below or at the curve $Y(K)$, for the sake of completeness we state the solution to the firm's dynamic programming problem above the curve. Here the optimal policy is to install a lump of capital instantaneously to move horizontally to the curve. Let the solution for K in

---

[3]In the social planner's problem of Chapter 9, Section 1.A, there were constant returns to capacity expansion in the industry, but a downward sloping demand; therefore the planner's objective function (social surplus) had diminishing returns.

terms of Y along the curve be $K(Y)$; this is just the inverse of the function $Y(K)$. Then the firm jumps from (K, Y) to $(K(Y), Y)$, and

$$W(K, Y) = W(K(Y), Y) - \kappa [K(Y) - K]. \tag{12}$$

Thus in fact we have $W_K = \kappa$ everywhere above the curve.

1.B   The Contingent Claims Approach

Now let us see how this investment problem can be solved using contingent claims methods. We will continue to view the stock of capital as a sequence of marginal projects. Each is an asset that contributes a marginal flow of profits. The steps to be followed when valuing each of these assets, along with the option to acquire it, are very familiar from Chapters 5–7.

We assume that the stochastic fluctuations of Y are spanned by assets traded in financial markets, and write μ for the appropriately risk-adjusted expected rate of return on this portfolio of spanning assets. The return shortfall or convenience yield on Y, namely, $\mu - \alpha$, is denoted by δ as before.

Now consider the $(K + dK)$th marginal unit of investment. Once installed, this unit will yield the marginal profit flow $Y H'(K) dK$ forever. Let $v(K, Y) dK$ denote the value of this installed unit. Now, consider a portfolio consisting of this unit, and a short position of n units of the asset (or portfolio of assets) that tracks Y. This portfolio yields a cash flow of $[Y H'(K) - n \delta Y]$ per unit time. (The second term of this cash flow is the amount the holder of the short position must pay to the holder of the corresponding long position.) The portfolio also has an expected capital gain or loss as Y fluctuates. Using Ito's Lemma we get

$$dv(K, Y) - n \, dY = \{\alpha Y [v_Y - n] + \tfrac{1}{2}\sigma^2 Y^2 v_{YY}\} \, dt + Y [v_Y - n] \, dz.$$

The choice $n = v_Y$ makes the portfolio riskless. Of course as Y and K change through time, the number of units n in the short position must be changed continuously (that is, a dynamic hedging strategy must be employed) to maintain this property. Since a riskless asset must earn the riskless return r, we have

$$[Y H'(K) - \delta Y] + \{\alpha Y [v_Y - n] + \tfrac{1}{2}\sigma^2 Y^2 v_{YY}\} = r v,$$

or

$$\tfrac{1}{2}\sigma^2 Y^2 v_{YY} + (r - \delta) Y v_Y - r v + Y H'(K) = 0. \tag{13}$$

As we have seen in Chapter 6, Section 1, this equation has the general solution

$$v(K, Y) = a_1(K) Y^{\beta_1} + a_2(K) Y^{\beta_2} + Y H'(K)/\delta.$$

The only new feature is that the constants of integration are now specific to the unit of capital under consideration, so they are functions of K. As in Chapter 6, we rule out the term corresponding to the negative root β_2 to ensure a finite value as $Y \to 0$, and that for the positive root to rule out a bubble as $Y \to \infty$, leaving only the fundamental term, or the discounted present value of profit,

$$v(K, Y) = Y\, H'(K)/\delta. \tag{14}$$

Next we value the option to invest in this incremental unit of capital. Denote the value by $f(Y, K)$. Retracing the steps of Chapter 6, we construct a dynamically rebalanced riskless portfolio consisting of the option and a short position of f_Y units of the asset that tracks Y. Setting its return equal to r yields the equation

$$\tfrac{1}{2}\sigma^2 Y^2\, f_{YY} + (r - \delta)\, Y\, f_Y - r\, f = 0.$$

This has the general solution

$$f(K, Y) = b_1(K)\, Y^{\beta_1} + b_2(K)\, Y^{\beta_2}.$$

The option is kept alive as $Y \to 0$ and must have a finite value there, so we eliminate the term corresponding to the negative root β_2. However, for some finite Y the option will get exercised and the option value will not be relevant as $Y \to \infty$, so we cannot infer the other term. This leaves

$$f(K, Y) = b_1(K)\, Y^{\beta_1}.$$

Then the constant $b_1(K)$ and the threshold $Y(K)$ for optimal exercise of the option are jointly determined from the familiar conditions of value matching and smooth pasting:

$$f(K, Y) = v(K, Y) - \kappa, \qquad f_Y(K, Y) = v_Y(K, Y).$$

Simple algebra yields

$$Y(K) = \frac{\beta_1}{\beta_1 - 1}\, \frac{\delta\, \kappa}{H'(K)}$$

and

$$b_1(K) = \left(\frac{\beta_1 - 1}{\kappa}\right)^{\beta_1 - 1} \left(\frac{H'(K)}{\beta\delta}\right)^{\beta_1}.$$

These are just the expressions for the investment threshold function and the marginal option value coefficient we found from the dynamic programming approach of the previous section. In fact the marginal increase in the Bellman value function that results upon investing the $(K + dK)$th unit is exactly equal to the fundamental value of having the unit in place minus the value of the option that is given up when the unit is installed:

$$W_K(K, Y) = v(K, Y) - f(K, Y).$$

Therefore the value-matching and smooth-pasting conditions of dynamic programming, $W_K = \kappa$ and $W_{KY} = 0$, coincide with those of option pricing just above.[4]

1.C Marginal q

We interpreted equation (9) as saying that the expected present value of the profits contributed by a marginal unit of capital had to equal a multiple of its purchase cost to justify its installation. This can be expressed in terms of Tobin's q. The new feature is that we must define the q appropriate for a marginal unit of capacity, or "marginal q." Recalling the distinction we made in Chapter 5, we take the "value-of-assets-in-place" concept. Applied to the marginal unit, this is just the ratio of the expected present value of the profits it contributes to its replacement cost, or

$$q(K) = Y\, H'(K)/(\delta \kappa).$$

Then $\beta_1/(\beta_1 - 1)$ is the threshold to which $q(K)$ must rise before investment in the marginal unit at K can be justified.

In Chapter 5, Section 2.C we defined another sense of Tobin's q, namely, one based on the value of the firm and taking into account the opportunity cost of exercising an option to invest. Similarly here, the marginal effect of capacity expansion on the value of the firm is the contribution to expected present value of profits, $v(K, Y)$, minus the value of the option to invest, $f(K, Y)$. Then the marginal q in the value-of-the-firm sense would be defined as $[v(K, Y) - f(K, Y)]/\kappa$, and its critical threshold would be 1. This is an exact analog of the corresponding observation for a discrete project in Chapter 5.

1.D The Effect of Uncertainty

Let us reexamine the solution for the investment threshold in equation (9). This formula shows two effects of uncertainty on investment. First, as in Chapters 5–7, if σ increases, the root β_1 decreases and the option value multiple

---

[4]Also compare the somewhat brief discussion of this issue in the social optimality model of Chapter 9, Section 1.A.

$\beta_1/(\beta_1 - 1)$ increases. This raises the threshold of Y for any given K. In this sense, greater uncertainty implies less willingness to invest.

It is important to understand the precise sense of the result. It says merely that some values of Y that would have justified a given increment of capacity for a low value of σ may be insufficient for a higher σ. It says nothing about how soon or how often the threshold will be reached as Y follows its stochastic process. Starting from a given initial value, a more volatile process will reach a given target level of Y sooner than will a less volatile process. To find the overall effect of increasing uncertainty, we must balance the effects of raising the threshold and raising the volatility of movements of Y. In the next section we will see how, in the context of an analytically tractable example, these forces can balance out on average over time.

The second effect of uncertainty that is apparent from equation (9) comes from the term δ. Recall that this is the "return shortfall" or convenience yield $\mu - \alpha$, and that μ is the risk-adjusted discount rate

$$\mu = r + \phi \, \rho_{YM} \, \sigma.$$

Here we are using the notation of Chapters 5 and 6, so ϕ is the market price of risk, and ρ_{YM} is the correlation coefficient between the asset that tracks Y and the market portfolio. Now the effect of an increase in σ depends on what else is held constant. If r and α are fundamental exogenous constants, then an increase in σ must increase μ and δ. On the other hand, if r and δ are basic constants, then α must adjust to offset the effect of σ on μ. In the first case the threshold will be affected in (9), in the second it will remain unchanged.

There is a third effect of uncertainty that does not appear in our formulation so far, because we have made the profit flow function linear in Y. More generally, we could have stipulated a function $\pi(K, Y)$. Now the determination of the threshold proceeds as in the general model of industry equilibrium expansion in Chapter 9. For notational simplicity we will adopt the dynamic programming approach with an exogenously fixed discount rate ρ, but parallel results can be obtained in the contingent claims valuation approach using the equivalent risk-neutral valuation procedure of Chapter 4, Section 3.

The marginal effect of capacity expansion on the profit flow is $\pi_K(K, Y)$. Holding K fixed, let the stochastic shock evolve along its random path $\{Y_t\}$ starting at the initial value Y. Calculate the discounted present value of the marginal profit flow,

$$\Pi_K(K, Y) = \mathcal{E} \int_0^\infty \pi_K(K, Y_t) \, e^{-\rho t} \, dt.$$

This will replace the marginal contribution $Y\,H'(K)/\delta$ in the firm's calculation. Therefore the value-matching condition (7) will become

$$W_K(K, Y(K)) = B_1'(K)\,Y(K)^{\beta_1} + \Pi_K(K, Y(K)) = \kappa,$$

and the smooth-pasting condition (8) will become

$$W_{KY}(K, Y(K)) = \beta_1\,B_1'(K)\,Y(K)^{\beta_1-1} + \Pi_{KY}(K, Y(K)) = 0.$$

Eliminating $B_1'(K)$ between the two, the threshold function $Y(K)$ is implicitly defined by

$$\Pi_K(K, Y(K)) - \frac{Y(K)}{\beta_1}\,\Pi_{KY}(K, Y(K)) = \kappa. \tag{15}$$

The profit flow is positively related to the stochastic variable Y, so Π_{KY} is positive. Therefore $\Pi_K(K, Y(K)) > \kappa$. In other words, the expected present value of the marginal contribution to the profit flow should exceed the cost of the marginal increase in capacity in order to justify the investment. The required excess is just the usual opportunity cost of exercising this marginal option to expand.[5]

Since Y enters nonlinearly on the left-hand side, greater uncertainty in the stochastic process of Y has an additional effect. Roughly speaking, if the marginal profit flow $\pi_K(K, Y)$ is a convex function of Y, greater uncertainty implies a larger marginal expected present value $\Pi_K(K, Y)$ and therefore a lower threshold, so that an increase in uncertainty encourages investment.

A simple example of this admits a closed-form solution that further clarifies the point. Suppose production involves a variable input (labor) that can be chosen optimally at each instant. Suppose the production function is Cobb-Douglas. Then

$$\pi(K, Y) = \max_L\,[\,Y\,K^\theta\,L^\nu - w\,L\,],$$

where w denotes the wage rate and $\theta + \nu < 1$ to ensure diminishing returns to scale. Then we find

$$\pi(K, Y) = C\,Y^{1/(1-\nu)}\,K^{\theta/(1-\nu)},$$

where C is a positive constant whose precise value is immaterial for our present purpose. Therefore

$$\pi_K(K, Y) = \frac{C\theta}{1-\nu}\,Y^{1/(1-\nu)}\,K^{-(1-\theta-\nu)/(1-\nu)}.$$

---

[5] Compare the similar general result in the social optimality framework of Chapter 9 [equation (11) there].

Since the power of Y is $1/(1-v) > 1$, we see that $\pi_K(K, Y)$ is convex in Y. In fact we can explicitly calculate the threshold for this case. A straightforward application of Ito's Lemma gives

$$\mathcal{E}[Y_t^{1/(1-v)}] = Y^{1/(1-v)} \exp\{[\alpha/(1-v) + \tfrac{1}{2}\sigma^2 v/(1-v)^2]t\}.$$

Then

$$\Pi_K(K, Y) = \frac{C\theta/(1-v)}{\rho - \alpha/(1-v) - \tfrac{1}{2}\sigma^2 v/(1-v)^2} \, Y^{1/(1-v)} \, K^{-(1-\theta-v)/(1-v)}.$$

Applying the formula (15) and solving for the threshold, we find

$$Y(K) = \left(\frac{\beta_1}{\beta_1 - 1/(1-v)}\right)^{1-v}$$

$$\cdot \left(\frac{\delta\kappa \, [\rho - \alpha/(1-v) - \tfrac{1}{2}\sigma^2 v/(1-v)^2]}{C\theta/(1-v)}\right)^{1-v} K^{1-\theta-v}.$$

We see that an increase in σ lowers the numerator in the expression within the second set of parentheses on the right-hand side, and therefore contributes to lowering the threshold. Of course the increase in σ lowers the root β_1 and therefore raises the option value multiple $\beta_1/[\beta_1 - 1/(1-v)]$; this contributes to raising the threshold. The balance depends on the other parameters ρ, α, and v.

1.E   Long-Run Average Investment

Following the optimal policy derived above, the firm invests in small bursts whenever the state (K, Y) hits the threshold curve from below. Although each instant of such a hit is random, we can calculate the average rate of growth of the firm's capital stock over a long interval of time. Doing so provides another useful way of looking at the effect of uncertainty on investment.

To do this, we consider the special (and analytically tractable) case of the Cobb-Douglas production function,

$$H(K) = K^\theta, \qquad 0 < \theta < 1.$$

In this case, equation (9) for the threshold can be written as

$$Y\,K^{-(1-\theta)} = \frac{\beta_1}{\beta_1 - 1} \, \frac{\delta\kappa}{\theta}.$$

We will abbreviate the left-hand side of this equation by M. The right-hand side is a constant; call it $\overline{M}$ for short. As Y fluctuates, so does M. The optimal policy is to increase K whenever M rises to $\overline{M}$, and this keeps M from rising any further.

In this calculation, we will denote the natural logarithms of all these variables by the corresponding lowercase variables; thus $y = \log Y$, etc. When $m < \overline{m}$, no investment is being made, so that K is constant, and m follows the same Brownian motion as y, namely, an absolute motion with drift parameter $\alpha - \frac{1}{2}\sigma^2$ and volatility parameter σ. At times, however, when m is equal to $\overline{m}$, investment takes place and K rises. Using the theory of Brownian motion, we can characterize the long-run distribution of m. We will omit the derivations, and refer the reader to Harrison (1985, p. 90), or Dixit (1993a, p. 61). The distribution exists only if $\alpha > \frac{1}{2}\sigma^2$, so we proceed on this assumption. Then the distribution is exponential, with density

$$\alpha' \, \exp[\alpha' \, (m - \overline{m})], \qquad -\infty < m < \overline{m},$$

where $\alpha' = 2\alpha/\sigma^2 - 1 > 0$. We will be interested in the part of this distribution where m is very close to $\overline{m}$.

To determine the long-run average growth rate of K, we treat the Brownian motion of m as a discrete random walk, in the manner discussed in Chapter 2, Section 2.B. Divide time into very short intervals of duration dt, and the range of m into very small steps of size $dh = \sigma \sqrt{dt}$. Now, given the exponential distribution above for m, we know that in long-run equilibrium, the probability that m lies in the step immediately to the left of $\overline{m}$ is $\alpha' \, dh$. Suppose that m does happen to lie just to the left of $\overline{m}$, and note that y can move either up or down. The probability that y will experience an upward move of size dh is given by $p = \frac{1}{2}[1 + \alpha'\sqrt{dt}/\sigma]$. If that happens, an offsetting increase in k prevents m from hitting $\overline{m}$. In that case,

$$dh - (1 - \theta) \, dk = 0, \qquad \text{or} \qquad dK/K = dk = dh/(1 - \theta).$$

Over a long time span, the average growth rate of capital is therefore given by the product of these probabilities and growth rate: the probability that m will be very close to $\overline{m}$ (which is $\alpha' dh$), times the probability that y has an upward move (p), times the percentage growth in K should an upward move in y occur [$dk = dh/(1 - \theta)$]. To get the growth *rate*, we divide the product by dt. The result is $\alpha' \, p \, (dh)^2/[dt \, (1 - \theta)]$. Recalling that $dh = \sigma \sqrt{dt}$, we find that the long-run average growth rate of K is

$$\tfrac{1}{2}\sigma^2 \, (2\alpha/\sigma^2 - 1)/(1 - \theta) = [\alpha - \tfrac{1}{2}\sigma^2]/(1 - \theta).$$

Thus in this Cobb-Douglas case, a larger σ means a lower long-run average growth rate of the capital stock, and thus less investment on average.

1.F Depreciation

Now we examine what happens if some of the capital installed by the firm gradually decays. Most theoretical treatments of the subject assume, for analytical convenience, that the decay occurs exponentially as a Poisson process. Thus suppose the firm's capital stock at time t is K. During the next small interval of time dt, each of these existing units will stop functioning with probability $\lambda \, dt$. Deaths of different units are independent events, so we can invoke the law of large numbers and say that exactly $\lambda \, K \, dt$ units die during this interval. If the firm installs dK_g new units (gross investment), the change dK in its capital stock (net investment) is given by

$$dK = dK_g - \lambda \, K \, dt. \tag{16}$$

Such depreciation complicates our conceptual device of treating different units of capital as different projects ranked by their order of installation. A unit that was installed as the $(K + dK)$th will take on a different label if some earlier units decay. Luckily this was only a conceptual device to allow us to introduce the concept of option value of a marginal unit in a clearer way. All units of capital are physically homogeneous and interchangeable in their productive potential, so no harm is done by abandoning their rank ordering.

Greater complication arises if each unit of capital has a given finite life, as in our earlier treatment of a single discrete project that depreciates by sudden death. Then, to describe the state of the firm, we must keep track not just of its total stock of capital, but also the age of each unit. However, this is a computational problem rather than a conceptual one, and our exposition of the underlying economic ideas can do without such added complexity.

We begin as usual, by finding the value of the firm's stock of initially installed capital K. Take the dynamic programming approach first. If the firm makes no new investments, the existing stock will decay as $dK = -\lambda \, K \, dt$, or $K_t = K e^{-\lambda t}$. The profit flow at time t will be $Y_t \, H(K e^{-\lambda t})$, and the expected present value calculated using the discount rate ρ will be

$$V(K, Y) = \mathcal{E} \int_0^\infty Y_t \, H(K e^{-\lambda t}) \, e^{-\rho t} \, dt. \tag{17}$$

We can differentiate (17) to get the value of the initial marginal unit of capital:

$$V_K(K, Y) = \mathcal{E} \int_0^\infty Y_t \, H'(K e^{-\lambda t}) \, e^{-(\rho+\lambda) t} \, dt. \tag{18}$$

This has an interesting interpretation. First, suppose only the earlier units of capital decay while the marginal one remains alive. Then its rank slides down from K to $K e^{-\lambda t}$, and its marginal product rises to $H'(K e^{-\lambda t})$. Second, recognize the probability that the marginal unit itself may die; this raises the discount rate from ρ to $\rho + \lambda$. Then (18) gives us the expected present value calculated taking both of these effects into account.

Alternatively, we can use the contingent claims approach. Here we should recognize the decay of capital as a negative dividend on the asset. Other than that, we follow the usual steps to get

$$\tfrac{1}{2} \sigma^2 Y^2 V_{YY}(K, Y) + (r - \delta) Y V_Y(K, Y) - \lambda K V_K(K, Y)$$
$$- r V(K, Y) + Y H(K) = 0. \tag{19}$$

Then (17) is the solution to this equation when we use the proper risk-adjusted rate of discount μ in place of ρ.

Next we consider the value of the firm's options to invest in additional capital, when the current stock is K and the current value of the stochastic shift variable is Y. We will denote the value of these options by $F(K, Y)$. As long as these options go unexercised, installed capital goes on decaying. Thus a short time dt later the firm will acquire back its option to invest the last marginal $\lambda K dt$ units of capital. This has value $-\lambda K F_K(K, Y)$; recall that $F(K, Y)$ is the value of future expansion options, so an increase in K means sacrificing some of these options at the margin, and hence F_K is negative. Now we can set up the usual risk-free portfolio to determine $F(K, Y)$: hold one unit of the option and sell short F_Y units of the asset spanning Y. This yields

$$\tfrac{1}{2} \sigma^2 Y^2 F_{YY} + (r - \delta) Y F_Y - \lambda K F_K - r F = 0.$$

Differentiating with respect to K, we get an equation for the value $f(K, Y) = -F_K(K, Y)$ of the marginal option:

$$\tfrac{1}{2} \sigma^2 Y^2 f_{YY}(K, Y) + (r - \delta) Y f_Y(K, Y)$$
$$- \lambda K f_K(K, Y) - (r + \lambda) f(K, Y) = 0. \tag{20}$$

This is a partial differential equation that generally would need to be solved numerically. However, for an interesting special case we can invoke an economic homogeneity argument to reduce it to an ordinary differential equation and solve it analytically. Suppose the dependence of the profit flow on the capital stock takes the special Cobb-Douglas form

$$H(K) = K^\theta, \qquad 0 < \theta < 1.$$

Now consider the expected present value $v(K, Y)$ of the profit flow that would result from the $(K + dK)$th marginal unit of capital. Using (18) above, this is

$$\mathcal{E} \int_0^\infty Y_t \, \theta \, [K \, e^{-\lambda t}]^{\theta-1} \, e^{-(\rho+\lambda)t} \, dt = Y \, K^{\theta-1} / (\rho + \lambda\theta - \alpha).$$

Now consider any two situations that differ in their initial values of K and Y but have the same value of $Y \, K^{\theta-1}$. Then the above formula will yield exactly the same expected value. The value of the opportunity to invest a marginal unit of capital should also be the same in the two situations. In other words, the option value $f(K, Y)$ should depend on just the single composite variable $y = Y \, K^{\theta-1}$. Write $f(K, Y) = g(y)$.

Then we can substitute $f_Y(K, Y) = K^{\theta-1} \, g'(y)$, etc., in (20) to get

$$\tfrac{1}{2}\sigma^2 \, y^2 \, g''(y) + [r - (\delta + \lambda(\theta - 1))] \, y \, g'(y) - (r + \lambda) \, g(y) = 0. \qquad (21)$$

This equation has a very familiar form, and yields the solution

$$g(y) = B \, y^{\beta_1}, \qquad (22)$$

where β_1 is the positive root of the standard quadratic associated with (21), namely,

$$\tfrac{1}{2}\sigma^2 \, \beta(\beta - 1) + [r - (\delta + \lambda(\theta - 1))] \, \beta - (r + \lambda) = 0.$$

We have eliminated the term corresponding to the negative root by the usual consideration of the limit as $y \to 0$. We will have $\beta_1 > 1$ if $r + \lambda > r - (\delta + \lambda(\theta - 1))$, or $\delta + \lambda\theta > 0$. Since we are assuming $\delta > 0$, this is assured.

We already obtained the value $v(K, Y)$ of the marginal unit once installed. Then the threshold $Y(K)$ that justifies installation (exercise of the option) is determined from the value-matching and smooth-pasting conditions

$$f(K, Y) = v(K, Y) - \kappa, \qquad f_Y(K, Y) = v_Y(K, Y).$$

This yields

$$Y(K) = \frac{\beta_1}{\beta_1 - 1} \frac{(\delta + \lambda\theta) \, \kappa}{\theta \, K^{\theta-1}}. \qquad (23)$$

This has the usual interpretation, slightly modified to take account of depreciation. It requires the value of the current marginal product $\theta \, Y \, K^{\theta-1}$ to be a multiple $\beta_1/(\beta_1 - 1)$ of the flow cost $(\delta + \lambda\theta)\kappa$. Note that the cost is no longer $\delta\kappa$ but is increased to reflect the possibility of decay of the marginal unit. The multiple is also modified to take into account the depreciation of it and earlier installed units. In particular, in the quadratic that defines β_1, the interest rate is increased from r to $r + \lambda$, which has the effect of increasing β_1 and thereby lowering $\beta_1/(\beta_1 - 1)$. Both these effects have exact parallels in the case of a single discrete depreciating project, namely equation (27) of Chapter 6, Section 4.

2 Increasing Returns and Lumpy Additions to Capacity

As a firm expands its capacity, we would expect it to eventually reach diminishing returns, if for no other reason than because of limits to organization and coordination within the firm. However, it is quite common for a firm to encounter an initial phase or phases of increasing returns. For example, a sizable amount of capital may be needed before any output can be produced at all. And later, capacity expansion may have to occur in discrete units corresponding to some minimum efficient plant scale. Sometimes laws of geometry dictate increasing returns, as when the amount of metal needed to construct a container varies as the square of its linear dimension, while its capacity varies as the cube. For all these reasons, it is important to extend our theory of incremental capacity expansion to cover situations in which there are increasing returns. To keep the complexities manageable and the new features that we introduce conceptually clear, we will work within as simple a structure as possible. Hence for now we will ignore depreciation.

Suppose $H'(K)$ is increasing over some range, and consider two units of investment located at K_1 and K_2 in this range. Label them so that $K_1 < K_2$, and therefore $H'(K_1) < H'(K_2)$. If we use the formula (9) to guess the thresholds Y_1 and Y_2 that will justify installation of these units, we will find $Y_1 > Y_2$. If Y is on a rising path from some low initial level, this says that the unit K_2 should be installed before the unit K_1. However, our labelling of the unit at K_2, and assigning it the marginal product $H'(K_2)$, presumes that all earlier units are already in place. Thus our guess of the thresholds based on equation (9) must be wrong for this range of increasing returns.

Looking at the situation the other way around, a threshold of Y that justifies installation of the unit at K_1 is also high enough to justify installation at K_2, and indeed the whole range in between. Therefore investment should be lumpy; a whole collection of our labelled units should be installed at once when a common threshold is reached. It remains to determine the size of the lump, and the appropriate threshold that triggers this large expansion of capacity.[6]

A rigorous derivation of the optimal investment policy turns out to be mathematically quite complicated, but the basic result can be understood intuitively. Therefore we will merely state the result and explain it; formal proofs are in Dixit (1993c), and we leave it to interested readers to pursue them.

Consider the simplest textbook form of increasing returns, where an initial range of increasing marginal product is followed by one of decreasing marginal product. The upper panel of Figure 11.2 shows this case for the production function $H(K)$. Note that the marginal product is at its maximum when K is at the point of inflection, which is labelled K^*. The average product is at its maximum when $K = K^{**}$, where a ray from the origin is tangent to the curve.

If the firm's initial stock of capital happens to exceed K^*, then returns to further expansion are diminishing. In this case, the basic theory developed in Section 1 applies, and the threshold is given by the formula (9). We will call this the right-hand branch of the investment threshold function for the present situation, and denote it by $Y_R(K)$.

Next, suppose the initial capital stock is $K_0 < K^*$, so that there are increasing returns to capacity expansion. Now, draw a line from the point on $H(K)$ corresponding to K_0 so that it is tangent to the production function at a point $K_1 > K^*$, as shown in the upper panel of Figure 11.2. With K_1 chosen in this way, the capacity increment from K_0 to K_1 has the property of maximizing the average product it contributes. Therefore it is worth considering as a candidate for the optimal amount of lumpy capacity expansion. In fact, that does turn out to be the optimal amount. The claim is that the threshold of Y that justifies the marginal unit at K_1, namely, $Y_R(K_1)$, is exactly the level that justifies capacity expansion from K_0 to K_1 instantaneously in a discrete lump.

Note that by construction, the average product of the added capacity is just the marginal product of the final unit:

$$[H(K_1) - H(K_0)]/[K_1 - K_0] = H'(K_1).$$

---

[6] In Chapter 2, Section 5 we considered an example that presented a trade-off between scale and flexibility. That does not arise here because scale economies pertain to the capital stock in the production function. If K_1 already exits and then $(K_2 - K_1)$ is installed, the same output flow commences as if the whole K_2 had been installed at once. That was not the case in the example of Chapter 2: two small plants were not equivalent to one large one.

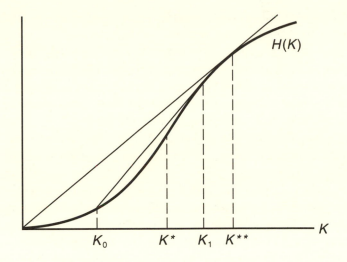

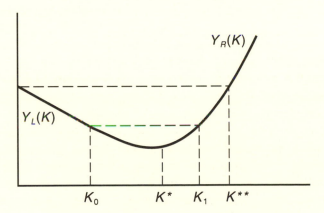

Figure 11.2. *Capacity Expansion with Increasing Returns*

Substituting in (9), we have

$$Y_R(K_1)\,[H(K_1) - H(K_0)] = \frac{\beta_1}{\beta_1 - 1}\,\delta\,\kappa\,[K_1 - K_0]. \tag{24}$$

In other words, at the instant the capacity expansion is made, the value of the additional output equals $\delta\,\beta_1/(\beta_1 - 1)$ times the cost of installation. Compare this with equation (9). That equation gave us the *marginal* condition for the unit invested under conditions of diminishing returns; now we have an exactly analogous *total* condition that is appropriate to the lump of capital invested under conditions of increasing returns.

The general idea should now become clear. Given any point K_0 in the range $(0, K^*)$, we can follow this tangency procedure to find the corresponding K_1, and construct the left-hand branch of the threshold function $Y_L(K)$ by defining $Y_L(K_0) = Y_R(K_1)$. The result is shown in the lower half of Figure 11.2. As K_0 is gradually decreased starting just to the left of K^*, the corresponding point K_1 gradually rises, and so does its $Y_R(K_1)$. Therefore the curve $Y_L(K)$ is downward-sloping. Finally, as K_0 falls to zero, K_1 rises to K^{**}, so $Y_L(0) = Y_R(K^{**})$.

The two branches $Y_L(K)$ and $Y_R(K)$ together comprise the investment threshold curve. In the region below this curve, the optimal policy is zero investment. If the initial capital stock K_0 is less than K^*, and Y rises to hit the curve at $Y_L(K_0) = Y_R(K_1)$, then capacity is immediately increased to K_1. To the right of K_1, the investment policy is the gradual one of barrier control as in Section 1. If the initial position is above the curve, then an immediate lumpy capacity expansion to move to the right-hand branch of the curve is optimal.

If the firm starts out without any initial capital, then it waits until Y rises to $Y_L(0) = Y_R(K^{**})$, and then installs capacity K^{**} at once: it is optimal to jump over the whole range of increasing average product. Therefore we will observe the firm with a capital stock in that range only if previous nonoptimal policies have left it there.

We considered a very special form of increasing returns, namely, a single initial region of increasing marginal product followed by one of decreasing marginal product. This allowed us to develop the idea in the context of the familiar textbook setting. However, the idea itself is perfectly general. Whatever the shape of the production function $H(K)$, given the initial K_0, we are to find a value K_1 to its right that maximizes the average incremental product $[H(K_1) - H(K_0)]/[K_1 - K_0]$. In more technical language, we seek the convex hull of the production function, but only to the right of the initial capital stock because investment is irreversible. By definition, returns at K_1 must be diminishing. The procedure of Section 1 can be employed to find the threshold of Y that would justify a marginal increment of capital at K_1. Then the same threshold applies to the whole discrete jump from K_0 to K_1. This idea works even when the production function is not differentiable; for example, it may have an initial portion where $H(K) = 0$ if some minimum amount of capital is needed to produce any output at all, and thereafter it may rise in steps corresponding to successive discrete-sized plants of minimum efficient sizes. All we need is that diminishing returns eventually prevail, and this is generally ensured by rising organizational costs within the firm.

We considered increasing returns that arise on the output side. However, lumpy capacity expansion might be optimal for cost reasons. Suppose the cost is not proportional to the amount of new capacity installed, but increases less than proportionately. There may be a lump-sum fixed cost of making any changes at all, or there may be economies of scale in a more general form. In the next section we will consider lump-sum costs, along with other kinds of costs that may be associated with capacity expansion.

3   Adjustment Costs

The theory of how firms make intertemporal choices gives us rules for determining the firm's desired or optimal capital stock at each point in time. The demand for gross investment during any one time period can then be calculated: gross investment equals the desired capital stock at the end of the period, minus the actual capital stock at the beginning, plus the depreciation that occurs during the period. Any shocks that occur, for example, demand shifts or interest rate changes, alter the desired capital stock. In theory, investment demand should immediately reflect this shock. In practice, the effects of such shocks on investment have been found to be more gradual and spread out over many future periods. Economists rationalized this by positing the existence of *adjustment costs*—costs of changing the capital stock too rapidly—and modifying their theories of investment to account for such costs.

In fact we need something stronger than the mere existence of adjustment costs to explain why a firm's investment choices might respond gradually to a shock. Specifically, we need costs that are a strictly convex function of the rate of investment. In other words, it would have to be the case that the marginal cost of investment is an increasing function of the rate of investment. Then the optimal rate of investment is determined at the point where the marginal cost of speeding up the adjustment of capital to its desired level is just equal to the marginal benefit of doing so.

The assumption of strictly convex adjustment costs became common in the theoretical and empirical literature on investment, but not without criticism from its earliest days. Rothschild (1971) is worth quoting at length on this question:

The arguments given as to why the cost of adjustment function should be convex are quite weak. Eisner and Strotz (1963) give two. The first is that, as the firm increases its demand for investment goods in a single period, pressure will be put on the supply of investment goods. Our model is that of a firm which is a price taker in factor markets; for it such considerations are clearly inappropriate. The second argument is that there are "increasing costs associated with integrating new equipment into a going concern: reorganizing production lines, training workers, etc." This is simply an assertion, and hardly a compelling one. Decreasing costs are just as plausible as increasing costs.... No reason is seen why training necessarily entails increasing costs. Training involves the use of information, which is a classic case of decreasing costs. ... Similarly, reorganizing production lines involves both the use of information as a factor of production ... and indivisibilities.

Alternative explanations of the observed gradual response of investment to changes in economic conditions were also offered. Of particular interest in the context of this book is the distinction between firm-level investment decisions and observations or data that are almost invariably at a more aggregate level. Suppose each firm adjusts its capital stock when the shock to its profitability reaches a threshold of the kind we have been calculating. Different firms differ in their technological or managerial abilities, local factor market conditions, and many other things. Therefore different firms have different action thresholds. Even firms that have equal thresholds may be at different historically determined initial conditions relative to this threshold. An aggregate shock will immediately push some firms over their threshold and they will invest, while other firms will merely get closer to their thresholds without crossing them. As time passes, some of these firms will experience other firm-specific shocks that will take them across their own thresholds and bring forth their investment responses. Thus the effect of the shock on aggregate investment will be spread out over time even though the action of each firm is concentrated at a point in time.

This idea is more intricate to work out in a simple model, because the aggregate response of investment depends on the relationship between aggregate and firm-specific shocks, and on the original location of firms relative to their action thresholds. Interesting theoretical and empirical work in this area has begun; see particularly Bertola and Caballero (1990, 1992).

For now we will develop the idea of strictly convex adjustment costs within a very general model that brings out its relationship with the approach we have followed in this book.

3.A Classification of Adjustment Costs

Let K denote the firm's capital stock, and Y denote a stochastic shift variable that affects its profits. Let $\pi(K, Y)$ denote the profit flow as a function of these state variables. Suppose existing capital depreciates at the rate λ. New capital can be added, and old capital can be removed (over and above the natural loss through depreciation), but these actions entail certain costs.

We will divide time into small intervals of length Δt. Suppose that during one such interval the firm takes deliberate action to change its capital stock by the amount ΔK. In other words, total gross investment (positive or negative as appropriate) during this time interval is ΔK, so that the stock at the end of the period is $(K - \lambda K \Delta t + \Delta K)$. There are three types of costs associated with this action.

First, there may be lump-sum costs for taking any action at all. These may be managerial decision costs, fixed costs of placing orders, or any such things. Call these "stock" fixed costs. There may also be costs that accrue as a given rate of flow over the time interval Δt where the action is being taken; call these "flow" fixed costs. Each kind may also be different depending on whether the capital stock is being increased or decreased. To be perfectly general, we let these costs be

$$\begin{cases} \Phi_+ + \phi_+ \, \Delta t & \text{if } \Delta K > 0, \\ \Phi_- + \phi_- \, \Delta t & \text{if } \Delta K < 0. \end{cases}$$

Next, there may be costs that vary linearly with the quantity of change in the capital stock, but do not depend on the (small) length of the time interval over which this change is accomplished. They will include primarily the actual prices paid for the capital goods purchased, but may have other components. We call these "linear" costs, and write them as

$$\begin{cases} \kappa_+ \, \Delta K & \text{if } \Delta K > 0, \\ \kappa_- |\Delta K| = -\kappa_- \, \Delta K & \text{if } \Delta K < 0. \end{cases}$$

Note the asymmetry; it captures the irreversibility that has been our central concern in this book. If $\kappa_- < 0$, then installed capital can be reduced by selling it at a price $-\kappa_-$ per unit. If $\kappa_- = -\kappa_+$, then the full cost of purchase can be recovered upon reselling, and investment is fully reversible. If $\kappa_+ + \kappa_- > 0$, or $-\kappa_- < \kappa_+$, the recovery is partial and there is some irreversibility. (We rule out the possibility $\kappa_- + \kappa_+ < 0$; otherwise the firm could make an infinite amount of money by quickly and repeatedly buying and selling large amounts of capital.) Of course we can also allow $\kappa_- > 0$; here the firm must pay to be allowed to reduce its capital stock, for example, site restoration costs when mines are shut down, or firing costs for workers associated with the machines that are being retired.

Finally, there may be adjustment costs that depend on the *rate* at which the capital stock is being changed, that is, that depend on $I = \Delta K / \Delta t$. This is the traditional category of "convex adjustment costs." Let $\Psi(I)$ denote the rate per unit time, or flow, with which these costs accrue. Then the adjustment cost during our time interval of length Δt is

$$\Delta t \, \Psi(\Delta K / \Delta t).$$

The function Ψ is convex, and satisfies $\Psi(0) = 0$ and $\Psi(I) > 0$ when $I \neq 0$. If the function Ψ is differentiable at zero, then we must have $\Psi'(0) = 0$. This is true in the commonly used case of quadratic adjustment costs; panel (a) of Figure 11.3 illustrates this case. However, the function could have a kink at zero, as illustrated in panel (b) of the same figure. Here the right-hand derivative of Ψ at zero, denoted by $\Psi'(0+)$, differs from the left-hand derivative, denoted by $\Psi'(0-)$. There can also be other more general asymmetry in the form of $\Psi(I)$ for positive and negative values of I.

Observe the nature of these costs. The flow rate at which the costs are incurred, namely, $\Psi(I)$, is a nonlinear function of the flow rate of gross investment, I. However, the total cost incurred over a time interval of length Δt is proportional to this length. To see how it costs more to change the capital

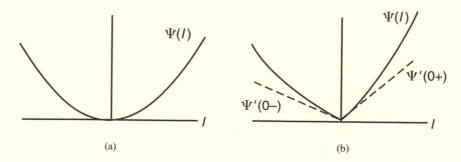

(a)   (b)

Figure 11.3.   Convex Adjustment Costs

stock more rapidly, hold ΔK fixed and vary Δt. The derivative of the cost with respect to Δt is

$$\Psi\left(\frac{\Delta K}{\Delta t}\right) - \frac{\Delta K}{\Delta t} \, \Psi'\left(\frac{\Delta K}{\Delta t}\right),$$

which is negative because Ψ is convex and satisfies $\Psi(0) = 0$. Thus reducing Δt increases the cost.

Each article in the voluminous literature on investment usually treated just one of these costs. This made it difficult to compare the results of different models based on different assumptions in this regard. Recently, Abel and Eberly (1993) have constructed a very general model that includes almost all of these costs (except stock fixed costs Φ_+ and Φ_-), thereby facilitating such comparisons and offering an improved understanding of the issues. Our treatment follows them.

3.B   The Bellman Equation

Now we are ready to examine the firm's optimal investment policy. For algebraic simplicity we will assume risk neutrality or an exogenously specified discount rate ρ, and use the dynamic programming approach. Let $W(K, Y)$ denote the value of the firm as a function of the state variables. Over the next short interval Δt of time, the firm chooses ΔK and restarts with a new capital stock $(K - \lambda K \Delta t + \Delta K)$ and a new random value of the stochastic variable, say, $(Y + \Delta Y)$. Write $C(\Delta K, \Delta t)$ for the costs of the action, which may include any or all of the components discussed above. To state this explicitly,

$$C(\Delta K, \Delta t) = \begin{cases} \Phi_+ + \phi_+ \Delta t + \kappa_+ \Delta K + \Delta t \, \Psi(\Delta K/\Delta t) & \text{if } \Delta K > 0, \\ 0 & \text{if } \Delta K = 0, \\ \Phi_- + \phi_- \Delta t - \kappa_- \Delta K + \Delta t \, \Psi(\Delta K/\Delta t) & \text{if } \Delta K < 0. \end{cases} \tag{25}$$

Then the Bellman equation can be written as

$$W(K, Y) = \max_{\Delta K} \left\{ \pi(K, Y) \Delta t + e^{-\rho \Delta t} \right.$$
$$\left. \cdot \mathcal{E}[W(K - \lambda K \Delta t + \Delta K, Y + \Delta Y)] - C(\Delta K, \Delta t) \right\}. \tag{26}$$

As in Abel and Eberly (1993), it is important to distinguish three cases according to whether the maximum on the right-hand side is achieved for ΔK positive, zero, or negative.

First, suppose the optimal ΔK is positive, that is, the firm is making positive gross investment. The first-order condition is

$$\mathcal{E}[W_K(K - \lambda K \Delta t + \Delta K, Y + \Delta Y)] - \kappa_+ - \Psi'(\Delta K/\Delta t) = 0.$$

The discrete time period Δt was introduced only for analytical convenience, and our real interest is in the continuous-time model. Therefore we take the limit as $\Delta t \to 0$. We assume for the moment that the rate of gross investment, $I = \Delta K / \Delta t$, is finite; we will soon check whether and when this can be valid. With this assumption the time path of K is continuous; since Y follows a geometric Brownian motion its time paths are also continuous. Therefore the condition in the limit becomes

$$W_K(K, Y) = \kappa_+ + \Psi'(I). \tag{27}$$

This determines the rate of investment as a function of the state variables.

Since we have various kinds of fixed costs, we must also consider a total condition that ensures the global optimality of the solution to the local first-order condition. For this, we need to compare the result of setting $\Delta K = I \, \Delta t$ where I is defined by (27) above, and that of setting $\Delta K = 0$. We need

$$\mathcal{E}[W(K + (I - \lambda K) \, \Delta t, Y + \Delta Y)] - \Phi_+ - \phi_+ \, \Delta t - \kappa_+ I \, \Delta t - \Delta t \, \Psi(I)$$
$$> \mathcal{E}[W(K - \lambda K \, \Delta t, Y + \Delta Y)].$$

Again our interest is in the limit as $\Delta t \to 0$.

The first point to note is that if there are stock fixed costs of investment ($\Phi_+ > 0$), they constitute the leading term in the total condition and in the limit we require $-\Phi_+ > 0$. That is a direct contradiction. Therefore if there is a stock fixed cost, that is, a one-time cost of making any positive gross addition to the stock of capital, then a finite rate of gross investment cannot be optimal. This makes good intuitive sense; such a policy would require incurring the stock fixed costs at every instant of the time interval over which the rate of investment is positive, which would be infinitely costly. The optimal policy will allow the capital stock to jump in discrete steps at isolated instants. It can be characterized using methods similar to those of Section 2 above.

Here let us assume that $\Phi_+ = 0$ and proceed. In this case, both sides of the total condition have leading terms of order Δt. So we must expand the values of W using Ito's Lemma and simplify. This gives

$$W_K(K, Y) I > \phi_+ + \kappa_+ I + \Psi(I). \tag{28}$$

To interpret this, we invoke the concept of Tobin's q. At any instant, the current state (K, Y) is known and therefore $W_K(K, Y)$ can be evaluated. This is just the marginal increase in the value of the firm that would result if it were given an additional marginal unit of capital. We could call it Tobin's marginal q using the value-of-the-firm-sense. The only difference is that it is now somewhat more convenient *not* to express it in ratio form, but to keep it as an absolute magnitude and compare it to the purchase cost of the marginal unit of capacity (including adjustment cost).

Now express equations (27) and (28) in this language. A rate of gross investment I sustained over a short time interval Δt contributes the marginal amount $I \Delta t$ to the capital stock. The first-order condition (27) sets the marginal benefit (increase in the value of the firm) of this action equal to its marginal cost, while the total condition (28) ensures that the total benefit exceeds its total cost.

We can illustrate and clarify these relationships using a diagram of a kind that is familiar from intermediate microeconomic theory, and is a modification of a figure in Abel and Eberly. In Figure 11.4 we show the marginal cost as a function of the rate of investment. For positive gross investment (to the right of the vertical axis) this is just the right-hand side of (27). The critical value $\bar{q}$ marks the point where the area between the vertical axis, a horizontal line at height q, and the marginal cost curve is exactly equal to the flow fixed cost ϕ_+. When $q = \bar{q}$, the I defined along the marginal cost curve satisfies both the marginal and the total conditions with equality. For $q > \bar{q}$ the total condition

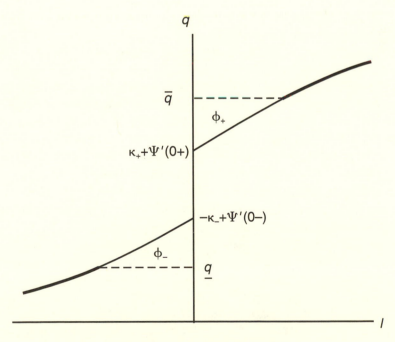

Figure 11.4. *The q Model of Investment*

is satisfied as an inequality. Therefore this portion of the marginal cost curve can be regarded as the firm's investment demand curve. This is shown thicker in the figure.

For negative gross investment the first-order condition is

$$W_K(K, Y) = -\kappa_- + \Psi'(I); \tag{29}$$

remember that $\Psi'(I)$ is negative when I is negative. Let $\underline{q}$ denote the critical value where the area trapped between the horizontal line and the marginal cost curve to the left of the vertical axis equals the flow fixed cost ϕ_- of negative gross investment. Then, for $q < \underline{q}$, the marginal cost curve becomes the firm's policy rule for negative gross investment. If q lies between the two critical levels $\underline{q}$ and $\overline{q}$, zero investment is optimal.

We now proceed to examine various implications of this analysis, and relate it to our earlier work.

3.C   The Range of Inaction

In the above analysis, zero gross investment is optimal over a range of values of $q = W_K(K, Y)$, and therefore over a corresponding region in the space of the underlying state variables (K, Y). There are three causes of this, and in the general model of Abel and Eberly, each is explained in terms of a different kind of adjustment cost. They appear below under the headings [1a], [1b] and [2].

[1] Note that the right-hand sides of the first-order conditions (27) and (29), corresponding to positive and negative gross investment, do not approach the same limit as $I \to 0$, and the marginal cost curve in Figure 11.4 has a discontinuity at the vertical axis. There are in turn two reasons for this. [1a] $\kappa_+ > -\kappa_-$, which is the irreversibility aspect we have emphasized throughout this book. [1b] A kink in the flow adjustment cost function, $\Psi'(0+) > \Psi'(0-)$, which also contributes to the discontinuity. The point here is that the marginal cost of even the first small amount of investment is positive; therefore positive gross investment is not made until Y rises sufficiently high relative to K to generate a compensating positive marginal benefit from having the extra capital. A similar situation holds for gross disinvestment.

[2] With a positive flow fixed cost ϕ_+, the critical value $\overline{q}$ exceeds the intercept of the right-hand branch of the marginal cost curve on the vertical axis. Similarly, a positive ϕ_- makes $\underline{q}$ less than the left-hand intercept. Both these effects widen the range of inaction.

A range of inaction exists as soon as any one of these three forces is in operation; the three operate in the same direction and reinforce each other as far as the optimality of zero gross investment is concerned.

Finally, note that we began by setting the stock fixed costs Φ_+ and Φ_- at zero. If those costs are positive, they are an even more powerful reason for taking no action most of the time, and choosing only isolated instants of time when the stock of capital is increased or decreased in discrete lumps.

When zero investment is optimal, the Bellman equation takes a particularly simple form. Expanding the right-hand side of (26) using Ito's Lemma and simplifying, we get

$$\tfrac{1}{2}\sigma^2 Y^2 W_{YY}(K, Y) + \alpha Y W_Y(K, Y)$$
$$- \lambda K W_K(K, Y) - \rho W(K, Y) + \pi(K, Y) = 0.$$

It is more convenient to convert this into an equation for $q(K, Y) = W_K(K, Y)$; recall that this is the marginal, value-of-the-firm, and absolute (not ratio) concept of Tobin's q. Differentiating with respect to K, we get

$$\tfrac{1}{2}\sigma^2 Y^2 q_{YY}(K, Y) + \alpha Y q_Y(K, Y) - \lambda K q_K(K, Y)$$
$$- (\rho + \lambda) q(K, Y) + \pi_K(K, Y) = 0. \tag{30}$$

This holds over the region of inaction in (K, Y) space, but the region itself must be determined as a part of the solution. Therefore this is a free-boundary problem. The boundary conditions vary somewhat from one model to the next. For example, when the only costs of adjustment are linear, the situation is like that of Section 1 of this chapter. Then at the conditions at the upper boundary (where I is about to become positive, in fact infinite) are $q = \kappa_+$ (value matching) and $q_Y = 0$ (smooth pasting). Similarly we have $q = \kappa_-$ and $q_Y = 0$ at the lower boundary.

3.D Barrier Control

If convex adjustment costs are relatively unimportant, so that $\Psi'(I)$ is very small for all I, then the marginal cost curve in Figure 11.4 is nearly flat. The critical values of q are approximately given by

$$\overline{q} = \kappa_+ \qquad \text{and} \qquad \underline{q} = -\kappa_-.$$

These are just the limits on $W_K(K, Y)$ that came out of our analysis of pure irreversibility earlier in this chapter. Moreover, as q reaches $\overline{q}$, the optimal rate of gross investment is very large, and likewise for the rate of gross disinvestment at $\underline{q}$. What happens in the limit if convex adjustment costs are absent altogether and only linear costs remain?

The answer is that an infinite rate of investment operates to increase or decrease the capital stock in small but rapid bursts, so as to prevent q

from ever rising above $\bar{q}$ or falling below $\underline{q}$. This is just the policy of "barrier control" that we obtained for the pure model that considered irreversibility on its own.[7] The rigorous demonstration of the limiting procedure would be mathematically too difficult and lengthy to attempt here, but we hope that the result is intuitively appealing, and that it clarifies the relationship between the irreversibility approach we have treated in detail, and the adjustment cost view that has been common in much of the previous literature on investment.

3.E   The Dynamics of q

When gross investment occurs at a nonzero rate, the optimal rate is defined by the first-order condition (27) or (29) as appropriate. Each defines I as a function of q, and the parameters that affect this relationship are κ_+ or κ_-, and the functional form of Ψ. In other words, for a given q the optimal rate of investment is determined entirely by the properties of adjustment costs.

The seemingly surprising thing is that the uncertainty, as captured in the parameter σ of the stochastic process of Y, does not enter into the picture at all, nor does the trend of Y, or the discount rate ρ. It would indeed be surprising if these aspects were irrelevant for investment. However, the surprise is only apparent, because this reasoning holds q fixed. The evolution of q is affected in a significant way by all of these parameters. For example, suppose (K, Y) is in a region where the rate of investment is positive. Let the investment function be $I = I(q)$. Expanding the right-hand side of the Bellman equation (26) and simplifying as usual, we have

$$\tfrac{1}{2}\sigma^2 Y^2 W_{YY} + \alpha Y W_Y + (I - \lambda K) W_K - \rho W - \phi_+ - \kappa_+ I - \Psi(I) + \pi = 0,$$

where we have omitted the arguments of functions to save notation. We can differentiate this with respect to K to get an equation for q, namely,

$$\tfrac{1}{2}\sigma^2 Y^2 q_{YY} + \alpha Y q_Y + (I - \lambda K) q_K - (\rho + \lambda) q$$
$$+ (I - \kappa_+ - \Psi'(I)) I'(q) q_K + \pi_K = 0.$$

The first-order condition simplifies this to

$$\tfrac{1}{2}\sigma^2 Y^2 q_{YY} + \alpha Y q_Y + (I - \lambda K) q_K - (\rho + \lambda) q + \pi_K = 0. \qquad (31)$$

The solution $q(K, Y)$ is affected by all relevant parameters.

----

[7]Barrier control uses infinite rates of investment at instants of time that sum to measure zero; that is how it generates a finite increase in the capital stock over a finite interval of time. See Harrison and Taksar (1983) for details. That is also why the flow fixed costs ϕ_+ and ϕ_- are irrelevant in this case; applied over time instants totalling to measure zero, they have zero effect.

3.F The Quadratic Cost Case

We will complete the solution to the adjustment cost model for a pure and simple special case.[8] Here we neglect all other aspects of costs, and suppose that the adjustment cost function is symmetric and quadratic, $\Psi(I) = \frac{1}{2} I^2$. Then there is no range of inaction, and the investment demand function is simply $I = q$ for all q. We also suppose that the flow profit function is linear in the capital stock and multiplicative in the shock, so $\pi(K, Y) = h K Y$. Then the equation for the dynamics of q becomes

$$\tfrac{1}{2} \sigma^2 Y^2 q_{YY} + \alpha Y q_Y + (q - \lambda K) q_K - (\rho + \lambda) q + h Y = 0.$$

This looks quite complicated, but economic intuition suggests the form of the solution. Since the profit flow is proportional to the capital stock, and adjustment costs do not depend on this stock, the maximized value $W(K, Y)$ should be a linear expression in K, so $W_K = q$ should depend on Y alone. Then we have an ordinary differential equation

$$\tfrac{1}{2} \sigma^2 Y^2 q_{YY} + \alpha Y q_Y - (\rho + \lambda) q + h Y = 0.$$

The solution is

$$q(Y) = h Y / (\rho + \lambda - \alpha). \tag{32}$$

The intuition is that when the capital stock produces profit flow at constant returns to scale and adjustment costs do not depend on the installed stock, we can regard each installed unit of capital quite independently of any other. It produces the profit flow $h Y$, but is subject to depreciation by a Poisson process with parameter λ. Then (32) gives just the expected present value of this uncertain profit flow. That must be the marginal value of this unit of capital to the firm.

Once q is known, the optimal investment policy follows immediately, and that is our main concern in this section. If desired, however, the solution for the value function itself can be obtained fairly easily; it is simply $q K$ plus the value of expansion options. For that, and for a more general version of this model, we refer the reader to Abel (1983).

4 Guide to the Literature

The model of this chapter has quite close links in some respects with the standard neoclassical theory of investment. That theory began by assuming

---

[8]This is Case II in Abel and Eberly (1993); see also Abel (1983).

competitive conditions, and ignoring uncertainty and irreversibility. The result was as if the firm could choose to rent any desired stock of capital for one period. The optimality condition was the same as that for any variable input: the marginal revenue product of the capital stock over the period was set equal to its rental cost, which equals interest plus depreciation (or minus capital gain, if any). Jorgenson (1963) is probably the most prominent and widely used model of this kind.

Such models implied a very rapid response of investment to changing economic conditions, whereas the response in reality was much more gradual. Several modifications of the neoclassical model were proposed in response to this observation; perhaps the most prominent was to introduce adjustment costs. Early models that adopted this approach include those of Lucas (1967) and Gould (1968).

Another feature that was introduced to make the model more realistic was irreversibility. Here Arrow (1968) is the early and prominent publication. In the context of certainty and perfect foresight, irreversibility implied stopping investment a little before the peak of potential profitability, bearing in mind the worse times to come.

Finally, uncertainty was introduced in a relatively simple way. The capital stock had to be chosen knowing only the probability distribution of a random variable, and other inputs like labor could be chosen after the realization of its actual value. A simple model by Hartman (1972) brought out the essential idea: the marginal product of capital was often a convex function of the random variable; therefore greater uncertainty implied a higher expected marginal product and therefore greater investment. Similar results in dynamic and stochastic contexts are in Abel (1984) and Craine (1989).

All of these earlier developments are surveyed and exposited in the excellent book by Nickell (1978).

More fully dynamic models combining uncertainty and adjustment costs were introduced by Abel (1983) and Hayashi (1982). Abel (1990) provides an excellent survey of some of this more recent work. A recent model by Abel and Eberly (1993) integrates many of the features of earlier treatments, and our exposition of adjustment costs is based on it.

Models that analyze variable capacity choice in the presence of irreversibility and uncertainty can be said to have begun with Pindyck (1988b) and Bertola (1988, Chapter 1) and (1989), although some glimpses of the idea can be found in Brennan and Schwartz (1985). Bertola and Caballero (1990) consider aggregation over firms in this context. Bertola (1988, Chapter 2) discusses the relation with Tobin's q.

Capacity expansion under increasing returns was studied extensively in the 1960s in the context of national planning. Weitzman (1970) is a prominent model of this kind. In much of this work, the focus was on finding the cost-minimizing path for meeting a given time path of demand, not on firm value maximization. Most of the work also assumed certainty and perfect foresight; Manne (1961) is a rare early exception.

Some dynamic programming problems we have encountered in this chapter have special features that make their rigorous mathematical theory quite difficult. Either the rate of investment is infinite so the paths of capital stock are nondifferentiable, or the capital stock itself makes discrete jumps, and so is at times discontinuous. In mathematical jargon, they are "singular" control problems. We treated them as if they were no different than ordinary dynamic programming. We proceeded heuristically, appealing to intuition and making the results appear reasonable. We hope to have succeeded in meeting the requirements of most readers, but some will demand more rigorous proofs. We can do no better than refer them to two classic articles, Harrison and Taksar (1983), which treats the nondifferentiable case (barrier or instantaneous control), and Harrison, Sellke, and Taylor (1983), which is about the discontinuous case (impulse control). Dumas (1991) also provides a different and insightful perspective on barrier control. At an intermediate level of rigor, Dixit (1991c) may be consulted. Dixit (1993a) is an exposition at about the same standard of heuristics as this book, but provides compact statements of the techniques and the results in fuller detail.

Chapter 12

Applications and Empirical Research

We hope that by this point we have made it quite clear that the "options" approach presented in this book is applicable to a broad range of investment problems. Our numerical calculations were guided by numbers typical of some specific industries, for example, copper mining in Chapters 7 and 8, and oil tankers in Chapter 7. However, for the most part our models were simple and stylized. In this chapter we present some examples that illustrate actual applications of the techniques, and their extension to other problems and issues.

We will begin with a problem faced regularly by companies in extractive resource industries—how to value an undeveloped resource reserve, and how to decide when to invest in the development and production of the reserve. As we have explained earlier in this book, an undeveloped resource reserve is best understood as an option, namely, an option to invest in development of the reserve and then produce the resource. By valuing this option we can value the reserve and determine when it should be developed. We will focus on the specific example of offshore oil reserves. Oil companies regularly bid hundreds of millions of dollars for offshore petroleum tracts auctioned off by the United States government, so it is clearly important to be able to correctly value these reserves and determine how best to exploit them.

Valuation and investment timing problems are also very important in the electric utility industry. Electric utilities make large and irreversible investments in new power plants, and face considerable uncertainty over the future

394

payoffs from such investments. For example, there is uncertainty over future fuel prices, over the future demand for electricity, over the future environmental regulations that will constrain the utility, and over the costs of alternative technologies to comply with those regulations. In Section 2 of this chapter we focus on a specific problem faced by many utilities with coal-burning power plants. The Clean Air Act calls for reductions in overall emissions of sulfur dioxide (SO_2), but to minimize the cost of these reductions, it gives utilities a choice. They can invest in expensive "scrubbers" to reduce emissions to mandated levels, or they can buy tradeable "allowances" that allow them to pollute. (This system reduces the total social cost of reducing air pollution by creating an incentive for utilities with the highest cost of emission reduction to buy allowances.) If the future prices of allowances were known, this would be a straightforward problem. However, there is considerable uncertainty over the future prices of allowances, and an investment in scrubbers is irreversible. The utility must decide whether to maintain flexibility by relying on allowances, or invest in scrubbers. We will see how this problem can be addressed using the options approach of this book.

The principles and analytical tools developed in this book have relevance that goes well beyond firms' investment decisions. As one example, in Section 3 we show how the tools can be applied to a general problem in environmental policy design—when should the government adopt a policy in response to a perceived threat to the environment? The standard framework by which economists evaluate environmental policies is cost-benefit analysis. Consider, for example, a carbon tax to reduce global warming. By distorting relative prices, this policy would impose an expected flow of costs on society in excess of the government tax revenues it generates. Presumably, it also yields an expected flow of benefits to society. Households and firms would burn less fuel, less carbon dioxide (CO_2) would accumulate in the atmosphere, global mean temperatures would not rise as much, and the damage caused by higher temperatures would be correspondingly smaller. The standard framework would recommend this policy if the present value of the expected flow of benefits exceeds the present value of the expected flow of costs.

This standard framework ignores three important characteristics of most environmental problems and the policies designed to respond to them. First, there is considerable uncertainty over the future costs and benefits of adopting a particular policy. With global warming, for example, there is uncertainty over how much average temperatures are likely to rise with or without reduced CO_2 emissions, and there is also uncertainty over the economic impact of higher temperatures. Second, there are usually important irreversibilities associated with environmental policy. These irreversibilities can arise with respect to environmental damage itself, but also with respect to the costs of adapting to policies to reduce the damage. Third, the adoption of an environmental policy is rarely a now-or-never proposition. In most cases the government can delay action and wait for new information. As a result, the same techniques that we used to determine the optimal timing of an investment can be used to determine the optimal timing of an environmental policy.

At the end of this chapter, we discuss some of the empirical implications of irreversibility and uncertainty for investment spending at the industry or country level. Although there is considerable anecdotal evidence that firms make investment decisions in a way that is at least roughly consistent with the theory developed in this book (for example, the use of hurdle rates that are much larger than the opportunity cost of capital as predicted by the CAPM), the task of more systematic econometric testing and application is still in its infancy. We review some work that exists, indicate the difficulties it encounters, and suggest topics for future research.

1   Investments in Offshore Oil Reserves

We begin with a model of offshore petroleum leases developed by Paddock, Siegel, and Smith (1988). The U.S. government regularly auctions off leases for offshore tracts of land, and oil companies typically perform valuations of such tracts as part of their bidding process. Because bids can involve hundreds of millions of dollars, it is important that these valuations be done accurately. In addition, oil companies must decide what to do with tracts that they succeed in leasing. How high should the price of oil be before they spend hundreds of millions of dollars more to develop the reserve and begin production?

It should be apparent that the failure to recognize and account for the optionlike nature of an oil reserve can lead to serious errors in its valuation. Suppose, for example, that one tried to value a reserve using a standard net present value approach. Depending on the current price of oil, the expected rate of change of price, and the cost of developing the reserve, one might construct a scenario for the timing of development and hence the timing (and size) of the future annual cash flows from production. One would then value the reserve by discounting these numbers forward and summing. In addition, since oil price uncertainty is not completely diversifiable, the greater is the perceived volatility of oil prices, the larger would be the discount rate, and the smaller the estimated value of the undeveloped reserve. However, this would underestimate the value of the reserve, and probably by a large amount.[1] The reason is that it ignores the flexibility that the owner has over when to actually develop the reserve, that is, the reserve's option value. Also note that because of this option value, the greater is the volatility of oil prices, the *larger* is the value of the reserve—just the opposite of what a standard NPV calculation would tell us.

As we discussed in Chapter 10, the valuation and exploitation of an off-shore oil tract can be viewed as part of a multistage investment problem. The first stage involves exploration—seismic and drilling activity to find out how much oil is present and the cost of extracting it. The second stage (which would only occur if the exploration results are favorable) involves development—the installation of the platforms and production wells that are needed to extract the oil. The last stage involves the extraction of the oil over some period of years. Since it is the development stage that involves the largest capital expenditures, it is the stage for which option value is most important.[2] Hence we will focus on the valuation of an undeveloped (but well delineated) reserve, and the decision as to when to develop it. In doing so, we must account for the fact that the option to develop the reserve is not a perpetual one; offshore leases are usually subject to *relinquishment requirements*, which limit the time the company can hold the tract before developing it.

The close connection between the value of an undeveloped reserve and a call option on a stock is illustrated in Table 12.1.[3] The underlying asset in the case of a call option is the stock price; for an undeveloped reserve it is the value of a developed reserve (which, as we will see, is in turn a function of the price of oil). The exercise price for the undeveloped reserve is the development cost, and the time to expiration is the relinquishment requirement. The value and optimal exercise rule for a call option depend on the stock's dividend rate; the higher the dividend, the greater the opportunity cost (in terms of foregone dividends) of holding the option rather than exercising. The analogous variable for the developed reserve is the net production revenue less the rate of depletion; one forgoes this by delaying development.

---

[1]This seems to be the way that the government arrives at its own valuations, which have been systematically too low. See Paddock, Siegel, and Smith (1988).

[2]When exploration generates information pertinent to later stages of decisions, it has an additional value, as we saw in Chapter 10. However, exploration expenditures are relatively small. As for the last stage, once a reserve is developed, extraction almost always proceeds at a more or less fixed rate.

[3]The analogy is with an *American* call option, that is, an option that can be exercised at any time up to and including the expiration date. A European option can only be exercised on its expiration date. The table is from Paddock, Siegel, and Smith (1988).

Table 12.1. *Comparison of a Call Option with an Undeveloped Oil Reserve*

Call option	Undeveloped reserve
Stock price	Value of developed reserve
Exercise price	Cost of development
Time to expiration	Relinquishment requirement
Volatility of stock price	Volatility of value of developed reserve
Dividend on stock	Net production revenue from developed reserve less depletion

1.A The Value of a Developed Reserve

We begin by characterizing the value of a developed reserve. Let B_t be the number of barrels of oil in a developed reserve, V_t be the value per barrel of the developed reserve, and let R_t be the return over an instant of time to the owner of the developed reserve. This return will have two components—the flow of profits from production, and the capital gain on the remaining oil. As a reasonable approximation, we can express production from a developed reserve as an exponential decline,[4] so that

$$dB_t = -\omega\, B_t\, dt, \tag{1}$$

that is, a fraction ω of the oil is produced each year. Then the return, R_t, can be written as

$$R_t\, dt = \omega\, B_t\, \Pi_t\, dt + d(B_t V_t)$$
$$= \omega\, B_t\, \Pi_t\, dt + B_t\, dV_t - \omega\, V_t\, B_t\, dt, \tag{2}$$

where Π_t is the after-tax profit from producing and selling a barrel of oil.

---

[4]This is a standard assumption that reflects geological constraints on the extraction rate. See McCray (1975).

We can also assume that the rate of return on the developed reserve follows a Brownian motion process:

$$\frac{R_t \, dt}{B_t V_t} = \mu_v \, dt + \sigma_v \, dz, \tag{3}$$

where μ_v is the risk-adjusted expected rate of return required by a competitive capital market. Combining equations (2) and (3) gives the following equation for the dynamics of V, the unit value of a developed reserve:

$$dV = (\mu_v - \delta_t) \, V \, dt + \sigma_v \, V \, dz, \tag{4}$$

where δ_t, the payout rate from a unit of producing developed reserve, is given by

$$\delta_t = \omega \, (\Pi_t - V_t)/V_t. \tag{5}$$

Note the close analogy here with our model of investment in Chapter 5, in which the value of a project follows a geometric Brownian motion. In Chapter 5, the value of the project was given by $dV = \alpha V \, dt + \sigma V \, dz$, with $\alpha = \mu - \delta$, where μ is the risk-adjusted expected rate of return. We called δ the rate of return shortfall, and explained that it could reflect the cash flows from the operating project. The same is true here, except that now the payout rate is net of depletion. In fact, the only significant difference between this model and the one in Chapter 5 is that here the option to invest (that is, to develop the reserve) does not last forever; there is a relinquishment requirement. Also, since the marginal cost of production is small (most of the cost of production is the sunk cost of development), and since oil can be extracted only slowly (ω is typically about 10 percent per year), $\Pi_t > V_t$, so that $\delta > 0$, and developed reserves will always be produced.

Before proceeding, it will be useful to roughly estimate the payout rate δ. The per-barrel value of a developed reserve typically equals about one-third of the market price of oil, per-barrel production costs are about 30 percent of the market price, and the corporate tax rate net of depreciation allowances is about 34 percent, so that the after-tax profit on a barrel of oil is about 46 percent of the price. Using $\omega = 0.1$ and letting P denote the market price of a barrel of oil, this gives

$$\delta = 0.1 \, (0.46P - 0.33P)/0.33P \approx 0.04.$$

Thus holding a developed reserve is like holding a stock that has a dividend yield of about 4 percent.

1.B The Value of an Undeveloped Reserve and the Optimal Development Rule

Given equation (4) for the value of a developed reserve, we can now determine the value of an undeveloped reserve as well as the optimal timing rule for its development. Since there is a variety of financial instruments that can be used to replicate fluctuations in the price of oil (for example, futures contracts, forward contracts, and the shares of oil companies), spanning clearly holds, and contingent claims methods can be used to value an undeveloped reserve. Let $F(V, t)$ denote the value of a one-barrel unit of undeveloped reserve. Using equation (4) and going through the usual steps, the reader can verify that $F(V, t)$ must satisfy

$$\tfrac{1}{2} \sigma_v^2 V^2 F_{VV} + (r - \delta) V F_V - r F = -F_t. \tag{6}$$

Note that equation (6) is a partial differential equation; since the option to develop the reserve expires at time T, the value of the option depends on the current time t.

Equation (6) must be solved subject to boundary conditions. Letting D be the per-barrel cost of developing the reserve (that is, the "exercise price" of the option), these conditions are:

$$F(0, t) = 0, \tag{7}$$

$$F(V, T) = \max [V_T - D, \ 0], \tag{8}$$

$$F(V^*, t) = V^* - D, \tag{9}$$

$$F_V(V^*, t) = 1. \tag{10}$$

Condition (8) just says that at expiration, the option to develop will be exercised if $V_T > D$. The other boundary conditions are standard.

Equation (6) cannot be solved analytically, but it is not difficult to obtain a solution numerically using finite difference methods. (See Chapter 10, especially the Appendix.) Figure 12.1 and Table 12.2 show solutions from Siegel, Smith, and Paddock (1987) based on the payout rate $\delta = 0.04$ discussed above, an after-tax real risk-free rate of interest r of 0.0125, and different values of σ_v. The value of σ_v is an important input to this model, and can be estimated in different ways. An estimate could be based on historical data, or obtained from an assessment by oil industry experts of, say, the 90-percent confidence interval for the price of oil at some time in the future. Estimates based on data over the past 30 years would put σ_v at about 0.15, but estimates based

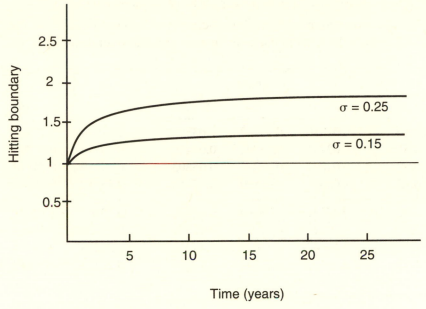

Figure 12.1. *Critical Value for Development of Oil Reserve*
(Shows V^*/D for $\delta = 0.04$ and $r = 0.0125$, where D is development cost)

on industry forecasts might be somewhat higher. A reasonable range for σ_v would be from 0.15 to 0.25.

Figure 12.1 shows the critical ratio V^*/D as a function of the number of years to expiration, for $\sigma_v = 0.15$ and 0.25. Note that at expiration, $V^*/D = 1$ [which follows from boundary condition (8)], so that the standard NPV rule applies. This critical ratio increases to 2 or more, however, when the firm can wait at least a few years before deciding whether to develop the reserve. This result is similar to those obtained for the simple "perpetual" option to invest in Chapter 5. Also, note that the critical ratio is not very sensitive to the time to expiration if that time is greater than one or two years. Hence for many such investments in oil reserves, it is a reasonable approximation to ignore the relinquishment requirement altogether, and simply treat the option to develop as perpetual.[5] Then the term F_t in equation (6) disappears, and the

---

[5]Compare the similar finding for our example of a depreciating machine in Chapter 4; a ten-year physical life was effectively infinite as far as the optimal abandonment rule was concerned.

Table 12.2. *Option Values per $1 of Development Cost*

(Note: Because option values are homogeneous in the development cost, total option value is the entry in the table times the total development cost.)

V/D	$\sigma_v = 0.142$			$\sigma_v = 0.25$	
	$T = 5$	$T = 10$	$T = 15$	$T = 5$	$T = 10$
0.80	0.01810	0.02812	0.03309	0.07394	0.10392
0.85	0.02761	0.03894	0.04430	0.09174	0.12305
0.90	0.04024	0.05245	0.05803	0.11169	0.14390
0.95	0.05643	0.06899	0.07458	0.13380	0.16646
1.00	0.07661	0.08890	0.09431	0.15804	0.19071
1.05	0.10116	0.11253	0.11754	0.18438	0.21664
1.10	0.13042	0.14025	0.14464	0.21278	0.24424
1.15	0.16472	0.17242	0.17599	0.24321	0.27349

Source: Siegel, Smith, and Paddock (1987).

equation can be solved analytically. (The solution is the same as the one we obtained in Chapter 5.)

Table 12.2 shows the value of an undeveloped reserve (that is, the value of the development option) per dollar of development cost, for $\sigma_v = 0.142$ [an estimate obtained by Paddock, Siegel, and Smith (1988)], and for $\sigma_v = 0.25$. When V/D is less than 1, that is, the value of the developed reserve is less than the development cost, we would not develop the reserve even using the standard NPV criterion. (In the parlance of financial options, the development option is "out of the money.") If V/D exceeds 1 (so that the development option is "in the money"), the standard NPV criterion would tell us to develop, but as Figure 12.1 shows, unless V/D is significantly greater than 1, this is not the optimal decision. The entries in the table show the value of the option per unit cost of development, that is, $F(V, t)/D$. For example, when $\sigma_v = 0.142$, $T = 10$, and $V/D = 1$, the option value is about nine cents for every dollar of development cost.

A simple example will help illustrate how these results can be used.[6] Consider an undeveloped reserve which, if developed, is expected to yield 100 million barrels of oil, and has a ten-year relinquishment requirement.

[6]This example is discussed in more detail in Siegel, Smith, and Paddock (1987).

Suppose that the value of the developed reserve is $12 per barrel, the payout rate (that is, net production revenues less depletion as a fraction of the reserve value) is 4 percent, that development takes three years (typical for an offshore reserve in the Gulf of Mexico), and that the present value of the development cost is $11.79 per barrel. Then we would value the undeveloped reserve as follows.

1. Since development takes three years, we must calculate the present value of the developed reserve. The correct discount rate is the payout rate, δ (that is, the difference between the risk-adjusted rate μ and the expected rate of growth of the reserve value, which is $\mu - \delta$). Since $\delta = 0.04$, the present value of the developed reserve is $V' = e^{-0.12}(\$12) = \$10.64$.
2. We next calculate the ratio of this developed reserve value to the present value of the development cost. That is $V'/D = \$10.64/\$11.79 = 0.90$. This is less than 1, so the development option is actually out of the money.
3. We can now use Table 12.2 to calculate the value of the undeveloped reserve. Assuming a standard deviation σ_v of 0.142, the option value per dollar of development cost is 0.05245, and the total development cost is ($11.79)(100 million) = $1,179 million. Hence the total value of the undeveloped reserve is (0.05245)($1,179 million) = $61.84 million.

Thus, although this undeveloped reserve could not be profitably developed given current oil prices, it is still worth about $62 million because of its option value. Furthermore, this value could rise substantially if conditions in world oil markets changed in a way that made the perceived volatility of oil prices higher. For example, as we can see from Table 12.2, if σ_v were to rise to 0.25, the value of the undeveloped reserve would rise to (0.14390)($1,179 million) = $169.66 million.

1.C Mean Reversion in the Price of Oil

We have assumed that the value of a developed oil reserve—like the price of oil—follows a geometric Brownian motion. However, as we have mentioned earlier in this book, one might argue that oil prices, and hence reserve values, follow some different stochastic process. For example, one might believe that over long periods of time, oil prices (and the prices of other commodities) are drawn back towards long-run marginal cost, and thus are mean reverting. Or, one might believe that the price of oil is best represented by a Poisson jump process, rather than a continuous Ito process.

Unfortunately, with limited amounts of data it is difficult to determine whether or not a price process is indeed mean reverting or has a significant jump component. For example, in principle one can perform a "unit root test" to test whether a price series is mean reverting or is a random walk. However, this is a weak test that for short time series (for example, 30 years or less) will often fail to reject the hypothesis of a random walk, even if the series is in fact mean reverting.[7] The reason is that any mean-reversion is typically very slow, and is therefore hard to discern in a short time series. In this case one might ask whether the results of an analysis are likely to change very much depending on whether one begins with a mean-reverting (or Poisson) process for the underlying stochastic state variable.

With regard to mean reversion, the numerical examples that we developed in Chapter 5 provide some guidance. Additional numerical results, for the oil reserve example of this section, were obtained by Wey (1993). As one would expect, the extent to which the answers change depends on the rate of mean reversion and the specific level to which the process is reverting.

Consider the following mean-reverting process, which we examined in Chapter 5, for the value of a developed oil reserve:

$$dV = \eta\,(\overline{V} - V)\,V\,dt + \sigma\,V\,dz. \tag{11}$$

Then the partial differential equation (6) for the value of the undeveloped reserve, $F(V, t)$, becomes

$$\tfrac{1}{2}\,\sigma_v^2\,V^2\,F_{VV} + [r - \mu + \eta(\overline{V} - V)]\,V\,F_V - r\,F = -F_t. \tag{12}$$

If the time until relinquishment is long enough (more than five years), we can ignore the time dependence of $F(V, t)$, so that the term $-F_t$ in equation (12) disappears and we have an ordinary differential equation identical to the one in Section 5(a) of Chapter 5. As we saw there, the solution can be written using the confluent hypergeometric function, which has a series representation. One can use this solution, with different values for η and $\overline{V}$, to determine the extent to which mean reversion matters for the valuation of the undeveloped reserve and for the optimal development rule.

Wey (1993) has shown, using a 100-year series for the real price of crude oil, that a reasonable estimate for η is about 0.3, and that using this value (and a value of σ_v of 0.20), the extent to which mean reversion matters depends on

---

[7]See Pindyck and Rubinfeld (1991) for an explanation of these tests and their limitations. That book provides an example (on pages 462–465) in which unit root tests are performed for the real (inflation-adjusted) prices of crude oil, copper, and lumber. The tests fail to reject a random walk when 30 years of data are used, but reject a random walk (in favor of a mean-reverting process) for crude oil and copper when used for data series covering a 117-year period.

the value to which V reverts, $\overline{V}$, relative to the development cost, D. As one would expect, if $\overline{V}$ is much larger than D, accounting for mean reversion gives a larger value for the undeveloped reserve when $V < D$ because V is expected to rise over time. Wey shows that if $\overline{V}$ is about twice as large as D, ignoring mean reversion can lead one to undervalue the reserve by 40 percent or more. On the other hand, if $\overline{V}$ is about as large as D, ignoring mean reversion will matter very little.

Paddock, Siegel, and Smith's (1988) original study was intended to illustrate the optionlike nature of an undeveloped oil reserve, and show that the use of standard NPV methods would lead to a substantial undervaluation of the reserve as well as premature development. That basic result still holds whether or not one accounts for mean reversion. Of course, for an oil company about to bid $500 million for offshore leases, a 10-percent valuation error adds up to a lot of money, so it would be worthwhile to do a careful analysis that accounts for mean reversion and any other characteristics of the price or developed reserve value process that are believed to be relevant.

2   Electric Utilities' Compliance with the Clean Air Act

Under the Clean Air Act Amendments of 1990, electric utilities in the United States are restricted in their emissions of SO_2. However, they can comply with the regulations in different ways. First, they can purchase tradeable emission allowances from other utilities, and then, with these allowances, continue to emit as much SO_2 as they did before. Alternatively, they can avoid the cost of buying allowances by sufficiently reducing their SO_2 emissions. This, too, can be done in different ways. One possibility is to pay a sunk cost of retrofitting the plant and then switching from high-sulfur to (more expensive) low-sulfur coal. The second possibility is to make a (sunk) investment in "scrubbers," that is, devices that remove the SO_2 before it is emitted.[8]

Each alternative involves costs that can change unpredictably over time. In particular, the emission allowances, which are traded on spot and futures markets,[9] will fluctuate in value as electricity demand fluctuates, as new technologies arrive for removing sulfur more cheaply and effectively,

---

[8] Scrubbers, technically referred to as flue gas desulfurizers, are vessels in which the SO_2 released from burning coal reacts with an alkali and is thereby "captured" before going up the smokestack.

[9] At the time of this writing, futures trading of emission allowances had not yet begun but was planned for the near future.

and as government regulations themselves change. Likewise, the cost differential between low-sulfur and high-sulfur coal fluctuates over time as supply
and demand conditions in coal markets change. Since switching to low-sulfur
coal and investing in scrubbers both involve sunk costs, the utility faces an
irreversible investment problem of the sort that we are now well equipped to
solve.

Herbelot (1992) recently examined this problem in detail, using the
options approach. He showed that because of the flexibility they provide,
purchasing emission allowances may be the preferred alternative even if the
present value of expected compliance costs is higher with allowances than it
is by installing scrubbers or switching to low-sulfur fuel. He also showed how
one can calculate the values of the options to install scrubbers or switch fuels,
and how these option values reduce the utility's true compliance cost. In this
section we use Herbelot's example to illustrate the solution to this investment
problem.

Under Phase II of the Clean Air Act Amendments, utilities will be able to
emit only 1.2 lbs of SO_2 per million BTUs (MMBTU) of fuel burnt.[10] A utility
that is able to emit less than 1.2 lbs of SO_2 per MMBTU can sell allowances
for the difference to other utilities. A utility that emits more than 1.2 lbs of
SO_2 per MMBTU must buy allowances to cover the difference. Of course the
utility can reduce its emissions (instead of buying allowances) by installing
scrubbers or switching fuels. The utility must determine when to optimally
install scrubbers or switch fuels, and must determine the present value of its
expected costs of compliance, taking into account these options.

2.A   The Model

We will consider two stochastic state variables, the price of an allowance, A,
measured in dollars per ton, and the price premium per MMBTU of low-
sulfur versus high-sulfur coal, D. We will assume that these variables follow
(correlated) geometric Brownian motions:

$$dA = \alpha_A A\,dt + \sigma_A A\,dz_A, \tag{13}$$

$$dD = \alpha_D D\,dt + \sigma_D D\,dz_D, \tag{14}$$

with $\mathcal{E}(dz_A dz_D) = \rho\,dt$. Let μ_A and μ_D be the risk-adjusted expected returns
on allowances and the price premium, respectively, and let the return "short-
falls" be denoted by $\delta_A \equiv \mu_A - \alpha_A$ and $\delta_D \equiv \mu_D - \alpha_D$. Herbelot shows that

---

[10]Under Phase I, utilities can emit 2.5 lbs of SO_2 per MMBTU. Phase II goes into effect in
the year 2000, but for simplicity we will assume it is in effect now.

reasonable "base case" parameter values are (on an annual basis): $\sigma_A = 0.12$, $\sigma_D = 0.14$, $\delta_A = \delta_D = 0.05$, and $\rho = 0.8$. Each allowance permits a utility to emit one ton of SO_2. In 1992, trading in allowances had not yet begun, but it was expected in the industry that they would be worth as much as $500 each. When trading began in 1993, prices were below $200. As for the coal price premium D, it has averaged about $0.45 per MMBTU during 1992 and early 1993.

We will assume that high-sulfur coal emits $x_H = 3.3$ lbs of SO_2 per MMBTU, and low-sulfur coal emits $x_L = 1.0$ lbs of SO_2.[11] We will consider an existing power plant that burns high-sulfur coal, is expected to last for another 20 years, has a capacity of 536,000 kilowatts, has a capacity factor of 80 percent, and a heat rate of 0.00898 MMBTU per kilowatt-hour of electricity. Hence the total number of MMBTUs of energy that the plant is expected to burn each year is given by

$$B = (536,000)(0.80)(365)(24)(0.00898) = 33.7 \times 10^6 \text{ MMBTU/year.} \quad (15)$$

First, suppose this utility had no option to switch to low-sulfur coal or to install scrubbers. Then its annual cost of complying with the allowed 1.2 lbs of SO_2 per MMBTU would be $B[(x_H - 1.2)/2000]A_t = 35{,}385 A_t$ per year,[12] and the expected present value of this flow of cost over the 20-year life of the plant would be

$$PV_0 = \int_0^{20} 35{,}385\, A_0\, e^{-\delta_A t}\, dt = 447{,}351\, A_0. \quad (16)$$

This is a "base case" cost of compliance, and we will compare it to the cost when the utility has the options to switch fuels or install scrubbers.

If the utility switches to low-sulfur coal, it will have to pay a one-time sunk retrofitting cost of $25 per kilowatt of capacity, which, for a 536,000-kilowatt plant, amounts to a sunk cost of $K_{sw} = \$13{,}400{,}000$. In addition, it will have to pay on an ongoing basis a coal price premium of D per MMBTU, as well as an increase in nonfuel operating costs of $0.50 per MMBTU. However, each year it will save having to buy $B\,(x_H - 1.2)/2000$ allowances, and in addition it will be able to sell $B\,(1.2 - x_L)/2000$ of these allowances, so the cost saving per year will be $A\,B\,(x_H - x_L)/2000$ dollars.

---

[11] There are a variety of different grades of low-sulfur coal with different sulfur contents, but this is a reasonable approximation.

[12] Pollution is measured in lbs per MMBTU, and the cost of allowances is in dollars per ton. The 2000 in the denominator converts pounds to tons.

If the utility installs a scrubber, it will have to pay a one-time sunk cost of $200 per kilowatt of capacity, which, for its 536,000-kilowatt plant, amounts to a sunk cost of $K_{scr} = \$107,200,000$. In addition, the scrubber requires energy and maintenance to operate. The operating cost is 0.73 cents per kilowatt-hour of electricity, which implies a total annual operating cost for the scrubber of $27,421,000. The flow cost saving can be calculated as above. Scrubbers are 90 percent effective, so $x_L = 0.1 x_H$ and the cost saving is $0.9 \, A \, B \, x_H/2000$ dollars per year.

Although in principle a utility could switch fuels more than once, in practice this is unlikely, so we will consider only the possibility of a single switch from high-sulfur to low-sulfur coal. Also, once the utility has switched to low-sulfur coal, there is no point to investing in scrubbers. As a result, we can proceed as follows. First, we determine the present value of the cost of compliance for a utility that is burning high-sulfur coal and has the option to switch to low-sulfur coal. Then, assuming that this option to switch fuels has not been exercised, we value the option to install scrubbers and determine the present value of the cost of compliance allowing for this option as well.

2.B   The Option to Switch Fuels

The utility can switch to low-sulfur coal at any time t, where $0 \leq t \leq T$ (and $T = 20$ years). If the utility switches at time t, the payoff, that is, the present value of cost savings from t to T, is

$$\Phi^{sw} = \int_t^T B \frac{x_H - x_L}{2000} A_t \, e^{-\delta_A(\tau - t)} \, d\tau$$

$$- \int_t^T B \, D_t \, e^{-\delta_D(\tau - t)} \, d\tau - \int_t^T 0.5 \, B \, e^{-r(\tau - t)} \, d\tau. \tag{17}$$

Substituting the values listed above for B, x_L, x_H, δ_A, and δ_D, and letting the risk-free rate, r, equal 0.05, we get

$$\Phi^{sw}(D_t, A_t, t) = [1 - e^{-0.05(T-t)}]$$
$$\cdot (775, 100 \, A_t - 674, 000, 000 \, D_t - 337, 000, 000). \tag{18}$$

During 1992–1993, D_t was about $0.45 per MMBTU and a reasonable range for A_t was $200 to $500 per ton. For this range of values, $\Phi^{sw}(D_t, A_t, t)$ is negative, so the option to switch fuels is clearly "out of the money." However, it could become "in the money" should A rise and D fall sufficiently, and we want to determine its value.

To value the option to switch fuels, we can assume that spanning holds and use contingent claims methods. The assumption of spanning is quite reasonable in this case because emission allowances are (or soon will be) traded on a futures market, and coal is traded on a variety of informal forward markets, and its price is partly correlated with the prices of other fuels. By going through the usual steps, the reader should be able to show that the value of the option to switch fuels, which we denote by $F^{sw}(A_t, D_t, t)$, must satisfy the following partial differential equation:

$$\tfrac{1}{2}\sigma_A^2 A^2 F_{AA}^{sw} + \tfrac{1}{2}\sigma_D^2 D^2 F_{DD}^{sw} + \rho\,\sigma_A\,\sigma_D\,A\,D\,F_{AD}^{sw} + (r - \delta_A)\,A\,F_A^{sw}$$
$$+ (r - \delta_D)\,D\,F_D^{sw} + F_t^{sw} - r\,F^{sw} = 0, \tag{19}$$

subject to the boundary conditions

$$F^{sw}(A, D, T) = 0, \tag{20}$$

$$F^{sw}(0, D, t) = 0, \tag{21}$$

$$F^{sw}(A^*(D, t), D, t) = \Phi^{sw}(A^*(D, t), D, t) - K_{sw}, \tag{22}$$

$$F_A^{sw}(A^*(D, t), D, t) = \Phi_A^{sw}(A^*(D, t), D, t). \tag{23}$$

Note the similarity of equation (19) to the partial differential equations that we examined in Chapter 10. Like those equations, equation (19) must be solved numerically.[13] There is a critical boundary, $A^*(D, t)$, that must be found as part of the solution, and the optimal investment rule is to switch fuels when $A > A^*$. In this case, we will have $\partial A^*(D, t)/\partial D > 0$ and $\partial A^*(D, t)/\partial t > 0$. (If the premium for low-sulfur coal rises, the allowance price must increase to make switching economical. Likewise, as time passes and the remaining life of the plant falls, the allowance price must rise to justify the capital cost of switching fuels.)

In equation (16) we found the present value of the utility's expected costs of compliance assuming that it could not switch fuels or install scrubbers. If we include the value of the utility's option to switch fuels, that present value at time $t = 0$ becomes

$$PV_0^{sw} = 447{,}351\,A_0 - F^{sw}(A_0, D_0, 0). \tag{24}$$

---

[13] Herbelot (1992) structures the problem using the binomial method as a way of obtaining numerical solutions. An alternative method of solution is to derive the partial differential equation as we have done here, and then solve it numerically using a finite difference method, along the lines discussed in the Appendix to Chapter 10.

Herbelot (1992) has calculated F^{sw} and shown that for a reasonable range of parameter values it is quite small (at most a few million dollars). This is not surprising; as we saw above, the option to switch fuels is far "out of the money" even for an allowance price, A, as low as $200.

2.C The Option to Install Scrubbers

Now consider the option to install scrubbers. The utility can install scrubbers at any time t, where $0 \leq t \leq T$. If it installs scrubbers at time t, the payoff, that is, the present value of cost savings from t to T, is

$$
\Phi^{\text{scr}} = \int_t^T B \, \frac{0.9 x_H}{2000} \, A_t \, e^{-\delta_A(\tau-t)} \, d\tau - \int_t^T 27,421,000 \, e^{-r(\tau-t)} \, d\tau
$$

$$
= [1 - e^{-0.05(T-t)}] \, (1,001,000 \, A_t - 548,420,000). \tag{25}
$$

Note that scrubbers entail a maintenance cost of $27,421,000 each year—which is certain and hence is discounted at the risk-free rate—that must be paid annually. If the utility installed scrubbers, it would also have to pay a capital cost $K_{\text{scr}} = \$107,200,000$ and would give up the option to switch fuels. If $t = 0$, $T = 20$, and $A = \$500$, the net cost savings would be negative; it is about −$155 million [less the value of the fuel switching option, $F^{\text{sw}}(A, D, t)$, which is fairly small]. Like the option to switch fuels, the option to install scrubbers is "out of the money" for the range of allowance prices we have considered, and only becomes "in the money" if the allowance price rises above $655.

To determine the value of the option to install scrubbers, which we denote by F^{scr}, and the optimal exercise rule, we can proceed as above. As long as we continue to account for the possibility of switching fuels, the net payoff from installing scrubbers depends on D_t, as well as A_t and t, and thus so does F^{scr}. As a result, F^{scr} will satisfy a partial differential equation similar to equation (19) for F^{sw}:

$$
\tfrac{1}{2} \sigma_A^2 \, A^2 \, F_{AA}^{\text{scr}} + \tfrac{1}{2} \sigma_D^2 \, F_{DD}^{\text{scr}} + \rho \, \sigma_A \, \sigma_D \, A \, D \, F_{AD}^{\text{scr}} + (r - \delta_A) \, A \, F_A^{\text{scr}}
$$

$$
+ (r - \delta_D) \, D \, F_D^{\text{scr}} + F_t^{\text{scr}} - r \, F^{\text{scr}} = 0. \tag{26}
$$

The boundary conditions are also similar:

$$
F^{\text{scr}}(A, D, T) = 0, \tag{27}
$$

$$
F^{\text{scr}}(0, D, t) = 0, \tag{28}
$$

$$F^{\text{scr}}(A^*(D, t), D, t) = \Phi^{\text{scr}}(A^*(D, t), D, t) - K_{\text{scr}}$$
$$- F^{\text{sw}}(A^*(D, t), D, t), \tag{29}$$

$$F_A^{\text{scr}}(A^*(D, t), D, t) = \Phi_A^{\text{scr}}(A^*(D, t), D, t)$$
$$- F_A^{\text{sw}}(A^*(D, t), D, t). \tag{30}$$

Herbelot obtains numerical solutions for F^{scr}, and shows that it is about \$15 million for the base case parameter values. This may seem small, but remember that the option is well "out of the money." Once we account for this option value, as well as the value of the option to switch fuels, the utility's expected cost of compliance at $t = 0$ becomes

$$PV_0^{\text{tot}} = 447{,}351\, A_0 - F^{\text{sw}}(A_0, D_0, 0) - F^{\text{scr}}(A_0, D_0, 0). \tag{31}$$

Herbelot also shows how this present value and its component option values depend on the various parameters of the problem.

2.D An Exercise for the Reader

We have said that the value of the option to switch fuels is quite small, so it would be a reasonable approximation to ignore the possibility of fuel switching. In addition, the option values and critical investment thresholds for a plant with a 20-year life are not very different from those for a plant with a 15- or 25-year life, so we could also simplify the problem by ignoring time. If we eliminate D_t and t as variables, the partial differential equation (26) for the value of the scrubber option becomes an ordinary differential equation that can be solved analytically. As an exercise, the reader can make these simplifications and then calculate the value of the option to install scrubbers and the critical threshold A^* that should trigger installation. The reader should also examine how this option value and critical threshold vary as parameters such as σ_A and δ_A are varied.

2.E Energy Conservation by Homeowners

Residential energy conservation became an important issue in the 1970s, and U.S. income tax law from 1978 to 1985 offered credits for investments that would promote this aim, for example, better attic insulation, double glazing, and some structural alterations. Empirical studies found that consumers' response to such policies was extremely low. If consumers were making their decisions on the basis of conventional net present value calculations, they must have been using very high discount rates. Various explanations, for example, fuel price distortions or lack of information, were offered for this "energy paradox."

The options approach suggests a different explanation. Most of these investments are irreversible, and the price of heating fuels (and therefore the savings from the investment) fluctuate randomly through time. Therefore consumers should rationally wait until the return to their investment is sufficiently above their opportunity cost of funds. Hassett and Metcalf (1992) find support for this explanation. The theory of investment is basically the model of Chapter 5 above. They consider the effect of a 15-percent tax credit. For the parameters of the fuel price process and the conservation technology, they find an option value multiple of 4.23. Thus the current rate of return must be over four times the cost of funds before a homeowner will make the energy-saving investment. They allow heterogeneity among households, so the responses to policy and price changes are distributed through time.

They calculate the mean increase in investment by simulating alternative realizations of price paths in a series of 1000 replications. If uncertainty in the price process is ignored and the traditional Marshallian criterion is employed, the effect of the tax credit is dramatic. Investment increases from about 27 percent of households to 43 percent immediately, and from 40 to 60 percent after five years. However, when uncertainty about future fuel prices is taken into account (with $\sigma = 0.093$), the credit is almost ineffective. Without the credit, very little investment is made because the price rarely hits the high threshold for action under uncertainty. In typical simulations, after 20 years only 5 percent of households adopt the energy-saving technology. However, the tax credit does not improve matters much. Compared to the no-policy baseline, investment increases by only 0.2 percent immediately, and by less than 3 percent after 20 years. The findings not only support the options approach, but also suggest that tax credits are not an effective policy to achieve energy conservation.

3   The Timing of Environmental Policy

As explained at the beginning of this chapter, environmental policy design has much in common with the design of an irreversible investment policy. When a firm makes an irreversible investment expenditure, it gives up the possibility of waiting for new information that might affect the desirability or timing of the expenditure, and this lost option value is an opportunity cost that must be included as part of the cost of the investment. The adoption of an environmental policy can also involve lost option value, but in this case there are two kinds of irreversibilities, and they work in opposite directions.

First, policies aimed at reducing ecological damage impose *sunk costs* on society. For example, such policies might force coal-burning utilities to install scrubbers, or firms to scrap existing machines and invest in more fuel-efficient ones. This creates an opportunity cost of adopting a policy now, rather than waiting for more information about ecological impacts and their economic consequences. This opportunity cost biases traditional cost-benefit analysis *in favor* of policy adoption. As with irreversible investment decisions, the sunk costs associated with policy adoption can make it preferable to wait rather than adopt the policy now.

Second, environmental damage can be partially or totally irreversible. For example, increases in greenhouse gas (GHG) concentrations are long-lasting. Even if radical policies were adopted in the future to drastically reduce GHG emissions, these concentrations (which have a natural decay rate of about one-half percent per year) would take many years to fall. In addition, the damage to various ecosystems from higher global temperatures (or from acidified lakes and streams, or from the clear-cutting of forests) can be permanent. This means that adopting a policy now rather than waiting has a *sunk benefit*, that is, a negative opportunity cost. This negative opportunity cost biases traditional cost-benefit analysis *against* policy adoption. Hence it may be desirable to adopt a policy now, even though the traditional analysis declares it uneconomical.

We will illustrate this interaction of uncertainty and irreversibility using a simple model, based on Pindyck (1993e), which in turn builds on Nordhaus (1991). Let M be the stock of an environmental pollutant (for example, atmospheric GHG concentration, or the acidity of a lake), and E the rate of emission of the pollutant. Then we can assume that M evolves as

$$dM/dt = \gamma\, E(t) - \lambda\, M(t), \tag{32}$$

where λ is the rate of natural decay of M. (Thus the smaller is λ, the more irreversible are the effects of emissions.) We will represent the flow of social cost (that is, negative benefit) associated with the stock of pollutant M_t by a function $B(M_t, \theta_t)$, where θ_t is a variable that shifts over time, perhaps stochastically, to reflect changes in tastes and technologies.[14] For simplicity,

---

[14]For example, if M is the GHG concentration, shifts in θ might reflect new agricultural techniques that reduce the cost of a higher M, or alternatively, demographic changes that raise the cost.

we will make $B(M_t, \theta_t)$ linear:

$$B(M_t, \theta_t) = -\theta_t \, M_t, \tag{33}$$

and we will assume that θ_t follows a geometric Brownian motion:

$$d\theta = \alpha \, \theta \, dt + \sigma \, \theta \, dz. \tag{34}$$

We will assume that until the policy is adopted, the rate of emissions E_t stays at the constant level E. Once the policy is adopted, E_t falls immediately to zero, where it remains. Finally, we will assume that the social cost of adopting the policy is completely sunk, and its present value at the time of adoption is K.[15]

The problem is to find a rule for policy adoption that maximizes the net present value function:

$$W = \mathcal{E}_0 \int_0^\infty B(M_t, \theta_t) \, e^{-rt} \, dt - \mathcal{E}_0 [K \, e^{-r\tilde{T}}], \tag{35}$$

subject to equation (32). Here, $\tilde{T}$ is the (in general, unknown) time that the policy is adopted, $\mathcal{E}_0$ as usual denotes the expectation based on information at time $t = 0$, and r is the discount rate. This is an optimal stopping problem, that is, we must find the optimal point at which to commit to spending K to reduce E_t to zero, given the (possibly stochastic) dependence of M_t on E_t, and given the stochastic evolution of θ_t.

We solve this problem using dynamic programming by defining the net present value function for each of two regions. Let $W^N(\theta, M)$ denote the value function for the "no-adopt" region (so that $E_t = E$), and let $W^A(\theta, M)$ denote the value function for the "adopt" region (in which $E_t = 0$). As the reader can confirm (as an exercise), $W^N(\theta, M)$ must satisfy the following Bellman equation:

$$r \, W^N = -\theta \, M + (\gamma \, E - \lambda \, M) \, W_M^N + \alpha \, \theta \, W_\theta^N + \tfrac{1}{2} \sigma^2 \, \theta^2 \, W_{\theta\theta}^N. \tag{36}$$

Likewise, $W^A(\theta, M)$ must satisfy the Bellman equation

$$r \, W^A = -\theta \, M - \lambda \, M \, W_M^A + \alpha \, \theta W_\theta^A + \tfrac{1}{2} \sigma^2 \, \theta^2 \, W_{\theta\theta}^A. \tag{37}$$

---

[15]Note that the policy might entail a *flow* of sunk costs over time (for example, expenditures for insulation on all new homes). All that matters is that adopting the policy implies a commitment to this flow of costs, so that we can replace the flow with its present value at the time of adoption. Also, if $B(M_t, \theta_t)$ is linear as in equation (33), it is always optimal to reduce E_t to zero if is optimal to reduce it at all.

These equations must be solved subject to the following boundary conditions:

$$W^N(0, M) = 0, \tag{38}$$

$$W^N(\theta^*, M) = W^A(\theta^*, M) - K, \tag{39}$$

$$W_\theta^N(\theta^*, M) = W_\theta^A(\theta^*, M), \tag{40}$$

where θ^* is the critical value of θ at or above which the policy should be adopted. In this case we can "guess" at a solution and then determine whether it works. The reader can confirm that the solutions for W^N and W^A are given by

$$W^N(\theta, M) = A\theta^\beta - \frac{\theta M}{r + \lambda - \alpha} - \frac{\gamma E \theta}{(r - \alpha)(r + \lambda - \alpha)}, \tag{41}$$

and

$$W^A(\theta, M) = -\frac{\theta M}{r + \lambda - \alpha}, \tag{42}$$

where A is a positive constant to be determined, and, from boundary condition (38), β is the positive root of the quadratic equation $\frac{1}{2}\sigma^2\beta(\beta-1)+\alpha\beta-r = 0$, that is,

$$\beta = \frac{1}{2} - \frac{\alpha}{\sigma^2} + \sqrt{\left(\frac{\alpha}{\sigma^2} - \frac{1}{2}\right)^2 + \frac{2r}{\sigma^2}} > 1. \tag{43}$$

W^N, the present value function that applies before adoption of the policy, has three components. The first term on the right-hand side of (41) is the value of the option to adopt the policy at some time in the future. The second term is the present value of the flow of social cost resulting from the current stock of pollutant, M. The third term is the present value of the flow of social cost that would result if emissions continued at the rate E forever. (Note that this social cost is reduced by the value of the option to reduce emissions, that is, the first term.) Once the policy has been adopted, $E = 0$ and W^A applies. Then the only social cost is from the current stock of pollutant.

There are still two unknowns, the constant A and the critical value θ^* at which the policy should be adopted, and they are determined from boundary conditions (39) and (40):

$$A = \left(\frac{\beta - 1}{K}\right)^{\beta-1}\left[\frac{\gamma E}{(r - \alpha)(r + \lambda - \alpha)\beta}\right]^\beta, \tag{44}$$

$$\theta^* = \left(\frac{K}{\beta - 1}\right)\left[\frac{(r - \alpha)(r + \lambda - \alpha)\beta}{\gamma E}\right]. \tag{45}$$

We can now see how the optimal timing of policy adoption depends on the degree of uncertainty over future costs and benefits, as well as other parameters. First, note that an increase in σ implies a decrease in β and hence an increase in θ^*. As we would expect, the greater the uncertainty over the future social cost of the pollutant, the greater the incentive to wait rather than adopt the policy now, and hence the greater must be the current cost in order to trigger adoption. Second, an increase in the discount rate r increases the value of the option to adopt the policy and thus also increases θ^*. This is analogous to the effect of a change in the interest rate on the value and optimal exercise point for a financial option; an increase in r implies a reduction in the present value of the cost K of policy adoption, so that the option to adopt is worth more but it should be exercised later. Third, an increase in λ, the rate of "depreciation" of the stock of pollutant, also increases θ^*; a higher λ implies that the environmental damage from emissions is less irreversible, so that the sunk benefit of adopting the policy now rather than waiting is reduced. Finally, an increase in the initial rate of emissions E reduces θ^*; the reason is that if E is higher, the social cost of waiting is higher, and since the cost K of adopting the policy is fixed, it pays to adopt earlier.

It is probably unrealistic, however, to assume that the cost of reducing emissions from E to zero is independent of E. The cost K should certainly be an increasing function of E, and probably convex in E. As a first approximation, however, we can assume that K is proportional to E:

$$K = kE. \tag{46}$$

In this case, θ^* becomes

$$\theta^* = \frac{k(r - \alpha)(r + \lambda - \alpha)\beta}{\gamma(\beta - 1)}. \tag{47}$$

Then, θ^* is independent of E. Also, in this case, we would never want to reduce emissions by anything less than 100 percent (assuming we would want to reduce them at all). The reason is that the value of the option to adopt the policy, $A\theta^\beta$, is independent of M and linear in E, so that W^N and W^A are linear in M and E.

A numerical example will illustrate this calculation and indicate the magnitudes involved. Suppose $\alpha = 0$ (so that the expected social cost per unit of M is constant), $r = \lambda = 0.02$, $\sigma = 0.20$, $\gamma = 1$, $E = 100{,}000$ tons per year, $\theta_0 = \$20$ per ton, and $K = \$2$ billion. Then $\beta = 1.62$,

$A = 7,681,000$, and $\theta^* = \$42$ per ton. Hence at the current value of $\theta_0 = 20$, the policy should not be adopted, but the value of society's option to adopt it, $A\theta^\beta$, is \$0.64 billion. The policy should only be adopted when θ reaches \$42 per ton; then $A\theta^\beta = \$2.1$ billion, and the reader can check that boundary conditions (39) and (40) are satisfied. We leave it to the reader to go through the calculations for, say, $\sigma = 0.4$, and show that it leads to a larger critical value θ^*.

Figure 12.2 shows the solution graphically for $M = 0$ (so that $W^A = 0$ for all values of θ). Note that θ^* is found at the point of tangency of W^N with the line $W^A - K$. [If M were greater than zero, we would have $W^A = -\theta M/(r + \lambda - \alpha)$, so we would simply rotate both $W^N(\theta)$ and the line $W^A - K$ downwards.] Figure 12.3 shows how the solution in Figure 12.2 changes

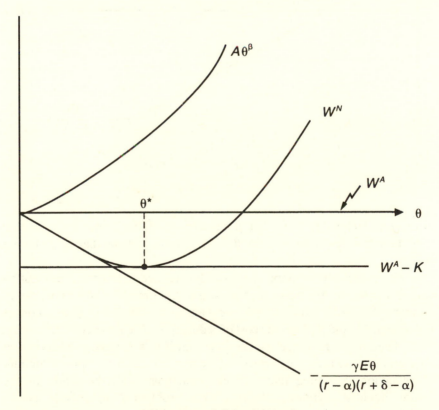

Figure 12.2. *Solution for $M = 0$*

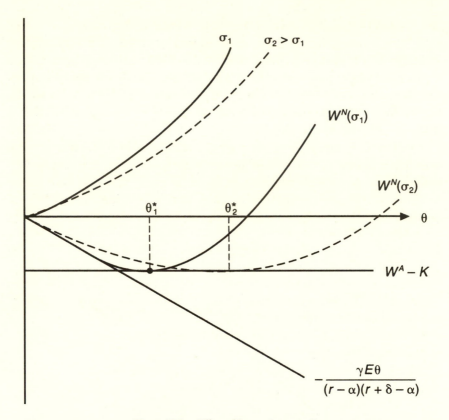

Figure 12.3. *Effect of Increasing σ on θ**

when σ is increased. Note that β falls to a number closer to 1, so that $A\theta^{\beta}$ becomes less convex, and $W^{N}(\theta)$ flattens out so that θ^{*} becomes larger.

This model is very simple, and is only intended to illustrate how option value can arise in public policy problems, as well as firms' investment problems. To make the model more realistic, we want to specify $B(M_t, \theta_t)$ as a convex function of M_t, and perhaps the cost of reducing E_t, $k(E)$, as a convex function of E. Then it will no longer be the case that if it is optimal to reduce E at all, it is optimal to reduce it to zero, and we could consider the optimal amount of reduction, assuming that further reductions could be made in the future should θ_t increase sufficiently. The problem then becomes exactly analogous to the incremental investment problems that we examined in Chapter 11.

4 Explaining Aggregate Investment Behavior

The explanation of aggregate and sectoral investment spending has been one of the less successful endeavors in empirical economics. For the most part, econometric models have not been very useful for explaining or predicting investment spending. The problem is not just that these models have been unable to explain and predict more than a small portion of the movements of investment. In addition, constructed quantities that in theory should have strong explanatory power—such as Tobin's q, or various measures of the cost of capital—in practice do not.[16]

The irreversibility of most investment expenditures may help to explain why neoclassical investment theory has failed to provide good empirical models of investment behavior. Effects of risk are typically handled by assuming that a risk premium (obtained, say, from the CAPM) can be added to the discount rate used to calculate the present value of a project. However, as we have seen throughout this book, the correct discount rate cannot be obtained without actually solving the option valuation problem, the discount rate need not be constant over time, and it need not equal the firm's average cost of capital. As a result, simple cost of capital measures may be poor explanators of investment spending.

4.A Models Based on Tobin's q

The problems that arise when irreversibility is ignored can be seen in the context of models based on Tobin's q. A good example is the model of Abel and Blanchard (1986), which is one of the more sophisticated attempts to explain investment in a q-theory framework; it uses a carefully constructed measure for marginal rather than average q, incorporates delivery lags and costs of adjustment, and explicitly models expectations of future values of explanatory variables. However, it does not treat irreversibility and option values. We will briefly review its structure.

The model is based on the standard NPV rule, "invest in the marginal unit of capital if the present discounted value of the expected flow of profits resulting from the unit is at least equal to the cost of the unit." Let $\pi_t(K_t, I_t)$ be the maximum value of profits at time t, given the capital stock K_t and investment level I_t, that is, it is the value of profits assuming that variable factors are used optimally. It depends on I_t because of costs of adjustment;

---

[16]For overviews and comparisons of traditional approaches to the econometric modelling of investment spending, see Chirinko (1991) and Kopcke (1985, 1993).

$\partial \pi / \partial I < 0$, and $\partial^2 \pi / \partial I^2 < 0$, that is, the more rapidly new capital is purchased and installed, the more costly it is. (See Chapter 11 for a discussion of adjustment costs.) Then the present value of current and future profits is given by

$$V_t = \mathcal{E}_t \sum_{j=0}^{\infty} \left[\prod_{i=0}^{j} (1 + \rho_{t+i})^{-1} \right] \pi_{t+j}(K_{t+j}, I_{t+j}), \qquad (48)$$

where ρ is the discount rate. Maximizing this with respect to I_t, subject to

$$K_t = (1 - \lambda) K_{t-1} + I_t,$$

(where λ is the depreciation rate), gives the following marginal condition:

$$- \mathcal{E}_t (\partial \pi_t / \partial I_t) = q_t, \qquad (49)$$

where

$$q_t = \mathcal{E}_t \sum_{j=0}^{\infty} \left[\prod_{i=0}^{j} (1 + \rho_{t+i})^{-1} \right] \left(\frac{\partial \pi_{t+j}}{\partial K_{t+j}} \right) (1 - \lambda)^j. \qquad (50)$$

Recall our discussions of q in Chapter 11. What we have here is marginal q; it pertains to the contribution of the marginal unit of capital being installed. However, it does not consider the effect of this unit on the whole value of the firm. Only the present value of the profit flows contributed by this unit is computed, and the opportunity cost of exercising the option to make this investment is ignored. Also, it is not expressed as a ratio to the purchase cost. Thus in the terminology used in Chapter 11, this is the marginal, value-of-assets-in-place, absolute concept of Tobin's q.

Equation (49) says that investment occurs up to the point where the cost of an additional unit of capital equals the present value of the expected flow of incremental profits resulting from the unit. Abel and Blanchard estimate both linear and quadratic approximations to q_t, and use vector autoregressive representations of ρ_t and $\partial \pi_t / \partial K_t$ to model expectations of future values. Their conclusion is simple and stark: "our data are not sympathetic to the basic restrictions imposed by the q theory, even extended to allow for simple delivery lags."

Throughout this book we have emphasized what amounts to a very different extension of the q theory, namely, one that recognizes the opportunity cost of exercising an option to invest. Abel and Blanchard's data for ρ_t are based on a weighted average of the rates of return on equity and debt. However, in our approach the discount rates ρ_t need not equal the average cost of capital. Instead, they can only be determined as part of the solution to the firm's optimal investment problem, and this involves valuing the firm's options to make (irreversible) marginal investments now or in the future. Thus the solution to the investment problem is more complicated than the first-order condition given by equations (49) and (50). For example, consider a project that has zero systematic risk. The use of a risk-free rate for ρ would lead to much too large a value for q_t, and might suggest that an investment expenditure should be made when in fact it should be delayed. Furthermore, there is no simple way to adjust ρ properly. The problem is that the calculation ignores the opportunity cost of exercising the option to invest.

Unfortunately, incorporating irreversibility into econometric models of aggregate investment spending is not simple. As we have seen, the equations describing optimal investment decisions are nonlinear, even for simple cases. Also, it can be difficult to measure (or statistically identify) the variables or parameters that reflect key components of risk. Additional problems arise if we want to explain the long-run equilibrium effects of uncertainty on investment spending. Although we know that irreversibility and uncertainty should raise the threshold (for example, the expected rate of return on a project) required for a firm to invest, we can say very little about the effects of uncertainty on the firm's *long-run average* rate of investment or average capital stock without making restrictive functional or parametric assumptions. We will say more about this below, but it means that tests cannot be based on simple equilibrium relationships between rates of investment and measures of risk, whether for firms, industries, or countries.

Finally, there are serious problems of aggregation. Our theory of optimal investment decisions applies most directly to a firm or similar decisionmaking unit. Different firms can have different technologies or managerial abilities, and they may be subject to different (idiosyncratic) shocks. Then they will have different action thresholds. Moreover, historical accidents may leave different firms with stocks of capital that are differently situated relative to their action thresholds. If our data pertain to industry aggregates, we must first develop the implications of our theory at the industry level before we can test them. If we wish to conduct the empirical analysis at the level of the micro decision units, we need data and specifications that can identify all these differences. All of this is a very difficult task. In the next section we will review some work that takes different approaches to it.

4.B Empirical Implications of Option Based Models

The models developed in this book suggest a much greater role for uncertainty as a determinant of investment than do traditional models. We saw in

Chapters 8 and 9 that although the mechanisms are different, for both a competitive industry and for a monopolist firm, uncertainty affects investment by affecting a critical threshold that triggers investment. That critical threshold can apply to the value of a completed project, to the price of the project's output, or, in the case of incremental investment, to the marginal profitability of capital. Through a variety of models, we saw that this threshold can be very sensitive to the volatility of the underlying stochastic state variable.

These models must be developed further to draw out their empirically testable implications. First, it is important to emphasize that the models do not describe investment per se, but rather the critical threshold required to trigger investment. In Chapter 11, for example, investment is implicitly defined as a stochastic process that will control the value of the marginal product of capital at a certain barrier. The models tell us that if volatility increases, the threshold increases. Only to the extent that we can also describe (or make assumptions about) the distribution across firms of the values of potential projects, or of the marginal profitability of capital, can we also derive a structural model that relates volatility to actual investment.

Without going this far, we can draw some inferences about how investment should respond in the short run to changes in volatility and other parameters. For example, a one-time increase in volatility should reduce investment at least temporarily, as project values that were above or close to what was a lower critical threshold are now below a higher one. Also, we have seen that holding everything else equal, an increase in the drift of, say, the output price lowers the critical threshold, and hence should be accompanied by an increase in investment, again in the short run. In the context of incremental investment at the firm or competitive industry level, increases in the volatility of the marginal profitability of capital, or decreases in its average growth rate, should lead to at least a temporary decrease in investment.

There is very little that can be said, however, about the effects of uncertainty on the long-run equilibrium values of investment, the investment-to-output ratio, or the capital-output ratio. To see this, note that although we know that an increase in volatility raises the *required return* needed to trigger investment, we do not know what it will do to the *average realized return*. The reason is that the firm requires a higher return to invest when volatility is higher, but it does so exactly because it is more likely to encounter periods of very low returns (when it will find itself holding more capital than it needs).

The same indeterminacy applies to the investment-to-output ratio, I/Q. In long-run equilibrium, we have $I/Q = \lambda K P_K / Q(K) P = (P_K/P) \cdot (\lambda K / Q(K))$, where λ is the depreciation rate. If the volatility of the marginal revenue product of capital increases, the required return increases, and investment falls for any given set of prices, so that the price of output P rises and P_K/P falls. Suppose the production technology is Cobb-Douglas with constant returns. Then $\lambda K / Q(K) = \lambda / A L^\alpha K^{-\alpha}$ rises. These two effects work in opposite directions, so we are unable to conclude what will happen to I/Q. Another way to see this is to note that, as before, an increase in volatility results in a higher threshold but also a greater frequency in which the firm holds more capital than it needs, so that the productivity of capital could fall on average, that is, I/Q could rise. Hence we cannot claim on theoretical grounds that countries with more volatile or more unstable economies should have, on average, lower ratios of investment to gross domestic proudct (GDP) or lower capital-output ratios than countries with more stable economies. In very specific models, for example the Cobb-Douglas case of Chapter 11, we do get clear results, but then their robustness is subject to question.

4.C Empirical Evidence

Given the difficulties outlined above, it is not surprising that there have been few attempts to statistically test the theory of irreversible investment under uncertainty. Here we briefly summarize some of the limited work that has been done to date.

One approach is to focus on the threshold that triggers investment, and see whether it depends on measures of risk in ways that the theory predicts. This has the advantage that the relationship between the threshold and risk is much easier to pin down than the relationship between investment and risk. The disadvantage is that the threshold cannot be observed directly. This approach was used in a recent study by Caballero and Pindyck (1992) of U.S. manufacturing industries. Caballero and Pindyck derived an expression for the required return needed to trigger investment in a competitive market with free entry, constant returns to scale, and a Cobb-Douglas production technology. They then framed tests in terms of this required return. Although the required return cannot be observed directly, one can obtain a proxy for it by using extreme values of the marginal profitability of capital — for example, the maximum over some period of time, or an average of the values in the highest decile or quintile. Caballero and Pindyck showed that for U.S. manufacturing data, such proxies indeed show a positive dependence on the volatility of the marginal profitability of capital, as the theory predicts.

Another approach is to examine how period-to-period movements in volatility affect investment. Pindyck and Solimano (1993) did this for a cross section of 30 countries, calculating a 28-year time series for the marginal profitability of capital for each country (again, assuming a Cobb-Douglas production technology with constant returns). They divided the sample up into three subperiods of nine years each, calculated the mean and sample standard deviation of annual log changes in the marginal profitability of capital, and the average investment-to-GDP ratio, for each subperiod and each country. They then ran panel regressions to determine the dependence of the investment-to-GDP ratio on this mean and standard deviation in each period. They found that the investment ratio indeed varies positively with the mean and negatively with the standard deviation, as the theory predicts.[17]

These studies are quite limited in scope. More ambitious "structural" models of investment spending, and of other irreversible decisions like spending on research and development, attempt to estimate the optimality conditions of the full stochastic dynamic programming problem, using method-of-moments estimators. The work of Rust (1987) is among the best known examples of this; pioneering attempts to use such methods in industrial organization include Pakes (1986). This is a promising approach, but still in early stages. Serious difficulties of specification and computation are only gradually being resolved. Specific applications often run up against unobserved state variables, and the approach can accommodate only very limited kinds of persistence over time (serial correlation) among these. The equilibrium of interactions among different firms poses further difficulties. Computational requirements remain formidable, although improvements in that technology are so rapid that this is not likely to remain an obstacle for long. Discussion of these matters would need at least one chapter and probably a monograph of its own. Therefore we merely refer interested readers to the very good surveys of the state of this art by Rust (1993) and Pakes (1993).

Short of full structural models, but more advanced in its attempt to tackle aggregation, is the work of Bertola and Caballero (1990, 1992). The first of these papers considers the demand for consumer durables. These are, of course, investment decisions. Grossman and Laroque (1990) had pointed out that a consumer facing transaction costs of purchase and resale would optimally follow threshold rules for the decision to purchase or trade durables like houses or automobiles. In the economy as a whole, different consumers have different thresholds and different historically determined initial positions

---

[17]In related work, Pindyck (1986, 1991a) studied aggregate U.S. investment using stock market data, on the grounds that when product markets become more volatile, stock prices should also become more volatile. This was indeed the case, for example, during the recessions of 1975 and 1980, and most dramatically during the Great Depression. He found that investment spending is negatively and significantly related to the variance of stock returns, even after accounting for the effects of mean returns, long- and short-term interest rates, and the growth rate of GNP.

relative to these thresholds. They are also subject to different (idiosyncratic) shocks as well as some common (economy-wide) shocks. Aggregation smooths out some of the all-or-nothing aspect of the threshold decision rules, but leaves substantial serial correlation in the aggregate expenditures on durables. In fact their simulations have such realistic time-series properties that Andrew Caplin, discussing their paper, concluded: "Bertola and Caballero have left us with the unusual problem of trying to rationalize a surprisingly successful empirical exercise." However, this is not a systematic econometric test of the real options hypothesis against specified alternatives.[18]

The gap between theory and empiricism in this area can be viewed in two ways. One would be a mixture of concern and skepticism — concern that theory has run ahead without empirical support (as indeed it often does), and hence skepticism about its validity. The other view is as an opportunity and challenge. The theory has several implications that are borne out in the real world, and throughout this book we have tried to spell them out at every available opportunity. We obtained numerical solutions for many of our models, using values for parameters such as the variance of the stochastic shocks that were representative of specific actual commodities or industries. We found qualitative implications, and several approximate quantitative ones, that conform to experience—the high hurdle rates used by business firms when they judge investment projects, the relative inefficacy of interest rate cuts as policies to stimulate investment, the significant and detrimental effect of policy uncertainty on investment, and so on. Thus there is much prima facie evidence that attests to the merit and significance of the theory. Then more serious empirical testing becomes a research opportunity. We hope that our book will spread and improve the understanding of the theory, and indirectly contribute to the progress of research on the empirical side.

5   Guide to the Literature

The use of option pricing models to value offshore oil reserves and determine when they should be developed was pioneered by Paddock, Siegel, and Smith (1988). Siegel, Smith, and Paddock (1987) provide a nontechnical exposition of their model and its application. The first section of this chapter draws heavily from these two articles. A predecessor is the study by Tourhinho (1979),

---

[18]Other good and promising empirical studies of consumer durables are Eberly (1991) and Lam (1989).

which first showed that resource reserves can be understood and valued as options. Related studies include Ekern (1985), Stensland and Tjostheim (1989, 1991), Jacoby and Laughton (1992), and Lund (1992). The book edited by Lund and Øksendal (1991) contains some general theory of real options in the context of natural resources, and some empirical studies of oil, fisheries, etc. Also, Morck, Schwartz, and Stangeland (1989), use these techniques to value forestry resources, and Brennan and Schwartz (1985) use them to value a copper mine and determine the rules for temporary closing or permanent abandonment. Applications have also appeared recently in the petroleum engineering literature [see, for example, Lohrenz and Dickens (1993) and Stibolt and Lehman (1993)] and on urban land valuation [see Quigg (1993)].

When examining an electric utility's problem of complying with the Clean Air Act, we did not discuss the numerical solution method, and we reviewed the characteristics of the solution and their dependence on various parameters only briefly. Interested readers can refer to Herbelot's (1992) thesis for more detail. Also, a related study is Martzoukos and Teplitz-Sembitzky (1992), which examines the implications of uncertainty over the future demand for electricity for investments in new transmission lines.

In Section 3 we examined the timing of environmental policy, and saw how the irreversibility of environmental damage creates an option value that can bias a traditional cost-benefit analysis against policy adoption. This option value was first noted by Arrow and Fisher (1974), Henry (1974a,b), and Krutilla and Fisher (1975), and has been elaborated upon by Hanemann (1989), Fisher and Hanemann (1987), and Lund (1991), among others.[19] Recent studies that are related to the analysis in Section 3 include Kolstad (1992) and Hendricks (1992). Kolstad developed a three-period model with learning about the net benefits from a lower stock of pollutant. He showed that with no sunk cost of policy adoption, the faster the rate of learning, the lower the first-period emission level should be, but if the costs of policy adoption are partly sunk, the effect of uncertainty is ambiguous. Also, Hendricks (1992) used a continuous-time model of global warming to study the timing of policies to irreversibly reduce emissions, allowing for a (partially) irreversible accumulation of the pollutant. He considered uncertainty over a parameter linking the global mean temperature to the atmospheric GHG concentration, allowed for learning by letting uncertainty

---

[19]This concept of option value should be distinguished from that of Schmalensee (1972), which is more like a risk premium needed to compensate risk-averse consumers because of uncertainty over future valuations of an environmental amenity. For a discussion of this latter concept, see Plummer and Hartman (1986).

over this parameter fall over time, and showed how the speed of learning affects the timing of policy. Finally, for a simple model of GHG emissions and global warming (the model on which the Hendricks study is based), see Nordhaus (1991).

Recent empirical research on irreversible investment includes Bizer and Sichel (1988) and Caballero (1991b). The latter, along with Bertola and Caballero (1990, 1992) is important in its development of aggregation when firm-specific and industry-wide shocks coexist. Empirical work using micro data, which aims to estimate the structural dynamic programming models of individual choice, is surveyed by Rust (1993) and Pakes (1993).

References

Abel, Andrew B. 1983. "Optimal Investment Under Uncertainty." *American Economic Review* 73 (March): 228–233.

_____. 1984. "The Effects of Uncertainty on Investment and the Expected Long-Run Capital Stock." *Journal of Economic Dynamics and Control* 7, 39–53.

_____. 1990. "Consumption and Investment." In *Handbook of Monetary Economics*, eds. Benjamin Friedman and Frank Hahn. New York: North-Holland.

_____, and Olivier J. Blanchard. 1986. "The Present Value of Profits and Cyclical Movements in Investment." *Econometrica* 54 (March): 249–273.

_____, and Janice C. Eberly. 1993. "A Unified Model of Investment Under Uncertainty." Unpublished working paper, The Wharton School, University of Pennsylvania, February.

Abramowitz, Milton, and Irene A. Stegun, eds. 1964. *Handbook of Mathematical Functions*. Washington D.C.: National Bureau of Standards.

Aitchison, J., and J.A.C. Brown. 1957. *The Lognormal Distribution*. Cambridge, England: Cambridge University Press.

Aizenman, Joshua, and Nancy Marion. 1991. "Policy Uncertainty, Persistence and Growth." NBER Working Paper No. 3848, September.

Akerlof, George A. 1970. "The Market for Lemons: Qualitative Uncertainty and the Market Mechanism." *Quarterly Journal of Economics* 84 (November): 488–500.

Appelbaum, Elie, and Chin Lim. 1985. "Contestable Markets Under Uncertainty." *Rand Journal of Economics* 16, Spring, 28–40.

Arnold, Ludwig. 1974. *Stochastic Differential Equations: Theory and Applications*. New York: John Wiley & Sons.

Arrow, Kenneth J. 1968. "Optimal Capital Policy with Irreversible Investment." In *Value, Capital and Growth, Essays in Honor of Sir John Hicks*, ed. James N. Wolfe. Edinburgh, Scotland: Edinburgh University Press.

————. 1970. *Essays in the Theory of Risk Bearing*. Amsterdam: North-Holland.

————, and Anthony C. Fisher. 1974. "Environmental Preservation, Uncertainty, and Irreversibility." *Quarterly Journal of Economics* 88, 312–319.

Arthur, W. Brian. 1986. "Industry Location Patterns and the Importance of History." Paper No. 84, Center for Economic Policy Research, Stanford University.

Baldwin, Carliss Y. 1982. "Optimal Sequential Investment when Capital is Not Readily Reversible." *Journal of Finance* 37 (June): 763–782.

Baldwin, Richard, and Paul Krugman. 1989. "Persistent Trade Effects of Large Exchange Rate Shocks." *Quarterly Journal of Economics* 104 (November): 635–654.

Bar-Ilan, Avner, and William C. Strange. 1992. "Investment Lags." Working Paper, Tel-Aviv University and University of British Columbia.

Becker, Gary S. 1962. "Investment in Human Capital: A Theoretical Analysis." *Journal of Political Economy*, 70, Supplement (October): 9–49.

————. 1975. *Human Capital*, second edition. New York: NBER and Columbia University Press.

————. 1980. *A Treatise on the Family*. Cambridge, MA: Harvard University Press.

Beddington, John R., and Robert M. May. 1977. "Harvesting Natural Populations in a Randomly Fluctuating Environment." *Science* 197, 463–465.

Bentolila, Samuel, and Giuseppe Bertola. 1990. "Firing Costs and Labor Demand: How Bad is Eurosclerosis?" *Review of Economic Studies* 57 (July): 381–402.

Bernanke, Ben S. 1983. "Irreversibility, Uncertainty, and Cyclical Investment." *Quarterly Journal of Economics* 98 (February): 85–106.

Bernstein, Peter L. 1992. *Capital Ideas: The Improbable Origins of Modern Wall Street*. New York: Free Press.

Bertola, Giuseppe. 1988. *Adjustment Costs and Dynamic Factor Demands: Investment and Employment Under Uncertainty*. Ph.D. Dissertation, Cambridge, MA: Massachusetts Institute of Technology.

————. 1989. "Irreversible Investment." Unpublished working paper, Princeton University.

_____, and Ricardo J. Caballero. 1990. "Kinked Adjustment Costs and Aggregate Dynamics." In *NBER Macroeconomics Annual 1990*, eds. Olivier Blanchard and Stanley Fischer. Cambridge, MA: MIT Press, 237–295.

_____, and _____. 1992. "Irreversibility and Aggregate Investment." Unpublished, Princeton University, June.

Bizer, David S., and Daniel E. Sichel. 1988. "Irreversible Investment: An Empirical Investigation." Unpublished, December.

Black, Fischer, and Myron Scholes. 1973. "The Pricing of Options and Corporate Liabilities." *Journal of Political Economy* 81, 637–659.

Bliss, Christopher J. 1968. "On Putty-Clay." *Review of Economic Studies* 35 (April): 105–132.

Bodie, Zvi, and Victor Rosanski. 1980. "Risk and Return in Commodity Futures." *Financial Analysts Journal* 36 (May): 27–40.

Brealey, Richard A., and Stewart C. Myers. 1992. *Principles of Corporate Finance*, fourth edition. New York: McGraw-Hill.

Brennan, Michael J. 1991. "The Price of Convenience and the Valuation of Commodity Contingent Claims." In *Stochastic Models and Option Values*, eds. D. Lund and B. Øksendal, New York: North-Holland.

_____, and Eduardo S. Schwartz. 1978. "Finite Difference Methods and Jump Processes Arising in the Pricing of Contingent Claims: A Synthesis." *Journal of Financial and Quantitative Analysis* 20, 461–473.

_____, and _____. 1985. "Evaluating Natural Resource Investments." *Journal of Business* 58 (January): 135–157.

Brock, William A., Michael Rothschild, and Joseph E. Stiglitz. 1988. "Stochastic Capital Theory." In *Joan Robinson and Modern Economic Theory*, ed. George R. Ferwel. New York: Macmillan.

Caballero, Ricardo J. 1991a. "Competition and the Non-Robustness of the Investment-Uncertainty Relationship." *American Economic Review* 81 (March): 279–288.

_____. 1991b. "On the Dynamics of Aggregate Investment." Discussion Paper No. 541, Columbia University, May.

_____, and Robert S. Pindyck. 1992. "Uncertainty, Investment, and Industry Evolution." NBER Working Paper No. 4160, September.

Carr, Peter. 1988. "The Valuation of Sequential Exchange Opportunities." *Journal of Finance* 43 (December): 1235–1256.

Carrier, George F., and Carl E. Pearson. 1976. *Partial Differential Equations: Theory and Technique*. New York: Academic Press.

Chirinko, Robert. 1991. "Business Fixed Investment Spending: A Critical Survey." Draft working paper, University of Chicago.

Chow, Gregory C. 1979. "Optimal Control of Stochastic Differential Equation Systems." *Journal of Economic Dynamics and Control* 1 (May): 143–175.

Clark, Colin W. 1976. *Mathematical Bioeconomics*. New York: John Wiley & Sons.

Copeland, Tom, Tim Koller, and Jack Murrin. 1991. *Valuation: Measuring and Managing the Value of Companies*. New York: John Wiley & Sons.

Cox, D. R., and H. D. Miller. 1965. *The Theory of Stochastic Processes*. London: Chapman and Hall.

Cox, John C., Jonathan E. Ingersoll, Jr., and Stephen A. Ross. 1985. "A Theory of the Term Structure of Interest Rates." *Econometrica* 53 (March): 385–407.

————, and Stephen A. Ross. 1976. "The Valuation of Options for Alternative Stochastic Processes." *Journal of Financial Economics* 3, 145–166.

————, ————, and Mark Rubinstein. 1979. "Option Pricing: A Simplified Approach." *Journal of Financial Economics* 7, 229–263.

————, and Mark Rubinstein. 1985. *Options Markets*. Englewood Cliffs, NJ: Prentice-Hall.

Craine, Roger. 1989. "Risky Business: The Allocation of Capital." *Journal of Monetary Economics* 23, 201–218.

Cukierman, Alex. 1980. "The Effects of Uncertainty on Investment under Risk Neutrality with Endogenous Information." *Journal of Political Economy* 88 (June): 462–475.

David, Paul A. 1985. "Clio and the Economics of QWERTY." *American Economic Review* 75, Papers and Proceedings (May): 332-337.

————. 1988. "Path-Dependence: Putting the Past into the Future of Economics." IMSSS Technical Report No. 533, Stanford University.

Davis, Steven J. and John Haltiwanger. 1990. "Gross Job Creation and Destruction: Microeconomic Evidence and Macroeconomic Implications." In *NBER Macroeconomics Annual 1990*, eds. Olivier Blanchard and Stanley Fischer, Cambridge, MA: MIT Press, 123–186.

Demers, Michel. 1991. "Investment Under Uncertainty, Irreversibility and the Arrival of Information Over Time." *Review of Economic Studies* 58 (April): 333–350.

Dertouzas, Michael, Richard K. Lester, and Robert Solow. 1990. *Made in America*. New York: Harper Paperback Edition.

Dickey, David A., and Wayne A. Fuller. 1981. "Likelihood Ratio Statistics for Autoregressive Time Series with a Unit Root." *Econometrica* 49, 1057–1072.

Dixit, Avinash. 1988. "Optimal Lay-up and Scrapping Decisions." Unpublished, Princeton University, July.

————. 1989a. "Entry and Exit Decisions under Uncertainty." *Journal of Political Economy* 97 (June): 620–638.

————. 1989b. "Hysteresis, Import Penetration, and Exchange Rate Pass-Through." *Quarterly Journal of Economics* 104 (May): 205–228.

————. 1989c. "Intersectoral Capital Reallocation Under Price Uncertainty." *Journal of International Economics* 26 (May): 309–325.

————. 1990. *Optimization in Economic Theory*, second edition. Oxford, UK: Oxford University Press.

————. 1991a. "Analytical Approximations in Models of Hysteresis." *Review of Economic Studies* 58 (January): 141–151.

————. 1991b. "Irreversible Investment with Price Ceilings." *Journal of Political Economy* 99 (June): 541–557.

————. 1991c. "A Simplified Treatment of the Theory of Optimal Control of Brownian Motion." *Journal of Economic Dynamics and Control* 15 (October): 657–673.

————. 1992. "Investment and Hysteresis." *Journal of Economic Perspectives* 6, Winter, 107–132.

————. 1993a. *The Art of Smooth Pasting*, Vol. 55 in *Fundamentals of Pure and Applied Economics*, eds. Jacques Lesourne and Hugo Sonnenschein. Chur, Switzerland: Harwood Academic Publishers.

————. 1993b. "Irreversible Investment and Competition Under Uncertainty." In *Capital, Investment, and Development*, eds. Kaushik Basu, Mukul Majumdar, and Tapan Mitra. Cambridge, MA: Basil Blackwell, forthcoming.

————. 1993c. "Irreversible Investment with Uncertainty and Scale Economies." *Journal of Economic Dynamics and Control*, forthcoming.

————, and Rafael Rob. 1993a. "Switching Costs and Sectoral Adjustments in General Equilibrium with Uninsured Risk." *Journal of Economic Theory*, forthcoming.

————, and ————. 1993b. "Risk-sharing, Adjustment, and Trade." *Journal of International Economics*, forthcoming.

Dothan, Michael U. 1990. *Prices in Financial Markets*. New York: Oxford University Press.

Dreyfus, Stuart E. 1965. *Dynamic Programming and the Calculus of Variations*. New York: Academic Press.

Duffie, Darrell. 1988. *Securities Markets: Stochastic Models*. San Diego, CA: Academic Press.

————. 1992. *Dynamic Asset Pricing Theory*. Princeton, NJ: Princeton University Press.

————, and Chi-fu Huang. 1985. "Implementing Arrow-Debreu Equilibria by Continuous Trading of a Few Long-Lived Securities." *Econometrica* 53, 1337–1356.

Dumas, Bernard. 1991. "Super Contact and Related Optimality Conditions." *Journal of Economic Dynamics and Control* 15, 675–695.

————. 1992. "Dynamic Equilibrium and the Real Exchange Rate in a Spatially Separated World." *Review of Financial Studies*, 5(2), 153–180.

Dutta, Prajit K., and Aldo Rustichini. 1991. "A Theory of Stopping Time Games with Applications to Product Innovation and Asset Sales." Discussion Paper No. 523, Department of Economics, Columbia University.

Eberly, Janice C. 1991. "Adjustment of Consumers' Durables Stocks: Evidence from Automobile Purchases." Working Paper No. 22–91, Rodney L. White Center for Financial Research, University of Pennsylvania.

Edleson, Michael and Kent Osband. 1988. "Competitive Markets with Irreversible Investment." Unpublished, Rand Corporation, Santa Monica, CA.

Eisner, Robert, and R. Strotz. 1963. "Determinants of Investment Behavior." In *Impact of Monetary Policy*. Englewood Cliffs, NJ: Prentice-Hall.

Ekern S. 1985. "An Option Pricing Approach to Evaluating Petroleum Projects." *Energy Economics*, 10, 91–99.

Fasano, A. and M. Primicerio (eds.). 1983. *Free Boundary Value Problems: Theory and Applications*, Vols. I, II. Marshfield, MA: Pitman Publishing Company.

Feller, William. 1968. *An Introduction to Probability Theory and Its Applications*, Volume I, third edition. New York: John Wiley & Sons.

————. 1971. *An Introduction to Probability Theory and Its Applications*, Volume II, second edition. New York: John Wiley & Sons.

Feynman, Richard P. 1949. "Space-Time Approach to Quantum Electrodynamics." *Physical Review* 76, 769.

Fine, Charles H., and Robert M. Freund. 1990. "Optimal Investment in Product-Flexible Manufacturing Capacity." *Management Science* 36 (April): 449–466.

Fisher, Anthony C., and W. Michael Hanemann. 1987. "Quasi-Option Value: Some Misconceptions Dispelled." *Journal of Environmental Economics and Management* 14 (July): 183–190.

Fleming, Wendell H., and Raymond W. Rishel. 1975. *Deterministic and Stochastic Optimal Control*. New York: Springer-Verlag.

Fudenberg, Drew, and Jean Tirole. 1985. "Preemption and Rent Equalization in the Adoption of New Technology." *Review of Economic Studies* 52 (July): 383–401.

Geske, Robert. 1979. "The Valuation of Compound Options." *Journal of Financial Economics* 7 (March): 63–81.

———, and H. E. Johnson. 1984. "The American Put Option Valued Analytically." *Journal of Finance* 39 (December): 1511–1524.

———, and Kuldeep Shastri. 1985. "Valuation by Approximation: A Comparison of Alternative Option Valuation Techniques." *Journal of Financial and Quantitative Analysis* 20 (March): 45–71.

Gibson, Rajna, and Eduardo S. Schwartz. 1990. "Stochastic Convenience Yield and the Pricing of Oil Contingent Claims." *Journal of Finance* 45 (July): 959–976.

———, and ———. 1991. "Valuation of Long-Term Oil-Linked Assets." In *Stochastics Models and Option Values*, eds. D. Lund and B. Øksendal. New York: North-Holland.

Gilbert, Richard J. 1989. "Mobility Barriers and the Value of Incumbency." *Handbook of Industrial Organization*, Vol. I. New York: North-Holland.

Goel, S. and N. Richter-Dyn. 1974. *Stochastic Models in Biology*. New York: Academic Press.

Goncalves, Franklin D. 1992. "Optimal Chartering and Investment Policies for Bulk Shipping." Unpublished Ph.D. thesis, Department of Ocean Engineering, Massachusetts Institute of Technology, September.

Gould, John P. 1968. "Adjustment Costs in the Theory of Investment of the Firm." *Review of Economic Studies* 35 (January): 47–55.

Grossman, Gene M., and Carl Shapiro. 1986. "Optimal Dynamic R&D Programs." *Rand Journal of Economics* 17, Winter, 581–593.

Grossman, Sanford J., and Guy Laroque. 1990. "Asset Pricing and Optimal Portfolio Choice in the Presence of Illiquid Durable Consumption Goods." *Econometrica* (January): 58, 25–52.

Guenther, Ronald B. and John W. Lee. 1988. *Partial Differential Equations of Mathematical Physics and Integral Equations*. Englewood Cliffs, NJ: Prentice-Hall.

Haberman, Richard. 1987. *Elementary Applied Partial Differential Equations*, second edition. Englewood Cliffs, NJ: Prentice-Hall.

Hamermesh, Daniel S. and Neal M. Soss. 1974. "An Economic Theory of Suicide." *Journal of Political Economy*, 82 (February): 83–90.

Hanemann, W. Michael. 1989. "Information and the Concept of Option Value." *Journal of Environmental Economics and Management* 16 (January): 23–37.

Harris, Milton. 1987. *Dynamic Economic Analysis*. New York: Oxford University Press.

Harrison, J. Michael. 1985. *Brownian Motion and Stochastic Flow Systems*. New York: John Wiley & Sons.

————, and David Kreps. 1979. "Martingales and Arbitrage in Multiperiod Securities Markets." *Journal of Economic Theory* 20, 381–408.

————, and Michael I. Taksar. 1983. "Instantaneous Control of Brownian Motion." *Mathematics of Operations Research* 8, 439–453.

————, Thomas M. Sellke, and Allison J. Taylor. 1983. "Impulse Control of Brownian Motion." *Mathematics of Operations Research* 8, 454–466.

Hartman, Richard. 1972. "The Effects of Price and Cost Uncertainty on Investment." *Journal of Economic Theory* 5 (October): 258–266.

Hassett, Kevin A. and Gilbert E. Metcalf. 1992. "Energy Tax Credits and Residential Conservation Investment." Working Paper No. 4020, National Bureau of Economic Research, Cambridge, MA.

Hawkins, Gregory D. 1982. "An Analysis of Revolving Credit Agreements." *Journal of Financial Economics* 10, 59–81.

Hayashi, Fumio. 1982. "Tobin's Marginal q and Average q: A Neoclassical Interpretation." *Econometrica* 50 (January): 213–224.

He, Hua, and Robert S. Pindyck. 1992. "Investments in Flexible Production Capacity." *Journal of Economic Dynamics and Control* 16 (August): 575–599.

Hendricks, Darryll. 1992. "Optimal Policy Response to an Uncertain Threat: The Case of Global Warming." Unpublished manuscript, Kennedy School of Government, Harvard University, March.

Henry, Claude. 1974a. "Option Values in the Economics of Irreplaceable Assets." *Review of Economic Studies* 41 (January): 89–104.

————. 1974b. "Investment Decisions under Uncertainty: The Irreversibility Effect." *American Economic Review* 64 (December): 1006–1012.

Herbelot, Olivier. 1992. "Option Valuation of Flexible Investments: The Case of Environmental Investments in the Electric Power Industry." Unpublished Ph.D. dissertation, Massachusetts Institute of Technology, May.

Huang, Chi-fu, and Robert H. Litzenberger. 1990. *Foundations for Financial Economics*. New York: Elsevier Science Publishers.

Hull, John. 1989. *Options, Futures, and Other Derivative Securities*. Englewood Cliffs, NJ: Prentice-Hall.

————, and Alan White. 1987. "The Pricing of Options on Assets with Stochastic Volatilities." *Journal of Finance* 42 (June): 281–300.

————, and ————. 1990. "Valuing Derivative Securities Using the Explicit Finite Difference Method." *Journal of Financial and Quantitative Analysis* 25 (March): 87–100.

Ingersoll, Jonthan E., and Stephen A. Ross. 1992. "Waiting to Invest: Investment and Uncertainty." *Journal of Business* 65 (January): 1–29.

Jacoby, Henry D., and David G. Laughton. 1992. "Project Evaluation: A Practical Asset Pricing Method." *The Energy Journal* 13: 19–47.

Jarrow, Robert A., and Andrew Rudd. 1983. *Option Pricing*. Homewood, IL: Irwin.

Johnson, Claes. 1990. *Numerical Solutions of Partial Differential Equations by the Finite Element Method*. Cambridge, England: Cambridge University Press.

Jorgenson, Dale. 1963. "Capital Theory and Investment Behavior." *American Economic Review* 53 (May): 247–259.

Judd, Kenneth L. 1985. "The Law of Large Numbers with a Continuum of IID Random Variables." *Journal of Economic Theory* 35 (February): 19–25.

———. 1992. *Numerical Methods in Economics*. Unpublished manuscript, Stanford University.

Kalish, Shlomo. 1983. "Monopolist Pricing with Dynamic Demand and Production Cost." *Marketing Science* 2 (March): 135–159.

Kamien, Morton I., and Nancy L. Schwartz. 1991. *Dynamic Optimization*, second edition. New York: North-Holland.

Karatzas, Ioannis, and Steven E. Shreve. 1988. *Brownian Motion and Stochastic Calculus*. Berlin: Springer-Verlag.

Karlin, Samuel, and Howard M. Taylor. 1975. *A First Course in Stochastic Processes*, second edition. New York: Academic Press.

———, and ———. 1981. *A Second Course in Stochastic Processes*, New York: Academic Press.

Kester, W. Carl. 1984. "Today's Options for Tomorrow's Growth." *Harvard Business Review* (March/April): 153–160.

Kogut, Bruce, and Nalin Kulatilaka. 1993. "Operating Flexibility, Global Manufacturing, and the Option Value of a Multinational Network." *Management Science* forthcoming.

Kolstad, Charles D. 1992. "Regulating a Stock Externality Under Uncertainty with Learning." Working Paper No. 92-0112, Department of Economics, University of Illinois at Urbana-Champaign, March.

Kopcke, Richard W. 1985. "The Determinants of Investment Spending." *New England Economic Review* (July): 19–35.

———. 1993. "The Determinants of Business Investment: Has Capital Spending Been Surprisingly Low?" *New England Economic Review* (January): 3–31.

Krugman, Paul R. 1988. "Deindustrialization, Reindustrialization, and the Real Exchange Rate." NBER Working Paper No. 2586, May.

———. 1989. *Exchange Rate Instability*. Cambridge, MA: MIT Press.

Krutilla, John V., and Anthony C. Fisher. 1975. *The Economics of Natural Environments*. Baltimore, MD: Johns Hopkins Press.

Krylov, N. V. 1980. *Controlled Diffusion Processes*, New York and Berlin: Springer-Verlag.

Kulatilaka, Nalin, and Alan J. Marcus. 1988. "General Formulation of Corporate Real Options." *Research in Finance* 7, 183–199.

———, and Enrico C. Perotti. 1992. "Strategic Investment Timing Under Uncertainty." Discussion Paper No. 145, Financial Markets Group, London School of Economics.

Kushner, Harold J. 1967. *Stochastic Stability and Control*. New York: Academic Press.

Kydland, Finn E., and Edward G. Prescott. 1982. "Time to Build and Aggregate Fluctuations." *Econometrica* 50, 1345–1370.

Lam, Pok-sang. 1989. "Irreversibility and Consumer Durables Expenditures." *Journal of Monetary Economics* 23 (January): 135–150.

Leahy, John. 1992. "Investment in Competitive Equilibrium: The Optimality of Myopic Behavior." Working Paper, Harvard University.

Lieberman, Marvin B. 1984. "The Learning Curve and Pricing in the Chemical Processing Industries." *The RAND Journal of Economics* 15, Spring, 213–228.

Lippman, Steven A., and R. P. Rumelt. 1985. "Demand Uncertainty and Investment in Industry-Specific Capital." Unpublished, University of California, Los Angeles, September.

Lohrenz, John, and R. N. Dickens. 1993. "Option Theory for Evaluation of Oil and Gas Assets: The Upsides and Downsides." *Proceedings of Society of Petroleum Engineers*, SPE 25837, 179–188.

Lucas, Robert E. Jr. 1967. "Adjustment Costs and the Theory of Supply." *Journal of Political Economy* 75 (August): 321–334.

———, and Edward C. Prescott. 1971. "Investment Under Uncertainty." *Econometrica* 39 (May): 659–681.

———, and ———. 1974. "Equilibrium Search and Unemployment." *Journal of Economic Theory* 32, 139–171.

Lund, Diderik. 1991. "Financial and Nonfinancial Option Valuation." In *Stochastic Models and Option Values*, eds. D. Lund and B. Øksendal. New York: North-Holland.

———. 1991b. "With Timing Options and Heterogeneous Costs, the Lognormal Diffusion is Hardly an Equilibrium Price Process for Exhaustible Resources." Unpublished, University of Oslo, November.

———. 1992. "Petroleum Taxation under Uncertainty: Contingent Claims Analysis with an Application to Norway." *Energy Economics* 14 (January): 23–31.

———, and Bernt Øksendal, eds. 1991. *Stochastic Models and Option Values*. New York: North-Holland.

MacKie-Mason, Jeffrey K. 1990. "Some Nonlinear Tax Effects on Asset Values and Investment Decisions Under Uncertainty." *Journal of Public Economics* 42 (August): 301–328.

———. 1991. "Sequential Investment Decisions with Asymmetric Learning." Working Paper, University of Michigan, September.

Majd, Saman, and Stewart C. Myers. 1986. "Tax Asymmetries and Corporate Income Tax Reform." NBER Working Paper No. 1924, May.

———, and Robert S. Pindyck. 1987. "Time to Build, Option Value, and Investment Decisions." *Journal of Financial Economics* 18 (March): 7–27.

———, and ———. 1989. "The Learning Curve and Optimal Production under Uncertainty." *RAND Journal of Economics*, Autumn, 20, 331–343.

Malliaris, A. G., and William A. Brock. 1982. *Stochastic Methods in Economics and Finance*. New York: North-Holland.

Manne, Alan S. 1961. "Capacity Expansion and Probabilistic Growth." *Econometrica* 29 (October): 632–649.

Manthy, Robert S. 1978. *Natural Resource Commodities: A Century of Statistics*. Baltimore, MD: Johns Hopkins Press.

Marcus, Alan J., and David M. Modest. 1984. "Futures Markets and Production Decisions." *Journal of Political Economy* 92 (June): 409–426.

Marglin, Stephen. 1963. *Approaches to Dynamic Investment Planning*. Amsterdam: North-Holland.

Martzoukos, Spiros H., and Witold Teplitz-Sembitzky. 1992. "Optimal Timing of Transmission Line Investments in the Face of Uncertain Demand: An Option Valuation Approach." *Energy Economics* 14 (January): 3–10.

Mason, Scott, and Robert C. Merton. 1985. "The Role of Contingent Claims Analysis in Corporate Finance." In *Recent Advances in Corporate Finance*, eds: E. Altman and M. Subrahmanyam. Homewood, IL: Richard D. Irwin.

McCray, Arthur W. 1975. *Petroleum Evaluations and Economic Decisions*. Englewood Cliffs, NJ: Prentice-Hall.

McDonald, Robert, and Daniel Siegel. 1984. "Option Pricing When the Underlying Asset Earns a Below-Equilibrium Rate of Return: A Note." *Journal of Finance* (March): 261–265.

————, and ————. 1985. "Investment and the Valuation of Firms When There is an Option to Shut Down." *International Economic Review* 26 (June): 331–349.

————, and ————. 1986. "The Value of Waiting to Invest." *Quarterly Journal of Economics* (November): 101, 707–728.

Merton, Robert C. 1971. "Optimum Consumption and Portfolio Rules in a Continuous-Time Model." *Journal of Economic Theory* 3, 373–413.

————. 1973. "The Theory of Rational Option Pricing." *Bell Journal of Economics and Management Science* 4, Spring, 141–183.

————. 1975. "An Asymptotic Theory of Growth Under Uncertainty." *Review of Economic Studies* 42, 375–394.

————. 1976. "Option Pricing when Underlying Stock Returns are Discontinuous." *Journal of Financial Economics* 3, 125–144.

————. 1977. "On the Pricing of Contingent Claims and the Modigliani-Miller Theorem." *Journal of Financial Economics* 5 (November): 241–249.

————. 1990. *Continuous-Time Finance*. Cambridge, MA: Basil Blackwell.

Metcalf, Gilbert and Kevin Hassett. 1993. "Investment with Uncertain Tax Policy." Work in progress.

Modigliani, Franco, and Merton H. Miller. 1958. "The Cost of Capital, Corporation Finance, and the Theory of Investment." *American Economic Review* 48 (June): 261–297.

Morck, Randall, Eduardo Schwartz, and David Stangeland. 1989. "The Valuation of Forestry Resources under Stochastic Prices and Inventories." *Journal of Financial and Quantitative Analysis* 24 (December): 473–487.

Mossin, Jan. 1968. "An Optimal Policy for Lay-up Decisions." *Swedish Journal of Economics* 70, 170–177.

Mussa, Michael. 1982. "Government Policy and the Adjustment Process." In *Import Competition and Response*, ed. Jagdish Bhagwati. Chicago, IL: University of Chicago Press, 73–120.

Myers, Stewart C. 1977. "Determinants of Corporate Borrowing." *Journal of Financial Economics* 5 (November): 147–175.

————, and Saman Majd. 1984. "Calculating Abandonment Value Using Option Pricing Theory." M.I.T. Sloan School of Management Working Paper No. 1462–83, January.

————, and Richard S. Ruback. 1992. "Discounting Rules for Risky Assets." M.I.T. Center for Energy and Environmental Policy Research Working Paper No. 93–001WP, November.

Newbery, David, and Joseph Stiglitz. 1981. *The Theory of Commodity Price Stabilization*. New York: Oxford University Press.

Nickell, Stephen J. 1978. *The Investment Decisions of Firms*. New York: Cambridge University Press.

Nordhaus, William D. 1991. "To Slow or Not to Slow: The Economics of the Greenhouse Effect." *The Economic Journal* 101 (July): 920–937.

Paddock, James L., Daniel R. Siegel, and James L. Smith. 1988. "Option Valuation of Claims on Real Assets: The Case of Offshore Petroleum Leases." *Quarterly Journal of Economics* 103 (August): 479–508.

Pakes, Ariel. 1986. "Patents as Options: Some Estimates of the Value of Holding European Patent Stocks." *Econometrica* 54 (July): 755–784.

———. 1993. "Dynamic Structural Models: Problems and Prospects. Mixed Continuous Discrete Controls and Market Interactions." In *Advances in Econometrics: Sixth World Congress*, eds. Jean-Jacques Laffont and Christopher Sims, Cambridge, UK: Cambridge University Press, forthcoming.

Pearson, Carl E. (ed.). 1990. *Handbook of Applied Mathematics*. New York: Van Nostrand Reinhold.

Pindyck, Robert S. 1984. "Uncertainty in the Theory of Renewable Resource Markets." *Review of Economic Studies* 51 (April): 289–303.

———. 1985. "The Measurement of Monopoly Power in Dynamic Markets." *Journal of Law and Economics* 28 (April): 193–222.

———. 1986. "Capital Risk and Models of Investment Behavior." M.I.T. Sloan School of Management Working Paper No. 1819–86, September.

———. 1988a. "Options, Flexibility and Investment Decisions." M.I.T. Center for Energy Policy Working Paper No. EL-88-018WP, March.

———. 1988b. "Irreversible Investment, Capacity Choice, and the Value of the Firm." *American Economic Review* 79 (December): 969–985.

———. 1991a. "Irreversibility and the Explanation of Investment Behavior." In *Stochastic Models and Option Values*, eds. D. Lund and B. Øksendal. Amsterdam: North-Holland.

———. 1991b. "Irreversibility, Uncertainty, and Investment." *Journal of Economic Literature* 29 (September): 1110–1152.

———. 1993a. "A Note on Competitive Investment Under Uncertainty." *American Economic Review* 83 (March): 273–277.

———. 1993b. "Investments of Uncertain Cost." *Journal of Financial Economics* 34 (August): 53–76.

———. 1993c. "The Present Value Model of Rational Commodity Pricing." *The Economic Journal* 103 (May): 511–530.

———. 1993d. "Inventories and the Short-Run Dynamics of Commodity Prices." *RAND Journal of Economics*, forthcoming.

————. 1993e. "Sunk Costs and Sunk Benefits in Environmental Policy." Unpublished working paper, Massachusetts Institute of Technology, May.

————, and Daniel L. Rubinfeld. 1991. *Econometric Models and Economic Forecasts*, third edition, New York: McGraw-Hill.

————, and Andrés Solimano. 1993. "Economic Instability and Aggregate Investment." *NBER Macroeconomics Annual* 8, 259–303.

Plummer, Mark L., and Richard C. Hartman. 1986. "Option Value: A General Approach." *Economic Inquiry* 24 (July): 455–471.

Quigg, Laura. 1993. "Empirical Testing of Real Option-Pricing Models." *Journal of Finance* 48 (June): 621–639.

Rawlinson, Richard, and Michael E. Porter. 1986. "The Oil Tanker Shipping Industry in 1983." Harvard Business School Case No. 9–384–034, July.

Roberts, Kevin, and Martin L. Weitzman. 1981. "Funding Criteria for Research, Development, and Exploration Projects." *Econometrica* 49, 1261–1288.

Rodrik, Dani. 1991. "Policy Uncertainty and Private Investment in Developing Countries." *Journal of Development Economics* 36 (October): 229–242.

Rothschild, Michael. 1971. "On the Cost of Adjustment." *Quarterly Journal of Economics* 85 (November): 605–622.

Ruback, Richard S. 1986. "Calculating the Market Value of Riskless Cash Flows." *Journal of Financial Economics* 15, 323–339.

Rubinstein, Mark. 1987. "Derivative Assets Analysis." *Journal of Economic Perspectives* 1, Fall, 73–94.

Rust, John. 1987. "Optimal Replacement of GMC Bus Engines: An Empirical Model of Harold Zurcher." *Econometrica* 55, 999–1034.

————. 1993. "Dynamic Structural Models: Problems and Prospects. Discrete Decision Processes." In *Advances in Econometrics: Sixth World Congress*, eds. Jean-Jacques Laffont and Christopher Sims. Cambridge, UK: Cambridge University Press, forthcoming.

Samuelson, Paul A. 1964. "Tax Deductibility of Economic Depreciation to Insure Invariant Valuation." *Journal of Political Economy* 72 (December): 571–573.

————. 1965. "Rational Theory of Warrant Pricing." *Industrial Management Review* 6, Spring, 41–50.

Sawhill, James W. 1989. "Evaluating Utility Investment Decisions—An Options Approach." M.S. thesis, M.I.T. Sloan School of Management, May.

Schmalensee, Richard. 1972. "Option Demand and Consumer's Surplus: Valuing Price Changes under Uncertainty." *American Economic Review* 62 (December): 813–824.

Scott, Louis O. 1987. "Option Pricing When the Variance Changes Randomly: Theory, Estimation, and an Application." *Journal of Financial and Quantitative Analysis* 22 (December): 419–438.

Siegel, Daniel R., James L. Smith, and James L. Paddock. 1987. "Valuing Offshore Oil Properties with Option Pricing Models." *Midland Corporate Finance Journal* 5, Spring, 22–30.

Slater, L. J. 1960. *Confluent Hypergeometric Functions*. Cambridge, U.K.: Cambridge University Press.

Smets, Frank. 1991. "Exporting versus FDI: The Effect of Uncertainty, Irreversibilities and Strategic Interactions." Working Paper, Yale University.

Smith, Clifford W., Jr. 1976. "Option Pricing: A Review." *Journal of Financial Economics* 3 (January): 3–51.

Solow, Robert M., James Tobin, Christian von Weizsacker, and Menachem Yaari. 1967. "Neoclassical Growth with Fixed Factor Proportions." *Review of Economic Studies* 33 (April): 79–115.

Spence, A. Michael. 1981. "The Learning Curve and Competition." *Bell Journal of Economics* 12, Spring, 49–70.

Spencer, Barbara, and James Brander. 1992. "Pre-commitment and Flexibility: Applications to Oligopoly Theory." *European Economic Review* 36, 1601–1626.

Stensland, Gunnar, and Dag B. Tjøstheim. 1989. "Optimal Investments Using Empirical Dynamic Programming with Application to Natural Resources." *Journal of Business* 62 (January): 99–120.

———, and ———. 1991. "Optimal Decisions with Reduction of Uncertainty Over Time—An Application to Oil Production." In *Stochastic Models and Option Values*, eds. D. Lund and B. Øksendal. New York: North-Holland.

Stibolt, R. D., and John Lehman. 1993. "The Value of a Seismic Option." *Proceedings of Society of Petroleum Engineers*, SPE 25821, 25–32.

Stokey, Nancy L., and Robert E. Lucas, Jr., with Edward C. Prescott. 1989. *Recursive Models in Economic Dynamics*. Cambridge, MA: Harvard University Press.

Summers, Lawrence H. 1987. "Investment Incentives and the Discounting of Depreciation Allowances." In *The Effects of Taxation on Capital Accumulation*, ed. Martin Feldstein. Chicago, IL: Chicago University Press.

Taggart, Robert A. 1991. "Consistent Valuation and Cost of Capital Expressions with Corporate and Personal Taxes." *Financial Management* 20, 8–20.

Tirole, Jean. 1988. *The Theory of Industrial Organization*. Cambridge, MA: MIT Press.

Tobin, James. 1969. "A General Equilibrium Approach to Monetary Theory." *Journal of Money, Credit and Banking* 1 (February): 15–29.

Tourinho, Octavio A. 1979. "The Valuation of Reserves of Natural Resources: An Option Pricing Approach." Unpublished Ph.D. dissertation, University of California, Berkeley.

Triantis, Alexander J., and James E. Hodder. 1990. "Valuing Flexibility as a Complex Option." *Journal of Finance* 45 (June): 549–565.

Trigeorgis, Lenos, and Scott P. Mason. 1987. "Valuing Managerial Flexibility." *Midland Corporate Finance Journal* 5, Spring, 14–21.

Van Wijnbergen, Sweder. 1985. "Trade Reform, Aggregate Investment and Capital Flight." *Economics Letters* 19, 369–372.

Varian, Hal S. 1987. "The Arbitrage Principle in Financial Analysis." *Journal of Economic Perspectives* 1 (Fall): 55–72.

————. 1991. *Microeconomic Analysis*, third edition. New York: W. W. Norton.

Weitzman, Martin L. 1970. "Optimal Growth with Scale Economies in the Creation of Overhead Capital." *Review of Economic Studies* 37 (October): 555–570.

————. 1979. "Optimal Search for the Best Alternative." *Econometrica* 47 (May): 641–654.

————, Whitney Newey, and Michael Rabin. 1981. "Sequential R&D Strategy for Synfuels." *Bell Journal of Economics* 12, 574–590.

Wey, Lead. 1993. "Effects of Mean-Reversion on the Valuation of Offshore Oil Reserves and Optimal Investment Rules." Unpublished undergraduate thesis, Massachusetts Institute of Technology, May.

Wiggins, James B. 1987. "Option Values Under Stochastic Volatility." *Journal of Financial Economics* 19, 351–372.

Zeira, Joseph. 1987. "Investment as a Process of Search." *Journal of Political Economy* 95 (February): 204–210.

Symbol Glossary

In a book as long as this, combining many different ideas and models, it is impossible to preserve completely consistent and unique notation throughout. We have tried to maintain consistency for the concepts that are most central and appear repeatedly in the core chapters 3–9. Even there, in a couple of places demands of standard notation in different uses conflict (for example, ρ as discount rate and correlation coefficient). In such cases, rather than switch to strange notation for one of the uses, we have risked some ambiguity. Luckily the same symbol does not need two different uses in close proximity, so in each case, the context clarifies which use is intended.

In Chapters 10–12, which treat some extensions of the core theory and discuss some applied literature, we take over the notation of the original articles we review, so some of our earlier notation sometimes has different meaning there. We have tried to minimize these occurrences, but pending the arrival of standardized notation and the use of Kanji characters in mathematical writing, some such problems are unavoidable.

Here we give a list, for easy reference, of our "global" notation, that is, usage (almost) consistent throughout the book. All other symbols are "local" to each chapter or even each section or subsection. They may denote different parameters or variables in different places; each of these is defined where used.

We should also clarify our notation for derivatives. For functions of a single variable, we generally use primes to denote the (total) derivatives. For example, $F(V)$ has derivatives $F'(V)$, $F''(V)$, etc. For functions of two or more variables, we use subscripts to denote the appropriate partial derivatives. For example, $F(V, t)$ has derivatives $F_V(V, t)$, $F_{VV}(V, t)$, $F_t(V, t)$ etc.

Uppercase Roman Letters

A, B Constants of integration in solutions of differential equation.
C Operating cost of a project.
F Value of the opportunity to invest; more generally, the value function in dynamic programming (also called the Bellman function).
I Capital cost of investment (Chapters 2, 5–9); rate of investment (Chapters 10–12).
K Stock of capital, either installed (Chapter 11) or remaining to the completion of the project (Chapter 10).
P Output price.
Q Industry output quantity.
T Terminal time.
V Value of asset in place.
W Total value of a whole range of capacity expansion opportunities, for the firm (Chapter 11) or for social optimality (Chapter 9).
X Firm-specific stochastic shock.
Y Industry-wide stochastic shock.

Lowercase Roman Letters

a, b Coefficients of diffusion process.
c Production cost function for a firm with variable output level (Chapter 9).
d Infinitesimal increment prefix (e.g., the differential dt).
m, n Short positions in replicating riskless portfolio.
p, q Probabilities in random walk representation.
q Tobin's q (Chapters 5, 6, 11, 12); a competitive firm's output level (Chapter 9).
dq Increment of a Poisson jump process (mainly Chapters 3, 4).
r Riskless interest rate.
t Current time.
u Control variable in theory of dynamic programming (Chapter 4); size of jump in basic Poisson process (Chapters 3, 4).
x General notation for the state variable of a stochastic process.
dz Increment of standard Wiener (Brownian motion) process.

Uppercase Greek Letters

Δ Prefix for finite but small increment (e.g., Δt).

Ω Terminal payoff function in dynamic programming.

Φ Value of replicating (riskless) portfolio, cumulative probability distribution function.

Lowercase Greek Letters

α Drift parameter of simple Brownian motion, or proportional growth rate parameter of geometric Brownian motion.

β Variable in fundamental quadratic. Its positive and negative roots are denoted by β_1 and β_2, respectively.

δ Rate of return shortfall or convenience yield.

λ Arrival rate of Poisson process; depreciation rate.

η Mean-reversion rate.

μ Risk-adjusted (CAPM) discount rate.

π Profit flow.

ϕ Market price of risk; probability density function of diffusion process variable.

ρ Exogenous discount rate in dynamic programming; correlation coefficient.

σ Variance parameter in Brownian motion.

τ General time variable (mainly used as variable of integration in expressions for present discounted values).

Calligraphic Letters

$\mathcal{E}$ Expectation operator.

$\mathcal{V}$ Variance operator.

$\mathcal{Q}$ Expression for the fundamental quadratic.

Author Index

Subject Index